OTHER BOOKS BY RONALD W. CLARK

Tizard
The Huxleys
J.B.S.
Einstein: The Life and Times
The Life of Bertrand Russell
The Man Who Broke Purple
Freud: The Man and the Cause
Lenin: A Biography

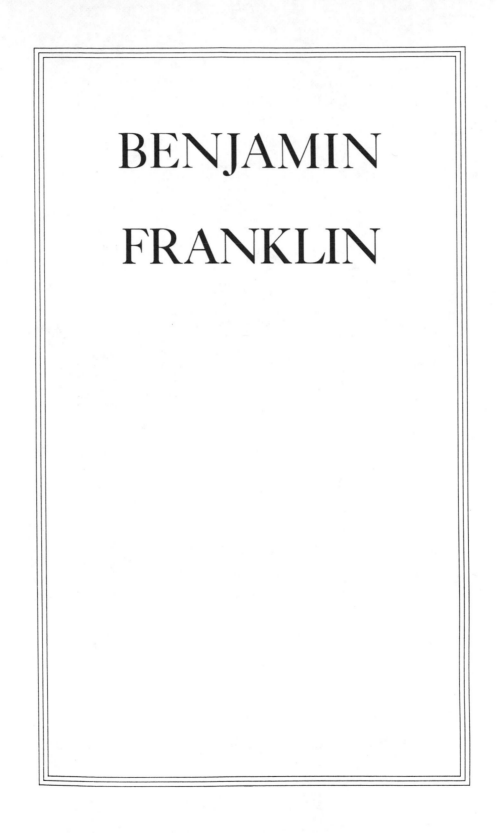

BENJAMIN

FRANKLIN

BENJAMIN

FRANKLIN

A Biography

RONALD·W·CLARK

A DA CAPO PAPERBACK

Library of Congress Cataloging in Publication Data

Clark, Ronald William.
  Benjamin Franklin.

(A Da Capo paperback)
  Reprint. Originally published: New York: Random House, 1983.
  Bibliography: p.
  Includes index.
  1. Franklin, Benjamin, 1706-1790. 2. Statesmen—United States—
Biography. 3. Scientists—United States—Biography. 4. Printers—
United States—Biography. I. title.
[E302.6F8C54 1989   973.3'092 [B]   89-11794
ISBN 0-306-80368-2

This Da Capo Press paperback edition of
Benjamin Franklin is an unabridged
republication of the edition published
in New York in 1983. It is reprinted
by arrangement with Random House, Inc.

Published by Da Capo Press, Inc.
A Subsidiary of Plenum Publishing Corporation
233 Spring Street, New York, New York 10013

ACKNOWLEDGMENTS

WISH TO THANK THE AMERICAN PHILO-sophical Society for permission to use material in its possession, and the owners who have provided letters for inclusion in *The Papers of Benjamin Franklin*, sponsored by the Society and Yale University and published by the Yale University Press. I also wish to thank Whitfield J. Bell, Jr., Executive Officer of the Society, for his kind advice concerning such material and William B. Willcox, the present editor of *The Papers*, for advice on a specific point.

While the opinions expressed in the text of *Benjamin Franklin: A Biography* are my own except where indicated, I would like to thank the following for reading parts of the manuscript: Hugh Brogan, of the University of Essex; Professor R. V. Jones, of Aberdeen University; Colonel John B. B. Trussell, Chief, Division of History, Bureau of Archives and History, Harrisburg, Pennsylvania; and Professor Esmond Wright, Director, Institute of United States Studies, University of London.

I also thank the Earl of Dartmouth for permission to consult and quote from the letters in the Dartmouth Papers held by the Staffordshire Record Office, Stafford; Mrs. Janet Dick-Cunyngham for permission to use Franklin's Prestonfield verses; the trustees of the Fitzwilliam Wentworth Estates and the Director of Sheffield City Libraries for permission to quote from letters in the Wentworth Woodhouse Muniments, in the Sheffield City Libraries; M. A. Guyot, of the Department of Archives and Documentation, French Foreign Ministry, Paris, for photocopies of material in the French Foreign Office; the Library of Congress for the loan of microfilms of its Franklin holdings; the Scottish Record Office for photocopies of material in the papers of Lord Kames; the Royal Society and the Royal Society of Arts for permission to consult documents in their possession; the Royal Society of Edinburgh for a photostat from the Library's Hume Manuscripts; and the staffs of the Public Record Office, Kew, and Chancery Lane, London, of the Science Museum, Kensington, and of the Reading Room and the Department of Manuscripts, British Library, Bloomsbury, for their unfailing help.

CONTENTS

ILLUSTRATIONS

THE

IMPORTANCE

OF BEING

FRANKLIN

ONE

═══════════════

PRINTER'S
APPRENTICE

O N M A Y 1 0 , 1 7 5 2 , T H E R E T O O K P L A C E I N Marly-la-Ville, a small village some twenty-five miles north of Paris, an experiment of crucial importance not only to science but to the history of the Western world. Nothing less than victory in America's War of Independence three decades later was to be linked with the events of that May afternoon.

In a walled garden on the outskirts of the village the French physicist Thomas-François Dalibard had erected a curious apparatus. At its center there rose a sharply pointed iron rod, an inch in diameter and some forty feet high. Resting on a wooden base which itself stood on four empty wine bottles, the rod was held in place by guy ropes which lashed it to three thirty-foot wooden supports forming a surrounding triangle. A small wooden shelter, big enough to accommodate a man, had been erected over the bottom few feet of the iron rod. Here, on duty during the early afternoon, was a retired French dragoon, Coiffier by name, a man who could be relied upon to carry out orders whatever the danger to life or limb.

Shortly after two o'clock the first rumbles of an approaching thunderstorm could be heard. The dragoon picked up a long brass wire, insulated in a glass bottle. As the storm came nearer Coiffier presented the wire to the rod. Sparks flew. A loud sizzling crackle could be heard and a smell of sulfur filled the air. To the dragoon there could be only one explanation, and he called out for M. Raulet, the Prior of Marly, to come urgently. If the Devil was around, then the local priest would be the best man to deal with him.

M. Raulet came at the run, accompanied by curious villagers, and through what developed into a sharp hailstorm. Having little fear of the Devil, the Prior of Marly grasped the bottle with its wire. "I repeated the experiment at least six times in about four minutes in the presence of many persons," he subsequently wrote, "and every time the experiment lasted the space of a *pater* and an *ave.*" He then touched the rod with his hand and received a severe shock. Nevertheless, he added later, he would have touched it a second time had the storm not passed.

The Prior sent a full account to Dalibard in Paris, and Dalibard prepared a report on the afternoon's events for the Royal Academy of Sciences. "M. Franklin's idea has ceased to be a conjecture," this stated; "here it has become a reality."

The reality, astounding to a world in which scientific investigation could still be equated with blasphemy, was that lightning was a form of electricity: that the fire from Heaven, which struck at random, set churches ablaze, demolished homes and killed good and bad without selection, was the same inexplicable spark-producing substance with which scientists had been playing dangerous parlor tricks for the past two decades.

Although there had been speculation about such an identity, there had never before been experimental proof, and the events at Marly were sufficient to send a shock wave through the European scientific community. In France the surprise was increased by the background of the man who had proposed the experiment. Dalibard's "M. Franklin" was not a Frenchman. He did not come from England or from Germany. He was, in fact, a Colonial from across the Atlantic, a man from that distant country on the edge of the wilderness where all effort, from what one heard, tended to concentrate on the problems of survival against the elements and the Indians rather than on the profundities of scientific research. M. Franklin, moreover, was not a scientist but, of all things, a retired printer. One or two of his experiments had, it is true, been described to the Royal Society in London, and a thin book of his had been translated and published in France with the support of Georges Louis Leclerc, Comte de Buffon, the eminent French naturalist. Even so, until the summer of 1752 there was one good reason for refusing to consider any ideas coming from this almost unknown amateur across the Atlantic: the Abbé Nollet, Preceptor in Natural Philosophy to His Majesty Louis XV, a man who had already demonstrated many electrical marvels, was unwilling to take them seriously.

Yet after May 10 it was difficult to doubt the implications of the dramatic experiment at Marly. A few days later M. de Lor, master of Experimental Philosophy, repeated it in the garden of his house in Paris. More ambitious than Dalibard, he raised a ninety-nine-foot iron bar. In the late afternoon, "a stormy cloud having passed over the bar, where it remain'd half an hour, he drew sparks from the bar. These sparks were like those of a gun when, in the electrical experiments, the globe is only rubb'd by the cushion, and they produced the same noise, the same fire, and the same crackling."

Before the end of the month an account of the French experiments was sent to Stephen Hales, Fellow of the Royal Society in London, who immediately passed on the news to a wide circle of friends. In July John Canton, a leading British investigator of electricity, found an opportunity for "trying mr. Franklin's experiment of extracting the electrical fire from the clouds." He did so "by means of a tin tube, between three and four feet in length, fixed to the top of a glass one, of about eighteen inches. To the upper end of the tin tube, which was not so high as a stack of chimnies on the same house, I fastened three needles with some wire; and to the lower end was solder'd a tin cover to keep the rain from the glass tube, which was set upright in a block of wood. I attended this apparatus as soon after the thunder began as possible, but did not find it in the least electrified, till between the third and fourth clap; when applying my knuckle to the edge of the cover, I felt and heard an electrical spark; and approaching it a second time, I received the spark at the distance of about half an inch, and saw it distinctly."

Benjamin Wilson, an Englishman who was later to argue that lightning conductors should end in knobs rather than points, tried the same experiment in the garden of a friend's house in Chelmsford. He used "no other apparatus than an iron curtain-rod, one end of which he put into the neck of a glass phial, and held this phial in his hand. To the other end of the iron he fasten'd three needles with some silk. This phial, supporting the rod, he held in one hand, and drew snaps from the rod with a finger of his other."

Elsewhere in Europe scientists were discussing the Marly experiment and soon began repeating it. They confirmed beyond all reasonable doubt that lightning and electricity were one and the same thing. *The Gentleman's Magazine* and *The London Magazine* both printed reports of the French experiment, that in *The Gentleman's Magazine* starting: "You must remember, Sir, how much we ridiculed Mr. *Franklin's* project for emptying clouds of their thunder, and that we could scarce conceive him to be any other than an imaginary Being. This now proves us to be but poor *virtuosi.*" And after describing events at Marly it ended: "Mean while you may assure the ladies in your part of the world, that we are doing our best here to secure them against thunder and lightning; not forgetting some of your pretty fellows, who, with all their courage, may possibly be no less terrified by thunder than the ladies."

In Philadelphia, Benjamin Franklin, originator and part owner of *The Pennsylvania Gazette,* received a copy of *The London Magazine*'s account and reprinted it in his issue of August 27. Pleased to be recognized in Britain, he was possibly surprised that he had become a hero in France. And not even Franklin could foresee the situation a quarter of a century later, when equipment of America's revolutionary forces would rest so largely on his fame, which had sprung from a May day's experiment.

To many Americans, Benjamin Franklin is the epitome of all that America should be, the patriot as responsible as Washington for prizing the young Colonies from the grip of the British, the successful businessman as well as that rare bird, the honest politician. The sensible advice of Franklin's *Poor Richard's Almanack*—"God helps them that help themselves"; "Having been poor is no shame, but being ashamed of it, is"—is compounded by the picture of the man himself, the homespun figure standing without wig or sword before Louis XVI at Versailles. The scintillating journey through life of the poor printer's apprentice from Boston becomes a log-cabin-to-White-House progress.

Yet there is a sizable minority who set a number of disagreeable facts against the glittering record which justifiably makes Franklin an American hero. He was, for a while, willing to acquiesce in the detested Stamp Act. At the time of the Boston Tea Party he was still assiduously lobbying the British Government in favor of a new colony on the Ohio which would have greatly enriched him and his family. His methods as a businessman were strictly within the law yet sometimes of a kind which has made some Americans as disliked in today's Europe as some British were disliked in Franklin's time. It was no doubt proper for the moralities of *Poor Richard's Almanack,* of which Franklin sold 10,000 copies a year, to be concentrated on prudence, hard work and horse sense.

The placid aphorisms of "Poor Richard" at times reflected "a shade of thrift seldom insensible to the profit side of the account." The errors of Franklin's theory of life, it is averred, "sprang from a defective early education, which made his morality superficial even to laxness, and undermined his religious faith. His system resolves itself into the ancient and specious dogma, of *honesty the best policy.* That nice sense which revolts at wrong for its own sake, and that generosity of spirit which shrinks from participating in the advantages of indirection, however naturally obtained, were not his." His pamphleteering and letter-writing, which earned the American cause a hearing in London, has been condemned as degrading literature. And his labors in France, which so strikingly made American victory possible in the War of Independence, merely transformed him in some eyes to a European. Thus with Franklin, as with many men whose genius keeps them at a full trot through life, vice or virtue frequently depends on the eye of the beholder.

As for the scientific curiosity which permeated his life from first days to last, this is often dismissed as nothing more than a utilitarian impetus very different from that which drove on Newton, Linnaeus or Einstein. And Franklin did once write that it was not of much importance to us to know the manner in which nature executes her laws. It was enough to know the laws themselves.

None of this detracts from his stature. But it does confirm the hodgepodge nature of great men in whom genius mingles with banality and in whom a perfect understanding of human means contrasts with a circumscribed view of human ends. All of it, in addition, makes Franklin a more complex figure than the popular picture of Rousseau-like sage, crossing the Atlantic to save the Old World from its follies. Unraveling his complexities is a task hindered rather than made easier by his famous *Autobiography*. The record dwelt on his early years, he told the Duc de la Rochefoucauld d'Enville, because the accounts were "of more general use to young readers, as exemplifying strongly the effects of *prudent* and *imprudent conduct* in the commencement of a life of business." His story therefore is tailored for a task, and the reader, even more than the reader of most autobiographies, must look about for both supporting evidence and for omissions in a book begun when the author was fifty-five and concluded when he was in his eighties.

Of all the ambiguities which stud Franklin's life, his attitude to Britain is perhaps the most remarkable, an ambiguity which surrounds a Founding Father rather unexpectedly. His pride in British ancestry and his love of Britain and her people until war broke out in 1775 were natural enough. But he boasted of feeling as much British as American until the British made fools of themselves. He for long worked toward a solution of Anglo-Colonial difficulties which would have brought America into confederation with an enlarged British Empire. And more than once, only chance prevented his settling in England for good; an event from which momentous consequences would almost certainly have flowed.

Like most people whose families have emigrated, Franklin was intrigued by his ancestors. Coming to England at the age of fifty-one, he soon took an opportunity to inspect the church register at Ecton, Northamptonshire, where his family had lived for at least three hundred years on a thirty-acre freehold supplemented by the income from a blacksmith's business. "By that Register," he later wrote, "I perceiv'd that I was the youngest Son of the youngest Son for 5 Generations back. My Grandfather Thomas, who was born in 1598, lived at Ecton till he grew too old to follow Business longer, when he went to live with his Son John, a Dyer at Banbury, in Oxfordshire, with whom my

Father serv'd an Apprenticeship. There my Grandfather died and lies buried."

His insatiable interest in his past led him to ask if the family had a coat of arms. "Your uncle Benjamin made inquiry of one skilled in heraldry, who told him there is two coats of armour, one belonging to the Franklins of the north, and one to the Franklins of the West," a relative told him. "However our circumstances have been such as that it hath hardly been worth while to concern ourselves much about these things, any farther than to tickle the fancy a little." The form which Franklin later adopted included two lions' heads, two doves and a dolphin. He allowed his brother John to use it as a bookplate; but he drew the line at letting his sister put it on the cakes of soap which she made and sold throughout the Colonies.

The records of the Franklin family give little indication that it was likely to sport a man of note. For generations indeed, the record appears to have been as featureless as the southern Midlands in which the Franklins were born, worked and died; a landscape of reddish earth, solid hedgerows and Tennyson's "immemorial elms." English poets have often caught its feeling and—for those who know that no hill in southern England rises more than 1,000 feet—no one better than Belloc with his "When I am living in the Midlands / That are sodden and unkind, / .... / and the great hills of the South Country / Come back into my mind."

The Franklins in Ecton appear to have survived the reign of Catholic Queen Mary without damage, despite their strong Protestant beliefs. "They had got an English Bible," Franklin wrote in his autobiography, "& to conceal & secure it, it was fastned open with Tapes under & within the Frame of a Joint Stool. When my Great Great Grandfather read in it to his Family, he turn'd up the Joint Stool upon his Knees, turning over the Leaves then under the Tapes. One of the Children stood at the Door to give Notice if he saw the Apparitor coming, who was an Officer of the Spiritual Court. In that Case the Stool was turn'd down again upon its feet, when the Bible remain'd conceal'd under it as before," a sleight of hand probably commonplace in those difficult times.

The only Franklin who seems to have given a hint of things to come was Benjamin's uncle Thomas, about whom he heard when visiting Ecton in 1758. There he found a decayed old stone building then still known as Franklin House, and there he was taken into the churchyard by his niece, who showed him several moss-covered gravestones of his ancestors.

While the party was unmossing the past, Franklin was told that his uncle had been something of a lawyer, clerk of the county courts and clerk to the archdeacon in his visitations. He had raised money to put chimes in the steeple, and his nephew now heard them play. "If Franklin says he knows how to do it, it will be done," the local people had said when Thomas proposed saving their water meadows from flooding.

At Ecton Franklin learned little about the emigration of his father, Josiah, from the familiar fields of the English Midlands to the perils of a new country across the Atlantic. It is known that Josiah sailed in 1683, and it is easy to assume that his motives, like those of so many other emigrants, were largely religious. Yet what little evidence has surfaced over the years suggests that economics, that spur for mass migration down the centuries, also played its part. Josiah Franklin had barely been keeping his head above water in England and presumably hoped to do better elsewhere.

The city of Boston, in which he landed after a rough seven-week voyage with his wife, Anne, and three children—Elizabeth, born in 1678; Samuel, born in 1681; and Hannah, born in 1683—was still imbued with the stern spirit of its Puritan founders. After 1640 the tide of emigrants from England had ebbed with the coming to power of Oliver Cromwell, but it increased after the restoration of the Stuarts in 1660. Even by the time of Josiah Franklin's arrival, a visitor could report of Boston: "The houses are for the most part raised on the Sea-banks and wharfed out with great industry and cost, many of them standing upon piles . . . their materials are Brick, Stone, Lime, handsomely contrived, with three Meeting Houses or Churches, and a Townhouse built upon pillars where the Merchants may confer." Already Boston was expanding toward the time, a quarter-century later, when 24,000 tons of shipping a year would pass through her harbor and the vessels' masts would appear to "make a kind of Wood of Trees like that which we see upon the River of Thames about Wapping and Limehouse. . . ."

Yet Boston was still almost an island, her connection with the mainland merely a three-hundred-yard-wide isthmus of sand.

And she was still at the edge of open country. At Muddy-River, two miles from the center of the town, there were rich farms where cattle were kept during the summer. There were plenty of horses, says a Frenchman in 1687. "There are even wild ones in the Woods, which are yours, if you can catch them. . . . As for wild Beasts, we have here plenty of Bears, and Wolves in great Number who commit Ravages among the Sheep, if good Precautions are not taken."

The Common, in the center of the town, was a parade ground for courting couples until the nine o'clock bell ordered them home, after which the local constables began their rounds to see that all was well and "to take up loose people." But the town and its immediate surroundings formed only an enclave, a small island of growing Colonial prosperity, psychologically looking eastward across the Atlantic to what many still called "home." Beyond it, to the west, there stretched the wilderness with its Indians, a huge territory of forest and river and mountain whose mysteries kept colonial settlement pressed firmly against the eastern seaboard of an unknown continent. More than half a century later, Lewis Evans, drawing the first maps of the Eastern states, marked the country beyond the Alleghenies "the Endless Mountains."

The Josiah Franklin who settled with his family in Boston in 1683 was a determinedly religious man, believing strongly in the accepted Christian virtues; believing also that only honest work did—or at least should—bring due reward; comfortably sure that the misfortunes of this world would be compensated by the fortunes of the next. For him there appear to have been many misfortunes. Unable to earn a living as a dyer, he became a tallow chandler—a distinct, if minor, step down the ladder in the later seventeenth century. His wife, after giving him three more children, of whom two survived, died in childbirth about five years after their arrival in Boston, her seventh child surviving only a fortnight. Josiah married again within the year, taking as his wife the considerably younger Abiah Folger, a Nantucket woman who bore him a succession of children. Her seventh—excluding one who died in infancy—was Benjamin, born on January 17 (O.S. January 6), 1706. His father had early decided that this child should become a minister, the family's tithe to the church. Events proved that there was much to be said for this. While Benjamin soon developed a dislike of dogma, he remained on comfortable terms with religion, especially, as he put it, when it remained useful. There was also the practical help of his uncle Benjamin, Josiah's brother, who lived with the family while Benjamin junior was growing up. He "propos'd to give me all his Shorthand Volumes of Sermons I suppose as a Stock to set up with . . ." Franklin later wrote.

The boy's upbringing in Boston was happy and unremarkable, being distinguished from that of most children only by the sober virtues of his parents, particularly his father. "He had an excellent Constitution of Body, was of middle Stature, but well set and very strong," the son later wrote. "He was ingenious, could draw prettily, was skill'd a little in Music and had a clear pleasing Voice, so that when he play'd Psalm Tunes on his Violin & sung withal as he sometimes did in an Evening after the Business of the Day was over, it was extreamly agreable to hear. He had a mechanical Genius too, and on occasion was very handy in the Use of other Tradesmen's Tools. But his great Excellence lay in a sound Understanding, and solid Judgment in prudential Matters, both in private & publick Affairs. In the latter indeed he was never employed, the numerous Family he had to educate & the straitness of his Circumstances, keeping him close to his Trade, but I remember well his being frequently visited by leading People, who consulted him for his Opinion in Affairs of the Town or of the Church he belong'd to & show'd a good deal of Respect for his Judgment and Advice. He was also much consulted by private Persons about their Affairs when any Difficulty occur'd, & frequently chosen an Arbitrator between contending Parties. At his Table he lik'd to have as often as he could, some sensible Friend or Neighbour, to converse with, and always took care to start some ingenious or useful Topic for Discourse, which might tend to improve the Minds of his Children."

It was with the ministry in view that Benjamin junior was sent to Boston's Latin school. The aim of life here was to train pupils in the use of sufficient Latin to pass into Harvard, the next and almost inevitable step along the path of theological progress in the Boston of those days. At first, it looked as if Josiah's plans were to be justified. Within a year his son had risen to be the head of his class. Then he was transferred to the next class above it so that he might enter the third class at the end of the year.

But Franklin never passed into the third class. Instead, he was taken from the Latin school and delivered into the hands of George Brownell, a well-known Boston teacher who ran a school for writing and arithmetic. Josiah took the step, according to his son, "from a View of the Expence of a College Education which, having so large a Family, he could not well afford, and the mean Living many so educated were afterwards able to obtain, Reasons that he gave to his Friends in my Hearing."

It seems unlikely that this was the real explanation, and Franklin's grandson, William Temple Franklin, recounts a telling story which is omitted from the *Autobiography*. "Dr. Franklin, when a child," this went, "found the long graces used by his father before and after meals very tedious. One day after the winter's provisions had been salted,—'I think, Father,' said Benjamin, 'if you were to say *Grace* over the whole cask—once for all—it would be a vast *saving of time.*'" It was hardly the remark expected of a devout young boy being prepared for the ministry. Josiah, who like the son was a practical man, knew that entrance to Harvard demanded a certain minimum of unquestioning devotion; a scholarship, for which he almost certainly hoped, demanded more. The father cut his losses and the son was sent to Mr. Brownell, where he would at least be assured of the instruction in writing and arithmetic so necessary if bright boys were to help their fathers' trades.

The years with Mr. Brownell were followed by apprenticeship to his father. Josiah Franklin had prospered and two years after Benjamin's birth had moved from the small rented premises where he had subsisted for a quarter of a century to a larger house on the corner of Hanover and Union streets. But although Josiah Franklin was a respected tradesman in the Boston community, he was still a tradesman and his son was employed on the most menial of tasks, "in cutting Wick for the Candles, filling the Dipping Mold, & the Molds for cast Candles, attending the Shop, going of Errands, &c.," as Benjamin remembered in later life. It was in many ways a miserable existence, hardly enlivened by the earnestness with which Josiah Franklin, while concentrating his family's attentions on those things which were "good, just, & prudent in the Conduct of Life," almost totally ignored many of those other things which made for civilized living. In his autobiography Franklin recalled that "little or no Notice was ever taken of what related to the Victuals on the Table, whether it was well or ill drest, in or out of season, of good or bad flavour, preferable or inferior to this or that other thing of the kind; so that I was bro't up in such a perfect Inattention to those Matters as to be quite Indifferent what kind of Food was set before me; and so unobservant of it, that to this Day, if I am ask'd I can scarce tell, a few Hours after Dinner, what I din'd upon." By a slightly warped comparison, he thought this an advantage, since his more sophisticated companions would often be unhappy with poor food.

Franklin led the normal life of a boy full of healthy animal spirits, playing around the tideways of Boston harbor and more than capable of looking after himself. "I remember that, when I was a boxing boy," he wrote years later, "it was allowed, even after an adversary said he had enough, to give him a rising blow." He was a keen swimmer and remained so. He was resolutely practical in this, as in most other occupations. The best way of learning how to swim, he wrote, was to choose a place where the water deepened gradually and to walk into it until it was up to one's breast. One should then turn around so that one faced the shore and throw an egg into the water between oneself and the shore. "It will sink to the bottom," he went on, "and be easily seen there, as your water is clear. It must lie in water so deep that you cannot reach it to take it up but by diving for it. To encourage yourself in undertaking to do this, reflect that your progress will be from deeper to shallower water, and that at any time you may by bringing your legs under you and standing on the bottom, raise your head far above the water. Then plunge under it with your eyes open, throwing yourself towards the egg, and endeavouring by the action of your hands and feet against the water to get forward till within reach of it. In this attempt you will find, that the water buoys you up against your inclination; that it is not so easy a thing to sink as you imagined; that you cannot, but by active force, get down to the egg. Thus you feel the power of the water to support you, and learn to confide in that power; while your endeavours to overcome it and to reach the egg, teach you the manner of acting on the water with your feet and hands, which action is afterwards used in swimming to support your head higher above water, or to go forward through it."

It was typical of Franklin's investigative mind that having learned how to swim he should consider practical ways of improving his performance. "I made two oval pallets, each about ten inches long, and six broad, with a hole for the thumb, in order to retain it fast in the palm of the hand," he wrote. "They much resembled a painter's pallets. In swimming I pushed the edges of these forward, and I struck the water with their flat surfaces as I drew them back. I remember I swam faster by means of these pallets, but they fatigued my wrists. I also fitted to the soles of my feet a kind of sandals, but I was not satisfied with them, because I observed that the stroke is partly given by the inside of the feet and the ancles, and not entirely with the soles of the feet."

There was also the occasion when he wanted to swim and to play with a toy kite at the same time. Lying on his back in the water and holding in his hands the stick to which the kite string was attached, he found himself being drawn across the water. While most boys might have stopped there, Franklin engaged another youngster to take his clothes to the far side of the lake and then made the crossing by kitepower. "I think it not impossible to cross in this manner from Dover to Calais," he noted when recollecting the incident years later. "The packet boat, however, is still preferable."

At the age of twelve, he was apprenticed to his elder brother James, who had recently set up as a Boston printer. This was a natural progress from the cutting of wicks, since Franklin had already taken to books as some men take to drink. He could never have enough of them and he was to enjoy printing them as much as he enjoyed reading them. The feel of a well-bound book, the sight of a well-laid-out page, continued to excite him throughout the whole of his life. However, books were not the sum of things in brother James's print shop. Comparatively little is known about the extent of his business, but an announcement in one of the local papers that he printed for a while stated: "The printer hereof, prints linens, callicoes, silks, etc. in good figures, very lively and durable colors, and without the offensive smell which commonly attends the linens printed here."

Franklin now set out on the profession of which he was to become a master. The uniform of the printer's apprentice then included "a pair of deerskin breeches coming hardly down to his knees, which, before they could be allowed to come into the presence of the ladies, at meeting, on the Sabbath, were regularly blacked up on the preceding Saturday night . . . in order to give them a clean and fresh appearance for the Sunday;

. . . a pair of blue woollen yarn stockings, . . . a thick and substantial pair of shoes well greased, and ornamented with a pair of small brass buckles, a present from his master for his good behaviour, . . . a speckled shirt all the week and a white one on Sunday, which was always carefully taken off as soon as he returned from meeting, folded up and laid by for the next Sabbath. . . . The leather breeches, after several years' wear, got greasy as they grew old, and were only flexible so long as they were on and kept warm by the superflux of youthful heat."

Printing was the profession of which Franklin was to be proud for the rest of his life. When, at the age of about twenty-two, he wrote his own mock epitaph, it read:

> The Body of
> B. Franklin, Printer,
> (Like the Cover of an old Book
> Its Contents torn out
> And stript of its Lettering & Gilding,)
> Lies here, Food for Worms.
> But the Work shall not be lost;
> For it will, (as he believ'd) appear once more,
> In a new and more elegant Edition
> Revised and corrected
> By the Author.

And the order in which he put his qualifications when making his will two-thirds of a century later is equally significant: "I, Benjamin Franklin, of Philadelphia, printer, late Minister Plenipotentiary from the United States of America to the Court of France, now President of the State of Pennsylvania."

The craft did not only demand a different order of thought and intelligence from the trade of tallow chandler. Printers dealt, to lesser or greater extent, with the stuff of dissent. In the Boston of the early eighteenth century even the humblest apprentice was brought into contact with pamphleteers, journalists and authors, men who by comparison with the devout circle of Josiah Franklin saw it as their duty to challenge rather than to obey, to question rather than to acquiesce.

Life had found its meaning. "I now had Access to better Books," he was later to write. "An Acquaintance with the Apprentices of Booksellers, enabled me sometimes to borrow a small one, which I was careful to return soon & clean. Often I sat up in my Room reading the greatest Part of the Night, when the Book was borrow'd in the Evening & to be return'd early in the Morning lest it should be miss'd or wanted." At this early age he also acquired skill in putting forward an argument in the most diplomatic way. He made a practice, he wrote, "of expressing my self in Terms of modest Diffidence, never using when I advance any thing that may possibly be disputed, the Words *Certainly, undoubtedly,* or any others that give the Air of Positiveness to an Opinion; but rather say, *I conceive, or I apprehend* a Thing to be so or so, *It appears to me,* or *I should think it so or so for such & such Reasons,* or *I imagine* it to be so, or *it is so if I am not mistaken.*"

There were two other printers in Boston, both well-established, and James Franklin had a hard struggle to survive. Pamphlets and ephemera provided some business, and when James found that his young brother could write topical ballads he seized on this new source of income. The first opportunity came in November 1718, when the keeper of a new lighthouse, built at the entrance to Boston's Outer Harbor, was swept to his death with wife and daughter. Benjamin swiftly produced "The Lighthouse Tragedy," a lurid piece of doggerel which he hawked along the quays and streets of Boston with great success. A few months afterward, the capture and death of a notorious British pirate brought forth "A Sailor's Song on the Taking of Teach or Blackbeard the Pirate." Years later Franklin himself wrote off the ballads as "wretched Stuff, in the Grubstreet Ballad Stile." Nevertheless, the success "flatter'd my Vanity," he admitted; "But my father discourag'd me, by ridiculing my Performances, and telling me Verse-makers were generally Beggars; so I escap'd being a Poet, most probably a very bad one."

Writing his two doggerel ballads, and proudly selling them on the Boston streets, generated in Franklin the first flutter of a self-confidence that never left him. A decade later he was certainly to write in *Articles of Belief and Acts of Religion* that the earth "on which we move, seems, even in my narrow Imagination, to be almost Nothing, and myself less than nothing, and of no sort of Consequence." But that was rarely the impression he created on those around him.

Franklin's high regard for himself soon came to the fore. In 1719 his brother became the printer of *The Boston Gazette.* After only two years the contract was taken elsewhere, and in 1721 James decided to start his own paper, *The New-England Courant,* named after the *London Daily Courant,* a journal renowned for maintaining the liberty of the press, and for the prosecutions its policy attracted.

The New-England Courant was important to Benjamin Franklin's development in at least three different ways. It brought him into touch with practicing writers, notably Nathaniel Gardner, who wrote regularly for the paper and has been called "perhaps the greatest single influence upon [his] prose style." It gave him an insight into the mechanics of journalism and particularly of pamphleteering journalism. Ever afterward, when it became expedient to persuade the public to support one cause or oppose another, Franklin would know how to phrase the argument, present the facts—or at least those favorable to his cause—and package his case in words that would persuade the ordinary reader. Possibly as important, the experience of *The New-England Courant* gave him an apprenticeship in opposing authority, an occupation which he thoroughly enjoyed and in whose practice he became a skilled operator.

The paper's first issue appeared on August 7, 1721. Four months earlier H.M.S. *Seahorse* had arrived in Boston from the West Indies, and within a few weeks it became evident that she had brought the smallpox with her. In Boston there had been no outbreak of the scourge since the first years of the century, and the precautions now taken were taken too late. By the end of the year no less than 6,000 of the town's 10,500 inhabitants had been struck down by the infection, and some 900 had died. Before the epidemic reached its height Cotton Mather, the most famous of all American Puritans and possibly the most influential opinion-former in Massachusetts, proposed inoculation. This method of warding off a disease had been practiced in China since the sixth century, and by the eighteenth was widely used in the Middle East. However, it was not until after the great English traveler Lady Mary Wortley Montagu had written her famous letter from Adrianople in 1717—"The small-pox, so fatal, and so general amongst us, is here entirely harmless by the invention of *ingrafting,* which is the term they give it"—that the practice became known in the West. Cotton Mather had read one of the first accounts in the *Philosophical Transactions* of the Royal Society of London. But public opinion, as backward then as today in most things, balked at an innovation which involved giving potential victims a minor dose of the infection. James Franklin, sensing where popularity lay, took up the antiinoculation cause and throughout the autumn of 1721 waged a bitter war against Mather and his supporters. James had, of course, supported the wrong side. Mather, whose witch-baiting and sanctimonious self-confidence make him one of the most disagreeable characters of early American history, had undoubtedly been right.

Cotton Mather's fulminations had a splendid vigor. "Notwithstanding God's hand is against us in his visitation of the smallpox, and the threatening aspect of the wet weather," he wrote, "we find a notorious, scandalous paper, called the 'Courant,' full freighted with nonsense, unmanliness, prophaneness, immorality, arrogance, calumnies, lies, contradictions and what not, all tending to quarrels and divisions, and to debauch and corrupt the minds and manners of New England." His father, Increase Mather, supported his son's attack. "Whereas a wicked Libel called the New-England Courant, has represented me as one among the Supporters of it," he wrote, "I do hereby declare, that altho' I had paid for two or three of them, I then, (before the last Courant was published) sent him word I was extremely offended with it: In special, because in one of his Vile Courants he insinuates, that if the Ministers of God approve of a thing it is a Sign it is of the Devil; which is a horrid thing to be related."

Despite the opposition of the Mathers, Franklin always remembered two ways in which Cotton Mather had influenced him. One was through Mather's book *Bonifacius,* later known from its subtitle as *Essays to Do Good,* a copy of which he had picked up secondhand. Some pages had been torn out; but the rest, he recollected almost three-quarters of a century later, had continued to affect him. "I have always set a greater value on the character of a *doer of good,*" he told Mather's son, "than on any other kind of reputation; and if I have been, as you seem to think, a useful citizen, the public owes the advantage of it to that book."

He also remembered the occasion on which he had visited Cotton Mather and had been led out of the house by a way he did not know. As they passed through a narrow passage, Franklin failed to notice a low heavy beam. Despite the warning of "Stoop, stoop," he hit his head on the beam. "You are young and have the world before you," he was told; "STOOP as you go

through it, and you will miss many hard thumps." Franklin took
the slightly ambiguous advice without qualification and at the
age of seventy-eight commented: "This advice, thus beat into
my head, has frequently been of use to me; and I often think of
it, when I see pride mortified, and misfortunes brought upon
people by their carrying their heads too high."

Mather appears to have noted down Franklin as a particularly
bright boy. The brightness was first to be demonstrated early in
1722. Franklin often listened to the young Bostonians who contributed to the *Courant* as they discussed their views and news
with the publisher. "I was excited to try my Hand among them,"
he has written; "But being still a Boy, & suspecting that my
Brother would object to printing any Thing of mine in his Paper
if he knew it to be mine, I contriv'd to disguise my Hand, &
writing an anonymous Paper, I put it in at Night under the Door
of the Printing House."

The following morning Franklin listened to the remarks as his
anonymous contribution was discussed. "They read it, commented on it in my Hearing, and I had the exquisite Pleasure,
of finding it met with their Approbation, and that in their different Guesses at the Author none were named but Men of some
Character among us for Learning & Ingenuity."

Franklin's contribution of about 1,000 words was published
on April 2, and at the end of it James Franklin printed a note
stating that further anonymous contributions from the same
source could be "deliver'd at his Printing-House, or at the Blue
Ball in Union-Street, and no Questions shall be ask'd of the
Bearer." Another thirteen contributions were printed at two- or
three-weekly intervals throughout the summer and early autumn. But if it was remarkable that a sixteen-year-old boy could
successfully hoodwink his brother with such ease, the contents
of the fourteen pieces were even more so. For these were the
Dogood Papers, the reminiscences and potted wisdom of "Silence
Dogood," a middle-aged widow of Franklin's invention who
lived on the outskirts of Boston and who gave her chatty advice
to all and sundry. More than a century was to pass before Franklin was thought to be the author, and it was only in 1868 that
John Bigelow, printing his edition of Franklin's autobiography
—which did not mention the *Dogood Papers*—printed also the
outline which Franklin had written when he had started his life
story. "My writing," it began. "Mrs. Dogood's letters."

The surname of Franklin's creation was taken from Cotton Mather's *Essays to Do Good,* and it has been suggested that "Silence" was derived from Mather's *Silentiarius. A Brief Essay on the Holy Silence and Godly Patience, that Sad Things are to be Entertained withal.* The form of the papers was modeled on Addison's *Spectator.* However, it was the worldly-wise knowledge embodied in the epistles from Mrs. Dogood as much as the natural journalistic skill with which they were pulled together that makes the *Dogood Papers* an omen of things to come.

Were I endow'd with the Faculty of Match-making, [Mrs. Dogood stated on August 20, 1722,] it should be improv'd for the Benefit of Mrs. Margaret [Aftercast, a widow], and others in her Condition: But since my extream Modesty and Taciturnity, forbids an Attempt of this Nature, I would advise them to relieve themselves in a Method of *Friendly Society;* and that already publish'd for Widows, I conceive would be a very proper Proposal for them, whereby every single Woman, upon full Proof given of her continuing a Virgin for the Space of Eighteen Years, (dating her Virginity from the Age of Twelve,) should be entituled to £500 in ready Cash.

But then it will be necessary to make the following Exceptions.

1. That no Woman shall be admitted into the Society after she is Twenty Five Years old, who has made a Practice of entertaining and discarding Humble Servants, without sufficient Reason for so doing, until she has manifested her Repentance in Writing under her Hand.

2. No Member of the Society who has declar'd before two credible Witnesses, *That it is well known she has refus'd several good Offers since the Time of her Subscribing,* shall be entituled to the £500 when she comes of Age; that is to say, *Thirty Years.*

3. No Woman, who after claiming and receiving, has had the good Fortune to marry, shall entertain any Company with Encomiums on her Husband, above the Space of one Hour at a Time, upon Pain of returning one half the Money into the Office, for the first Offence; and upon the second Offence to return the Remainder.

I am, Sir, Your Humble Servant, SILENCE DOGOOD.

Any sixteen-year-old precocious enough to create Silence Dogood had an interesting future. Mrs. Dogood, moreover, was not identified: Franklin was not found out.

Throughout the first half of 1722 *The New-England Courant* continued to criticize the ecclesiastical and civil authorities in

Boston. Eventually, in June, the Governor could stand no more. James Franklin was summoned before the Governor's Council, and for printing what was alleged to be a sentence critical of the authorities, was sentenced to prison for a month. On his release, moreover, it was ordered that *"James Franklin should no longer print the Paper called the New-England Courant."*

The verdict had critical repercussions, and not only in Boston. In Philadelphia, for instance, the *Mercury* stated: "By private letters from Boston, we are informed, that the bakers were under great apprehensions of being forbid baking any more bread, unless they will submit it to the Secretary as supervisor-general and weigher of the dough, before it is baked into bread and offered to sale."

The order from the Governor's Council was greatly to affect Benjamin's life. "There was a Consultation held in our Printing House among [James's] Friends what he should do in this Case," he wrote. "Some propos'd to evade the Order by changing the Name of the Paper; but my Brother seeing Inconveniences in that, it was finally concluded on as a better Way, to let it be printed for the future under the Name of *Benjamin Franklin.* And to avoid the Censure of the Assembly that might fall on him, as still printing it by his Apprentice, the Contrivance was, that my old Indenture should be return'd to me with a full Discharge on the Back of it, to be shown on Occasion; but to secure to him the Benefit of my Service I was to sign new Indentures for the Remainder of the Term, wch were to be kept private." Thus James would technically retain a legal hold on his brother's services while evading the Council's judgment.

The *Courant,* published again under new management, led off with a typically ironic Benjamin Franklin item: "Long has the press groaned in bringing forth an hateful brood of pamphlets, malicious scribbles and billingsgate-ribaldry." For the next few months the paper ran without trouble. But while the arrangement may have hoodwinked the authorities, it was not a happy one as far as the Franklin brothers were concerned. This is hardly to be wondered at. "The two made up an ill-mated pair," it was once said. "From disagreements they passed to insults. Insults led to quarrels. Quarrels to blows, and with blows they parted." No one knows what the issue was, but Benjamin himself later wrote: "Perhaps I was too saucy & provoking." Whatever the cause, Benjamin now left brother James, confident that the latter would not wish to invoke the new and secret indentures and thus reveal the trick which had been played on the authorities. "It was not fair in me to take this Advantage," Benjamin piously admitted years later.

Franklin now embarked on a venture not particularly uncommon even today. He left home. The enterprise turned out successfully and this, together with his talent for survival and the vivid account that he later wrote of it, has made the exploit one of America's most famous runaway-makes-good stories.

James, deserted by his apprentice, found it easy to block his employment by any other Boston printer even without invoking the secret indentures, and the boy decided that salvation might be found in New York. There was an additional reason for leaving the city where he had been born and brought up: "my indiscrete Disputations about Religion begun to make me pointed at with Horror by good People, as an Infidel or Atheist."

Josiah Franklin had no wish to part with his son, so it was necessary for Benjamin to smuggle himself out of Boston. He left late in September 1723. He was in New York within three days, but after this successful start, everything seemed to go wrong. William Bradford, the printer with whom he hoped to find work, and who was soon to start New York's first newspaper, was working part-time and could only suggest that the youth travel on to Philadelphia, where Bradford's son might be able to offer work.

The first leg of the journey, from New York to the New Jersey shore, was more arduous than expected, since a storm first prevented the small craft he had taken from entering the Kill, then drove it back on to Long Island. There followed a night on the water, in a gale "without Victuals, or any Drink but a Bottle of filthy Rum," and it was more than thirty hours before Franklin landed at Perth Amboy. And he was still fifty miles from Burlington on the Delaware, the town from which he was told he could take a boat downstream to Philadelphia. He set out on foot, in heavy October rain, a miserable youth, soon soaked through, and beginning to wish he had never left home. He had little money and, arriving in Burlington on a Saturday, was appalled to find that there would apparently be no boat until the following Tuesday. But walking by the river he spotted an unscheduled vessel and succeeded in joining it. The crew were soon unable to discover how far downstream they had come and it was after a night's camping out that Franklin finally set foot in Philadelphia.

On that October morning few people would have credited that the dirty, disheveled boy would become its best-known citizen. "I was in my Working Dress, my best Cloaths being to come round by Sea," he later wrote. "I was dirty from my Journey; my Pockets were stuff'd out with Shirts & Stockings; I knew no Soul, nor where to look for Lodging. I was fatigued with Travelling, Rowing & Want of Rest. I was very hungry, and my whole Stock of Cash consisted of a Dutch Dollar and about a Shilling in Copper."

Franklin's arrival in Philadelphia is famous. But for more than two centuries the image of the sage, producing wise sayings at will, much as the conjuror pulls rabbits from a hat, has tended to obscure the picture of the youth. Yet when he stepped ashore at Market Street Wharf, Franklin had characteristics which more than outweighed his poverty. He was only an inch or two less than six feet in height, thickset and muscular, with dark brown hair above friendly hazel eyes. He was obviously able to look after himself, a distinct advantage in the rougher eighteenth century, and of use even today. These physical attributes were compounded by a nimbleness of mind, so that in argument as well as in action he tended to be off the mark quicker than most men. Above all, and largely concealed by his instinctive hail-fellow-well-met nature, there was a steely determination to succeed and some impatience with those who got in his way.

On arrival in Philadelphia he was so tired that, resting in the Quaker Meeting House, he fell asleep for a while. Next day he was off to the office of William Bradford's son, Andrew. Once again, there was no work, but printers always helped each other, and Benjamin was passed on to a Samuel Keimer, who was willing to employ him, at first part-time and soon afterward full-time. "These two Printers," wrote Franklin, "I found poorly Qualified for their Business. Bradford had not been bred to it, & was very illiterate; and Keimer tho' something of a Scholar, was a mere Compositor, knowing nothing of Presswork." Franklin's bumptious words were no more than the truth. He was not only a cut above the other apprentices but also a cut above their masters and would almost certainly have come to the top even without the unexpected—and at first apparently disastrous—intervention of Pennsylvania's governor, Sir William Keith.

Early in 1724, when Franklin had been in Philadelphia a few months, he received a letter from his brother-in-law Robert Homes, the master of a sloop trading between Boston and Delaware. Homes told the young man that his parents were worrying about him. Franklin replied, giving his "Reasons for quitting Boston fully, & in such a Light as to convince him [he] was not so wrong as [Homes] had apprehended." Captain Homes opened the letter when Sir William was visiting him and the Governor was impressed when he read it.

The upshot was that Sir William called at Keimer's printing house. Keimer, expecting that the distinguished visitor wished to see the master himself, was astounded when his new assistant was asked for. "I was not a little surpriz'd," Franklin later recorded, "and Keimer star'd like a Pig poison'd."

The Governor proposed that the young man should set up in business on his own. He promised to use his influence to send him public printing, and it was arranged that Franklin should return to Boston on the next boat, with a letter from Sir William seeking his father's approval. The offer of support was not disinterested. Sir William was at odds with "the Proprietors," the Penn family who under a Royal Charter effectively controlled Pennsylvania and who had appointed him six years previously. He badly needed a first-class printer to spread his views.

In due course Franklin returned to Boston, armed with the letter from the Governor to his father which said "many flattering things of me to my Father, and strongly recommending the Project of my setting up at Philadelphia, as a Thing that must make my Fortune." However, Franklin the elder was not impressed and refused to allow his son to start business on his own at the tender age of eighteen. When Benjamin returned to Philadelphia some weeks later it was merely as assistant to Samuel Keimer once more.

The Governor appeared little disturbed at Josiah Franklin's refusal. "And since he will not set you up," he said on hearing the news, "I will do it my self. Give me an Inventory of the Things necessary to be had from England, and I will send for them. You shall repay me when you are able; I am resolv'd to have a good Printer here, and I am sure you must succeed." Franklin estimated that the necessary printing equipment would cost about £100, and the Governor thereupon suggested that he should sail to London to buy the equipment. It would, it was assumed, be bought on letters of credit provided by the Governor, who would also give the young man introductions to useful people in England.

Before the *London Hope* sailed from Philadelphia on November 5, 1724, Franklin called on the Governor but found him engaged. He was told that when the ship anchored off New Castle, down the Delaware, Sir William would be there; but another hitch occurred. "The Governor was there," Franklin later recalled, "But when I went to his Lodging, the Secretary came to me from him with the civillest Message in the World, that he could not then see me being engag'd in Business of the utmost Importance; but should send the Letters to me on board, wish'd me heartily a good Voyage and a speedy Return, &c." Franklin's suspicions were not aroused, although he described himself as a little puzzled, and he later expected that a colleague of the Governor who came aboard at New Castle had brought the expected letters. This was not so.

The seven-week transatlantic voyage, the first of eight which Franklin was to make, involved hardships that have almost completely disappeared during the last two hundred and fifty years. The small vessel, a blunt-nosed packet difficult to control, sailed east through the winter storms from one deep trough of waves to the next, buffeted on the intervening crests before the stomach-turning lurch that followed. Salt pork, salt beef, hard biscuit formed the staple diet. Through the long nights the passengers, battened down below deck in a near-darkness relieved only by a swinging oil lamp, could console themselves with one thought: every miserable hour that passed brought nearer the end of their 3,000-mile journey.

Eventually, on Christmas Eve, the *London Hope* docked at Gravesend, a few miles down the Thames from London. Shortly afterward, Franklin learned from Thomas Denham, a friendly Quaker merchant with whom he had struck up an acquaintance on the ship, that he should not expect the promised letters from Governor Keith. He "let me into Keith's Character, told me there was not the least Probability that he had written any Letters for me, that no one who knew him had the smallest Dependance on him, and he laught at the Notion of the Governor's giving me a Letter of Credit, having as he said no Credit to give." Denham was right. There were no letters.

Franklin's reliance on the governor whom no one else trusted was one indication that he was as yet little versed in the ways of the world. Another was his faith in a colleague, James Ralph, who traveled on the ship with him. Only after they had arrived in London did Franklin discover that Ralph had no intention of returning to America, but was deserting his wife and child in Philadelphia.

The two young men took lodgings in Little Britain, a street of houses to the north of St. Paul's, and Franklin found work with Palmer's, a well-known firm of printers in St. Bartholomew Close. It was here that he was alerted to the dangers of lead poisoning. Some compositors, he learned, had lost the use of their hands, apparently by breathing in fumes when they heated their wet cases of leaden type. But colleagues said that it was not the effluvia but the particles of metal swallowed by workmen who did not wash their hands before eating. Franklin noted the information, considered it briefly, and then pigeonholed it for future use.

He worked at Palmer's for a year, then moved to the larger firm of Watts. Here he might have remained had not Mr. Denham, who had enlightened him about the Governor, sought him out and explained that he was returning to Philadelphia. "He propos'd to take me over as his Clerk, to keep his Books (in which he would instruct me) copy his Letters, and attend the Store. He added, that as soon as I should be acquainted with mercantile Business he would promote me by sending me with a Cargo of Flour & Bread, &c. to the West Indies, and procure me Commissions from others; which would be profitable, & if I manag'd well, would establish me handsomely." The £50 a year offered was less than Franklin was earning as a printer. But he was homesick—"I was grown tired of London, remember'd with Pleasure the happy Months I had spent in Pennsylvania, and wish'd again to see it." He accepted the offer and sailed for Philadelphia on July 22, 1726.

Franklin had been in the London of Swift, Defoe, Fielding and Samuel Richardson for only eighteen months, but the experience had consolidated the foundation on which he was to build his future. The work in Palmer's and Watts had fleshed out the principles he had learned in Boston and Philadelphia and from now on he was to have the craft of printer at his fingertips. But there had been other incidents which were omens for the future. One was his approach to a young woman whom his friend Ralph had met in London, had begun living with and had then abandoned. "I grew fond of her Company," Franklin subsequently wrote, "and being at this time under no Religious Restraints, & presuming on my Importance to her, I attempted Familiarities . . . which she repuls'd with a proper Resentment, and acquainted [Ralph] with my Behaviour." It is not certain how frequently, or how successfully, Franklin attempted such familiarities throughout a long and active life. He fathered an illegitimate son at about the age of twenty-four, and in his seventies his entertainment by distinguished French women, innocent as it almost certainly was, tended to shock the austere American community by whom he was employed. There is little indication that this was vice rather than vivacity, yet it was to be significant. The records of the times suggest that a useful diplomatic qualification was Franklin's "way with the ladies," his ability to switch on the charm as one can today turn on electricity.

During his brief stay in London Franklin also showed his ability to write controversial polemic. At Palmer's he was employed on setting the third edition of William Woollaston's *Religion of Nature Delineated,* in which the author outlined his "intellectual" theory of morality. "Some of his Reasonings not appearing to me well-founded," Franklin subsequently wrote, "I wrote a little metaphysical Piece, in which I made Remarks on them." This was *A Dissertation on Liberty and Necessity, Pleasure and Pain,* of which Franklin himself printed one hundred copies. The dissertation, which he later considered to be an error, contained his *"present* Thoughts of the *general State of Things* in the Universe," argued that since God was all-powerful and all-wise, and allowed the world to continue as it did, then there could be no place in the universe for free will or for virtues or vices. He agreed that the reasoning, which brought men "down to an Equality with the Beasts of the Field!" would not be popular. And eventually he destroyed most of the copies he had printed.

Yet publication of a pamphlet written by a journeyman printer was distinctly unusual and helped him push his way into the society of educated men. He met James Lyons, the surgeon, author of *The Infallibility of Humane Judgment, Its Dignity and Excellency,* and Bernard Mandeville, the author of *The Fable of the Bees, or Private Vices, Public Benefits.* He tried, unsuccessfully, to meet Sir Isaac Newton. He wrote to Sir Hans Sloane, the founder of the British Museum, was invited to his house in Bloomsbury

Square, and sold him a purse brought from Philadelphia, made of asbestos, whose fire-resistant properties were known but not yet exploited.

He also came within an ace of taking up an unexpected profession. At Watts's printing house he taught one of his colleagues to swim. Some of the young man's relatives accompanied him and Franklin on a trip up the river Thames to Chelsea. "In our Return," Franklin wrote, "at the Request of the Company . . . I stript & leapt into the River, & swam from near Chelsea to Blackfryars [a distance of about three and a half miles], performing on the Way many Feats of Activity both upon & under Water, that surpriz'd & pleas'd those to whom they were Novelties."

Some while afterward he was sent for by Sir William Wyndham, a former secretary of state for war, who had heard of the exploit. "He had two Sons about to set out on their Travels," Franklin wrote; "he wish'd to have them first taught Swimming; and propos'd to gratify me handsomely if I would teach them. They were not yet come to Town and my Stay was uncertain, so I could not undertake it. But from this Incident I thought it likely, that if I were to remain in England and open a Swimming School, I might get a good deal of Money. And it struck me so strongly, that had the Overture been sooner made me, probably I should not so soon have returned to America."

But Denham's offer had been accepted, and Franklin sailed from London on July 23, 1726, in the *Berkshire* on a voyage to Philadelphia that was to take about ten weeks. As they worked their way down the Thames and along the Channel coast, he went ashore with the handful of other passengers wherever possible. He took a poor view of Gravesend, where he saw "the chief dependence of the people [as] being the advantage they make of imposing upon strangers. If you buy any thing of them, and give half what they ask, you pay twice as much as the thing is worth." Portsmouth, and the small towns of Cowes, Newport and Yarmouth on the Isle of Wight, were all more pleasant, and Franklin, always interested in new experiences, did a good deal of simple sightseeing. Only after the winds at last changed and the *Berkshire* was able to beat out westward to the open sea did boredom begin. It was relieved when dolphins followed the ship, to be caught if possible and eaten; when flying fishes could be reported; and when there was an eclipse first of the sun and then of the moon.

For most of the voyage the story was monotonous enough. "I rise in the morning and read for an hour or two perhaps," Franklin reported in his "Journal," "and then reading grows tiresome. Want of exercise occasions want of appetite, so that eating and drinking affords but little pleasure. I tire myself with playing at draughts, then I go to cards; nay, there is no play so trifling or childish, but we fly to it for entertainment."

He did, however, find time to write out what he later called a *"Plan . . . for regulating my future Conduct in Life."* Although the plan itself has been lost, the four main points were presumably similar to those printed nearly a century later.

"1. It is necessary for me to be extremely frugal for some time, till I have paid what I owe. 2. To endeavour to speak truth in every instance, to give nobody expectations that are not likely to be answered, but aim at sincerity in every word and action: the most amiable excellence in a rational being. 3. To apply myself industriously to whatever business I take in hand, and not divert my mind from my business by any foolish project of growing suddenly rich; for industry and patience are the surest means of plenty. 4. I resolve to speak ill of no man whatever, not even in a matter of truth; but rather by some means excuse the faults I hear charged upon others, and, upon proper occasions, speak all the good I know of everybody."

Franklin does not appear to have had any copy of the plan when he reported it in his autobiography. However, he claimed that it had been "pretty faithfully adhered to quite thro' to old Age."

He had sketched out the plan on the *Berkshire* before one of the crew, climbing aloft on October 9, shouted down the longed-for word, "Land." Within an hour it was possible to see from the heaving deck what looked like tufts of trees on the distant horizon. "I could not discern it so soon as the rest," wrote Franklin; "my eyes were dimmed with the suffusion of two small drops of joy." The *Berkshire* anchored in the Delaware and Franklin expected a lengthy wait before he could get ashore; but a party out on a spree hove in sight and agreed to take him upriver. On October 11 he once again set foot in Philadelphia.

TWO

A TALENT TO
SUCCEED

RANKLIN ARRIVED BACK IN PHILADELPHIA
in the autumm of 1726 a good deal more sophisticated
than the ingenuous youth who had sailed away less
than two years previously. He had consolidated his professional
position; he was now a better printer than most and he was fully
aware of it. What is more, he had made himself acceptable in
London to men whose counterparts in Philadelphia would
barely have noticed him. It is true that he had been singled out,
although unfortunately, by Governor Keith, but that was a circumstance not likely to be repeated. In Philadelphia he had been
merely a printer's apprentice. In London he had been drawn on
to the periphery of that rumbustious society of authors and
pamphleteers, polemicists and scientists, which made the city an
intellectual center of eighteenth-century Europe. If in 1726 any
one man was determined to make his mark in Philadelphia, it
was the confident Benjamin Franklin, aged just twenty.

But if Franklin was ready for Philadelphia, Philadelphia was by
now ready for him. It was less than fifty years since some twenty-

six million acres lying between the Delaware and the Alleghenies had been granted to William Penn, son of Admiral William Penn and a dedicated Quaker. When the Admiral had died in 1670 he had been owed £16,000 by the British Crown, and the American territory was granted in settlement of the debt. Penn wished to call the area Sylvania because of its great tracts of forest. However the king, to whom Penn had to deliver two beaver skins each year plus one-fifth of the Colony's gold and silver, insisted on the name being prefixed with "Penn."

William Penn himself had landed in 1682 from the *Welcome* after a voyage from England in which nearly a third of the three hundred settlers and crew had died from smallpox. But no time had been lost in building, along the orderly lines that he had laid down, a township in the wilderness. In those early days it was the abundance of wildlife on the peninsula between the Delaware and Schuylkill rivers which impressed all comers. Fish, fowl and animals, Penn wrote, were of "divers Sorts, some for Food and Profit, and some for Profit only; For Food, as well as Profit, the Elk, as big as a small Ox, Deer bigger than ours, Beaver, Racoon, Rabbits, Squirrels, and some eat Young Bear and commend it. Of Fowl of the Land, there is the Turkey (Forty and Fifty Pound Weight) which is very great; Pheasants, Heath-Birds, Pigeons, and Partridges in Abundance." Wild pigeons, wrote one of the early settlers, "were like clouds, and often flew so low as to be knocked down with sticks." Another wrote that he and his family had "peaches by cartloads. The Indians bring us 7 or 8 fat bucks of a day. Without rod or net we catch abundance of herrings, after the Indian manner, in pinfolds [pens or traps]. Geese, ducks, pheasants are plenty." Swans abounded and so did excellent oysters, six inches long.

The caves along the Delaware which the advance guard of the settlers had improvised into temporary homes quickly gave way to log huts, and then, as Penn's plans began to be carried out, were superseded by brick and stone houses on the nine streets running east and west between the two rivers, each road named after a local tree. Numbered north-south roads completed the gridiron pattern of what was soon a swiftly expanding town. Each plot, Penn proudly wrote, had "room enough for a House, Garden and small Orchard, to the great Content and Satisfaction of all here concerned."

Although religious freedom was guaranteed in Philadelphia,

as it was in the rest of Pennsylvania, Penn's aim had been the foundation of a Quaker colony, and Quakers formed a majority of the immigrants who flooded in from Europe during the last years of the seventeenth century. They formed a majority of the administration, and their influence percolated all aspects of life, public and private. But during the first years of the eighteenth century the balance began to change once more. Just as the township on the fringe of the wilderness had been transformed into Penn's "city of brotherly love," so did it now in turn begin to change from the center of a religious experiment into the prosperous commercial center of the Eastern Seaboard.

In 1696 the Governor of Pennsylvania reported that within the previous fourteen years Philadelphia had drawn equal with the city of New York in trade and riches. During the first years of the eighteenth century flour mills, paper mills and steel furnaces were started along the two rivers bounding the town, while in the year that Franklin returned from London the first shipyards were opened on the Delaware. With the growth of commerce there grew up also a new merchant class, formed of men who sometimes appeared to have little in common with their immigrant ancestors and whose links with the ruling Quakers were tenuous or nonexistent. Here was the ideal environment for any ambitious young man anxious to make his mark.

At first, Franklin worked in the store which Mr. Denham had opened on Water Street. "I attended the Business diligently," he remembered, "studied Accounts, and grew in a little Time expert at selling." It is uncertain how long a natural-born printer with fingers itching to set type and hands ready to operate a press would have remained satisfied with this. However, chance stepped in less than four months later. Early in February 1727, Franklin fell ill with pleurisy, in those days frequently fatal, but eventually recovered. His employer fell ill with "a distemper" and died.

Franklin now once again took work with Samuel Keimer, although in circumstances very different from those of earlier days. Like many printers of the time, Keimer had opened a stationer's shop. While he was to devote his attention to the shop, Franklin was to supervise and train the semiskilled printing staff that Keimer employed.

This situation, with a first-class printer employed by a third-rater, was unlikely to last long without trouble. It came after a few months. Franklin was sacked, then reemployed when Keimer won a contract for printing currency for the neighboring state of New Jersey. Only Franklin, Keimer knew, could do the tricky work involved.

However, Franklin had by this time been approached by Hugh Meredith, one of Keimer's apprentices, who explained that his father was prepared to set up Franklin in business. Despite the warning experience with Governor Keith, Franklin agreed and equipment was ordered from London. While waiting for it he carried on work with Keimer without, of course, revealing his plans.

Franklin was to play an important part in printing the New Jersey money. Just how important it is difficult to say since the only account is by Franklin himself, who rarely made less than the most of his own achievements. "I contriv'd a Copper-Plate Press for it, the first that had been seen in the Country," he has written; "I cut several Ornaments and Checks for the Bills. We went together to [the State printing works at] Burlington, where I executed the Whole to Satisfaction, & he [Keimer] received so large a Sum for the Work, as to be enabled thereby to keep his Head much longer above Water."

The job took three months, and as members of the New Jersey government had to ensure that no more than the specified number of notes was printed, Franklin was brought into touch with many of them, including the secretary of the Province and the surveyor-general. "My Mind having been much more improv'd by Reading than Keimer's, I suppose it was for that Reason my Conversation seem'd to be more valu'd," he remembered when writing his autobiography more than forty years later. "They had me to their Houses, introduc'd me to their Friends and show'd me much Civility, while he, tho' the Master, was a little neglected."

This was but the beginning of Keimer's discomfiture. Soon after he and Franklin returned from Burlington to Philadelphia, the equipment which had been ordered from London arrived up the Delaware. Franklin and his colleague handed in their notices. A few weeks later they set up their own printing shop in opposition, a business from which Franklin was soon to buy out his partner and which was to be the foundation of his financial success.

The rise of Franklin the printer was due partly to the thrusting character of the man. Concentration, determination, the belief that financial success was among the most important things in life, all ensured survival, although they also created weapons with which he would later be attacked. Yet something more was needed.

One word for this extra ingredient without which Franklin would not have succeeded so often is genius. Another is obsession. Once he turned his mind to a project, be it the success of a printing business, investigation of electricity or reconciliation of American and British interests, all else tended to take second place. Furthermore, few of the unwritten rules of conduct were then allowed to operate unduly as deterrents to success. From his youth he was accustomed to playing a rough game in what was, admittedly, a rough age. But he tended to dissimulate, and to carry a homemade halo for use as necessary. Perhaps this, as much as anything else, was responsible for the dichotomy of views about him. "We admire, I think, the lusty good sense of the man who triumphs in the world that he accepts," wrote John William Ward, "yet at the same time we are uneasy with the man who wears so many masks that we are never sure who is there behind them."

To the basic characteristics which were to impel him up the ladder, Franklin added skill as a craftsman, an innate ability to publicize his own ideas and an unerring instinct for seizing any luck which fate pushed his way.

The last two requirements for business success were exemplified by his printing of Pennsylvania's currency. In 1723, when the Colony had begun to supplement the coinage with paper notes, only a small amount of money had been printed, and in 1728 there was much discussion as to whether more should be issued. In general, the wealthy were against notes, believing they led to depreciation of the currency; the poor, less likely to be affected, tended to take the opposite view. There is no doubt that Franklin sincerely believed that an influx of fresh paper money would be economically useful and he put forward this view, at length but anonymously, in *A Modest Enquiry into the Nature and Necessity of a Paper-Currency.* The modest enquiry left the reader in little doubt that paper money was the thing and that he should extol its virtues to the lawmakers. "I think," the author ended up, "it would be highly commendable in every one of us, more fully to bend our Minds to the Study of *What is the true Interest of Pennsylvania;* whereby we may be enabled, not only to reason pertinently with one another; but, if Occasion requires, to transmit Home such clear Representations, as must inevitably convince our Superiors of the Reasonableness and Integrity of our Designs." The pamphlet was well received by the common people in general, Franklin later wrote; "but the Rich Men dislik'd it; for it increas'd and strengthen'd the Clamour for more Money; and they happening to have no Writers among them that were able to answer it, their Opposition slacken'd, & the Point was carried by a Majority in the House." This was not all. "My Friends there," says Franklin, "who conceiv'd I had been of some Service, thought fit to reward me by employing me in printing the Money, a very profitable Jobb, and a great Help to me. This was another Advantage gain'd by my being able to write." Here, in recollection, Franklin slightly gilded the lily. It was Andrew Bradford who gained the contract, although Franklin won the next one, for a further issue of notes two years later.

One thing led to another. Printing the paper money led to other government orders. Franklin soon began to pay off his debts, and to give Philadelphia the correct impression of a sober young man on his way to the top. America's first public relations man is hardly too brash a description, judging by his own statement. "In order to secure my Credit and Character as a Tradesman, I took care not only to be in *Reality* Industrious & frugal, but to avoid all *Appearances* of the Contrary. I drest plainly; I was seen at no Places of idle Diversion; I never went out a-fishing or Shooting; a Book, indeed, sometimes debauch'd me from my Work; but that was seldom, snug, & gave no Scandal: and to show that I was not above my Business, I sometimes brought home the Paper I purchas'd at the Stores, thro' the Streets on a Wheelbarrow. Thus being esteem'd an industrious thriving young Man, and paying duly for what I bought, the Merchants who imported Stationary solicited my Custom, others propos'd supplying me with Books, & I went on swimmingly."

It was not only in his business philosophy that Franklin was maturing. The confident unorthodoxy of *Liberty and Necessity* of three years earlier was by now considered a mistake and was replaced by *Articles of Belief and Acts of Religion,* "a whole Book of Devotions for my own Use," as he was later to describe it. The nub of his argument now was that "since Men are endued with

Reason superior to all other Animals that we are in our World acquainted with; Therefore I think it seems required of me, and my Duty, as a Man, to pay Divine Regards to Something." It is not certain that Franklin's close brush with death, when he and his master had been ill, was a factor in this turnabout; but it was a change which remained for the rest of his life. From now on he believed in "Something," although always ready to direct his fire on what he regarded as the more questionable aspects of religion. The use of prayer was one of them and when, some years later, his brother John was sailing with the Colonial forces for an attack on the French—and therefore Catholic—fortress of Louisburg, Franklin revealed his views in the following letter. "You have a fast and prayer day [to ensure victory]; in which I compute five hundred thousand petitions were offered up to the same effect in New England, which added to the petitions of every family morning and evening, multiplied by the number of days since January 25th [the date when the expedition was approved], make forty-five millions of prayers; which, set against the prayers of a few priests in the garrison, to the Virgin Mary, give a vast balance in your favor. If you do not succeed, I fear I shall have but an indifferent opinion of Presbyterian prayers in such cases, as long as I live. Indeed, in attacking strong towns I should have more dependence on *works,* than on *faith.*"

The same skeptical strain runs through much of his writings. Religion was frequently useful. But some of its manifestations should be viewed with caution.

In the autumn of 1728, when Franklin wrote his *Articles of Belief,* there was only one newspaper in Philadelphia. This came from Bradford's press and was, in Franklin's words, "a paltry thing, wretchedly manag'd, & no way entertaining; and yet ... profitable to him." Confident that a good paper would drive out bad, Franklin decided to start his own, but then let the news of the project slip out. Samuel Keimer prepared to forestall him with a publication of his own. But even in his early twenties, Franklin was not a man to be crossed. Without delay he began writing for Bradford's paper; "To wreck his rival's enterprise," as one of his early biographers described it. "By this means," he himself later wrote, "the Attention of the Publick was fix'd on that Paper, & Keimers Proposals which we burlesqu'd & ridicul'd, were disregarded. He began his Paper however, and after carrying it on three Quarters of a Year, with at most only 90

Subscribers, he offer'd it to me for a Trifle, & I having been ready some time to go on with it, took it in hand directly, and it prov'd in a few Years extreamly profitable to me."

Keimer's paper had the lumbering title of the *Universal Instructor in all Arts and Sciences: and Pennsylvania Gazette."* Franklin pared the title down to *The Pennsylvania Gazette* and proceeded to make a fortune from it. A note in the first number of the paper revealed both percipience and arrogance in its twenty-three-year-old owner. "The Author of a Gazette (in the Opinion of the Learned)," he said, "ought to be qualified with an extensive Acquaintance with Languages, a great Easiness and Command of Writing and Relating Things cleanly and intelligibly, and in few Words; he should be able to speak of War both by Land and Sea; be well acquainted with Geography, with the History of the Time, with the several Interests of Princes and States, the Secrets of Courts, and the Manners and Customs of all Nations. Men thus accomplish'd are very rare in this remote Part of the World; and it would be well if the Writer of these Papers could make up among his Friends what is wanting in himself." It was, at the very least, one way of obtaining a flow of contributions.

From the start *The Pennsylvania Gazette* had all the hallmarks of success, and of an owner who was critical, outspoken—and admiring of the British to what now seems a surprising extent. It was natural enough that a third of a century later Franklin should enjoy the sophisticated London society that thought something of him; that the pleasure of exercising influence should affect his regard for the environment in which it was exercised; and that, gregarious man that he was, he should begin to see himself as a propagandist of Empire. Certainly in the 1750s Franklin, as surely as A. C. Benson, the author of Britain's "Land of Hope and Glory," a century and a half later, hoped for Britain: "Wider still and wider shall thy bounds set; / God who made thee mighty, make thee mightier yet." Yet these chauvinistic sentiments, so explicitly set down by Franklin in his fifties, if sometimes fudged by his biographers, were quite as strong in his younger days. Thus in 1729, discussing the Massachusetts Assembly in *The Pennsylvania Gazette,* he concluded: "Their happy Mother Country will perhaps observe with Pleasure, that tho' her gallant Cocks and matchless Dogs abate their native Fire and Intrepidity when transported to a Foreign Clime (as the common Notion is), yet her SONS in the remotest Part of the Earth, and even to the third and fourth Descent, still retain that ardent Spirit of Liberty, and that undaunted Courage in the Defence of it, which has in every Age so gloriously distinguished BRITONS and ENGLISHMEN from all the Rest of Mankind.''

Franklin himself wrote much of most issues of *The Pennsylvania Gazette,* personally chose the news which the paper reported, added the nonnews items which took his fancy, and did not shun the unexpected or racy. Thus "The Drinker's Dictionary" listed more than two hundred words and phrases for drunkenness, including such delights as "He's as Drunk as a Wheel-Barrow," "He's as Dizzy as a Goose," "Loose in the Hilts," "He's got his Top Gallant Sails out," and "The Malt is above the Water." A mildly radical paper which benefited from Franklin's strong and clear prose, *The Pennsylvania Gazette* steadily became influential, not only in Philadelphia but throughout the whole of the province. And just as the papers of the nineteenth- and twentieth-century newspaper barons exercised influence in the wider social and political worlds, so did the *Gazette* steadily bring Franklin to an influential position in Pennsylvania.

In printing and newspaper production, as in so much else, he understood the benefits to be gained from independence. He bought rags and traded them with papermakers for the finished paper. He also encouraged the Colonies to set up their own paper mills, thus becoming less dependent on Britain, and once told a visitor that he "had established about 18 mills." He also purchased a lampblack factory, and was soon making and selling his own printer's ink, and in the days before specialization sometimes cast his own type and cut ornaments for title pages.

With his printing and newspaper business beginning to flourish at the end of the 1720s, Franklin needed only one addition to complete the picture of the up-and-coming Philadelphian. The requirement was a wife, and he set about filling it with his customary efficiency and zeal. Mrs. Godfrey, who with her husband lodged in the house he rented as his printer's premises, had as relative a suitable young girl. She was frequently invited to meet Franklin, who has said that "a serious Courtship on my Part ensu'd, the Girl being in herself very deserving." However, being deserving was not quite enough. "I let her [Mrs. Godfrey] know that I expected as much Money with [the girl] as would pay off my Remaining Debt for the Printinghouse, which I believe was not then above a Hundred Pounds," Franklin has written.

"She brought me Word they had no such Sum to spare. I said they might mortgage their House in the Loan Office." The parents then replied that they did not approve the match, a decision which appears to have surprised the ambitious suitor. The reaction was perhaps only that of a couple unwilling to pawn their house in order to marry off a daughter.

Franklin looked elsewhere; he found no one willing to put up money for giving away a presentable offspring. This was perhaps strange. He himself was distinctly presentable, a well-set-up young man in his early twenties, lacking the plumpness of his later years and radiating an apparently inexhaustible energy. As for his prospects, they were obviously good and almost as obviously improving. Why, then, was it so difficult for the promising young thruster to find a bride? A clue to the answer lies in Franklin's cold-blooded demand for cash from Mrs. Godfrey. A dowry was no more unusual in Philadelphia than it was elsewhere; but the episode, even as Franklin recalled it decades later, when the rough edges might have been smoothed off by time, suggests a young man whose ambition to succeed could at times become offensive. The trait, which appears regularly throughout a long life, was to provide a handy weapon for the enemies that any ambitious man makes. Yet in another way this concentration on the main chance does Franklin's memory a disservice. There are times when motives for his actions in politics, trade or intercolonial relations appear—and probably were—impeccably objective; yet it is usually difficult to ignore the question, "How would they affect the fortunes of Benjamin Franklin?"

After his first failure to find a wife he went a-whoring for a while. Not that he admitted it quite like that. Instead, "that hard-to-be-govern'd Passion of Youth, had hurried me frequently into Intrigues with low Women that fell in my Way, which were attended with some Expence & great Inconvenience, besides a continual Risque to my Health by a Distemper which of all Things I dreaded, tho' by great good Luck I escaped it." The statement was made some forty years later. Franklin did not refer to subsequent sexual encounters, and the frequent assumption that he lived a generally randy life until age quenched lust is an assumption for which there is no firm evidence. The point would be of less interest if Franklin had not spent a good deal of his life extolling virtue. "The issue," it has been pointed out, "is whether or not Franklin was a hypocrite because he worked out, in terms of the utilitarian philosophy of his day, a system of conduct which expressed his ideals rather than his attainment, and then proceeded to violate it on occasion. [D. H.] Lawrence objects to the code, Mrs. Grundy to its violation; they agree in the matter of hypocrisy. In either case Franklin is condemned on ethical grounds."

Within the context of the age this is a little hard. Certainly in Britain, where Franklin had spent a formative eighteen months, and where he was to spend many years, bastards were as thick on the family trees as fruit in a good year. He was to have his own, William, believed to have been born in 1731; William, carrying on the tradition, fathered an illegitimate son in England, William Temple Franklin, before marrying and sailing to America as the royal governor of New Jersey. And William Temple carried on the tradition while serving as his grandfather's secretary in Paris.

The bastardy of Franklin's own son has remained covered in mystery. It was first claimed in a political pamphlet that the mother was a young servant in the Franklin household; then, in London's *The Morning Post, and Daily Advertiser,* that he "had this son by an oyster wench in Philadelphia, whom he left to die in the streets of disease and hunger." The second statement, written at a time when Franklin was considered by many Englishmen as a traitor about whom any calumny might be spread, need not be taken too seriously. Considerably later Professor John Bach McMaster noted that "the law of bastardy [being] then rigidly enforced against the woman and not against the man, she was, in all likelihood, one of that throng who received their lashes in the market-place and filled the records of council with prayers for the remission of fines."

There is also the unscotched rumor that William Franklin was in fact the son by Franklin of the Deborah Read whom Benjamin married in September 1730. Miss Read had first seen Benjamin when he had landed, bedraggled and hungry, on Philadelphia's Market Street Wharf in the autumn of 1723. Shortly afterward, working for Keimer, he had lodged with the Reads and "made some Courtship during this time to Miss Read." But there then came the journey to London, and of the period before he left he wrote: "I had a great Respect & Affection for [Miss Read] and had some Reason to believe she had the same for me: but as I was about to take a long Voyage, and we were both very young, only a little above 18, it was thought most prudent by her Mother to prevent our going too far at present, as a Marriage if it was to take place would be more convenient after my Return, when I should be as I expected set up in my Business."

It is unclear how close Franklin's relations then were with Miss Read. In his autobiography he carefully smudges the involvement, whether by intent or by genuine loss of memory, saying of his time in London, "I by degrees [forgot] my Engagements wth Miss Read, to whom I never wrote more than one Letter, & that was to let her know I was not likely soon to return."

When he did so, in the autumn of 1726, it was to find that Deborah had married during his absence. Her husband was a Mr. Rogers. But to the fact that Mr. Rogers had disappeared soon after the marriage there were added two suggestions: one was that he already had a wife at the time of his marriage to Deborah Read; the other that he had died shortly after his disappearance. Together, these rumors left the way open for Franklin. "Our mutual Affection was revived," he wrote. And he and Deborah Read were married on September 1, 1730—but by common law and without a ceremony since there remained the embarrassing possibility that a nonbigamous Rogers might turn up and claim his due.

That did not happen and Deborah became, in Franklin's words, "a good & faithful Helpmate." A carpenter's daughter, she turned out to be an ideal assistant in the mundane work of the business which Franklin was building up. At a different level she was not such a success; not very literate, as she herself knew, she preferred to remain in the Philadelphia background rather than be a brake on a husband already to be noted in the Colonial firmament, a star determined to go on rising.

The headquarters for what was to become a new force in Pennsylvania was humble enough, "the New Printing Office, near the Market." Here there lived Franklin and his wife; Deborah's mother, widow Sarah Read; William Franklin of the unidentified mother; and Francis Folger Franklin, "young Franky," born in 1732 and much-beloved of his father. "Young Franky" was to die in 1736 of smallpox. His father was by then a supporter of inoculation, and known to be; therefore it was quickly spread about that the young Franklin was one of the few who had died after treatment. His father killed the idea by an announcement in *The Pennsylvania Gazette* of December 23 to December 30, 1736, saying: "I do hereby sincerely declare, that he was not inoculated, but receiv'd the Distemper in the common Way of Infection: And I suppose the Report could only arise from its being my known Opinion, that Inoculation was a safe and beneficial Practice; and from my having said among my Acquaintance, that I intended to have my Child inoculated, as soon as he should have recovered sufficient Strength from a Flux with which he had been long afflicted."

No. 139 Market Street was the first of half a dozen houses which Franklin was to occupy on or near the main street running down to the wharf where he had stepped ashore in 1723. Seven years later, in the words of *The Pennsylvania Gazette*, Franklin "removed from the House he lately dwelt in, four Doors nearer the River, on the same side of the Street," then, some years later, to the corner of Race Street and Second Street before moving back after two years to a site higher up Market Street. While he himself was absent in England in 1761 the family moved to another home on the opposite side of the street. This was to be the last move from one rented home to another before the Franklin family moved in 1765—with Franklin himself again in England—to the next-door site which he had bought in the early 1760s, and where, in the spring of 1763, he had begun to build his own house.

These houses, it will be noted, were all in the same area of Philadelphia. Each was probably slightly better equipped than its predecessor, but there is little indication that as Franklin's position and fortune increased his living conditions moved up the scale at an equal speed. In old age, when he was one of the most influential living Americans, comfort rather than splendor was the characteristic of his home.

And in 1731 he joined the recently formed Freemason's Lodge of St. John's in Philadelphia, the first in the United States. The Masonic brotherhoods of Europe in the Middle Ages had been important craft guilds but their character had changed over the years, and after the Grand Lodge had been founded in London in 1717 an increasing number of its officials were men of aristocratic origin. In London Franklin had noted the importance and influence of the Freemasons and after the St. John's Lodge had been set up in 1727 decided that membership would be of use to a journalist and printer. But even after he began to print favorable stories about the Masons in *The Pennsylvania Gazette* there was delay in his joining. On December 8, 1730, however, he printed a lengthy report which began: "By the Death of a Gentleman who was one of the Brotherhood of FREEMASONS, there has lately happen'd a Discovery of abundance of their secret Signs and Wonders, with the mysterious Manner of their Admission into that Fraternity." Although the paper went on to claim that there were, in fact, no secret signs, it was clear that Franklin was in a position to stir up trouble. Within two months he was invited to join; within another three, now a member of the Lodge, he admitted that his December report was wrong.

This was the start of an involvement with the Masons that lasted the whole of Franklin's life. In 1732 he helped draft the Lodge's bylaws and in 1734 printed the *Constitutions,* the first Masonic book to be printed in America, and also became Grand Master of the Lodge. Fifteen years later he was for a while Grand Master of the Province; and when in France in the 1770s he became first a member and then Grand Master of the influential Nine Sisters Lodge in Paris. Membership certainly helped in the string-pulling which brought desperately needed arms to the struggling United States.

However much Franklin's success was to be helped along by Masonic friendships, Mr. Denham's earlier instruction in salesmanship was another factor. And from the start he sold everything that his printing business could produce, as well as many other goods. An advertisement for October 27, 1729, gives a list of the items that could even then be found in the shop which formed part of his establishment. They included: "Bibles, Testaments, Psalters, Psalm Books, Accompt-Books, Bills of Lading bound and unbound, Common Blank Bonds for Money, Bonds with Judgment, Counterbonds, Arbitration Bonds, Arbitration Bonds with Umpirage, Bail Bonds, Counterbonds to save Bail harmless, Bills of Sale, Powers of Attorney, Writs, Summons, Apprentices Indentures, Servants Indentures, Penal Bills, Promisory Notes, &c., all the Blanks in the most authentick Forms, and correctly printed, may be had at the Publishers of this Paper; who perform all other Sorts of Printing at reasonable Rates."

There were also pamphlets, and books, six hundred of the latter being listed in one of his catalogues. "I would not have you be too nice in the Choice of Pamphlets you send me," he once wrote to William Strahan, the London printer who was his supplier and who became one of his closest friends. "Let me have everything, good or bad, that makes a Noise and has a Run: for I have Friends here of Different Tastes to oblige with the Sight of them. . . . Whatever [James] Thomson writes, send me a Dozen Copies of. I had read no Poetry for several years, and almost lost the Relish of it, till I met with his *Seasons*. That charming Poet has brought more Tears of Pleasure into my Eyes than all I ever read before. I wish it were in my Power to return him any Part of the Joy he has given me."

Franklin always remembered bookselling as a chancy business and half a century later commiserated with a friend whose book had not been as much talked about as might have been expected. "This however is a Matter that is subject to Accidents," he warned. "The Death of a Prince, a Battle or any other important Event happening just on the Publication of a new Book, tho' a very good one, occasion it to be little spoken of and for some time almost forgotten. We Printers & Booksellers are well acquainted with this."

More than a bookseller, newspaper publisher, printer and stationer, Franklin also sold from his shop iron stoves and cakes of the Crown soap that members of his family made in Boston. "It was a shop which defies description, hard by the marketplace in High Street," it has been claimed. "There were to be had imported books, legal blanks, paper and parchment, Dutch quills and Aleppo ink, perfumed soap, Rhode Island cheese, Chapbooks such as the peddlers hawked, pamphlets such as the Quakers read, live-geese feathers, bohea tea, coffee, very good sack, and cash for old rags."

In addition, tucked in between Franklin's other multifarious activities was his work as the poor man's moneylender. Carefully marked down in his business books were loans as small as two shillings, others ranging up to £200, and a loan of twenty-five shillings made to his brother-in-law John Read.

The Pennsylvania Gazette was soon flourishing. But there were other indications of Franklin's success as a printer. In 1741 he published the earliest American medical treatise, Cadwallader Colden's *Essay on the Iliac Passion*. Three years later his press produced the first novel to be printed in America, Samuel Richardson's *Pamela*. *The Pennsylvania Gazette* published the first detailed account of the Niagara Falls—sent from Albany by the

Swedish traveler Peter Kalm, who asked Franklin to turn it into better English before printing it. And Franklin's own successful general magazine—*The General Magazine and Historical Chronicle for all the British Plantations in America*—published America's first magazine advertisement. "There is a FERRY kept over Potomack (by the Subscriber)," this said, "being the Post Road and much the nighest way from Annapolis to Williamsburg, where all Gentle-men may depend on a ready Passage in a good new Boat with able Hands. By Richard Brett, Deputy-Post-Master at Potomack." And from 1733 on, there was *Poor Richard's Almanack*, which made Franklin famous throughout North America.

In all that he printed he showed the spirit of the enthusiastic craftsman. Nearly half a century later, when ambassador of the infant United States to the Court of Versailles, he set up his own press in Passy, a useful instrument for the printing of propaganda material to be used in the war with Britain. Visiting the establishment of the greater printer François Ambroise Didot in 1780, he operated one of the famous man's presses with a familiarity which surprised everyone. "Do not be astonished, Sirs," said Franklin, "it is my former business." And in *Poor Richard's Almanack* the printer who abhorred bad work could not refrain from quoting a salutary story about printers' errors. "I have heard," he wrote there, "that once, in a new Edition of the 'Common Prayer,' the following Sentence, 'We shall all be chang'd in a Moment, in the Twinkling of an Eye'; by the Omission of a single Letter, became, 'We shall all be hang'd in a Moment, &c.' to the no small Surprize of the first Congregation it was read to."

Almanacs were popular in the American colonies during the first half of the seventeenth century, and Philadelphia alone had no less than six when, on December 28, 1732, *The Pennsylvania Gazette* announced the publication of: "POOR RICHARD: AN AL-MANACK containing the Lunations, Eclipses, Planets Motions and Aspects, Weather, Sun and Moon's rising and setting, Highwater &c. besides many pleasant and witty Verses, Jests and Sayings, Author's Motive of Writing, Prediction of the Death of his Friend Mr. Titan Leeds, Moon no Cuckold, Batchelor's Folly, Parson's Wine and Baker's Pudding, Short Visits, Kings and Bears, New Fashions, Game for Kisses, Katherine's Love, Different Sentiments, Signs of a Tempest, Death a Fisherman, Conjugal Debate, Men and Melons, H. the Prodigal, Breakfast in Bed,

Oyster Lawsuit, &c. by RICHARD SAUNDERS, Philomat." "Richard Saunders" was, of course, a pseudonym, like the worldly-wise Silence Dogood, while "Philomat" gave him the distinction of being a lover of learning. Produced as *Poor Richard* from 1733 until 1748, and as *Poor Richard improved* from then onward until 1758, the *Almanack* helped to make Franklin's name known for the first time to many thousands of ordinary readers.

The range of its contents was somewhat above the average, since most almanacs were hard-pressed to produce the necessary maxims, jokes and other fillers which padded out the required calendar, list of inns, dates of fairs, dates of eclipses and weather forecasts. More remarkably, Franklin was able to keep up the standard until he left for London in 1757. From the first, *Poor Richard* overwhelmed its opposition and was soon selling 10,000 copies a year throughout the Colonies, an enormous number for the time.

Success was largely due to Franklin's flair for touching the ordinary reader. "Daring and prodigality, marks of the aristocrat, had no personal or professional value for the butcher, the baker, the candlestick-maker," it has been said of the almanac. And Franklin, son of a candlemaker, knew what the most diligent readers of almanacs wanted. "He's a Fool that makes his Doctor his Heir" (1733); "He that drinks fast, pays slow" (1733); "The Bell calls others to Church, but itself never minds the Sermon" (1754); "To be intimate with a foolish Friend, is like going to bed with a Razor" (1754); "*Mine* is better than *Ours*" (1756); "Love your Enemies, for they tell you your Faults" (1756); "A Change of *Fortune* hurts a wise Man no more than a Change of the *Moon*" (1756); "Be civil to *all;* serviceable to *many;* familiar with *few;* Friend to *one;* Enemy to *none*" (1756)— it was with such aphorisms that Franklin built up the popularity of *Poor Richard.* "I consider'd it," he was later to explain, "as a proper Vehicle for conveying Instruction among the common People, who bought scarce any other Books. I therefore filled all the little Spaces that occurr'd between the Remarkable Days in the Calendar, with Proverbial Sentences, chiefly such as inculcated Industry and Frugality, as the Means of procuring Wealth and thereby securing Virtue, it being more difficult for a Man in Want to act always honestly, as (to use here one of those Proverbs) *it is hard for an empty sack to stand upright.*" Readers of the *Almanack* were therefore warned that "He that riseth late must trot all day," that "reading makes a full man, meditation a profound man, discourse a clear man."

Franklin kept *Poor Richard* going year after year. He started a literary weekly that was not a success. He tried to serve the considerable German-speaking population of Philadelphia and its surroundings with publication of *Die Philadelphische Zeitung*. In the first issue he announced that he would wait for three hundred subscriptions at ten shillings a year before deciding to publish regularly; after six weeks the second, and last, issue announced that only fifty subscriptions had come in. His experiences with the *Zeitung* no doubt strengthened his normal business caution. This was exemplified six years after the *Zeitung* failure when he was asked to print the *Zionitischer Weyrauchs Hügel* (Zionitic hill of incense). This was a collection of 650 hymns designed for use by the Separatists of the province. The religious community at Ephrata founded by Conrad Beissel was to help in the typesetting and Christopher Saur of Germantown was to provide type and ink. "When the type was set and the presses were ready, it was found that there was no paper on which to run off the 791 pages of print," it has been written. "Benjamin Franklin controlled the whole stock of printing paper in the province, and he demanded cash. He distrusted queer people. Saur did not have the ready money, and neither did the [Community]." The situation was saved only by Conrad Weiser, Pennsylvania's chief interpreter between the Colonists and the native Indians, traveling to Philadelphia and organizing the deal. In the not entirely unbiased words of Weiser's biographer, he "saved the publication . . . from disaster at the hands of Benjamin Franklin."

A decade later, an attempt to publish America's first bilingual paper, *Die Hoch Teutsche und Englische Zeitung* (The High-Dutch and English gazette), was little more successful than the *Zeitung*, failing after thirteen issues. But such failures were exceptional. Franklin prospered, and when his business had extended to the limits of Philadelphian possibilities, franchises were set up elsewhere: not only in Pennsylvania, but as far afield as Georgia, Rhode Island, South Carolina, New York, Antigua and Jamaica. In these places he established young printers, supplied them with type and presses, paid one-third of their expenses and took one-third of their profits.

It was all good business. Yet it was also something more.

Franklin had an almost religious belief in the value of the written word. It had begun in his youth, when he voraciously read practically every book on which he could lay hands. It grew stronger as he spread his views on public affairs through the columns of *The Pennsylvania Gazette* and it continued into old age, when as a pamphleteer he supported the cause of American independence first in Britain, then in France. He therefore encouraged printers and printing not only as being good for business but also as part of the moral good.

This dichotomy of motives permeates a good deal of Franklin's actions, and is disarmingly revealed in an "Apology for Printers," which he published in the June 10, 1731, issue of *The Pennsylvania Gazette*. "Printers," he wrote there, "are educated in the Belief, that when Men differ in Opinion, both Sides ought equally to have the Advantage of being heard by the Publick." They cheerfully served, he went on, "all contending Writers that pay them well, without regarding on which side they are of the Question in Dispute."

However, there were limits to this belief, at least according to one story which must have come from Franklin himself. In the early days of *The Pennsylvania Gazette* a contribution was brought into the office with the request that Franklin publish it. According to Isaiah Thomas's history of printing in America, Franklin asked that the piece should be left to the following day, when he would decide about printing it. "The person returned at the time appointed," Thomas has written, "and received from Franklin this communication: 'I have perused your piece, and find it to be scurrilous and defamatory. To determine whether I should publish it or not, I went home in the evening, purchased a twopenny loaf at the baker's, and with water from the pump made my supper; I then wrapped myself up in my great-coat, and laid down on the floor and slept till morning, when, on another loaf and a mug of water, I made my breakfast. From this regimen I feel no inconvenience whatever. Finding I can live in this manner, I have formed a determination never to prostitute my press to the purposes of corruption, and abuse of this kind, for the sake of gaining a more comfortable subsistence.'"

The printing business did not absorb all Franklin's talents for organization and man-management, and from the early 1730s on he nurtured into existence societies, libraries, schools and hospitals that all helped to build Philadelphia into the flourishing city that became the focus for American resistance during the War of Independence; all were steps along the road which was to lead Franklin to a position almost as important as that of the governor of Pennsylvania.

One of the first had been taken in 1727 when he formed a number of his colleagues into the Junto, "a Club for mutual Improvement." They met every Friday evening, went on country excursions once a month in the summer and held an annual dinner in the winter. Each member had to "produce one or more Queries on any Point of Morals, Politics or Natural Philosophy, to be discuss'd by the Company, and once in three Months produce & read an Essay of his own Writing on any Subject he pleased." Typical questions discussed were: "Have you lately heard how any present rich man, here or elsewhere, got his estate?" "What unhappy effects of intemperance have you lately observed or heard? of imprudence? of passion? or of any other vice or folly?" "Do you think of any thing at present, in which the Junto may be serviceable to *mankind*? to their country, to their friends, or to themselves?" "Is there any man whose friendship you want, and which the Junto or any of them, can procure for you?" and "What benefits have you lately received from any man not present?"

Many of the dozen founder members who discussed such questions were young apprentices and, because of this, the Junto was at first known as the Leather Apron Club. Franklin chose them with care. William Coleman, a merchant's clerk, became a merchant in his own right and a provincial judge. Nicholas Scull, a surveyor, became surveyor-general. Joseph Breintnal, a copier of deeds for the scriveners, brought Franklin printing work from the Quakers. Indeed, in his autobiography, Franklin names some members of the Junto before adding: "But my giving this Account of it here, is to show something of the Interest I had, every one of these exerting themselves in recommending Business to us." When the Junto reached what Franklin considered to be the satisfactory maximum of members, subsidiary groups—the Vine, the Union, the Band—were formed on the outskirts of Philadelphia or beyond, and reported regularly to the Junto.

From this group, motivated by the wish to do good and an inclination for making profit, there was to grow a variety of public institutions. The first was Philadelphia's public library. In

1730 Franklin proposed to the Junto that since members' books were often consulted about the questions they discussed, "it might be convenient to us to have them all together where we met, that upon Occasion they might be consulted; and by thus clubbing our Books to a common Library, we should, while we lik'd to keep them together, have each of us the Advantage of using the Books of all the other Members, which would be nearly as beneficial as if each owned the whole." This idea failed "for want of due Care of [the books]," but Franklin then proposed something more ambitious: a subscription library which could be joined by anyone prepared to pay an entrance fee and an annual subscription. Fifty subscribers each willing to pay an entrance fee of £2 were soon found, and early in 1732 the first order of books to supplement the existing stock was sent off to Peter Collinson, a London Quaker who had acquaintances in Philadelphia.

The books were at first kept in the house being used as the Junto's headquarters. But the library, and its use, soon grew. Nonsubscribers were allowed to borrow books at 8d. a week for a folio volume, sixpence for a quarto, and 4d. a week for smaller books. A separate building was put up to house them and here there were kept fossils, stuffed animals, the robes of Indian chiefs and other items which gave the library the air of a museum. Thomas Penn, the Proprietor, who virtually ran Pennsylvania and who had presented the city with a plot of land for the building, gave telescopes and globes.

Franklin carried through the library project successfully with the help of a technique he was to use for other enterprises. To start with there came discussion in the Junto. If the idea was favorably received, it was further discussed in the subsidiary clubs. If the reaction was still good, Franklin started to use the columns of *The Pennsylvania Gazette* as a sounding board.

The next public innovation which he sponsored concerned the City Watch, which, he wrote, "I conceiv'd to want Regulation." The system was that certain householders were warned by the constable of each ward in turn for watch duty each night, but could buy exemption for six shillings a year. The money was theoretically for hiring substitutes, but it was more than was needed for the purpose and the constableships thus became places of profit. And the constable, "for a little Drink," Franklin explained, "often got such Ragamuffins about him as a Watch,

that reputable Housekeepers did not chuse to mix with. Walking
the rounds too was often neglected, and most of the Night spent
in Tippling." Franklin read a paper in the Junto criticizing the
system and proposed a regular force of watchmen who would be
paid by householders, the payment being proportional to their
property. The paper was read in the Junto's subsidiary clubs,
supported by *The Pennsylvania Gazette* and its proposals eventually implemented, although only after the lapse of a few years.

Franklin's proposals for a local fire brigade brought more
results more quickly. In 1736 he proposed the formation of a
thirty-man brigade whose members would meet once a month
"& spend a social Evening together, in discoursing and communicating such Ideas as occur'd to us upon the Subject of Fires
as might be useful in our Conduct on such Occasions." The
Union Fire Company was set up on December 7, 1736. Other
companies were formed in Philadelphia, and Franklin was eventually able to claim that the city had the best fire services in the
world.

Much the same practice of first sounding out informed opinion
through the Junto and *The Pennsylvania Gazette* was followed when
he proposed improving the paving, lighting and cleaning of
streets, the foundation of a city hospital and of the College which
eventually became the University of Pennsylvania. More important, however, was the American Philosophical Society, an intercolonial Junto, as it was at first considered. During the first half of
the eighteenth century scientific societies flourished not only in
London but in Edinburgh, Paris, Vienna, Madrid and St. Petersburg, and in 1728 Cadwallader Colden, the doctor and botanist
of New York, had suggested "a Voluntary Society for the advancing of Knowledge." Nothing came of this and it was not until May
1743 that Franklin sent to his friends, Colden among them, a
circular letter. After noting the long, narrow stretch of country in
North America that had been settled by the British, he commented that its geography prevented men from easily passing on
newly discovered facts. He proposed, therefore,

That One Society be formed of Virtuosi or ingenious Men, residing in
the several Colonies, to be called *The American Philosophical Society*, who
are to maintain a constant Correspondence.

That Philadelphia being the City nearest the Centre of the Continent[al]-Colonies, communicating with all of them northward and

southward by Post, and with all the Islands by Sea, and having the Advantage of a good Growing Library, be the Centre of the Society.

That at Philadelphia there be always at least seven Members, viz. a Physician, a Botanist, a Mathematician, a Chemist, a Mechanician, a Geographer, and a general Natural Philosopher, besides a President, Treasurer, and Secretary.

The members were to meet at least once a month and discuss the correspondence received. Their subjects, it appears from Franklin's letter, covered almost the entire field of human knowledge, ranging from botany to geology, art and industry. And to make sure that nothing had gone by default they were to consider "all philosophical Experiments that let Light into the Nature of Things, tend to increase the Power of Man over Matter, and multiply the Conveniences or Pleasures of Life." Franklin himself offered to serve as secretary until someone else could be found.

That the American Philosophical Society should have come into existence owing to Franklin's efforts is not surprising, since a genuine interest in the natural sciences permeated the whole of his life. The word "genuine" is necessary, since the purely utilitarian side of his interests is often stressed to the exclusion of all else. It is true that the Franklin stove is the best-known spinoff from his nonelectrical work; it is true that he is apt to be recalled as the inventor of bifocal glasses and of a multiplicity of gadgets. Writing to a friend of the magic squares which he constructed—each square containing rows of whole numbers so arranged that their sum was the same whether they were added up horizontally, vertically or diagonally—he said he was "rather ashamed to have it known I have spent any part of my time in an employment that cannot possibly be of any use to myself or others." And even as enthusiastic an admirer of Franklin as Bernard Cohen has admitted: "In point of fact, most American scientists do not even appreciate Franklin's major stature in the development of physical thought and would be hard pressed to explain how Franklin could ever have been considered a 'Newton' save in jest." There is a lot to be said for that attitude. Nevertheless, even at the height of Franklin's dedication to the main chance, to winning each battle in his business campaigns, he could easily be drawn away into speculation about natural phenomena that had not yet been reasonably explained. This was true not only of his more significant years when, in London and Paris, he wrestled with the problems of American independence, but of the two decades when he was a successful Philadelphia printer.

Franklin's lust for learning was also to produce the University of Pennsylvania. His first proposals, for an Academy, were drawn up in 1743, but his involvement in defending Philadelphia from French and Spanish marauders caused these to be put aside for a few years. "Peace being concluded, and the [defense] Business therefore at an End," he later wrote, "I turn'd my Thoughts again to the Affair of establishing an Academy. The first step I took was to associate in the Design a Number of active Friends, of whom the Junto furnished a good Part: the next was to write and publish a Pamphlet, intitled 'Proposals relating to the Education of Youth in Pennsylvania.' " From these proposals there rose the Academy and from the Academy there rose in due course the University.

One sign of the scientific mind was Franklin's determination to question, to seek explanations of natural phenomena that could be checked by experiment or observation. Another was his habit of quantifying. When, for instance, the preacher George Whitefield held an open-air meeting in Philadelphia, Franklin came not only to listen, but also to settle a doubt in his mind. He paced back down the street as long as Whitefield could be heard clearly. He then imagined a semicircle with a radius of the distance he had paced, allowed each potential listener two square feet, and estimated that more than 30,000 could have heard the words. "This," he wrote, "reconcil'd me to the Newspaper Accounts of his having preach'd to 25,000 People in the Fields, and to the antient Histories of Generals haranguing whole Armies, of which I had sometimes doubted."

If it was the processes of the natural world which intrigued him, it was their practical effect on human life which he tried to elucidate. Thus he invoked the rotation of the earth to account for the fact that the Atlantic could be crossed more quickly from America to Europe than in the reverse direction. But before his theory could be published he found that it was incorrect and that the discrepancy was due to the Gulf Stream.

His interest in meteorology led him to the discovery that the northeast storms which sweep the Eastern Seaboard of America in the summer begin first in the southwest. This occurred when he was trying to observe an eclipse of the moon from Philadelphia. He was prevented from doing so, he wrote, "by a North-East storm, which came on about seven, with thick clouds as usual, that quite obscured the whole hemisphere. Yet when the post brought us the Boston newspaper, giving an account of the effects of the same storm in those parts, I found the beginning of the eclipse had been well observed there, though Boston lies N.E. of Philadelphia about 400 miles." When preparations were being planned to record the transit of Mercury in 1753, James Alexander, the astronomer in charge, thought that Franklin was the best man to persuade the various colleges of North America to take part. And it was at Franklin's suggestion that on two occasions the Philadelphia merchants sent ships in search of the Northwest Passage.

Another by-product of his scientific bent was the Pennsylvania Fire Place, later better-known as the Franklin stove. By the 1740s the growing population of the Colonies was making noticeable inroads on the great forests which supplied fuel. The heating of houses was growing more expensive, while the wood was used very inefficiently, much of the heat—five-sixths, Franklin estimated in many cases—being lost up the chimney. The Pennsylvania Fire Place dealt with the problem by incorporating a number of passages and vents so that the apparatus drew in cold fresh air from outside the building and, after warming the air in passages kept hot by the escaping gases of the fire, finally discharged it into the room.

The main advantage, Franklin maintained, was that "your whole room is equally warmed, so that people need not crowd so close round the fire, but may sit near the window, and have the benefit of the light for reading, writing, needle-work, &c. They may sit with comfort in any part of the room, which is a very considerable advantage in a large family, where there must often be two fires kept, because all cannot conveniently come at one."

He devised the first of the Fire Places, made of the cast iron which could easily be obtained in Pennsylvania, at the start of the 1740s, but it was not until 1744 that he began to popularize them. He gave one of the early models to Robert Grace, an old friend from the Junto, who owned an iron foundry and who, Franklin claimed, found the casting of the necessary material very profitable. Although Franklin could have patented the ingenious device, he refused to do so since he believed, as he wrote, *"That as we enjoy great Advantages from the Inventions of others, we should be glad of an Opportunity to serve others by any Invention of ours, and this we should do freely and generously."*

What Franklin did do to help Grace's sales was write a propaganda pamphlet with the imposing title: "An Account of the New-Invented Pennsylvania Fire Places: Wherein their Construction & manner of Operation is particularly explained; their Advantages above every other Method of warming Rooms demonstrated; and all Objections that have been raised against the Use of them answered & obviated. &c." In this he quoted from numerous authorities to support and explain the claims made for the stove, and the pamphlet illustrated Franklin's skill as a publicist, particularly for Benjamin Franklin. Although he began with a simple but convincing explanation of how the Fire Place did its job, he quickly went on to point out that women sat more in a house than men and were thus particularly susceptible to the effects of drafts, bad heating and all the disadvantages of conventional fireplaces. Very big fires, moreover, had their own bad effects, since they helped "to damage the eyes, dry and shrivel the skin, and bring on early the appearances of old age." This was sufficient argument to win over the women. He next turned to the menfolk, explaining how easily the Fire Place could be built and enumerating its advantages in a hard-hitting selling prospectus.

However, the efficient advertising man, the innovator, the successful newspaper proprietor already shaping up into the patron saint of getting on, was also something else. The municipal benefactor was also the creator of Mrs. Dogood, and from the foundation of *The Pennsylvania Gazette* onward had written more than one humorous satirical piece. Among the first was *A Witch Trial at Mount Holly,* which poked fun at the witch trials still taking place. And the defense speech of Polly Baker, allegedly prosecuted for bearing a fifth bastard—a speech that in Franklin's hoax was so moving that the judge married her the next day—was convincing enough to deceive more than one reader.

The most famous of these lighter pieces were Franklin's *A Letter to the Royal Academy at Brussels* and his *Advice to a Young Man on the Choice of a Mistress,* both published anonymously. *Advice to a Young Man on the Choice of a Mistress,* reprinted many times—

and under a variety of titles—before its authorship was publicly acknowledged, began by saying that marriage was best. "But if you will not take this Counsel, and persist in thinking a Commerce with the Sex inevitable, then I repeat my former Advice, that in all your Amours, you should *prefer old Women to young ones.*" Franklin provided eight reasons for giving this advice. 1) Because they had more knowledge of the world: 2) "Because when Women cease to be handsome, they study to be good. To maintain their Influence over Men, they supply the Diminution of Beauty by an Augmentation of Utility": 3) Because there was no hazard of children: 4) Because they were more discreet in conducting an affair: 5) While an older woman could be distinguished from a younger one by her face, "regarding only what is below the Girdle, it is impossible of two Women to know an old from a young one": 6) "Because the Sin is less. The debauching a Virgin may be her Ruin, and make her for Life unhappy: 7) Because the Compunction is less. The having made a young Girl *miserable* may give you frequent bitter Reflections; none of which can attend the making an old Woman *happy:* 8) [thly and Lastly] They are *so grateful!!*"

The letter, ridiculing a Prize Question set by a learned academy, proposed another: "To discover some Drug, wholesome and not disagreeable, to be mixed with our common Food, or Sauces, that shall render the natural discharges of Wind from our Bodies not only inoffensive, but agreeable as Perfumes." The proposal was followed up in detail, ending with the suggestion that the "generous Soul, who now endeavours to find out whether the Friends he entertains like best Claret or Burgundy, Champagne or Madeira, would then enquire also whether they chose Musk or Lilly, Rose or Bergamot, and provide accordingly."

Such *jeux d'esprit* were in strong contrast to Franklin's growing reputation as a sober, successful man of business and public figure. In 1736 he became clerk of the Pennsylvania Assembly and the following year postmaster in Philadelphia. The second appointment was most obviously of benefit to him. "I . . . found it of great Advantage," he later wrote, "for tho' the Salary was small, it facilitated the Correspondence that improv'd my Newspaper, encreas'd the Number demanded, as well as the Advertisements to be inserted, so that it came to afford me a very considerable Income." But as in so many fields, it was not only

Franklin himself who benefited; detailed investigation into his postmastership during recent years shows that he made the first intelligent reorganization of the service. One small but typical example is that he had printed, in local papers, the names of those who had letters waiting for them in the post office.

Franklin's appointment as clerk of the Assembly also "secur'd to [him] the Business of Printing the Votes, Laws, Paper Money, and other occasional Jobbs for the Public that on the whole were very profitable." But it was of far greater significance in other ways. When he became clerk, Franklin took the first step on a road that was to lead him into the heart of Pennsylvania politics and the warfare that raged almost continuously between the Assembly and the Proprietors, the Penn family. From there he was to move on into the relationship between the Colonies and Britain, and so into the maelstrom of British miscalculation that led to war and to American independence.

The royal grants under which the American Colonies had been set up were of five kinds. Property might be given to personal proprietors while the government and jurisdiction remained with the Crown, as in the Carolinas and the Jerseys. Property and government might remain with the Crown, as in Virginia and New York. Property might rest in the people and their representatives while government remained with the Crown, as in Massachusetts Bay. Property and government might rest in the governor and company, called the Freemen of the Colony, as in Connecticut and Rhode Island. Or both property and government might rest with one or more personal proprietors and their heirs and assigns, as in Pennsylvania.

The charter under which William Penn and his successors ran the Colony laid down that English laws should operate until the passing of new ones, which could be reviewed by the Crown. This process was begun by the first Assembly, held in 1682, and was continued throughout the following decades. But Penn, and subsequently his heirs, remained "the Proprietors." In practice they ruled through a governor who was appointed by them, who had to obey their instructions and who could be sacked by them. In reality, the reigning Penn was the governor and his appointee was deputy governor, even though the latter was always known throughout the Colony simply as Governor, with Penn being known as the Proprietor.

The arrangement was unsatisfactory, and it was almost inevitable that disagreements would arise between the Assembly on one hand and the Proprietor and his Governor on the other. This likelihood was increased by the privileges accorded to the Penns in the charter—notably the exemption of their lands from taxation. This exemption had been a source of controversy almost since the Colony's foundation, but the argument grew more heated during the later 1740s and 1750s as wars between Britain and France put the Colonies at increasing risk of attack from the French in their Canadian settlements to the north. The routine became familiar. The Assembly would pass a money bill for defense, which involved taxing the Penn estates. The bill would be amended by the Governor so that the Penn estates were exempted. The Assembly might acquiesce or might redraft the bill; but if the new draft failed to accord with instructions the Governor had received from the Proprietor, then back it would go to the Assembly once again, unsigned. Almost inevitably, the Assembly was always forced to give in.

The situation was exacerbated in Franklin's time by the fact that Thomas Penn, the more important of the two "young Proprietors" who succeeded on William Penn's death, chose to remain in London, an absentee landlord who in the opinion of many Pennsylvanians lived in luxury on the fruits of his huge and untaxed lands. This wealth was often grossly exaggerated by opponents, including Franklin, who had raised to a high level of sophistication the practice of presenting facts and figures to suit his own convenience. But in his day the situation was also confused by the changing balance of power in the Assembly and by the changing faith of the Proprietors. The Assembly had for long been dominated by English Quakers or their descendants, but the influx of Germans, Scots and Irish during the first decades of the eighteenth century steadily eroded their majority. Meanwhile the young Penns had been slipping away from the true faith, and in 1743 Thomas was able to write to the Governor, "I felt obliged to solicit the ministry against the Quakers, or at least I stated I did not hold their opinion concerning defense. I no longer continue the little distinction in dress." This distinction was the Quaker simplicity of dress—no lace, no wide cuffs, no lapels and no sartorial extravagances of any sort.

Within this Byzantine situation the duty of the clerk of the Assembly was nominally to record the votes and proceedings of the House. In practice Franklin's duties went far beyond this. At the opening of each session he had to call over the election returns, read the forms on which members listed their qualifications for their seats and make a record of those qualifications. Occasionally he was required to draft bills, and a detailed account of the Assembly's organization suggests how the post put his fingers on the levers of influence. "By order of the House," it says, "he had frequently to amend bills, transcribe copies of particular acts, make a copy of the sessional laws for the printer, search the journals for precedents, prepare an account of unfinished business, and, in the Speaker's absence, adjourn the House."

It says a lot for Franklin's unquenchable energy that during dull debates he beguiled the time by making magic squares "and, at length, had acquired such a knack at it, that I could fill the cells of any magic square, of reasonable size, with a series of numbers as fast as I could write them."

This self-confident, and by now well-rounded, figure regarded Pennsylvania's lawmakers with perceptive eyes and judged them with an even more perceptive mind. In the two decades since he had landed at Market Street Wharf, a youngster in search of a future, he had forced his way through the crowd of men seeking fame and fortune in this bustling city. He had reached his position of influence by hard work, an appreciation of what counted in the race for success and a belief that it was the letter of the law, rather than its spirit, which had to be obeyed. But he had made more than his fair quota of enemies in the upward struggle. He had his devoted supporters. But he was in many quarters respected more than liked and this had made his path a rugged one. It was to have the same effect in the political arena he was now entering and in the greater world across the Atlantic to which the chances of history were now inexorably leading him.

THREE

THE
PROFESSIONAL
AMATEUR

I N 1 7 4 8, AFTER FRANKLIN HAD BEEN
serving as the Assembly's clerk for eleven years, and
three years after the death of his father, he finally
retired from the personal management of his printing business
and began a formal partnership with David Hall, sent to him five
years earlier by William Strahan. He had found Hall a good
worker, had soon promoted him to the post of foreman, and had
increasingly let him manage the business. At the same time
Franklin moved with his family to a new rented house on the
corner of Race and Second streets.

The retirement presented no financial problem. After the reorganization of the business into Franklin and Hall, Franklin still
received half the profits. The printing operations he had set up
elsewhere were all successful and he also owned land in Philadelphia, where property values were steadily rising. His income
when he decided to abandon the career of successful businessman is not certain; but in a Colony where the governor was paid
only £1,000 a year, Franklin was a man of substance.

To Cadwallader Colden in New York he explained why he had retired. "I [have] remov'd to a more quiet Part of the Town, where I am settling my old Accounts, and hope soon to be quite a Master of my own Time, and no longer (as the Song has it) *at every one's Call but my own.* If Health continues, I hope to be able in another Year to visit the most distant Friend I have, without Inconvenience." He had, he went on, discouraged an appeal to serve as a member of the Assembly, a statement it would be unwise to take at its face value. "Thus you see I am in a fair Way of having no other Tasks than such as I shall like to give my Self, and of enjoying what I look upon as a great Happiness, Leisure to read, study, make Experiments, and converse at large with such ingenious & worthy Men, as are pleas'd to honour me with their Friendship or Acquaintance, on such Points as may produce something for the common Benefit of Mankind, uninterrupted by the little Cares & Fatigues of Business."

When he wrote to his mother after giving up the cares and fatigues—of which he had decided to retain only editorship of *The Pennsylvania Gazette* and of *Poor Richard*—he appeared to be living the life outlined to Colden. "At present I pass my time agreably enough," he wrote. "I enjoy (thro' Mercy), a tolerable Share of Health; I read a great deal, ride a little, do a little Business for my self, more for others; retire when I can, and go [into] Company when I please; so the Years roll round, and the last will come, when I would rather have it said, 'He lived usefully,' than, 'He died rich.' "

By now he had two surviving children. First there was the illegitimate William, for whom Franklin had a soft spot but whom Deborah seems only to have tolerated. There was also Sarah, known as Sally, born in 1743, seven years after the death of Franky, whose loss Franklin was to feel for the rest of his life. Sally was always the adored daughter whom he missed on his travels. Sally could do no wrong, as her granddaughter made clear. "On one occasion [Franklin] saw her endeavoring to make a proper button-hole," she has written. "After many efforts she gave up the task in despair. Not one word or look of reproach came from her father at her failure to accomplish her object, but the next day he said: 'Sally, I have made an arrangement with my tailor to have you go to him every day at a fixed hour. He will teach you to make button-holes.''

The fortunes of Sally, and of William, were never far from his thoughts and at first it seems strange that Franklin should retire from active business at the age of forty-two when the prospects of increased success looked so good; strange, however, only if his statements are taken at their face value. Indeed, it is difficult to know how much of what he said about retirement was believed by the man himself.

One hint lies in his comment on "experiments." For by the time he had pulled out from the business world Franklin had already started the electrical experiments that within the next few years were to bring him international fame. The leisure to devote more time to probing the mysteries of this extraordinary phenomenon was almost certainly an important factor in his decision.

In the twentieth century it is not easy to appreciate how thick was the veil of mystery which in Franklin's day still cloaked electricity. Some understanding of the situation is necessary before the nature of his achievement can be appreciated.

It is true that since earliest times men had speculated on the forces which enabled amber to attract lightweight objects when it was rubbed, a phenomenon so mysterious that for centuries its investigation was regarded as little less than sacrilege. But at the end of the sixteenth century the English scientist William Gilbert demonstrated that this inexplicable property of attraction was also a characteristic of resins, sealing wax, sulfur, glass and many other materials. Gilbert christened the phenomenon electricity from the Greek word for amber and showed how its intensity could be measured by means of a free-moving iron needle.

The intensity was very slight and it remained so until, toward the end of the seventeenth century, the German physicist Otto von Guericke mechanized the production of electricity. Von Guericke found that if a globe of sulfur was mounted on a shaft, rotated by a crank and simultaneously stroked with the hand, then electricity would be accumulated on the sulfur. This could be discharged, as electricity, and more could then be accumulated again. The method was progressively improved over the years. One or more globes of various materials were mounted on an axle; around this passed a cord which also passed over a large-diameter wheel. When the latter was cranked by hand the globes or cylinders revolved at up to 1,000 revolutions a minute. In Franklin's homely phrase, "we turn the sphere like a common grindstone."

This development, which put larger quantities of electricity under control of the experimenter, opened the way for theoretical and practical advances during the first decades of the eighteenth century. As early as 1720 Stephen Gray in London wrote a paper for the Royal Society's *Philosophical Transactions* suggesting investigations which led to discovery of the principle of conduction and insulation, as well as of the fact of induction, a paper used to support the claim that Gray laid the foundation of electricity as a science. "Altho' these Effects are at present but in *minimis*," he later wrote, "it is probable, in Time there may be found out a Way to collect a greater Quantity of it; and consequently, to increase the Force of this Electrick Fire, which, by several of these Experiments . . . seems to be of the same Nature with that of Thunder and Lightning."

Gray lived at the London Charterhouse, where charity boys were available for the parlor tricks frequently used to demonstrate the effects of electricity. "One caught an urchin," it has been written, "hung him up with insulating cords, electrificed him by contact with rubbed glass, and drew sparks from his nose."

A decade after Gray was writing, the Frenchman Charles François de Cisternay Du Fay concluded that there might be two kinds of electricity. "This Principle is, that there are two distinct Electricities, very different from one another; one of which I call *vitreous Electricity*, and the other *resinous Electricity*. The first is that of Glass, Rock-Crystal, Precious Stones, Hair of Animals, Wool, and many other Bodies: The second is that of Amber, Copal, Gum-Lack, Silk, Thread, Paper, and a vast Number of other Substances. The Characteristick of these two Electricities is, that a Body of the *vitreous Electricity*, for Example, repels all such as are of the same Electricity; and on the contrary, attracts all those of the *resinous Electricity*."

These experimenters had all noted the production of sparks in their experiments, and in Germany Andreas Gordon, a Scots Benedictine monk, professor of philosophy at Erfurt, found how to augment and multiply the phenomenon. Gordon used a glass cylinder eight inches long and four inches wide and had it revolved at 680 revolutions a minute. According to the Abbé Nollet, writing later in the century, Gordon "increased the electric sparks [produced by the electricity] to such a degree that they were felt from a man's head to his foot, and small birds could be killed by them."

While scientists in Europe were thus groping toward an understanding of electricity, many of them were also transforming the science into an entertainment. Typical was the German George Mathias Bose. "He invited guests to an elegant supper-table loaded with silver and glass and flowers and viands of every description, and, as they were about to regale themselves, caused them to stand transfixed with wonder at the sight of flames breaking forth from the dishes and the food and every object on the board. The table was insulated and received the discharge from a huge glass retort which was revolved in another room. He introduced his ardent pupils to a young woman of transcendent attractions, and as they advanced to press her fair hand, a spark shot from it accompanied by a shock which made them reel." And in Berlin Christian Friedrich Ludolff gave a dramatic demonstration of electricity at the opening of the Royal Academy of Sciences, setting alight a container of sulfuric ether with an electrical spark drawn from the sword of a Court cavalier.

So far, however, no one had devised any satisfactory way of storing large quantities of this puzzling electricity. The answer came only in 1746, and, as so often happens, the discovery was made almost simultaneously by two men, neither of whom knew of the other's work. However, credit is usually given to Pieter van Musschenbroek of Leyden, who described the experience in a dramatic letter to René de Réaumur, the French physicist. "I wish to inform you of a new, but terrible experiment, which I advise you on no account to attempt personally," van Musschenbroek began. "I am engaged in research to determine the strength of electricity. With this object I had suspended by two blue silk threads, a gun barrel, which received electricity from a glass globe which was rapidly turned on its axis by one operator, while another pressed his hands against it. From the other end of the gun barrel hung a brass wire, the end of which entered a glass jar, which was partly full of water. I held this jar in my right hand, while with my left I tried to draw sparks from the gun barrel. Suddenly I received in my right hand a shock of such violence that my whole body was shaken as by a lightning stroke. The vessel, although glass, was not broken, nor was the hand displaced by the commotion: but the arm and body were affected in a more terrible way than I can describe. In a word, I believed that I was done for."

The essence of van Musschenbroek's device, soon to be known as the Leyden jar, was a glass jar, filled with either water or lead shot, whose inner and outer surfaces were coated with a conducting material. A wire pierced an insulating cork which filled the open top of the jar. If the wire was brought into contact with a charged body the jar could accumulate a considerable amount of electricity.

The significance of this new ability to store electricity was shown the same year by the Abbé Nollet, the formidable French experimenter who was to become one of Franklin's most persistent enemies. Commanded by Louis XV to demonstrate the wonders of electricity, Nollet set up his apparatus in the Palace of Versailles. Here, 148 French Guards were paraded in the Grande Galerie, and ordered to link hands with the men on either side. The first and the last in the line then each grasped a metal wire which was attached to Nollet's apparatus. When all was ready the accumulated charge was sent through the wire; all 148 guardsmen jumped simultaneously as they felt the shock. The demonstration was surpassed when a group of Carthusian monks in Paris were formed up for Nollet in a line nine hundred feet long, each man being connected to the next by a length of iron wire. As with the guardsmen, when the current was applied all simultaneously gave a sudden jump. "The exclamations of surprise were simultaneous," reported Nollet, "even though they came from two hundred mouths."

Nollet had shown that the unexplained phenomenon—the invisible electric charge—appeared to be felt at the same time at all points along the circuit. Shortly afterward William Watson, doctor, naturalist and experimental physicist, gave a comparable demonstration in London, using the 1,200-foot-wide river Thames at Westminster to show that an electric charge could instantaneously be sent across the river and back. Thus by 1746 it was known in Europe that the inexplicable electricity stored in a Leyden jar could be transmitted over considerable distances, and that it produced a startling shock in human beings. Almost everything else was speculation.

In the American Colonies electricity had been mentioned in

a science course at Harvard at the end of the seventeenth century and it was possibly discussed after a chair of Natural Philosophy and Mathematics was set up at William and Mary College in 1712. Some lectures and demonstrations on the subject were given by Isaac Greenwood in Boston and Philadelphia in 1740, and interest, once aroused, grew quickly. After 1746, the date at which Franklin enters the scene, scientific information began to arrive more regularly from Europe, and even as staunch a supporter of Franklin's individual genius as Professor Cohen has stated: "It is no exaggeration to say that Watson was Franklin's master and guide in the study of electricity. Franklin studied each of Watson's writings with care and they influenced his own concept of electrical action in a variety of ways."

At first glance Franklin, a man trained in the arts of survival within the worlds of competitive Colonial printing and hard-hitting Colonial politics, seemed an unlikely candidate as scientist. But in two ways his background helped. The electrical experimenter of the eighteenth century had frequently to improvise, to alter and improve many parts of his equipment. The successful printer had to deal with similar practical handyman problems. More important, Franklin's tough upbringing had taught him the value of skepticism, of taking nothing for granted, of always asking yet one more question—the hallmark of the scientist down the ages.

The introduction of this practical Philadelphian to the esoteric mysteries of electricity appears to have been almost by chance. In his autobiography he stated: "In 1746, being at Boston, I met there with a Dr Spence, who was lately arrived from Scotland, and show'd me some electric Experiments. They were imperfectly perform'd, as he was not very expert; but being on a Subject quite new to me, they equally surpriz'd and pleas'd me. Soon after my Return to Philadelphia, our Library Company receiv'd from Mr Peter Collinson, F.R.S. [Fellow of the Royal Society] of London a Present of a Glass Tube, with some Account of the Use of it in making such Experiments." However, after Collinson's death in 1768, his son Michael received a letter from Franklin telling him that his father had in 1745 "sent an account of the new German experiments in electricity, together with a glass tube and directions for using it, so as to repeat the experiment. This was the first notice I had of that curious subject which I afterwards prosecuted with some diligence, being encouraged by the friendly reception he gave to the letters I wrote to him upon it."

Research during the century that followed Franklin's death showed that "Dr. Spence" was Dr. Archibald Spencer, from Edinburgh, who between 1743 and 1751 lectured in various cities along the Eastern Seaboard of North America. It is almost certain that Franklin met Spencer at Boston in 1743, not three years later, a fact which at first glance makes his letter to Michael Collinson seem curious. Recently, however, N. H. de V. Heathcote of the Department of the History and Philosophy of Science, University College, London, has thrown fresh light on the discrepancy. Spencer's experiments, he has suggested, covered a variety of subjects. Only three years later, having received the gift from Collinson, did Franklin realize that some of them were electrical. Writing to Michael Collinson much later, he could thus truly say that the first notice of electricity had come from Peter Collinson in 1746. As Heathcote has said, "Spencer introduced Franklin to an experiment with a glass tube and leaf-brass; Collinson introduced him to *electricity.*"

The introduction was a five-page translation in *The Gentleman's Magazine* of an article from the Dutch *Bibliothèque raisonnée* describing the work of George Mathias Bose, Christiani August Hausen and Johann Heinrich Winkler, written by Albrecht von Haller, the naturalist. Thus Franklin's first serious knowledge of electricity came, as it has been noted, from "the work of Leipzig academicians as reported by a Swiss at Göttingen in a review run by professors in Holland." After describing the work of the German naturalists, von Haller continued: "And from the year 1743 they discover'd phenomena, so surprising as to awaken the indolent curiosity of the public, the ladies and people of quality, who never regard natural philosophy but when it works miracles. Electricity became all the subject in vogue, princes were willing to see this new fire which a man produced from himself, and which did not descend from heaven. Could one believe that a lady's finger, that her whale-bone petticoat, should send forth flashes of true lightening, and that such charming lips could set on fire a house? The ladies were sensible of this new privilege of kindling fires without any poetical figure, or hyperbole, and resorted from all parts to the publick lectures of natural philosophy, which by that means became brilliant assemblies."

The Gentleman's Magazine article, reprinted in the Colonies, greatly increased the existing interest in electricity and the *Boston Evening Post* was soon reporting that William Claggett, a watchmaker of Newport, Rhode Island, had "fixed a Machine, by which a great Variety of those Experiments have been repeated, to the Astonishment of the Spectators." Before the end of the year, moreover, Mr. Claggett had "at last succeeded so far in the Electrical Experiments, as to set Fire to Spirits of Wine, the most satisfactory and difficult of all."

Franklin's concern with the subject was more than just another item in what for some while was a fad, hobby or entertainment rather than a scientific investigation. First he bought some of the equipment he had seen used by Dr. Spencer—presumably duplicate apparatus which was surplus to requirements, since the doctor went on lecturing. He also ordered better apparatus to be made in Philadelphia. And he and his friends now embarked on the formation of a "school" which, operating independently of those in England and on the Continent, helped to lay the groundwork of electrical science. His house, he wrote in his autobiography, "was continually full for some time, with People who came to see these new Wonders. To divide a little this Incumbrance among my Friends, I caused a Number of similar Tubes to be blown at our Glass-House, with which they furnish'd themselves, so that we had at length several Performers."

Within a few months he had carried out one simple but crucial experiment from which he was able to draw two vital deductions. In it he used three helpers, two of whom were insulated from the ground by standing on a layer of insulating wax. If one of the insulated observers held a glass tube and then rubbed it, an electric charge accumulated on the glass; if the second insulated observer then touched the glass the charge was communicated to him; furthermore, either of the insulated observers was then able to transmit the charge to the third observer. However, if the two insulated men touched each other before being approached by the third, then neither appeared to have any electricity to transmit to number three. Franklin believed this was because the first observer, rubbing the glass, collected on himself a charge equal in amount to, but in some way opposite to, the charge generated on the glass.

With this experiment Franklin effectively overthrew the concept of two different kinds of electricity, vitreous and resinous.

Instead, he maintained that it consisted of a subtle fluid and that the different reactions of different materials depended only on whether they had an excess or a deficiency of the fluid. "We say *B* (and bodies like circumstanced) is electrised *positively; A, negatively.* Or rather, *B* is electrised *plus; A, minus.* And we daily in our experiments electrise bodies *plus* or *minus* as we think proper."

In other words, Franklin believed that when two materials with differing quantities of electricity were brought either near to each other, or together, then the fluid would flow from the material that had the excess into the material that had the deficiency. Today it is known that electricity is the flow of the subatomic particles known as electrons; but electrons are negatively charged, and in an electrical circuit the flow of current is from the negative terminal to the positive, the reverse of what Franklin had proposed. Nevertheless, his concept was a remarkable step forward.

The excitement with which he carried on his experiments is revealed in a letter to Peter Collinson, whom he regularly kept informed on the work. "I never was before engaged in any study that so totally engrossed my attention and my time as this has lately done," he wrote as early as March 28, 1747, "for what with making experiments when I can be alone, and repeating them to my Friends and Acquaintance[s], who, from the novelty of the thing, come continually in crouds to see them, I have, during some months past, had little leisure for any thing else."

The fame of the experiments spread to New York and on August 3, 1747, Cadwallader Colden wrote: "Some Gentlemen here are desirous to go on Electrical experiments. We hear that you have the whole Apparatus sent over from England. They would purchase the like if they can be made at Philadelphia from what you have sent to you. Please to let me know whether any of your Artists can do it & what may be the price."

The Philadelphia group whose fame spread so quickly through the Colonies was very different from its counterparts in Europe. None of its members were scientists in the accepted sense of the word and none of them exercised any proprietorial rights in the suggestions which they put into the common pool during the sessions in Franklin's Market Street home. It was Philip Syng, a silversmith, who built the group's first machine to collect electricity for the Leyden jar, using in the process one of the cannonballs acquired by the Philadelphians for defense against French or Spanish forays up the Delaware. Thomas Hopkinson, president of the American Philosophical Society, first noted that pointed objects threw off electricity, Franklin having only reported that they drew it off. And Ebenezer Kinnersley, a Baptist minister and Philadelphian friend of Franklin, devised many of the experiments.

The equipment that Franklin used was not so much crude as of an extraordinary simplicity. "He could make an experiment with less apparatus and conduct his experimental inquiry to a discovery with more ordinary materials than any other philosopher we ever saw," Lord Brougham once said. "With an old key, a silk thread, some sealing-wax, and a sheet of paper, he discovered the identity of lightning and electricity."

Of equal importance was the clarity with which Franklin described his discoveries, a clarity which was to be of cardinal significance in his subsequent political writings. "He has endeavoured to remove all mystery and obscurity from the subject," commented Sir Humphry Davy. "He has written equally for the uninitiated and the philosopher; and he has rendered his details as amusing as well as perspicuous, elegant as well as simple. Science appears in his language in a dress wonderfully decorous, the best adapted to display her native loveliness. He has in no instance exhibited that false dignity, by which philosophy is kept aloof from common applications; and he has sought rather to make her a useful inmate and servant in the common habitations of man, than to preserve her merely as an object of admiration in temples and palaces."

Franklin had much of the proselyte in his approach to electricity and once it was evident that experiments could be repeated without fear of failure he proposed that Kinnersley give public demonstrations not only in Philadelphia but throughout the Colonies. Their nature can be judged from the headings of the lectures, prepared by Franklin. They included:

The Force of the Electrical Spark, making a fair hole thro' a Quire of Paper.
Small Animals killed by it Instantaneously.
Spirits kindled by Fire darting from a Lady's Eyes (without a Metaphor).

Spirits of Wine also kindled by a Spark after it has passed thro' ten Foot of Water. Also by Fire issuing out of a cold Egg.
An extinguished Candle lighted again by a Flame issuing out of cold Iron.
An Electrical Mine Sprung.
The amazing Force and Swiftness of the Electrical Fire in passing thro' a Number of Bodies at the same Instant.
A Piece of Money drawn out of a Persons Mouth in spite of his Teeth, yet without touching it, or offering him the least Violence.
The Salute repuls'd by the Ladies Fire.
Eight musical Bells rung by an electrisied Phial. Also by an electrisied Picture.
A Battery of eleven Guns discharged by Fire issuing out of a Man's Finger.

Quite apart from Kinnersley, there was Samuel Domien, described variously as a Greek priest and as a native of Transylvania, whom Franklin appears to have started on an almost full-time career as lecturer and demonstrator. "I taught him the use of the tube; how to charge the Leyden phial, and some other experiments," Franklin explained to John Lining, the Charleston physician who made some important contributions to early American science. "[Domien] wrote to me from *Charles-Town,* that he had lived eight hundred miles upon Electricity, it had been meat, drink and cloathing to him. His last letter to me was, I think, from *Jamaica,* desiring me to send the tubes you mention, to meet him at the *Havanah,* from whence he expected to get a passage to *La Vera Cruz;* designed travelling over land through *Mexico* to *Acapulco;* thence to get a passage to *Manilla,* and so through *China, India, Persia,* and *Turkey,* home to his own country; proposing to support himself chiefly by Electricity. A strange project! But he was, as you observe, a very singular character."
Franklin wrote to Collinson:

The first [matter to be noted] is the wonderful effect of pointed bodies, both in *drawing off* and *throwing off* the electrical fire. For example:
Place an iron shot of three or four inches diameter, on the mouth of a clean dry glass bottle. By a fine silken thread from the cieling, right over the mouth of the bottle, suspend a small cork-ball, about the bigness of a marble; the thread of such a length, as that the cork-ball

may rest against the side of the shot. Electrify the shot, and the ball will be repelled to the distance of four or five inches, more or less, according to the quantity of Electricity. When in this state, if you present to the shot the point of a long slender sharp bodkin, at six or eight inches distance, the repellency is instantly destroy'd, and the cork flies to the shot. A blunt body must be brought within an inch, and draw a spark, to produce the same effect. To prove that the electrical fire is *drawn off* by the point, if you take the blade of the bodkin out of the wooden handle, and fix it in a stick of sealing wax, and then present it at the distance aforesaid, or if you bring it very near, no such effect follows; but sliding one finger along the wax till you touch the blade, and the ball flies to the shot immediately. — If you present the point in the dark, you will see, sometimes at a foot distance, and more, a light gather upon it like that of a fire-fly or glow-worm; the less sharp the point, the nearer you must bring it to observe the light; and at whatever distance you see the light, you may draw off the electrical fire, and destroy the repellency. . . .

This largely theoretical work, the attempt to discover the fundamental facts about electricity, was only one side of the coin. The other was represented by the efforts of Franklin and his friends to find practical uses for the new phenomenon they were slowly beginning to understand. Franklin's detractors have tended to stress such applications; to maintain that he was primarily concerned with the utilitarian aspects of electricity and that the theory—the realm of the scientists rather than of the inventor—followed on much as the coach follows the horses. To others the rules were reversed, with scientist Franklin seeking and finding a new theory of electricity and not being overconcerned about its practical results. Both claims reflect the contemporary gulf between engineers and scientists, between applied and pure science and, in English terms, between "gentlemen" and "players." It is doubtful if Franklin or his colleagues thought very much along such lines. Certainly he, like Matthew Arnold's Shakespeare, "self-schooled, self-scanned, self-honoured, self-secure," was able to move with ease from one class of society to another, from one occupation to another, and from the theory of negative and positive electricity to the most practical way of putting up a lightning conductor. He got on with the job, trying to explain his experimental results and then thinking up more experiments to test new ideas.

Many of them suggest a convivial lightheartedness. Thus Franklin was delighted to show his friends how a candle, just blown out, could be relit by causing a spark to pass through the smoke between the wire and the snuffers—a forerunner of the later method of lighting gas by means of the spark from a spark-coil passing through a jet of gas. Philip Syng contrived little pasteboard wheels which were driven like windmills by the invisible force of electricity, while Kinnersley publicly demonstrated what *The Pennsylvania Gazette* called "A curious Machine acting by means of the Electric Fire, and playing Variety of Tunes on eight musical bells." There was also the artificial spider. "We suspend by fine silk thread a counterfeit spider, made of a small piece of burnt cork, with legs of linnen thread, and a grain or two of lead stuck in him to give him more weight," Franklin wrote. "Upon the table, over which he hangs, we stick a wire upright as high as the phial and wire, two or three inches from the spider; then we animate him by setting the electrified phial at the same distance on the other side of him; he will immediately fly to the wire of the phial, bend his legs in touching it, then spring off, and fly to the wire in the table; thence again to the wire of the phial, playing with his legs against both in a very entertaining manner, appearing perfectly alive to persons unacquainted. He will continue this motion an hour or more in dry weather."

More intriguing was the treatment which could be given to a framed portrait of King George II. First it had to be dismantled, then reassembled so that part of the picture was in front of the glass and part behind, while a surrounding layer of gilt had to be added in a certain way. Next, a gilt crown was put on the King's head. "If now the picture be moderately electrified," Franklin wrote, "and another person take hold of the frame with one hand, so that his fingers touch its inside gilding, and with the other hand endeavour to take off the crown, he will receive a terrible blow, and fail in the attempt. If the picture were highly charged, the consequence might perhaps be as fatal as that of high-treason; for when the spark is taken through a quire of paper laid on the picture, by means of a wire communication, it makes a fair hole through every sheet; that is, through 48 leaves, (though a quire of paper is thought good armour against the push of a sword or even against a pistol bullet) and the crack is exceeding loud. The operator, who holds the picture by the upper-end, where the inside of the frame is not gilt, to prevent its falling, feels nothing of the shock, and may touch the face of the picture without danger, which he pretends is a test of his loyalty. If a ring of persons take the shock among them, the experiment is called, *The Conspirators.*"

The minor shocks received in these early experiments soon led Franklin and his friends to investigate the effect of larger ones, especially after they had discovered an easier way of accumulating the electric charge. They used, Franklin told Collinson, "what we call'd an *electrical-battery,* consisting of eleven panes of large sash-glass, arm'd with thin leaden plates, pasted on each side, placed vertically, and supported at two inches distance on silk cords, with thick hooks of leaden wire, one from each side, standing upright, distant from each other, and convenient communications of wire and chain, from the giving side of one pane, to the receiving side of the other; that so the whole might be charged together, and with the same labour as one single pane."

A chicken, the Philadelphians discovered, could be killed outright when electrocuted with the charge which could be accumulated in two six-gallon jars. A turkey, however, was merely stunned and recovered in about fifteen minutes, although unable to survive the shock from five jars. In describing these experiments Franklin made two points. One was that the birds died more quickly than when killed by normal methods, a fact of which he approved on humanitarian grounds, noting that this might "operate as a motive with compassionate persons to employ it for animals sacrificed for their use." The second was that birds killed in this way "eat uncommonly tender."

The dangers of electricity were thus soon appreciated. In practice, Franklin seems to have been rather casual about avoiding them, although he did warn that "the operator must be very circumspect, lest he should happen to make the experiment on his own flesh, instead of that of the fowl."

Despite the cautionary note he nearly killed himself at least twice. On one occasion there were a number of people in the room with him and, he says, "I was obliged to quit my usual standing, and placed myself inadvertently under an iron hook which hung from the ceiling down to within two inches of my head, and communicated by wire with the outside of the jars. I attempted to discharge them, and in fact did so; but I did not perceive it, though the charge went through me, and not through the persons I intended it for. I neither saw the flash, heard the report, nor felt the stroke. When my senses returned, I found myself on the floor. I got up, not knowing how that had happened. I then again attempted to discharge the jars; but one of the company told me they were already discharged, which I could not at first believe, but on trial found it true. . . . A small swelling rose on the top of my head, which continued sore for some days; but I do not remember any other effect, good or bad."

He failed to learn by experience and on Christmas Day 1750 reported what seems to have been an even more dangerous adventure. "I have lately made an Experiment in Electricity that I desire never to repeat," he began. "Two nights ago being about to kill a Turkey by the Shock from two large Glass Jarrs containing as much electrical fire as forty common Phials, I inadvertently took the whole thro' my own Arms and Body, by receiving the fire from the united Top Wires with one hand, while the other held a Chain connected with the outsides of both Jars. The Company present (whose talking to me, and to one another I suppose occasioned my Inattention to what I was about) Say that the flash was very great and the crack as loud as a Pistol; yet my Senses being instantly gone, I neither Saw the one nor heard the other; nor did I feel the Stroke on my hand, tho' I afterwards found it raised a round swelling where the fire enter'd as big as half a Pistol Bullet by which you may judge of the Quickness of the Electrical Fire, which by this Instance Seems to be greater than that of Sound, Light and animal Sensation."

Franklin seems to have been as casual in his experiments with others as he was with himself. "The knocking down of the six men was performed with two of my large jarrs not fully charged," he explained to John Lining. "I laid one end of my discharging rod upon the head of the first; he laid his hand on the head of the second; the second his hand on the head of the third, and so to the last, who held, in his hand, the chain that was connected with the outside of the jarrs. When they were thus placed, I applied the other end of my rod to the prime-conductor, and they all dropt together. When they got up, they all declared they had not felt any stroke, and wondered how they came to fall; nor did any of them either hear the crack, or see the light of it." He had also seen a young woman struck down, by accident, he went on, but she complained of nothing. "Too great a charge," he admitted, "might, indeed, kill a man, but I have not yet seen any hurt done by it." And then, as if in consolation for such an awkward event, he added: "It would certainly, as you observe, be the easiest of all deaths."

The lighthearted nature of much of this work is shown by Franklin's letter to Collinson of April 29, 1749. The warm weather, unconducive to experiments, would soon be starting, and it was therefore agreed to suspend operations throughout the summer. But first there would be a party on the banks of the Schuylkill River. Here inflammable liquids on one bank were to be set on fire by an electric spark activated through the water from the other bank. In the letter, published in the first, 1751, edition of *Experiments and Observations on Electricity*, Franklin described the experiment as follows: "Spirits, at the same time, are to be fired by a spark sent from side to side through the river, without any other conductor than the water; an experiment which we some time since performed, to the amazement of many." In subsequent editions of *Experiments and Observations*, Franklin added the following explanatory footnote: "As the possibility of this experiment has not been easily conceived, I shall here describe it. Two iron rods, about three feet long, were planted just within the margin of the river, on the opposite sides. A thick piece of wire, with a small round knob at its end, was fixed to ["on" in 1774 edition] the top of one of the rods, bending downwards, so as to deliver commodiously the spark upon the surface of the spirit. A small wire fastened by one end to the handle of the spoon, containing the spirit, was carried a-cross the river, and supported in the air by the rope commonly used to hold by, in drawing the ferry-boats over. The other end of this wire was tied round the coating of the bottle; which being charged, the spark was delivered from the hook to the top of the rod standing in the water on that side. At the same instant the rod on the other side delivered a spark into the spoon, and fired the spirit. The electric fire returning to the coating of the bottle, through the handle of the spoon and the supported wire connected with them."

A turkey was to be killed electrically for dinner and roasted on a spit turned by electricity over a fire which had been kindled by "the *electrified bottle.*" And then, Franklin concluded, "the healths of all the famous electricians in *England, Holland, France* and *Germany,* are to be drank in *electrified bumpers,* under the discharge of guns from the electrical battery."

It was not all jollification. As early as 1743 Johann Gottlob Krüger of Halle had told students that if electricity "must have some practical use, it is certain that none has been found for it in Theology or Jurisprudence, and therefore where else can the use be than in Medicine?" Collinson had told Franklin of "3 Instances of the Electrical power on Human Bodies By filling the Electrical Phyal with a purgative Portion [*sic*] and Transferring it into a Patient and it had all the Effects as if taken into the Stomach." From Europe there came other reports of shock treatment for various ailments, and Franklin found a number of paralytics coming to him for treatment. "My method," he later wrote, "was, to place the patient first in a chair, on an electric stool, and draw a number of large strong sparks from all parts of the affected limb or side. Then I fully charged two six gallon glass jars, each of which had about three square feet of surface coated; and I sent the united shock of these through the affected limb or limbs, repeating the stroke commonly three times each day." There were some results. "A man, for instance, who could not the first day lift the lame hand from off his knee, would the next day raise it four or five inches, the third day higher; and on the fifth day was able, but with a feeble languid motion, to take off his hat." But there was no further improvement after the fifth day and the patients, who tended to fear the shocks, invariably stopped the treatment at that point.

When Franklin began his electrical experiments the War of the Austrian Succession, known in America as King George's War, was still being fought between Britain—which included the American Colonies—on one side and France and Spain on the other. French and Spanish ships were marauding up the Delaware to within a few miles of Philadelphia. There was intermittent warfare with French-supported Indians on the frontier, little more than a hundred miles away, and it was inevitable that Franklin should consider the military uses of the startling phenomena he and his colleagues were investigating. They therefore considered firing gunpowder "by the electric flame." Explaining how this could be done, Franklin told Collinson, "A small cartridge is fill'd with dry powder, hard rammed, so as to bruise some of the grains. Two pointed wires are then thrust in, one at each end, the points approaching each other in the middle of the cartridge, till within the distance of half an inch: then the cartridge being placed in the circle, when the four jars are discharged, the electric flame leaping from the point of one wire to the point of the other, within the cartridge among the powder, fires it, and the explosion of the powder is at the same instant with the crack of the discharge." Thus a cannon could be fired by what would now be called remote control.

Meanwhile, as he worried out a visible theory to explain electrical phenomena, and set lecturers on the road, Franklin moved nearer to immortality: to showing how lightning and electricity were manifestations of the same force, and to demonstrating how this terror of the ages might be brought under control.

Until the start of the eighteenth century, lightning had remained as much a mystery as it had been in the days of the legendary Prometheus who drew fire from Heaven. But as primitive electrical experiments began, similarities were noted between it and the sparks of electrical machines. As early as 1705, Francis K. Hauksbee carried out an experiment which produced light which "darted thick from the Crown of the included Glass, *like Flashes of Lightning,* of a very pale colour, and easily distinguishable from the rest of the Light produc'd. These Flashes I have observ'd to be darted, *sometimes Horizontally,* sometimes *inclining upwards,* at other times downwards." Four years later Samuel Wall reported in the Royal Society's *Philosophical Transactions* that when amber was rubbed "it produc'd a Light but no Crackling; but by holding one's Finger at a little distance from the Amber, a large Crackling is produc'd, with a great flash of Light succeeding it, and, what to me is very surprizing, upon its eruption it strikes the Finger very sensibly, wheresoever apply'd, with a push or puff like wind . . . and it seems, in some degree, to represent Thunder and Lightning." In the year that Franklin began his experiments the Englishman John Freke stated bluntly that lightning is "intirely the same with Electricity; for it will kill without a Wound, and pass through every thing, as this seems to do." And in Germany Johann Heinrich Winkler said much the same, adding, "the only difference exists in the relative strengths and weaknesses of their operation."

In fact *The Gentleman's Magazine* article of 1745, which had become so well known in the Colonies, said of electricity: "Lightening has pretty much the same qualities, for it generally runs over the whole length of the solid bodies which it strikes, and it has been seen to descend along the wire of a steeple-clock from top to bottom, and the threads of the wire have been found at the bottom of the steeple, melted into thousands of small bits. This is not the only property which lightening has in common with electricity." In 1748 the Abbé Nollet had made a list of the similarities between lightning and electricity, and the following year his friends at the Bordeaux Academy made them the subject of its essay competition. "Electricity in our hands," wrote the winner, a Dijon doctor taking a phrase from the Abbé Nollet's writings, "is the same as thunder in the hands of nature."

Yet despite these conjectures no one in Europe proposed how they might be checked or, if they were found correct, how lightning might be dealt with. This was left to Franklin.

From the first he, too, had had his suspicions, writing to Collinson of one experiment that produced "fire . . . like a flash of lightning." In another letter, written shortly afterward, he describes "a vivid flame, like the sharpest lightning," which was the outcome of another experiment. Two years later he appeared convinced of the electrical nature of lightning and, after noting how clouds are "jostled and mixed by the winds," speculated on the huge energies that could be involved. "When the gun-barrel (in electrical experiments) has but little electrical fire in it, you must approach it very near with your knuckle, before you can draw a spark," he points out. "Give it more fire, and it will give a spark at a greater distance. Two gun-barrels united, and as highly electrified, will give a spark at a still greater distance. But if two gun-barrels electrified will strike at two inches distance, and make a loud snap, to what a great distance may 10,000 acres of electrified cloud strike and give its fire, and how loud must be that crack!"

Later in 1749 he listed in his notebook various characteristics which were true both of lightning and of electricity. They both gave out light of the same color and had crooked direction and swift motion. Both were conducted by metals, made a noise, "subsisting" in water and ice, and could tear apart materials that they went through. In addition, both could kill animals, melt metals, set fire to inflammable substances and produce a sulfurous smell. This hardly broke new ground, however. That came with the last four sentences in the notebook. "The electric fluid," he ended, "is attracted by points. —We do not know whether this property is in lightning. —But since they agree in all the particulars wherein we can already compare them, is it not probable they agree likewise in this? Let the experiment be made."

With that last sentence Franklin took his place in history. He himself was usually modest about the circumstances. Asked how he first came to think of proposing the experiment, he replied, "I cannot answer better than by giving you an extract from the minutes I used to keep on the experiments I made, with memorandums of such as I purposed to make, the reasons for making them, and the observations that arose upon them, from which minutes my letters were afterwards drawn. By this extract you will see that the thought was not so much 'an out-of-the-way one,' but that it might have occurred to any electrician."

But what could the experiment be? Franklin answered that question in the summer of 1750 in a dissertation sent to Collinson and entitled "Opinions and Conjectures, Concerning the Properties and Effects of the Electrical Matter, arising from Experiments and Observations, made in Philadelphia, 1749."

If lightning was shown to be no longer an inexplicable mystery, what then? Franklin had an answer:

if these things are so, may not the knowledge of this power of points be of use to mankind, in preserving houses, churches, ships, &c. from the stroke of lightning, by directing us to fix, on the highest parts of those edifices, upright rods of iron made sharp as a needle, and gilt to prevent rusting, and from the foot of those rods, a wire down the outside of the building into the ground, or down round one of the shrouds of a ship, and down her side till it reaches the water? Would not these pointed rods probably draw the electrical fire silently out of a cloud before it came nigh enough to strike, and thereby secure us from that most sudden and terrible mischief!

. . . To determine the question, whether the clouds that contain Lightning are electrified or not, I would propose an experiment to be try'd where it may be done conveniently. On the top of some high tower or steeple, place a kind of sentry-box, big enough to contain a man and an electrical stand. From the middle of the stand, let an iron rod rise and pass bending out of the door, and then upright 20 or 30 feet, pointed very sharp at the end. If the electrical stand be kept clean and dry, a man standing on it when such clouds are passing low, might be electrified and afford sparks, the rod drawing fire to him from a cloud. If any danger to the man should be apprehended (though I think there would be none) let him stand on the floor of his box, and now and then bring near to the rod the loop of a wire that has one end fastened to the leads, he holding it by a wax handle; so the sparks, if the rod is electrified, will strike from the rod to the wire, and not affect him.

This was the proposal he was making public when he sent "Opinions and Conjectures" to Collinson. For from the start of the correspondence, Collinson had passed on Franklin's letters to other Fellows of the Royal Society. The first had been referred to in detail when William Watson read a paper to the Society on January 21, 1748. Watson pointed out that he had put forward the one-fluid theory of electricity before Franklin had done so. But he then went on to emphasize that the theory had been proposed "upon the other Side of the *Atlantic Ocean* before this Gentleman [Franklin] could possibly be acquainted with our having observed the same Fact here, and as he seems very conversant in this Part of Natural Philosophy, I take the Liberty of laying before you his own words."

The same attitude was taken when Franklin's description of the similarities between lightning and electricity reached England. "Part of a paper containing a new theory of thunder-gusts by Mr. Franklin, communicated by Mr. Watson, was read," says the *Journal Book* of the Royal Society. "But the same being long, the residue was defer'd till next meeting." On November 16, "The remainder of a paper entitled 'Observations and suppositions towards forming a new hypothesis for explaining the several phenomena of thunder-gusts, by Mr. Franklin of Philadelphia in Pennsylvania and transmitted by him to Dr. Mitchel, F.R.S., part of which had been read at the last meeting, was now read. Thanks were ordered to Dr. Mitchel and to Mr. Franklin for this communication."

Franklin was certainly being noticed. But, so far, noticed only by the relatively small number of men who read and discussed the Royal Society's *Philosophical Transactions.* The change came after Collinson had shown Franklin's letters to Edward Cave, publisher of *The Gentleman's Magazine,* who agreed to print them. Then, rightly sensing that he had something more important than a journal contribution, Cave decided to publish the letters separately.

Before doing so, however, he gave his readers a taste of things to come: in January 1750, a brief résumé of Franklin's experiments as explained to Collinson, and described merely as "lately made in Philadelphia"; then, four months later, a suggestion for lightning conductors, printed under the heading "A curious Remark on ELECTRICITY; from a Gentleman in America; whose ingenious Letters on this Subject will soon be published in a separate Pamphlet, illustrated with Cuts."

Only then came the letters, published as *Experiments and Observations on Electricity, made at Philadelphia in America, by Mr. Benjamin Franklin, and Communicated in several Letters to Mr. P. Collinson, of London, F.R.S.* Sometimes described as a pamphlet, they formed a book of eighty-six pages which was to mark a turning point in Franklin's life. It was prefaced by Dr. John Fothergill, a prominent British Quaker who was to become one of Franklin's closest friends and who felt that the letters "said more sensible things on the subject [of electricity] and let us see more into the nature of this delicate affair than all the other writers put together." They described Franklin's early experiments, repeated the conclusion that lightning was an electrical phenomenon and the proposal for testing this hypothesis; and they also described a lightning rod to protect buildings. The book was republished three years later, and again in 1760, 1769 and 1774, Franklin adding fresh material to some of these later editions; on the Continent it was published in French, German and Italian.

It was in France that the crucial development now took place. A copy of Franklin's book came into the hands of the naturalist the Comte de Buffon, whether by chance or at Franklin's request is not clear. Buffon proposed a French translation, not only because he saw the merit of the work but because he realized that publication would embarrass the Abbé Nollet as well as other French scientists with whom he was in dispute. To carry out the translation he used Thomas-François Dalibard, an old friend who knew little of electricity but had a good knowledge of English. Dalibard was coached in how best to make the experiments by De Lor, a demonstrator in experimental philosophy, and news of their activities reached the ears of Louis XV. The Duc d'Ayen offered his château at St. Germain and here, on February 3, 1752, Buffon, Dalibard and De Lor repeated before the King the experiments carried out in Franklin's Philadelphia home. The King's interest, combined with publication of Dalibard's translation, which appeared in March, now induced the Frenchmen to plan the vital experiment which would provide evidence of the character of lightning.

The Marly experiment followed, so did its repetition elsewhere, and Dalibard's report to the Academy of Sciences, which concluded: "Perhaps only a hundred or so iron rods, so arranged and deployed in different quarters and in the highest places, would suffice to preserve the entire city of Paris from thunderstorms."

A grateful King ordered that Franklin should be thanked and Peter Collinson subsequently passed on the message. "If any of thy Friends . . . should take Notice that thy Head is held a little higher up than formerly," wrote Collinson, "let them know; when the Grand Monarch of France strictly commands the Abbé Mazéas to write a Letter in the politest Terms to the Royal Society, to return the King's Thanks and Compliments in an express Manner to Mr. Franklin of Pennsilvania for the useful Discoveries in Electricity, and Application of the pointed Rods to prevent the terrible Effects of Thunder-storms. I say, after all this, is not some Allowance to be made, if the Crest is a little Elevated? . . . I think, now I have stuck a Feather on thy Cap, I may be allowed to conclude in wishing thee long to wear it."

Dalibard's experiment made Franklin famous throughout Europe and forever afterward he was to be lauded by authors and poets as the patron saint of lightning protection. Thomas Campbell wrote in "The Pleasures of Hope" of those who would "With Franklin grasp the lightning's fiery wing," while in Byron's "The Age of Bronze" Franklin was to have a double entry: "While Franklin's quiet memory climbs to heaven, / Calming the lightning which he thence hath riven," and then, "And stoic Franklin's energetic shade, / Robed in the lightnings which his hand allayed." The French economist and statesman Anne Robert Jacques Turgot, inscribing a bust of Franklin, wrote that he had "snatched the lightning shaft from heaven, and the sceptre from tyrants," while Gordon Forrest of Boston put the matter more simply if less mellifluously: "Some write in blood a name / Which fame is ever brightening; / But Franklin had a heavenly aim, / And wrote his name with lightning."

Yet the Marly experiment tends to be overshadowed today by something very different: the experiment in which a toy kite, flown into thundery air, attracted electricity down to a metal key on the line from which it was being flown. A good deal of mystery still surrounds the event.

The only detailed account is that given by Joseph Priestley in his history of electricity published in London in 1767. Here he provides "particulars which I have from the best authority," and since Franklin was both a friend of Priestley's and in London while the book was being written, there is little doubt that Franklin himself provided the details. In June 1752 he was, according to this account, awaiting the completion of the Christ Church steeple in Philadelphia, believing that only such a tall building would enable him to confirm his lightning theory. Then, according to Priestley, it occurred to Franklin that with a kite, "he could have a readier and better access to the regions of thunder than by any spire whatever." Exactly where and when the experiment was carried out is not known, but one theory locates it on the high ground near the junction of what are now Eighteenth and Spring Gardens streets, a site where the wind was likely to be strong and where Franklin would have the seclusion he wanted.

"Preparing, therefore, a large silk handkerchief, and two cross-sticks, of a proper length, on which to extend it; he took the opportunity of the first approaching thunder storm to take a walk into a field, in which there was a shed convenient for his purpose," says Priestley. "But dreading the ridicule which too commonly attends unsuccessful attempts in science, he communicated his intended experiment to no body but his son, who assisted him in raising the kite. The kite being raised, a considerable time elapsed before there was any appearance of its being electrified. One very promising cloud had passed over it without any effect; when, at length, just as he was beginning to despair of his contrivance, he observed some loose threads of the hempen string to stand erect, and to avoid one another, just as if they had been suspended on a common conductor. Struck with this promising appearance, he immediately presented his knuckle to the key, and (let the reader judge of the exquisite pleasure he must have felt at that moment) the discovery was complete. He perceived a very evident electric spark. Others succeeded, even before the string was wet, so as to put the matter past all dispute, and when the rain had wet the string, he collected electric fire very copiously. This happened in June 1752, a month after the electricians in France had verified the same theory, but before he heard of any thing they had done."

Franklin published a brief account of the experiment in *The Pennsylvania Gazette* of October 19, 1752, but he did not claim to have made the experiment himself: "As frequent Mention is made in the News Papers from Europe of the Success of the Philadelphia Experiment for drawing the Electric Fire from Clouds by Means of pointed Rods of Iron erected on high Buildings, &c. it may be agreeable to the Curious to be inform'd, that the same Experiment has succeeded in Philadelphia, tho' made in a different and more easy Manner, which any one may try, as follows." He then explained how to make a kite from "two light Strips of Cedar, the Arms so long as to reach to the four Corners of a large thin Silk Handkerchief when extended," and how to carry out the experiment.

This account left many questions unanswered. To such an extent indeed that a few days later Cadwallader Colden, writing to Franklin from New York, added a P.S., saying that he had seen the newspaper account of the kite experiment and continuing, "I hope a more perfect & particular account will be published in a manner to preserve it better & to give it more Credit than it can obtain from a common News paper." It is possible that Franklin was put off by the description of his beloved *Pennsylvania Gazette* as a "common News paper"; but he does not appear to have fulfilled Colden's hope.

Priestley's is the only version mentioning that Franklin's son, William, was present, although he is included in later sketches or engravings of the incident. Strangely enough, most of them show the son as a small boy, even though he was then aged twenty-one; and Benjamin West's famous painting, *Franklin Drawing Electricity from the Sky,* executed about 1805, shows Benjamin Franklin not as the vigorous forty-six-year-old which he was at the time, but as a wrinkled patriarch with white hair streaming in the wind.

It seems unlikely that fresh light will ever be thrown on the famous kite experiment. It was no doubt inspired by Franklin and there is every possibility that he himself carried it out. But it is not inconceivable that it was performed by another member of the group who had been working on electricity with him for the previous six years. The event was certainly extraordinary for one reason. By the summer of 1752 Franklin knew that man-collected electricity could be a killer, at least of poultry. He had, moreover, commented on the huge charges that might be accumulated in the upper atmosphere. Yet here he was, preparing to collect in the most casual manner a charge of unknown but potentially tremendous size, an operation which seems to be explained either by extreme ignorance or extreme recklessness. The dangers were in fact to be demonstrated within little more than a year.

On August 6, 1753, Professor Georg Richmann of St. Petersburg tried with a colleague, M. Sokolaw, engraver to the Academy at St. Petersburg, to attract the lightning. He attached a wire to the top of his house and led it down to an iron bar suspended above "the electrical needle" and a bowl of water partly filled with iron filings. "The Professor," stated a letter from Moscow which Franklin published in *The Pennsylvania Gazette,* "judging from the Needle that the Tempest was at a great Distance, assured M. Sokolaw that there was no Danger, but that there might be at the Approach. M. Richmann stood about a Foot from the Bar, attentively observing the Needle. Soon after M. Sokolaw saw, the Machine being untouched, a Globe of blue and whitish Fire, about four inches Diameter, dart from the Bar against M. Richmann's Forehead, who fell backwards without the least Outcry. This was succeeded by an Explosion like that of a small Cannon which also threw M. Sokolaw on the Floor, feeling as it were some Blows on his Back. It has since been found that the Wire breaking, some Bits had hit him behind, and left the Marks of Burning on his Clothes." Professor Richmann was killed—"his body [being] found in the midst of his apparatus, like an artilleryman dead under the wreck of his gun." To Priestley, he was martyr in a good cause—the "justly envied" Richmann.

So far, however, it was only the readers of the learned journals who could be saved from the effects of lightning which this experiment demonstrated. Kinnersley, it is true, had in his lectures spoken of the similarity between lightning and electricity and stated that lightning rods could give protection. This, however, was more general, and of far less influence than the announcement that now appeared in the 1753 issue of *Poor Richard.* It was headed "How to secure Houses &c. from LIGHT-NING" and continued as follows:

"It has pleased God in his Goodness to Mankind, at length to discover to them the Means of securing their Habitations and other Buildings from Mischief by Thunder and Lightning. The

Method is this: Provide a small Iron Rod (it may be made of the Rod-iron used by the Nailers) but of such a Length, that one End being three or four Feet in the moist Ground, the other may be six or eight Feet above the highest Part of the Building. To the upper End of the Rod fasten about a Foot of Brass Wire, the Size of a common Knitting-needle, sharpened to a fine Point; the Rod may be secured to the House by a few small Staples. If the House or Barn be long, there may be a Rod and Point at each End, and a middling Wire along the Ridge from one to the other. A House thus furnished will not be damaged by Lightning, it being attracted by the Points, and passing thro the Metal into the Ground without hurting any Thing."

Two matters should be noted. The first is the practicality of the instructions. The Rod could be obtained from the Nailers, and fixed with a few Staples. Franklin's utilitarian approach may or may not be a debit when he is judged as a scientist, but it is certainly commendable in other ways. Secondly, "God in his Goodness" is given credit for the new device. Until long after Franklin's day lightning was considered an expression of divine wrath, to be warded off only by prayer or by the ringing of church bells, many of which bore the words *"Fulgura frango"* ("I break up the lightning"). But bell ringing during storms was a hazardous business, and Johann Nepomuk Fischer's *Beweis dass das Glockenläuten bey Gewittern mehr schädlich als nützlich ist,* published in Munich in 1784, recorded that during the previous thirty-three years lightning had hit 386 church steeples and killed 103 bell ringers.

The belief that lightning rods were no less than sacrilegious attempts to interfere with the decisions of God remained strong, and Kinnersley in his lectures made a point of stating that their erection was "not chargeable with presumption, nor inconsistent with any of the principles either of natural or revealed religion." A Boston clergyman opposed such safety devices on the grounds that lightning was a means of punishing mankind and of warning them from the commission of sin: it was therefore impious to prevent its full execution. A different objection came from those who believed that if the lightning was led down into the bowels of the earth, the result would be an outbreak of earthquakes.

Despite all warnings of the wrath to come, Franklin practiced what he preached and in September 1752 set up a lightning conductor on the new house to which he had moved in Philadelphia. His aim was to carry out experiments as much as to protect the building, and he equipped the device with two bells which would ring when the apparatus was electrified. "I found the bells rang sometimes when there was no lightning or thunder, but only a dark cloud over the rod," he told Collinson; "that sometimes after a flash of lightning they would suddenly stop; and, at other times, when they had not rang before, they would, after a flash, suddenly begin to ring; that the electricity was sometimes very faint, so that when a small spark was obtain'd, another could not be got for some time after; at other times the sparks would follow extremely quick, and once I had a continual stream from bell to bell, the size of a crow-quill: Even during the same gust there were considerable variations."

One result of Franklin's success, as demonstrated at Marly-la-Ville, was a blast from the Abbé Nollet, who refused to take the experiment seriously. He was an important man and Franklin was at first determined to refute him. He repeated all the Abbé's own experiments and, as he wrote to Cadwallader Colden on January 1, 1753, found that they answered "exactly as they should do on my Principles, and in the material Part quite contrary to what he [Nollet] has related of them; so that he has laid himself extreamly open, by attempting to impose false Accts of Experiments on the World, to support his Doctrine. . . . I conclude to write a civil Letter to the Abbé myself in which, without resenting his Chicanery or any thing else in his Letters, I shall endeavour to set the disputed Matters in so clear a Light, as to satisfy every one that will take the Trouble of Reading it."

There was one point in Nollet's arguments which particularly worried Franklin, as he confessed to Colden a few months later. "In one or two Places he seems to apply to the superstitious Prejudices of the Populace, which I think unworthy of a Philosopher. He speaks as if he thought it Presumption in man, to propose guarding himself against the *Thunders of Heaven*! Surely the Thunder of Heaven is no more supernatural than the Rain Hail or Sunshine of Heaven, against the Inconveniences of which we guard by Roofs & Shades without Scruple."

However, the protest to Nollet was never finished, for reasons which Franklin set out toward the end of the year, after receiving a note from M. Dalibard. The Frenchman, Franklin told his friend James Bowdoin, was "preparing an Answer, not only to the Abbé, but to some others that have wrote against my Doctrine, which will be publish'd the Beginning of this Winter. This, with a good deal of Business, and a little natural Indolence, have made me neglect finishing my Answer, till I shall see what is done by him. Perhaps it may then appear unnecessary for me to do any thing farther in it. And will not one's Vanity be more gratify'd in seeing one's Adversary confuted by a Disciple, than even by one's self?"

The adversary was in fact to be confuted by history. The events of the summer of 1752, William Watson noted in Britain, enabled philosophers to show, as never before, the nature and effects of thunder, "a phaenomenon hitherto almost inaccessible to their inquiries." Baron von Humboldt, one of the world's greatest naturalists, was to put the transformation more succinctly. "From this epoch," he wrote, "the electric process passed from the domain of speculative physics to that of the cosmical contemplation of nature—from the chamber of the student to the open field."

The most spectacular result of the Philadelphia experiments carried out by Franklin and his friends between 1746 and 1752 was the confirmation that lightning and electricity were one and the same thing and that lightning conductors could safeguard life and property. Less dramatic but more important was Franklin's concept of electricity as one "fluid" rather than two, his substitution of "positive" and "negative" for what had previously been described as vitreous and resinous electricities, and his demonstration of what became known as the law of conservation of charge.

Appreciation of what had been achieved came first from Harvard, which awarded him the honorary degree of Master of Arts in July 1753. Yale followed two months later. And in November there came the award of the Royal Society's Copley Medal. Its Council, said the President, Lord Macclesfield, "could not overlook the merit of Benjamin Franklin, of Pensilvania; for though he not a Fellow of this Society, nor an inhabitant of this island, is a subject of the Crown of Great Britain, and must be acknowledged to have deserved well of the philosophical world, and of this learned body in particular." Three years later Franklin was elected a Fellow of the Society, and in 1760 was voted onto its Council. Only then did he learn the circumstances of his election. It was, he told his son, "by a unanimous vote; and, the honour being voluntarily conferred by the Society, unsolicited by me, it was thought wrong to demand or receive the usual fees or composition; so that my name was entered on the list with a vote of council, *that I was not to pay any thing.*"

At the age of fifty Franklin had moved into new territory. His success in the commercial and political worlds of Pennsylvania was one thing; entrance into the scientific world of the Royal Society, and subsequently into that of the French Académie des Sciences, was to be vastly more important not only for him but also for America. Britain's relations with her Colonies, soon to be simmering, were largely governed by a small and close-knit group of men who had at least some contact with the world of science. To them, therefore, Franklin was, in the two decades ahead, not entirely the unknown outsider. Far more significant was the reputation which he had gained in France, a reputation which by a quirk of fate was to put him in a unique position of influence as Anglo-American relations collapsed a quarter of a century later.

FOUR

===

"TRIBUNE OF
THE PEOPLE"

F RANKLIN'S INTERNATIONAL FAME AS A
scientist, quickly achieved once he had begun his electrical experiments, was equaled at a different level by
the fame, not to say notoriety, which he also began to acquire
throughout Pennsylvania as an agile politician. The two roles
tended to supplement each other. His Fellowship of the Royal
Society, and the valuable contacts that followed from it, offered
him potential influence were he ever to leave America for the
imperial capital of London; his involvement in Pennsylvania
politics made it increasingly likely that the Assembly would send
him there if a crisis arose. During these years he found himself
sailing, with his hand on the tiller, in the stormy seas where the
Governor, the Proprietors, and even His Majesty's Government
across the Atlantic, were all jockeying for position. For the first
time he experienced what it was to have the power to influence
events. He liked the sensation.

The decade that followed his retirement thus witnessed something very different from what might have been expected. Frank-

lin the successful printer was revealed to be the chrysalis not only of a scientist but of a character with potential for world-wide fame. Franklin the businessman, drawn into politics by the needs of the day, was brought to consider in a new light the relationship of the American Colonies to what he still thought of as the "mother country." Thus there emerges in the later 1740s and the 1750s the multifaceted Franklin who is able to play a diversity of parts not only in Pennsylvania but on that wider stage where the fate of Europe and of North America was to be decided.

Throughout this decade it was his work on electricity that established his fame in Europe. But it was only one of the scientific subjects on which he exercised his brain. There were many others, mostly of a speculative nature, and his thoughts on them are intermingled in his letters and other writings, with indications, at times, of an almost alarming restlessness. While one part of his mind was grappling with the problem of disruptive Proprietors or the difficulties of frontier defense, another was frequently trying to explain a puzzling natural phenomenon he had observed.

Some of his speculations were far in advance of their time. A generation before Hutton founded the science of geology with his *Theory of the Earth,* and a century before Lyell confirmed uniformitarianism (the belief that geological processes are due to causes or forces operating uniformly in the past and present), Franklin was cogitating on the early history of the world in a way which many of his contemporaries would have considered both crazy and blasphemous. "Now I mention Mountains, it occurs [to me] to tell you," he wrote in July 1747 to Jared Eliot, the Connecticut clergyman and writer on agricultural problems, "that the great Apalachian Mountains, which run from York River back of these Colonies to the Bay of Mexico, show in many Places near the highest Parts of them, Strata of Sea Shells, in some Places the Marks of them are in the solid Rocks. 'Tis certainly the *Wreck* of a World we live on! We have Specimens of those Sea shell Rocks broken off near the Tops of those Mountains, brought and deposited in our Library as Curiosities. If you have not seen the like, I'll send you a Piece. Farther, about Mountains (for Ideas will string themselves like Ropes of Onions) when I was once riding in your Country, Mr. Walker show'd me at a Distance the Bluff Side or End of a Mountain, which appeared striped from top to Bottom, and told me the Stone or Rock of that Mountain was divided by Nature into Pillars."

Once cataclysmic changes in the earth's surface appeared a possibility, Franklin slotted the information away for reinforcement or denial at a later date. Years later he found reinforcement in England when he studied oyster shells mixed in the stone of a mountain slope. Moreover, after visiting a coal mine at Whitehaven in northern England, he was to note: "The slate, which forms the roof of this coal mine, is impressed in many places with the figures of leaves and branches of fearn, which undoubtedly grew at the surface when the slate was in the state of sand on the banks of the sea. Thus it appears, that this vein of coal has suffered a prodigious settlement." Also "part of the high county of Derby being probably as much above the level of the sea, as the coal mines of Whitehaven were below it, it seemed a proof that there had been a great *boulversement* in the surface of that island, some part of it having been depressed under the sea, and other parts, which had been under it, being raised above it. Such changes in the superficial parts of the globe, seemed to me unlikely to happen, if the earth were solid to the centre. I therefore imagined, that the internal parts might be a fluid more dense, and of greater specific gravity than any of the solids we are acquainted with, which therefore might swim in or upon that fluid. Thus the surface of the globe would be a shell, capable of being broken and disordered by the violent movements of the fluid on which it rested." To his brother Peter, he wrote: "It is evident from the quantities of sea-shells, and the bones and teeth of fishes found in high lands, that the sea has formerly covered them. Then, either the sea has been higher than it now is, and has fallen away from those high lands; or they have been lower than they are, and were lifted up out of the water to their present height, by some internal mighty force, such as we still feel some remains of, when whole continents are moved by earthquakes."

Franklin's interest in the geological history of the earth continued all his life. So did his concern with electricity, and with the other scientific riddles of the day. But the time he could devote to such work and conjectures was steadily if unexpectedly decreased by the repercussions of one event: the death in October 1740, without male issue, of the Emperor Charles VI of Austria. This imperial oversight was to start a chain reaction which led to some fifteen years of useless warfare in Europe and North America. These began with the War of the Austrian Succession, known in America as King George's War, which lasted from 1740 until the Peace of Aix-la-Chapelle in 1748. After a period during which sporadic fighting and privateering still continued, there followed the Seven Years' War, formally declared in 1756 and ended only by the Peace of Paris in 1763. The wars led, at the hands of the British, to the end of the French dominion in North America which had long threatened the American Colonies, but they had to be paid for. And the attempts of a near-bankrupt Britain to recoup from the Colonies the cost of defending the northern frontiers led, almost with the inevitability of Greek tragedy, to the Stamp Act; after its repeal, to the Townshend Acts; to the Boston Tea Party; the fusillades at Concord, Bunker Hill and the end of the first British Empire. Franklin was to be progressively involved in these events or their repercussions.

In Pennsylvania, the first nub of trouble was presented by the Quaker-dominated Assembly's reluctance to vote money for war. In 1745, the Pennsylvania Assembly had refused to grant Governor George Thomas any money for defense, and had only reluctantly voted him £4,000 for the purchase of "Bread, Beef, Port, Flour, Wheat or other Grain." In what seems to have been the contemporary spirit of genial misrepresentation when necessary, Thomas interpreted the word "grain" as meaning "gunpowder." This was a sleight of oratory similar to that of Franklin, asking for arms in a Quaker community that did not approve of them. "If we fail," he said, "let us move the Purchase of a Fire Engine with the Money; the Quakers can have no Objection to that: and then if you nominate me, and I you, as a Committee for that purpose, we will buy a great Gun, which is certainly a *Fire-Engine.*"

When England decided to support Austria in 1742, she was immediately brought into conflict with France, already at war with the Austrians. At first this made little difference in North America, since it was clear that the spreading war would be won or lost in Europe. But the French, securely in control of Canada, began systematically to recruit the Indians for raids across the Alleghenies into the rear areas of the Colonies. At sea, the threat became even more dangerous. In 1745, it is true, New England troops supported by an English squadron had captured Louis-burg, the fortress on Cape Breton Island at the mouth of the St. Lawrence whose position had given it the title of "the key to Canada." But in return French, and Spanish, ships began to maraud along the coast. In 1747 they put ashore a French raiding party only forty miles from Philadelphia and sailed up the Delaware, virtually unopposed, to within twenty miles of the city. Philadelphia was for all practical purposes completely defenseless.

The Assembly had repeatedly refused to pass a militia act even though a French force could have sacked Philadelphia with impunity. But now, in the autumn of 1747, Franklin took a decisive step. "I determined," he later wrote, "to try what might be done by a voluntary Association of the People." The smoothness of the words disguises the real intent, an intent which was to rouse the Proprietor to a paroxysm of fury. Franklin had determined that if the Assembly would not defend Philadelphia, then he would take the law into his own hands and form an independent militia to do so.

He used the arm of propaganda, having first gained the support of his friend William Coleman of the Junto, Thomas Hopkinson of the American Philosophical Society, and the attorney-general, Tench Francis. To start with, preparatory, pro-defense material was published in *The Pennsylvania Gazette.* This was followed, on November 17, by *Plain Truth: or, Serious Considerations On the Present State of the City of Philadelphia, and Province of Pennsylvania. By a Tradesman of Philadelphia.* It was a hard-hitting propaganda piece, pointing out that those living on the frontiers did not believe that attack up the Delaware would affect them; that those living by the river felt that a frontier war would not affect them; and that many were reluctant to contribute men or money for defense as long as the Quakers held aloof. " 'Till of late," Franklin wrote almost despairingly, "I could scarce believe the Story of him who refused to pump in a sinking Ship, because one on board, whom he hated, would be saved by it as well as himself."

In *Plain Truth* Franklin not only called for a people's defense militia but lashed out at both of the main groups which had for years been contending for power in the Colony. The Quakers —the "wealthy and powerful Body of People, who have ever since the War governed our Elections"—were told that *"Protec-*

tion is as truly due from the Government to the People, as *Obedience* from the People to the Government." The Proprietors came off no better, they and their supporters being described as "Great and rich Men, Merchants and others, who are ever railing at *Quakers* . . . but take no one Step themselves for the Publick Safety."

Franklin called a meeting for November 21, 1747, to discuss the militia project. So great was the response that a second meeting was called two nights later, by which time he had drawn up the articles of association. "The House was pretty full," he wrote; "I had prepared a Number of printed Copies, and provided Pens and Ink dispers'd all over the Room. I harangu'd them a little on the Subject, read the Paper, & explain'd it, and then distributed the Copies, which were eagerly signed, not the least Objection being made."

Franklin claimed that more than 1,200 men signed that night, although contemporary evidence suggests that the number was much smaller. But after more copies of the articles of association had been printed and distributed throughout the Colony, 10,000 signatures were obtained. The men armed themselves, formed themselves into units, elected their own officers and met weekly for military instruction.

Franklin's achievement was significant, since Pennsylvania was the only Colony in America that did not have a militia organization. His Association reflected the effort to evade Quaker objections; and, being voluntary, it was not technically a militia, since militia service in the literal sense—and in the sense that it existed everywhere else in America—was mandatory. It was also significant that the provincial government approved, even if only tepidly, since it stated that formation of the Association was not disapproved; and although officers were to be elected by the members, their commissions had to be approved and issued by the government.

Franklin knew that the first need was defense of the Delaware below Philadelphia. With no money available for artillery, he ran a lottery and with the receipts, plus some £1,500 from local merchants, began to acquire cannon. Some came, through what channels is not clear, from Boston. Others arrived from New York, whose Governor Clinton was visited personally by Franklin and three other members of the Association. "He at first refus'd us peremptorily," Franklin later recalled; "but at a Dinner with his Council where there was great Drinking of Madeira Wine, as the Custom at that Place then was, he soften'd by degrees, and said he would lend us Six. After a few more Bumpers he advanc'd to Ten. And at length he very good-naturedly conceded Eighteen."

The cannon were shipped to Pennsylvania and mounted in the battery which Franklin helped site and whose establishment is sometimes considered as marking the end of the Quakers' complete control of Philadelphia. "It is proposed to breed gunners by forming an artillery club, to go down weekly to the battery and exercise the great guns," he wrote during the first week of December to James Logan, an eminent Quaker. Franklin, who took his turn at the batteries when they were manned during the night, believed he had put himself in favor by the work, recollecting later: "My Activity in these Operations was agreable to the Governor and Council; they took me into Confidence, & I was consulted by them in every Measure wherein their Concurrence was thought useful to the Association."

It appears likely, however, that the Governor, whose ineffectiveness had been highlighted by Franklin's "private army," thought differently. Certainly this was the case with Thomas Penn, who was quite certain that Franklin's proposed militia was illegal. "The paper called 'Plain Truth' . . . I am afraid has done much mischief, as such a spirit raised in a people cannot be of any service, but under proper and legal regulations," he wrote to Lynford Lardner, a friend of Richard Peters, the provincial secretary. "I am sure the people of America are too often ready to act in defiance of the Government they live in, without associating themselves for that purpose. 'The Association,' as printed, I have seen; and I admire that any man used to thinking seriously could imagine such a military establishment legal and proper, but I shall send the President and Council the Attorney or Solicitor General's opinion upon it." And to Richard Peters he maintained: "Mr. Franklin's doctrine that obedience to governors is no more due them than protection to the people, is not fit to be in the heads of the unthinking multitude. He is a dangerous man and I should be glad if he inhabited any other country, as I believe him of a very uneasy spirit. However, as he is a sort of tribune of the people, he must be treated with regard."

The military progress of the people's tribune was to be ended by the Peace of Aix-la-Chapelle, an event which, Franklin told

Collinson, might enable him and his friends to resume their electrical experiments since it offered "a Prospect of being more at Ease in our Minds." However, it was an uncertain peace and Franklin, together with many others in Pennsylvania, looked on it more as an armistice. Certainly on the northern frontiers of the American Colonies, French pressure on the Indians, whom they had suborned to attack the Colonists wherever the chance of pillage seemed likely, could not be stopped at a moment's notice. Vigilance was still necessary for survival.

Franklin had now learned that he was a leader able to influence Pennsylvania as readily by action as by propaganda. It was a salutary lesson, and his "retirement" was soon being ended by a multitude of new duties and interests. He became, in succession, a justice of the peace, a member of the city's Common Council and, soon afterward, an alderman. By 1751 he had considered his prospects in the Assembly with sufficient care, acceded to friends' demands that he should stand for election, and on August 13 backed with a dignified step into the limelight and took his seat in the Assembly. As a member, he had to vacate the clerkship. It was passed over to son William.

Franklin was obviously to be a workhorse, fully used for a variety of tasks. On the day he took his seat he was voted onto a committee to prepare a bill. Within little more than four weeks he was working on committees to inspect the accounts, to consider a petition of bakers, to examine the rules governing fees, to consider a bill relating to dogs and to see the Great Seal affixed to laws. He was competent to handle any task entrusted to him and soon began to exercise a dominating influence in the Assembly. It was natural, therefore, that he should be picked as one of the three men chosen in September 1753 to meet an Indian delegation in the small settlement of Carlisle, founded on the frontier only two years previously.

To the north there lived the Indians and to the north of them there lived the French, who from their bases in Canada were able to harass everyone in the Ohio Valley whom they regarded as unfriendly. The Indians were now appealing to the Colonists for protection; and appealing with the implied threat that if no protection was forthcoming, they might decide to throw in their lot with the French.

Franklin, Isaac Norris (the Speaker) and Richard Peters arrived in Carlisle after four days' hard riding. Their brief was "to treat with the said Indians now at Carlisle, or with their or any or every of their Chiefs or Delegates, and with them to renew, ratify, and confirm the Leagues of Amity subsisting between Our said Province of Pennsylvania and the said Nations of Indians." In other words, they had to keep the Indians on their side. It was probably Franklin's first visit to the ill-defined frontier separating the settled part of Pennsylvania from the wilderness which stretched nearly 2,500 miles to the Pacific Coast. Despite this, his comments on it are sparse, an indication no doubt that if, for Philadelphians, the threat from the interior was usually out of sight, it was never out of mind.

It is clear from *A Treaty held with the Ohio Indians, at Carlisle, In October, 1753*, printed by Franklin and Hall, that Franklin was intrigued by the mechanics of the diplomacy exercised before the existing agreement could be confirmed. The £800-worth of presents that the delegation had brought was ceremonially presented to the tribes. There was bargaining about the number of trading posts to be allowed in Indian territory, about the sale of rum, about the prices charged by Pennsylvania traders. Even for Franklin it was a new exercise—but in principle not so very different from the negotiations in which he was later to become an expert in London and Paris.

Back in Philadelphia he soon learned of another success. Two years previously he had heard that Elliott Benger, the deputy postmaster general for North America, was dying. The post, the most senior in America, was held under the British Crown and Franklin decided that it could provide yet another opening for his talents. To Peter Collinson he wrote invoking him to pull, in England, whatever strings could be pulled. To more than one friend in Pennsylvania he suggested that lobbying for his appointment in London would be a kindly gesture. Elliott Benger was two years a-dying, and it was not until the summer of 1753 that his post became vacant. But Franklin had laid his lines well and on August 10 he and William Hunter were appointed as deputy postmaster-general and manager, respectively, for North America.

His first act after appointment was to install his son, William, as postmaster at Philadelphia, a post later filled by Joseph Read, a relative of his wife, and then by his own brother. Few of the Franklin or Read families failed to profit over the next few years from their kinsman's zeal for public service, but in an age when nepotism was the order of the day this is less startling than it seems. Nevertheless, even such a normally uncritical writer as Albert Henry Smyth, who edited Franklin's works at the start of the present century, felt it necessary to record: "He looked after them all: brothers, and cousins, and nephews, and brothers-in-law drew salutary incomes from public offices. It may be true that Franklin, as he says, never debated the question of salary, but it is quite evident that he had a wary eye for the incidental income arising from office, and was industrious in filling the choicer seats with members of his own family. . . . In fact, the student of Franklin must, with however much reluctance, come to the conclusion that was expressed by some wicked wag who said that Franklin so loved truth that he was rather sparing in the use of it."

The Deputy Postmaster's partiality for relatives was more than balanced by Franklin's concentration on improving the service and his imagination in doing so. As Philadelphia postmaster he had, typically, introduced the first local delivery service. Now he prepared to set out with Hunter on a journey "to regulate the Post offices, and . . . Travel at least 3,000 Miles before we sit down at home again." This was the first move in a twenty-year tenure of the post during which Franklin introduced great improvements in the postal services. There was ample room for them. In 1753 news from South Carolina was frequently received in Philadelphia by way of Rhode Island, while three years later Franklin still found that the quickest way of sending a letter from Virginia to Philadelphia was by the sea route to New York and then overland back to its destination.

The one man who could have blocked Franklin's appointment as deputy postmaster was Thomas Penn. He, however, was in favor of it. For the moment he overlooked *Plain Truth* and the founding of the militia, which for practical purposes had dissolved after the peace treaty signed at Aix-la-Chapelle. And he overconfidently assumed that his attitude to the post office appointment would win him Franklin's support for the Proprietor's party in the Assembly. On his side, Franklin's relationship with the Proprietors was still ambivalent. The Penns had helped him in more than one of his municipal enterprises and he had not yet turned against them. In the Assembly he was becoming powerful and the Penns, for their part, still believed that it was possible to conscript that power on their own behalf. It was

natural, therefore, that Franklin should be one of the four commissioners from Pennsylvania sent to the Congress—sometimes
called the Convention—held at Albany in June 1754. The others
were John Penn, grandson of William Penn, Isaac Norris and
Richard Peters. Maryland, New York and the four New England
states were also represented.

Ostensibly the Congress, requested by Britain, was held to
make an intercolonial treaty with the Iroquois Indians. But there
were hopes of more far-reaching agreements, and attendance at
the Congress was to mark a watershed in Franklin's life. In
politics, and in the great drama that was starting to be played
out, before being fought out, between Britain and the Colonies,
he had so far been confined to the limited role he could play in
the Pennsylvania Assembly. Albany altered all that.

The plan for union which emerged from the Congress was, it
is true, finally rejected. But it was to lie at the heart of two
decades of argument. The plan itself was very largely Franklin's,
and discussion of it inevitably led him progressively into discussion of the plans and proposals put forward as the British made
increasing demands that the Colonies pay for their own defense
and as the Colonies began to sink their differences and think of
themselves as potentially united states.

The problem of intercolonial union was as old as the foundation of the first British Colonies. It had grown during the wars
with France, and in the early 1750s, as the Treaty of Aix-la-
Chapelle appeared to have ushered in an armed truce rather
than peace, its resolution became one of the British Government's more pressing needs.

Franklin had devised his own ambitious solution as early as
March 20, 1751, when he outlined it to James Parker, whom he
had set up as a printer in New York. "Were there a general
council form'd by all the colonies," it stated, "or in some manner to concur with and confirm their acts, and take care of the
execution; every thing relating to Indian affairs and the defence
of the colonies, might be properly put under the management.
Each colony should be represented by as many members as it
pays sums of . . . hundred pounds into the common treasury for
the common expences; which treasury would perhaps be best
and most equitably supply'd, by an equal excise on strong liq-
uors in all the colonies, the produce never to be apply'd to the
private use of any colony, but to the general service. Perhaps if

the council were to meet successively at the capitals of the several colonies, they might thereby become better acquainted with the circumstances, interests, strength or weakness, &c., of all, and thence be able to judge better of measures propos'd from time to time: at least it might be more satisfactory to the colonies if this were propos'd as a part of the scheme: for a preference might create jealousy and dislike."

From this scheme there was to develop during the next two decades Franklin's vision of an English-speaking union, an empire that could be "the greatest Political Structure Human Wisdom ever yet erected." Yet in spite of such enthusiasm he never ceased to excoriate what he saw as folly or injustice in British actions. As early as 1751 he was lambasting proposals from London that convicts should be dumped into the American Colonies, even while proposing intercolonial union under a governor appointed by the Crown.

Writing as "Americanus" in *The Pennsylvania Gazette* for May 9, 1751, he suggested a suitable countermove. "In some of the uninhabited Parts of these Provinces," he said, "there are Numbers of these venomous Reptiles we call RATTLE-SNAKES; Felons-convict from the Beginning of the World. These, whenever we meet with them, we put to Death, by Virtue of an old Law: *Thou shalt bruise his Head.* But as this is a sanguinary Law, and may seem too cruel; and as however mischivous those Creatures are with us, they may possibly change their Natures, if they were to change the Climate; I would humbly propose that this general Sentence of *Death* be changed for Transportation. In the Spring of the Year, when they first creep out of their Holes, they are feeble, heavy, slow, and easily taken; and if a small Bounty were allow'd per Head, some Thousands might be collected annually, and *transported* to Britain. There I would propose to have them carefully distributed in *St. James's Park,* in the *Spring-Gardens* and other Places of Pleasure about *London;* in the Gardens of all the Nobility and Gentry throughout the Nation; but particularly in the Gardens of the *Prime Ministers,* the *Lords of Trade* and *Members of Parliament;* for to them we are *most particularly* obliged."

Despite such suggestions, which reflected much current feeling, the thoughts of Colonial politicians continued to be dominated in the early 1750s with the French-sponsored Indian threat and plans for meeting it through intercolonial measures. The British were soon considering a plan of their own. However, in London it was appreciated that if the Colonies banded together to improve their defenses, they might well band together for other purposes. Thus the Duke of Newcastle, appointed prime minister six months previously, was warned of the "ill consequence to be apprehended from uniting too closely the Northern colonies with each other; and Independency upon this Country being to be apprehended from such an Union."

By the summer of 1753 the "ill consequence" was being increasingly counterbalanced by actions of the French. The governor of Virginia told Lord Halifax, president of the Board of Trade in London, that they were now building a line of forts along the Ohio which would join the defenses of the Mississippi with those on the St. Lawrence, effectively penning in all the British in North America. The British now decided to act. On August 28, 1753, the Earl of Holderness, secretary of state, wrote to the governors of those Colonies already threatened by the French, or likely to be in the not too distant future. They should, it was suggested, plan mutual military assistance to prevent, if possible, further Indian support for the French. On September 18 the Board of Trade followed this up with a request that the Colonies should "enter into articles of union and confederation with each other for the mutual defence of His Majesty's subjects and interests in North America, as well in time of peace as war," and it was agreed that a Congress should be held at Albany the following year.

New York, New Hampshire, Massachusetts, New Jersey, Pennsylvania, Maryland and Virginia had been invited, but while Virginia and New Jersey failed to send delegates, Rhode Island and Connecticut did so without having received invitations. Final resolutions were sent not only to all these but also to North and South Carolina. In the various plans which were subsequently proposed there was some lack of definition as to who would become involved, but the majority—and certainly Franklin—hoped if not expected that all the Colonies would eventually cooperate in any plan that was finally adopted.

As Franklin was in May making final preparations to leave Philadelphia for the Congress, he received disturbing news. "Mr. *Ward*, Ensign of Capt. *Trent*'s Company," said a message from Major George Washington, the commander on the northern frontier, "was compell'd to surrender his small Fort in the Forks of Monongahela to the French on the 17th past, who fell down from Venango with a Fleet of 360 Batoes and Canoes, upwards of 1,000 Men, & 18 Pieces of Artillery, which they planted against the Fort; and Mr. *Ward* having but 44 Men, and no Cannon, to make a proper defence, was obliged to surrender on Summons, capitulating to march out with their Arms &c. . . ."

The action restored to the French control of the Ohio Valley and once more gave them a line of communication between their forces in Canada and those in Louisiana, some 1,200 miles to the south. " 'Tis farther said," continued Washington's message, which was published in *The Pennsylvania Gazette,* "that besides the French that came down from Venango, another Body of near 400, is coming up the Ohio, and that 600 French Indians of the Chippaways and Ottaways, are coming down Siola River from the Lake, and many more French are expected from Canada; The Design being to establish themselves, Settle their Indians, and build Forts, just on the Back of our Settlements in all our Colonies; from which Forts, as they did from Crown Point, they may send out their Parties to kill and Scalp the Inhabitants, and ruin the Frontier Counties." Already, he concluded, settlers in some parts were pulling back from the frontier areas, abandoning their lands and moving toward the coast, where protection could better be given.

Franklin now used *The Pennsylvania Gazette* to spread his views, and on May 9 the paper published a leading article and a cartoon which Franklin may have drawn himself. This showed a snake, cut into eight parts, each of which was marked with the initials of one of the eight northern colonies. Below were the words: "Join, or Die."

He left Philadelphia for Albany on June 3, 1754. From New York he sent to James Alexander, a member of the American Philosophical Society, a sketch headed *Short Hints towards a Scheme for Uniting the Northern Colonies*—the association he had outlined in *The Pennsylvania Gazette* article—asked his friend to look over them and pass them to Cadwallader Colden, who was requested to "forward the whole to Albany." *Short Hints,* an amplification of the plan he had outlined to Parker four years previously, was presented to the Congress together with plans drawn up by the commissioners from the other colonies. First the Congress agreed on the wisdom of forming a union. Then it set up a seven-man committee, including Franklin, to consider the various proposed plans and "to digest them into one general Plan for the Inspection of this Board." The "general plan" was drawn up, debated, and finally agreed upon. This was the "Albany Plan of Union," adapted from Franklin's *Short Hints,* greatly expanded, and incorporating almost all his basic points. Its central idea was, as recorded in the words of the Pennsylvania Provincial Council *Minutes:*

That humble Application be made for an Act of the Parliament of Great Britain, by Vertue of which one general Government may be formed in America, including all the said Colonies, within and under which Government each Colony may retain its present Constitution, except in the particulars wherein a Change may be directed by the said Act, as hereafter follows.

President General   That the said general Government be adminis-
& Grand Council   tred by a President General to be appointed and supported by the Crown, and a Grand Council to be chosen by the Representatives of the People of the several Colonies met in their respective Assemblies.

Five months later he was to tell Peter Collinson, "tho' I projected the Plan and drew it, I was oblig'd to alter some Things contrary to my Judgment, or should never have been able to carry it through."

Before dealing with the fate of the Albany Plan it is necessary to note that John Penn and Richard Peters made their own treaty with the Six Nations—the Indian confederacy of the Cayugas, Mohawks, Oneidas, Onondagas, Senecas and Tuscaroras—also buying from them for £400, plus a further £400 to be paid later, an enormous stretch of territory which extended Pennsylvania territory almost to Lake Erie. Franklin, who witnessed the treaty, had already agreed with developers in New England to negotiate for enough land for two new colonies. Those involved genuinely believed that they would be killing not two but three birds with one stone. "One large step over the mountains," as Thomas Pownall, later lieutenant governor of New Jersey and governor of Massachusetts, had described such a move to Lord Halifax, would provide an outer defense against the French; fresh colonies would, in any case, consolidate the British position in North America; and with luck a profit might be made by all.

Although this example of private enterprise was successful, larger hopes aroused at the Congress were quickly doused. Not a single Colony approved the plans drawn up by their delegates. One reason was that the prospect of a new tier of intercolonial legislators inevitably diminished the power and influence of those on the existing tier. In addition to this understandable, if parochial, feeling there was the belief that Franklin's plan—for such it was, for most practical purposes—would give too much power to the British Crown.

Franklin was distressed that the individual Colonies had rejected his ideas but still hoped that they might be enforced from Britain. "I doubt not but they will make a good [plan]," he wrote to Peter Collinson, "and I wish it may be done this Winter." There was no chance of that. The Albany Plan arrived in London during the first days of October and reached the desk of the Duke of Newcastle, by now prime minister, on October 12. For the next three weeks he was too busy even to look at it. Then, on November 2, he wrote to Charles Townshend, the Lord of the Admiralty, who was to resign the following year in protest against Newcastle's inept policies. "There is a Representation from the Commissioners, who met at Albany, which may forward our Work of engaging the Colonels [sic] to take some Care of Themselves. I have not had Time to examine it, But if I am not mistaken, It is so far conformable to your own Idea that they themselves propose that what they would have done should be by Act of Parliament here." But finally the Crown found itself at one with the individual Colonies. It totally rejected the Plan.

Franklin never doubted that acceptance of the Albany Plan might have averted the War of Independence. "On Reflexion," he wrote thirty-five years later, "it now seems probable, that if the foregoing plan, or something like it, had been adopted and carried into execution, the subsequent separation of the colonies from the mother country might not so soon have happened, nor the mischiefs suffered on both sides have occurred, perhaps, during another century. For the colonies, if so united, would have really been, as they then thought themselves, sufficient to their own defence, and being trusted with it, as by the plan, an army from Britain, for that purpose, would have been unnecessary. The pretences for framing the stamp act would then not have existed, nor the other projects for drawing a revenue from America to Britain by acts of parliament, which were the cause of the breach, and attended with such terrible expense of blood and treasure; so that the different parts of the empire might still have remained in peace and union."

In his new role as deputy postmaster Franklin traveled from the Congress down to New York before embarking on a long tour of New England post offices. He had two encounters of interest, one in New York and the other in Boston, which for a while was the base for his post office work.

In New York he met by chance Robert Hunter Morris, "the rashest and most indiscreet Governor that I have known," as he described him. A corresponding member of the American Philosophical Society, and former chief justice of New Jersey, Morris had recently been appointed governor of Pennsylvania as replacement to Governor Hamilton, who had retired when no longer able to stand the strain of being torn between the Assembly and the Proprietors. "Mr. Morris asked me," Franklin later wrote, "if I thought he must expect as uncomfortable an administration. I said, No, you may on the contrary have a very comfortable one, if you will only take care not to enter into any dispute with the assembly. My dear friend, said he, pleasantly, how can you advise my avoiding disputes? You know I love disputing, it is one of my greatest pleasures; however, to show the regard I have for your counsel, I promise you I will, if possible, avoid them."

The second meeting was in Boston with William Shirley, governor of Massachusetts, who revealed to Franklin his own plan for colonial defense. The details can only be inferred from Franklin's correspondence with Shirley, and it is not clear whether the Governor's plan had been worked out after suggestions from Britain. From a letter which Franklin wrote on December 22, 1754, it appears that a key part of the plan was for Colonial representatives to sit in the Westminster Parliament. As long as they were present in "reasonable" numbers, Franklin wrote, the idea would probably be acceptable to the Colonies. "I should hope too," he went on, "that by such an union, the people of Great Britain and the people of the Colonies would learn to consider themselves, not as belonging to different Communities with different Interests, but to one Community with one Interest, which I imagine would contribute to strengthen the whole, and greatly lessen the danger of future separations." But the plan, which involved Colonial organization of a combined defense force paid for by Britain, but with the cost later being recouped from the Colonies, rested on the presence of Colonial Members of Parliament. In the British climate of 1754 that could be little more than a pipe dream.

In Boston Franklin stayed with his brother John, whom he had recently appointed as the local postmaster. Here he met for the first time Catharine Ray. A relative by marriage of John Franklin, Catharine was one of the many attractive young women who formed part of Franklin's circle of friends throughout long periods of a long life. On this occasion they traveled together the seventy miles from Boston to Newport, Rhode Island, where Franklin inspected the post office and Catharine completed her journey by boat to lonely Block Island. Although they were to meet only four more times, their correspondence contains more than a hundred letters in which the young girl, who married her second cousin, William Greene, three years after meeting Franklin, poured out her problems and received in return from Franklin a running commentary on events. Their relationship raised eyebrows, but almost certainly without reason.

From Newport, Franklin continued his leisurely journey back to Philadelphia. At Newbury, which became Newburyport, Massachusetts, in 1764, he was delighted to come across an example of what his lightning rods could do. Here, he later reported to James Birkett, "I saw an Instance of a very great Quantity of Lightning conducted by a Wire no bigger than a common Knitting Needle." The spire of the church steeple, seventy feet high above the belfry, he went on, "was split all to pieces and thrown about the Street in Fragments; from the Bell down to the Clock plac'd in the Steeple 20 foot below the Bell there was the small wire above mention'd which communicated the Motion of the Clock to the Hammer striking the Hour on the Bell. As far as the Wire extended no Part of the Steeple was hurt by the Lightning nor below the Clock as far as the Pendulum Rod reach'd: but from the End of the Rod downwards the Lightning rent the Steeple surprizingly. The Pendulum Rod was about the thickness of a small Tobacco Pipe Stem, and conducted the Whole without Damage to its own Substance, except that the End where the Lightning was accumulated it appeared melted so much [as] made a small Drop. But the Clock Wire was blown all to Smoke and smutted the Wall where it passed in a broad black Track, and also the Cieling under which it was carried horizontally. No more of it was left than about an Inch and half next the Tail of the Hammer, and as much joining to the Clock. Yet this is observable that tho' it was so small, as not to be sufficient to conduct the Quantity with Safety to its own Substance yet it did conduct it so as to secure all that part of the Building."

When Franklin arrived back in Philadelphia early in 1755 events had already begun to overtake the Albany discussions. Britain and France were not yet at war again but the British had decided to send to North America two regiments to occupy the Monongahela valley and penetrate to the Ohio, already partially occupied by the French. The justification for this, according to the Duke of Newcastle's ministry, was that the government was entitled to aid British subjects in the defense of British territory and Colonial frontiers—a "soothing fiction," as one historian has called it. War was formally declared between Britain and France only in May 1756, a renewal of the struggle for Europe in which the Colonial dispute at first played only a minor part.

Franklin was to be deeply involved long before this. Late in December 1754, Governor Morris had urged the Assembly to increase the Colony's defenses and had supported his plea by two letters from Sir Thomas Robinson, secretary of state in London. In the second letter Sir Thomas said that two regiments were being sent to America and that two others were to be raised there. As official printers to the Assembly, Franklin and Hall would be forced to print these letters in the record of the Assembly proceedings if they were formally submitted. Franklin proposed that this should not be done. The French, if they had not known, which they probably did, would know now. Governor Morris insisted. As a result, Sir Thomas's statement of future intent was read into the record and printed for all to see.

This incident incensed Thomas Penn, apparently unaware that the situation had arisen from his own governor's intransigence. "I think with you," he wrote to Governor Morris some months later, "that Mr. Franklin's having signed that vile Report upon our answer to the Address of the Assembly, and printed the Secretary of State's Letter contrary to your order shews plainly he is not to be depended upon to assist in promoting the Publick Service in a way the most agreable to the Government.

I make no doubt he differs from the Quakers about the Militia Law, but believe he has no great desire to lessen the power of the Assembly."

Franklin was to be closely involved with the British force whose coming had been reported by Sir Thomas Robinson. It landed in Virginia in the spring of 1755 under the command of General Edward Braddock, a brisk, self-confident Coldstream Guards officer. It was agreed that Braddock should meet the governors of the Colonies in which he would be operating. He would need to keep in touch with them as securely as possible, and the task of ensuring this fell on Franklin as deputy postmaster.

On April 9, only recently returned from almost a year's journeying on post office business, he rode out from Philadelphia to meet Braddock. With him were Governor Morris, Governor Shirley of Massachusetts, Governor De Lancey of New York and Franklin's son, William. An incident during the final part of the journey shows the reputation that Franklin had by this time gained. In Maryland the party was joined by Colonel Tasker, a local landowner. Shortly afterward a whirlwind could be seen in a neighboring valley. Franklin spurred his horse toward the whirlwind, succeeded in getting close to it, and returned to the rest of the party with a detailed account of what he had seen. Were whirlwinds, he then asked, at all common in Maryland? *"No, not at all common,"* the Colonel replied; *"but we got this on purpose to treat Mr. Franklin."*

The party reached Frederick Town (now Frederick), Maryland, General Braddock's headquarters, on April 21 and found him awaiting the return of officers sent out to collect the horses and wagons needed to move his force inland. He had resented the Pennsylvania Assembly's apparent reluctance to vote money for defense but was quickly mollified by Franklin.

Then his officers returned. They had been able to collect only twenty-five wagons, although at least one hundred and fifty were needed. Braddock, and some of his staff, declared that the expedition would have to be abandoned, and many cursed the incompetence of ministers in Britain who had landed them in such a quandary. Franklin now casually mentioned that the force should have been landed in Pennsylvania, where almost every farmer had his wagon. Braddock responded with: "Then you, Sir, who are a Man of Interest there, can probably procure them for us, and I beg you will undertake it."

Franklin, retired printer, accepted the invitation and took on the task of getting George II's army under way. His method demonstrates very well how he so often worked. Into the local paper he inserted a letter "To the Inhabitants of the Counties of Lancaster, York & Cumberland" which started, "Friends and Countrymen." He began by explaining that the army was lacking horses and carriages "thro' the Dissentions between our Governor and Assembly"—a polite indication that the Governor was at fault. "It was proposed," he went on, "to send an armed Force immediately into these Counties, to seize as many of the best Carriages and Horses as should be wanted, and compel as many Persons into the Service as would be necessary to drive and take care of them. I apprehended that the Progress of a Body of Soldiers thro' these Counties on such an Occasion, especially considering the Temper they are in, and their Resentment against us, would be attended with many and great Inconveniences to the Inhabitants; and therefore more willingly undertook the Trouble of trying first what might be done by fair and equitable Means."

Having set himself up as the fair-minded tribune of the people, Franklin stressed the advantages of cooperation. Upwards of £30,000 would be paid out in hire fees, the service to be demanded of the horses and carriages would be light and easy, and the horses et cetera would always be "plac'd where they can be most secure, whether on a March or in Camp." He himself had no particular interest in the affair "(except the Satisfaction of endeavouring to do Good and prevent Mischief)."

Then he added what most propagandists will consider to have been a touch of genius. "If this Method of obtaining the Waggons and Horses is not like to succeed, I am oblig'd to send word to the General in fourteen Days; and I suppose *Sir John St. Clair* the Hussar, with a Body of Soldiers, will immediately enter the Province for the Purpose aforesaid of which I shall be sorry to hear, because I am, very sincerely and truly your Friend and Well-wisher, B. Franklin." Many of Pennsylvania's Germans and Dutch well knew that European hussars were notorious for the ways in which they obtained the supplies they needed and William Shirley, Jr., Governor Shirley's eldest son, whom Braddock employed as secretary, commented: "I can but honour, Franklin for ye last clause of his Advertisemts."

It is not known whether the attraction of £30,000 or fear of the Hussars—a unit which did not in fact then exist in the British army—was the stronger. But within two weeks Franklin had hired the one hundred fifty wagons, at 15s. a day for each wagon, four good horses and driver; sufficient packhorses with saddle at 2s. a day; and sufficient unsaddled packhorses at 1s. 6d. a day. Braddock had supplied him with £800, but Franklin himself added a necessary additional £200. More important, since few farmers had heard of General Braddock, it was Franklin who gave his bond for return of horses and wagons, a gesture which, a few months later, he feared would ruin him. The need for his work was graphically described in a note by Deborah Franklin to Peter Collinson. Her husband was in the Back Counties, she wrote, getting wagons and horses for the army, "which tho' so much out of his Way, he was obliged to undertake, for preventing some Inconveniencies that might have attended so many raw Hands sent us from Europe, who are not accustomed to necessary Affairs."

One thing was still wanting. In Britain's eighteenth-century army the subalterns provisioned themselves, and in the Colonial wilderness they would have difficulty in doing so. Once Franklin became aware of the situation, he sent son William back to Philadelphia, where there existed a committee which had, as he later put it, "the Disposition of some public Money." A letter from Franklin described the subalterns as a deserving cause, and within a few days William was back at Frederick Town with twenty pack animals laden with supplies. One critical version of the incident was that the Assembly "gave sweetmeats, Horses and Presents to conciliate themselves to the King's officers, who threatened us with Fire and Sword if we sat idle." The "sweetmeats, Horses and Presents" were in fact supplemented with hams, butter, sugar, chocolate, biscuits and wine and spirits.

Judging by a letter written to Braddock on June 4 by Governor Morris, provisioning was still on a rather hit-and-miss basis. "I have bought fifty fat Oxen at the Expense of the little Government of the Lower Counties, which I shall send forward tomorrow with a Parcel of fat Sheep, the particular Number I cannot yet say," wrote Morris. "I have put 'em under the Care and Direction of a very careful Man, but the Heat of the Season will make their Progress very slow; this small Supply in behalf of that Government I must desire your Acceptance of for the Use of the army under your immediate Command. . . . How consistent the furnishing Cannon and Stores of War may be with the non-resisting Principles of my Quaking Assembly I can't pretend to say, but from their past Conduct I dare not venture to promise that they will enable me to comply with your Demand, tho' the Accounts they have from England of their Conduct being disapproved by the Ministry and by the Quakers in general, may possibly put 'em into better Temper."

All was now ready. Braddock's first aim, he explained to Franklin, was to regain from the French the area around what was to become Fort Duquesne. "I am to proceed to Niagara," he said, "and, having taken that, to Frontenac, if the Season will allow time; and I suppose it will, for Duquesne can hardly detain me above three or four Days; and then I see nothing that can obstruct my March to Niagara."

Franklin was a natural townsman who rarely went beyond Philadelphia without good reason. But he had spent most of the previous three decades little more than a few days' ride from the frontier, and to him the Indian threat was a background to life as ever-present as the threat of storm and tempest to the seaman. He pointed out to Braddock that on the march his line would be some four miles long and vulnerable to Indian ambush.

"He smil'd at my Ignorance," Franklin wrote later, "& reply'd, 'These Savages may indeed be a formidable enemy to your raw American Militia; but upon the King's regular & disciplin'd Troops, Sir, it is impossible they should make any Impression."

Shortly afterward Braddock began the march north. On July 8 he reached the Monongahela River. From there he pushed on with some 1,300 picked troops toward Fort Duquesne. So far he had apparently heeded American warnings, putting out flank and advance guards, and he now crossed the river twice in order to avoid dangerous defiles.

Then, a few miles from the fort, Indians and French attacked. The accounts of the battle given by either side are very different; surprisingly, the French claimed that "success [was] long doubtful," while the English accounts suggest that from the moment of attack there was little they could do.

Braddock ordered his troops to fight in line, according to the rule book, thus laying them open to deadly fire from Indians who had known how to use the best cover since they had learned to walk. Confusion soon took control, with British troops firing

on their own men. At places Indians appeared as if from nowhere, scalped a man, then disappeared. Braddock was forced
to flat-saber some units in an effort to prevent withdrawal. Four
horses were shot under him until, on a fifth, he was mortally
wounded. *"We shall better know how to deal with them another time"*
were his last words. As the British force lost all cohesion, split-
ting into small leaderless groups which vainly tried to escape
from the nearly invisible enemy, many wagoners cut the traces
of their teams, chose the fittest horse and made for home. Then,
through the blinding smoke and disorder, the survivors heard
the drums sounding the retreat.

"The rout was complete," reported a French eyewitness of
the engagement. "We remained in possession of the field with
six brass twelves and sixes, four howitz-carriages of 50, 11 small
royal grenade mortars, all their ammunition, and, generally,
their entire baggage. . . . We have had 3 officers killed; 2 officers
and 2 cadets wounded." The British also left on the field one
particularly important wagon. It contained Braddock's papers,
including secret instructions for the proposed plan of attack on
the French in Canada.

By this time Franklin had returned to Philadelphia from Frederick Town. He was putting the finishing touches to what was to
become his famous *Observations Concerning the Increase of Mankind*
when on July 18 the first news of the disaster was brought into
Philadelphia. Further news trickled in and then, on the twenty-
third, there came a report printed in the *Lancaster Post* two days
earlier confirming that about 1,000 men had been lost as well
as the artillery train and the baggage train. William Franklin,
one of the survivors of the debacle, was later to claim: "The
shocking news of the strange, unprecedented and ignominious
defeat of General Braddock had no more effect upon Governor
Morris than the miracles of Moses had on the heart of Pharaoh."

Nevertheless, the Governor had to do something. As was
becoming the habit in Philadelphia, he sent for Franklin and
asked for advice. It was, after all, Franklin who had made the
expedition possible—and who was soon to find bills for
£20,000-worth of wagons and horses arriving at his door. Franklin's sensible proposal was that Colonel Dunbar, now in charge
of the remaining British forces, should be ordered to man the
frontier posts and "hold the fort" until a new expedition could
be mounted. But Dunbar was already on his way back to Phila-

delphia, apparently with little idea of what he could do with his surviving troops. "[We] have lost a Number of brave Men, and all our Credit with the Indians," Franklin wrote to Jared Eliot. The disaster appeared to be complete. It was to have one effect. It "gave us Americans," Franklin wrote, "the first Suspicion that our exalted Ideas of the Prowess of British Regulars had not been well-founded," a suspicion of some importance two decades later.

There now followed not the urgent rush to protect the frontier that might have been expected, but weeks of discussion and delay. For Franklin they were weeks of frustration and worry. Only with difficulty did he induce the British authorities to accept responsibility for the £20,000-worth of claims which began to come in when the extent of Braddock's defeat was known. And in the bitter political warfare which continued despite the threat from beyond the frontiers, he had other problems. "I am supposed," he told Collinson, "to have had a principal Share in prevailing with the House to make their late generous Grants to Braddock and Shirley, and the Bill for giving £50,000, and the Governor, with his few Friends are angry with me for disappointing them by that means, of a fresh Accusation against Quakers. A Number of Falshoods are now privately propagated to blast my Character, of which I shall take no Notice 'till they grow bold enough to show their Faces in publick. Those who caress'd me a few Months since, are now endeavouring to defame me every where by every base Art. But it happens that I have the means of my full Defence and their effectual Defeat, in my Power, and shall use those means in due time. Let me know if you learn that any of their Slanders reach England. I abhor these Altercations; and if I did not love the Country and the People, would remove immediately into a more quiet Government, Connecticut, where I am also happy enough to have many Friends."

Even now, with the enemy metaphorically at the gates, exemption of the Penn property from taxation remained a stumbling block to defense.

The seriousness of the situation was admitted by the Governor, who on July 28 sent the Assembly a message stating: "The Removal of the Army from the Frontiers will leave the Back Settlements entirely exposed to the Incursions of the French and Indians, who are flushed by their late Victory, and will be encouraged by the Retreat of the Forces to penetrate deep into the Province, and the People being defenceless, will immediately quit their Habitations."

Once the Assembly was told of Braddock's defeat it resolved to raise the £50,000 for defense by a general land tax. Within a few days the Governor had refused to approve the measure unless the Penn estates were excluded. The resulting back-and-forth between Governor and Assembly filled no less than the first two entire pages of *The Pennsylvania Gazette* for August 14. There followed a three-month indecisive lull, ended when increased Indian attacks forced the Assembly to make another attempt to raise money. This time its members voted for £60,000, again to be raised by a tax on estates and once again including the Penn properties. Over a period of some days the bill was presented to the Governor, returned to the Assembly, re-presented, and then again returned. Once again the argument monopolized the pages of *The Pennsylvania Gazette,* which on October 2 stated: "We are once more under a Necessity of postponing the News till next Week, being obliged to publish these Proceedings between the Governor and Assembly; which we hope our Readers will be kind enough again to excuse."

Only on November 24 did the Penns offer a voluntary £5,000 for defense. The Assembly then altered the bill to exclude the Penn estate. It was passed three days later—before the Assembly discovered that the £5,000 was not quite what it had seemed. The money was to come, in effect, from the Penns' bad debts.

It was not only money that was required. There was still need for a militia. The Quakers, however, were unwilling to serve and others found this an excuse for not doing so. Attempts by Franklin and others to push a militia bill through the Assembly continued to fail.

Meanwhile the Indians descended on all but the best-defended frontier settlements. It was alleged that families were being scalped within eighty miles of Philadelphia and as an argument for action the mutilated bodies of a murdered family were taken round the city in an open wagon and laid out before the State House. The pattern of events is typified by a letter which Franklin wrote to Richard Partridge, Pennsylvania's agent in London. "We have this Day the bad News that the Enemy have last Week surpriz'd and cut off eight Families in this Province," he said; "13 grown Persons were killed and scalped, and

12 Children carried away. They were new Settlers at a Place called Penn's Creek near Shamokin. This is a natural Consequence of the loose manner of Settling in these Colonies, picking here and there a good Piece of Land, and sitting down at such a distance from each other, as that a few Indians may destroy a Number of Familys one after the other, without their being even alarm'd or able to afford one another any Assistance."

Eventually, as the threat sidled closer, Franklin did succeed in pushing a militia bill through the Assembly. But the bill had its limitations. No militiaman could be compelled to go more than three days' march beyond the inhabited parts of Pennsylvania. None could be kept in a garrison for more than three weeks without a special engagement. Moreover, Quakers were exempted, a fact which created much ill-will. Franklin doused it effectively with an ingenious contribution to *The Pennsylvania Gazette* in which three gentlemen, X, Y and Z, discussed the militia bill, the crafty Mr. X winning the argument for the bill despite all objections. The article was, according to William Peters, writing to Thomas Penn, "a Defence and Explanation by way of Dialogue, of our late Militia Law, supposed to be his [Franklin's] performance and intended to pave the way for the Meetings this Week of some of our Citizens for choosing their Officers in compliance with that part of the Act, and which is expected to be a precedent for the rest of the Province."

The law, which could be construed as setting up a private army, was an important factor in widening the rift between the Proprietor and Franklin. Many factors were involved in this, but their enmity seems almost inevitable as Franklin at last lost patience with the Proprietor's exemption from taxation and as Thomas Penn increasingly saw Franklin as trying to wrest control of Pennsylvania from his hands. His belief was certainly nourished by Governor Morris, who on November 22, 1755, wrote to him:

Since Mr. Franklin has put himself at the head of the Assembly they have gone greater lengths than ever, and have not only discovered the warmth of their Resentment against your Family but are using every means in their Power, even while their Country is invaded, to wrest the Government out of your hands, and to take the whole powers of it into their own. To which end Mr. Franklin and others have sent Arms and

Ammunition into the several countys and distributed them to such People as they thought proper without my knowledge or consent. This I esteem a very extraordinary measure, as the people will be thereby taught to depend upon an Assembly for what they should only receive from the Government, and if it is not criminal I am sure it ought to be so.

They have also given presents to the Indians without my privity or Consent, and by a Bill they have sent me this Session, under pretence of regulating the Indian Trade, they propose not only to take that whole Trade into their own hands and manage it by a Committee, but to take the Indians entirely out of the hands of the Government, and least the trade itself should not give them all the Influence they may have occasion for, the profits of it are to be given by the Assembly in presents to the Indians.

Nevertheless circumstances forced Governor Morris's hand and during the last days of November he approved the militia bill, excusing himself to Thomas Penn on the grounds that it was "impossible to carry it into execution, and is therefore no more than waste Paper."

While the first militiamen were being drilled for duty, disturbing news arrived from the Moravian county of Northampton, some ninety miles from Philadelphia. On the night of November 24 a party of Shawnees had raided Gnadenhütten, burned the village and murdered the inhabitants. Nearby villages were considered to be in extreme danger, and it was essential that some action should be taken. Governor Morris turned to the man who had successfully forced through the militia bill. He did so with great distaste, since he was a loyal supporter of the Penns, who as long ago as August had warned Sir Thomas Robinson, "I think it my Duty to observe to You, that Mr. Benjamin Franklin, who holds an office of profit under the General Post Office, is at the head of these extraordinary measures taken by the Assembly, writes their Messages and directs their motions."

But this embryonic rebel, this archenemy of the Proprietor, was to be of considerable use. The Governor "prevail'd with me," Franklin was later to write, "to take Charge of our Northwestern Frontier, which was infested by the Enemy, and provide for the Defence of the Inhabitants by raising Troops, & building a Line of Forts. I undertook this military Business, tho' I did not conceive myself well-qualified for it." The account, like many of

Franklin's, tends to emphasize the importance of Franklin. In fact he was, to begin with, only one of three commissioners appointed to inspect the frontier areas and propose what should be done. The others were the former governor, James Hamilton, and Joseph Fox, a member of the Assembly for nearly twenty years. None of the commissioners had military experience, and it was lucky that Franklin's son, William, who had served in Braddock's ill-fated expedition, accompanied the party.

On December 17 Franklin paid the next half-year's rent for his house, bought a cask of wine for the wagon train, and, ever the newspaperman, drew up an announcement for the following day's issue of *The Pennsylvania Gazette,* which ran: "This Day the Honourable James Hamilton, Esq. and Benjamin Franklin, and Joseph Fox, Esquires set out for the Frontiers, in order to settle Matters for the Defence of the Province."

They left on time the following morning, accompanied by one hundred and fifty cavalry and a wagon train that must have been particularly vulnerable to attack. One officer gives an idea of their problems during the worst season of the year. "Part of our Route, this day," wrote Ensign Thomas Lloyd, "was through the worst country I ever saw. Hills, like Alps, on each side, and a long narrow defile, where the road scarcely admitted a single wagon. At the bottom of it a rapid creek with steep banks, and a bridge made of a single log, so situated that the Indians might with safety to themselves, from the caverns in the rocks, have cut us all off, notwithstanding all human precaution." That they failed to do so was probably the result of William's experience, since presumably it was he who ensured that their flanks were guarded by scouts and that the dangers of ambush were reduced to a minimum. During the fifty days that the expedition lasted it experienced no more than occasional desultory sniping by isolated Indians.

The column camped on the night of the eighteenth and reached the outskirts of Bethlehem on the afternoon of the nineteenth. "Opposite them, across the swiftly coursing Lehigh, there rose the irregular group of houses which formed the Unitas Fratrum, the settlement which Count Zinzendorf and his Moravian colleagues had founded fifteen years before. On the eminence above the stream appeared the castellated turrets of the Brother House, the less imposing Sister House, and the red frame structure where dwelt the Bishop. The mill tower stood hard by the bank of the Monokasy creek, and behind it a winding lane mounted to the cattle house, the storeroom and the multifarious buildings which housed the varied husbandry of the thrifty Brotherhood. And far to the northward, silhouetted in the wintry rays of the setting sun, loomed the ominous snow-capped summits of the savage mountains which sheltered a still more savage foe. Perhaps as Franklin gazed he realized the extent of his responsibility. Upon the measures of defense which he would arrange in the next few weeks might largely depend whether the arrogant white flag of the Bourbons would float over the Bishop's House of Bethlehem."

Franklin and the officers spent the night at the Crown Inn and the following day marched on to Easton, the settlement at the eastern extremity of Pennsylvania. Here, where they remained for ten days, Franklin came into his own. Although head of the Assembly's Committee of Safety, and appointed by the Governor to lead the expedition, he had obtained only verbal instructions. Until arriving at Easton the column was in charge of Hamilton, the former governor. Then, however, the roles were reversed. On arrival, Hamilton had written to Governor Morris, somewhat despondently reporting: "We found the Country under the greatest Consternation, & every thing that has been said of the distress of the inhabitants, more than verified upon our own views. The country along the River is absolutely deserted from this place [Easton] to Broadhead's, nor can there be the least Communication between us and them but by large Parties of Armed Men every body being afraid to venture without that security, so that we have had no accounts from them for several days."

It was Franklin, however, who now ordered the clearing of scrub around the town so that its defenders would have a clear field of fire if attacked, and it was Franklin who organized a local guard and brought the inhabitants into a state of defense. It was he, moreover, who had already issued instructions for defense that no one had yet thought of issuing. "If Dogs are carried out with any Party, they should be large, strong, and fierce; and every Dog led in a Slip-String, to prevent their tiring themselves by running out and in, and discovering the Party by Barking at Squirrels, &c. Only when the Party come near thick Woods and suspicious Places, they should turn out a Dog or two to search them. In Case of meeting a Party of the Enemy, the dogs are then to be all turn'd loose and set on. They will be fresher and fiercer for having been previously confin'd, and will confound the Enemy a good deal, and be very serviceable. This was the Spanish method."

Franklin would presumably have stayed longer in Easton but for the need to rendezvous with Governor Morris in Reading on New Year's Day. He arrived there on time, finding a settlement whose description, given by Richard Peters to Thomas Penn, highlights the precarious frontier situation through which the troops were moving. From being "a flourishing Town full of people and with a good business and a well frequented thorofare, [it] is become a most wretched village, the men of substance having chiefly deserted their houses and the rest being poor and frightened. Would you believe the panic is so intolerably great that Mr. Jones Seeley a magistrate and a man of good sense (who by marrying Hartley's widow became your tenant at the Widow Finney's Plantation, bought of Mr. Lawrence) actually quitted the house, tho close to the outstreets of the town and ran away from it and took a house in the centre of the town.

"The Country people expect the Indians in ten days to fall on some part of the County, that being their time of the moon but I hope they are not too prophetic."

Here among the alarmingly nervous inhabitants, Franklin, Hamilton, Fox and Governor Morris settled down to decide the next move. They had barely begun their discussions when there came news from Gnadenhütten. The Indians had struck there for a second time, surprising the small garrison which had been left in charge after the earlier massacre and forcing it to retreat. The Lehigh Gap, through which the Indians had access to the settled areas, and for which Gnadenhütten had been a forward outpost, was once again quite unprotected. Someone had to be sent back to reorder its local defenses.

Franklin was the man picked for the task. That he should be "chosen over the heads of younger men more experienced in military affairs," it has been stated, "is as surprising as that he should have accepted the charge with such unselfish alacrity." Yet Franklin was not particularly favored by Governor Morris and there is some evidence that he was disliked by the former governor, Hamilton. These gentlemen are unlikely to have been unduly concerned at sending him on the journey and on January

5 the Governor signed Franklin's new commission. "I do hereby authorize and empower you, to take into your Charge the County of Northampton, to dismiss all Persons who have been Commissionated by me to any Military Command, and to put other's into their Places," it went, "and to fill up the Blank Commissions herewith delivered, with the Names of such persons as you shall judge fit for his Majesties Service; hereby ratifying all your Act's and Proceedings, done in Virtue of this Power, and approving the Expences accruing thereupon. And I do further order and enjoin all Officers and Soldiers to yield Obedience to you, in the Execution of this Power, and all Magistrates, Sheriffs, and others, in any kind of Civil Authority, and all his Majesties Liege Subjects, to be aiding and assisting to you in the Premisses. Given under my hand and Seal, at Reading this 5th Day of January 1756."

The problems of Franklin's mission became apparent a few days later. His letter to Governor Morris from Bethlehem not only gives a graphic account of the situation but also indicates just how well Franklin the sedentary printer was able to handle the perils of military command.

As we drew near this Place [he wrote], we met a Number of Waggons, and many People moving off with their Effects and Families from the Irish Settlement and Lehi Township, being terrified by the Defeat of Hays's Company [in Gnadenhütten], and the Burnings and Murders committed in the Township on New Year's Day. We found this Place fill'd with Refugees, the Workmen's Shops and even the Cellars being crouded with Women and Children; and we learnt that Lehi Township is almost entirely abandoned by the Inhabitants.

Soon after my arrival here, the principal People of the Irish Settlement, as Wilson, elder Craig, &c., came to me and demanded an Addition of 30 Men to Craig's Company, or threatned they would immediately one and all leave their Country to the Enemy. Hays's Company was reduc'd to 18 Men, (and those without Shoes, Stockings, Blankets or Arms,) partly by the Loss at Gnadenhütten, and partly by Desertion. Trump and Aston had made but slow Progress in building the First Fort, complaining for want of Tools, which it was thought the People in those Parts might have supply'd them with. Wayne's Company we found posted at Nazareth agreeable to your Honour's Orders. I immediately directed Hays to compleat his Company, and he went down to Bucks County with Mr. Beatty, who promised to assist him in

Recruiting. His Lieutenant lies here lame with frozen Feet, and unfit for Action; But the Ensign with the 18 Men is posted among the present Frontier Inhabitants to give some Satisfaction to the Settlement People, as I refus'd to increase Craig's Company. In my turn, I have threaten'd to disband or remove the Companies already posted for the Security of particular Townships, if the People would not stay on their Places, behave like Men, do something for themselves, and assist the Province Soldiers. The Day after my Arrival here, I sent off 2 Waggons loaded with Bread, and some Axes, for Trump & Aston, to Nazareth, escorted by Lieut. Davis, and the 20 Men of McLaughlin's that came with me; I ordered him to remain at Nazareth to guard that Place while, Capt. Wayne whose Men were fresh proceeded with the Convoy. To secure Lyn and Heidleberg Townships, whose Inhabitants were just on the Wing, I took Trexler's Company into Pay, (he had been before commission'd by Mr. Hamilton) and I commission'd Wetterholt, who commanded a Watch of 44 Men before in the Pay of the Province, ordering him to compleat his Company. I have also allow'd 30 Men to secure the Township of Upper Smithfield, and commission'd Van Etten and Hinshaw as Captain and Lieutenant. And in order to execute more speedily the first Design of erecting a Fort near Gnadenhütten, to compleat the Line, and get the Rangers in Motion, I have rais'd another Company under Capt. Charles Foulk, to join with Wayne in that Service; and as Hays, I hear, is not likely soon to recruit his Company, I have ordered Orndt to come up from Rockland in Bucks County to strengthen this Part of the Province, convoy Provisions, &c. to the Companys, who are and will be at work over the Mountains, and quiet the Inhabitants who seem terrified out of their Senses.

The Arms and Blankets wrote for to New York are not yet arriv'd; but I hear that 100 Guns and 150 Blankets are on the Road, sent me by Mr. Colden; those of Mr. Walton's being sold before. I have consulted Mr. Parsons, and if the Waggons come to-Day it is proposed that I proceed tomorrow with Wayne's Company, which is return'd, Foulk's, and the 20 Men of McLaughlin's, to Gnadenhütten to lay out the intended Fort, and endeavor to get it dispatch'd. Capt. Wayne tells me that Trump expects the first Fort will be finished next Week; I hope to get this done as soon, having more Tools; tho' at this Season it seems to be fighting against Nature. But I imagine 'tis absolutely necessary to get the Ranging Line of Forts compleated, that the People may be secur'd as soon as possible in their Habitations, and the inter-

nal Guards and Companies dismiss'd, otherwise the Expence and Loss
to the Province will be intolerable.

I want much to hear the Event of the proposed Treaty, and the
Determination your Honour and the Commissioners may have come
to, for the Encouragement of Volunteer Scalping Parties.

After thus reorganizing the defenses of Bethlehem, Franklin
marched his column on toward Gnadenhütten. "We arrived
. . . about 12 o'clock and immediately employed our men in
forming a camp and raising a breast-work to defend it," wrote
Ensign Thomas Lloyd. "Here all round appears nothing but one
continued scene of horror and destruction. Where lately flourished a happy and peaceful village, it is now all silent and desolate, the houses burnt; the inhabitants butchered in most
shocking manner; their mangled bodies, for want of funerals,
exposed to birds and beasts of prey; and all kinds of mischief
perpetrated, that wanton cruelty can invent." The column buried the murdered inhabitants and started to build a fort.

Franklin's letter, written from Gnadenhütten on the evening
of January 25, and recorded in the *Minutes* of the Provincial
Council of Pennsylvania, describes the work. Before five o'clock
on the afternoon of their arrival, he says, "[we] had inclosed our
Camp with a Strong Breast work, Musket Proof, and with the
Boards brought here before by my Order from Drucker's mill,
got ourselves under some shelter from the Weather. Monday
was so dark with a thick Fog all day, that we cou'd neither look
out for a Place to build or see where Materials were to be had.
Tuesday morning we looked round us, Pitched on a Place,
mark'd out our Fort on the Ground, and by 10 o'clock began to
cut Timber for Stockades and to dig the Ground. By 3 in the
afternoon the Logs were all cut and many of them halled to the
Spot, the Ditch dug to set them in 3 Feet deep, and that Evening
many were pointed and set up. The next Day we were hinder'd
by Rain most of the Day. Thursday we resum'd our Work and
before night were pretty well enclosed, and on Friday morning
the Stockado was finished and part of the Plat form within
erected, which was compleated the next morning, when we dismissed Foulk's and Wetterholt's Companies, and sent Hays'
down for a Convoy of Provisions. This Day we hoisted your Flag,
made a general Discharge of our Pieces, which had been long

loaded, and of our two Swivels, and nam'd the Place Fort Allen, in Honour of our old Friend [William Allen, chief justice]. It is 125 Feet long, 50 wide, the Stocadoes most of them a Foot thick; they are 3 Foot in the Ground and 12 Feet out, pointed at the Top." All this on the site where Weissport stands today.

Throughout these operations Franklin and his officers benefited from his forethought and ate well. "We have enjoyed your roast beef," he wrote to Deborah, "and this day began on the roast veal. All agree that they are both the best that ever were of the kind. Your citizens, that have their dinners hot and hot, know nothing of good eating. We find it in much greater perfection when the kitchen is four score miles from the dining room. The apples are extremely welcome, and do bravely to eat after our salt pork; the minced pies are not yet come to hand, but I suppose we shall find them among the things expected up from Bethlehem on Tuesday; the capillaire [a syrup flavored with orange flower water] is excellent, but none of us having taken cold as yet, we have only tasted it."

By the end of January Franklin's work was done. He had stitched together a defense of sorts and was unlikely to get men or money to do more—"at present the Expence in this County is prodigious," he had told the Governor when reporting that he had 522 men on the payroll. He now turned for home and arrived in Philadelphia late on the night of February 5, in considerable secrecy. "The People happen to love me," he explained to Peter Collinson. "Perhaps that's my Fault. When I was on the Frontier last winter, a great Number of the Citizens, as I was told, intended to come out and meet me at my Return, to express their thankful Sense of my (small) Services. To prevent this, I made a forc'd March, and got to Town in the Night, by which they were disappointed, and some a little chagrined."

He is perhaps a little ingenuous. But he had every reason to be proud of his performance—and for having carried it out without making a penny for himself, a circumstance almost unknown in those times. "You cannot but have heard of the Zeal and Industry with which I promoted the Service in the Time of General Braddock, and the Douceurs I procur'd for the Officers that serv'd under him," he wrote a decade later. "I spent a Summer in that Service without a Shilling Advantage to myself, in the Shape of Profit, Commissions, or any other way whatsoever."

On his return Franklin was relieved to learn that Governor Morris had appointed four commissioners to "audit, liquidate, adjust and settle" the wagon accounts that had hung like a financial millstone around his neck since the summer. Governor Morris gave other signs that he now saw Franklin in a less unfriendly light than his employer, Thomas Penn, might have wished, since he made Franklin two offers, the first of a general's commission if he would lead a force to capture Fort Duquesne. Franklin turned it down, very wisely no doubt; despite his commonsense management of the foray to Gnadenhütten, he was no soldier and he knew it. The second offer, which he accepted, was the more nominal appointment as Colonel of the Regiment of Philadelphia.

This, following hard on Franklin's success in the field, concentrated the enmity of the Proprietor. "The Governor," he had been told by Richard Peters, "will, I think, lose all character by approving the choice of field officers of the City Regiment and giving such an important commission to Mr. Franklin, which he is determined to do against all reason and without advice." Penn, replying, was uncompromising: "I much wonder the Governor would appoint Mr. Franklin, Colonel. He should never have any commission given to him till it is certain he has changed his sentiments." Nevertheless, Franklin was commissioned by Governor Morris, and it was Richard Peters before whom he took the prescribed oath on February 28.

In London rumors were soon circulating that the new Colonel might even be sent to Britain as an agent, an idea which made Penn anxious. "I think Mr. Franklin will not engage in so foolish a project as to come over here," he told Richard Peters. "I am sure that he will meet with a very cool reception and that I have no reason to be uneasy from anything that he may do." Maybe so. But Penn was nevertheless already prepared to take spoiling action, as he showed in a letter to William Peters, secretary of the provincial land office, written less than a fortnight after Franklin's triumphant return to Philadelphia and before the news of it could have reached England.

"I shall entrust you with a secret no one knows but Sir Everard Falconer and myself nor shall not for I copy this letter," he wrote. "I have spoke to Sir Everard about Franklin (as I have to the Duke of Cumberland and to the Secretary of State) and desired him to write a letter which goes by this packet to tell

Franklin that all the King's officers and himself in particular are expected to assist the Governor on all occasions and to recommend him to do it. If this has any good effect I shall proceed no further but if it has not I shall desire he may be removed from his Postmastership."

Franklin, unperturbed by the passions which he knew he had aroused, set off in March for a two-month tour of the Colonies, ostensibly to carry out post office business but probably with the secondary aim of testing feeling outside Pennsylvania on the controversial subject of defense and how it should be concerted and paid for. Between thirty and forty officers of the City Regiment escorted him to the frontier with Maryland, an event which gravely disturbed the Proprietor, who saw this as confirming his fear that Franklin was now heading an illegal armed force.

After two months in Virginia, Franklin sailed north to New York, then returned overland to Philadelphia. Here he found that Governor Morris had resigned. It has been said that a Pennsylvania governor had to serve three masters, "the proprietaries who could take away his office, the Assembly who could withhold his salary, and the King of England who could cut off his head." Morris, like Hamilton before him, had been unable to stand the three-way strain any longer. "Change of devils," noted Franklin's son, "according to the Scotch proverb, is blithesome."

The Duke of Cumberland, George II's influential second son, long known as "Bloody Cumberland" for his treatment of the Scottish Highlanders after the battle of Culloden, first considered as Morris's successor the young Thomas Pownall, who had already held a number of appointments in the Colonies. Since Pownall was already a friend of Franklin, whom he had met at the Albany Congress, the proposal was received less than warmly by Thomas Penn. Eventually he settled for William Denny, who had served with Cumberland in Flanders and who was now given a commission as lieutenant colonel in America only. "By this compromise," it has been said, "Penn saved his rights and the colony its self-government, but how unsatisfactory the settlement was Denny's subsequent difficulties showed."

The new governor arrived in mid-August 1756 and was inaugurated on the twentieth with the customary hoisting of flags, roaring of batteries, ringing of bells and lighting of bonfires. A handsome banquet was organized by the Assembly in the Masonic Lodge and here Denny presented Franklin with the Royal Society's Copley Medal, which had been awarded three years earlier. "I know not whether any of your learned Body have attain'd the ancient boasted Art of *multiplying* Gold," wrote Franklin in his acknowledgment to the Society, "but you have certainly found the Art of making it infinitely *more valuable.*"

When the official ceremonies were over, Denny drew Franklin aside and said he hoped that they would work agreeably together. "He said much to me also," Franklin later wrote, "of the Proprietor's good Dispositions towards the Province, and of the Advantage it might be to us all, and to me in particular, if the Opposition that had been so long continu'd to his Measures, were dropt, and Harmony restor'd between him and the People, in effecting which it was thought no one could be more serviceable than my self, and I might depend on adequate Acknowledgements & Recompences, &c. &c." Franklin made it clear that he was not bribable.

Within a few months it was obvious that Governor Denny had been given a facsimile of his predecessor's instructions. In November 1756 the Indians overcame the garrison of Franklin's Fort Allen and burned to the ground the village and the stockade. But when the Assembly voted the defense funds for the coming year the Governor refused to approve the vote. There was the traditional back-and-forth, but consultations failed to find a compromise and the Governor thereupon told the Assembly that "he would not give his consent to it, and there being no person to judge between the governor and the House in these parts, he would immediately transmit to his Majesty his reasons for so doing." Only on February 3, 1757, did the Assembly reluctantly agree to pass a £100,000 supply bill, which exempted the Proprietors' estates from taxation. Even then, the Governor continued to protest over details and the bill remained blocked.

This time the Proprietors' intransigence had finally exhausted the Assembly's patience and its members resolved: "That a Commissioner, or Commissioners, be appointed to go Home to England, in Behalf of the People of this Province, to solicit a Removal of the Grievances we labour under by Reason of Proprietary Instructions &c."

Three days later Franklin warned his printer friend, William Strahan: "Our Assembly talk of sending me to England speedily. Then look out sharp, and if a fat old fellow should come to your printing house and request a little smouting [free-lance printer's work], depend upon it 'tis your affectionate friend and humble Servant [B. Franklin]."

The Assembly now set up a Committee of Aggrievances, which in February listed five heads of complaint against the Proprietors. First, they had "so abridged and restricted their late and present Governor's Discretion in Matters of Legislation, by their illegal, impracticable, and unconstitutional Instructions and Prohibitions, that no Bill for granting Aids and Supplies to our most gracious Sovereign . . . unless it be agreeable thereto, can meet with his Approbation." Secondly, and specifically, the Proprietors had prevented the Assembly from giving the necessary aid to defense of the Colony. The next two complaints were linked; since the Proprietors did not pay taxes, they should have no power over the way in which the taxpayers' money was spent, but they themselves should, in fact, be taxed. Lastly, while judges should hold their jobs only during their "good Behaviour, and no longer," they had been appointed by the governors to hold them during the governors' "Will and Pleasure."

At first it was proposed that Franklin and the Speaker of the Assembly, Isaac Norris, should travel to England and present their case to the Proprietors in London. Norris soon withdrew on the grounds of age and ill-health, and the delicate task now remained with Franklin alone. His enemies had little objection. He would, after all, be removed from the political arena of Philadelphia at least for some months, and he would be traveling on a mission which had only a very slim chance of success. Nevertheless, there was opposition, typified by Dr. John Kearsley, Jr.'s letter to ex-Governor Morris. "They talk of Sending the Electrician home which is a new delay," he wrote. "He Jumps at going. I am told his office [of deputy postmaster general] shakes. However though he would not go but to Support this falling interest of his own, he is artfully Insinuating that he goes on his Countrys Service. Most Certain I am that he will go at his Country's Expence for he is wicked enough to Blind the people."

The Assembly's resolution did in fact offer an opportunity for which Franklin had been waiting. As far back as 1748 he had contemplated a voyage to England and had told his mother in 1749 that it "might be of service to me, in the matter of getting in my debts." The following month he confided to William

Strahan that he had not given up the idea and believed he would travel in 1750 "if nothing extraordinary occurs."

Seven years later the Assembly's decision opened the way, and he prepared to sail from New York as soon as possible. However, before Franklin could leave Philadelphia, Lord Loudoun, recently appointed British commander in America, arrived in the city. Loudoun, a regular soldier who had fought under Cumberland against Charles Edward Stuart in the Forty-five, had sensibly come to Philadelphia hoping to arrange a compromise between the Assembly and the Governor. "In behalf of the Assembly I urg'd all the Arguments that may be found in the publick Papers of that Time, which were of my Writing, and are printed with the Minutes of the Assembly," Franklin wrote, "& the Governor pleaded his Instructions, the Bond he had given to observ them, and his Ruin if he disobey'd: Yet seem'd not unwilling to hazard himself if Lord Loudoun would advise it. This his Lordship did not chuse to do, tho' I once thought I had nearly prevail'd with him to do it; but finally he rather chose to urge the Compliance of the Assembly; and he entreated me to use my Endeavours with them for that purpose; declaring he could spare none of the King's Troops for the Defence of our Frontiers, and that if we did not continue to provide for that Defence ourselves they must remain expos'd to the Enemy."

Franklin, according to his own account, then intervened with the Assembly and succeeded in pushing through a compromise bill which the Governor was able to approve. This was one part of the truth. What he failed to mention, writing some fourteen years later, was that the Governor had also been swayed by a false report of a huge enemy force preparing to attack Fort Augusta, on the Susquehanna. Unless military expenses were approved immediately, the whole of Pennsylvania might be open to attack. Denny passed the news to Loudoun, who persuaded him to waive his instructions and pass the £100,000 bill as it stood.

Early in April Franklin set out for New York with his son, William, and two black servants. "I leave Home," he wrote to Deborah from Trenton, "and undertake this long Voyage more chearfully, as I can rely on your Prudence in the Management of my Affairs, and Education of my dear Child; and yet I cannot forbear once more recommending her to you with a Father's tenderest Concern."

He expected to be away for less than a year and his absence would therefore be very similar to the months-long separations which had been part of his task as postmaster. But with the exception of a two-year break, Franklin was not to return home for seventeen years. Although he did not know it, he was all but pulling himself up by the roots.

THE

AMBIVALENT

AMERICAN

FIVE

FIGHTING THE
PROPRIETORS

RANKLIN HOPED TO SAIL FROM NEW YORK
by mid-April 1757. In fact, it was mid-June before he
was able to leave. There was now gathering off New
York a fleet to carry 6,000 British regular troops for an assault
on Louisburg, given back to the French after the Treaty of
Aix-la-Chapelle, and Loudoun did not wish to move until all was
ready. The civilian packets would sail with the assault force part
of the way, since it was essential that they get as much protection
as possible from attacks by French privateers during their crossing of the Atlantic.

Franklin thus found himself kicking his heels in New York for
two months. As was his habit when he could find no urgent work,
he let his mind speculate on subjects which sprang from the
observations he believed formed the basis of science. Possibly
shivering in whistling winds, he wrote to John Lining on the
business of keeping warm. By "a constant supply of fuel in a
chimney, you keep a warm room, so, by a constant supply of
food in the stomach, you keep a warm body; only where little

exercise is used, the heat may possibly be conducted away too fast; in which case such materials are to be used for cloathing and bedding, against the effects of an immediate contact of the air, as are, in themselves, bad conductors of heat, and consequently, prevent its being communicated thro' their substance to the air. Hence what is called *warmth* in wool, and its preference, on that account, to linnen; wool not being so good a conductor: And hence all the natural coverings of animals, to keep them warm, are such as retain and confine the natural heat in the body, by being bad conductors, such as wool, hair, feathers, and the silk by which the silk-worm, in its tender embrio state, is first cloathed. Cloathing, thus considered, does not make a man warm by *giving* warmth, but by *preventing* the too quick dissipation of the heat produced in his body, and so occasioning an accumulation." It was a subject which was to intrigue him for the rest of his life.

Franklin's observations of the world about him rarely ceased. This was demonstrated as the fleet of more than one hundred ships eventually sailed up the coast of New England and toward Halifax, where Loudoun was to be reinforced with the additional 6,000 troops—and where, for little apparent reason, he abandoned the attack on Louisburg and returned to New York.

Franklin noticed that while the wakes of most vessels were ruffled by the wind, those of two appeared remarkably smooth. "The cooks [of those vessels]," the captain of his own ship told him, "have, I suppose, been just emptying their greasy water through the scuppers, which has greased the sides of those ships a little." The explanation did not satisfy Franklin. Neither did any of the others that he received over the years. But he continued to look for one, observing that "For a new appearance, if it cannot be explain'd by our old principles, may afford us new ones, of use perhaps in explaining some other obscure parts of natural knowledge."

Franklin's persistence in hanging on to unsolved riddles was well exemplified by this question of how oil calmed the waters. Arrived in England, he was soon carrying out his own experiments and, observing a pond whose waters had been roughened by the wind, dropped on it a little oil from a cruet. "I saw it spread itself with surprizing swiftness upon the surface; but the Effect of smoothing the waves was not produced; for I had applied it first on the leeward side of the pond, where the waves were largest, and the wind drove my oil back upon the shore. I then went to the windward side, where they began to form; and there the oil though not more than a tea spoonful, produced an instant calm over a space several yards square, which spread amazingly, and extended itself gradually till it reached the lee side, making all that quarter of the pond, perhaps half an acre, as smooth as a looking-glass. After this, I contrived to take with me, whenever I went into the Country, a little Oil in the upper hollow joint of my bamboo Cane, with which I might repeat the Experiment as Opportunity should offer; and I found it constantly to succeed."

It not only succeeded but later gave Franklin an addition to the repertoire of party tricks with which he impressed friends. The Abbé Morellet describes one such incident when Franklin was among the guests of Lord Shelburne at Wycombe. A fresh breeze was ruffling the waters of a little stream which flowed through the park. Franklin "ascended a couple of hundred paces from the place where we stood and, making what appeared to be several magic passes, shook three times upon the stream a cane which he carried in his hand. A moment later the waves diminished and soon the surface was smooth as a mirror."

Franklin was not the only man to know the secret of surreptitiously spreading oil upon the waters—St. Aidan was reported by Bede in his *Ecclesiastical History* to have done the same in the seventh century—but he, alone, appears to have been given the credit for it. William Small, writing to him from Birmingham, reported that Matthew Boulton, the engineer who worked with James Watt on the steam engine, had "astonished the rural philosophers exceedingly by calming the waters *à la Franklin.*"

During the voyage to London in 1757, the third of his eight Atlantic crossings, Franklin continued the observations he had made on the first two, taking the temperature of the water, noting the weather and recording the fishes and birds which followed the vessel.

He also wrote what was to become one of his most famous pieces. Needing a preface for the *Poor Richard* of 1758 but preoccupied as he had been during recent months, he was short of fresh material. He therefore fell back on the familiar practice of rewriting what had been used years previously. It was ingeniously done, with a venerable Father Abraham being asked by a village crowd to give them good advice. Father Abraham replied by stringing together many of the aphorisms that had appeared in *Poor Richard* over the years. Franklin had no previous issues with him and therefore altered and improved his earlier versions. The result was a recipe for a successful financial life.

"Methinks," said Father Abraham, "I hear some of you say, *Must a man afford himself no leisure?* I will tell thee, my friend, what Poor Richard says, *Employ thy time well if thou meanest to gain leisure;* and, *since thou art not sure of a minute, throw not away an hour.* Leisure, is time for doing something useful; this leisure the diligent man will obtain, but the lazy man never; so that, as poor Richard says, *A life of leisure and a life of laziness are two things.* Do you imagine that sloth will afford you more comfort than labour? No, for as poor Richard says, *Trouble springs from idleness, and grievous toil from needless ease. Many without labour, would live by their* wits *only, but they break for want of stock.* Whereas industry gives comfort, and plenty, and respect: *Fly pleasures, and they'll follow you. The diligent spinner has a large shift;* and *now I have a sheep and a cow, every body bids me good morrow;* all which is well said by poor Richard."

As *The Way to Wealth,* it was later printed as a separate publication, and eventually went through seventy editions in English, fifty-six in French, eleven in German, and nine in Spanish. In addition it was translated into Danish, Swedish, Welsh, Polish, Gaelic, Russian, Bohemian, Dutch, Catalan, Chinese and Greek. When Franklin arrived in France in 1776 as representative of the United States, the intelligentsia knew him for his scientific work on electricity. Thousands of ordinary Frenchmen and Frenchwomen knew him as the author of *The Way to Wealth.*

More than once during the crossing, as Franklin scribbled out his ideas, what were suspected to be French vessels were seen on the horizon and evasive action had to be taken. Off the Scillies, and coming up the western reaches of the Channel, it was thought prudent to sail at night, and at one point the ship barely escaped destruction on the rocks. The following morning, after a voyage of some five weeks, soundings showed that the vessel was nearing land, although a thick fog covered the sea and the coast.

"About 9 a'Clock the Fog began to rise," Franklin recorded, "and seem'd to be lifted up from the Water like the Curtain at a Play-house, discovering underneath the Town of Falmouth, the Vessels in its Harbour, & the Fields that surrounded it. A most pleasing Spectacle to those who had been so long without any other Prospects, than the uniform View of a vacant Ocean! And it gave us the more Pleasure, as we were now freed from the Anxieties which the State of War occasion'd."

From Falmouth Franklin took the coach to London, where he arrived on the evening of July 26 and was met by Peter Collinson, the man so largely responsible for presenting his electrical discoveries to the world. He stayed at the Bear Inn in the City but was soon taken out to Collinson's splendid house at Mill Hill, a few miles north of London.

Franklin was not only an emissary from the Pennsylvania Assembly, a body of little more than parochial interest in England, but also the American whose electrical experiments had made him famous throughout Europe. He was something of a showpiece and at Mill Hill was visited by many men who were to become close friends. Among them was Dr. John Fothergill, the Quaker physician who had written the preface to *Experiments and Observations* a few years earlier. So well known that his postal address was for long simply "Dr. Fothergill, London," and soon to be elected a Fellow of the Royal Society, Fothergill was the owner at Upton, Essex, of one of the finest botanical gardens in Europe, and an artist so skilled that his botanical drawings were bought by the Empress of Russia. He now became Franklin's doctor but, more significantly, was to help arrange the first meeting between Franklin and the Penns.

Another visitor to Mill Hill was William Strahan, Franklin's correspondent for more than thirty years. There had been half-serious consideration by the two men that Strahan's son William might marry Sally Franklin, and before leaving America for England, Franklin had written to Strahan: "It gives me great pleasure to hear so good an account of our son Billy. In return, let me tell you, that our daughter Sally is indeed a very good girl, affectionate, dutiful, and industrious, has one of the best hearts, and though not a wit, is for one of her years, by no means deficient in understanding. She already takes off part of her mother's family cares. This must give you and Mrs. Strahan pleasure. So that account is partly balanced."

Now that Franklin and Strahan met for the first time, the latter was quick to sing Franklin's praises to Deborah: "For my own part, I never saw a man who was, in every respect, so perfectly agreeable to me. Some are amiable in one view, some in another, he in all." And son William was "one of the prettiest young gentlemen I ever knew from America."

Franklin was aware that his mission would involve meetings not only with the Penns but also with the British authorities who would be involved in any changes of relationship between the Proprietors and the Assembly. It was essential to acquire a base in the center of London, and with the help of Robert Charles, the Pennsylvania agent in London, he moved before the end of July to the quarters that were eventually to become almost a second home. This was No. 7 Craven Street—or "Judas's office in Craven Street," as Franklin's denigrators were to call it.

The house formed part of a double line of terrace dwellings at the western end of the Strand, running down from the site of the present Trafalgar Square to the river Thames near today's Hungerford Bridge. In Franklin's times it was the home of numerous barristers from Gray's Inn, and a local ditty ran: "For the Lawyers are just at the top of the street / And the Barges are just at the bottom; / Fly, honesty, fly to some safer retreat / For there's craft in the river and craft in the street."

The owner of No. 7 was Mrs. Margaret Stevenson, a widow who occupied it with her daughter Mary, often known as Polly. Miss Stevenson married a Dr. William Hewson a few years after Franklin arrived in London and therefore appears in his correspondence as Mary Stevenson, Polly Stevenson, Mary Hewson and Polly Hewson. The correspondence was considerable, since Margaret Stevenson's daughter had, for her time, a rare feminine interest in science. After she moved to live with relatives on the outskirts of London, her inquiries to Franklin were intelligent and frequent while his replies were more than simple explanations to a young girl. With her he discussed the cause of waterspouts, the absorption of heat by different-colored cloths and the cause of tides in rivers. Eight of his letters to her were included in a new edition of *Experiments and Observations on Electricity* published in 1769.

He was soon settled in with the Stevensons as naturally as on his native heath and twenty-five years later was able to write of his relations with the family: "Our Friendship has been all clear Sunshine, without the least Cloud in its Hemisphere." He occupied a second-floor front room as bedroom, with a second room at the back of the house where he could continue his electrical experiments. William Franklin had his own room above while the Franklins' two servants—one of whom was soon to run away —occupied a garret.

Franklin was now, in his early fifties, an imposing figure, not so much by height or by girth—although a shadow of the portliness which came later could by now be seen—as by the air of self-confidence which he exuded. London society was more sophisticated than that of Philadelphia. Its customs and rules were different and rooted in a tradition which went back almost a thousand years rather than a couple of hundred. But Franklin quickly learned, adapted, and almost as quickly became a part of the landscape. At the very top levels of society he was for long to be handled only with very long tongs. But at all other levels he was soon to be exercising influence: first as a, and later as the, unofficial spokesman for the American Colonies. He loved it.

For William, whose name had been entered on the books of the Middle Temple by Strahan in 1751, the delights of London were never-ending. "For some Time after my Arrival at this great Metropolis," he wrote in an affectionate letter to Elizabeth Graeme, a young Pennsylvania girl to whom he had become engaged but whom he would soon desert, "the infinite Variety of new Objects; the continued Noise and Bustle in the Streets; and the Viewing such Things as were esteem'd most curious, engross'd all my Attention. Since then, frequent Engagements among Politicians, Philosophers, and Men of Business; making Acquaintances with such Men as have it in their Power to be of Service in settling our unhappy Provincial Disputes; and now and then partaking of the publick Diversions and Entertainments of this bewitching Country, have found full Employment for almost every Hour. Even the present Hour is stolen from Sleep; the Watchman's hoarse Voice calling Past two aClock and a Cloudy Morning."

Franklin himself soon acquired the additional necessities of London life and his account book for August 1757 lists purchases of spectacles and a glass (£1 0. 6.), a watch at auction (£4), mourning swords and buckles (£1 10. 6.), two pairs of silver shoe and knee buckles (£2 12. 6.) and a sword knot for 8/6. As quickly as his son, he became absorbed in the new and exciting world of London life, but not before he had gone to the press in Lincoln's Inn Fields where he had worked in 1724, bought a gallon of beer for the workers and drunk with them to the toast of: "Success to Printing."

He appears to have felt strongly about the parting from his family. "I have made your Compliments to Mrs. Stevenson," he wrote to Deborah shortly after his arrival. "She is indeed very obliging, takes great Care of my Health, and is very diligent when I am any way indispos'd; but yet I have a thousand times wish'd you with me, and my little Sally with her ready Hands and Feet to do, and go, and come, and get what I wanted. There is a great Difference in Sickness between being nurs'd with that tender Attention which proceeds from sincere Love."

He had brought with him to England a small portrait of Sally and another of his young son who had died of smallpox. Even after he had been years in London his mind was often filled with thoughts "of my Son Franky, tho' now dead thirty-six Years, whom I have seldom since seen equal'd in every thing, and whom to this Day I cannot think of without a Sigh." He also proposed that Deborah might have another portrait of Sally painted by a relation of a John Reynolds who he believed was in Philadelphia. "Send it me with your small Picture," he said, "that I may here get all our little Family drawn in one Conversation Piece." But six months later he abandoned the idea, since family pieces "never look well, and are quite out of Fashion."

Portraits provided him with some solace. He expected the same reaction in others and when he fell ill during his first autumn in London had a miniature of himself painted for Deborah. There had been one earlier portrait of Franklin, commissioned by his brother John and executed by Robert Feke in the late 1730s or early 1740s. Here there was Franklin the printer and newspaper proprietor in suit of green and with dark-green waistcoat. An immaculate brown wig, simple enough to satisfy a Quaker, avoided ostentation, but in Feke's portrait Franklin looks what he was, the successful businessman preparing for even better times.

The London miniature of 1757 was executed by an artist still identified only as "C. Dixon." Showing Franklin in reddish dressing gown which covers a yellow waistcoat and white shirt, and with a turbanlike cap as substitute for wig, it was dispatched by warship to Philadelphia via New York. This was to be the first of innumerable portraits executed in London. Franklin, it has been said, "gave prints, paintings and sculptures of himself to friends more freely than almost anyone else of the time, and always with the feeling that it was done in the nature of a personal visit, a form of vicarious intimacy, just as the portraits of others around him brought their lives and friendship closer to him. Those whom he approached in this way responded with an answering warmth, elders regarding the image with reverence and affection, young women kissing it as ardently as they might the original."

There was in 1757, and there remained for two decades, a considerable ambivalence in Franklin's attitude to his family in Philadelphia and particularly to his wife. It is difficult not to believe that he would have been, at the least, mildly disconcerted if Deborah had agreed, as he proposed more than once, to follow him across the Atlantic. Indeed, as early as January 1758 he had told her: "I am sure there is no inducement strong enough to prevail with you to cross the seas." She herself had adamantly declared the same thing to his friend William Strahan, and in a letter to David Hall, Strahan had said, "I have received Mrs. Franklin's Letter, to whom I beg you will give my sincere Respects, and tell her I am sorry she dreads the Sea so much that she cannot prevail on herself to come to this fine place, even tho' her Husband is before her. There are many Ladies here that would make no Objection to sailing twice as far after him, but there is no overcoming Prejudices of that kind."

This was the reaction when Franklin saw that his mission would be a long one. It was mid-August before Fothergill was able to arrange Franklin's first meeting with Thomas Penn in London. According to Penn, the "Heads of Complaint" document was "neither dated, Signed or addressed to any Person." A few days later, at a second meeting, Franklin handed over the document duly completed. He now learned, however, that the Penns expected him to deal not with themselves but with their lawyer, Ferdinand John Paris, a course to which he strongly objected.

At this point he fell ill. The illness, the symptoms of which included vertigo, a humming tinnitus and a vision of faint twinkling lights, lasted for seven weeks and was treated by Dr. Fothergill. Franklin was a bad patient, refusing to follow Fothergill's instructions and relapsing more than once after a partial recovery. Eventually he was, as he reported to Deborah, "cupped me on the back of the head" and thereafter made a slow recovery. Whether the trouble was psychosomatic or the result of high blood pressure brought on by frustration is uncertain. But in the struggle that was now developing it is evident that the Proprietors had the advantages of experience. As was to be more obvious when Franklin began to approach the authorities, he did not yet know how matters were managed in Britain. He learned quickly, but during the first exchanges the Proprietors were justified in their confidence and, when the time came, in sending their reply not to Franklin, still in London, but to the Assembly in Philadelphia.

There were further meetings after Franklin's recovery—in November, and then again in January 1758. On the latter occasion Penn riled Franklin more than usual when he spoke of William Penn's charter of privileges. Franklin said that the original charter expressly stated that the Pennsylvania Assembly should have all the power and privileges of an assembly, as was the right of the freeborn subjects of England, and as was usual in any of the British plantations in America. "Yes!" Penn replied, according to Franklin's account of the meeting which he sent to Isaac Norris a few days later, "but if my father granted privileges he was not by the royal charter empowered to grant; nothing can be claimed by such grant."

Franklin's letter to Norris reveals his astonishment at the claim. "I said," he wrote, "if then your father had no right to grant the privileges he pretended to grant, and published all over Europe as granted, those who came to settle in the province, on the faith of that grant, and in expectation of enjoying the privileges contained in it, were deceived, cheated and betrayed. He answered they should have themselves looked to that, that the royal charter was no secret; they who came into the province, on my father's office of privileges, if they were deceived, it was their own faults, and that he said with a kind of triumphing, laughing insolence, such as a low jockey might do, when a purchaser complained that he had cheated him in a horse. I was astonished to see him thus meanly give up his father's character, and conceived at that moment a more cordial and thorough contempt for him, than I ever before felt for any man living, a contempt that I cannot express in words, but I believed my countenance expressed it strongly, and that his brother, who was looking at me, must have observed it. However, finding my self grow warm, I made no other answer to this, than that the poor people were no lawyers themselves, and confiding in his father, did not think it necessary to consult any."

Norris appears to have treated the letter rather casually, although later denying to Franklin that this was so. Certainly it fell into the hands of Richard Peters, the provincial secretary, who immediately had a copy sent to Thomas Penn in London. Whatever slim hopes of a compromise had previously existed were now removed; above all, no doubt, by the phrase "low jockey."

Once Franklin realized he was unlikely to get quick satisfaction from the Penns, he knew that his enemies in Philadelphia would complain. "I make no doubt but Reports will be spread by my Enemies to my Disadvantage, but let none of them trouble you," he wrote to his wife. "If I find I can do my Country no Good, I will take care, at least, not to do it any Harm. I will neither seek nor accept any thing for my self; and though I may perhaps not be able to obtain for the People what they wish and expect, no Interest shall induce me to betray the Trust they have repos'd in me; So make yourself quite easy with regard to such Reports." Natural words, maybe, but it is slightly strange that Franklin should find it necessary to reassure his own wife that he was not about to betray his friends. But perhaps she had passed on the Philadelphia rumors that he was to be knighted and given a seat in the House of Commons.

There was, of course, no need to restrict the attack on Franklin to political innuendos, to suggestions that he was either failing in his efforts to bring the Proprietors to heel or was giving way to their blandishments. Franklin's fame in Europe had arisen from his earlier electrical work, and the Reverend William Smith, provost of the Philadelphia College and Academy, and at this time one of Franklin's most implacable enemies, put into blunt words the rumors that others had been circulating for some time. Kinnersley, he wrote in the October 1758 issue of *The American Magazine*, "is well qualified for his profession; and has moreover great merit with the learned world in being the chief inventor . . . of the *Electrical* apparatus, as well as author of a considerable part of those discoveries in *Electricity*, published by Mr. Franklin to whom he communicated them."

Kinnersley replied in *The Pennsylvania Gazette* the following month, admirably summarizing the situation during the years that followed 1745. "As to [Franklin's] *not being careful to distinguish between the particular Discoveries of each* [of his colleagues]; this perhaps was not always practicable; it being sometimes impossible to recollect in whose Breast the Thought first took Rise, that led to a Series of Experiments, which at length issued in some unexpected important Discovery. But had it been always practicable to distinguish between the particular Discoveries of each, it was altogether unnecessary; as, I believe, none of Mr. Franklin's electrical Friends had the least Thought of ever appearing as Competitors for any of the Honours that they have beheld, with Pleasure, bestowed on him, and to which he had an undoubted Right, preferable to the united Merit of all the Electricians in America, and, perhaps, in all the World."

While the campaign of mumblings and grumblings continued in Pennsylvania, Franklin in London cultivated the Quaker community, lobbied those in the government who he believed would be of use to him, and kept his ear close to the ground. Evidence that he was well informed of the Penns' plans came early in 1758 when he wrote to his wife telling her that the removal of Governor Denny was being planned. "It was to have been kept a Secret from me, that the Proprietors were looking out for a new [governor]," he wrote; "because they would not have Mr. Denny know any thing of it till the appointment should be actually made, and the Gentleman ready to embark. So you may make a Secret of it too, if you please, and oblige all your Friends with it."

If Denny were to be replaced it was even more certain that a long battle lay ahead. From the summer of 1758 Franklin ceased to regard his mission as one that would end that year and warned Deborah that there was little chance of her seeing him home before the spring of 1759.

His difficulties were spelled out by John Fothergill in a letter to Israel Pemberton, Jr., of Philadelphia. Franklin, he wrote in June 1758, had not yet been able to make much progress. "Reason is heard with fear, the fairest representations are considered as the effects of superior art," he continued; "and his reputation as man, a philosopher, and a statesman, only serve to render his situation more difficult and perplexing. Such is the unhappy turn of mind of most of those who constitute the world of influence in this country. You must allow him time and without repining. He is equally able and solicitous to serve the Province, but his obstructions are next to insurmountable. Great pains had been taken, and very successfully, to render him odious and his integrity suspected to those very persons to whom he must first apply. These suspicions can only be worn off by time and prudence."

With the prospects of a long stay ahead, Franklin began to hire his own carriage at twelve guineas a month. It had apparently been on the persuasion of his wife, since he had written to her: "Your kind Advice about getting a Chariot, I had taken some time before; for I found that every time I walk'd out; I got fresh Cold; and the Hackney Coaches at this End of the Town, where most People keep their own, are the worst in the whole City, miserable dirty broken shabby Things, unfit to go into when dress'd clean, and such as one would be asham'd to get out of at any Gentleman's Door."

If he was to be rooted in London for a while, he wanted at least the familiar food of home. "Pray remember to make me as happy as you can, by sending some Pippins for my self and Friends, some of your small Hams, and some Cranberries," he implored Deborah. In due course they all arrived, the first of a long series of food parcels delivered by accommodating captains.

However, this was to be only one part of a two-way traffic. Much as he enjoyed the cozy society into which he had settled down, part of Franklin's heart still remained in Pennsylvania. And he was assiduous in choosing from the apparently unexpected treasure-house of England domestic goods and furnishings for the home to which he was always expecting to return in a few months' time. One consignment shipped across the Atlantic contained a variety of items, beginning with china.

To show the Difference of Workmanship, there is something from all the China Works in England. . . . The same Box contains 4 Silver Salt Ladles, newest, but ugliest, Fashion; a little Instrument to Core Apples; another to make little Turnips out of great ones; Six coarse diaper Breakfast Cloths; they are to spread on the Tea Table, for no body breakfasts here on the naked Table, but on the Cloth set a large Tea Board with the Cups; there is also a little Basket, a Present from Mrs. Stephenson to Sally, and a Pair of Garters for you which were knit by the young Lady her Daughter, who favour'd me with a Pair of the same kind, the only ones I have been able to wear; as they need not be bound tight, the Ridges in them preventing their Slipping. We send them therefore as a Curiosity for the Form, more than for the Value. . . .

In the great Case, besides the little Box, is contain'd some Carpeting for the best Room Floor. There is enough for one large or two small ones; it is to be sow'd together, the Edges being first fell'd down, and Care taken to make the Figures meet exactly; there is Bordering for the same. This was my Fancy. Also two fine Flanders Bed Ticks, and two pair large superfine Blankets, 2 fine Damask Table Cloths and Napkins, and 43 ells of Ghentish Sheeting Holland; these you ordered. There is also 56 Yards of Cotton printed curiously from copper Plates a new Invention, to make Bed and Window Curtains; and 7 Yards Chair Bottoms printed in the same Way, very neat; these were my Fancy; but Mrs. Stevenson tells me I did wrong not to buy both of the same Colour. Also 7 Yards of printed Cotton, blue Ground, to make you a Gown; I bought it by Candlelight, and lik'd it then, but not so well afterwards: if you do not fancy it, send it as a Present from me to Sister Jenny. There is a better Gown for you of flower'd Tissue, 16 Yards, of Mrs. Stevenson's Fancy, cost 9 Guineas; and I think it a great Beauty; there was no more of the Sort, or you should have had enough for a Negligée or suit. There is also Snuffers, a Snuff Stand, and Extinguisher, of Steel, which I send for the Beauty of the Work; the Extinguisher is for Sperma Ceti Candles only, and is of a new Contrivance to preserve the Snuff upon the Candle. . . .

I forgot to mention another of my Fancyings, viz. a Pair of Silk Blankets, very fine. They are of a new kind, were just taken in a French Prize, and such were never seen in England before: they are called Blankets; but I think will be very neat to cover a Summer Bed instead of a Quilt or Counterpain. I had no Choice, so you will excuse the Soil on some of the Folds; your Neighbour Forster can get it off. I also forgot among the China, to mention a large fine Jugg for Beer, to stand in the Cooler. I fell in Love with it at first Sight; for I thought it look'd like a fat jolly Dame, clean and tidy, with a neat blue and white Calico Gown on, good natur'd and lovely, and put me in mind of—Somebody [presumably his wife, Deborah]. It has the Coffee Cups in its Belly, pack'd in best Chrystal Salt, of a peculiar nice Flavour, for the Table, not to be powder'd.

Franklin was always solicitous about domestic matters, telling his wife that if the noise from bells on his lightning conductor disturbed her, then there was a simple remedy. She could, he said, "tie a Piece of Wire from one Bell to the other, and that will conduct the lightning without ringing or snapping, but silently. Tho' I think it best the Bells should be at Liberty to ring, that you may know when the Wire is electrify'd, and, if you are afraid, may keep at a Distance."

It was plain to Deborah that her husband now expected to be absent for some time, just as it was evident to him that he would have to master the techniques of agency-lobbying. He did so, quickly, and as though born to the game. The Colonial agents carried out their work by methods governed as by the rules of a dance or of a religious ceremony. In the case of petitions, whose presentation formed much of an agent's business, each one had first to be submitted to the relevant secretary of state. The agent could discuss it with members of the Cabinet or send it to the president of the Privy Council, who would in turn refer it to the Board of Trade. At this point the advice of legal counsel would be sought. When it was given, the petition would make the return journey to the anxiously awaiting agent. All this took time. It also took money, and it was not only legal fees which were involved. At every point, and at almost every level, tips or bribes were at least helpful, often necessary, if a petition was to be kept on the move from desk to desk.

The agents were briefed and paid by the individual Colonies. They worked for those separate Colonies alone and until the outbreak of war with the French in 1756, united action was unusual. This had been taken in the case of the Molasses Act of 1733 and the Currency Act of 1744, both of which affected all the Colonies, but these were exceptions and it was only in 1756 that there arose the threat that should have united them at once. It did so only slowly. Some of the agents were helped by connections with the few great families who dominated the government of Britain. Some were funded, openly or otherwise, by important City interests. While Franklin could draw on neither of these advantages, he had his Fellowship of the Royal Society, which in the eighteenth century was a society of some political importance. Through it he became a close friend of John Pringle, later doctor to Queen Charlotte, consort of George III, and to some of the most powerful politicians in the country. His friend Collinson was not only an important link with other Fellows but introduced him to the influential Hanburys, and through them to rich City merchants and to Lord Granville, lord president of the Council. In practice, science partly made up for the social and political connections which Franklin lacked.

If he quickly learned the art of lobbying as played by English rules, he was already a past master of one technique much in favor during his years in London. This was the use of letters, articles and essays, often pseudonymous, printed not only in the political broadsheets but in the more popular papers of the day. One of his first was the strongly antiproprietorial letter, signed A.B., inveighing against the Penns and published in the September 19, 1758, issue of William Strahan's *London Chronicle,* the first of at least thirty-two contributions to the paper. Strahan also eased Franklin's way into *The Citizen* and *The Gentleman's Magazine.* He held shares in the *Public Advertiser,* in which at least thirty-three of Franklin's essays have been discovered; in the *Public Ledger* and *Lloyd's Evening Post;* and he printed Ralph Griffiths's *Monthly Review,* the literary magazine favorable both to America in general and to Franklin in particular. Franklin therefore had no difficulty in mobilizing much of the London press to considerable effect, both in his argument with the Penns and in the later disputes which ended in the revolt of the Colonies. Nearly twenty pseudonyms have been traced back to him, and it seems likely that the full number could be twice as many.

Much of Franklin's personal lobbying was carried along on a swift stream of wining and dining. As he was to put it to the Assembly, "being myself honour'd with visits from persons of quality and distinction, I was obliged for the credit of the province to live in a fashion and expense, suitable to the publick character I sustain'd, and much above what I should have done if I had been consider'd merely as a private person."

For a man of Franklin's sociable character this was no hardship. It was he, after all, who noted to the Abbé Morellet "that God wants us to tipple, because he has made the joints of the arm just the right length to carry a glass to the mouth, without falling short of or overshooting the mark." Dining out six nights a week, for six or seven weeks, and quite capable of finishing his second bottle of claret, was a pattern that fitted comfortably into the shape of eighteenth-century London society.

Like many of his contemporaries, he appears to have paid a price in gout, that endemic disease of the eighteenth century. It was not only gout that troubled him, however, and during his long stay in England he was frequently to inform his wife that he had, or was expecting, a bout of illness that would only be cured by a spell of traveling. "I am at present meditating a Journey somewhere. Perhaps to Bath and Bristol," she was told on one occasion, "as I begin to find a little Giddiness in my Head, a Token that I want the Exercise I have yearly been accustomed to." There may have been something in this, although it seems unlikely that Franklin would be wined and dined less generously when visiting the eminent, which was usually the case, than he would have been in London. He himself was later to give an impression of his health rather different from the picture he presented to Deborah. "I had enjoyed continued health for near 20 years," he wrote from Passy, outside Paris, in 1778, "except once in two or three years a slight fit of the gout, which generally terminated in a week or ten days, and once an intermitting fever got from making experiments over Stagnate waters. I was sometimes vexed with an itching on the back, which I observed particularly after eating freely of beef. And sometimes after long confinement at writing with little exercise, I have felt sudden pungent pains in the flesh of different parts of the body, which I was told were scorbutic. A journey used to free me of them." However, the little all-for-the-good-of-my-health missives to Philadelphia would tend to quieten the fears, both of a loving wife, and of the Assembly, for a Pennsylvania agent living a high life in London. But in the eighteenth century a high life helped in getting things done even more than it sometimes does in the twentieth.

Once he saw that he would have to play a waiting game, Franklin began to utilize the opportunities that this offered. In May 1758 he visited Cambridge with his son, carried out a number of experiments on evaporation with John Hadley, the chemist and physician, and for a week was "entertained with great kindness by the principal people, and shown all the curiosities of the place."

On his return he remained in London for only a few weeks. He had found the Cambridge trip "advantageous to my health, increasing both my health and spirits, and therefore, as all the great folks were out of town, and public business at a stand, I the more easily prevailed with myself to take another journey." It began with a further visit to Cambridge during which Franklin and William dined in hall and were present at the ceremonies when degrees were conferred on graduates. That done, they moved on north for a tour in search of ancestors.

Franklin had already gathered a good deal of information and at Wellingborough, thirty-five miles to the west of Cambridge, he expected to find the descendants of his cousin Mary Fisher, the married daughter of Thomas, his father's eldest brother.

Instead, he found Mary and her husband. "They are wealthy, have left off business, and live comfortably," he noted. But it was Ecton, a few miles outside Wellingborough, that was Franklin's main goal. Here, where his father, grandfather and great-grandfather had all been born, he came upon the old stone building still known as Franklin House. And here the local rector showed him the church register containing details of the births, marriages and deaths of his ancestors for the past two hundred years. Outside, in the churchyard, there were the gravestones. The rector's wife sent for scrubbing brush and pail of water, and as the Franklins' black servant, Peter, washed the moss from the stones William took down their inscriptions.

From Ecton they made their way to Birmingham, and were there able to trace a number of Deborah's relatives before returning to London, where Franklin compiled detailed genealogical trees for his own and his wife's families. He had been impressed by Ecton and, as he later wrote to his sister Jane Mecom, "had some Thoughts of re-purchasing the little [estate] in Northamptonshire that was our Grandfather's."

As the summer of 1758 turned to autumn, settlement of the Assembly's complaints against the Penns looked no nearer. Nevertheless, Franklin was preparing the ground, and not only with newspaper articles. Soon after the illness of his first few months in London he had begun planning what was to become *An Historical Review of the Constitution and Government of Pennsylvania.* Printed by Strahan and issued anonymously, it was generally attributed to Franklin, which was hardly surprising, since it was very largely a polemic against the Penns. "The Proprietor is enrag'd, . . ." Franklin told Isaac Norris. "He supposes me the author, but he is mistaken. I had no hand in it. It is wrote by a gentleman said to be one of the best pens in England, and who interests himself much in the concerns of America, but will not be known. Billy afforded great assistance, and furnish'd most of the materials. . . . I look'd over the manuscript, but was not permitted to alter every thing I did not fully approve."

Franklin's "I had no hand in it" must be taken with reserve, and certainly Mrs. Deborah Logan, widow of his friend Dr. George Logan (grandson of William Penn's secretary) and "the Female Historian of Pennsylvania," believed otherwise, writing: "I have no doubt but that [Franklin] had a considerable hand in writing the 'Historical Review.' There is a great deal of his acumen in it. But it was utterly unworthy of him, for party purposes, to violate truth and candor, as is done in that work. It is founded on false views, and does the greatest injustice to the memory of the virtuous dead."

The actual writer was in fact Richard Jackson—"omniscient Jackson," as he was known—Pennsylvania agent in London, later a Member of Parliament and a Lord of the Admiralty. Many of the facts in the "history," presumably those gathered by the helpful William, were later to be queried, and not only by Thomas Penn. Certainly the work was as much propaganda as fact, and Franklin saw that it was distributed in Pennsylvania as widely as possible. Hall was sent five hundred copies as soon as they were available and told that fifty of them were for distribution among members of the Assembly.

The argument with the Penns continued to hang fire throughout the spring and summer of 1759 and the issue was no farther forward when, early in August, Franklin and his son began a three-month tour that was to take them through the Midlands to Scotland. They left a few days after William learned that he had become the father of an illegitimate son, the William Temple Franklin who was to be of such great use to his grandfather in Paris two decades later, and whose mother has never been identified.

Once the tour was under way Franklin told Deborah that the journey was agreeing very well with him "and will probably be many ways of use to me." He did, no doubt, benefit from the break with his demanding London work but he was also moved by an innate and insatiable curiosity. This was particularly strong in regard to Scotland, which he persistently regarded as an English colony, a Gaelic Pennsylvania whose strange sights were to be savored and for whose intellectuals he had high regard.

He had been commissioned by Hall to buy new type for *The Pennsylvania Gazette* and stopped in Birmingham to visit John Baskerville, the finest printer in modern times, as he has been called. He decided against buying Baskerville's new type and made a similar decision in Glasgow, where he visited the type foundry of Alexander Wilson, one of Strahan's major suppliers. Eventually he settled for what was already the traditional Caslon.

Franklin did, however, become an enthusiastic supporter of John Baskerville, who in 1760 brought out the famous edition of the prayerbook, using his new type. Among Franklin's friends there was one who was highly critical, claiming that the type would be "a Means of blinding all the Readers in the Nation." When the friend arrived in Craven Street one evening, Franklin could not resist producing a page set in the traditional Caslon, saying it was Baskerville's, and asking for its poor points to be explained. "He readily undertook [the task]," Franklin subsequently explained to Baskerville, "and went over the several Founts, shewing me every where what he thought Instances of that Disproportion; and declared, that he could not then read the Specimen without feeling very strongly the Pain he had mentioned to me. I spared him that Time the Confusion of being told, that these were the Types he had been reading all his Life, with so much Ease to his Eyes; the Types his adored Newton is printed with, on which he has pored not a little; nay, the very Types his own Book is printed with, for he is himself an Author; and yet never discovered this painful Disproportion in them, till he thought they were yours."

After the visit to Baskerville in 1759, the Franklin party took in Derby, Sheffield and Liverpool and also visited Manchester. Here Franklin was told of the huge subterranean salt mines at Northwich. He insisted on visiting them and on climbing down into the caverns. William, accompanying his father, acquired a great stalactite of rock salt which he later dispatched to his uncle Peter in Newport.

In Edinburgh, where William Strahan had arrived to ensure that the Franklins would see all they wished, they stayed for a while with Sir Alexander Dick, president of the College of Physicians of Edinburgh. Most of the notables sought a meeting with the visitors, David Hume and Adam Smith among them. The latter, it has been suggested, was influenced by Franklin when writing *The Wealth of Nations.* The evidence is sparse. But although the book was not published until 1776, when Franklin had left Britain for good, Smith had been collecting material for years and, judging by the comments of Mrs. Deborah Logan, writing it as well. "Dr. Franklin," she has said, "once told my husband that the celebrated Adam Smith, when writing his 'Wealth of Nations,' was in the habit of bringing chapter after chapter, as he composed it, to himself, Dr. Price and others of the *literati* of that day, with whom he was intimate; patiently hearing their observations, and profiting by their discussions and criticisms: nay, that he has sometimes reversed his positions and re-written whole chapters, after hearing what they had to remark on the subject before them."

Whether or not Franklin did have any significant effect on Smith, his Edinburgh visit introduced him to a wide range of northern society. Included in it was the Scottish divine Alexander Carlyle, who records one dinner and implies that the Scots' view of the Colonial situation was not always Franklin's. "Franklin's son," he later wrote, "was open and communicative, and pleased the company better than his father; and some of us observed indications of that decided difference of opinion between father and son which, in the American war [of Independence], alienated them altogether."

In Edinburgh, Franklin made his first acquaintance with Lord Kames, the Scottish judge and author, who was to become a friend for life, and he visited Scone, where in earlier centuries the Scottish kings had been crowned on the "Stone of Destiny." According to the probably apocryphal record, Franklin looked and commented: "Who knows but St. James's [then the regular residence of the British sovereign] may, some time or other, lie in ruins as Scone does now?" Then he traveled on to St. Andrews to be installed as Doctor of Laws at the university which had conferred the degree on him earlier in the year.

Franklin was later to describe his weeks in Scotland as among the happiest of his life. Certainly they increased his affection for Britain and led him on toward the position where only chance prevented him from settling in the country for good. And on his way back to London, reaching Coldstream on the border between Scotland and England, he stopped to write the following lines to Lady Dick:

1.

Joys of Prestonfield Adieu!
Late found, soon lost, but still we'll view
The engaging Scene—oft to these eyes
Shall the pleasing Vision rise!

2.

Hearts that warm towards a friend,
Kindness on kindness without end,
Easy converse, sprightly wit
These we found in *Dame* and *Knight*.

3.

Chearfull meals, balmy rest,
Beds that never buggs molest,
Neatness and Sweetness all around
These at *Prestonfield* we found

4.

Hear O Heaven a stranger's prayer,
Bless the hospitable pair!
Bless their sweet Bairns, and very Soon
Give these a *Brother*—Those a *Son*.

A second visit to Scotland was to leave him with less elevated opinions. "I have lately made a Tour thro' Ireland and Scotland," he would write in January 1772 to Dr. Joshua Babcock. "In those Countries a small Part of the Society are Landlords, great Noblemen, and Gentlemen, extreamly opulent, living in the highest Affluence and Magnificence: The Bulk of the People Tenants, extreamly poor, living in the most sordid Wretchedness, in dirty Hovels of Mud and Straw, and cloathed only in Rags."

By the time that Franklin and his son arrived back in London in the autumn of 1759, Pitt's determined leadership had given the British forces the upper hand over France. Louisburg had fallen to Lord Amherst after Loudoun's failure. Fort Duquesne had been destroyed by the French, who had then withdrawn up the Allegheny River, thus allowing the British to build Fort Pitt nearby, on the site of what was to become Pittsburgh. And Wolfe had scaled the cliffs to reach the Plains of Abraham and bring Quebec—and with it all Canada for practical purposes—under British control.

Peace was not to be signed for another three years, but by the beginning of 1760 it was obvious that Canada could be permanently taken from the French. There would be other alternatives, and between 1760 and 1763 the competing claims of Canada and of Guadeloupe became the subject of a pamphleteering war into which Franklin was drawn. Hostilities were opened with *A Letter Addressed to Two Great Men, on the Prospect of Peace; And on the Terms necessary to be insisted upon in the Negociation.* Favoring the acquisition of Canada, it was attributed to Lord Bath but was more probably written by John Douglas, a favorite of Bath's and later bishop of Salisbury. The admonition to the two men—William Pitt and the Duke of Newcastle—was answered in *Remarks on the "Letter Addressed to Two Great Men" In a Letter to the Author of that Piece,* almost certainly the work of William Burke, a former secretary of Guadeloupe, who not unexpectedly stressed the value of the great sugar plantations on the island. Canada, by contrast, was considered little more than a vast tract of unexplored forest and wilderness stretching north to the Arctic Circle. "Some," Pitt declared, "are for keeping Canada; some Guadeloupe; who will tell me which I shall be hanged for not keeping?"

Franklin now entered the argument with a pamphlet full of an empire-builder's blazing enthusiasm. Richard Jackson had a hand in Franklin's *The Interest of Great Britain Considered, With Regard to her Colonies, And the Acquisitions of Canada and Guadaloupe,* but the pamphlet left no doubt about the author's feelings. They were expressed even more unreservedly in a letter from Franklin to Lord Kames. "No one can rejoice more sincerely than I do on the Reduction of Canada; and this, not merely as I am a Colonist, but as I am a Briton. I have long been of Opinion, that the Foundations of the future Grandeur & Stability of the British Empire, lie in America; and tho', like other Foundations, they are low and little seen, they are never the-less, broad & strong enough to support the greatest Political Structure Human Wisdom ever yet erected. I am therefore by no means for restoring Canada. If we keep it, all the Country from St. Laurence to Missisipi, will in another Century be fill'd with British People; Britain itself will become vastly more populous by the immense Increase of its Commerce; the Atlantic Sea will be cover'd with your Trading Ships; and your naval Power thence continually increasing, will extend your Influence round the whole Globe; & awe the World!" Here, with a vengeance, was the logical outcome of Franklin's Albany Plan.

There were dangers, of course, but Franklin's Canada pamphlet dismissed them. Some men in England, it admitted, even had warms the Mind, enlivens the Imagination, and is continually starting fresh Game that is immediately pursu'd and taken, and which would never have occur'd in the duller Intercourse of Epistolary Correspondence. So that whenever I reflect on the great Pleasure & Advantage I receiv'd from the free Communication of Sentiments in the Conversation your Lordship honour'd me with at Kaims, and in the little agreeable Rides to the Tweedside, I shall forever regret that unlucky premature Parting. ——

No one can rejoice more sincerely than I do on the Reduction of Canada; and this, not merely as I am a Colonist, but as I am a Briton. —— I have long been of Opinion, that the Foundations of the future Grandeur & Stability of the British Empire, lie in America; and tho', like other Foundations, they are low and little seen, they are nevertheless, broad & strong enough to support the greatest Political Structure Human Wisdom ever yet erected. I am therefore by no means for Restoring Canada. —— If we keep it, all the Country from St Laurence to Missisipi, will in another Century be fill'd with British People; Britain itself will become vastly more populous by the immense Increase of its Commerce; the Atlantic Sea will be cover'd with your Trading Ships; and your naval Power thence continually increasing, will extend your Influence round the whole Globe, & awe the World. —— If the French remain in Canada, they will continually harrass our Colonies by the Indians, impede if not prevent their Growth; your Progress to Greatness will at best be slow, and give room for many Accidents that may forever prevent it. —— But I refrain, for I see you begin to think my Notions extravagant, and look upon them as the Ravings of a mad Prophet. Your

Excerpt from Franklin's letter to Lord Kames, London, January 3, 1760
[Reproduced with the approval of the Keeper of the Records of Scotland, Scottish Record Office, Ref. T/134 G/180/1/4]

the fear that the Colonies might, if they became too prosperous, rise against Britain. But for that fear Franklin, who was to sign the Declaration of Independence sixteen years later, had what in 1760 appeared to be an uncontestable reply. "If [the Colonies] could not agree to unite for their defence against the *French* and *Indians,* who were perpetually harassing their settlements, burning their villages, and murdering their people," he wrote, "can it reasonably be supposed there is any danger of their uniting against their own nation, which protects and encourages them, with which they have so many connections and ties of blood, interest and affection, and which 'tis well known they all love much more than they love one another? . . . I will venture to say, an union amongst them for such a purpose is not merely improbable, it is impossible; and if the union of the whole is impossible, the attempt of a part must be madness: as those colonies that did not join the rebellion, would join the mother country in suppressing it."

However, he added a warning. "When I say such an union is impossible, I mean without the most grievous tyranny and oppression."

Franklin's Canada pamphlet was printed not only in London in 1760 but also in Dublin, in Philadelphia by William Bradford, grandson of the William to whom Franklin had applied for work in New York in 1723, and in Boston by Franklin's nephew, Benjamin Mecom, son of his favorite sister, Jane. Yet another edition appeared in London six years later when Franklin was lobbying for repeal of the Stamp Act. It increased interest in the subject both by its sober marshaling of arguments and by its typically Franklinian readability, although it is impossible to assess its effect on the outcome of the argument; nevertheless, when the Treaty of Paris was signed in 1763, Guadeloupe was returned to France and Canada became British.

With Franklin's plea for keeping Canada there was also printed in 1760 his *Observations concerning the Increase of Mankind, Peopling of Countries, &c.* Started in 1750, and inspired by British restrictions on the manufacture of iron in Pennsylvania, it had been published in Boston five years later. It was reprinted now because on its economic and demographic arguments there depended the role which Franklin believed should be played by the American Colonies in a grand imperial scheme designed in London. His belief was that Britain had nothing to fear from expansion of the Colonies, which already contained about a million inhabitants. They would inevitably increase more quickly than the inhabitants of Britain. "This million doubling, suppose but once in 25 years," he wrote, "will in another century be more than the people of England, and the greatest Number of Englishmen will be on this side the water, What an accession of power to the British empire by sea as well as land! What increase of trade and navigation! What numbers of ships and seamen! We have been here but little more than 100 years, and yet the force of our privateers in the late war, united, was greater, both in men and guns, than that of the whole British navy in Queen Elizabeth's time.— How important an affair then to Britain, is the present treaty for settling the bounds between her colonies and the French, and how careful should she be to secure room enough, since on the room depends so much the Increase of her people?"

When Franklin's polemic on Canada was printed with his essay on the expected increase of the American population, the unresolved problem of the Pennsylvania Assembly's right to tax the Penn lands was at last moving toward a climax. Only during the first weeks of 1759 had the Assembly received an answer to the list of grievances which Franklin had presented to the Penns in the summer of 1757. The Penns' lawyer, Ferdinand John Paris, pointed out that Franklin had been given no authority by the Assembly to settle drafts of bills while in London. "Had such Power been lodged here, it is possible many of the Seeming Differences would have been settled," he went on. In effect, the Proprietors brushed aside the Assembly's complaints.

However, British operations against the French were still demanding more money and in April 1759 the Assembly passed a bill enabling it to raise £100,000 by taxing all land, including that of the Penns. Governor Denny, acting in defiance of instructions, approved the bill and the money was issued. This was too much for the Penns and in January 1760 Thomas Penn asked the Privy Council to oppose eleven of nineteen acts which the Assembly had passed in 1758 and 1759. There followed, during 1760, a series of hearings, first by the Board of Trade, then by the Privy Council's Committee for Plantation Affairs. Franklin's counsel—both he and the Penns were allowed two each—argued of the April 1759 bill that since the £100,000 had been issued, repeal of, or alteration to, the bill would only cause chaos. And they denied the Penns' allegation that Denny had been bribed by the Assembly to approve the bill. However, when the Board reported in June, it effectively disallowed the bill. The reason was that while the Proprietors could legitimately be taxed, the Assembly's money bill was too badly drafted to be approved.

But the Board's recommendations had finally to be considered by the Privy Council's Committee for Plantation Affairs. During these final hearings, toward the end of August 1760, there took place, while the lawyers were still arguing, a meeting between Franklin and Lord Mansfield, an important member of the committee. Franklin was later to claim that Mansfield approached him; other evidence suggests that Franklin approached Mansfield. Whatever the truth, there is no doubt about the outcome. Franklin promised on behalf of the Assembly that if the money bill was approved, he would acquiesce in the bill being condemned in principle though passed in practice; and he promised that the proprietary lands would be fairly taxed —this being understood to mean that the Proprietors' unsurveyed land would not be taxed at all, and that the rest would be taxed no higher than anyone else's.

Early in September the Privy Council reported. The money law was "fundamentally wrong and unjust, and ought to be Repealed." But as Franklin had given certain guarantees on behalf of the Assembly, the bill should be allowed through. Thus, for the first time, it was agreed in Britain that the Penn estates should be taxed. As for the amendments which Franklin had promised on the Assembly's behalf, "the Assembly," he recalled in his autobiography, "did not think them necessary." And it was, in fact, only in 1764 that the Assembly grudgingly approved the amendments that Franklin had promised on their behalf.

The eleven acts opposed by the Penns varied considerably in importance. Six of them were disallowed by the Privy Council and five were approved. It was thus possible to assess the result of the hearings as a victory, or a defeat, for either side. Nevertheless, Franklin had been successful in a main object of his mission: it had now been agreed by the Privy Council, and was confirmed by the King, that the Penn estates were taxable. Nothing that could be put into the scales was quite as weighty as that.

Now, it might have been expected, he would make for home. In fact, it was another two years before he did so. Once the vital decisions had been made by the Privy Council, Franklin left London with his son for a leisurely tour of Wales and the West Country. In Bath he learned of the accession to the throne of George III, following the death of his grandfather, George II. By November he was back in London. But even now he made no preparations to leave England for America.

Earlier in the year he had told his wife that the business with the Penns was on its way to a conclusion and that after that he would "be able to fix a Time for [his] Return." Later in 1760, William Strahan, still hoping for a match between Sally Franklin and his son, wrote a personal letter to Sally. Franklin passed it on to his wife with a revealing note. There were, he said, two reasons against the whole Franklin family uprooting themselves and coming to England. "One," he said, "my Affection to Pensilvania, and long established Friendships and other Connections there: The other, your invincible Aversion to crossing the Seas. And without removing hither, I could not think of parting with my Daughter to such a Distance. . . . You need not deliver the Letter to Sally, if you do not think it proper."

But there were at least three reasons for not recrossing the Atlantic just yet. One was that having won a victory over the Proprietors, Franklin now contemplated raising his sights. Would it not be possible, he speculated, either to change the Charter, which he saw as being such an impediment to the government of the Colony, or to claim that it had been irregularly manipulated at some stage between the seventeenth century and the present day? He began to investigate, but failed to make much progress.

The other two reasons for hanging on in London were financial. The Privy Council's ruling had been followed by an award to Pennsylvania of some £26,000 as compensation for its expenses in the war. Franklin had to bank this in his own name and then meet the calls made upon it. This alone would have caused worry enough, but he unwisely ignored warnings and put some of the money into government stock, hoping that its value would rise when peace came. When it was seen that peace rumors were premature, he found himself in perilous financial waters and was saved from disaster only by a last-minute loan from a friendly firm of merchants. Even so, the Assembly lost some of its money. Thomas Penn proposed, as might have been expected, that Franklin should make good the loss out of his own pocket. The Assembly disagreed—but took care to restrict his management of the remaining funds.

Quite apart from the need to continue handling Pennsylvania's finances, Franklin also found it useful to remain in London for another reason. He had already become involved in the first of numerous plans for new settlements beyond the Alleghenies. Delicate lobbying was needed, and for the moment he found London a more suitable place than Philadelphia.

For a while he appeared to be taking things easy, regularly visiting the Royal Society and bringing back Fellows to Craven Street to witness experiments on a more powerful electrical machine. He also amused himself with developing the armonica —later the harmonica, a name subsequently given to other instruments, including one kind of mouth organ—a primitive instrument of which he had heard at the Royal Society. During the previous century an ingenious Nuremberg inventor had created a musical instrument which was "played" with a moistened finger run along differently-sounding glasses. In 1746 the composer Gluck, and in 1750 an Irishman named Puckeridge, had in London played various airs on a row of glasses, tuned by filling each with different quantities of water. The idea had been taken up by a Mr. Delaval of the Royal Society and Franklin decided that there was a case for improvement.

The result was a row of glass hemispheres, the largest nine inches in diameter, the smallest three inches. There were thirty-seven glasses in all, mounted on a horizontal spindle which could be turned by a foot treadle rather as a spinning wheel is turned. "This instrument is played upon," Franklin explained to Father Giambatista Beccaria, professor of experimental physics in Turin, "by sitting before the middle of the set of glasses as before the keys on a harpsichord, turning them with the foot, and wetting them now and then with a spunge and clean water. The fingers should be first a little soaked in water, and quite free from all greasiness; a little fine chalk upon them is sometimes useful, to make them catch the glass and bring out the tone more readily. Both hands are used, by which means different parts are played together. —Observe, that the tones are best drawn out when the glasses turn *from* the ends of the fingers, not when they turn *to* them."

The instrument never wanted tuning and the tones which could be drawn from it were attractive. In Miss Marianne Davies he found an excellent performer and for more than a decade she played the instrument with success not only in London but on the Continent. No improvement ever appears to have been made on Franklin's original instrument; and it finally fell into disuse not through lack of audiences but because of its effect on performers: drawing sounds from the fingertips caused attacks of nervousness and even fainting fits.

To some, Franklin appeared to be frittering away his time. Thomas Penn was particularly scathing, writing on April 13, 1761, to Governor Hamilton, reappointed governor as Denny's successor, "He has spent most of his time in Philosophical, and especially in Electrical Matters, having generally Company in a Morning to see those Experiments, and Musical performances on Glasses, where any one that knows him, carrys his Friends."

In the summer of 1761 Franklin made his usual therapeutic journey, this time through Belgium and Holland in company with his son and his fellow agent, Richard Jackson. William proudly wrote to his sister after their return that they had been received in The Hague by the British ambassador, Sir Joseph Yorke, and by Count Bentinck, president of the College of Deputies of the States General. "Att Brussels," he wrote, "we were at Prince Charles of Lorrains, in whose Cabinet, which is full of Art and Nature, we saw an Apperatus for trying my Father's Experiments in Electricity. The Magnificence and Riches of The Roman Catholic Churches here and at Ghent, and Bruges and Antwerp, particular the latter, surpass'd any thing I had ever seen before or Conceived." And in Leyden they met Pieter van Musschenbroek, whose Leyden jar had been a starting point for the electrical experiments a decade and more previously.

Franklin's greatest surprise came with the comparison of Flanders with New England in the matter of Sunday observance. In America Sunday travel could bring punishment. But in Flanders, Franklin explained to Jared Ingersoll, "every one travell'd, if he pleas'd, or diverted himself any other way; and in the Afternoon both high and low went to the Play or the Opera, where there was plenty of Singing, Fiddling and Dancing." According to Puritan beliefs this should have brought down the wrath of God, but Franklin found this singularly absent. "The cities were well built and full of inhabitants," he wrote, "the Markets fill'd with Plenty, the People well favour'd and well clothed; the Fields well till'd, the Cattle fat and strong; the Fences, Houses, and Windows all in Repair; and *no Old Tenor* anywhere in the Country; which would almost make one suspect, that the Deity is not so angry at that Offence as a New England Justice."

The Franklin party's return to Britain was accompanied by a great storm which almost prevented them from attending a ceremony on which Franklin had set his heart: the coronation of George III. Father appears to have watched from outside, but William had secured a ticket which enabled him "to walk in the Procession quite into the Abbey."

Franklin's monarchial enthusiasm continued. "I am of Opinion," he was to write to William Strahan of George III, "that his Virtue, and the Consciousness of his sincere Intentions to make his People happy, will give him Firmness and Steadiness in his Measures, and in the Support of the honest Friends he has chosen to serve him; and when that Firmness is fully perceiv'd, Faction will dissolve and be dissipated like a Morning Fog before the rising Sun, leaving the rest of the Day clear, with a Sky serene and cloudless. Such, after a few of the first Years, will be the future Course of his Majesty's Reign, which I predict will be happy and truly glorious."

With such sentiments, it is not surprising that as he began to make plans for returning to America during the first months of 1762, some friends should have felt that the journey was merely to wind up his affairs there before permanently settling in London. Certainly he left with his friend John Pringle the belief that he would be coming back.

But whatever the future might hold for him, either in Pennsylvania or in England, Franklin knew it would be wise to deal with the opposition steadily building up against him in Philadelphia. The attitude of Chief Justice William Allen, who had blocked Franklin's handling of a second installment of the Province's government grant, typified the feeling of many. "One would," he wrote, "fain hope [Franklin's] almost insatiable ambition is pretty near Satisfied by his parading about England &c. at the province's Expense for these five years past, which now appears in a different Light to our Patriots than formerly especially, as he has already stayed near two years longer; than they expected;

a sample of which is their refusing to put the Second Sum received from the Crown into his Hands—a matter to which I did not a little contribute."

In Britain there was as yet no particular animosity toward Franklin except from those who opposed him on the issue with the Penns. Indeed, while making preparations to return he learned that the University of Oxford had voted to confer on him the honorary degree of Doctor of Civil Law. He accepted it at a special convocation on April 30, his son, William, being given a Master of Arts degree at the same ceremony.

Although Franklin had no doubts about returning to Philadelphia, for some while if not for good, his contradictory letters show that he half-hoped, half-feared, that he would be returning to Britain before long. "I fancy," he wrote to Mary Stevenson, "I feel a little like dying Saints, who in parting with those they love in this World, are only comforted with the Hope of more perfect Happiness in the next. I have, in America, Connections of the most engaging kind; and, happy as I have been in the Friendships here contracted, *those* promise me greater and more lasting Felicity. But God only knows whether those Promises shall be fulfilled."

Certainly there were many friends in Britain who were loath to see him go. Among them was David Hume, who sent his famous letter of regret. "I am very sorry, that you intend soon to leave our Hemisphere," it said. "America has sent us many good things, Gold, Silver, Sugar, Tobacco, Indigo, &c. But you are the first Philosopher, and indeed the first Great Man of Letters for whom we are beholden to her: it is our own Fault, that we have not kept him: Whence it appears, that we do not agree with Solomon, that Wisdom is above Gold; For we take care never to send back an ounce of the latter, which we once lay our Fingers upon."

SIX

A PENNSYLVANIA INTERLUDE

RANKLIN ARRIVED AT PORTSMOUTH FROM London early in August 1762. Although fighting between the British and the French had virtually come to a standstill, the Treaty of Paris had not yet been signed and a convoy had to be gathered before the Philadelphia packet sailed. Then, when the ships had gathered, contrary winds held them back until mid-August. Franklin used the time to write farewell letters to Mary Stevenson, Sir Alexander Dick and Lord Kames. And here, separated from his London haunts, with Philadelphia far beyond the horizon, he wrote a revealing letter to William Strahan. "I cannot, I assure you," he said, "quit even this disagreable Place without Regret, as it carries me still farther from those I love, and from the Opportunities of hearing of their Welfare. The Attraction of *Reason* is at present for the other Side of the Water, but that of *Inclination* will be for this side. You know which usually prevails. I shall probably make but this one Vibration and settle here for ever. Nothing will prevent it, if I can, as I hope I can, prevail with Mrs. F. to accompany me;

especially if we have a Peace." These were not passing sentiments.

The voyage was calm but took ten weeks, since the ships were limited by the speed of the slowest, some of them regularly being forced to shorten sail or lay by. At Madeira the journey was broken to replenish stores and since it was harvesttime bunches of fine grapes were brought on board, first to adorn the ceilings of the ships' cabins and then to provide dessert for many nights afterward. Of Madeira, Franklin later wrote to Richard Jackson, "I shall only mention that it produces not only the Fruits of the hot Countries, as Oranges, Lemons, Plantains, Bananas, &c. but those of the cold also, as Apples, Pears and Peaches in great Perfection. The Mountains are excessively high, and rise suddenly from the Town, which affords the Inhabitants a singular Conveniency, that of getting soon out of its Heat after they have done their Business, and of ascending to what Climate or Degree of Coolness they are pleased to chuse, the Sides of the Mountains being fill'd with their Country Boxes at different Heights." The passengers "had pleasant Weather and fair Winds, and frequently visited and dined from Ship to Ship," Franklin told Strahan, while to Lord Kames he described sailing in convoy as "like travelling in a moving Village, with all one's Neighbours about one."

He arrived back in Philadelphia on November 1 to the joy of his admirers and the fears of his enemies. Even while he was still at sea, the case so often to be made against him was set out by Governor Hamilton. "Your Friend Mr. Franklin, and mine if he pleases, (for it will much depend on himself) is dailey expected from England," he wrote to Jared Ingersoll. "I cannot find that his five years negotiation at a vast expence to the province, hath answered any other purpose with respect to the publick, than to get every point that was in controversy, determined against them. Yet what is this to Mr. Franklin? Hath it not afforded him a life of pleasure, and an opportunity of displaying his talents among the virtuosi of various kingdoms and nations? And lastly hath it not procured for himself the Degree of Doctor of Laws, and for the modest and beautiful Youth, his son, that of master of Arts, from one of our most famous universities? Let me tell you, those are no small acquisitions to the public, and therefore well worth paying for."

The modest and beautiful son was soon to add fuel to the fire which the Proprietary party always kept alight beneath the father. On the packet which followed Franklin's there came news that William, aged about thirty-one, had been appointed royal governor of New Jersey. This had come about shortly after the new ministry under Lord Bute had been formed, and the obvious conclusion was that the government in London was now more favorable to Franklin and his causes. "Every body concludes that this must have been brought about by some strong Interest his Father must have obtained in England," Hamilton wrote to Thomas Penn, "but with whom no Body here pretends to know. If you do, I beg You will be pleased to inform me." John Penn (soon to succeed Hamilton as governor of Pennsylvania) was livid. "It is no less amazing than true, that Mr. William Franklin, son of Benjamin Franklin, of Philadelphia, is appointed to be Governor of the Province of New Jersey!" he wrote to Lord Stirling. "The warrant for his commission was ordered to be made out last Wednesday. The whole of this business has been transacted in so private a manner, that not a tittle of it escaped until it was seen in the public papers; so that there was no opportunity of counteracting, or, indeed, doing one single thing that might put a stop to this shameful affair. I make no doubt but the people of New Jersey will make some remonstrance upon this indignity put upon them. You are fully as well acquainted with the character and principles of this person as myself, and are as able to judge of the impropriety of such an appointment. What a dishonour and disgrace it must be to a country to have such a man at the head of it, and to sit down contented! Surely that will not be the case—at least, I should hope that some effort would be made, before our Jersey friends would put up with such an insult. If any *gentleman* had been appointed, it would have been a different case—but I cannot look upon the person in question in that light, by any means. How this matter will turn out, I know not, but I should be very sorry to see him first in that Government, as there cannot, in my opinion, any good result from it—but, on the contrary, dishonour and disgrace to the country, and hatred of the people to himself. I may, perhaps, be too strong in my expressions, but I am so extremely astonished and enraged at it, that I am hardly able to contain myself at the thoughts of it."

Speculation has persisted as to how the matter had been arranged but Thomas Penn's version is the most likely. The Franklins, father and son, were friends of Dr. John Pringle. Pringle was Lord Bute's physician and it would have been the simplest of things—and the most natural in those days—for Pringle to carry out a minor and successful piece of lobbying on William's behalf. Bute, an accomplished dabbler in natural philosophy, had a special interest in electricity and owned what was possibly the finest collection of electrical machines in the country. Few details exist of the contacts between him and Franklin before the latter's departure for Philadelphia in 1762. Franklin was in North America during Bute's eleven-month tenure of office as prime minister. And after that brief spell of power, Bute went into near-retirement. Nevertheless, there is little doubt that contacts between the two men paved the way for son William's appointment. In eighteenth-century Britain, no less than in that of today, it was whom one knew, rather than what one knew, that really mattered.

William Franklin arrived in Philadelphia in February 1763, with the wife he had married in the fashionable St. George's, Hanover Square, shortly after his appointment as governor. A few years earlier his father had hoped that he might marry Mary Stevenson; but Mary moved to the country and William became engaged to someone else. That engagement was broken off and in the summer of 1762 William announced his betrothal to Elizabeth Downes, the daughter of a rich sugar planter from Barbados. Then, shortly before his marriage, he had, following his father's example, become the father of an illegitimate son whose mother has remained unknown.

Although Thomas Penn was as shocked as John Penn at William Franklin's gubernatorial appointment, he believed that it might help him in his running fight with the new governor's father. "I am told," he wrote to Governor Hamilton, "you will find Mr. Franklin more tractable, and I believe we shall, in matters of prerogative; as his son must obey instructions, and what he is ordered to do the father cannot well oppose in Pennsylvania."

This was but wishful thinking and suggests that the Penns had begun to lose touch with the situation on the ground. If any one simple fact emerges from the two years that Franklin was now to spend in Philadelphia it is that the rift between him and the Penns became unbridgeable. It is hardly surprising, since Franklin had returned to Philadelphia quite convinced that Pennsylvania would be better run as a royal colony than as a sinecure of the Penns. The belief was reinforced by a rather naive view that the government at Westminster would be prepared either to renege on its legal obligations to the Penns or to buy them out at enormous cost.

The situation was, it is true, to be confused by the complex currents and countercurrents which in the early 1760s swept through the Alice-in-Wonderland world of Pennsylvania politics. The Presbyterians tended to support the Penns—now, it must be remembered, no longer Quaker supporters—if only on the grounds that while the Quakers were overrepresented in the Assembly by the city constituencies, the Presbyterians, concentrated in the back-county areas, were underrepresented. There was the reluctance of the Quakers to vote for defense supplies and a dogged effort of the Governor to squeeze money from the Assembly on his own terms rather than the Assembly's. The last point became temporarily less important after the Treaty of Paris had been signed in February 1763, but it was to reappear in full strength before very long.

This, then, was the situation as Franklin settled down once more in Philadelphia. He had succeeded in the Assembly's mission, although there were men ready to dispute this, and others ready to claim that if he had in fact succeeded, the cost had been too great. He was a man of political importance and in the eyes of those who had barely seen the Atlantic, let alone crossed it, he had all the authority of one who had not only traveled but who had walked with the great. Little wonder that many speculated that if Pennsylvania did become a royal colony, Benjamin Franklin would be its first royal governor.

First he rendered his accounts to the Assembly. They had voted him £1,500 in 1757 and he now gave a figure of £714 10s. 7d. for expenses. To the initial £1,500 it was decided to add a similar sum, making a total of £600 a year for five years. Unfortunately, there is no meaningful way of converting these sums into contemporary values; but the *Dictionary of American Biography*'s entry on Thomas Hutchinson—later governor of Massachusetts —estimates that in 1763 a common family could live comfortably in Boston on £40 a year.

Back home for less than five months, Franklin then set out on a long tour of the Colonies' post offices. Canada's incorporation within the empire certainly made it necessary to reorganize the service, but Franklin almost gives the impression of wanting to bring the organization up to date before returning across the Atlantic. His attachment to England remained strong and emerges forcibly from a letter to Mary Stevenson written in March 1763, before he left for what was to be a seven-month tour: "Of all the enviable Things England has, I envy it most its People," he wrote. "Why should that petty Island, which compar'd to America, is but like a stepping Stone in a Brook, scarce enough of it above Water to keep one's Shoes dry; why, I say, should that little Island, enjoy in almost every Neighbourhood, more sensible, virtuous and elegant Minds, than we can collect in ranging 100 Leagues of our vast Forests."

A month later he was off with John Foxcroft, first down to Virginia, then back to Philadelphia and, after a short rest, north to New York and then on to New England. In New York he was joined by his daughter, Sally, and in Boston he stayed with his sister Jane Mecom. In between he visited Catharine Ray Greene and her family, now settled in Warwick, and recovered there from a bad fall from his horse.

He had nearly fifty offices to visit on his tour and he seems to have pressed himself hard, almost as if wishing to see the shores of England again as soon as possible. "No Friend can wish me more in England than I do my self," he wrote to Strahan. "But before I go every thing I am concern'd in must be so settled here as to make another Return to America unnecessary." And, after hearing of the convulsions that followed the arrest of John Wilkes on the charge of libeling George III: "If the stupid brutal Opposition your good King and his Measures have lately met with should as you fear become general, surely you would not wish me to come and live among such People; you would rather remove hither, where we have no Savages but those we expect to be such. But I think your Madmen will ere long come to their Senses; and when I come I shall find you generally wise and happy."

At times he continued to put forward his wife's reluctance to emigrate as preventing his own move back to England. "God bless you and let me find you well and happy when I come again to England; happy England!" he wrote to Strahan. "In two Years at farthest I hope to settle all my Affairs in such a Manner, as that I *may* then conveniently remove to England, provided we can persuade the good Woman to cross the Seas. That will be the great Difficulty; but you can help me a little in removing it."

When it came to contradictory statements about returning to England it is difficult to know whether he was deceiving his friends or deceiving himself. He knew that the chances of persuading Deborah to uproot herself were nonexistent; but he could hardly admit that he might be contemplating leaving her for good, so the fiction had to be kept up. Moreover he could always claim, if half-heartedly, that there would be difficulties in his own emigration. "Don't let them tell you 'old trees cannot safely be transplanted,'" wrote Mary Stevenson after he had pointed this out. "I have lately seen some fine tall firs remov'd from Kensington to the Queen's Palace without injury, and Why should not the valuable North American plants flourish here?" Conflicting emotions pulled Franklin in two directions. But there is little doubt that throughout most of this visit to Philadelphia he was willing to seize any chance of returning to London. One was to be offered sooner than he may have expected.

The end of the war with the French had lowered the political temperature in Pennsylvania. Now, surely, there would be an end to the wranglings over defense bills, since they would no longer be necessary. But if peace had been signed with the French, it had not been signed with the Indians, even though they no longer had active French support. In the spring of 1763 Pontiac, chief of the Ottawa Indians, who was said to have led the attack against Braddock's forces in 1755, opened a coordinated attack on the forts guarding the northern frontiers of the Colonies. At Detroit, where the assault was led by Pontiac himself, the British commander had been forewarned and a five-month siege followed. Elsewhere the Indians were successful; eight forts were taken and their defenders massacred. Once more, as in 1755, the whole northern frontier was ablaze with marauding parties of Indians ranging almost at will across the countryside.

When Franklin arrived back in Philadelphia in the autumn of 1763 the blind vengeance of the white inhabitants was already rising to the surface.

There was more than one massacre of peaceful Indians, and in December a score of quiet innocents, old and young, women and children, were slaughtered at Conestoga by a group of settlers known as the Paxton Boys. Once the mob had tasted blood, their fury was quickly augmented. Several hundred men joined the Paxton Boys and by February 1764 were marching on Philadelphia, where large numbers of their prey had sought refuge.

The Assembly, and many other Philadelphians, were now alarmed not only by the threat from the Indians but by the frustrated whites, who believed the authorities in Philadelphia had failed to support them. Indeed, warrants had been issued for the arrest of those who had murdered Indians, a move which many of the settlers felt to be little less than treason. But the Assembly had at last agreed to give the British commander, Lord Amherst, the 1,000 men he had long been demanding for defense of the frontier; had passed an "Act for Preventing Tumults and Riotous Assemblies"; and had even gained the Governor's approval for money without the usual haggling disputes.

This was the more remarkable as the governor was now John Penn, nephew of Thomas, who had replaced Hamilton in November 1763. But John Penn was so worried that when "the March of the Paxton Boys" neared Philadelphia, he sought advice from, and refuge with, the detested enemy, Benjamin Franklin. Thus it was Franklin who led a deputation which marched out to meet the nearly rebellious white colonialists, faced them at Germantown, eight miles from Philadelphia, and, with what must have been a *tour de force* of oratory, persuaded them to disband and return home.

His own version of these incidents was given in a letter to John Fothergill describing the new militia forces. "The Governor offer'd me the Command of them, but I chose to carry a Musket and strengthen his Authority by setting an Example of Obedience to his Orders," he wrote. "And, would you think it, this Proprietory Governor did me the Honour, on an Alarm, to run to my House at Midnight, with his Counsellors at his Heels, for Advice, and make it his Head-Quarters for some time. And within four and twenty Hours, your old Friend was a common Soldier, a Counsellor, a kind of Dictator, an Ambassador to the Country Mob, and on their Returning home, *Nobody* again." Franklin revealed his state of mind during this episode in a letter to Richard Jackson. "You may judge what Hurry and Confusion we have been in for this Week past," he wrote. "I was up two Nights running, all Night, with our Governor; and my Rest so broken by Alarms on the other Nights, that the whole Week seems one confus'd Space of Time, without any such Distinction of Days, as that I can readily & certainly say, on such a Day such a thing happened."

Once the crisis had passed, however, Governor Penn reverted to the Proprietor's normal hostility to Franklin, a change that was unseemly, dishonorable and unwise. More revealingly, Governor Penn, descendant of the unflinchingly pacifist William Penn, now offered a bounty for Indian scalps, male or female.

Even by the start of these sickening events Franklin's thoughts of a return to England were hardening, apparently under the pressure of William Strahan, to whom he wrote in December 1763: "I have a great Opinion of your Wisdom (Madeira apart; [Strahan apparently did not share Franklin's taste for the wine]) and am apt enough to think that what you seem so clear in, and are so earnest about, must be right. Tho' I own, that I sometimes suspect, my Love to England and my Friends there, seduces me a little, and makes *my own* middling Reasons for going over; appear very good ones. We shall see in a little Time how Things will turn out."

He would see how things turned out. Meanwhile, he had begun planning a new house. During the preceding thirty years he had acquired more than one parcel of land on the south side of High (Market) Street and he now set about building on them. Samuel Rhoads, an old friend from the early days of the Junto, was commissioned as an agent to supervise the work—and subsequently was to be ordered, as best as could be, through letters to Deborah. One of the first had come when Franklin was in New York on his postal tour and Rhoads had been asked to "send me an Invoice of such Locks, Hinges and the like as cannot be had at Philadelphia, and will be necessary for my House."

Now, early in 1764, bitter that no genuine attempt was being made to apprehend the murderers of Conestoga, Franklin attacked the Proprietors again. The Assembly supported his renewed call for a change to royal rather than proprietorial government, and the way was opened for the election of 1764, an election distinguished by its torrents of insult, obloquy and libel, large even when measured against the robust practices of the times.

Early in 1764 Franklin had written *A Narrative of the Late Massacres, in Lancaster County. . . .* It was a sober recapitulation of events, a statement that Indians on the warpath gave no

justification for murdering others who had always lived peace-
ably among the white settlers. "What," Franklin asked, "could
Children of a Year old, Babes at the Breast, what could they do,
that they too must be shot and hatcheted? Horrid to relate! and
in their Parents' Arms! This is done by no civilised Nation in
Europe. Do we come to America to learn and practise the Manners of *Barbarians*? But this, *Barbarians* as they are, they practise
against their Enemies only, not against their Friends."

His description of potential supporters as barbarians, justified
though it was, did little to help him or his party—the Old Party,
as it was called—in the autumn election campaign. As a result
he was, he confided to Strahan, "much the Butt of Party Rage
and Malice, express'd in Pamphlets and Prints, and have as many
pelted at my Head in proportion, as if I had the Misfortune of
being your Prime Minister."

Months before the autumn campaign got under way, the situation had altered in two respects. Relations between the Assembly and the Governor had reached a new low ebb after John
Penn had refused to pass a money bill except on the exact terms
which Franklin had guaranteed to the Privy Council—that "the
Located uncultivated Lands belonging to the Proprietaries shall
not be assessed higher than the lowest Rate at which any
Located uncultivated Lands belonging to the Inhabitants shall
be assessed." And the Assembly had warned the Governor that
any ill results of his action would undoubtedly add to "that Load
of Obloquy and Guilt the Proprietary Family is already bur-
dened with, and bring their Government (a Government which
is always meanly making Use of public Distress, to extort something from the People for its own private Advantage) into (if
possible) still greater Contempt."

Franklin now wrote his *Cool Thoughts on the Present Situation of
Our Public Affairs,* an impassioned plea for change. It was produced at breakneck speed and on the night of April 12 was thrust
beneath house doors or thrown in through open windows.

When the Assembly reconvened in May the Governor still
refused to budge. Reluctantly, the Assembly had to pass the
money bill on the Governor's terms and in conformity with the
terms of Franklin's agreement with the Privy Council. But this
time the Governor had overreached himself. Once the money
bill was under way the Assembly appointed a committee empowered to draw up a petition to George III asking him to take over

the Colony. The Speaker, Isaac Norris, who disagreed with the decision, found himself too ill to fulfill his duties. Franklin was chosen by the Assembly as a replacement.

On June 1 Franklin sent the petition to Jackson, the agent for the Colony in London, and ordered him to present it to the King-in-Council. On the face of it this was an indication that he was not angling for another spell in London; yet by mid-June William Franklin was informing William Strahan that his father now appeared to be preparing in earnest for a voyage to England.

Throughout the summer, with the Assembly adjourned, opposition to a change from proprietorial government to royal began to develop. With it, a campaign against Franklin was soon being stepped up by the Penns.

There was a brief session of the Assembly in September, and decks were then cleared for the election to be held on October 1. As an example of uninhibited scurrility the campaign on both sides has considerable interest. Those who supported the Proprietor's party included most of Philadelphia's aristocracy, whose members were excoriated by Isaac Hunt, father of the poet Leigh Hunt and one of Franklin's main propagandists. Hunt, who emigrated to England before his son was born, devoted what has been called "thirteen verses of scurrilous billingsgate" to William Allen, the province's chief justice. He followed up with the genealogy of Philadelphia's leading families, which purported to show that they were descended from "London fishwives, huckstering salt sellers, and daughters of convict servants." The Proprietary party was no less uninhibited. Franklin's alleged extravagances in London were among its lesser points. His son's illegitimacy was made much of, as was his own reported immorality in London and elsewhere. "A Letcher" who "Needs nothing to excite him, / But is too ready to engage, / When younger Arms envite him" was among the less venomous doggerels touted abroad. His electrical results were described as largely those of others, and he was told that he should restrict himself to "measuring how many quarts of fire were contained in a watery cloud, instead of attempting once more to set this province on fire." He was also caricatured as a cynical master of bear-baiting, speaking the lines: "Fight dog, fight bear, you're all my friends: / By you I shall attain my ends; / For I can never be content / Till I have got the government; / But if from this attempt I fall, / Then let the devil take you all!'' On the pros and cons of continuing proprietary government or of changing to the rule of George III comparatively little was said or written.

But the virulence of the campaign more than made up for any serious discussion of the issues, as a report of the election in Philadelphia reveals. "The poll was opened about nine in the morning, the first of October, and the steps so crowded, till between eleven and twelve at night, that at no time a person could get up in less than a quarter of an hour from his entrance at the bottom, for they could go no faster than the whole column moved. About three in the morning, the advocates for the new ticket moved for a close, but (O! fatal mistake!) the old hands kept it open, as they had a reserve of the aged and lame, which could not come in the crowd, and were called up and brought out in chairs and litters, &c., and some who needed no help, between three and six o'clock, about two hundred voters. As both sides took care to have spies all night, the alarm was given to the new ticket men; horsemen and footmen were immediately dispatched to Germantown &c., and by nine or ten o'clock they began to pour in, so that after the move for a close, seven or eight hundred votes were procured; about five hundred or near it of which were for the new ticket, and they did not close till three in the afternoon, and it took them till one next day to count them off."

Only then was it realized that Franklin would have done better had he let the poll close earlier: after fourteen years in the Assembly, he had lost his seat by 25 votes in a poll of 4,000.

But if the Old Party had lost Philadelphia, it had won a majority throughout Pennsylvania. And on October 26 the results were made plain when the Assembly "Resolved That Benjamin Franklin Esq. be, and is hereby appointed to embark, with all convenient Dispatch, for Great-Britain, to join with and assist Richard Jackson, Esq., our present Agent, in representing, soliciting and transacting the Affairs of this Province for the ensuing Year." So the appointment was, in effect, for a year. But it would at least get him back to England, and who knew what might happen once he was there.

The Assembly had no money immediately available to fund the appointment but passed a resolution "That the Expence attending the Voyage . . . and the Execution of the Trust reposed in him, [should] be provided for in the first Bill prepared by this House for raising Money to defray the public Debts." Meanwhile, it was decided, he should have one year's advance payment for his passage in consideration of the disruption of his private affairs. There was, in any case, to be no immediate financial problem. Within two hours of the Assembly decision the Philadelphia merchants who were anxious to see the end of proprietary government had subscribed £1,100. Franklin calculated that he need take only £500 with him and confidently noted to his nephew, Jonathan Williams, "any Sum is to be had, that I may want."

There was, nevertheless, strong opposition, and ten of the eleven Assembly members who had voted against Franklin's appointment drew up a seven-point protest. Franklin had been, they maintained, the chief author of those measures in the Assembly which had caused such uneasiness and distraction in the province; his fixed enmity to the Proprietors would prevent all settlement of the disputes with them; he was unfavorably thought of by several of his Majesty's ministers; his appointment was disagreeable to a great number of the most serious and reputable inhabitants of the province, and he had been rejected at the last election after having been in the Assembly for fourteen years; moreover, the House had acted far too hastily in his appointment. Furthermore, it was claimed that when the money he had lost in stock investments was added to his fees and expenses, the amount he had cost the Colony came to £11,000, and had made his an agency too expensive to be repeated; finally, the mischiefs apprehended by his appointment could be obviated by some other assistant to Mr. Jackson, and if some gentleman of integrity, abilities and knowledge (such as Dr. Fothergill) were appointed, those signing the protest would pay him at their own expense.

The protest was, for all practical purposes, totally ignored. But it enabled Franklin to issue a formal reply which put the protesters smartly in their place. Dated November 5, it concluded: "I am now to take Leave (perhaps a last Leave) of the Country I love, and in which I have spent the greatest Part of my Life. ESTO PERPETUA. I wish every kind of Prosperity to my Friends; and I forgive my Enemies."

Despite the all-embracing wording of his appointment, Franklin had two main tasks to carry out in England. The first, and most important as it still appeared, was to present, and gain acceptance of, the Assembly's petition for a change from proprietary to royal government. The present government was weak, it stated, and as a result there had been "great Riots ... armed Mobs marching from Place to Place, and committing violent Outrages, and Insults on the Government with Impunity, to the great Terror of your Majesty's Subjects." The King was therefore asked if he would be "graciously pleased to resume the Government of this Province; making such Compensation to the Proprietaries for the same as to your Majesty's Wisdom and Goodness shall appear just & equitable, and permitting your dutiful Subjects therein to enjoy under your Majesty's more immediate Government and Protection, those Civil and Religious Priviledges, which, to encourage the Settlement of this Province have been granted and confirmed to them, by your Royal Predecessors."

To this task, which had considerably less chance of success than anyone in Philadelphia seems to have realized, there was added another. This was to represent Pennsylvania's interests if the British Government began to implement plans to raise money in the Colonies, a move which had been vaguely rumored earlier in the year. Britain's war with France had been enormously expensive and her national debt had risen from £70 million at the beginning of the war to £150 million in 1763. In Britain it seemed reasonable that the Colonies should now produce some of the money which had been spent on the war, and it had been proposed that the amount might be raised by laying a stamp duty on legal documents and newspapers.

Protesting against the proposal demanded some twisting and turning from both the Assembly and Franklin. For this objectionable idea, which drove a coach and horses through the principle of "no taxation without representation," was a brainchild of George III's government—the very George III whose control of Pennsylvania would, it was argued, be so very much better than that of the Penns. At the least, Franklin's second task thus laid him open to the charge that by calling for an end to proprietary rule he was supporting taxation from Britain.

However, he lost no time and on November 7 rode to Chester, down the Delaware, where *The King of Prussia* was waiting at anchor. He was, noted *The Pennsylvania Gazette,* "accompanied by a great Number of the reputable Inhabitants, from both City and

County." Despite this show of support he had no illusions about the number or strength of the enemies he was leaving in Philadelphia. As his ship stood off Reedy Island, preparing to move out into the open sea the next morning, he warned his daughter, Sally, that his enemies were "very bitter ones; and you must expect their Enmity will extend in some degree to you, so that your slightest Indiscretions will be magnified into crimes, in order the more sensibly to wound and afflict me. It is therefore the more necessary for you to be extreamly circumspect in all your Behaviour, that no Advantage may be given to their Malevolence."

Franklin was not exaggerating. While he was on the high seas Chief Justice William Allen was writing to a friend in England of the recent political struggles in Pennsylvania. "I have hereby drawn on me," he wrote, "the Resentment of the contentious, particularly of the grand Incendiary, Franklin, who, the day before he left Town, published a very abusive paper, chiefly levelled against me. . . . He has filled his papers with Sundry other infamous Falsehoods. He is so bad a man that I hope he will not receive any Countenance from honest Men in England."

SEVEN

HOLDING
THE SCALES

RANKLIN'S TRANSATLANTIC CROSSING in the winter of 1764 was very different from the voyage of August 1762. He described *The King of Prussia* as "a miserable vessel, improper for those northern seas (and which actually foundered in her return)." If the weather was bad, the food was worse, and he came ashore at Portsmouth on December 10 with "scarce strength to stand."

This time he had a home waiting for him. He drove to London and was soon at the door of Mrs. Stevenson's in Craven Street. "Your good Mama," he wrote to Mary Stevenson, "was not at home, and the Maid could not tell where to find her, so I sat me down and waited her Return, when she was a good deal surpriz'd to find me in her Parlour." He was unwell for a few weeks after his arrival, possibly an automatic reaction to the hardships of the voyage, but an enforced rest gave him the opportunity to take things easy for a while. There was, in any case, no chance of immediately getting down to official business since Parliament would not be assembling until January and most men of importance were out of London. For the time being he could occupy himself with settling down into his old haunts.

Once again he went to the Royal Society. Once again he met Dr. Priestley and John Pringle, the latter soon to be created a baronet by a grateful George III. Peter Collinson visited him in Craven Street. So of course did William Strahan, with whom Franklin now had an additional link. Before he left England in 1762 he had accepted Strahan's offer to care for William Franklin's illegitimate son. Strahan had found a foster home and now brought the boy to Craven Street to meet his grandfather. Franklin took over from Strahan, and he sent William Temple Franklin to a school in Kensington, whence he came to Craven Street during the school holidays three times a year.

Franklin had been in London only two months when he informed his wife that Mrs. Stevenson "wishes you would come over and bring Sally." Yet in the same letter he hopes "to be able to return about the End of Summer." Five days later he writes: "A few Months, I hope, will finish Affairs here to my Wish, and bring me to that Retirement and Repose with my little Family, so suitable to my Years, and which I have so long set my Heart upon." Similar conflicting statements were to be sent across the Atlantic at regular intervals during the next eleven years. At best they suggest that Franklin was perpetually in an anxious and worried state of mind, torn between the attractions of London and of Philadelphia; at worst, that he thought it wise to impress on his wife that he was genuinely anxious to be home and would be coming soon. Certainly he never gave any serious indication that he expected his family to join him in London; indeed, he had known for years that Deborah ruled out any such possibility, and he gave every sign of being happy to settle back once again into the cozy Stevenson ménage.

Two questions raise their awkward heads. The first asks whether Franklin was really prepared to remain in England and never see his wife again. It seems very doubtful if even Franklin knew the answer. He was content to be carried on the tide of events as long as it carried him forward. At times he was lonely and at times he was homesick. His letters to Deborah were by no means only letters tailored to create the right impression. But when they had been written and sent, there was usually some interesting political, social or scientific diversion to which he could turn. What an exciting and beguiling place London was!

The second question concerns Deborah herself, uncomplaining, obedient. What was her reaction? There is a simple answer. She put up with it. There was no alternative.

Franklin's appointment from the Assembly was, it is true, only for a year, but extreme good luck would be needed if the petition for the Penns' replacement by the Crown was to be presented and then passed through the complex machinery of government in anything like that time. As for taxation of the Colonies, Franklin was by now experienced enough to know that that subject could stretch out almost indefinitely.

Reasons for remaining in London were also strengthened as his status slowly but subtly changed. While he remained as an agent for Pennsylvania, he was also appointed agent for Georgia and for Massachusetts by their respective Houses of Representatives. The new governor of Pennsylvania and the Massachusetts governor both refused formally to confirm the appointments, an indication of Franklin's attitude in the emerging Colonial confrontation. Yet despite this he slowly but perceptibly began to exercise an almost ambassadorial influence as the spokesman in London for the Assemblies of the American Colonies. This was important during the repercussions which followed the Stamp Act, but it became more so as feelings across the Atlantic hardened, as the British Government began to view events in North America first as insurrection, then as rebellion, and as the specter of American independence rose above the horizon and began to overshadow British politics.

Even so, none of this entirely explains the fact that Franklin was to remain in Britain—except for holiday journeys on the Continent—not for a year but for more than a decade: and that he was in fact to leave only after the Hutchinson letters affair had in 1774 destroyed his effectiveness as an American advocate. But for that, it appears almost certain that he would have remained in Britain, probably for the rest of his life, with results which would certainly have affected the course of history.

To the official tasks of replacing the Penns by the Crown, and of dissuading the Crown from imposing fresh taxes on the Colonies, there were added the private tasks connected with the ambitious land-speculation schemes in which he was involved and which he hoped might bring a fortune to him and his family. This fortune would be won in projects that were also in the public interest, a considerable attraction, since Franklin was ever anxious to weld public good to private profit. New opportunities now presented themselves, since the government controlled huge areas ripe for settlement, development and exploitation, a situation very different from that of 1762, when Franklin had sailed for Philadelphia. With the Paris Treaty of 1763 the country had gained control over huge territories of the West and of Canada. What was to be done with them? What, in particular, was to be done with the vast and potentially rich lands of the Mississippi and Ohio valleys, the lands behind the Alleghenies?

"How," Clarence Alvord has asked in his study of the Mississippi Valley and British politics, "could there be a reconciliation between the various interests clamoring for consideration? The Indians' rights must be protected; the claims of various colonies to the West must be considered; the influence of the great land companies of different colonies must not be neglected; there were the fur traders who opposed western colonization; and these latter were supported by British and American speculators in eastern lands who feared the effects of opening the West; and last of all there were the imperial interests to be conserved."

These factors combined to create a situation too tempting to be ignored by Franklin's mercantile instincts. Throughout the greater part of his residence in London between 1764 and 1775 he was actively concerned in promoting a succession of land-speculation companies whose success or failure in successive crises rested very largely on the whim of British ministers. As C. P. Snow has pointed out, "In times of crisis, as all kinds of men have found out, from Trotsky downwards, the first mistake is to absent oneself." Franklin had no intention of doing that.

His official duties began in earnest on February 2, 1765, when George Grenville, the Chancellor of the Exchequer, invited him and three other Colonial agents to discuss their objections to the Stamp Act, by now drawn up and already passing through Parliament. The need for it sprang directly from the precarious situation in North America following the peace of 1763. It had been decided that a permanent establishment of about 10,000 men would be necessary to meet a potential threat from the French, who despite the end of their rule in Canada still had strong roots there. About a third of the cost could be met by an act which demanded that all legal documents, newspapers and playing cards would have to be stamped. A university degree, for instance, would have to bear a £2 stamp before it was valid. When it came to arguing against the bill Franklin found that one stumbling block was the popular misconception of the way in which the Colonies had been founded in the previous century. There was, as he wrote to his friend Lord Kames, the "mistaken Notion . . . that the Colonies were planted at the Expence of Parliament, and that therefore the Parliament has a Right to tax them, &c." The truth was very different. Private adventurers had been given charters by the Crown allowing them to settle in North America and yet remain British subjects even though they had taken up residence in a foreign country—a country which, as Franklin expressed it, "had not been conquer'd by either King or Parliament, but was possess'd by a free People." He nevertheless offered to consider alternative ways of raising the money. But it seemed obvious to him as well as to his colleagues that the government was set on passing the bill. Perhaps it was regrettable. But to Franklin approval of the petition from the Assembly, for which he was still trying to drum up support, was vastly more important. On the principle of losing a sprat to catch a mackerel he accepted the Stamp Act as a fact of life. And, curiously out of touch with feeling across the Atlantic, he expected it to be accepted there without undue protest.

The act was finally approved by the House of Commons on February 27, 1765, by the House of Lords on March 8, and was to come into operation on November 1. "We might as well have hinder'd the sun's setting," he wrote to Charles Thomson. "That we could not do. But since it is down, my Friend, and it may be long ere it rises again, Let us make as good a Night of it as we can. We may still Light Candles. Frugallity and Industry will go a great way towards indemnifying us. Idleness and Pride Tax with a heavier Hand than Kings and Parliaments. If we can get rid of the former we may easily bear the Latter."

Certainly Franklin was willing to "make as good a Night of it as we can" for himself and his friends. Initially, it had been expected that it would be possible for paper to be stamped in the United States, but this option was later ruled out, as Franklin put it, "notwithstanding all I could do." Previously, however, he had sent David Hall, his former assistant and partner, a quantity of unstamped paper. Had Hall been able to use it, he was told by Franklin, he "would have had great Advantage of the other Printers, since if they were not provided with such Paper, they must have either printed but a half sheet common Demi, or paid for two Stamps on each Sheet." However, as events turned out, this attempt to make one stamp serve for two sheets was too clever by half. The newsprint had to be returned to Britain for stamping and Hall was unable to make the hoped-for windfall profit.

Franklin seems to have been taken aback by the opposition that the act began to arouse. As deputy postmaster he appointed his old friend John Hughes one of the detested stamp distributors. Enforcing the act "may make you unpopular for a Time," Hughes was told, "but your Acting with Coolness and Steadiness, and with every Circumstance in your Power of Favour to the People, will by degrees reconcile them. In the mean time, a firm Loyalty to the Crown and faithful Adherence to the Government of this Nation, which it is the Safety as well as Honour of the Colonies to be connected with, will always be the wisest Course for you and I to take, whatever may be the Madness of the Populace or their blind Leaders, who can only bring themselves and Country into Trouble, and draw on greater Burthens by Acts of rebellious Tendency." Few of George III's subjects could have been more loyal or more obedient.

By late summer Franklin began to realize that he was backing the wrong horse. "In short," David Hall told him, "there seems to be a general Discontent all over the Continent, with that Law, and many thinking their Liberties and Privileges, as English Men lost, or at least in great Danger, seem Desperate. What the Consequences may be, God only knows; but, from the Temper of the People, at Present, there is the greatest Reason to fear, that the Passing of that Law will be the Occasion of a great Deal of Mischief."

As summer turned to autumn, the situation grew steadily worse. "I am so verey poor a writer that I donte undertake to say aney thing a bought the dis[order] in this porte of the world," Deborah wrote to her husband, "but to me it semes we air verey wicked and so is the pepel in in [sic] London and other plases on your sid the watter I pray god mend us all." Stamp agents resigned in numbers, mainly for their own safety. Some, including Hughes, were hanged in effigy, and Franklin must have experienced a considerable shock when he heard from his friend Thomas Wharton of events in Philadelphia. "This day," Wharton wrote on October 5, "the Letters per the August

packet came to Hand as well as the Vessell with the Stamp'd
Paper came up to town, but such confusion and disorder it
Created as thou never saw with Us, the Inhabitants collected to
the State house by beat of Drum, and nothing Less than the
distruction of our dear Friend J. Hughes or the surrender of his
Office were the Objects, [and ?] finding Matter, thus Circum-
stanc'd, and He being reduced to a very low State by a severe
Indisposition, He at last Promisd that He would resign on Second day next."

Then James Parker followed with a letter saying a "black
Cloud seems to hang over us; but whether it will blow past, or
the Thunder break in upon us all, is what he alone, who guides
it, can tell . . . the People are all running Mad; and say it is as
good to dye by the Sword as by the Famine." The next month
Wharton gave Franklin a graphic account of the New York
crowds burning the Governor's coach, forcing him to give up
the stamp papers and destroying the property of a British officer
who had said he would enforce the act.

If public opinion vented itself on the wretched agents, it did
not spare Franklin, a fact which the Proprietor no doubt observed with pleasure. He could, of course, capitalize on Franklin's campaign for a change to the government of a monarch
now applying the Stamp Act. "The Matter of the Prop^y Party
against my Father, on Account of his wanting to bring about a
Change of Government, is beyond all Bounds," the still-dutiful
son, William, wrote to Strahan. "They glory in saying and doing
Things to destroy his Character that would make even Devils
blush." Even before the wrath had mounted, a cartoon showed
a Devil whispering in Franklin's ear, "Thee shall be agent, Ben,
for all my dominions," with, below it, the lines: "All his designs
concenter in himself, / For building castles and amassing
pelf. / The public 'tis his wit to sell for gain, / Whom private
property did n'er maintain."

It is doubtful if Franklin worried much about attacks of this
sort; not only had he become inured to them over the years, but
he himself was a past master at mounting propaganda campaigns. Soon, however, his home was under threat and his beloved daughter, Sally, was forced to leave Philadelphia. "I was
for 9 day keep in one Contineued hurrey by pepel to removef,"
Deborah informed him, "and Salley was porswaided to go to
burlington for saiftey but on munday laste we had verey graite

rejoysing on a Count of the Chang of the Ministrey and a preyperaition for binfiers att night and several houses thretened to be puled down. Cusin Davenporte Come and told me that more than twenty pepel had told him it was his Duty to be with me. I sed I was plesed to reseve Civility from aney bodey so he staid with me sum time to words night I sed he shold fech a gun or two as we had none. I sente to aske my Brother to Cume and bring his gun all so so [*sic*] we maid one room into a Magazin. I ordored sum sorte of defens up Stairs such as I Cold manaig my self. I sed when I was advised to remove that I was verey shuer you had dun nothing to hurte aney bodey nor I had not given aney ofense to aney person att all nor wold I be maid unesey by aney bodey nor wold I stir or show the leste uneseynis but if aney one Came to disturbe me I wold show a proper resentement. . . . I was told that thair was 8 hundred men readey to asiste aney one that shold be molisted."

A good deal of this was probably occasioned as much by the bitter political infighting of the previous few years as by the Stamp Act itself. "In the Heat of Party, Abuse is receiv'd greedily, and Vindications coldly," Franklin wrote to David Hall. "And it is my Opinion, that if I had actually prevented the Stamp Act, (which God knows I did all in my Power to prevent) neither the Malice of the bigotted Abettors of Indian Murder, nor the Malice of the interested Abettors of Proprietary Injustice, would have been in the least abated towards me."

By November 1, when a copy of the act was buried at Portsmouth, New Hampshire, in a coffin on whose lid was written "*Liberty* aetas 145, *Stamp'd*," the act had clearly become unenforceable and crowds were marching the streets singing: "He who for a Post or Base sorded Pelf / His Country Betrays, Makes a Rope for himself. / Of this an Example, Before you we Bring / In these Infamous Rogues, Who in Effigy Swing."

In Philadelphia *The Pennsylvania Gazette* appeared on November 7 without its usual printed title and in its place the words: "No *Stamped Paper* to be had." Among its news was the item: "On Friday and Saturday last, the DREADFUL FIRST and SECOND Days of November, our Bells were rung muffled, and other Demonstrations of Grief Shewn." The following week, the next issue, No. 1925, also appeared on unheaded paper. The written title was "Remarkable *Occurrences*": the news of how America was reacting to the Stamp Act.

Her inhabitants were already demonstrating that the act would be unenforceable without troops. And it was now realized in Britain, where so few facts about the Colonies had been realized, that even if troops succeeded in making the detested stamped paper available, there was no practicable means of ensuring its use. The Americans could, if they preferred, continue as before and damn the consequences. They could, in fact, do much more. Years before independence was even a thought, Franklin had encouraged the idea of Colonial industrial independence. Now, under the propagandist effect of the Stamp Act, company after company along the Eastern Seaboard began canceling orders from England and setting out along the road to self-sufficiency. Before the end of 1765 it was estimated in London that deliveries of some £700,000-worth of goods had already been canceled by Colonial firms and that some £4 million-worth were involved. Belatedly, it was recognized that the Stamp Act, which it had been estimated would raise £60,000, could cut Britain's commercial throat.

Franklin saw this more quickly than most men. He realized that the tide would be turning and made sure that he would then be swimming with it. To the obvious charge of being a turncoat he had a very adequate defense. Early in 1765 the Stamp Act had rated a lower priority than the petition to the King. Now, with British opinion appreciating the disastrous impact of the act, support for its repeal might help in the continuing battle with the Penns.

The battle had got off to a very bad start. The petition from the Assembly did not arrive at the end of the long bureaucratic tunnel and reach the Privy Council until November 4, some eleven months after Franklin's return to England. Eighteen days later the Council, moving with comparative speed, reported that it could not consider passing the petition to the King. Yet Franklin continued to hope that this was not, as it turned out to be, the end of the line.

His standing in Pennsylvania had been lowered by his acquiescence in the Stamp Act, temporary though this was. That he well knew how equivocal he might appear is suggested in a letter from William Strahan to David Hall. "I saw Dr. Franklin yesterday, and found him under deep Concern for the present distracted State of America," Strahan wrote. "No Father can be under more Anxiety for his Children. I don't know what People with you think of him, but I can assure you, from my own Knowledge, that some of those in Power, to whom he is known, and admit and even admire his natural Sagacity, and his Knowledge of American Affairs, think him too partial to his own Country; and yet his Enemies, I am told, look upon him as a Betrayer of its Interests. — This is truly provoking, and is enough to cool the zeal of the warmest Patriot—But if I know anything of his Disposition, he is not to be diverted by any Insult or Injury done himself, from following the Dictates of his Conscience, which as he possesses an Understanding enlightened in no common Degree, I dare say will always prompt him to advise such Measures (as far as he is consulted) as most directly tend to heal the Divisions, secure the Liberty, and restore the Happiness, Commerce, and Tranquillity of America."

While Franklin considered, during the last weeks of 1765, how it might be possible to have the anti-Penn petitions resubmitted, opposition to the Stamp Act increased. Before the end of the year petitions for repeal of the act were on their way from the Stamp Act Congress, an intercolonial meeting called in New York to plan joint action against the law. Organizations for boycotting British goods were already being set up in most of the Colonies and Franklin could sincerely warn in Britain of the potentially disastrous economic consequences. It might, he began to realize, even lead to a future total separation between the Colonies and the mother country, a prospect which filled him with dismay.

To further his aims he now embarked on a press campaign for which he was almost uniquely qualified. He wrote under the pen names of "Homespun," "Pacificus" and "Traveller." He adapted his writing to a wide variety of audiences and was, as required, reportorial, historical or satirical. When he wished to suggest that America was not entirely dependent on British wool he went far to justify Balzac's description of him as "the inventor of the lightning rod, the hoax and the republic." The British woolen industry had no chance, for instance, against the American, he implied, since "The very Tails of the American Sheep are so laden with Wool, that each has a Car or Waggon on four little Wheels, to support and keep it from trailing on the Ground." Much the same technique was used when it was rumored that a cod and whale fishery was being set up on the inland lakes. Tongue-in-cheek, Franklin said it was difficult to deny such reports even though the lakes were fresh-water and the cod and the whale were salt-water fish and animal. The cod, Franklin explained, "like other Fish, when attacked by their Enemies, fly into any Water where they think they can be safest; . . . Whales, when they have a Mind to eat Cod, pursue them wherever they fly; and . . . the grand Leap of the Whale in that Chace up the Fall of Niagara is esteemed by all who have seen it, as one of the finest Spectacles in Nature."

It can be questioned whether Franklin's propaganda affected the issue of the Stamp Act very much. There was, in fact, little need for it to do so since by the beginning of 1766 business organizations in no fewer than twenty-five British cities, including London, Bristol and Glasgow, were petitioning the government for its repeal. It was quickly decided that the House of Commons, sitting as a committee, should take evidence on the situation, and during a fortnight of hearings which began on February 3 thirty witnesses were heard. On the tenth day Franklin was called. His interrogation was, as Edmund Burke put it, like that of a master examined by a panel of schoolboys.

There could have been few better witnesses. He had the facts and figures at his fingertips. He oozed sweet reason, and he had a presence. "He was fat, square built, and wore his own hair, thin and gray; but he looked healthy and vigorous," was how he appeared even a decade later to Mrs. Deborah Logan. "His head was remarkably large in proportion to his figure, and his countenance mild, firm, and expressive. He was friendly and agreeable in conversation, which he suited to his company, appearing to wish to benefit his hearers. I could readily believe that he heard nothing of consequence himself but what he turned to the account he desired, and in his turn profited by the conversation of others." If Franklin deplored the Stamp Act, his concern seemed more for the harm it would do Britain than for its affront to the Colonies. But with respect for Britain there went a steely resolution that left Members in no doubt that, failing repeal, great trouble lay ahead. These sentiments were exemplified by two questions and answers in the middle of the interrogation, and by two others as it closed.

Asked whether the Americans would submit to the stamp duty if it were moderated, Franklin replied: "No, never, unless compelled by force of arms." Then, asked what the temper of America had been toward Britain before 1763, he replied: "The best in the world. They submitted willingly to the government of the Crown, and paid, in all their courts, obedience to acts of Parliament. Numerous as the people are in the several old provinces, they cost you nothing in forts, citadels, garrisons, or armies, to keep them in subjection. They were governed by this country at the expence only of a little pen, ink and paper. They were led by a thread. They had not only a respect, but an affection for Great-Britain, for its laws, its customs and manners, and even a fondness for its fashions, that greatly increased the commerce. Natives of Britain were always treated with particular regard; to be an Old-England man was, of itself, a character of some respect, and gave a kind of rank among us."

And, at the end of the hearing, there came two significant questions and answers. "What used to be the pride of the Americans?" to which the answer was: "To indulge in the fashions and manufactures of Great Britain." And "What is now their pride?" "To wear their old clothes over again, till they can make new ones."

The House finished its hearings in February. Within a few weeks repeal of the act had been drafted, after a proposal to explain and amend it rather than repeal it had been defeated by 275 votes to 167. It had been a busy time for Franklin. "My dear child," he wrote to his wife on February 22, "I am excessively hurried, being every Hour that I am awake either abroad to speak with Members of Parliament or taken up with People coming to me at home, concerning our American Affairs, so that I am much behind-hand in answering my Friends' Letters. . . . I am well; 'tis all I can say at present, except that I am just now made very happy by a Vote of the Commons for the Repeal of the Stamp Act." George III signed the repeal on March 18, 1766. "The Marquis of Rockingham told a Friend of mine a few Days after," William Strahan wrote to David Hall, "That he never knew Truth make so great a Progress in so very short a Time."

Parliament's capitulation had been brought about, very largely, by the reaction of mercantile magnates who saw their profits melting away under the vigor of American decisions to suspend trade with Britain until the Stamp Act was repealed. But to that reaction there was added the somber, quiet-voiced answers of Franklin and the threat which they enclosed: that if Parliament persisted, the Stamp Act could be imposed on an unwilling population only by bayonets.

The repeal was considered a political defeat by the die-hards, however great a sigh of relief it brought from the business community. Franklin was among the men who had swayed the balance; and from now on, as disagreement between Britain and the Colonies hardened first to disruption and then to what was increasingly seen as preparation for rebellion, his position changed into that of a potentially treasonable Colonial agent. He himself, among the most far-sighted of men on either side, argued to the last minute of the last hour, and with an almost pathetic intensity, that Britain and the Colonies should not part and go their different ways. In much of Britain the imperial vision which had been so evident in his letters to Lord Kames was brushed aside; an arrogant ignorance clouded the obvious fact that the world was changing and that if the Colonies were not given satisfactory status they would take it as of right.

In Pennsylvania, also, there was little understanding that if their agent was firm he was also, by nature, conciliatory. There he was now praised for, as it was believed, defeating the detested Stamp Act almost single-handed. "We have heard by a round about way that the stamp act is repeal'd," Sally Franklin wrote to him only a week after the King had signed the repeal; "the People seem ditermined to beleave it, tho it came from Ireland to Maryland. The bells rang we had bonfires and one house was illumanited, indeed I never heard so much noise in all my life the very Children [in the surrounding houses] seem distracted."

Confirmation, in fact, came only two months later. "Upon its Arrival agreable to your Advice," Joseph Galloway told Franklin, "Our Friends exerted their utmost Endeavours to prevent any indecent Marks of Triumph and Exultation. We opposed the Intended Fire Works Illuminations, firing of Canon &ca. and Advised more Temperate and Private rejoicing on this great Occasion."

However, judging by John Watson's 1844 *Annals of Philadelphia and Pennsylvania in the Olden Time*, Galloway's account told only half of the story. "When the news of 'Stamp Act Repealed' arrived in 1766," says Watson, "the gentlemen at the coffeehouse sent a deputation to Captain Wise, by whose brig the news came, to invite him up to drink punch, and at the same time to give his whole crew presents. All was joy and hilarity. At the coffee-house the punch was made common, and a gold-laced hat was presented to the captain as a token of their gratitude. The same night every street in the city was illuminated. A large quantity of wood was given for bonfires, and many barrels of beer to the populace. Next day the governor and mayoralty gave a great feast for 300 persons, at the State-house gallery. At the same place it was unanimously resolved to dress themselves at the approaching birthday [of George III] in new suits of English manufacture, and to give their homespun and patriotic garments to the poor!"

On the great day, Watson continues, "a great number of the inhabitants of the Northern Liberties and Southwark met on the banks of the Schuylkill, then a place of arborescent shade, where 430 persons were dined in a grove. The Franklin barge, of 40 feet, and the White Oak barge, of 50 feet, both decorated with many flags, were then used with much parade. One was rowed up the Schuylkill, firing her salutes; and the other was drawn through the streets of the city, also firing her salutes *en passant*. Fireworks were exhibited at night. The whole scene was a joyous occasion, and the crowds were great."

Now it was surely time for Franklin to return home. One part of his mission had been successfully accomplished; as for the other, the Assembly's petition for royal government had been rejected, and there would have to be lengthy consideration before another effort was made. Yet for another nine years he was regularly to say that he hoped to be returning soon and just as regularly found it necessary to remain.

It is difficult to judge how sincerely Franklin believed in the series of statements he made during the decade that followed the Stamp Act controversy. A random selection serves to illustrate the fluctuating feelings behind his outwardly imperturbable presence in Britain. In the summer of 1767 he told Joseph Galloway he hoped to be returning to America the following spring and in May 1768 he told him: "I am preparing for my return." But shortly afterward he implied to his son that he would be "gone in a few weeks"—unless, that is, he gained a government post which might now be in the offing and which would be better than that of deputy postmaster. In 1770 he told

Pierre Samuel Du Pont de Nemours, the French economist: "I purpose returning to America in the ensuing Summer, if our Disputes should be adjusted, as I hope they will be in the next Session of Parliament." And the following summer he answered Deborah's inquiry about his return with the words: "I purpose it firmly after one winter more here." In the summer of 1773 he told his friend Jonathan Shipley, the bishop of St. Asaph, that he was homesick and longed to see his family but mentioned, rather curiously, his plans for "visiting" America. In July he talked of leaving England in September, but in September told his Dutch friend Jan Ingenhousz that "some Events in our Colony Affairs induc'd me to stay here another Winter." A week later he told his wife that "positively nothing shall prevent, God willing, my Returning in the Spring."

Franklin's conflicting feelings are well brought out in a letter to his son written in 1772, a letter in which, significantly, he does not rule out returning to Britain after a visit to Philadelphia, despite the fact that he knows his wife will not accompany him. "I have of late great Debates with my self whether or not I should continue here any longer," he told William. "I grow homesick, and being now in my 67th Year, I begin to apprehend some Infirmity of Age may attack me, and make my Return impracticable. I have also some important Affairs to settle before my Death, a Period I ought now to think cannot be far distant. I see here no Disposition in Parliament to meddle farther in Colony Affairs for the present, either to lay more Duties or to repeal any; and I think, tho' I were to return again, I may be absent from hence a Year, without any Prejudice to the Business I am engag'd in, tho' it is not probable that being once at home I should ever again see England. I have indeed so many good kind Friends here, that I could spend the Remainder of my Life among them with great Pleasure, if it were not for my American Connections, and the indelible Affection I retain for that dear Country, from which I have so long been in a State of Exile."

There were certainly personal inducements to return. In Philadelphia, Deborah informed him as early as the autumn of 1765, work was continuing on his new house, part of which was almost ready. "Now for the room we Cale yours," she wrote, "thair is in it your Deske the armonekey maid like a Deske a large Cheste with all the writeings that was in your room down stairs the boxes of glases for musick and for the Elicktresatecy and all your close and the pickters as I donte drive nailes leste it shold not be write. . . . The Blewroom has the Armoneyca and the Harpseycord in it the Gilt Sconse a Carde tabel a seet of tee Chaney I bought sens you wente from home the worked Chairs and Screen a verey hansom mohoganey Stand for the tee kittel to stand on and the orney mental Chaney but the room is not as yit finished for I think the paper has loste much of the blume by paisteing of it up their-fore I thought beste to leve it tell you Cume home."

For his part, Franklin certainly maintained a close interest in the building and fitting out of his new house. "I could have wished to have been present at the Finishing of the Kitchen, as it is a mere Machine, and being new to you, I think you will scarce know how to work it," he wrote to his wife when this stage of the work had been reached. "The several Contrivances to carry off Steam and Smell and Smoke not being fully explain'd to you. The Oven I suppose was put up by the written Directions in my former Letter. You mention nothing of the Furnace. If that Iron One is not set, let it alone till my Return, when I shall bring a more convenient copper one."

Two months later he was inquiring: "Let me have the Breadth of the Pier, that I may get a handsome Glass for the Parlour. I want also the Dimensions of the Sash Panes in the Buffets of the little North Room: and the Number of them. Also the Dimensions of the Windows for which you would have me bring Curtains, unless you chuse to have the Curtains made there."

Quite apart from his obvious interest and enjoyment at creating a new home, Franklin was not entirely unaffected by Deborah's sometimes rather pathetic attempts to coax him back home and by her anxiety for news of him—"as I partake of none of the divershons I stay at home and flatter myself that the next packit will bring me a letter from you." Nevertheless the attractions of London were considerable and they included more than charms of life at Craven Street.

It was, of course, agreeable to have the willing services of the Stevensons, who tried, usually with success, to anticipate his wishes and to remove from day-to-day life any of the minor annoyances which might have irked their distinguished visitor. But there was also the friendly atmosphere at the Royal Society and his nearness to its headquarters in Crane Court, adjoining

Fetter Lane, which enabled him to learn, without trouble, of the latest developments in electricity. He himself was to make no more discoveries and to write no more papers on the subject, but his deep interest produced one important result: the writing of Joseph Priestley's 735-page *History and Present State of Electricity*. Franklin encouraged Priestley in the work and lent him much of the material he required.

In the final pages of his book Priestley described how he had repeated an experiment made by Franklin twelve years previously. When a silver pint can standing on an insulated stand was electrified, and a cork ball lowered into it on a silk thread, it was found that the ball was attracted to neither one side nor the other. "You require the reason," Franklin had written at the time; "I do not know it. Perhaps you may discover it, and then you will be so good as to communicate it to me."

Now, having carried out the same experiment, Priestley asked: "May we not infer from this experiment that the attraction of electricity is subject to the same laws as that of gravitation, and is therefore according to the squares of the distances; since it is easily demonstrated, that were the earth in the form of a shell, a body in the inside of it would not be attracted to one side more than another?" Thus from Franklin's initial experiment there was produced the first statement of the inverse square law of electrostatics, afterward verified by direct measurement by John Robinson and by Charles Augustin de Coulomb.

With the help of his friends at the Royal Society Franklin was also able to learn, more readily than in North America, the progress of the campaign for lightning conductors that had followed his work in the 1750s. In England itself few conductors had been erected and in many places church bells were still rung to ward off the lightning. "Probably the vestries of our English churches are not well acquainted with [the] facts," Franklin wrote to John Winthrop, the Harvard astronomer; "otherwise, since as Protestants, they have no faith in the blessing of bells, they would be less excusable in not providing this other security for their respective churches, (more exposed than common buildings by their greater height,) and for the good people that may happen to be assembled in them during a tempest."

Improvement came, if slowly, and five years later he was able to report: "Many country seats are provided with [lightning conductors], some churches, the powder magazines at Purfleet, the Queen's house in the park, &c. and M. Le Roy, of the Academy of Sciences at Paris, has lately given a Memoir recommending the use of them in that kingdom, which has been long opposed and obstructed by Abbé Nollet."

London also offered access to fine libraries and an almost continuous stream of invitations to the homes of the near-great, occasionally to those of the great. Franklin himself described the situation as he saw it in a letter to his son which reveals as much of Franklin as of his surroundings. "As to my situation here," he wrote, "nothing can be more agreeable, especially as I hope for less embarrassment from the new minister. A general respect paid me by the learned, a number of friends and acquaintance[s] among them with whom I have a pleasing intercourse; a character of so much weight that it has protected me when some in power would have done me injury, and continued me in an office they would have deprived me of; my company so much desired that I seldom dine at home in winter, and could spend the whole summer in the country houses of inviting friends, if I chose it. Learned and ingenious foreigners that come to England, almost all make a point of visiting me, for my reputation is still higher abroad than here; several of the foreign ambassadors have assiduously cultivated my acquaintance, treating me as one of their *corps*, partly I believe from the desire they have from time to time of hearing something of American affairs, an object become of importance in foreign courts, who begin to hope Britain's alarming power will be diminished by the defection of her Colonies; and partly that they may have an opportunity of introducing me to the gentlemen of their country who desire it. The K[ing] too, has lately been heard to speak of me with great regard."

This last was pitching the story rather high. It has been remarked that Franklin was never taken to any of the great clubs —Brooks' or Almacks, for instance. He was not a member of the inner circle and in the outer one he was still regarded with qualifications. Despite his Fellowship of the Royal Society he was still an outsider; but he would have been less than human had he not hoped that a year or so longer in England might alter all that.

Moreover, the possibility of obtaining a post under the Crown more important than that of deputy postmaster general in America seems to have been very real. In the mid-eighteenth century, virtually all such appointments were politically motivated, a situation which as far as Franklin was concerned had its advantages as well as the reverse: the anomaly of a deputy postmaster general for America living in London was counterbalanced by the fact that there was no political reason for moving him. By 1768 Franklin was, as he wrote to his son, "grown so old as to feel much less than formerly the spur of ambition." Yet he also reported that the Duke of Grafton, now the acting prime minister, while considering Franklin's long residence in London a disqualification for his postmaster's appointment, had added: "if I chose rather to reside in England, my merit was such in his opinion, as to entitle me to something better here, and it should not be his fault if I was not well provided for." Franklin had, he continued, so great an "inclination to be at home, and at rest, that I shall not be sorry if this business falls through, and I am suffered to retire with my old post; nor indeed very sorry if they take that from me too on account of my zeal for America, in which some of my friends have hinted to me I have been too open." He may have been writing in the knowledge, or at least the belief, that his letters to America would be opened. But, reporting that he had told the authorities he was going home, he added: "(which I still say to every body, not knowing but that what is intimated above [Grafton's approach] may fail of taking effect)." It thus seems likely that had the British offered him a plum job in the later 1760s Franklin might well have accepted it. But the British mishandled this possibility as they were to mishandle almost all their other relations with the American Colonies.

Franklin therefore remained in Britain as the representative of the Pennsylvania Assembly and later of the Massachusetts Bay and Georgia Assemblies—even though Governor Hutchinson of Massachusetts had refused to confirm the Assembly's nomination. He was in an ambiguous position for at least three reasons. He was, after all, an absentee deputy postmaster general of the British Government. Throughout most of the later 1760s and early 1770s he was negotiating with Crown officers for land concessions which would have vastly enriched him and his family. And as Colonial discontent changed first to revolt and then to revolution he found that his views, although increasingly distancing him from the Colonial governors, who with few exceptions remained loyal to the Crown, were more moderate than those of the men who were to force the pace and bring about the revolution. Thus the conflicting personal emotions and feelings which simultaneously drew him to Philadelphia and to London were compounded by an intellectual struggle in which hopes for an imperial future which included America were steadily extinguished by the arrogant stupidity of British governments.

However, a crucial factor behind Franklin's failure to take the first available packet home after 1766 was his instinctive, and correct, belief that the Stamp Act argument had been merely one battle in what would be a long campaign; that relations between Britain and the American Colonies were in a dangerous state of flux and that he, more than most men, could affect the course that they took.

The need for him was to continue, and two years later Dr. Fothergill, Franklin's Quaker friend who had written an introduction to his book of electrical experiments, was writing to James Pemberton in Philadelphia: "I took the liberty to urge your agent B. Franklin to stay here another winter. Much time will be spent on affairs of election [*electioneering*] this session; but America will nevertheless engross the attention of the public. I already perceive a spirit of bitterness against you prevails through most ranks except the Merchants and the wiser mechanics. Country Gentlemen are almost totally against you, full, as I said before, of the spirit of John Bull."

Fothergill's pessimistic caution was to be fully justified; the later 1760s were to witness a series of disorders and riots produced as much by the blundering legislation of British governments incapable of learning the lessons of the time as by American intransigence. The repeal of the Stamp Act, forced on the government more by mercantile common sense than by American indignation, had not been followed by the tacit admission that taxation without representation was not practicable. Indeed, it had produced the reverse. A Declaratory Act, passed on the very day of the Stamp Act's repeal, reaffirmed Britain's right to tax the Colonies—even though, it was implied, there was no intention of doing so at present.

Before the end of the decade, and an omen of things to come, New York's State Assembly refused to enforce a Quartering Act under which the new British commander in America—General Thomas Gage, who had survived Braddock's disastrous rout in

1755—could demand lodgings for his troops. Under pressure from Gage, the Governor dissolved the Assembly; a new Assembly willing to enforce the act was eventually elected. To this new turn of the screw the Americans reacted much as they had reacted against the Stamp Act. Boycotts of imports from Britain were organized, plans to increase Colonial self-sufficiency went ahead, and once again it was hoped that Britain's policy would be changed by pressure on her pocket.

Franklin supported these Colonial measures for a number of reasons. When traveling in Yorkshire he had made a point of discussing production with the mill owners and had, he told Thomas Cushing, the Speaker of the Massachusetts Assembly, become "more and more convinced of the natural impossibility there is that, considering our increase in America, England should be able to much longer supply us with Clothing." And writing to the Committee of Merchants in Philadelphia he praised their proposals for the use of home-produced goods, which would result in the country being "enrich'd by its industry and frugality, those virtues will become habitual"; he went on, "farms will be more improved, better stock'd, and render'd more productive by the money that used to be spent in super-fluities; our artificers of every kind will be enabled to carry on their business to more advantage; gold and silver will become plenty among us, and trade will revive after things shall be well settled, and become better and safer than it has lately been; for an industrious frugal people are best able to buy, and pay best for what they purchase." It was a policy he was to urge with great intensity a decade later when the Colonies were struggling to survive during the early months of the War of Independence.

That war had been brought critically nearer in August 1766 by the appointment of Charles Townshend as chancellor of the exchequer. Early in 1767 he presented his first budget, openly supported the principle of the repealed Stamp Act and "pledged himself to find a revenue in America nearly sufficient for the purposes that were required." Then, in May, there occurred in the House of Commons at Westminster an incident in the long line of events leading to the War of Independence which would be farcical had its results not been tragic. Townshend virulently criticized his opponents in a speech whose quality can be judged by its fame as the "champagne speech." George Grenville, one of those attacked, shouted that while Townshend might make great claims he dare not tax the Americans. A week later the Chancellor replied by putting duties on glass, red and white lead, painters' colors, paper and tea. The act was passed on June 29, 1767, and repercussions followed swiftly.

The results of Townshend's actions can be judged from the statement of the historian A. F. Pollard. "[He] was one of those statesmen whose abilities are the misfortune of the country they serve," Pollard has written. "He impressed his contemporaries as a man of unrivalled brilliance, yet to obtain a paltry revenue of £40,000 he entered a path which led to the dismemberment of the empire."

Franklin's reaction to the deteriorating situation was "The Causes of the American Discontents before 1768." Printed in William Strahan's *The London Chronicle,* it set out the American position in almost conciliatory terms. It is true that he later complained to his son that the editor, Griffith Jones, had "drawn the teeth and pared the nails of my paper, so that it can neither scratch nor bite. It seems only to paw and mumble." Yet even the unedited version, later published in America, was animated by reason and a spirit of economic necessity. In fact, he went so far as to tell Lord Kames that the article had been "written to palliate a little the late offensive Behaviour of the Boston People relating to the use of the Manufactures of this Country." "Let us," he said in *The London Chronicle,* in reference to the economic war then developing, "unite in solemn resolutions and engagements with and to each other, that we will give these new officers as little trouble as possible, by not consuming the British manufactures on which they are to levy the duties. Let us agree to consume no more of their expensive gewgaws. Let us live frugally; and let us industriously manufacture what we can for ourselves." Franklin, percipient businessman that he was, clearly saw how vulnerable Britain was.

While London was discussing Franklin's view of the American discontents, Samuel Adams and James Otis in Boston persuaded the Massachusetts Assembly to approve a circular calling for united action by all the Colonies. This was considered seditious and Thomas Hutchinson, then acting governor, dissolved the Assembly. Dissolution of Colonial Assemblies by loyal royal governors was becoming almost a habit and it might have been expected that the British Government would take some measures to cool the air. Instead, following a riotous attack on Customs officials in Boston, it was decided to send two regiments of troops to the city. "It seems," Franklin wrote to George Whitefield, "like setting up a smith's forge in a magazine of gunpowder." The consequence of the decision is described by Josiah Quincy in his account of the troops' arrival in fourteen men-of-war whose broadsides were turned toward the town to cover the disembarkation: "With muskets charged, bayonets fixed, drums beating, fifes playing, and a complete train of artillery, the troops took possession of the common, the state-house, the court-house, and Faneuil hall. The main-guard, with two pieces of artillery, was stationed at the state-house with their guns pointed towards it. The town wore the aspect of a garrison. Counsellors as they entered the council-chamber, citizens, as they passed and repassed on their private business, were challenged by sentinels."

Within little more than a year there came the "Boston Massacre." A snowball attack on a British sentry led to a riot and the death of five Bostonians. The behavior of the troops called out to quell the riot was defended by no less staunch an American than John Adams, later second President of the United States. The troops appear to have fired only in self-defense, and Adams feared that unless they were properly defended they might be condemned and executed, an outcome that could have disgraced Massachusetts. The shootings increased tensions, hardened attitudes all round and made more difficult the task of reconciling the two sides, which Franklin saw as his main mission in life.

His way of working, which changed little in manner although it improved in efficiency during his eleven-year stay in Britain, was well described in a letter which William Strahan wrote to David Hall when the repeal of the Stamp Act was the issue. He says that he does not know how agents for the other Colonies work, before continuing: "But the Assiduity of our Friend Dr. Franklin is really astonishing. He is forever with one Member of Parliament or other (most of whom by the bye seem to have been deplorably ignorant with regard to the Nature and Consequence of the Colonies) endeavouring to impress them; first, with the Importance of the present Dispute; then to state the Case clearly and fully, stripping it of every thing foreign to the main Point; and lastly, to answer Objections arising from either a total Ignorance, a partial Knowledge, or a wrong Con-

ception of the Matter. To inforce this repeatedly, and with Propriety, in the Manner he has done for these two Months, I assure
you is no easy Task. By this means, however, when the Parlt. re-
assembles, many Members will go into the House properly instructed, and be able to speak in the Debates with Precision and
Propriety, which the Well-wishers of the Colonies have hitherto
been unable to do. —This is the most necessary and essential
Service he could possibly perform on this Occasion; and so
effectually hath he done this, and I will venture to say, he hath
thrown so much true Light upon the Subject, that if the Legislature doth not now give you ample Redress, it is not for want of
the fullest and most distinct Information in respect to the real
Merits of the Case. All this while, too, he hath been throwing out
Hints in the Public Papers, and giving Answers to such Letters
as have appeared in them, that required or deserved an Answer.
—In this Manner is he now employed, with very little Interruption Night and Day."

What Franklin did for the repeal of the Stamp Act he did for
all the applications that ended up in Craven Street. While the
most important concerned the looming threat of confrontation
between the Colonies and Britain, there were many others which
occupied his time. He had, for instance, been appointed agent
of the Georgia Assembly for only a few weeks before being asked
to find out why two acts passed by the Assembly had been
repealed in London: one "An Act for the better Ordering and
Governing Negroes and other Slaves in this Province and to
prevent the inveigling or carrying away Slaves from their Masters or Employers," the second for a grant of £1,815 in London
which would be used to encourage emigration to Georgia.

To a man with an uncompartmentalized mind, one thing often
led to another, and this was so when the Board of Customs at
Boston complained to the Treasury in London that mail packets
sailing from Falmouth to New York were taking a fortnight
longer on the voyage than merchant ships sailing from London
to Rhode Island. Since the ships from London had to sail down
the Thames estuary and then west along the whole south coast
of England before passing Falmouth and making for the open
sea, it suggested a curious state of affairs. The Treasury turned
to Franklin for advice.

Franklin raised the matter with Timothy Folger, a distant
cousin and a sea captain. "He told me," Franklin later wrote,

"he believed the fact might be true; but the difference was owing to this, that the Rhode Island captains were acquainted with [the Gulf Stream] which those of the English packets were not. We are well acquainted with that stream, said he, because in our pursuit of whales, which keep near the sides of it, but are not to be met with in it, we run down along the sides, and frequently cross it to change our side; and in crossing it have sometimes met and spoken with those packets, who were in the middle of it, and stemming it. We have informed them that they were stemming a current that was running against them at the rate of three miles an hour, and advised them to cross it and get out of it; but they were too wise to be counselled by simple American fishermen." Folger added that on a calmish day a vessel might be carried back by the current more than it was carried forward by its sails.

There had been vague reports of a "Gulf Stream" centuries earlier, and Juan Ponce de León, who discovered Florida in 1513, had noted the force of the current against which his ships had tried to sail south along the coast. Almost a century later Marc Lescarbot, cruising off the Newfoundland Banks, reported: "I have something remarkable upon which a natural philosopher should meditate." On the eighteenth of June, 1606, in latitude 45, 120 leagues east of the Newfoundland Banks, he and his crew found themselves in the midst of very warm water, despite the fact that the air was cold. But on the twenty-first of June they were suddenly in so cold a fog that it seemed like January, and the sea was extremely cold, too. The existence of this "river in the sea," as it was sometimes called, was common knowledge throughout the seventeenth and eighteenth centuries. Yet although its importance to navigation must have been appreciated, there was no attempt to plot its course; the nearest approach was made by two charts of the 1730s, one covering the Gulf of Florida, the other Chesapeake Bay; but neither mentioned the Gulf Stream or showed any continuous current, and they limited their information to suggestions of a current in specific areas.

Now the quite extraordinary gap was to be closed by Franklin, who asked his cousin to mark the current on an existing chart. This Folger did, adding directions for avoiding it in sailing from Europe to North America. "I procured it to be engraved by order from the general post-office, on the old chart of the Atlantic at Mount & Page's, Tower-hill," Franklin later explained, "and copies were sent down to Falmouth for the captains of the packets, who however slighted it; but it is since printed in France."

He did not let matters rest there. Franklin was to cross the Atlantic in 1775, 1776 and 1785, and on each occasion carried out experiments which enabled him to show the course and depth of the stream more accurately. This was done with comparative ease since it was known that the water in the stream was warmer than that on either side of it. "The weather being perfectly calm," he reported of his work on August 14, 1775, "an empty bottle, corked very tight, was sent down 20 fathoms, and it was drawn up still empty. It was then sent down again 35 fathoms, when the weight of the water having forced in the cork, it was drawn up full; the water it contained was immediately tried by the thermometer, and found to be 70, which was six degrees colder than at the surface."

The ease with which Franklin turned from the niceties of taxation and the complexities of politics to the riddles of natural philosophy made him a formidable opponent but it also made him good company, and during the years that followed repeal of the Stamp Act he had no difficulty in arranging long summer breaks that served at least three purposes. They provided the change from London life that he insisted was necessary to his good health; they enabled him to sound out public opinion; and they frequently added fresh evidence on the philosophical problems that engaged him.

In the summer of 1766, barely recuperated after the long strain of lobbying against the Stamp Act, he visited Germany. "This Excursion," William Strahan confided to David Hall, "tho' otherwise well, Dr. Fr. needs very much, as he has by no means recovered his late Fatigue, which was very considerable indeed, both in body and mind." Franklin thought the same, writing to his wife on June 13, "I am now nearly well again, but feeble. Tomorrow I set out with my Friend, Dr. Pringle (now Sir John) on a Journey to Pyrmont, where he goes to drink the Waters, but I hope more from the Air and Exercise, having been us'd, as you know, to make a Journey once a Year, the Want of which last Year has, I believe, hurt me, so that tho' I was not quite to say sick, I was often ailing last Winter, and thro' this Spring."

At Bad Pyrmont both Franklin and Sir John took the waters. There followed visits to Göttingen, even then one of Germany's most important university cities, and to Hanover. In Göttingen Franklin met the great classical scholar Johann David Michaelis, whose account of a dinner with Franklin reveals the blunt views on American independence that Franklin then held. "I said," Michaelis later wrote, "that when I was in London in 1741 I might have learned more about the condition of the Colonies by English books and pamphlets, had I then thought seriously of what I had even then expressed to others, that they would one day release themselves from England. People laughed at me but I still believed it. He answered me with earnest but expressive face: 'Then you were mistaken. The Americans have too much love for their mother country.' I said, 'I believe it, but almighty interest would soon outweigh that love or extinguish it altogether.' He could not deny that this was possible, but secession was impossible, for all the American towns of importance, Boston, New York and Philadelphia, could be destroyed by bombardment. This was unanswerable." Franklin and Sir John were made members of the Hanoverian Royal Society of Sciences, attended a meeting and then, in Hanover, visited the Royal Hospital, where its director, Johann Friedrich Hartmann, demonstrated his electrical apparatus.

The following year they went to Paris, a journey begun in rather bad shape, judging by the report which Mrs. Stevenson sent to Deborah after Franklin had left. "I think it a Duty Incumbent in me [to] Tell you how he was when he sete out from me," she wrote. "His Backe was full of small Blind Boils soe call'd, that for severl days made him verey unessey; in other ways in good health. He wrott me from Calais of the 30 Augt they had a pleasant Pasage over the Water But says my Complants ar not lessan'd by my Journy. My ill Humors Have yet found no Vent, so he told me he had a grat mind to vent them upon me."

Despite the ill humors, Franklin was able to give a light enough account of the Channel crossing to Mary Stevenson, saying that they had set sail from Dover with a number of passengers who had never before been at sea. "They would previously make a hearty Breakfast, because if the Wind should fail, we might not get over till Supper-time, Doubtless they thought that when they had paid for their Breakfast they had a Right to it, and that when they had swallowed it they were sure of it. But they had scarce been out half an Hour before the Sea laid Claim to it, and they were oblig'd to deliver it up. So it seems there are Uncertainties even beyond those between the Cup and the Lip."

In Paris Franklin and Sir John were received rather grandly and, as far as Franklin was concerned, not only because of his reputation in science. He had been courted by the French since the arrival in London of M. Durand, the new ambassador, who had been charged with making the greatest possible effect on him. He "has desired to have all my political writings," William Franklin was told by his father, "invited me to dine with him, was very inquisitive, treated me with great civility, makes me visits, &c. I fancy that intriguing nation would like very well to meddle on occasion, and blow up the coals between Britain and her colonies; but I hope we shall give them no opportunity." The attention no doubt sprang from the interest of Etienne François, duc de Choiseul, the foreign minister. At the height of his power, Choiseul had already sent an emissary to America, briefed to discover American military resources and the strength of any movement for independence. The Treaty of Paris was already four years old and the French were happy to investigate any way of harassing their former enemies.

On September 9 Franklin and Sir John were presented to Louis XV at Versailles and on the same day attended the Grand Couvert, where the royal family supped in public. It was no doubt for this occasion that Franklin visited his tailor and wig-maker, who "transformed [him] into a Frenchman. Only think what a Figure I make in a little Bag Wig and naked Ears!" Louis questioned Sir John about the British royal family and also had conversation with Franklin. "That's saying enough," Franklin wrote to Mary Stevenson, "for I would not have you think me so much pleas'd with this King and Queen as to have a Whit less Regard than I us'd to have for ours. No Frenchman shall go beyond me in thinking my own King and Queen the very best in the World and the most amiable." As the decade of independence approached, Franklin remained more loyal and more royal than many Englishmen.

And, like most Englishmen, he could easily be critical of anything beyond the Channel. "Versailles has had infinite Sums laid out in Building it and Supplying it with Water: Some say the Expence exceeded 80 Millions Sterling," he told Mary Stevenson. "The Range of Building is immense, the Garden Front most magnificent all of hewn Stone, the Number of Statues, Figures, Urns, &c. in Marble and Bronze of exquisite Workmanship is beyond Conception. But the Waterworks are out of Repair, and so is great Part of the Front next the Town, looking with its shabby half Brick Walls and broken Windows not much better than the Houses in Durham Yard. There is, in short, both at Versailles and Paris, a prodigious Mixture of Magnificence and Negligence, with every kind of Elegance except that of Cleanliness and what we call *Tidyness.*"

While Durand in London had for diplomatic reasons paved the way for Franklin's reception, there was of course no need to introduce him to the scientific society of Paris. Many physicists were known as Franklinists, the visitor was asked to write a paper explaining how the Americans safeguarded their houses from lightning, and Franklin and Pringle were the guests of Dalibard, whose experiment had made Franklin famous fifteen years earlier. The men spent much time together and, back in London, Franklin wrote of his stay in Paris that it "seems now to me like a pleasing Dream, from which I was sorry to be awaked by finding my self again at London."

In Paris he discovered confirmation of his views on lead poisoning—the "dry bellyache" or "colica pictorum"—of which he had first become aware in London in 1724. Sir John had visited La Charité, the hospital particularly famous for dealing with the complaint, and had brought away a pamphlet containing the professions or trades of those cured in the hospital. Examining the list, Franklin found that nearly all the patients, being plumbers, glaziers or painters, would have had some contact with lead in the course of their daily work. But there were two exceptions. Some patients were stonecutters and others were soldiers. "These," Franklin later wrote, "I could not reconcile to my notion, that lead was the cause of that disorder." That might have been enough for most men but Franklin, undeterred, persisted in his inquiries. The stonecutters, he was told by a doctor at the hospital, were continually using melted lead to fix the ends of iron balustrades in stone; the soldiers had been employed by painters, as laborers, in the grinding of colors.

Two years later he was once more in Paris, having received an enthusiastic invitation from Joseph Etienne Bertier, the author of *Letters on Electricity.* "To crown your work," Bertier had written, "you should again make a journey to France. It is your country as much as England is. You would be here in the midst of Franklinists, a father in his own country, where the country is inhabited by his children. I was a Franklinist without knowing it; now that I do know it, I shall not fail to name the founder of my sect."

Franklin, once again traveling with Sir John, kept his eyes open, observing the mundane as well as the extraordinary. "When I was there," he reported on his return to Samuel Rhoads, now supervising construction of his new home in Philadelphia, "I took particular Notice of the Construction of their Houses; and I did not see how one of them could well be burnt. The Roofs are Slate or Tile; the Walls are Stone; the Rooms generally lin'd with Stucco or Plaister instead of Wainscot; the Floors of Stucco, or of sixsquare Tiles painted brown; or of Flag Stones, or Marble; if any Floor were of Wood, it was Oak Wood, which is not so inflammable as Pine. Carpets prevent the Coldness of Stone or Brick Floors offending the Feet in Winter. And the Noise of Treading on such Floors overhead is less inconvenient than that on Boards."

On this journey Franklin took the opportunity of finding out how the French viewed the prospects of the American Colonies. "In short," he reported to the Reverend Samuel Cooper, "all Europe (except Britain) appears to be on our side the Question. But Europe has its Reasons. It fancies itself in some Danger from the Growth of British Power, and would be glad to see it divided against itself. Our Prudence will, I hope, long postpone the Satisfaction our Enemies expect from our Dissensions." "Our enemies," it should be noted, were the Continental Europeans, while the "our" of the dissensions were the combined British and Americans.

This pronouncement, which tends to underline how resolutely Franklin still looked on Britain and the Colonies as being one and indivisible, was written after his expected one year in London had been extended to nearly five. He was already an ambivalent American and in comparing America and Britain could say: "Being born and bred in one of the countries and having lived long and made many agreeable connections of friendship in the other, I wish all prosperity to both." But, he added, "I do not find that I have gained any point, in either country, except that of rendering myself suspected of my impartiality; in England, of being too much an American, and in America, of being too much an Englishman." Indeed, it required no abnormal suspicion in Pennsylvania to feel that the British were once again using their traditional tactic of absorbing a potential rebel into their Establishment.

By now Franklin's constant reiterations that he would soon be coming home were beginning to look mildly implausible. He certainly missed his daughter, Sally, and after she had married Richard Bache and produced a son, Benjamin Franklin Bache, he was constantly asking Deborah for news of the boy. In general, his letters to his wife not unnaturally played down the pleasures of life in London. What a thankless role he had to play, he appeared to be complaining, a complaint that would do no harm, he must have realized, if it came to the ears of the Assembly. Typical was one message which recalls the apocryphal first cable that every foreign correspondent is supposed to send after arriving in a new country. "I live here as frugally as possible," he wrote, "not to be destitute of the Comforts of Life, making no Dinners for any body, and contenting my self with a single Dish when I dine at home; and yet such is the Dearness of Living here in every Article, that my Expences amaze me."

As far as she was able, the faithful Deborah continued to lessen the frugality with a regular supply of home goodies which crossed the Atlantic in the care of friendly sea captains. "The Buckwheat and Indian Meal are come safe and good," Franklin acknowledged on one occasion. "They will be a great Refreshment to me this Winter. For since I cannot be in America, every thing that comes from thence comforts me a little, as being something like Home. The dry'd Peaches too are excellent, those dry'd without the Skin: The Parcel in their Skins are not so good. The Apples are the best I ever had and came with the least Damage. The Sturgeon you mention did not come: but that is not so material."

Frugality can be measured in various ways, and a letter in which Franklin described his health to Mary Stevenson suggests that he took a liberal view of the subject. "As to my own Head, which you so kindly enquire after," he wrote, "its Swimming has gradually wore off, and today for the first Time I felt nothing of it on getting out of Bed. But, as this speedy Recovery is, (as I am fully persuaded) owing to the extream Abstemiousness I have observed for some Days past at home, I am not without

Apprehensions, that being to dine abroad this Day, tomorrow, and next Day, I may inadvertently bring it on again."

He knew that more exercise would be a remedy and he took it when possible. In bad weather, even walking up and down stairs at Craven Street was an exercise to profit by. "The dumb bell is another of the latter compendious kind," he told his son. "By the use of it I have in forty swings quickened my pulse from 60 to 100 beats in a minute, counted by a second watch; and I suppose the warmth generally increases with quickness of pulse."

He was something of a fatalist about his health, as was probably the case with most two-bottles-a-meal men. "In the Easter Holidays, being at a Friend's House in the Country," he told Deborah on one occasion, "I was taken with a Sore Throat, and came home half strangled. From Monday till Friday I could swallow nothing but Barley Water and the like. I was bled largely and purged two or three times. On Friday came on a Fit of the Gout, from which I had been free Five Years. Immediately the Inflammation and Swelling in my Throat disappeared; my Foot swelled greatly, and I was confined about three Weeks; since which I am perfectly well, the Giddiness and every other disagreeable Symptom having quite left me." For Deborah herself he often had good advice, telling her on another occasion: "Eat light Foods, such as Fowls, Mutton, &c and but little Beef or Bacon, avoid strong Tea, and use what Exercise you can; by these Means you will preserve your Health better, and be less subject to Lowness of Spirits."

Cold baths had for long been the vogue but Franklin considered the shock to be too violent. "I have found it much more agreeable to my constitution to bathe in another element, I mean cold air," he told his French colleague, Jacques Barbeu-Dubourg. "With this view I rise almost every morning, and sit in my chamber without any clothes whatever, half an hour or an hour, according to the season, either reading or writing. This practice is not in the least painful, but, on the contrary, agreeable; and if I return to bed afterwards, before I dress myself, as sometimes happens, I make a supplement to my night's rest of one or two hours of the most pleasing sleep that can be imagined. I find no ill consequences whatever resulting from it, and that at least it does not injure my health, if it does not in fact contribute much to its preservation. I shall therefore call it for the future a *bracing* or *tonic* bath."

The tonics were supplemented not only by the summer tours abroad but by shorter journeys made, as Franklin was perpetually reminding his wife, mainly to improve his health. Moreover, in the autumn of 1770 the Craven Street routine was broken by an interlude which appears to have had a distinctly bracing effect on Franklin. In June Mary Stevenson had married William Hewson, the doctor and anatomist. Three months later, her mother, Margaret Stevenson, was invited to spend a holiday with friends in Kent. With her was to go Sarah Franklin, Benjamin's distant relative, who was a frequent visitor to Craven Street. During Mrs. Stevenson's absence, Mary and William Hewson moved in to take care of Franklin.

One outcome was the 2,500-word *Craven Street Gazette,* in which Franklin cast Mrs. Stevenson in the role of Queen, Mary Hewson as Cook, Lady Chamberlain of the Household, Lady of the Bedchamber and First Ministress, while William Hewson became Groom, Porter and First Minister. The tone of the *Gazette,* which reveals Franklin at his best spoof-rumbustious, can be gathered from the start of the first issue, which states: "This morning Queen Margaret, accompanied by her first maid of honor, Miss Franklin, set out for Rochester. Immediately on their departure, the whole street was in tears—from a heavy shower of rain."

Later it is reported that "this morning a certain great person was asked very complaisantly by the mistress of the household, if he would choose to have the blade-bone of Saturday's mutton, that had been kept for his dinner to-day, *broiled* or *cold*? He answered gravely, *If there is any flesh on it, it may be broiled; if not, it may as well be cold.* Orders were accordingly given for broiling it. But when it came to table, there was indeed so very little flesh, or rather none at all (puss having dined on it yesterday after Nanny) that, if our new administration had been as good economists as they would be thought, the expense of broiling might well have been saved to the public, and carried to the sinking fund."

The next year was remarkable for a series of journeys: first a spring tour to Leeds, Manchester and Lichfield; in the autumn to Ireland and Scotland; with, in addition, two visits to his friend Jonathan Shipley, the bishop of St. Asaph, at his home at Twyford, near Winchester in Hampshire.

The Bishop's brother William had been a founder of the Society of Arts in London. Franklin had joined the Society before leaving Philadelphia, and it was probably through William that he met Jonathan, one of the few bishops who from the first had supported the American Colonies rather than the British Government. In 1771 Franklin spent first a week, then a longer period, with the Bishop at his country home. And here, during the second visit, probably prompted by the Bishop's young daughters, he sat down to write the first part of what was to become one of the most famous autobiographies in the English language.

He first made a rough draft of the subjects he wished to cover. "My writing," it began. "Mrs. Dogoods Letters. Differences arise between my Brother and me (his temper and mine) their Cause in General . . ." This was in fact the first confirmation that he was the author of the Dogood articles in the *Courant* of almost half a century ago.

"Dear Son," the autobiography started, "I have ever had a Pleasure in obtaining any little Anecdotes of my Ancestors. You may remember the Enquiries I made among the Remains of my Relations when you were with me in England; and the Journey I took for that purpose." He continued, at the rate of about 2,000 words a day, until the time came to leave Twyford. He had reached only 1730 and his foundation of the Philadelphia Library. Thirteen years were to pass before he continued the story, then another four before a third installment was written, while the fourth was finished only in 1789, a few months before his death.

As completed in 1789, the autobiography ceased with Franklin's arrival in London in 1757. Most of it was written without access to documents and as a detailed record of events it has to be taken with caution. Its extraordinary fascination lies, rather, in the light which it throws on Franklin's ideas and ideals. By the time he wrote even the first portion he had made his mark in the world. He had no need to prevaricate, to excuse. The result is a textbook on how to win without actually cheating. It has been claimed, with some reason, that he implied advancement to be merely "a matter of keeping an eye on the main chance. It requires calculation and may even mean using one's friends, flattering one's superiors, and suppressing one's opinions if they seem likely to offend influential people. The good life, according to the *Autobiography*, is not the pursuit of simple saint-liness or spiritual serenity but the attainment of economic inde-pendence and social position. The aura of finagling and of elasticity of conviction which surrounds the *Autobiography* offends many sensitive readers and is the justification for the castigation of Franklin by such critics as D. H. Lawrence."

However, an amount of sly humor can be detected in the pages of the *Autobiography*. There are places where the author appears to be suggesting that his counsels of thrift and prudence should not always be taken too seriously. Franklin, moreover, often failed to live down to his principles, and generosity and kindliness then overwhelmed business instincts.

He intended to leave Twyford for London on July 12 but had been persuaded by the Bishop's wife to stay a day longer so that everyone could celebrate the birthday of Franklin's absent grandson. "At Dinner, among other nice Things, we had a Float-ing Island, which they always particularly have on the Birth Days of any of their own Six Children; who were all but one at Table, where there was also a Clergyman's Widow now above 100 Years old," he told Deborah the following month. "The chief Toast of the Day was Master Benjamin Bache, which the vener-able old Lady began in a Bumper of Mountain [a variety of Malaga wine, made from the grapes grown on the mountains, which was popular in England in the eighteenth century]. The Bishop's Lady politely added, *and that he may be* as good a *man as his Grandfather*. I said I hop'd he would be *much better*. The Bishop, still more complaisant than his Lady, said: We will com-pound the Matter; and be contented if he should not prove *quite so good*."

To Franklin, his stay with the Bishop was a memorable one, and four years later he wrote: "How happy I was in the sweet retirement of Twyford, where my only business was a little scri-bling in the Garden Study, and my pleasure, your conversation, with that of your family!"

EIGHT

THE FATAL ERROR

S FRANKLIN WHILED AWAY THE SUMMER
afternoons on his autobiography in Bishop Shipley's
Hampshire garden, he was still immersed in the problems of Anglo-Colonial relationships which had obsessed him
for at least two decades.

At times he was optimistic, and in the summer of 1769 had
written to Noble Wymberley Jones, Speaker of the Georgia
House of Commons, saying that no new Townshend taxes were
contemplated and that the existing ones might be lifted. "Possibly," he went on, "we may not at first obtain all we desire or all
that ought to be granted to us, but the giving Ground to us in
some degree has a good Aspect and affords room to hope that
gradually every Obstruction to that cordial Amity, so necessary
for the Welfare of the whole Empire, will be removed. Indeed
I wish, as I think it would be best, that this could be done at once.
But 'tis perhaps too much to expect, considering the Pride natural to so great a Nation, the Prejudices that have so universally

prevail'd here with regard to the Point of Right, and the Resentment at our disputing it."

His optimism at first appeared to be justified, and in April 1770 the Townshend duties, with the sole exception of that on tea, were repealed. But by the summer of 1771 doubts were beginning to creep in and on May 15 Franklin wrote to Boston: "I think one may clearly see, in the system of customs to be exacted in America by Act of Parliament, the seeds sown of a total disunion of the two countries, though, as yet, that event may be at a considerable distance."

The continually changing prospects for reconciliation were reflected by the weathercock attitude of those with whom Franklin had to deal, notably Lord Hillsborough, who had become secretary of state for the Colonies in 1768. On the morning of January 16, 1771, Franklin had called upon Hillsborough to tell him formally of his appointment by the House of Representatives of Massachusetts Bay as their agent in Britain. The House had in fact made a first choice of Franklin, and a second choice of Arthur Lee if Franklin failed to take up the offer. What eventually happened was that although Franklin became agent, Lee also operated as such. The youngest of the four famous sons of Thomas Lee of Virginia, he had been educated at Eton and the University of Edinburgh, had returned to Virginia, come back to England and some years later was to be called to the English bar. His appointment by the Massachusetts House aroused a jealousy of Franklin that grew throughout the following years. Eventually it was to imperil Franklin's efforts in Paris at the start of the War of Independence. The Minister denied that Franklin had been appointed and followed his denial by declaring that the governor, Thomas Hutchinson, had refused to give assent to the necessary bill and had written to inform him of the fact. Franklin maintained that no bill was necessary for the appointment, asked to see the letter and found that it apparently did not exist. The two men then exchanged a few frosty remarks and Franklin left.

At least, that is the story as told by Franklin. It is uncertain how much he knew at the time or how much he had forgotten when he wrote the relevant part of his autobiography many years later. Nevertheless, Hutchinson had indeed written to Hillsborough almost two months before the interview, on November 20, 1770. "The Council," he said, "have renewed their choice of Mr. Bollan [William Bollan, an English solicitor] and the House have chosen Doctor Franklin and in case of his absence or refusal, Doctor Lee. Distinct Standing Agents for each or either of the two Branches of the Legislature appear to me unnecessary, irregular and unconstitutional. I have expressed my readiness to consent to an Agent chosen by the two Houses, and the Council proposed to the House to join in the choice, but the House declined. As soon as the several Laws can be prepared I will transmit them with Remarks upon them." Governor Hutchinson's refusal to accept Franklin as agent was no passing fancy. "The two Houses," he informed Hillsborough in 1772, "renewed their grants of 900£ sterl. to Mr. Bollan and 600£ to Mr. Franklin, which were laid before me and I refused to assent to them."

To Franklin it seemed that Hillsborough's attitude was based on something more substantial than Governor Hutchinson's disclaimer and he felt himself to be "not only on bad Terms with Lord Hillsborough, but with the *Ministry in general.*" He was therefore astounded when, in the autumn of the same year, the Minister appeared in a very different light. Franklin had left London in mid-August for one of his longer tours, which was to take him to Dublin, where he was to be honored by the Irish Parliament, then on to Edinburgh and back to London at the end of November. In Ireland he and Hillsborough accidentally met. Hillsborough, far from being aloof, invited him home and treated him as an honored guest. His eldest son, Lord Kilwarling, drove "me a Round of Forty Miles, that I might see the Country, the Seats, Manufactures, &c. covering me with his own Cloak, lest I should take Cold," as Franklin recalled.

The guest was mildly bemused at the change of stance. It might be a case of genuine good will at last. "But," Franklin informed Thomas Cushing, "if he takes no Step towards withdrawing the Troops, repealing the Duties, restoring the Castle, or recalling the offensive Instructions, I shall think all the plausible Behaviour I have describ'd and the Discourse related, concerning Manufactures, &c., as meant only, by patting and stroaking the Horse, to make him more patient, while the Reins are drawn tighter and the Spurs set deeper into his Sides."

The real feelings of Hillsborough, as of other ministers, remained enigmatic. Franklin was still optimistic, continuing to see himself in the role of bridge-builder, one who, by successful lobbying, would eventually persuade the Westminster government to establish a framework within which satisfied colonies could develop and move along their own chosen paths to individual destinies within the empire. But the suspicions of his enemies in Pennsylvania had a good deal on which to feed. Franklin still held his deputy postmaster's appointment from the Crown, and it is unlikely that his willingness to accept something more important had remained unknown across the Atlantic. Son William was the royal governor of New Jersey. There was, moreover, Franklin's involvement in what was known variously as the Grand Ohio or Vandalia Scheme. This was a plan for the settlement of a fresh colony behind the Alleghenies in which a number of Colonial businessmen, a number of British ministers and an odd clutch of supporters, including both Franklin and his son, aimed to make large fortunes at comparatively little risk. It was a scheme which required government approval, but the fact that the ministers who would profit included those who had to give approval was considered irrelevant in those robust days.

The Grand Ohio Scheme was to occupy much of Franklin's time between 1766 and his departure from England in 1775 and was the culmination of an interest in land settlement which had begun much earlier. His motives for creating new colonies to the west of those already existing were varied. The chance of making money from such transactions was a constant spur. But like many men of his times Franklin saw the western frontiers in terms of defense against the Indians forever waiting only just over the horizon. Thus each settlement that helped push back the frontier made the coastal Colonies that much more secure. There was also a third inducement, revealed in Franklin's letter to the Reverend George Whitefield. "I sometimes wish that you and I were jointly employ'd by the Crown, to settle a Colony on the Ohio," he wrote. "I imagine we could do it effectually, and without putting the Nation to much expence. But I fear we shall never be called upon for such a Service. What a glorious Thing it would be, to settle in that fine Country a large strong Body of Religious and Industrious People! What a Security to the other Colonies; and Advantage to Britain, by Increasing her People, Territory, Strength, and Commerce. Might it not greatly facilitate the Introduction of pure Religion among the Heathen, if we could, by such a Colony, show them a better Sample of Christians than they commonly see in our Indian Traders, the most vicious and abandoned Wretches of our Nation? . . . In such an Enterprise I could spend the Remainder of Life with Pleasure; and I firmly believe God would bless us with Success, if we undertook it with a sincere Regard to his Honour, the Service of our gracious King, and (which is the same thing), the Publick Good."

Franklin made his first attempt to earn the blessing as early as 1763, when he became interested in the purchase of titles to lands to the south of Virginia and persuaded Richard Jackson to search for the title deeds. The scheme came to nothing, possibly because the title to the land was found inadequate.

The next year, however, something more tangible was proposed when Jackson suggested that Franklin might be interested in a grant of land in Nova Scotia. "As I have some Money to spare," he replied, "I know not how better to dispose of it for the Advantage of my Children." The idea prospered and in February 1766 Franklin "humbly [prayed] that His Majesty will be graciously pleased to grant him twenty thousand Acres of Land in such part of the Province of Nova Scotia as the Petitioner or his Agent shall choose upon the same terms and conditions on which Lands have been granted within the said Province, in order to make a Settlement thereupon." The Board of Trade and the Privy Council approved and in June the governor of the Province granted Franklin his 20,000 acres.

The Nova Scotia estate, which Franklin was to leave to his son nearly a quarter of a century later, was a small affair when compared with the grandiose scheme for establishing a new colony on the Ohio. It had arisen when a group of Pennsylvanians conceived the plan as one method of gaining compensation for their losses in the Indian Wars. Franklin joined the board of the company which was subsequently formed and given authority to bring on to it "such Gentlemen of Character and Fortune in England" as he thought would be most likely to promote the undertaking.

At first, the prospects looked good for a grant of 1,200,000 acres lying roughly between the Wisconsin and the Ohio, the Wabash and the Mississippi rivers. Pitt's administration, formed in the summer of 1766, favored replacing proprietorial governments in the Colonies with royal governments, and all members of what was at first called the Illinois company were strong antiproprietorial Philadelphians; and Franklin's main task in

London was to end the Penn regime. In addition Lord Shelburne, who had helped repeal the Stamp Act and was generally well-intentioned toward the Colonies, now came to power as secretary of state for the southern department, one of the two groups (northern and southern) through which Britain then administered her foreign affairs before they were amalgamated into the Foreign Office.

In August 1767, Franklin dined with Shelburne. The conversation turned—or, perhaps more accurately, was turned by Franklin—to the expenses which Britain had to incur in the Colonies. "I took the opportunity of urging [the settlement company] as one means of saving expence in supporting the out-posts, that a settlement should be made in the Illinois country," Franklin wrote to his son; "expatiated on the various advantages, viz. furnishing provisions cheaper to the garrisons, securing the country, retaining the trade, raising a strength there which on occasion of a future war, might easily be poured down the Mississippi upon the lower country, and into the Bay of Mexico, to be used against Cuba or Mexico itself &c. I mentioned your plan [for a new settlement], its being approved by Sir William Johnson, the readiness and ability of the gentlemen concerned to carry the settlement into execution with very little expence to the crown, &c. &c. The Secretaries appeared finally to be fully convinced, and there remained no obstacle but the Board of Trade, which was to be brought over privately before the matter should be referred to them officially."

However, progress was slower than Franklin had expected and in 1769 two supporters of the plan, Samuel Wharton and William Trent, arrived in London from Pennsylvania in the hope of speeding matters up. By this time Shelburne had been superseded by Lord Hillsborough—in the newly created post of secretary for the Colonies. He referred the petitioners to the Treasury but at the same time advised them to be more bold, and to ask for 20,000,000 acres. Such an enlargement of the enterprise had one advantage: its potential profits would now be big enough to attract various ministers and officials. As a result Lord Hertford, the lord chamberlain, became a shareholder, followed by Lord Camden, the lord chancellor, and Lord Rochford, secretary of state for the northern department.

On December 27, 1769, Franklin and seventeen others met in the Crown and Anchor Tavern to formalize a new petition for

20,000,000 acres to be settled by the Grand Ohio Company, frequently called the Walpole Company after the banker who was one of its directors. But by the time that the petition arrived on Lord Hillsborough's desk he was having second thoughts. One reason, it was believed, was that he owned large estates in Ireland, and any spate of new settlements across the Atlantic might make it more difficult for him to retain Irish labor.

From now on Franklin was the man who had to wet-nurse the scheme through government, and his letters to his son regularly contain reports of progress. By the summer of 1771 he was optimistic, although warning that "many things happen between the Cup & the Lip." But not until March 1772 did the Board of Trade begin to consider the petition; and on April 29 it turned down the idea in a report to the Privy Council. However, Lord Gower, a shareholder no doubt unwilling to let such a potentially profitable scheme disappear without a fight, announced that the Council was willing to hear evidence against the Board of Trade's decision. On June 5 Franklin, Walpole and other interested parties gave evidence before a committee of the Council in the Cockpit, Whitehall, a room where Franklin was to be present in very different circumstances some eighteen months later.

The Privy Council agreed to forward the petition. Hillsborough resigned and was replaced by Lord Dartmouth, generally friendly to the Americans. It was a convenient development but did not necessarily reflect any particular views about the Grand Ohio Scheme. Some of Hillsborough's colleagues were anxious that he should go, and the overturning of his decision left him with little alternative but to resign. As Edmund Burke wrote shortly afterward, "if we were to consider the principal actors, one might be inclined to think, what was at first generally conjectured, that this opposition to Lord Hillsborough on the Grant had been a Manuevre of the friends of the late Duke of Bedford; in hopes of getting Lord Weymouth into some Office acceptable to him in the Jumble and confusion created by such a controversy."

However, the outcome of this political "jumble" was a greatly increased chance that the new colony—tentatively named Indiana, Pittsylvania and then Vandalia because Queen Charlotte was said to be a descendant of the royal line of the Vandals— would eventually be founded to the considerable profit of all concerned. It was not to be so. For one thing, the company's claims were contested by Virginia and Pennsylvania as well as by the Indians. As far as government policy was concerned, it was stressed that the new colony would be cut off from the sea by intervening colonies and would produce nothing to compensate for the cost of its defense. Thus the prospects for the Grand Ohio Company stood still while relations between Britain and her Colonies worsened. And before a single new emigrant could be settled—"at least one white Protestant person for every Hundred acres" was called for—Britain and the Colonies were at war. Franklin's own healthy connection with the scheme suffered a relapse early in 1774 when he was under political attack and Thomas Walpole induced him to cut his links with the company. At least, that was the apparent outcome; in fact, his acquiescence with Walpole's proposal was tailored only to remove his colleagues' embarrassment, and his connection continued for another three years.

In October 1772, before his affairs had begun to slip down the slope, he suffered a minor personal upheaval. From the summer of 1757 his home had, with the exception of a single break, been in No. 7 Craven Street, a house subsequently renumbered No. 36. But Mrs. Stevenson decided in the autumn of 1772 that her daughter and son-in-law should take over the house while she moved to another home in the same street. Franklin went to the country for a month while the change was taking place. This removed him from the hurly-burly. Nevertheless, as he reported to Deborah: "The Removing has been a troublesome Affair."

By mid-November he was securely ensconced once more in Craven Street. And now, whether by accident or intent, he was to set in motion the train of events which made his presence in Britain no longer of use to the American cause. This was the affair of the Hutchinson letters.

It would be unjust to judge Franklin's actions in the affair other than in the context of the times. A century and a half later Henry Stimson, trying to close down the American counter-intelligence and decipherment department known as the Black Chamber, commented that "gentlemen do not read each other's mail." That was hardly the spirit in which eighteenth-century government was carried on. Franklin's letters to the Colonies were opened, read and resealed—an undetectable method of copying the seals being used—and he knew that this was so. He himself could not be too finicky in his methods, as he revealed in a draft letter to Thomas Cushing. "Politicians on our Side the Water should take Care what they write to Ministers if they wish the World may never know it," he advised. "For Great Men are sometimes very careless of such Papers. One of them not long since gave a great Quantity of American Letters to his Footman who sold them for Waste Paper. By chance an Acquaintance of mine saw them, bought for a Trifle and sent them to me; and they have Afforded me abundance of Amusement." Franklin struck these sentences from the letter sent, probably because he expected it to be opened by the British; and, conditions being what they were, the "By chance an Acquaintance of mine saw them" could well be read as "luckily, one of my men had his eyes open and was able to get his hands on them."

Yet if there were few inhibitions about the ways in which correspondence was read it was still unwise to be caught *in flagrante delicto*. Whether Franklin fully understood this, or whether he made a serious error of judgment, is not known. But it is certain that the case of the Hutchinson letters was to mark a turning point in his life. Moreover it was to be maintained by John, 1st Baron Campbell, a later lord chancellor, that the case "mainly conduced to the civil war [of Independence] which soon followed, and to the dismemberment of the empire, — by exciting over-weening arrogance on one side, and rankling revenge on the other. Had Franklin been soothed, instead of being insulted, America might have been saved. As yet, though eager for the redress of the wrongs of his transatlantic brethren, he professed, and I believe he felt, respect and kindness for the mother country, and a desire that all differences between them might be honourably reconciled."

The calamitous affair—and it was no less, since Lord Campbell's judgment seems fully justified—began in the winter of 1772. Franklin was, he claimed, discussing with "a gentleman of character and distinction" the sending of British troops to Boston and their behavior in the town, acts which he maintained showed that Britain no longer had a parental regard for the Colonies. On the contrary, he was told, these actions had been taken on the specific recommendation of members of the Massachusetts administration in Boston. If blame there were, it lay with the Americans themselves. Franklin, unable to believe that Americans could have adopted what might today be called a Quisling attitude, asked for proof.

Shortly afterward he was, he said, presented by the same unidentified gentleman of character and distinction with a number of letters written to a British Member of Parliament, Thomas Whately, by Thomas Hutchinson, now governor of Massachusetts, and by Andrew Oliver, his deputy. These letters could be construed to show that the Americans, Hutchinson and Oliver, had encouraged the British to impose harsher conditions on the people of Massachusetts. It appeared, Franklin wrote in the aftermath of the disaster which his actions were to bring about, "my *duty* to give my constituents intelligence of such importance to their affairs; but there was some difficulty, as this gentleman would not permit copies to be taken of the letters; and, if that could have been done, the authenticity of those copies might have been doubted and disputed. My simple account of them, as papers I had seen, would have been still less certain; I therefore wish'd to have the use of the originals for that purpose, which I at length obtained, on these express conditions: that they should not be printed; that no copies should be taken of them; that they should be shown only to a few of the leading people of the government; and that they should be carefully returned."

There is at least one remarkable point about the story as related later by Franklin: while the owner of the letters was unwilling to let them be copied, for what he no doubt considered very good reasons, he apparently agreed to let them be sent across the Atlantic to the place where they could presumably do most damage. The "apparently" is necessary in view of Franklin's somewhat mysterious "at length obtained."

On December 2, 1772, Franklin sent the letters to Thomas Cushing in Boston. He justified the action to himself on the grounds that they had no doubt circulated among members of the government in London; that they dealt with affairs of public concern and thus could be considered in a different category from private letters; and that their contents would be read in Boston only by the Colonial equivalents of those who had already seen them in London.

The restrictions on how the letters should be used grew less with surprising speed if Franklin's correspondence with Cushing is taken at its face value. "I can only allow them to be seen by yourself, by the other Gentlemen of the Committee of Correspondence, by Messrs. Bowdoin, & Pitts, of the Council, and Drs. Chauncey, Cooper, and Winthrop, with a few such other Gentlemen as you may think it fit to show them to," he had said in his initial letter. A few months later he was writing "that they may be shown or read to whom and as many as you think proper." John Adams, moreover, was later to say: "I was permitted to carry [the letters] with me upon a circuit of our Judicial Court, and communicate them to the chosen few." In addition, an account of the affair which Franklin began to write on an unknown date in 1774 but never completed or published, says that there were "three gentlemen here [i.e., in Britain] to whom I had communicated the matter."

Cushing told Franklin that his colleagues in Boston thought the letters "ought to be retained on this side the water to be hereafter improved as the Exigency of our affairs may require or at least that authenticated Copies ought to be taken before they are returned."

On July 7, 1773, Franklin wrote an extremely revealing letter to Samuel Cooper. "You mention," he said, "the Surprize of Gentlemen to whom those Letters have been communicated, at the Restrictions with which they were accompanied, and which they suppose render them incapable of answering any important End. The great Reason of forbidding their Publication, was an Apprehension that it might put all the Possessors of such Correspondence here upon their Guard, and so prevent the obtaining more of it. And it was imagined that showing the Originals to so many as were named, and to a few such others as they might think fit, would be sufficient to establish the authenticity, and to spread thro' the Province so just an Estimation of the Writers, as to strip them of all their deluded Friends, and demolish effectually their Interest and Influence. The Letters might be shown even to some of the Governor's and Lieutenant Governor's Partizans; and spoken of to every body; for there was no Restraint proposed to Talking of them, but only to copying. And possibly, as distant Objects seen only through a Mist appear larger, the same may happen from the Mystery in this Case. However this may be, the Terms given with them, could only be those with which they were received. There is still some Chance of procuring more, and some still more abominable."

The letter casts doubt on Franklin's integrity and on his sincerity. It must have been obvious to him that however many times he asked for the letters not to be copied, their contents would, for all practical purposes, soon become public property. And even though he intended to throw responsibility for the deteriorating situation on Americans rather than the British, the destruction of Thomas Hutchinson, who had refused to confirm his appointment as agent for Massachusetts Bay, is unlikely to have been entirely absent from his mind.

The letters began to circulate immediately after their arrival in Boston. When the Assembly met at the end of May it was common knowledge that some allegedly explosive material had arrived from England, and on June 2, in the words of the official *Journal* of the House, it

was inform'd by one of its Members that he had matters that greatly concern'd the Province to communicate with the Leave of the House, and the same Member moved that the Galleries be cleared.

Upon a Motion ordered that the Members be injoyned to attend.

Then Mr. [Samuel] Adams acquainted the House, that, he had perceiv'd the minds of the People to be greatly agitated with a prevailing Report that Letters of an extraordinary Nature had been written and sent to England greatly to the prejudice of this Province: That he had obtained certain Letters with different Signatures, with the consent of the Gentleman from whom he received them that they should be read in the House under certain Restrictions, namely that the said Letters be neither printed nor copied in whole or in part; and that they be return'd sometime during the Session, and accordingly he offered them for the consideration of the House.

It was moved that the Letters be read in the House under the said Restrictions and the Question being put, pass'd in the affirmative, and they were read accordingly, being severally sign'd And^W. Oliver, Tho. Hutchinson, Cha^S. Paxton, Thomas Moffat, Robert Auchmuty, Nath. Rogers, G. Rome.

Upon a Motion Resolv'd, that at three of the Clock, this afternoon, the House will resolve into a Committee of the whole House, to take the Letters now read into consideration.

After the letters had been read and discussed, the House voted by 101 to 5 that "the tendency and design of the letters . . . was to overthrow the Constitution of this Government and to introduce Arbitrary Power into the Province." *The Massachusetts Spy* declared the following day that the letters brought "many *dark* things to *light*—gain many proselytes to the cause of freedom—make tyrannical rulers tremble."

Although the House had been told that the letters should be neither printed nor copied they had, of course, been read into the record. However, Adams, no doubt wishing to cover himself against charges of perfidy, now declared that copies of the letters had been received from a second source and that the original restrictions therefore no longer applied. On hearing of Adams's statement, Franklin immediately pronounced it to be impossible; and he, of all men, would know. By this time, however, the letters had been published, first by the Boston printers Edes and Gill, who in an introduction observed that "the judicious Reader will discover the fatal Source of the Confusion and Bloodshed in which this Province especially has been involved, and which threatned total Destruction to the Liberties of all America."

Cushing, virtually apologizing to Franklin for what he considered a breach of faith, explained away the breach; "Considering the Number of Persons who were to see them (not less than Ten or Fifteen), it is astonishing they did not get Air before," he wrote. ". . . I have done all in my Power strictly to conform to your Restrictions; but, from the Circumstances above related, you must be sensible it was impossible to prevent the Letters being made publick and therefore hope I shall be free from all Blame respecting this Matter."

If Cushing felt a trace of guilt, the Reverend Samuel Cooper felt none. "Nothing," he wrote, "could have been more seasonable, than the arrival of these Letters. They have had great effect; They make deep impressions wherever they are known; They strip the mask from the writers who, under the Professions of Friendship to their Country, now plainly appear to have been endeavoring to build up themselves and their Families upon its ruins. They and their adherents are shock'd and dismay'd; the confidence repos'd in them by many is annihilated; and Administration must soon see the Necessity of putting the Provincial Power of the Crown into other Hands."

What, in fact, were these letters which Franklin had surreptitiously acquired, which were to bring about his downfall in Britain, wreck the chances of any compromise between Britain and the Colonies, and, in Lord Chancellor Campbell's words, lead on to the War of Independence?

They consisted of six letters, written in the aftermath of the Stamp Act disturbances, by Thomas Hutchinson between June 18, 1768, and October 1769, four by Andrew Oliver, the lieutenant governor during the same period, one from Robert Auchmuty to Hutchinson and other trivial ones from Charles Paxton, Nathaniel Rogers, Thomas Moffat and G. Rome. All the letters were written before Hutchinson became governor and were addressed to Thomas Whately when he was not a member of the British Government, facts which severely undercut Franklin's argument that they were public rather than private.

To the extent that they criticized the revolutionary elements in Massachusetts and called for the enforcement of law and order, they were of course offensive to the Assembly. But even in their original form—and the printing used italicizing and the alteration of punctuation to reinforce statements wherever this was considered salutary—the letters did no more than repeat the views of Hutchinson and Oliver that they had aired many times over the years.

The one letter in which Hutchinson appeared to have laid himself open to attack was that written to Whately on January 20, 1769. "I never think of the measures necessary for the peace and good order of the colonies without pain," he said. "There must be an abridgment of what are called English liberties. I relieve myself by considering that in a remove from the state of nature to the most perfect state of government, there must be a great restraint of natural liberty. I doubt whether it is possible to project a system of government in which a colony, 3000 miles distant from the parent state, shall enjoy all the liberty of the parent state. I am certain I have never yet seen the projection. I wish the good of the colony when I wish to see some further restraint of liberty rather than the connexion with the parent state should be broken; for I am sure such a breach must prove the ruin of the colony. Pardon me this excursion, it really proceeds from the state of mind into which our perplexed affairs often throws me."

There was to be considerable exegesis on the words "an abridgment of . . . English liberties," and it was even alleged that Hutchinson had been responsible for the sending of troops to Boston in 1768. The troops had, in fact, been dispatched nearly four months before the letter was written, but this was a point easily ignored by those wishing to make the most of the case. Hutchinson himself was later to write: "To a candid mind the substance of the whole paragraph was really no more than this: 'I am sorry the people cannot be gratified with the enjoyment of all they call English liberties, but in their sense of them, it is not possible for a Colony at three thousand miles distance from the parent state to enjoy them, as they might do if they had not removed.'"

However, candid minds were in comparatively short supply in the Assembly which on June 25 "Resolved that if His Majesty in his great Goodness, shall be pleased to remove His Excellency Thomas Hutchinson Esq., and the Honble Andrew Oliver Esq., from the Offices of Governor and Lieutenant Governor, it is the humble opinion of this Board, that it will be promotive of His Majesty's Service, and the Good of his loyal and affectionate People of this Province."

The following day Hutchinson wrote to Lord Dartmouth.

The greatest part of the present session of the General Court has been spent in considering a number of Letters wrote by the Governor & Lieut. Governor & others to a Gentleman in England so long ago as the years 1767–68 & 69 all of them relating to the then public occurrences. The person's name to whom they were directed has been erased but they were undoubtedly wrote to Mr. Whately and since his death they have by some evil minded person been sent over here to be used against the persons who wrote them. Every art has been practised to inflame the minds of the people & to cause them to believe the Letters to be highly criminal. I was satisfied that neither the House nor Council properly had any business with them, nevertheless as I was the principal Subject of the debates founded upon them I thought it advisable to let them take their course for if I had put an end to the session the construction would have been that I was conscious of my guilt. I know of no misrepresentation in any of the Letters nor of any expression in either mine or the Lieut.^t Governor's to which any just exception can be taken. They were private & confidential & all but the last wrote at a time when I had no share in the Administration here, the Governor being in the Province, & the Gentleman to whom they were wrote had no share in the Administration in England. Both House & Council, notwithstanding, after putting a very injurious and forced construction upon some parts of them voted that His Majesty be addressed to remove the Governor & the Lt. Governor from the Government for ever, and the Addresses I suppose are to be sent by this ship.

After four years in which every difficulty has attended me that can well be imagined they complain of no one act of male [sic] administration but have recourse to Letters wrote before that time in my private charactic [sic] which are in every part true and in no part unfriendly to the Province.

The chief Actor, in these debates, which are publick, declared that the principal design of their Resolves was to represent me in an odious light to the people the consequence of which must be my removal. In this way they said, they had succeeded against Governor Bernard and the King would never keep a Governor in place after the people in general should be dissatisfied and wish him removed. It is certain that such a general discontent as they have raised, which they could not have done in any other way, will lessen the prospect of further usefulness.

The Addresses having no support but the Letters must, I humbly conceive, appear upon the face of them to be groundless & vexatious; and their offering them after the censure upon the proceedings against Sir Francis Bernard rending them more inexcusable. [In 1769 Sir Francis Bernard, Hutchinson's predecessor, had been recalled to England following pressure by the Assembly after a number of his letters to Lord Hillsborough had been made public. The charges made against him by the Assembly were dismissed in London; but Sir Francis remained in England.] I hope there fore both the Lieut.^t Governor & myself shall be honorably acquitted without any trouble or being held to answer but I had rather even make a voyage to England at my advanced time of life than my reputation & character should suffer.

It is not improbable, My Lord, that it may be of advantage to me in my private affairs to make a voyage to England in the Fall and it may appear to me to be for His Majestys Service. I therefore humbly beg your Lordship's favour in obtaining leave from His Majesty for my absence from the Province for six or nine months in case that I shall find it necessary for either of the reasons which I have mentioned. The Lieuten^t. Governor is in as good health as he has been for several years, and I know no danger of any inconvenience from my absence.

As Hutchinson had expected, the petition for his removal and his letter to Lord Dartmouth crossed the Atlantic on the same ship and arrived in England in mid-August. It naturally fell to

Franklin to deliver the Assembly's petition and he did so without delay—but not, in all probability, before Dartmouth had received Hutchinson's warning of what was on the way.

With the petition Franklin sent an explanatory letter. "I have the pleasure of hearing from [Massachusetts]," he said, "by my late letters, that a sincere disposition prevails in the people there to be on good terms with the Mother Country; that the Assembly have declared their desire only to be put into the situation they were in before the stamp act; they aim at no novelties. And it is said, that, having lately discovered, as they think, the authors of their grievances to be some of their own people, their resentment against Britain is thence much abated. This good disposition of their's (will your Lordship permit me to say) may be cultivated by a favourable answer to this Address, which I therefore hope your goodness will endeavour to obtain."

Dartmouth replied by return with an emollient letter saying that the petition would be laid before George III "the next time I shall have the Honor of being admitted into his presence," and concluding: "I cannot help expressing to you the pleasure it gives me to hear that a sincere disposition prevails in the People of that Province to be on good terms with the Mother Country, and my earnest hope that the time is at no great distance, when every ground of uneasiness will cease, and the most perfect tranquillity and happiness be restored to the breasts of that people."

It was not essential that the petition should go to the King, and Dartmouth's motives for thus keeping the pot a-boil are obscure. "The Executive Government," Lord Campbell has sagely noted, "ought quietly to have disposed of it, either by refusing [the Assembly's] prayer, or by transferring the parties complained against to some other sphere, where their services would be more available for the public good: but it was thought that a glorious opportunity had occurred of publicly inveighing against the colonists, and of heaping odium on their champion."

It cannot be established when this opportunity was seen and seized, and Campbell's illuminating hindsight does not necessarily mean that Dartmouth was yet planning Franklin's humiliation. By now, indeed, Franklin had some grounds for what looks like ingenuous overconfidence. Soon he was telling Cushing that Hutchinson had already asked to be allowed to resign and that some provision should be made for him in Britain. It is curious that Franklin, in London, should be informing Cushing, in Boston, of what Hutchinson had decided in Boston. The least unlikely explanation is that his information came from garbled reports of Hutchinson's letter to Dartmouth. Whatever the truth, at this point Franklin could feel that good use had been made of the letters he had so mysteriously acquired and passed on.

However, if Dartmouth was willing to reassure Franklin, he was equally willing to reassure his opponent, and in August he sent a pleasant note to Hutchinson. "With regard to those proceedings & resolutions I shall only say at present, that I see no ground for any apprehensions on your part that your character or reputation may suffer by your not coming to England: your request however to have The King's permission for that purpose, in case you should find it necessary, has been humbly submitted to His Majesty; and altho' the giving Governors in the Plantations leave to come to England at their own request is not compatible with a general Rule that has been laid down, yet His Majesty is graciously pleased in consideration of the peculiar circumstances of your Case, to dispense in the present instance with that Rule; and inclosed I send you His Majesty's Sign Manual, allowing you to come to England, and to remain here during His Majesty's Pleasure, in case it shall be necessary either on account of His Majesty's Service or your own private affairs."

At the same time the issue appeared to be losing momentum in Massachusetts. "The flame which was raised with so much art by means of the private Letters of the Governor and Lt. Governor and the Resolves of Council and Assembly," Hutchinson informed Dartmouth, "appears to me to have been much subsided for several weeks past, the most sensible people in all parts of the Province when they came to read the Letters being convinced that they gave no grounds for the Resolves and the prejudice which now remains is principally upon the minds of the lower classes of the people and I cannot but flatter myself that the notice which shall be taken in England of so very irregular and unwarrantable proceedings will tend to convince even them, altho' in all Governments they are most susceptible of Impressions to the disadvantage of their Rulers."

Hutchinson wrote this early in August, by which time it must have appeared to Franklin, as well as to the Governor, that the outcry in Boston was beginning to die down. If this was so, then surely something else might be done to keep the Anglo-Colonial dispute in the public eye. Unless Franklin was a man with a particularly blind spot—and there is no evidence of this—he must have known that by sending the Hutchinson letters to Boston he would destroy Hutchinson politically. That outcome is unlikely to have drawn tears from his eyes. But it would be unfair to claim that he acted from personal motives alone. The events of the last few years had taught him to believe that the Anglo-Colonial situation was deteriorating so badly that only a major row or confrontation could resolve it. Stirring the pot with the letters so opportunely to hand might bring this about. But now it appeared that the opportunity might have been lost.

As usual when hard-pressed, Franklin picked up the weapon he used with the greatest confidence: his pen. First there came "Rules by which a Great Empire may be reduced to a Small One," published in *The Public Advertiser* on September 11; next, "An Edict by the King of Prussia," published in the same paper eleven days later. While the first demanded that its readers should look at the British Government's actions through Colonial eyes, the second almost hoaxed its readers into believing that they were colonists from another great empire. As the editors of Franklin's papers have noted, he "was almost as busy as the Bostonians themselves in antagonizing Whitehall, and he seems to have been no more concerned than they were with the danger of reprisal."

The "Rules" were twenty in number. Their flavor can be gathered from brief quotation. The first rule stated that a great Empire, "like a great Cake, is most easily diminished at the Edges. Turn your Attention therefore first to your remotest Provinces; that as you get rid of them, the next may follow in Order." As to taxes, said Rule IX, "never regard the heavy Burthens those remote People already undergo, in defending their own Frontiers, supporting their own provincial Governments, making new Roads, building Bridges, Churches and other public Edifices, which in old Countries have been done to your Hands by your Ancestors, but which occasion constant Calls and Demands on the Purses of a new People." The fifteenth rule enjoined readers to "Convert the brave honest Officers of your Navy into pimping Tide-waiters and Colony Officers of the Customs." And the last rule began with the instruction "Invest the General of your Army in the Provinces with great and unconstitutional Powers, and free him from the Controul of even your own Civil Governors."

The "Edict" was by contrast a straight hoax, purporting to be a statement issued from Dantzick by Frederick II of Prussia. The British Isles, it maintained, had been colonized from Germany and had "flourished under the Protection of our august House, for Ages past, have never been *amancipated* therefrom, and yet have hitherto yielded little profit to the same." Therefore, the edict ran, a duty of 4½ percent would in future be levied by Prussia on all exports from and imports into Britain. As printed, the concoction had a plausibility that was illustrated to Franklin himself, who was staying with Lord le Despencer, formerly Sir Francis Dashwood, at High Wycombe when the "Edict" appeared. Paul Whitehead, the satirist, another guest, broke the news to the rest of the party with the words: "Here's news for ye! *Here's the King of Prussia, claiming a right to this kingdom!*" Everyone stared. "I as much as any body," Franklin wrote to his son, "and he went on to read it. When he had read two or three paragraphs, a gentleman present said, *Damn his impudence, I dare say, we shall hear by next post that he is upon his march with one hundred thousand men to back this*. Whitehead, who is very shrewd, soon after began to smoke it, and looking in my face said, *I'll be hanged if this is not some of your American jokes upon us*. The reading went on, and ended with abundance of laughing, and a general verdict that it was a fair hit. And the piece was cut out of the paper and preserved in my Lord's collection."

The two September pieces were, Franklin wrote to his son, "designed to expose the conduct of this country towards the colonies, in a short, comprehensive, and striking view, and stated therefore in out-of-the-way forms, as most likely to take the general attention." The following month William was told: "Such papers may seem to have a tendency to increase our divisions, but I intend a contrary effect, and hope by comprizing in little room, and setting in a strong light the grievances of the colonies, more attention will be paid to them by our administration, and that when their unreasonableness is generally seen, some of them will be removed to the restoration of harmony between us." And to Jane Mecom he observed: "I have held up a Looking-Glass in which some Ministers may see their ugly Faces, & the Nation its Injustice." The two pieces certainly kept up the pressure, but there was not the slightest chance of diverting government policy from its course. However, if Franklin was by this time suspected to be at the root of the Hutchinson letters furor, which may well have been the case, these pinpricks would have made Dartmouth even more determined to discover the truth.

But by late autumn the matter still appeared to be stationary and Franklin began to feel that the petition for removing Hutchinson and Oliver would be forgotten. "I imagine that it will hardly be complied with," he told Cushing in November, "as it would embarrass government to provide for them otherwise, and it will be thought hard to neglect men who have exposed themselves by adhering to what is here called the interest and rights of this country." As far as Franklin was concerned it must have appeared that despite earlier threats the episode of the Hutchinson letters was now sliding to a standstill. In fact, it was sliding out of control.

It was known that the Hutchinson letters had been written to Thomas Whately. But it was not known how they had come into the hands of whoever had sent them to Boston and it was not yet known that that person was Franklin, since Cushing, the fountainhead of the letters once they had arrived in Boston, had kept cautiously silent on this point. However, there was a suspicion that on Thomas Whately's death they had passed into the hands of his brother William, and that William Whately had granted access to them to John Temple, former surveyor general of the customs in Massachusetts.

Part of the rumor appeared to be supported when on December 11 a letter from William Whately was published in London's *Public Advertiser*. Mr. Temple had, he declared, inspected some of his brother's letters. But none of them had been taken away by him. "Mr. Temple assured me in Terms the most precise," he went on, "that (except some letters from himself and his Brother, which he had from me by my Permission), he had not taken a single Letter, or an Extract from any I had communicated to him. I saw him twice afterwards on the same Subject, and the same Assurances were invariably repeated by him, and confirmed by him in the most solemn Manner."

But despite the treble confirmation, Mr. Temple found he was not believed and in the gentlemanly manner of the times challenged Whately to a duel. It took place in Hyde Park and was a curious affair. Whately arrived armed only with a sword, so

Temple handed him one of his own pistols. Both men deliberately fired wide of the mark. The duel then assumed a farcical air. The antagonists drew their swords. "Temple, who was not unskilled in the use of his weapon, discovering, at once, that Whately was completely at his mercy, endeavored to wound his sword arm, and thus end the combat. Whately, however, inexpert as he was, made a vigorous defense, laying about him with a wild energy that baffled the scientific thrusts of his antagonist. It became a tumultuous and even ridiculous struggle, during which Whately, in his furious contortions, repeatedly exposed himself to a fatal lunge. Temple, kindling at length, aimed a thrust which would have transfixed the banker if it had taken effect. Whately, however, caught at the blade with his left hand, and so diverted the stroke that it pierced his side without touching a vital part. The wound was somewhat severe, though not dangerous, and Whately uttered words indicating a desire to end the fight. But Temple, who was extremely deaf, did not hear him, and snatching away the sword, thrust again. Whately slipped, fell forward, and received the point of the sword in the back part of one of his shoulders." The combat ended with Whately injured twice, Temple unhurt, and neither satisfied.

On hearing of the duel Franklin stepped in. His motives in the Hutchinson letters affair certainly appear more complex than he tried to make out at the time: his method—the use of purloined correspondence—can hardly be justified. Nevertheless, he now moved into the open, exposing himself to his enemies in the belief that by so doing he would prevent a repetition of the duel and thus almost certainly save a life.

On December 25 he wrote a statement published in *The Public Advertiser* two days later: "Finding that two Gentlemen have been unfortunately engaged in a Duel about a Transaction and its Circumstances, of which both of them are totally ignorant and innocent, I think it incumbent on me to declare (for the Prevention of farther Mischief, as far as such a Declaration may contribute to prevent it), that I alone am the Person who obtained and transmitted to Boston the Letters in question. Mr. W. could not communicate them, because they were never in his Possession; and, for the same Reason, they could not be taken from him by Mr. T. They were not of the Nature of *private Letters between Friends:* They were written by public Officers to Persons in public Stations, on public Affairs, and intended to procure public Measures; they were therefore handed to other public Persons who might be influenced by them to produce those Measures; Their Tendency was to incense the Mother Country against her Colonies, and, by the Steps recommended, to widen the Breach, which they effected. The chief Caution expressed with regard to Privacy was, to keep their Contents from the Colony Agents, who the Writers apprehended might return them, or Copies of them, to America. That Apprehension was, it seems, well-founded; for the first Agent who laid his Hands on them thought it his Duty to transmit them to his Constituents."

The first government reaction to the petition for Hutchinson's removal had come at the end of November, and on December 3 John Pownall, Lord Dartmouth's secretary, told the clerk of the Privy Council that the Assembly's petition for the removal of Hutchinson and Oliver had been presented to George III. The King had decided that it should be laid before the Privy Council. Franklin had not yet been openly named as the source of the letters, but since his correspondence was frequently opened and read, the Crown may already have known of his involvement and, were this the case, would have had little difficulty in bringing the facts into the open at a Privy Council hearing. However, any problems were removed by Franklin's letter to *The Public Advertiser* after the Whately-Temple duel. Franklin had named himself as the man who had passed on what were generally considered private letters, acquired by means that although unknown were certainly dubious.

On January 5, Franklin reported to Cushing that he had seen Lord Dartmouth and had learned that the Assembly's petition had been presented to the King. But Dartmouth, who had known for at least a month what the next step would be, had not been particularly forthcoming, since Franklin continued to Cushing: "No subsequent step had yet been taken upon it: but his lordship said, the King would probably refer the consideration of it to a committee of Council, and that I should have notice to be heard in support of it. By the turn of his conversation, though he was not explicit, I apprehend the petition is not likely to be complied with; but we shall see."

He was to see only three days later. On January 8 he was informed that the Lords of the Committee of His Majesty's Privy Council for Plantation Affairs would be considering the Assembly's petition in three days' time and that his attendance was required as agent for the Assembly. He wasted no time in suggesting Mr. Bollan, the barrister employed by the Council of Massachusetts as their London agent, to support the petition. Then, less than twenty-four hours before the hearing was due to start, he learned that Israel Mauduit, a friend of Hutchinson and Oliver, had obtained leave for a hearing by counsel. Counsel was to be Alexander Wedderburn, the solicitor general, and on hearing the news Franklin realized that trouble was approaching.

Wedderburn, later 1st Baron Loughborough and 1st Earl of Rosslyn, was a Scottish advocate whose character and method of operation is suggested by the fact that he had been dismissed from the Scottish bar after insulting the Lord President in open court. One of Franklin's early biographers, James Parton, has described him as "sharp, unprincipled . . . destined to scale all the heights of preferment which shameless subserviency could reach," and if this reveals the bias of a Franklin hagiographer it is true that the ferocity of his attack sometimes produced sympathy for his victim which would otherwise have been nonexistent.

On the eleventh Mr. Bollan was barred from speaking on the ground that he was the agent of the Council of Massachusetts, not of the Assembly, and therefore had no right of a hearing on behalf of the Assembly. Franklin asked if Mr. Mauduit would surrender his right to be heard by counsel. But Mauduit replied that Hutchinson and Oliver wished to "have a hearing in their own justification, that their innocence may be fully cleared, and their honour vindicated; and have made provision accordingly. I do not think myself at liberty therefore to give up the assistance of my Counsel, in defending them against this unjust accusation."

The Council then adjourned for three weeks, during which time Franklin found suitable counsel, John Dunning, later 1st Baron Ashburton, and John Lee, an English barrister who was to become attorney general in 1783. In the same interval, however, news arrived from America which was to strengthen still further the official tide now running against Franklin. Late in November a shipment of East India Company tea had arrived in Boston harbor and the inhabitants had stopped its unloading. The vessels did not sail away, as others had done under similar conditions at New York and Philadelphia, a reluctance to give in which was supported by the authorities, possibly because two sons and a nephew of Governor Hutchinson had been appointed agents by the company and would make a considerable profit if the tea could be landed and sold. Deadlock continued until the evening of December 16, after which date the customhouse officers would legally be entitled to seize the cargo by force. "Under these Apprehensions," said a letter which Franklin now received from Cushing, "the Teas on the Evening of the 16th Instant, were destroyed by a Number of Persons unknown and in disguise." The persons unknown were in fact members of the Sons of Liberty—led by Samuel Adams, who with Cushing and two others signed the letter to Franklin. Disguised as Mohawk Indians, they had boarded the ships and dumped overboard 342 chests of tea.

Franklin was outspoken in his condemnation of the Boston Tea Party, news of which quickly spread throughout Britain. "If War is finally to be made upon us, which some threaten, an Act of violent Injustice on our part, unrectified may not give a colourable Pretence for it," he warned Cushing. "A speedy Reparation will immediately set us right in the Opinion of all Europe. And tho' the Mischief was the Act of Persons unknown, yet as probably they cannot be found or brought to answer for it, there seems to be some reasonable Claim on the Society at large in which it happened."

Franklin himself offered to pay for the destruction of the tea provided the acts made against Massachusetts were repealed, a qualification which of course made the offer impossible to accept. "I still think," he told David Hartley years later, "it would have been wise to have accepted it." He had every reason to be embarrassed, since the incident greatly increased opposition to America and Americans just as the date for the Privy Council hearing approached.

The place chosen for what was certain to be a confrontation between Franklin and the authorities on January 29, 1774, was the Cockpit, in which the Grand Ohio Scheme had been approved in 1772. There was great competition for admission, and it was purely by chance that Franklin's friend Dr. Priestley got in after a lucky encounter with Edmund Burke, the politician, who had been a supporter of the Colonists since he had first spoken in the House of Commons in 1766, and who had later become the London agent for the province of New York. "When we got to the anti-room," Priestley later wrote, "we found it quite filled with persons as desirous of getting admission as ourselves." But Burke took his arm and the couple were first into the Council chamber.

A large bow window occupied one side of the room. Facing it, a deep fireplace enclosed two recesses, one on either side of the chimney. A long table ran below the window and here sat the members of the Privy Council. There were no less than thirty-six, among them Lord President Gower; nine other earls, including Dartmouth, Hillsborough and Rochford; and nine other peers of the realm. The archbishop of Canterbury was there as well as the bishop of London.

Among the spectators were the young Jeremy Bentham and Dr. Edward Bancroft, the American who was to play so traitorous a role in Franklin's Paris ménage a few years later. "Of the President's chair the back parallel to and not far distant from the fire," Bentham later recorded; "the chimney-piece, projecting a foot or two from that side of the apartment, formed a recess on each side. Alone in the recess, on the left hand of the President, stood Benjamin Franklin in such position as not to be visible from the situation of the president, remaining the whole time like a rock in the same posture, his head resting on his left hand; and in that attitude abiding the pelting of the pitiless storm."

"The Doctor," said Bancroft, "was dressed in a full dress suit of spotted Manchester velvet, and stood *conspicuously erect,* without the smallest movement of any part of his body. The muscles of his face had been previously composed, so as to afford a placid, tranquil expression of countenance, and he did not suffer the slightest alteration of it to appear during the continuance of [Wedderburn's] speech in which he was so harshly and improperly treated.— In short, to quote the words which he employed concerning himself on another occasion, he kept his 'countenance as immovable as if his features had been made of *wood.*' "

The proceedings started quietly enough, with the attending clerk reading Franklin's covering letter to Lord Dartmouth, the Assembly's petition, the resolutions of the Assembly and then the letters from Hutchinson, Oliver and the others. Wedderburn offered no objection, either when these documents were being read or when first Dunning and then John Lee emphasized that the Assembly was merely asking the King for a favor which could be granted or refused.

Alexander Wedderburn then rose. He spoke for an hour, with what has been called "the energy of a bold, bad man who saw a coronet glittering in the eager eyes of the magnates whom he addressed." The Solicitor General first lauded Governor Hutchinson's record, then maintained that it was Franklin's aim to supplant him, an assertion he must have found it difficult to support with any plausibility. He next emphasized the case for the letters being private. Then he came to the core of his attack: the manner in which Franklin had come into possession of the letters.

The writers did not give them to him; nor yet did the deceased correspondent, who from our intimacy would otherwise have told me of it: Nothing then will acquit Dr. Franklin of the charge of obtaining them by fraudulent or corrupt means, for the most malignant of purposes, unless he stole them, from the person who stole them. This argument is irrefragable.

I hope, my Lords, you will mark (and brand) the man, for the honour of this country, of Europe, and of mankind. Private correspondence has hitherto been held sacred, in times of the greatest party rage, not only in politics but religion. He has forfeited all the respect of societies and of men. Into what companies will he hereafter go with an unembarrassed face, or the honest intrepidity of virtue. Men will watch him with a jealous eye; they will hide their papers from him, and lock up their escrutoires. He will henceforth esteem it a libel to be called *a man of letters*; *homo* trium *litterarum*!

—a reference to Plautus, *Aulularia*, 2:325: "Tun, trium litterarum homo me vituperas? fur." "Do you find fault with me? You, a man of three letters—thief!"

The Earl of Shelburne described to Chatham the conclusion of Wedderburn's performance as "a most scurrilous invective" and the editors of Chatham's correspondence give the following as the end of Wedderburn's speech:

Amidst these tranquil events, here is a man who, with the utmost insensibility of remorse, stands up and avows himself the author of all. I can compare him only to Zanga, in Dr. Young's "Revenge": "Know, then, 'twas I— / I forged the letter—I dispos'd the picture— / I hated —I despis'd—and I destroy."

I ask, my Lords, whether the revengeful temper attributed to the bloody African, is not surpassed by the coolness and apathy of the wily American?

Wedderburn then said he was ready to examine Franklin as a witness. Franklin declined to put his head in that particular noose. Thus the hearing ended, with the recommendation of the Privy Council a foregone conclusion.

As was to be the case more than once during the coming struggle with the Colonies, the British had thoughtlessly handed a weapon to their opponents, and almost a century and a half later a historian of the period could write: "The methods by which [Franklin] had obtained, and the use he had made of, the letters is wholly indefensible. But Wedderburn's violent attack on him and the indecency with which the tribunal showed their approval of his coarse invective were positively criminal."

The Privy Council's judgment, dated the day of the hearing, gave Hutchinson and Oliver a clean bill of health. "The Lords of the Committee do agree humbly to Report, as their Opinion to Your Majesty," it ran, "that the said petition is founded upon Resolutions formed upon False and Erroneous Allegations, and that the same is groundless, Vexatious and Scandalous and calculated only for the Seditious Purpose of keeping up a Spirit of Clamour and Discontent in the said province. And the Lords of the Committee do further humbly report to Your Majesty that nothing has been laid before them, which does or can, in their Opinion in any manner or in any Degree, Impeach the Honour, Integrity or Conduct, of the said Governor or Lieutenant Governor. And their Lordships are humbly of Opinion that the said Petition ought to be Dismissed."

Reactions to Wedderburn's attack tended to follow party lines: those who supported the American cause criticized what they saw as the unnecessary brutality of the Solicitor General's words, and almost thirty years later—when in 1803 the French renewal of war was being debated—Charles James Fox reminded the House of Commons "how all men tossed up their hats, and clapped their hands in boundless delight, at Mr. Wedderburn's speech against Dr. Franklin, without reckoning the cost it was to entail upon them." Many appreciated the lines quoted by Horace Walpole:

Benjamin Franklin, by the sculptor Jean-Antoine Houdon, possibly drawn during
the voyage to Philadelphia in 1785, when Houdon, commissioned to make a bust of
Washington, sailed on the same ship as Franklin [Sotheby's]

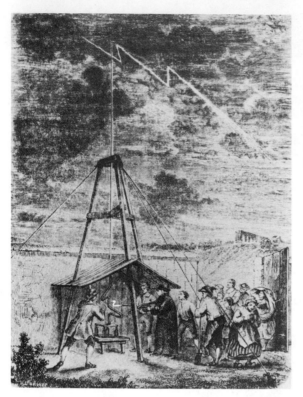

The experiment at Marly-la-Ville on May 10, 1752, carried out for Thomas-François Dalibard, which confirmed Franklin's theory that lightning was a form of electricity [An engraving from Figuier's *Les Merveilles de la Science*, reproduced in J. L. Heilbron's *Electricity in the 17th and 18th Centuries* (Berkeley and Los Angeles: University of California Press, 1979)]

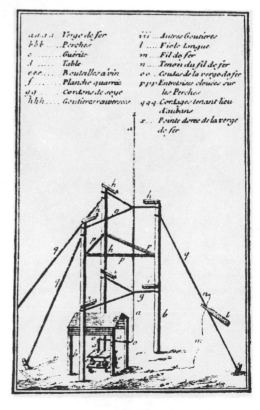

Diagram of the Marly-la-Ville experiment [T.-F. Dalibard, *Expériences et Observations sur le Tonnerre, Relatives à Celles de Philadelphie*, in *Neudrucke von Schriften und Karten über Meteorologie und Erdmagnetismus*, ed. G. H. Hellmann (Berlin: A. Asher & Co., 1897)]

Benjamin Franklin in London, working as a printer, 1724 [*The Printing Times and Lithographer* (London), June 15, 1876]

Diagrams illustrating Franklin's Philadelphia Fire Place [William Temple Franklin, *Memoirs of the Life and Writings of Benjamin Franklin* (London, 1818)]

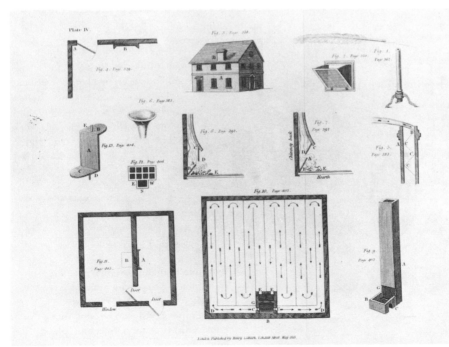

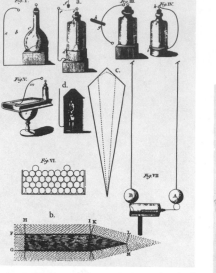

Diagram illustrating some of Franklin's early electrical experiments [William Temple Franklin, *Memoirs of the Life and Writings of Benjamin Franklin* (London, 1818)]

14.1 (a) Franklin's demonstration of the opposite electrifications on the coatings of a Leyden jar (b) his depiction of the statics of electrical atmospheres (c) his form of Wilson's fish (d) the sentry box for collecting lightning. From EO^b.

Peter Collinson, F.R.S., the British naturalist and antiquary to whom Franklin sent his first letter describing his electrical experiments [Emmet Collection (#3204), Art, Prints and Photographs Division, The New York Public Library, Astor, Lenox and Tilden Foundations]

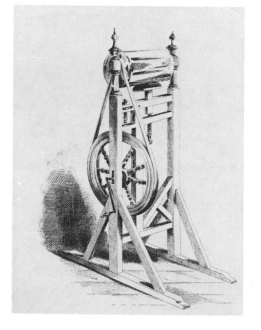

Benjamin Franklin's original machine for producing electricity [Emmet Collection (#3202), Art, Prints and Photographs Division, The New York Public Library, Astor, Lenox and Tilden Foundations]

"Join, or Die," the cartoon urging the American Colonies to unite in defense, published in Franklin's *Pennsylvania Gazette* on May 9, 1754 [The New-York Historical Society]

Benjamin Franklin's home in Craven Street, London, 1757–1762 [Emmet Collection (#3218), Arts, Prints and Photographs Division, The New York Public Library, Astor, Lenox and Tilden Foundations]

Dr. John Fothergill, Franklin's Quaker friend and doctor; painted by John Flaxman [Ex-Barlow Collection, The Courtauld Institute of Art]

William Strahan, printer, Franklin's friend over many years, by Joshua Reynolds [National Portrait Gallery, London]

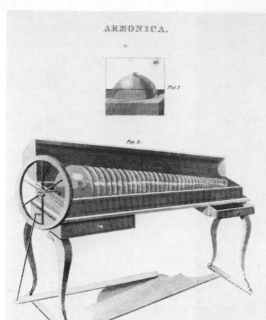

ARMONICA.

Fig. 1.

Fig. 2.

An early drawing of Franklin's armonica [William Temple Franklin, *Memoirs of the Life and Writings of Benjamin Franklin* (London, 1818)]

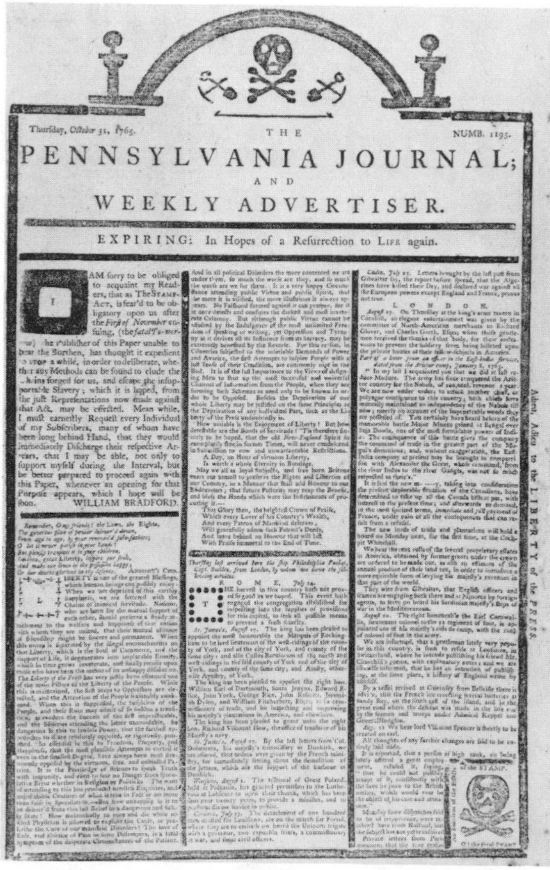

The front page of *The Pennsylvania Journal; and Weekly Advertiser* for Thursday, October 31, 1765, with its black border to mark the introduction of the Stamp Act which came into operation the following day. Down the right margin of the page there is printed: "Adieu, Adieu to the Liberty of the Press." [Rare Book Collection, Rare Books and Manuscripts Division, The New York Public Library, Astor, Lenox and Tilden Foundations]

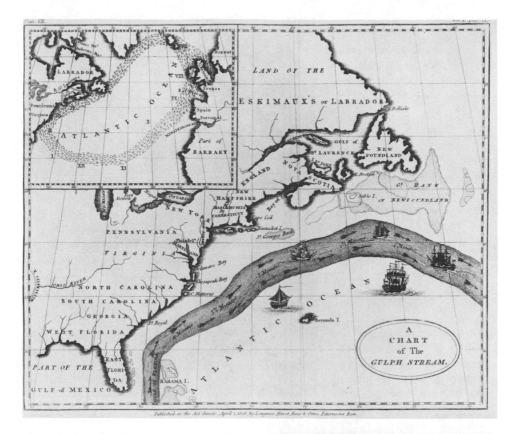

An early chart showing the Gulf Stream, printed in the *Memoirs of the Life and Writings of Benjamin Franklin*, edited by his grandson William Temple Franklin (London, 1818)

Engraving of Franklin by François Nicolas Martinet, 1773, from a painting by Mason Chamberlin [Trustees of the British Museum]

Alexander Wedderburn, whose attack on Franklin in the Cockpit marked a watershed in Franklin's life; painted by William Owen [National Portrait Gallery, London]

The confrontation between Franklin and Alexander Wedderburn *(center)* in the Cockpit, Whitehall, January 29, 1774; a painting by Christian Schuessle [The Huntington Library, San Marino, California]

Admiral Lord Howe; a relief by John Flaxman [National Portrait Gallery, London]

Franklin medallion, 1777, by Jean Baptiste Nini after a drawing by Thomas Walpole [National Portrait Gallery, London]

The Billopp House, Staten Island, where Franklin, John Adams and Edward Rutledge met Admiral Howe in September 1776 [Engraving in *Appleton's Journal* 11(February 7, 1874): 161–63; here copied from *Adams Family Correspondence,* ed. L. H. Butterfield (Cambridge, Mass.: The Belknap Press of the Harvard University Press, 1963), vol. 2]

Late-nineteenth-century drawings (from the *Century Illustrated Monthly Magazine* [vol. 57 (n.s. 35), 1898–99]) showing *(clockwise):* Franklin asleep in the Quaker Meeting House on his first arrival in Philadelphia; Franklin's return in 1758 to Watts's Printing House, London, where he had worked more than thirty years previously; Franklin, discussing at dinner in France the Abbé Raynal's theory of degenerate Americans, and finding that he is taller than most men present; Franklin unknowingly applauding his own praises at the French Academy; Franklin's return to Philadelphia in 1785

Benjamin Wilson's 1759 portrait of Franklin, stolen from Philadelphia by Major André in 1778 and restored to the United States in 1906 by the 4th Earl Grey, then governor general of Canada [Trustees of the British Museum]

Diogenes with his lantern, holding a portrait of Franklin, by Van Loo, a print made in July 1780. A Latin inscription below the portrait says: "Nations! Stop and wonder: Diogenes has found a man."
[Trustees of the British Museum]

The treaty between the United States and France, February 1778, signed by Conrad Alexandre Gérard, Franklin, Silas Deane and Arthur Lee [National Archives, Washington, D.C.]

Sarcastic Sawney, swol'n with spite and prate
On silent Franklin poured his venal hate.
The calm philosopher, without reply,
Withdrew, and gave his country liberty.

Edmund Burke, writing to the Marquis of Rockingham a few days later, said that Wedderburn had "replied in a very well-performed invective against the assembly, and all the town meetings of New England; justifying the governor, and laying on most heavily, indeed beyond all bounds and measure, on Dr. Franklin." Those who believed that American unrest was being irresponsibly fomented felt that no words were too strong to condemn a man who acquired private letters by means he was unwilling to disclose and then allowed the contents to be spread abroad. There were a few exceptions. General Gage, in London from Boston, showed a grudging respect when he observed: "I suppose no Man's Conduct and Character was before so mangled and torn as Dr. Franklin's was at this time. People wondering he had Confidence to stand it, with the contemptuous Looks of the audience upon him." On the other side, David Hume appears to have had doubts, writing to Adam Smith: "Pray, what strange Accounts are these we hear of Franklyn's Conduct? I am very slow in believing that he has been guilty in the extreme Degree that is pretended; tho' I always knew him to be a very factious man, and Faction, next to Fanaticism, is, of all passions, the most destructive of Morality. How is it suppos'd he got Possession of these Letters? I hear that Wedderburn's Treatment of him before the Council, was most cruel, without being in the least blameable. What a pity!" According to John Adolphus, apologist for George III and a historian whose works fill twenty volumes, Franklin "had sufficient self-command to suppress all display of feeling; but the transactions of the day sunk deeply into his mind, and produced an unextinguishable rancour against this country which coloured all the acts of his subsequent life, and occasioned extensive and ever memorable consequences."

There is a good deal of evidence to support Adolphus's view. But although Wedderburn's attack conditioned Franklin's view of the political situation, his personal reaction was distinctly sophisticated. "You know that in England," he wrote in mid-

March to Jan Ingenhousz, "there is every day in almost every Paper some Abuse on public Persons of all Parties, the King himself does not always escape; and the Populace, who are used to it, love to have a good Character cut up now and then for their Entertainment. On this occasion it suited the Purposes of the Ministry to have me abused, as it often suits the Purposes of their Opposers to abuse them. And having myself been long engag'd in Publick Business, this Treatment is not new to me, I am almost as much used to it as they are themselves, and perhaps can bear it better."

At times he was no doubt bitter—but possibly with the bitterness of a man who knew that he had made a mistake. Openly, he took a different line, telling Priestley, who breakfasted with him at Craven Street the next morning, that he had a good conscience: "if he had not considered the thing for which he had been so much insulted, as one of the best actions of his life, and what he should certainly do again in the same circumstances, he could not have supported it."

The first repercussion came the following day when Franklin received an official notice that the King had "found it necessary" to remove him from his post as deputy postmaster of North America. According to the editors of Burke's correspondence, his removal "seems to have been the object government had in view, in bringing forward the petition after it had lain by so long." It may be true, but it would seem to be only part of the answer. Once Franklin had revealed his hand in the affair, the government must have found it difficult to resist using this new weapon to bring about his destruction in Britain.

Before the week was out, Dartmouth had written to Hutchinson telling him that it would take some days before the Order in Council on the Assembly's petition was promulgated. "In the meantime," he wrote on February 5, 1774, "it will be a satisfaction to you to know that there has been a Hearing upon it before a Committee more numerous than was ever known to attend upon any Occasion and that their report to the King is conceived in terms that reflect the highest Honor upon your Conduct, & express very just Indignation at the Falsehood and Malevolence of the Charge brought against you."

The effect of the Cockpit confrontation on public opinion was considerable, and a letter from London dated February 14, printed in *The Pennsylvania Gazette* two months later, accurately sums up the reaction. "You will have heard before this reaches you," it said, "how infamously Dr. Franklin has been treated by Administration; and you will soon see in what light they behold American Petitions. There is not a more obnoxious Character here, at present, than that of a Friend to America. The Colonies should, therefore, be more particularly attentive in cultivating Union and Harmony among themselves. The Spirit of this Country is extremely hostile to them; and they have nothing to depend upon, but their own Union and Firmness."

In America, news of the Cockpit encounter, and its outcome, aroused rebellious protest. *The Pennsylvania Gazette* reported on May 4:

Yesterday, about Four o'clock in the Afternoon, the effigies of Alexander Wedderburn, Esq., convicted of traducing the American Colonies, and insulting their Agent before his Majesty's Privy Council for doing his Duty; and of Thomas Hutchinson, Esq., Governor of Massachusetts-Bay convicted of an attempt to incense Great Britain against her Colonies, were put in a Cart, and conducted through the Streets of this City. . . .

He [Wedderburn] availed himself of the Licence of the Bar to insult the venerable Dr. Franklin, whose Knowledge in Philosophy, universal Benevolence, just Sentiments of Liberty, and indefatigable Labours to promote Harmony between Britain and her Colonies, entitle him to the Esteem of the Learned of every Nation, the Love of all good Men and the sincere Affection of every *honest* Briton and American.

But the base born SOLLICITOR who attempted to turn his Learning, Benevolence and Patriotism into Ridicule is (like Hutchinson) a Paricide of the first Rank, who would sacrifice his Country, his Liberty and his God, and delight in the Carnage of the most faithful British Subjects in America, to gain Promotion at Court. Such horrid Monsters are a Disgrace to human Nature and justly merit our utmost Detestation and the Gallows, to which they are assigned, and then burnt by Electric Fire. With several others and the following lines from Hudibras:

> "So a wild Tartar, when he spies
> A man that's handsome, valiant, wise
> If he can kill him, thinks t'inherit
> His Wit, his Beauty, and his Spirit:
> As if just so much he enjoy'd
> As in an other is destroy'd."

On Governor Hutchinson's breast was fixed the following label. "Governor Hutchinson, whom we now consign to the Gallows and Flames, as the only proper Reward for Double-Dealing and Treachery to his native Country."

After being exposed for several Hours, they were hung, and burnt, in the Evening, amidst a vast Concourse of People who testified their Resentment against the Originals with the loudest Acclamations.

Later reports maintained that the bonfire beneath the effigies had, symbolically, been fired electrically by Franklin's old collaborator, Ebenezer Kinnersley.

If this was the response of the radicals, government supporters reacted as fiercely in the opposite direction. On March 12, 1774, the governor of Georgia, Sir James Wright, wrote to Dartmouth, pointing out that he could not accept the reappointment by the Georgia Assembly of Franklin as their agent in London. He had no need to cite the circumstances of the former deputy postmaster's dismissal. Instead, he based his refusal on the fact that the whole legislative body had to make such appointments, adding that the Assembly's action "seems to me to be a pretty extraordinary attempt in the Lower House of Assembly and I wish it may not lead to something further." This was only the beginning, and Franklin was to claim that he had lost a total of £1,500 a year from the Cockpit verdict: £300 from the Post Office, £500 from Pennsylvania, £400 from Massachusetts, £100 from New Jersey and £200 from Georgia. However, he later admitted that some of the Colonies had never paid him at all.

The man at the heart of the Hutchinson letters theft—for it appears to have involved nothing less than theft whoever was the prime mover—has remained only inconclusively identified, although the case against John Temple is greater than it is sometimes claimed to be. Franklin's letter to *The Public Advertiser* certainly appeared to have cleared Temple, although it should be noted that all he denied was that Temple had taken them specifically from William Whately.

The main evidence usually cited against Temple is his own letter to Franklin, now in the Library of Congress, written on July 9, 1781, when Temple was in Amsterdam and Franklin was the American ambassador in Paris. "I am now upon the Continent of Europe & at Liberty to write an Innocent Letter to a Friend in another Kingdom without running the Risk of having

Mr. Wedderburn's very extraordinary Talents at *Constructive Treason* exercised upon it," he stated. He had been in Philadelphia, where he had spoken to Cushing and the others involved in the affair of the Hutchinson letters. "I told them," he continued, "that I had been privy to the whole transaction: that it was through my means that you were able to Obtain [the letters]: that they were obtained in the most honourable way, of which the Minister has not, nor could not have, any knowledge, unless from the [unclear] but to save an Innocent person, who might be Suspected by the Minister, the most positive injunct from you at my request, Accompanied those Letters, which injunction they thought necessary to violate." Cushing and others in Boston took Temple's statement at its face value. But Temple was, in 1781, trying to build up in Boston a reputation for being pro-American; thus this evidence must certainly be suspect.

However, there is a letter from Governor Hutchinson, written some seven years before to Lord Dartmouth, and today in Lord Dartmouth's papers, which appears to confirm Temple's involvement, although in a manner not spelled out.

"My Lord," he wrote on August 16, 1774—having arrived in Britain at the end of June—"After a solemn declaration made by Mr. Temple to the contrary, I could not help being astonished when I heard the information, which had been given to your Lordship, at his own acknowledgment that he had seen the Letters among Mr. Whateley's files, and that he had them in his possession in a packet directed to Doctor Franklin. Will it be too much trouble for your Lordship, when you see the Gentleman again, to desire him to recollect whether Temple expressed himself in such manner as would not consist [*sic*] with his receiving the letters from Franklin and sending them back again without saying anything of his seeing them himself among Whateley's files? I should be ashamed to ask this trouble of your Lordship if it was not upon an affair very interesting; for if the declaration made to me is false, I shall think Mr. Temple a most dangerous man, and guard against the most distant acquaintance with him; if it is not false I should wish he might not suffer from a charge or suspicion not sufficiently found."

Even if Temple's implication can be taken for granted, as is almost certainly the case, the manner in which the letters came into Franklin's hands has remained unclear. In September 1773 he wrote to his son of the letters: "They fell into my hands, and

I thought it my duty to give some principal people [in Boston] a sight of them." Here there is nothing about the long negotiations necessary before permission could be obtained to send the letters abroad; nor any comment on the curious fact that while the man involved allegedly banned copying of the letters he was willing to allow the originals to be sent abroad. And the phrase "fell into my hands" is reminiscent of the letters which, as Franklin at first intended to tell Cushing in the autumn of 1772, had been salvaged from a dustbin by a footman. Moreover if the Hutchinson letters had been acquired by a lucky quirk of fate, then this itself might well account for the somewhat random nature of the collection.

With so little known about the machinery which brought the letters to Craven Street from the files of Mr. Whately, there is another possibility, Machiavellian maybe, but no more so than other incidents in what were, in a gentlemanly way, Machiavellian times. It was well known that Governor Hutchinson had refused to confirm Franklin's appointment as Massachusetts agent. Franklin's capacity for intrigue in support of good causes —among which he included the survival of Benjamin Franklin —was also well known. Many men must have had a shrewd suspicion of what his reaction would be if the Hutchinson letters came into his hands—and of what might follow. It is not inconceivable, therefore, that the letters were made accessible to Franklin by someone who hoped that he might make, in his use of them, the false step that he did make. Nevertheless, John Temple was, and remains, the chief suspect.

Whatever the real details of the Hutchinson letters affair, Franklin was pointedly ostracized by the Establishment by the early spring of 1774. With his use to the Colonies severely circumscribed, if not entirely at an end, it might have been thought that the time had at last come for him to sail for home. Indeed, three weeks before the events in the Cockpit, when he was expecting that the Hutchinson affair would blow over, Franklin had told his son: "I am now seriously preparing for my departure to America. I purpose sending my luggage, books, instruments, &c. by All or Falconer [captains of two transatlantic packets], and take my passage to New York in one of the spring or summer packets." Before the end of April, with the Cockpit episode behind him, he was telling his wife: "I hoped to have been on the Sea in my Return by this time; but find I must stay a few Weeks longer, perhaps for the Summer Ships." In June he told Cushing that he had been expecting to leave before the end of the month and had handed over the agency to Arthur Lee. But Lee was now making a tour of Europe and Franklin felt himself "under a kind of Necessity of continuing till you can be acquainted with this Circumstance, and have Time to give farther Orders."

An additional reason for delay in leaving had been provided by the Parliament at Westminster. In March it passed the Boston Port Bill, which closed the harbor, except for the handling of military supplies, until damages had been paid for the tea destroyed in December. In May there came the Quebec Act and the Massachusetts Government Act. The first extended Canada's frontiers to the Ohio, thus taking in territory claimed by Connecticut, Massachusetts and Virginia, and also restored a number of French rights to French Canadians. The second virtually suspended the Massachusetts charter, moved the Colony's capital from Boston to Salem and ordained that members of the Council would be appointed by the King rather than elected by the House of Representatives. The Quartering Act was extended and the Administration of Justice Act ordained that serious crimes would no longer be tried in provincial courts but in those of another Colony or in England. These acts encouraged the moves for a Congress at which all the Colonies should be represented and plans were soon announced. It was "thought by the great Friends of the Colonies here," Franklin wrote to his son from London, "that I ought to stay till the Result of the Congress arrives, when my Presence here may, they suppose, be of Use."

So by the end of the summer he was still in England. There were, in fact, two events which might have hastened his departure. The first was the issue of a chancery writ by William Whately on January 7, some three weeks before the confrontation in the Cockpit. Whately, administrator of his brother's estate, alleged that Franklin had caused the Hutchinson letters to be printed abroad, and called for their return. The writ was transparently a device to force from Franklin the manner in which he had secured the letters, and throughout 1774 the lawyers on both sides made the preparatory moves for a court hearing—Whately's urging hurry, Franklin's ensuring delay. Once the case was heard Franklin would have two choices: he could reveal how he had acquired the letters; or by refusing to do so he could lay himself open to a charge of contempt and the imprisonment that would almost inevitably follow.

More important, and more dangerous, was a move by Dartmouth in the summer of 1774. In spite of support from the government, Hutchinson had found it impractical to remain as governor and was replaced by General Gage. And on June 3 Dartmouth wrote to Gage. Proof of "dangerous and unwarrantable" correspondence between people in England and "the Leaders of the Faction at Boston" had come to his knowledge, he said, "by a confidential communication of the Copies of two Letters, the one from Dr. Franklin dated 7th July 1773, the other from Mr. Arthur Lee dated 25 December 1773." He had, in fact, been sent a copy of Franklin's letter by Governor Hutchinson in October 1773, but the original was needed for prosecution.

"Both these Letters have I understand been publickly read in the Assembly, and are expressed in such Terms as makes it very much to be wished that such Evidence could be obtained of the authenticity of them as might be the grounds of a proper Proceeding thereupon; you will therefore use your best Endeavours with that Secresy and Caution the nature of the Case requires, to procure either the Originals, or some regular attested Copies of those Letters & transmit them to me by the first opportunity."

Following a suggestion from Cushing, Franklin had sent him two letters on July 7, one containing information for his own eyes alone and marked "Private," the other containing material for the Assembly. He made drafts of each letter, the drafts ending up in the Library of Congress. The original of the private letter is now held by the Public Record Office in London, having presumably been seized by the British from Cushing's house in 1775. The original of the second has not been found, but a copy exists in Lord Dartmouth's papers. It was this second letter, in which Franklin discussed the future relationship between the Colonies and Britain, which laid him open to possible prosecution. It might perhaps, he said, be "best and fairest for the Colonies, in a general Congress now in Peace to be assembled, (or by means of the Correspondence lately proposed) after a full and solemn Assertion and Declaration of their Rights, to engage firmly with Each Other that they will never grant Aids to the Crown in any General War, till those Rights are recognised by the King and both Houses of Parliament; communicating at the same time this their Resolution to the Crown." Whether this constituted treason or merely incitement to treason is uncertain; but Dartmouth's intention of getting the letter suitably authenticated for a "proper proceeding" has an ominous ring.

There is no evidence that Gage had any quick success. But in December he sent Dartmouth "a printed extract of a letter said to be a performance of Dr. Franklin and written to Cushing." In his covering letter he said: "I mention another letter to his Lordship dated in September, which Cushing talked of before Mr. Flucker and others as from Dr. Franklin and told the Contents of it. I have not mentioned the Doctor's name as I could not prove it upon him; but he is certainly capable of any mischief, and I believe the Author of the Disturbances in this Province, and, I may add now, of the Continent."

When British troops occupied Boston the following year there seems to have been competition in the search for incriminating correspondence. In October Gage wrote to Dartmouth: "I transmit your Lordship a packet of Letters that were picked out from a Number of Papers scattered about Cushing's house. They contain no Intelligence of present Transactions, but shew the nature of the Correspondence that the two Lees [the brothers Arthur and William], Doctor Franklin and others kept up with the Leaders of this Rebellion."

The following month General Howe sent Dartmouth his own contribution. "The enclosed are original Letters that were found in Mr. Cushing's house in this Town," he said. "They are from Dr. Franklin and Mr. Stephen Sayre [later arrested in London and charged with plotting to overthrow the British Government, but discharged for lack of evidence], of a Nature that points out the Train carried on by these Gentlemen, to blow up this Country into Rebellion."

Thirteen of Franklin's letters eventually found their way into the British State Paper office, a prefatory note to them saying: "These letters are perhaps now only precious or Important so far as they prove and discover the Duplicity Ingratitude and Guilt of this Arch Traitour whom they unveil and really unmask Displaying Him as an accomplished proficient in the blacker Arts of Dissimulation and guile." Some letters are individually annotated, a typical comment being: "A Scurrilous and very

wicked letter being highly Defamatory of the Earl of Hillsborough and contains the most Criminal Insinuations and Insti-
gations against the Authority of the British Parliament in North
America."

In the autumn of 1774 Franklin was not yet the "arch traitor,"
although he was regarded with increasing suspicion by the government as relations between Britain and the North American
Colonies continued to deteriorate. In Boston, General Gage was
fortifying the neck of land which was then the only connection
between Boston and its hinterland, an ominous indication that
a siege was in someone's mind. Elsewhere, throughout the province, local militia began to appear, some of them groups of
"Minutemen," ordered to remain in constant readiness for action. By September, the situation had become so bad that Grey
Cooper of the Treasury received a message from Boston which
was later summarized as: "Removal of Province's powder at
Lt.-General Gage's order brought on plan to intimidate Lieut-
Governor Oliver and Councillors. I escaped to Boston with difficulty. Lt.-Governor's conduct is considered sole cause of
disgrace of troops. Several of Council have resigned. Justice and
civil power are at an end. Salem is as refractory as Boston. If
Great Britain yields, consequence will be fatal. Extirpation of
episcopal clergy is intended. Quebec Act has increased clamour."

In Britain, also, feelings were hardening and tempers rising.
Wedderburn supported the moves so dogmatically that Burke
had been forced to reply, "The learned gentleman's speech
demands blood; the sword must convince the Americans and
clear up their clouded apprehensions! The learned gentleman's
logical resources surely desert him if he is obliged to call such
a coarse argument as an army to his assistance. Not that I mean
to cast any personal reflection upon him: I always respect, and
sometimes dread his talents." Dr. Johnson was preparing to
write his *Taxation no Tyranny* and was to claim that the Americans
"are a race of convicts, and ought to be thankful for anything we
allow them short of hanging" and to proclaim that he was "willing to love all mankind *except an American.*"

The rising tide of anti-Americanism, following the drubbing
in the Cockpit, reinforced the change which now began to
suffuse Franklin's attitude to Anglo-Colonial relations. He was

still anxious to avert rebellion and war if they could be averted on honorable terms. But the imperial vision which he had revealed to Lord Kames only a few years previously had now evaporated, as was only too evident when he reviewed a new plan for union, drawn up by Joseph Galloway, somewhat like the Albany Plan of 1754.

When I consider the extreme corruption prevalent among all orders of men in this old rotten state, and the glorious public virtue so predominant in our rising country [he said], I cannot but apprehend more mischief than benefit from a closer Union. I fear they will drag us after them in all the plundering Wars, which their desperate circumstances, injustice and rapacity, may prompt them to undertake; and their wide-wasting prodigality and profusion is a gulf that will swallow up every aid we may distress ourselves to afford them.

Here numberless and needless places, enormous salaries, pensions, perquisites, bribes, groundless quarrels, foolish expeditions, false accounts or no accounts, contracts and jobs, devour all revenue, and produce continual necessity in the midst of natural plenty. I apprehend, therefore, that to unite us intimately will only be to corrupt and poison us also. . . . However I would try any thing, and bear any thing that can be borne with safety to our just liberties, rather than engage in a war with such relations, unless compelled to it by dire necessity in our own defence.

Now, at almost the last minute of the last hour, some men in England, and even a few members of the government, saw the precipice toward which the country was moving and did their best to prevent it from going over the brink. Franklin, though detested in many quarters, appeared in others as the man who could most usefully help, and it was Franklin who from late August 1774 until the middle of March 1775 was at the center of individual but overlapping efforts to halt the ominous progress of events. The historian George Otto Trevelyan was later to write that acceptance of *Hints for Conversation,* a report which Franklin prepared during these fruitless months, would "have had a merit rare among the celebrated instruments in history, that of terminating a sharp and extended controversy rationally, equitably, permanently and without derogation to the self-esteem of either of the contracting parties." Franklin himself was to remark years afterward to David Barclay, the prominent Quaker banker who was a key figure in the abortive negotiations: "How much might have been done, and how much mischief prevented, if his, your, and my joint endeavours, in a certain melancholy affair, had been attended to."

Franklin wrote his own 24,000-word account of the events after they had ended, the only detailed account that has survived. While he appears to hold the balance fairly enough, his comment in *Poor Richard's Almanack* should be remembered: "Historians relate, not so much what is done, as what they would have believed." In the long account, written on the Atlantic as he returned to Philadelphia, he implored both houses of Parliament "not to suffer, by their little misunderstandings, so glorious a fabric as the present British empire to be demolished by these blunderers," "misunderstandings" being a mild enough word after the Boston Massacre and the Boston Tea Party. And, perhaps more surprisingly, when it came to independence, he assured Lord Chatham that "having more than once travelled almost from one end of the [American] continent to the other, and kept a great variety of company, eating, drinking and conversing with them freely, I never had heard in any conversation from any person drunk or sober, the least expression of a wish for a separation, or hint that such a thing would be advantageous to America."

It was Chatham who, in August 1774, arranged for Franklin to call upon him and to outline the situation in America as he saw it. Although in retirement, Chatham still exercised an enormous influence. However, it appears that the Byzantine series of moves which took place during the next few months were blessed by Dartmouth and possibly even by Lord North, both desperately anxious that war with the Colonies should be avoided but as equally desperate that independence should not be offered them. It would have been unwise for either man to approach Franklin direct. They therefore adopted the strategy of indirect approach, first using Lord Hyde, chancellor of the Duchy of Lancaster. Hyde invoked the aid of Dr. Fothergill, friend of Franklin since 1757, and David Barclay, now organizing a petition from London merchants who feared that events were leading to the complete wrecking of their trade with America. Another line of attack was through the Howe brothers: Richard, Admiral Lord Howe, and William, General Lord Howe.

Their widowed sister was an ardent chess player and Franklin was inveigled to play with her and thus to meet her brother the admiral.

After a series of opening talks during which each side assessed the other's position, Franklin met Fothergill and Barclay on December 3 and was persuaded—rather reluctantly, since he was waiting to hear what had been proposed by the Continental Congress in Philadelphia—to draw up a series of heads for discussion. Seventeen in all, these proposed payment for the tea destroyed in Boston Harbor and the repeal of the Tea Duty Act. That was followed by suggestions that all acts regulating trade with the Colonies or restraining manufacture there should be reconsidered, that British troops should not be quartered in any Colony without the consent of the legislature, and that various other acts which limited Colonial activities should be altered or abrogated. But nowhere was there the word "independence." These "HINTS FOR CONVERSATION upon the Subject of Terms that might probably produce a Durable Union between Britain and the Colonies" were copied and made available to Lord Dartmouth and Lord Hyde. Franklin contends that he expected his paper to go no further and that its authorship should remain anonymous.

Shortly afterward, there arrived from the Continental Congress a petition outlining American grievances, with instructions that it should be presented to the King. It was consigned not only to Franklin but also to Edmund Burke, Charles Garth, Arthur Lee and Paul Wentworth, agent for New Hampshire. According to a note from Thomas Pownall in Lord Dartmouth's papers, the instructions were that it should be sent to the King either by these five and a number of British merchants or by Lord Dartmouth. Congress favored the first option, Franklin the second. "They were to meet today at Waghorn's Coffee house," Pownall stated, "but Paul Wentworth (from whom I have these particulars) declines acting, and says the Petition is an assertion of all their claims in a very high tone and with very offensive expressions."

It eventually reached the King via Dartmouth, but not before Franklin had shown a copy to Chatham, whom he had promised to keep informed. There followed another meeting with Lord Howe, his sister's addiction to chess again allowing the encounter to go unpublicized. On this occasion Franklin found Howe in possession of his "Hints for Conversation" and obviously aware of its authorship. That was only the first surprise. Howe did not believe that the proposals in the "Hints" were acceptable. But he felt that Franklin might try again—and then added that if he were successful he "might with reason expect any reward in the power of government to bestow." To Franklin that was nothing less than bribery, or, as he called it, "what the French vulgarly call 'spitting in the soup.'" Nevertheless, he provided an amended paper. It was no more acceptable than its predecessor.

At this point Chatham reappeared on the scene, inviting Franklin to attend the Lords on the second parliamentary sitting after the Christmas recess. And here Franklin heard Chatham propose "that immediate orders may be despatched to general Gage for removing his Majesty's forces from the town of Boston, as soon as the rigour of the season, and other circumstances indispensable to the safety and accommodation of the said troops may render the same practicable." During his speech in support of the motion Chatham warned: "The nation of America, who have the virtues of the people they sprung from, will not be slaves." And it was reported that he ended his speech with a remarkable prophecy: "If the Ministers thus persevere in misadvising and misleading the King, I will not say, that they can alienate the affections of his subjects from his crown; but I will affirm, *that they will make the crown not worth his wearing.* I will not say, that the King is betrayed; but I will pronounce, *that the kingdom is undone.*"

But Chatham's motion was rejected by 77 votes to 18. "Sixteen Scotch peers, and twenty-four bishops, with all the lords in possession or expectation of places, when they vote together unanimously, as they generally do for ministerial measures," wrote Franklin, "make a dead majority, that renders all debating ridiculous in itself, since it can answer no end."

During the debate a number of lords had proposed that Chatham, criticizing the current method of handling American affairs, should produce his own plan. This he now proceeded to do, discussing it with Franklin, who on January 27, 1775, drove again to Chatham's home in Hayes, on the outskirts of London. Two days later Franklin received the former prime minister at Craven Street. He was especially proud of this latter visit, made, as he pointed out, "on the very day twelve months that the ministry had taken so much pains to disgrace me before the Privy Council." "He stayed with me near two hours, his equipage waiting at the door; and being there while people were coming from Church, it was much taken notice of, and talked of, as at that time was every little circumstance that men thought might possibly any way affect American affairs. Such a visit from so great a man, on so important a business, flattered not a little my vanity."

On Wednesday, February 1, watched by Franklin, whom he had invited, Chatham presented his plan to the House of Lords. It was rejected, but not before Lord Sandwich had maintained that it could not have been the work of any British peer. It appeared to him to be the work of some American and, turning toward Franklin, he "said, he fancied he had in his eye the person who drew it up, one of the bitterest and most mischievous enemies this country had ever known. This drew the eyes of many Lords upon me; but as I had no inducement to take it to myself, I kept my countenance as immovable as if my features had been made of wood."

There were to be further exchanges, in private and in public. Both Dartmouth on one side and Franklin and his supporters on the other were reluctant to let go the last chance of reconciliation. But the virtual inevitability of defeat shone out clearly from the letter which Fothergill wrote to Dartmouth on February 6. "I wish it had been in my power to have informed my Noble Friend that our negotiation had been successful," he began. "But it is not—And this not owing to our want of attention or willingness to promote a reconciliation; nor to any opposite or refractory disposition. Our difficultys arose from the American acts. The Boston Port Bill, the Government of the Massachusetts, and the Quebec Act. . . . Should the King's servants happily concede in adopting the simple plan of pacification which our Noble Friends so generously concurred in, and include the repeal of the acts above mentioned, we have not the least doubt but America would immediately return to every just expression of duty, both in language and conduct. The party we conferred with should thus be tacitly consented to, would have not the least objection to petition for the restoration of peace—offer on the part of Boston to pay the East India Company for the tea, tho' at the risque of his own private fortune and concert every means of a lasting and reciprocally beneficial union."

It was a generous offer—although Franklin must have known that there was not the slightest chance of its being accepted.

Meetings later in the month confirmed the obvious: that neither side was, in practice, willing to budge. Franklin still wanted to preserve peace. But, as he told Lord Hyde, "if any supposed I could prevail with my countrymen to take black for white, and wrong for right, it was not knowing either them or me; they were not capable of being so imposed on, nor was I capable of attempting it."

Britain had committed herself to a disastrous war and to the loss of a great part of her empire. So far, however, few Britons were aware of the fact.

FOUNDING

FATHER

NINE

INDEPENDENCE CLAIMED

EFORE THE FIRST FEW WEEKS OF 1775 were over, Franklin knew that his work in London for the Colonies was finished. The scene in the Cockpit a year earlier had opened his eyes more widely to the way that the game of politics was played in Britain, and he had few hopes left. They had been kept alive for a while by the protracted negotiations with Chatham, Howe, Hyde, Barclay and Dr. Fothergill, but the failure of the discussions seemed to mark the end of the line.

The decision to reinforce the troops in Boston increased, moreover, Franklin's constant fear that mischance or misunderstanding would lead to disaster. "I am in perpetual Anxiety lest the mad Measure of mixing Soldiers among a People whose Minds are in such a State of Irritation, may be attended with some sudden Mischief," he had written to Thomas Cushing in the autumn of 1774; "For an accidental Quarrel, a personal Insult, an imprudent Order, an insolent Execution of even a prudent one, or 20 other things, may produce a Tumult, unforeseen, and therefore impossible to be prevented, in which such a Carnage may ensue, as to make a Breach that can never afterwards be healed." That danger now loomed larger each day.

As Franklin at last prepared to leave the country which had been his home, with one brief break, for almost eighteen years, he still hoped against hope that war could be avoided; and he still believed that if the worst came to the worst Britain would eventually be forced to release her grip on the Colonies. Priestley, both a younger man to whom he could unburden himself and a crony with whom he could discuss electricity, has left one record of his state of mind. "I was seldom many days without seeing him, & being members of the same club, we constantly returned together," he wrote. "The difference with America breaking out at this time, our conversation was chiefly of a political nature, and I can bear witness that he was so far from promoting, as was generally supposed, that he took every method in his power to prevent, a rupture between the two countries. He urged so much the doctrine of forbearance, that for some time he was unpopular with the Americans on that account, as too much a friend of Great Britain. His advice to them was to bear every thing for the present as they were sure in time to out-grow all their grievances; as it could not be in the power of the country to oppress them long. He dreaded the war, and often said that if the difference should come to an open rupture, it would be a war of *ten years,* and he should not live to see the end of it."

Yet Franklin was confident in the future of America and sometimes subtle in expressing that confidence. John Adams was to recall a dinner party at which it was being deplored that fables involving animals were so widespread that no more could be invented. Franklin thought briefly, then declared: "Once upon a time an eagle scaling round a farmer's barn, and espying a hare, darted down upon him like a sunbeam, seized him in his claws, and remounted with him in the air. He soon found that he had a creature of more courage and strength than a hare; for which, notwithstanding the keenness of his eyesight, he had mistaken a cat. The snarling and scrambling of the prey was very inconvenient; and what was worse, she had disengaged herself from his talons, grasped his body with her four limbs, so as to stop his breath, and seized fast hold of his throat with her teeth.

'Pray,' said the eagle, 'let go your hold and I will release you.'
'Very fine,' said the cat; 'I have no fancy to fall from this height,
and be crushed to death. You have taken me up, and you shall
stoop and let me down.' The eagle thought it necessary to stoop
accordingly."

It was still not known whether Britain would be willing to
stoop within the next few months or only after the tribulations
of war; yet Franklin felt assured that the day would come. But
now at last, after so many abandoned attempts, he began preparations for leaving Britain.

Before they were complete he heard, on February 20, that his
wife, Deborah, had died of paralysis two months earlier. It was
eleven years before that he had left her, expecting, or at least
claiming to expect, that they would be parted only for a year or
so at the most. Now she was gone forever. In 1768 she had
suffered a partial palsy of the tongue and had begun to lose her
memory. Her doctor, Thomas Bond, warned Franklin that although she had recovered, her constitution seemed impaired.
Two years later her memory failed completely and William
Franklin told his father that every day she was becoming "more
and more unfit to be left alone." There had been talk of Sally
coming to England, but if so, William hoped that Franklin would
arrange for someone to take over the care of his wife. The slow
disintegration compounded the problems that already existed.
Franklin had ordered his bankers in Philadelphia to allow her
£30 a month—but when she failed to send him accounts he had
refused to increase the sum. Eventually he justified his attitude
—at least to himself—with the statement that her memory was
"too much impair'd for the Management of unlimited Sums,
without Danger of injuring the future Fortune of your Daughter
and Grandsons." As a result, she started to borrow from his
friends.

Franklin's feelings for his wife have remained something of an
enigma. On her part, there was regret at his continued absence
but a loyal resignation to put up with it. "She told me," William
Franklin wrote to his father after he had attended her funeral,
". . . that she never expected to see you unless you returned this
winter, for that she was sure she should not live till next summer.
I heartily wish you had happened to have come over in the fall,
as I think her disappointment in that respect prayed a good deal
on her spirits."

Franklin himself had a firm theoretical attitude to marriage and in 1783, toward the end of his life, reaffirmed his views to a friend: "The married state is, after all our jokes, the happiest, being comformable to our natures. Man and woman have each of them qualities and tempers, in which the other is deficient, and which in union contribute to the common felicity. Single and separate, they are not the compleat human being; they are like the odd halves of scissars; they cannot answer the end of their formation." But Franklin himself seems not to have been too unhappy in a partial simulation of the simple and separate state. Certainly his letters to Deborah from England were genuinely, if mildly, affectionate and often tinged with homesickness. Certainly he appears to have made at least some show of encouraging her to cross the Atlantic and to start a new life in Europe. Certainly she would, in London, have satisfied his creature comforts more fully and more conveniently than by provisioning him with hampers of the food he could not find in London. Yet it is difficult to feel that there was very much urgency, very much impassioned pleading on his part. Franklin, ensconced in Craven Street, a notable lion in the care of the Stevenson family, survived tolerably well with his wife 3,000 miles away across the Atlantic. Nevertheless, if he ever regretted the months spent wrangling with the Penns and the government, it was probably now.

His son felt that his father should return to Philadelphia immediately. "If there was any prospect of your being able to bring the people in power to your way of thinking, or those of your way of thinking being brought into power, I should not think so much of your stay," William wrote. "But as you have had by this time pretty strong proofs that neither can be reasonably expected, and that you are looked upon with an evil eye in that country, and are in no small danger of being brought into trouble for your political conduct, you had certainly better return while you are able to bear the fatigues of the voyage, to a country where the people revere you and are inclined to pay a deference to your opinions."

Franklin was beginning to feel somewhat the same. The transformation in the Cockpit had begun to make him think at times that he was no more a genuine Englishman than the roughest backwoods settler who had never seen the Atlantic, let alone crossed it. Yet Franklin was a tough-skinned political operator.

He could not help being mortified by the confrontation with Wedderburn, but the mortification wore off more quickly than one is sometimes led to believe. Far from preparing to leave Britain forever, he told his friends in March 1775 that he would possibly be returning in the autumn; and he later wrote to his lawyer saying that he had planned to come back in October. It was plain that he still hoped to be bringing proposals from Congress that would be acceptable to the British. Even the insults from Wedderburn were less important than the prospects of a settlement. Thus the passage which he now booked for mid-March did not necessarily mark his departure forever. Indeed, a remark to Lord Howe that following the death of his wife, "in whose hands [he] had left the care of [his] Affairs . . . it was become necessary for [him] to return thither as soon as conveniently might be," suggests a temporary rather than a permanent return to America.

The day before leaving London he went to Priestley's house. The two men discussed not only the mysteries of electricity and the new wonders still to be discovered, but also the steadily deteriorating relations between Britain and the Colonies. Much of the time, Priestley later wrote, "was employed in reading American newspapers, especially accounts of the reception which the 'Boston Port Bill' met with in America, and as he read the addresses to the inhabitants of Boston, from the places in the neighbourhood, the tears trickled down his cheeks." The editors of his papers go so far as to suggest, after commenting on his ties with Britain, that "The tears may not have been due entirely to the news." It seems clear that Franklin hated leaving England. Yet although his departure was to be a pivotal moment in his life, it is clear from his plans for a return that he himself was unaware of the moment's full importance. His distress, it is true, was not only at the trials and tribulations which he saw looming ahead for America. There was distress also at the collapse of the plans for Anglo-American reconciliation at which he had labored so long and which now might have disintegrated forever. It would not be true to claim that this complex man loved England as he loved America; but as his letters make plain —particularly his letters of this period—it was agonizing to him that the two countries should now be heading toward each other on a collision course. And there was perhaps one matter especially galling to a man so confident of himself as Franklin usually was; what might have happened had he not sent the Hutchinson letters across the Atlantic and thereby created just the weapon which the British Establishment was seeking?

The following day Franklin and his grandson William Temple posted southwest from the capital, across the wilds of Hindhead, with its grisly gibbet and its swinging warning of what happened to those who broke the law, then across the South Downs and into Portsmouth. They sailed on the *Pennsylvania Packet* on March 21, without fuss and without recognition, but with a note from Dr. Fothergill: "Farewel," it said, "and befriend this infant, growing Empire with the utmost exertion of thy abilitys, and no less philanthropy, both of which are beyond my powers to express. A happy, prosperous voyage!"

A fortnight out, Franklin noted: "When you intend a long voyage, you may do well to keep your intentions as much as possible a secret, or at least the time of your departure; otherwise you will be continually interrupted in your preparations by the visits of friends and acquaintance, who will not only rob you of the time you want, but put things out of your mind, so that when you come to sea, you have the mortification to recollect points of business that ought to have been done, accounts you intended to settle, and conveniences you had proposed to bring with you, &c., all which have been omitted through the effect of these officious friendly visits."

On this occasion there were other good reasons for keeping his plans secret. William Whately, whose lawyers had not yet succeeded in bringing his chancery writ to court, had feared that Franklin might escape him and had proposed that he should be held. The authorities had refused, possibly on the ground that the government might be charged with persecution. Nevertheless, Franklin had little time to spare. On May 13, eight days after he had arrived in Philadelphia, an order for his arrest was made in England. Had the order come two months earlier Franklin would never have arrived in France for the work which made American victory possible.

The crossing took six weeks—"the weather constantly so moderate that a London wherry might have accompanied us all the way," as Franklin later told Priestley—and he might have been expected to use the voyage for rest. Instead, he settled down in the confined space of a small cabin to describe the negotiations of the last few months, writing a total of some 250 foolscap pages of dispassionate prose that are a clear guide to what went on during that crucial period.

However, mere writing was not enough for the scientist in his seventieth year. Once the ship was on the high seas he began methodically sampling the ocean, recording its temperature, color and phosphorescence and increasing his knowledge of the Gulf Stream. On the evening of May 5 the ship anchored in the Delaware off Philadelphia, and Franklin went at once to the new home in Market Street which he had never seen, even though his family had moved in nine years previously.

He had sailed from a country at peace; he landed in a country at war. During his weeks on the Atlantic the Colonies had gone through a series of traumatic experiences which were to change the world. Two days after Franklin had sailed from Portsmouth, Patrick Henry, the lawyer and orator who had made his name in attacks on the Stamp Act and was to become governor of Virginia, had called in Virginia's House of Burgesses for the setting up of an armed militia. "The next gale that sweeps from the north," he declaimed, "will bring to our ears the clash of resounding arms! Our brethren are already in the field! Why stand we here idle? What is it that gentlemen wish? What would they have? Is life so dear, or peace so sweet, as to be purchased at the price of chains and slavery? Forbid it, Almighty God! I know not what course others may take; but as for me, give me liberty, or give me death!"

The words were echoed from New York to Georgia as men began to believe that the explosion could not be averted much longer. It came on April 19—the "sudden Mischief" that Franklin had so long feared. General Gage in Boston had decided to take over the military stores being accumulated by radical leaders at Concord, twenty miles away. British security was almost nonexistent and on the evening of the eighteenth Paul Revere, who had taken part in the Boston Tea Party, rode out to warn the countryside. Revere, despite the legend created by Longfellow's famous poem, was turned back by a British patrol. But a colleague got through. When the British reached Lexington the following morning they found a handful of Minutemen facing them.

As the two groups confronted each other, a shot rang out—

Emerson's "shot heard round the world." More than two centuries later, passionate debate still rages as to whether it came from the Americans or the British and even a summary of the arguments would fill many pages. But in the exchange which followed eight Americans were killed and ten wounded. Then the British marched on to Concord, to find most of the military stores already removed. There was a brief encounter with armed farmers, and the British, frustrated, began the twenty-mile march back. But the march was through a countryside now alive with insurgents, and the survivors of what had been a 700-strong British force reached Boston with 99 men dead or missing and 174 wounded. There were different versions of exactly what had happened, with the British action being described as almost everything between wanton vandalism and military necessity. But while General Gage sent his account of the operation to London in the *Sukey,* a loaded merchant ship, the Americans sent theirs in the *Quero,* sailing in ballast. It left Boston four days after the *Sukey* but arrived in London twelve days earlier; thus the story first heard in Europe was the American version.

Franklin's warning about the spark setting the tinder ablaze had been justified. It was General Gage who had drawn the sword, he told Bishop Shipley, "and a war is commenced, which the youngest of us may not see the end of." Later he added: "I found at my arrival [in Philadelphia] all America from one end of the 12 united Provences, to the other, busily employed in learning the use of arms. The attack upon the country people near Boston by the army had roused everybody and exasperated the whole Continent. The tradesmen of [Philadelphia] were in the field twice a day, at 5 in the morning, and six in the afternoon, disciplining with the utmost diligence, all being volunteers. We have now three Battalions, a troop of Light Horse, and a company of Artillery, who have made surprising progress. The same spirit appears everywhere and the unanimity is amazing."

He found that Joseph Reed, a friend of Lord Dartmouth and previously an ardent supporter of agreement with Britain, had "banished from his mind all anxiety or hope for a compromise." The Philosophical Society was searching its books to find the best way of making saltpeter for the manufacture of gunpowder, while even the Quakers, who had rigidly held aloof from all warlike activities, were considering how best to help the population of Boston.

Franklin's unique position was indicated by the *Pennsylvania Packet,* which, on May 8, lauded him with the following lines:

> Welcome! Once more
> To these fair western plains—thy native shore.
>
> Here live beloved, and leave the tools at home
> To run their length, and finish out their doom.
> Here lend thine aid to quench their brutal fires,
> Or fan the flame which Liberty inspires,
> Or fix the grand conductor, that shall guide
> The tempest back, and 'lectrify their pride.
> Rewarding Heaven will bless thy cares at last,
> And future glories glorify the past.
>
> Why stayed the apostate, Wedderburn, behind,
> The scum—the scorn—the scoundrel of mankind?
> Whose heart at large to every vice is known,
> And every devil claims him for his own;
> Why came he not to take the large amount
> Of all we owe him, due on thine account?

Some eighteen months were now to pass before Franklin left Philadelphia for the nine years in France which were to be the climax of his career. During those months he was engaged in a muster of duties extraordinary in their range even for a man of his diverse talents. On the day following his arrival he was nominated by the Pennsylvania Assembly as one of their delegates to the Second Continental Congress, about to meet in Philadelphia. This was merely the beginning and Franklin was soon serving on a multiplicity of committees which from the summer of 1775 to the summer of 1776 helped transform a country of settlers and farmers into an armed nation which could challenge the might of Britain on land and at sea. Notably, he served as president of the Committee of Safety, which the Pennsylvania Assembly set up at the end of June.

"My time was never more fully employed," he was soon writing. "In the morning, at six, I am at the Committee of Safety, appointed by the Assembly to put the province in a state of defence, which Committee holds till nine, when I am at the Congress, and that sits till after four in the afternoon. Both these bodies proceed with the greatest unanimity, and their meetings are well attended. It will scarce be credited in Britain that men can be as diligent with us, from zeal for the public good, as with you for thousands per annum. Such is the difference between uncorrupted new states, and corrupted old ones."

But the wearying work in Assembly and Congress formed only part of Franklin's tasks before he finally set out for France. He led a diplomatic mission to Canada through the ravages of an exceptionally hard winter and nearly succumbed to the effort. He led a final last-minute delegation to Lord Howe, with whom he had unsuccessfully negotiated in London some two years previously and who by the summer of 1776 was in control of New York, and hoping to end the war in its early stages. And he was one of the men whose efforts at raising foreign aid laid the foundations of the State Department.

As Franklin was emerging as the most important of the American rebels—with the possible exception of Washington, commander of America's new Continental army—the Battle of Bunker Hill removed the last chance of confining the conflict. Two months later George III declared the Colonies in a state of rebellion: Franklin's hopes had at last been destroyed, his worst fears realized.

He had by this time settled into his new home, happy to be cared for by his daughter, Sally, and her husband. He was only slowly recovering from the effects of the Atlantic crossing, on which he had been forced to eat a lot of salt meat, and in Congress found himself sitting ten or twelve hours a day without exercise. He had, as he recalled, "frequent giddinesses."

One personal problem was soon presented by his son. More than once in the early seventies he had been asked by William to suggest to the British ministry that his governor's salary might be raised. Franklin had refused to help and, although continuing to hold office as deputy postmaster, had shown distaste that his son should beg for more money from the British.

Now, back in Philadelphia, he found waiting for him a note from William rejoicing in the fact that his governorship had not been affected by his father's misfortune. William received a brisk reply. "I don't understand it as any favour to me or to you, the being continued in an office, by which with all your Prudence, you cannot avoid running behind hand, if you live suitably to your Station. While you are in it, I know you will execute it with Fidelity to your Master, but I think Independence more honourable than any Service, & that in the State of American Affairs, which from the present arbitrary measures is likely soon to take place, you will find yourself in no comfortable Situation, & perhaps wish you had soon disengaged yourself." Shortly afterward William arrived in Philadelphia. Franklin failed to change his son's views, and the Governor returned soon afterward to Perth Amboy, taking with him his own son, William Temple.

The ease with which a royal governor could visit and leave the headquarters town of the rebellious Congress was an indication of the curious situation that was maintained throughout the later months of 1775. Communications between North America and Britain were not entirely cut, and Franklin continued to receive uncensored—but intercepted—letters from London. One came from Mrs. Stevenson, describing how happy she would be when Franklin was back in England, confirming the expectation of return which he mentioned in a letter to his lawyer, Thomas Life: "I did then [in March 1775] propose returning in October." Another came from Dr. Bancroft, the American who had written admiringly of Franklin after the confrontation in the Cockpit. "I strongly hope however," it said, "that the ill success which I am persuaded will attend all the attempts of the Army & Navy in America this summer may at the commencement of next winter compel the present ministry to quit the helm, which they have so unwisely and wickedly conducted and that they may be succeeded by others who will contribute to a permanent and equitable reconciliation between Great Britain and the Colonies. I shall be happy at all times to hear of your welfare & to receive & execute any commands with which you may think fit to honour me."

Not only did mail continue to flow west across the Atlantic; Franklin himself was still able to write to England. One of his first letters was to Edmund Burke.

You will see by the papers, that General Gage called his assembly to propose Lord North's pacific plan; but before they could meet, drew the sword and began the war. His troops made a most vigorous retreat, —twenty miles in three hours, —scarce to be paralleled in history; the feeble Americans, who pelted them all the way, could scarce keep up with them.

All people here feel themselves much obliged by your endeavours to serve them. I hear your proposed resolves were negatived by a great majority, which was denying the most notorious truths, and a kind of national lying, of which they may be convicted by their own records.

The congress is met here pretty full. I had not been here a day before I was returned a member. We dined together on Saturday, when your health was among the foremost. With the sincerest esteem. . . .

For his part, Burke was impressed, writing to Count Patrick D'Arcy, *maréchal-de-camp* in the French army, "What say you to your friend and brother Philosopher Franklin, who at upwards of seventy years of age, quits the Study of the Laws of Nature, in order to give Laws to new Commonwealths; and has crossed the Atlantick ocean at that time of Life, not to seek repose but to plunge into the midst of the most laborious and most arduous affairs that ever were. Few things more extraordinary have happened in the history of mankind."

Franklin also wrote to Priestley and to other friends. He advised against investment in the Colonies, presumably on the ground that an American victory would mean loss of the investment, settled his finances in Britain without trouble and instructed his bankers to clear his account with John Sargent, one of his colleagues in the Grand Ohio Company. "It may possibly soon be all I shall have left," he told Sargent in explaining how the money would be paid, "as my American Property consists chiefly of Houses in our Seaport Towns, which your Ministry have begun to burn, and I suppose are wicked enough to burn them all. It now requires great Wisdom on your Side [of] the Water to prevent a total Separation; I hope it will be found among you. We shall give you one Opportunity more of recovering our Affections and retaining the Connection; and that I fear will be the last."

The following month he was even more despairing when he wrote to Priestley. Britain "has begun to burn our seaport towns; secure, I suppose, that we shall never be able to return the outrage in kind," he said. "She may doubtless destroy them all; but, if she wishes to recover our commerce, are these the probable means? She must certainly be distracted; for no tradesman out of Bedlam ever thought of increasing the number of his customers, by knocking them on the head, or of enabling them to pay their debts, by burning their houses. If she wishes to have us subjects, and that we should submit to her as our compound sovereign, she is now giving us such miserable specimens of her government, that we shall ever detest and avoid it, as a complication of robbery, murder, famine, fire, and pestilence.''

This criticism of the war and the way in which the British were waging it was not confined to Franklin and to those in the Colonies who thought like him. In the papers of Lord Dartmouth there exists a remarkable letter of protest from no less a person than John Wesley. ''All my prejudices are against the Americans,'' he wrote to Dartmouth on June 14, 1775, ''for I am an High Churchman, the son of a High Churchman, bred up from my childhood in the highest notions of passive obedience and non-resistance; and yet in spite of all my rooted prejudice, I cannot avoid thinking (if I think at all) that an oppressed people asked for nothing more than their legal rights and that in the most modest and inoffensive manner which the nature of the thing would allow. But waiving this, waiving all considerations of Right and Wrong, I ask, is it common sense to use force toward the Americans? . . . O my Lord, if your Lordship can do anything, let it not be wanting! For God's sake, for the sake of the King, of the nation, of your lovely family, remember Rehoboam! Remember Philip the Second! Remember King Charles the First!''

While Franklin protested with the best, his protests were made with a moderation which his enemies at times misunderstood. Sir Henry Barkly, who for two years acted as a successful British spy in Philadelphia, reported back to Grey Cooper in Whitehall on June 19: ''By all I can learn Mr. Franklin is among those who are for moderation, and bringing about reconciliatory measures, but he is a deep designing man, and it is not easy coming at his real intentions, but hitherto (my friends tell me), he appears on the side of moderation: the Americans has a high Opinion of his principals and penetration, by which means he will have great influence on their deliberations.''

Hugh Finlay, on H.M.S. *Kingfisher* stationed off Sandy Hook on the Jersey shore, south of Long Island, also reflected the view that some Englishmen still held of Franklin and his beliefs. ''They say that Doctor Franklin is come over with a hearty intention to do every thing in his power to heal the wounds that the false friends of America have given her,'' he wrote to his brother-in-law. ''He is justly esteem'd a man of sense and penetration and it is confidently said that he will leave no stone unturned to show the Americans the right path. Heaven grant him success in this righteous Fatherly intention.''

Both Barkly and Finlay were justified when they emphasized Franklin's essential moderation, his perpetual hope of a compromise even after the fighting had begun. But the line between honest compromise and a weakness for surrender is at times rather slim, and in the summer of 1775 Franklin knew that he could easily be misunderstood. On July 5, it is true, John Dickinson had drawn up the "Olive Branch Petition," repeating Colonial grievances but asking for the King's intervention and an end to hostilities until a reconciliation could be worked out—a petition which George III refused to receive. But Franklin felt it necessary to distance himself from too conciliatory a stance and on the day that the Olive Branch Petition was signed he wrote a singular letter to his old friend William Strahan. Both men had long supported different attitudes to the Colonial problem but both agreed to differ in a civilized way. As far back as November 1770 Strahan had told David Hall, Dr. Franklin "and I differ widely in our American politics, which I am heartily sorry for, as I esteem him highly. —But tho' we *differ* we do not *disagree;* and must ever be good Friends, as I trust we aim at both the same End, tho' we differ in the Means." But now it appeared that that phase had ended. "Mr. Strahan," went Franklin's letter, "You are a Member of Parliament, and one of that Majority which has doomed my Country to Destruction—You have begun to burn our Towns, and murder our People. —Look upon your Hands! They are stained with the Blood of your Relations! —You and I were long Friends: —You are now my Enemy, —and I am, Yours, B. Franklin."

In the same month, William Bradford, Jr., wrote to James Madison: "The suspicions against Dr. Franklin have died away; whatever his design at coming over here, I believe he has now chosen his side, and favors our cause." Franklin did favor the cause, but the Strahan letter was hardly evidence of this for one very good reason. It was never sent.

Perhaps more significant is the fact that Franklin and Strahan maintained their correspondence as long as was possible throughout 1775. Strahan long believed that his old friend might return to Britain, "invested with full Powers to terminate all Differences upon reasonable and solid terms. Believe me," he continued, "I think so well of this office that I hope it is actually reserved for you, and that the successful conclusion of so important a Treaty will crown the Operations of a Life spent in the Investigation of every useful Branch of Knowledge, and in the service of his Country in particular."

Three months later Strahan was warning that in a few years of fighting America was likely to suffer more than "the Amount of all the Taxes the British Parliament (always considering themselves as the representative of every British Subject) would probably have imposed upon them for a Century to come." And in October, using the last regular packet from England to America, Strahan delivered to Franklin what appeared to be his final judgment. "I am still of the opinion that the Ministry of this Country was never disposed to fleece or oppress you, that this unnatural Civil War has been chiefly, if not wholly, occasioned by our wicked Factions at Home, whose Struggles for Places & Power have by degrees carried them such daring lengths as have induced & encouraged you to increase your Demands much beyond what you at first dreamt of. . . . I am sorry to differ from you, *toto coelo*," he concluded, "in this great Political Dispute; but I can nevertheless subscribe myself with great Truth, Dear Sir, Your affectionate humble Servant, Will Strahan."

The tone of Franklin's response to these friendly letters was very different from that of the "my enemy" letter. He wrote from Philadelphia on October 3:

Since my arrival here, I have received Four Letters from you, the last dated August 2, all filled with your Reasonings and Persuasions, and Arguments and Intimidations on the Dispute between Britain & America, which are very well written, and if you have shewn them to your Friends the Ministers, I dare say they have done you credit. In Answer I can only say that I am too fully engaged in actual Business to write much; and I know your opinions are not easily changed. You wish me to come over with Proposals of Accommodation. Your Ministers have made that impracticable for me, by prosecuting me with a frivolous Chancery Suit in the name of Whately, by which, as my Sollicitor writes me, I shall certainly be imprisoned if I appear again in England. Nevertheless, send us over hither fair Proposals of Peace, if you choose it, and no body shall be more ready than myself to promote their Acceptation: For I make it a Rule not to mix personal Resentments with Public Business. They have voted me here 1000 Dollars an annum as Postmaster General, and I have devoted the whole Sum to the Assistance of such as have been disabled in the Defence of their Country, that I might not have, or be suspected to have the least interested Motive for keeping the Breach open. My love to Mrs. Strahan and Peggy. I am ever

Dear Sir, Your affectionate humble Servant.

B. FRANKLIN

Present my respectful compliments to my dear Friend Sir John Pringle; and To Mr. Cooper when you see him.

It was the love rather than the enmity which was remembered and in 1778 Franklin and his colleague Silas Deane, both serving in Paris, were glad to accept a large Stilton cheese sent across the Channel from William Strahan in London.

None of this continuing friendship was publicized in Philadelphia and it seems inescapable that the aborted "you are my enemy" letter was a successful piece of propaganda. It certainly removed any doubts that the more radical Colonists may have had about the man who had lived in England so happily, so long.

While Franklin's attitude had in some quarters been under suspicion—a suspicion nourished by the political residues of a quarter century, questionings about what the Vandalia affair had really meant and the fact that his son was the still staunchly loyal governor of New Jersey—no one had doubted his administrative ability. One of the first measures approved by Congress had been to appoint a six-man committee under Franklin's chairmanship to consider the best means of establishing posts for conveying letters and intelligence throughout North America. Congress adopted his plan and appointed him postmaster general, a move which dismayed the British in New York. There was great confusion there, John Antill wrote from the city in a secret note to Anthony Todd in Whitehall. "I think the storm thickens, the Congress has appointed Doctor Franklin Postmaster-General of North America and the different Posts will be soon Established so that I suppose in a few days we shall have nothing to do. God only knows what will be the end of it. All Business is Stopped & there seems nothing going forward but exercising." One of Franklin's first acts was to appoint his son-in-law, Richard Bache, as his secretary.

In August, Congress adjourned for a few weeks and Franklin took the opportunity of visiting his loyal governor son at Perth Amboy. He tried to win William from the loyalist cause. He was unsuccessful and in less than a year was to witness his son branded as a traitor to America and placed under house arrest.

He arrived back in Philadelphia in time for resumption of the debates in Congress, where his new vigor was at once noticed by enemies as well as friends. To Sir Henry Barkly, he was now "a daring arteful insinuating incendiary" and Sir Henry, who warned London that he was obliged "to use the greatest precaution in forwarding my letters, for fear of being discovered," was able to report: "The disguise Mr. Franklin put on for some time after his arrival, is in a great degree thrown off, he appears now openly for independency, and I believe has all along in his heart been of those principles, but he artefully at the beginning lead the people such lengths that he knows now that they cannot retract."

This was only a partial truth. Two days before Sir Henry wrote, Franklin warned David Hartley in words that mingled resolution with regret: "I am persuaded the body of the British people are our friends; but they are changeable, and by your lying Gazettes may soon be made our enemies. Our respect for them will proportionally diminish; and I see clearly we are on the high road to mutual enmity, hatred, and detestation. A separation will of course be inevitable. 'Tis a million of pities so fair a plan as we have hitherto been engaged in for increasing strength and empire with *public felicity*, should be destroyed by the mangling hands of a few blundering ministers. It will not be destroyed: God will protect and prosper it: You will only exclude yourselves from any share in it. We hear that more ships and troops are coming out. We know you may do us a great deal of mischief, but we are determined to bear it patiently as long as we can; but, if you flatter yourselves with beating us into submission, you know neither the people nor the *country*."

Much the same feeling that events had passed the point of no return was being expressed on the other side. "If the Boston Port Bill had not furnished a Pretence for a Rebellion something else would have brought it forth," General Gage informed Lord Dartmouth on October 15, 1775.

Yet even at this late stage, while Franklin was writing of a separate course as "inevitable," and while Gage was stressing that only force could be relied on, there was still, in the Colonies, a strong reluctance to sever all links with Britain except as a last resort. "We cannot in this country conceive that there are Men in England so infatuated as seriously to suspect the Congress, or people here, of a Wish to erect ourselves into an independent State," John Adams wrote early in October 1775. "If such an Idea really obtains amongst those at the Helm of Affairs, one Hour's residence in America would eradicate it. I never met one Individual so inclined, but it is universally disavowed. Whatever Views the Delegates from the Massachusetts may have, inspired by a keen Sense of Miseries their Country has endured, they have never disclosed Sentiments favourable to an Independancy on [sic] Great-Britain."

By this time there had been set up the first of the two congressional committees on whose success the war was to depend. This was the Secret Committee of Congress, created to buy war supplies under the chairmanship of Thomas Willing. Franklin was one of its members and early in October was appointed with Thomas Lynch of South Carolina and Benjamin Harrison of Virginia to visit General Washington in his Cambridge headquarters to discover the army's needs.

They arrived on October 16 and heard Washington's views on the formation and equipping of a 20,000-man army of twenty-six regiments, as well as on the methods to be followed in selling prize captures and in exchanging prisoners in the long and bloody war which was now seen as inevitable.

One man was particularly impressed by Franklin. He was General Nathanael Greene, commander of the forces from Rhode Island, and a distant relative by marriage of Catharine Greene, whom Franklin had first met years earlier as Catharine Ray. "I had the honor," he wrote, "to be introduced to that very great man Dr. Franklin, whom I viewed with silent admiration the whole evening. Attention watched his lips, and conviction closed his periods."

Back in Philadelphia, Franklin was appointed with Benjamin Harrison, Thomas Johnson, John Dickinson and John Hay to the diplomatic equivalent to the Secret Committee of Congress, the Committee of Secret Correspondence, a title it was to hold until April 1777, when it became the Committee for Foreign Affairs. The direct forerunner of the State Department, it had the aim of "corresponding with our friends in Great Britain, Ireland, and other parts of the world" and of "lay[ing] their correspondence before Congress when directed."

In 1775 the Colonies still had little industry, certainly no arms industry, no navy, and a military tradition limited largely to frontier warfare. As they began to confront the military forces which had defeated the French Empire a decade previously, their credit-worthiness was small, and the success of the war thus rested very largely on the success of the two "secret" committees whose names are often confused and whose functions certainly tended to overlap. Franklin was not only a member of both committees but also far more experienced than any other member in the ways of Europe, where the Colonies' salvation obviously lay. He had a formidable reputation in France, the most obvious of the potential sources of arms and equipment, and it was very largely he who was to sustain the enterprise in the difficult days ahead.

Before this episode in his life was to begin, he was given another responsibility, one which would have stretched the abilities of any man. This was the virtually hopeless task of saving American prospects in Canada. It had been clear to General Washington since the outbreak of hostilities that the British in Canada, holding their fortresses on the St. Lawrence, were a standing threat to the security of the Colonies. An audacious British general could well lead a force south through the long trench in which lay Lakes Champlain and George, reach the Hudson and invest New York from the north. To counter such a move two small American forces were sent north in October. Sir Guy Carleton, the British commander in Montreal, made a strategic withdrawal downstream to Quebec, and the American forces under Richard Montgomery entered an undefended Montreal in November. After that, things began to go wrong. An assault on Quebec failed. The Americans found themselves short of provisions, short of munitions and living among French-Canadians who stubbornly refused to throw in their lot with the Americans and help fight the British. Then, to make matters worse, smallpox broke out.

The situation looked desperate, and on February 15, 1776, Congress resolved that a committee of three, two of whom were to be members of Congress, should visit Canada. Congress then did what the Pennsylvania Assembly had done more than once in a tight corner: asked Franklin to use his good offices.

In March 1776, he set out with three companions for the testing journey; with him went the Protestant Samuel Chase, the Catholic Charles Carroll and John Carroll, a Jesuit priest who was to become the first Roman Catholic archbishop of the United States. Charles Carroll was from Maryland and reputed to be among the richest men in America, worth between £150,000 and £200,000. Educated in France, he spoke French perfectly and, as John Adams put it, was "yet a warm, a firm, a zealous Supporter of the Rights of America, in whose Cause he has hazarded his all." Opposition from the Canadians had been partly on religious grounds—the Catholics in the province of Quebec numbered 150,000, the Protestants 360—and it was felt that they might be more easily converted to the American cause by the arguments of two Catholics.

The British had been well warned of what was afoot. Lord George Germain, secretary of state for the Colonies, was to receive a letter dated March 28 of which the P.S. read: "I have just heard that two of the delegates (Dr. Franklin and Mr. Chace) have passed through Woodbridge this Morning in their Way to Canada, accompanied by a Mr. Carrol, a Roman Catholic Gentleman of great Estate in Maryland, and a Romish Priest or two. It is suggested that their principal Business is to prevail on the Canadians to enter into the Confederacy with the other Colonies and to send Delegates to the Continental Congress. It is likewise reported that a great Number of the Continental Troops have returned to Albany, not being able to cross the Lakes, several Soldiers, Carriages etc. having fallen in, and some Lives lost, by the Breaking of the Ice." The warning of Franklin's mission came from Perth Amboy and was signed by the Governor, Franklin's son.

The French, also, knew the significance of the move, and on May 17 M. Garnier, the French chargé d'affaires in London, told the French foreign minister, Charles Gravier, Comte de Vergennes, of Franklin's mission: "The sending of this man, who may be regarded as the best intellect of the Continental Congress, shows us," he wrote, "that the Americans attach the greatest importance to gaining the minds of the Canadians, and to show[ing] them their interests sufficiently to induce them to make common cause." Vergennes, who had watched the British remove Canada from the French Empire, must have had mixed feelings. So must Franklin, who seventeen years earlier had so strongly urged that Britain should take Canada from the French; now he was to urge that it should be taken back again—but into American rather than French hands.

He and his companions arrived early in April in New York,

where they were joined by Frederick William Baron de Woedtke, sent from Philadelphia to accompany them on their mission. It was a very different city now from the one he had once known, "no more the gay, polite place it used to be esteemed," John Carroll wrote to his mother. It had, he went on, "become almost a desert unless for the troops. The people were expecting a bombardment, and had therefore removed themselves and their effects out of the town; and on the other side the troops were working at the fortifications with the utmost activity."

At five on the afternoon of April 2 Franklin and his party set sail up the Hudson for Albany. From the first, almost everything that could go wrong did go wrong, and they reached their destination only after their mainsail had been torn to pieces by storms. From Albany they continued north by road. But at Saratoga, where General Schuyler received them, it was obvious that their difficulties were just beginning. Before moving on, Franklin wrote to Josiah Quincy in a mood that, for him, was something like despair: "I am here on my way to Canada, detained by the present state of the Lakes, in which the unthawed ice obstructs navigation," he wrote. "I begin to apprehend that I have undertaken a fatigue that at my time of life may prove too much for me; so I sit down to write to a few friends by way of farewell."

It took the party thirty-six hours to cover the twenty-six-mile length of Lake George. Then their improvised boat had to be drawn overland by oxen to the shores of Lake Champlain. Somewhere en route Franklin picked up a warm, soft, shapeless cap of marten fur. A useful protection from the bitter weather, it was, a year and more later in France, to become a symbol of the homespun philosopher. On April 29 they reached Montreal. "We . . . were received at the landing by General Arnold and a great body of officers, gentry &c., and saluted by firing of cannon, and other military honours," John Carroll wrote. "Being conducted to the general's house, we were served with a glass of wine, while people were crowding in to pay their compliments, which ceremony being over, we were shown into another apartment, and unexpectedly met in it a large assembly of ladies, most of them French. After drinking tea, and sitting some time, we went to an elegant supper, which was followed with the singing of the ladies, which proved very agreeable, and would have been much more so, if we had not been so much fatigued with our journey."

Franklin was more than fatigued. "On the passage," he later wrote, "I suffered much from a number of large boiles. In Canada my legs swelled, and I apprehended dropsy." If his personal condition was poor, that of the cause was worse. "Our misfortunes in Canada, are enough to melt an Heart of Stone," John Adams wrote to his wife when he learned of the situation a few weeks later. "The Small Pox is ten times more terrible than Britons, Canadians and Indians together. This was the cause of our precipitate Retreat from Quebec. . . . There has been Want, approaching to Famine, as well as Pestilence. And these Discouragements seem to have so disheartened our Officers, that none of them seem to Act with Prudence and Firmness."

Above all, there was the shortage of money that was to hamper the Americans until the last days of the war. "We have tried in vain to borrow some hard money here, for the immediate occasion of the army, either on the public, or on our own private credit," the Commissioners wrote back to Congress. "We cannot even sell sterling bills of exchange, which some of us have offered to draw. It seems it had been expected, and given out by our friends, that we should bring money with us. The disappointment has discouraged everybody, and established an opinion that none is to be had, or that the Congress has not credit enough in their own colonies to procure it. Many of our friends are drained dry; others say they are so, fearing, perhaps, we shall never be able to reimburse them." Franklin did what he could, advancing the army commander, General Arnold, £353 in gold out of his own pocket.

Worse was to come. A week after the Commissioners arrived in Montreal there came bad news from Quebec. A British fleet had arrived off the city and was disembarking strong reinforcements. It was decided that Chase and Charles Carroll should remain in Montreal but that Franklin should return with John Carroll, first to New York and then on to Philadelphia. The British soon knew of the decision. On May 25 the naval commander at Quebec, Captain Charles Douglas of H.M.S. *Isis,* noted in a report to the Admiralty: "A Triumvirate, consisting of Dr. Franklin and other Members of the Rebel Congress, went away in a great hurry on hearing of the flight of their Army (of 3,000 Men) from before Quebec."

From the note that Franklin sent back to Montreal from New York, where he arrived with Carroll on May 27, the reason for his return seems obvious: "As to myself," he said, "I find I grow daily more feeble, and think I could hardly have got along so far but for Mr. Carroll's friendly assistance and tender care of me. Some symptoms of the gout now appear, which makes me think my indisposition has been a smothered fit of that disorder, which my constitution wanted strength to form completely. I have had several fits of it formerly." To all except the most optimistic it must have seemed that Franklin, aged and ailing, had performed his last service for America.

He was in bad shape when he regained Philadelphia, and spent the next few weeks getting back his strength on a friend's farm outside the city. His illness kept him from Congress, unusual for him, and on June 21 he wrote to Washington that he knew "little of what has pass'd there, except that a Declaration of Independence is preparing."

By that date Franklin had in fact been appointed—with Thomas Jefferson, John Adams, Roger Sherman of Connecticut and Robert R. Livingston of New York—to draw up a declaration that could be formally announced to the world. Opinion had moved slowly and would no doubt have moved even more slowly had it not been for British activities which progressively weakened any remaining chance of conciliation. British attacks on American coastal towns; attempts to enlist slaves into British service and to use the Ohio Indians as they had been used by the French; and, in Europe, preparations to enlist thousands of mercenaries—all slowly convinced the Americans that their only hope lay in complete independence.

Another factor in crystallizing the American attitude was a fortuitous result of Franklin's benevolent help to all and sundry. In the autumn of 1774 he had been brought into contact with a young Quaker dismissed from the excise service for demanding better pay. The young man wanted to start a new life in America, and Franklin wrote a note for his son-in-law, Richard Bache, introducing Mr. Thomas Paine, "a Grub Street writer in London, when he fell into the Doctor's Way," according to one of Dartmouth's correspondents. After a year's journalism in Philadelphia, Paine was introduced to Benjamin Rush, already one of America's best-known doctors and a man who had met Franklin while completing his training in Edinburgh. Rush had intended to write a pamphlet supporting independence but feared the publicity might harm his profession, and proposed that Paine should do so.

The result was *Common Sense,* a forty-seven-page pamphlet that appeared in January 1776 and advocated independence in terms that ordinary men and women could understand. It sold some 120,000 copies within a few months, opened up the discussion and made the task that much easier for the five-man committee now appointed to draw up the Declaration of Independence. Its members acted quickly. Within less than three weeks, Jefferson had prepared a draft and submitted it to Franklin and Adams. Jefferson and Adams later gave differing accounts about what happened next—by no means remarkable, since both men were recollecting events many years after they happened. Various alterations were made, and it appears that Franklin changed the description of certain truths from "sacred & undeniable" to "self-evident," but it is clear from Carl Becker's *The Declaration of Independence* that uncertainty surrounds the details.

On July 1 Congress debated the Declaration of Independence for nine hours. Pennsylvania and South Carolina opposed it, the Delaware delegation was divided, while the New York delegation still awaited its instructions. The debate was postponed until the following day. Agreement came on July 4. On July 6 the Declaration, in which the phrase "United States of America" was used for the first time, was published in the Pennsylvania *Evening Post,* and on July 8 it was read in the State House yard, the royal coat of arms torn down and burned, the Liberty Bell rung.

Only on August 2 was the Declaration of Independence formally signed. John Hancock, the president, signed first, in large letters, it is said, so that George III could read his name without putting on spectacles. Legend asserts that he warned: "We must be unanimous; there must be no pulling different ways; we must all hang together," and that Franklin replied: "Yes, we must, indeed, all hang together, or most assuredly we shall all hang separately." No contemporary record substantiates the story, which first surfaced in 1840 when Jared Sparks recorded it as "another anecdote related of Franklin."

He might, it is true, have made such a witticism, even though he knew better than most men in Congress that the Declaration was more a hope for the future than a reinforcement of the present. And a reinforcement was increasingly necessary. Boston had been evacuated by British troops, but even while the details of the Declaration were being hammered out, these same troops were coming ashore on Staten Island against negligible resistance. Soon afterward strong reinforcements were being landed there. By August Washington's 18,000 men were facing a well-equipped professional army of 32,000.

Yet the British were by no means happy at the prospects of unlimited war opening up before them. Surely, they vainly hoped, it was still possible to avert what a growing number of Britons saw as a catastrophe. The task of the British commanders two Howes, was therefore not only to land troops which would help drive Washington from New York, but—as commissioners—also to offer proposals which, it was almost pathetically hoped, would pave the way to peace. So optimistic was Admiral Howe that at Halifax, on his journey to New York, he had told Admiral Arbuthnot that peace with America "would be made within ten days of his arrival."

He cast anchor in the *Eagle* off New York on the day that Congress adopted the Declaration of Independence. But once again the government in London had grossly misjudged the situation. Howe was authorized to grant pardons to "the rebels," with certain exceptions, but was not officially authorized even to discuss terms of peace. His first difficulty lay in starting a peace initiative. He could not write to Congress, regarded as an illegal body by George III. A letter sent to George Washington, Esq., instead of to General Washington, was returned as wrongly addressed. Next Howe wrote to Franklin, who had already received from David Barclay a hint that an approach would be made: "I could not with any satisfaction," Barclay wrote, "avoid informing my Friend Doctor Franklin that Lord Howe continues as respectable a Character at this hour, as when we last parted—a Hint, that I thought, in every point of view, consistent for me to communicate to my respectable Friend, at this critical Conjuncture; with this addition, that whatever the mission of Lord Howe may prove, I am firmly persuaded that it will not be for want of inclination in him, should the Ollive Branch not rise superior to the direful din of war."

There was some delay before Congress authorized Franklin to

answer Howe's "Olive Branch." His reply was as uncompromising as he could make it. "Directing pardons to be offered the Colonies, who are the very parties injured, expresses indeed that opinion of our ignorance, baseness and insensibility which your uninformed and proud nation has long been pleased to entertain of us," he said, "but it can have no other effect than that of increasing our resentment. It is impossible we should think of submission to a government that has with the most wanton barbarity and cruelty burnt our defenseless towns in the midst of winter, excited the savages to massacre our farmers and our slaves to murder their masters, and is even now bringing foreign mercenaries to deluge our settlements with blood." The last point was particularly significant. Not many Englishmen were willing to take up arms and sail 3,000 miles to fight their compatriots; but there were small German states whose authoritarian rulers were willing to sell their subjects to Britain's forces at so much a head. Howe's forces outside New York already included 6,000 Hessians.

Franklin's letter, in which he recapitulated his own long and sincere efforts to prevent war breaking out, ended with a backhanded compliment to Howe, written no doubt with the letter from David Barclay in mind. "I know your great motive in coming hither," he wrote, "was the hope of being instrumental in a reconciliation; and I believe, when you find *that* impossible on any terms given you to propose, you will relinquish so odious a command, and return to a more honorable private station."

But Howe, like Franklin, knew where duty lay. Howe replied from the *Eagle* on August 16, 1776, ending: "I will only add, that as the dishonour to which you deem me exposed by my military situation in this country, has effected no change in your sentiments of personal regard towards me; so shall no difference in political points alter my desire of proving how much I am your sincere and obedient humble Servant, HOWE."

There followed the Battle of Long Island on August 27, 1776, and Washington's skillful withdrawal on the twenty-ninth and thirtieth. During the fighting General John Sullivan was captured by the British and was then sent by Howe to Philadelphia to request a private conversation with members of Congress. Howe appears totally to have misunderstood the situation, believing that after Washington's withdrawal his opponents would welcome terms of surrender if they could be worked out in a gentlemanly way. This was by no means the case. Only after some discussion did Congress decide that while "it was improper to appoint any of their Members to confer, in their private Characters with his Lordship . . . they would appoint a Committee of their Body, to wait on him, to know whether he had Power, to treat with Congress upon Terms of Peace and to hear any Propositions, that his Lordship may think proper to make."

Almost inevitably, Franklin was the leader of the committee. Its other members were John Adams and Edward Rutledge of South Carolina. On their way to meet Howe they spent the night at New Brunswick and here there occurred a slightly farcical incident that nevertheless illustrates Franklin's persistence at hammering home his ideas. There were many troops on the march, accommodations were scarce and John Adams and Franklin were forced to spend the night in a small room which had only one window.

"The Window was open," Adams subsequently wrote, "and I, who was an invalid and afraid of the Air in the night blowing upon me, shut it close. 'Oh!' says Franklin, 'don't shut the Window. We shall be suffocated.' I answered I was afraid of the Evening Air. Dr. Franklin replied: 'The Air within this Chamber will soon be, and indeed is now worse than that without Doors: come! open the Window and come to bed, and I will convince you: I believe you are not acquainted with my Theory of Colds.' Opening the Window and leaping into Bed, I said I had read his Letters to Dr. Cooper in which he had advanced, that Nobody ever got cold by going into a cold Church, or any other cold Air but the Theory was so little consistent with my experience, that I thought it a Paradox: However I had so much curiosity to hear his reasons, that I would run the risque of a cold. The Doctor then began a harrangue upon Air and cold and Respiration and Perspiration, with which I was so much amused that I soon fell asleep, and left him and his Philosophy together; but I believe they were equally sound and insensible, within a few minutes after me, for the last Words I heard pronounced as if he was more than half asleep. . . . I remember little of the Lecture, except, that the human Body, by Respiration and Perspiration, destroys a gallon of Air in a minute; that two such Persons as were now in that Chamber, would consume all the Air in it, in an hour or two: that by breathing over again the matter thrown off, by the Lungs and the Skin, We should imbibe the real Cause of Colds, not from abroad but from within."

From New Brunswick the members of the committee rode on to Perth Amboy, from whose governor's house William Franklin had recently been taken by the revolutionary forces. From Staten Island, across the narrow waters of Arthur Kill, there came Howe's barge, carrying a British officer whom Howe had offered to leave in Perth Amboy as hostage for the committee's safe return from a company in which all three were, technically, treasonable felons. To this gentlemanly act the committee gave a gentlemanly response: they took the hostage back across the waters with them. Howe, appreciating the gesture, was notably cordial but led the three men through a double line of Hessian troops—no doubt a psychologically significant touch—to a house where they sat down to a cold lunch and, in effect, a discussion as to whether the War of Independence could be called off.

A brief account of the meeting, held in the Billopp House, or the "Manor of Bentley," overlooking Raritan Bay, was sent back by Howe to Lord George Germain, the British secretary of state for the Colonies (George Sackville Germain, known as Lord George Sackville from 1720 until 1770, then as Lord George Germain until 1782, when he was created Viscount Sackville). "The Three Gentlemen," this ran, "were very explicit in their Opinions that the associated Colonies would not accede to any Peace or Alliance, but as free and independent States; and they endeavored to prove that Great Britain would derive more extensive and more durable Advantages from such an Alliance, than from the Connection it was the object of the Commission to restore. Their Arguments not meriting a serious Attention, the Conversation ended, and the Gentlemen returned to Amboy."

Neither Franklin's own account nor that of Henry Strachey, secretary to Howe, differ very much. Franklin was the natural leader of the Americans, and not only because he was, in effect, carrying on the negotiations he had tried to open some two years previously after the games of chess in Miss Howe's London house. But from the first there was little chance of success. "Forces have been sent out and towns have been burnt," he emphasized. "We can not now expect happiness under the domination of Great Britain. All former attachments are obliterated.

America can not return to the domination of Great Britain, and I imagine that Great Britain means to rest it upon force." Even had this not been so, the men on Staten Island were virtually powerless to affect events. Howe's commission, as John Adams interpreted it, authorized him "to grant Pardons upon Submission, and to converse, confer, consult and advise with such Persons as he may think proper, upon American Grievances, upon the Instructions to Governors and the Acts of Parliament, and if any Errors should be found to have crept in, his Majesty and the Ministry were willing they should be rectified." In his report to Lord George Germain, Lord Howe pointed out that that was, in fact, the extent of his commission, noting that "for very obvious Reasons, we could not enter into any Treaty with their Congress, and much less proceed in any Conference or Negociation, upon the inadmissable Ground of Independency; a Pretension which the Commissioners had not, nor was it possible they ever should have, Authority to acknowledge." Franklin and his colleagues could of course accept nothing less.

At the water's edge there was a courteous parting and the Americans landed from the Admiral's barge onto New Jersey soil once again. As an Englishman was to remark shortly afterward: "They met, they talked, they parted, and now nothing remains but to fight it out."

"It was an agreable Excursion," John Adams informed his wife after his arrival back in Philadelphia. "His L[ordshi]p is about fifty Years of Age. He is a well bred Man, but his Address is not so irresistable, as it has been represented. I could name you many Americans, in your own Neighbourhood, whose Art, Address, and Abilities are greatly superiour. His head is rather confused, I think."

Confused as the Admiral's head may have been, he had every reason for believing that ultimate British success was inevitable. The Royal Navy commanded the seas. If Britons hardly leapt to arms unbidden, there was a satisfactory supply of foreign troops whose services could be bought from their continental owners. Quite as important, the rebellious Americans lacked the strong industrial and economic foundations which were necessary if arms and ammunition were to be made or bought. In the autumn of 1776 American prospects looked exceedingly bleak.

It was this prospect to which Congress addressed itself after Franklin and his two companions returned to Philadelphia.

TEN

BATTLE
FOR ARMS

Y THE SUMMER OF 1776 CONGRESS HAD already, if only reluctantly, turned to France for help; many members remembered the wars in which the French had encouraged Indian atrocities against their enemies —just as the British were now doing. But France, it was rightly believed, would not be averse to encouraging the Americans against what Louis XVI's foreign minister, the Comte de Vergennes, had described as the restless and greedy England. Secret aid might be all that could be expected to start with, but that would be better than nothing.

A complex series of undercover negotiations on which the arming of the American forces was to depend had begun in the autumn of 1775; only in February 1778, with the signing of treaties between the Americans and the French, did the covert operations come into the light of day. A number of factors had made them even more tortuous than might have been expected. On the French side, Vergennes had, of course, been bitter at the loss of the French Empire during the succession of wars with the British. And what could be a better revenge than aiding the Colonists in a war of attrition that might liquidate British possessions in North America just as the Seven Years' War had liquidated the French? But there were at least three qualifications to the position as it was seen from Paris. For one thing, France and Britain were ostensibly on good diplomatic terms with each other, and French supply of arms to the Colonists would consequently have to be circumspect. Secondly, the Americans might not win; their chances, indeed, looked poor, and backing a loser is rarely good diplomatic policy. Moreover if the Americans, in revolt against George III, had a certain distaste for begging help from an absolute monarch, the French themselves were not entirely free from ideological doubts. Whatever the economic motives behind the Stamp Act or the Boston Tea Party, it was plain that across the Atlantic ordinary people were in revolt against their king, an act which it might be dangerous to encourage. Apart from anything else, the disease could be catching.

For their part the Americans, desperately short of equipment, had no wish to let the French know how short they really were. Private French entrepreneurs were agreeable to supplying what the French Government was unwilling openly to supply, but like most entrepreneurs they wanted to be sure of their money; and the Americans were as short of money as of arms. These impediments were increased by the fact that Congress in Philadelphia was to be constantly suspicious that its representatives in Paris were lining their own pockets, and was innocently ignorant of the fact that without a certain minimum of "sweeteners" they could expect to receive very little indeed. All this was compounded by two further unfortunate facts. The British already had an excellent intelligence service in France; and the Americans sent to Paris to procure money and arms were constantly riven by jealousy and distrust of each other.

The first move on the French side came when in the autumn of 1775 Vergennes agreed to the proposal of the French ambassador in London that Achard de Bonvouloir, a Frenchman who had already visited America, should now sound out the situation there. He arrived in Philadelphia in October and made contact with Franklin and later with other members of the Secret Committee. The meetings were conspiratorial and they were unsatisfactory, since the Americans were uncertain of the Frenchman's authority and he himself seems to have been almost as uncertain.

But the Americans now made a move that was to have important long-range consequences; they sent a message to Arthur Lee, Pennsylvania agent in London, appointed him their member in England and instructed him to discover the attitude to America of the main European powers. At least this would be a useful cross-check on Bonvouloir's statements. If it seems strange that this was possible, it should be remembered that the Colonies were as yet more in a state of revolt than a state of war and that hundreds of Americans were still loyal to the Crown. Lee had not yet shown his hand.

However, when he received the Secret Committee's message at the end of 1775, Lee had already made contact with one of the more unexpected figures among the potential arms suppliers who were to keep the American forces in the field. This was the dramatist Pierre Augustin Caron de Beaumarchais, author of *The Marriage of Figaro*. Confident of American victory, he had the ear of Vergennes. He was eager to act as entrepreneur, for the benefit not only of the Americans and of France but of Caron de Beaumarchais. And he had met Arthur Lee in the London home of John Wilkes earlier in 1775.

Vergennes eventually agreed that Beaumarchais should set up a commercial firm that would provide the Americans with munitions or with money to buy them. "But," he added, "the operation must have essentially in the eyes of the British Government, and even in the eyes of the Americans, the aspect of an individual speculation, to which we are strangers. That it may be so in appearance, it must be so to an extent in reality. We will give you secretly a million [livres]. We will endeavour to persuade the Court of Spain to unite in giving you another. With these two millions you shall found a great commercial establishment, and at your own risk and peril you shall furnish to America arms and everything else necessary to sustain war. Our arsenals will deliver to you arms and munitions, but you shall pay for them. You will not demand money of the Americans for they have none; but you can ask return in their staple products."

This was the scheme whose details Beaumarchais passed on to Lee, who in turn informed Congress that a gift of two million livres was on its way. The firm of Rodrique Hortalez and Company was set up in Paris and before the end of 1776 the first arms shipments were being prepared. By that time it had become unclear to most of those concerned whether their contents had to be paid for in kind or came as a gift.

While Beaumarchais and Arthur Lee were organizing these initial supplies, the Secret Committee decided that they should have their own man in Paris. He was the Connecticut congressman Silas Deane, who in March 1776 set out for France, armed with introductions from Franklin to M. Dubourg and to M. Le Roy at the Louvre, still one of the great royal palaces but by this time less favored than Versailles. "By conversing with them," said his instructions, "you will have a good opportunity of acquiring Parisian French, and you will find in M. Dubourg a man prudent, faithful, secret, intelligent in affairs, and capable of giving you very sage advice." Deane was to have need of all this, and more.

"I arrived at Bordeaux on the 6th of June . . . in full expectation of finding several vessels there which the Committee had encouraged me should be sent out with cargoes to enable me to execute the commission I was intrusted with," he later reported. "Unfortunately none had arrived." In Bordeaux he posed as a merchant from Bermuda and attempted to pick up the background for his role before moving on to Paris later in June. He arrived there when, he was later to claim, the news from America was at its blackest. "Unknown and unconnected in Europe," he later told Congress, "I was without personal credit, and the accounts of our misfortunes in America, with the confident assurances of the British Ministry by their ambassadors and partisans at Paris, that everything would be finished, as they expressed themselves, that campaign, left me as little credit on the public account as my own."

Deane's first report back to Philadelphia was depressing. "Were it possible I would attempt to paint to you the heartrending anxiety I have suffered in this time through a total want of intelligence," he began; "my arrival here, my name, my lodgings, and many other particulars have been reported to the British Administration, on which they sent orders to the British ambassador to remonstrate in high terms, and to enforce their remonstrance they despatched Wedderburn from London and Lord Rochford from Holland as persons of great interest and address here to counteract me. They have been some time here, and the city swarms with Englishmen, and as money purchases everything in this country, I have had, and still have, a most difficult task to avoid their machinations."

There were other and more obvious difficulties for the man who has been called the United States' first diplomat. After he had told a friend that he did not "open his mouth before English-speaking people," it was reported that he must be the most silent man in France, since he could barely speak six consecutive words of French. And it has been said that he "would not say nay to any Frenchman who called himself Count or Chevalier."

Poorly equipped for the task in hand, Deane now found himself responsible for the shipments being planned under the cover of Hortalez and Company, of which he heard for the first time when he received a letter from Beaumarchais on July 18. The Frenchman explained that since leaving London his correspondence with Arthur Lee had been "difficult and in code and I have received no reply to my last letter in which I fixed certain matters in this great and important business." However, a meeting the following day straightened out a number of problems, and Beaumarchais carried on business with Deane rather than with Arthur Lee, who continued to remain in London.

"I made out an invoice or estimate of clothing for thirty thousand men," Deane later wrote, "and for other necessaries in proportion, together with an invoice for two hundred pieces of brass cannon, four pounders, and of twenty-eight mortars; the cannon and mortars he [Beaumarchais] told me he could purchase out of the King's arsenals, and could possibly obtain a credit of eight months, or perhaps longer. I added an invoice, or order, for thirty thousand fusees [light muskets], for two thousand barrels of powder, for ball, lead, flints, four thousand tents, and other articles in proportion. He told me that he hoped to purchase also a part of the fusees from the arsenals."

Throughout 1776, as the Declaration of Independence was drawn up and signed, Deane did his best to implement the plans so enthusiastically worked out by Beaumarchais. In August, as Washington was forced to retreat from Long Island, it appeared that the French might be having second thoughts. "Sir," wrote Vergennes to Lord Stormont, the British ambassador in Paris, "I am deeply touched by the attention of your Excellency in permitting me to share with you the joy you feel at the happy news of the successes of the British arms in Connecticut and in New York. I beg your Excellency to accept my thanks for this proof of friendship, and my sincere congratulations upon an event so likely to contribute towards the re-establishment of peace in that quarter of the globe." But the message turned out to be only what has been called "one of the most curious specimens of diplomatic lying in history," and Beaumarchais's plans apparently suffered no particular setback. In fact three months later Deane could tell the Committee of Secret Correspondence: "I should never have completed what I have, but for the generous, the indefatigable and spirited exertions of Monsieur Beaumarchais, to whom the United States are on every account greatly indebted; more so than to any other person on this side the water; he is greatly in advance for stores, clothing and the like."

Nevertheless, it was increasingly felt in Philadelphia that support was needed in Paris. Almost inevitably Congress decided Franklin should provide part of it. "I am old and good for nothing," he is alleged to have remarked to Dr. Rush, sitting nearby, when the Congress's decision was announced, "but as the store-keepers say of their remnants of cloth, I am but a fag end, and you may have me for what you are pleased to give." Thomas Jefferson was also elected but refused the appointment on account of his wife's health. His place, it was decided, would be taken by Arthur Lee, now ordered to move from London to Paris. This final choice demonstrates congressional ignorance of what was happening on the far side of the Atlantic. Lee, already angry that he had, as he saw it, been supplanted in the Beaumarchais schemes by Deane, was now obliged to work with him, a circumstance which Franklin's presence alone prevented from becoming disastrous.

Franklin was aged seventy. He was frail, and he was sometimes crippled by attacks of gout which could immobilize him for upward of a fortnight at a time. These handicaps would seem to make him a curious choice for a mission which would take him across the Atlantic, at the mercy of capture by British forces for whom he was no better than a traitor, to a country still technically neutral, and one where all the wiles and guiles of diplomacy would be needed. His duties, moreover, would inevitably increase unless the mission were to be a sudden failure. As the *Revolutionary Diplomatic Correspondence* has stated, he was also "in the negotiation of our loans from France and the disbursement of the funds thus obtained, a secretary of the treasury; while, in concerting allied campaigns, he was to some extent secretary of war, and in directing our navy in European waters to some extent secretary of the navy. In each of these capacities his arguments and those of his associates were based on finance and war."

Much of Franklin's success in France was due to character, to a homely exterior which fascinated the sophisticated French court but concealed a high ability for intrigue. A great deal rested on his knowledge of American administration and also on the way in which the political game was played in Britain. But perhaps the most important factor in his success—which between 1777 and 1782 attracted some 26 million francs from the coffers of France into the service of the American Revolution—was the reputation he had acquired a quarter of a century earlier. Franklin in France was the man whom the savants knew as a pioneer of electricity; to ordinary people he was the man who had tamed lightning by thinking up the newfangled conductors which were by this time largely accepted as safeguards. John Adams may have been guilty of hyperbole when he maintained that "there was scarcely a peasant or a citizen, a *valet de chambre*, coachman or footman, a lady's chambermaid or a scullion in a kitchen, who was not familiar with [Franklin's name], and who did not consider him as a friend to human kind," but the testimonial was basically true. That this remarkable genius was an American, that he came from a country still often thought of as the home only of backwoodsmen, gave the American Revolution a head start when it came to arguing for arms, or money, or both.

Before Franklin set out he withdrew between £3,000 and £4,000 from the bank and lent it to Congress for the more efficient prosecution of the war. He also wrote to a friend, possibly Priestley. Luckily for the Americans, he gave no detail of military operations, since the letter was captured by the British. "As to our public affairs, I hope our people will keep up their courage," he began. "I have no doubt of their finally succeeding by the blessing of God, nor have I any doubt that so good a cause will fail of that blessing. It is computed that we have already taken a million sterling from the enemy. They must soon be sick of their piratical project. No time should be lost in fortifying three or four posts on our extended coast as strong as art and expense can make them. Nothing will give us greater weight and importance in the eyes of the commercial states, than a conviction that we can annoy, on occasion, their trade, and carry our prizes into safe harbors; and whatever expense we are at in such fortifying, will soon be repaid by the encouragement and success of privateering."

One more thing had to be settled. The Secret Committee appears to have made no provision for staff. Franklin knew that he would be hard-pressed and that his grandson William Temple, staying with his stepmother at Perth Amboy following the house arrest of his father, could be turned into a useful assistant. "Dear Temple, I hope you will return hither immediately," Franklin now wrote, "& that your [step]mother will make no Objection to it, something offering here that will be much to your Advantage if you are not out of the way. I am so hurried that I can only add Ever your affectionate Grandfather."

In due course William Temple arrived. Soon afterward Franklin decided that his other grandson, Benjamin Franklin Bache, living in Philadelphia, should also sail with him to France.

Before he left, always an optimist, preparing for the best if expecting the worst, he drafted a brief outline of the terms on which peace with Britain might be possible, and showed it to the other members of the Secret Committee. The first requirement —and the one upon which all else rested—was that Britain would "renounce and disclaim all pretence of right or authority to govern in any of the United States of America." She would also have to cede, to a United States of America, the provinces or colonies of Quebec, St. John's, Nova Scotia, Bermuda, East and West Florida, and the Bahama Islands, "with all their adjoining and intermediate territories now claimed by her." America would pay to Britain in return, in annual installments, a sum which would be agreed by negotiation and would grant a free trade to all British subjects throughout her territories. Only a man of Franklin's determination would in 1776 have considered such proposals as less than crazy.

On October 26 he and his two grandsons, William Temple Franklin, nearly seventeen, and seven-year-old Benjamin Franklin Bache, left Philadelphia in secret for Chester, down the Delaware. Here they spent the night. The next morning they drove on another three miles to Marcus Hook, where the 16-gun sloop

Reprisal, commanded by Captain Lambert Wickes, was waiting, already loaded with 3,000 pounds of indigo, to be sold in Europe at as high a price as possible. As soon as Franklin was on board, Wickes opened his sealed orders from the Committee of Secret Correspondence. "The Honourable Doctor Franklin being appointed by Congress one of their Commissioners for negotiating some publick business at the court of France," he read, "you are to receive him and his suite on board the Reprisal, as passengers, whom it is your duty and we dare say it will be your inclination, to treat with the greatest respect and attention, and your best endeavours will not be wanting to make their time on board the ship perfectly agreable."

The *Reprisal* was soon down the Delaware, past Cape May and on to the high seas, lashed by the first of the winter storms and with a careful lookout being kept for British vessels. Franklin still believed that his departure was secret. In fact, even before the *Reprisal* had sailed on the twenty-ninth, Grey Cooper had written from New York: "The Arch ——— Dr. Franklin, has lately eloped under a cloak of plenipotentiary to Versailles."

Captain Wickes's orders were clear: escape pursuit if escape was possible, and fight only if it was unavoidable. The crossing was rough but quick. Despite the weather, Franklin took his soundings as opportunity offered, measuring the temperature of the water and estimating whether or not they were sailing in the waters of his old friend the Gulf Stream. The speed was as well, since the fowl taken as provision was too tough for Franklin's teeth and he was forced to survive on salt beef. The result, he noted, was that "boils continued to vex me, and the scurff extending all the small of my back, on my sides, my legs, and my arms besides what continued under my hair."

On the morning of November 27 they sighted, then captured, an Irish brig only a day out from Bordeaux; in the afternoon a British vessel was taken, also without a fight. The following morning the lookout on the masthead sighted land ahead— Belle Ile off the Brittany coast—and on December 4, the *Reprisal* anchored in Quiberon Bay, the first regularly commissioned vessel of the American navy to reach Europe. Franklin expected that another day or two would bring them to Nantes. But now the wind changed and after waiting for four days Captain Wickes hailed a fishing boat, which landed the Franklin party at the small town of Aunoy.

No post chaises were available and it was not until the next day that one arrived from Vannes. "The carriage was a miserable one, with tired horses," Franklin reported, "the evening dark, scarce a traveler but ourselves on the road; and to make it more *comfortable,* the driver stopped near a wood we were to pass through, to tell us that a gang of eighteen robbers infested that wood, who but two weeks ago had robbed and murdered some travelers on that very spot."

In Nantes Franklin wrote to John Hancock, president of Congress. "Our voyage," he admitted, "though not long, was rough, and I feel myself weakened by it, but I now recover strength daily, and in a few days shall be able to undertake the journey to Paris. I have not yet taken any public character, thinking it prudent first to know whether the court is ready and willing to receive ministers publicly from the Congress, that we may neither embarrass on the one hand, nor subject ourselves to the hazard of a disgraceful refusal on the other."

The desire for anonymity was logical; it was also unavailing. In Nantes there were many friends of America, and Franklin was received as the guest of honor at a hastily organized dinner. He was complimented on his safe arrival, feted as a celebrity, and felt himself at the center of French enthusiasm for the American cause. After a few days' rest he posted to the capital, sleeping at Versailles en route and arriving on December 22 at the Hôtel d'Hambourg in the Rue de l'Université, where Silas Deane was already living.

"Nothing has, for a long time, occasioned greater speculation than this event," Deane informed the Committee of Secret Correspondence on hearing of Franklin's arrival in France, "and our friends here are elated beyond measure, as this confirms them you will not negotiate with England; and for me, I will not attempt to express the pleasure I feel on this occasion, as it removes at once difficulties under which I have been constantly in danger of sinking." On the same day he wrote to Beaumarchais, telling him that Franklin, Arthur Lee and himself had been appointed joint commissioners to the Court of France, a letter which brought an anxious inquiry. "Does the appointment of a number of agents," Beaumarchais asked, "affect the power of the first of them; and shall I have to recommence with the new ones what I have already arranged with you?"

Deane reassured him. At the same time he wrote to Lee in London, advising him to come to Paris as soon as possible since in view of Franklin's journey the British might prevent him leaving England. Lee arrived in Paris the day after Franklin, but whether this was owing to enthusiasm for the cause or to anxiety to be hard on Franklin's heels is not certain. He had been successful in launching Beaumarchais's schemes. He had been jealous of Franklin in London some years earlier. And he may have been suspicious that Franklin would now try, with Silas Deane's aid, to reap where he had sown.

The British were well informed of what was going on, but were frequently unable to exploit their intelligence, and it was typical that Sir Grey Cooper had not ensured that the *Reprisal* be intercepted. Their interpretation of events was often wide of the mark. Horace Walpole, the famous author and litterateur, who had good friends in Paris, was told as early as November 26—when the *Reprisal* was still a day off landfall—that Franklin had arrived in France, "no equivocal step," as he described it to Sir Horace Mann. He correctly assumed that Franklin must have left Philadelphia a few days after Washington's retreat from New York, but he added that it was "natural to conclude that he is come to tell France, that she must directly interpose and protect the Americans, or that the Americans must submit to such terms as they can obtain. If I am not wrong in my reasons," he continued, "the question is thus brought to a short issue, and there I leave it."

Other Englishmen had a more accurate assessment of Franklin, of the prospects that were now opening up and of the need for countermeasures. General Howe, writing to the British foreign secretary shortly after Franklin left Philadelphia, was quite confident of what should be done. "The enemy, though much depressed at the success of his Majesty's arms," he wrote, "are encouraged by the strongest assurances from their Leaders of procuring Assistance from Foreign Powers, for which end it is understood that Dr. Franklin is gone to France to solicit aid from that Court. I do not presume to point out a way of counteracting him; but were that effected and the force I have mentioned sent out [33,000 men, including 15,000 mercenaries from Europe] it would strike such terror through the country that little resistance would be made to the progress of His Majesty's arms in the provinces of New England, New York, the Jerseys and Pensilvania, after the Junction of the Northern and Southern Armies."

In England, also, there were those not particularly happy that Franklin had reached Paris. The Marquis of Rockingham, hearing of the landing in France, gave an unidentified correspondent an acutely understanding forecast of the future.

In regard to this event, I cannot refrain from paying my tribute of admiration to the vigour, magnanimity, and determined resolution of the *Old Man.* The horrid scene at a *Privy Council,* is in my memory, though, perhaps not in his. It may not excite his conduct. It certainly deters him not.— He boldly ventures to cross the Atlantic in an American little frigate, and risks the dangers of being taken, and being once more brought before an implacable tribunal. The sight of Banquo's ghost could not more offend the eyes of Macbeth, than the knowledge of this old man being at Versailles, should affect the minds of those who were principals in that horrid scene.

Depend upon it he will plead forcibly. He has but to combat a degree of folly in a very few in France. He is so armed with proofs of the *facility* with which France and Spain may now give a deadly blow to this country, that I can no longer enjoy the chief comfort I had in the reliance, that though the political conduct of this country was weak or infatuated beyond all bounds—yet the Courts of France and Spain were still more weak and blind.

I am very curious to know what reception your information will meet from the Ministers. Inwardly they will tremble at it. They may appear to think slightly of the effects it will have. They will cherish a fond hope that France will not listen. In the meantime they will try to raise more and more indignation *here* against the Americans for this strong effort of application to France.

This I am confident you will see. It cannot be otherwise. There is no man who has access to his Majesty who has integrity and magnanimity of mind sufficient to enable him to go and say to his Majesty, the measures and policy of the Ministers towards America are erroneous; the adherence to them is destruction. What can now be done to avert impending ruin, must be a matter of great difficulty, and even uncertainty, in regard to its execution; *of this,* at least, we are certain, that *force, violence,* and cruelty have brought the country into this direful situation. The reverse of such measures is the *only thing* left to try.

Among the men with the best judgment was Lord Stormont, whose main task was now to frustrate Franklin's activities. "I learnt Yesterday Evening," he wrote to Lord Weymouth, secretary of state for the southern department, "that the famous Doctor Franklin is arrived at Nantes, with his two grand children; . . . Some people think that either some private Dissatisfaction or Despair of Success have brought him into this Country. I cannot but suspect that He comes charged with a secret Commission from the Congress, and as he is a subtle artful Man, and void of all Truth, He will in that Case use every Means to deceive, will avail himself of the Genl Ignorance of the French, to paint the Situation of the Rebels in the falsest Colours, and hold out every lure to the Ministers to draw them into an open support of that Cause. He has the advantage of several intimate Connexions here, and stands high in the General opinion. In a word, My Lord, I look upon him as a dangerous Engine, and am very sorry that some English Frigate did not meet with Him by the Way."

Since that had not happened Stormont was reduced to making the empty threat to Vergennes that he would leave Paris if Franklin were allowed to set foot in the city. The Foreign Minister's reply exemplified the attitude he was to adopt during the next few months. He had, he claimed, already sent a messenger to Nantes, but the messenger might miss Franklin since no one knew which route he was taking to the capital. If the American did arrive in Paris, then he, Vergennes, would like to send him away. However, he went on, "If the doctor were once in Paris, the Government, notwithstanding its desire to comply as far as possible with the views of the Court of London, would not like to send him away because of the scandalous scene this would present to all France, should we respect neither the laws of nations nor of hospitality."

If Stormont was worried about the effect of Franklin's presence, Franklin himself left Charles James Fox, in Paris when Franklin arrived, in no doubt about the resolution with which the Colonies would fight the war. "I recollect," Fox later said, "that conversing with him [there] on the subject of the impending hostilities, he, while he predicted their ruinous consequences, compared their principle and their consequences to those of the ancient Crusades. He foretold that we should expend our best blood and treasure in attempting an unattainable object; and that like the *holy* war of the dark ages, while we carried slaughter and desolation over America, we should finally depopulate, enfeeble and impoverish Great Britain."

Franklin appears to have recovered quickly from his Atlantic crossing and on the twenty-third, the very day after arriving in Paris, wrote to Vergennes. He came to the nub of his mission in the first sentence of a letter signed by himself, Silas Deane and Arthur Lee. "Sir," he began, "We beg leave to acquaint your Excellency that we are appointed and fully empowered by the Congress of the United States of America to propose and negotiate a treaty of amity and commerce between France and the United States."

William Temple Franklin was now given his first task, that of delivering the letter to Versailles. M. Gérard of the Foreign Office was absent when he arrived on the twenty-fourth, so the young man delivered it personally to Vergennes. The Foreign Minister put it in his pocket and told Temple to call for a reply at nine the following morning.

Five days later the Foreign Minister received Franklin and Deane. Their subsequent report to the Committee of Secret Correspondence ably sums up the state of the game during the first months of 1777: "In our first conversation with the minister, after the arrival of Mr. Franklin," it began, "it was evident that this court, while it treated us privately with all civility, was cautious of giving umbrage to England, and was therefore desirous of avoiding an open reception and acknowledgment of us, or entering into any formal negotiation with us as ministers from the Congress. To make us easy, however, we were told that the ports of France were open to our ships as friends; that our people might freely purchase and export, as merchandise, whatever our States had occasion for, vending at the same time our own commodities; that in doing this we should experience all the facilities that a Government disposed to favour us could, consistent with treaties, afford to the enemies of a friend. But though it was at that time no secret that two hundred field-pieces of brass and thirty thousand fusils, with other munitions of war in great abundance, had been taken out of the King's magazines for the purpose of exportation to America, the minister, in our presence, affected to know nothing of that operation, and claimed no merit to his court on that account. But he intimated to us that it would be well taken if we communicated with no other person about the court concerning our affairs but himself, who would be ready at all convenient times to confer with us."

Franklin, following the military maxim of reinforcing success, quickly made an audacious proposal. It was signed by Franklin, by Deane and by Arthur Lee, but its wording has the mark of Franklin the propagandist at his best. "The Congress, the better to defend their coasts, protect their trade and drive off the enemy," it began, "have instructed us to apply to France for eight ships of the line, completely manned, the expense of which they will undertake to pay. As other princes of Europe are lending or hiring their troops to Britain against America, it is apprehended that France may, if she thinks fit, afford our independent States the same kind of aid, without giving England any first cause of complaint. But if England should on that account declare war, we conceive that by the united force of France, Spain and America, she will lose all her possessions in the West Indies, much the greatest part of that commerce which has rendered her so opulent, and be reduced to that state of weakness and humiliation which she has, by her perfidy, her insolence, and her cruelty, both in the east and the west, so justly merited."

The proposal, as Franklin must have expected, was politely turned down. At this date the French were unwilling to provoke the British too far. Aid for the Americans, maybe, but only aid which could be explained away if the British discovered it or could be ignored if they did not. Nevertheless, Franklin had made a good first impression, as Vergennes revealed on January 10 to the Marquis de Noailles, the new French ambassador in London.

"I tell you nothing, M. le Marquis, of Dr. Franklin," he wrote. "He behaves very modestly in Paris, where he finds a few friends and more idle callers. He has paid me a visit which I have returned. His conversation is gentle and honest, he appears to be a man of much talent: Lord Stormont affirms that he will deceive us as he has deceived three English Ministries. I do not know whether that is his intention, but he has not yet taken any steps to carry it out, besides, we act here upon principle."

ELEVEN

FIGHT FOR
SURVIVAL

RANKLIN REMAINED IN THE HÔTEL d'Hambourg for only a few weeks after his arrival in Paris. "I have taken a lodging at Passy, where I shall be in a few days," he wrote on January 29 to Charles Dumas, an old Swiss friend living in Holland, "and hope there to find a little leisure, free from the perpetual interruption I suffer here by the crowds continually coming in, some offering goods, others soliciting offices in our army, etc. I shall then be able to write to you fully."

If there was no Stevenson family to cosset Franklin at Passy, there was nearly everything else. One mile from Paris, seven from Versailles, the little village on the lower slopes of the hill of Chaillot was in the 1770s one of the most exclusive suburbs of the capital. "To the west," says a description of the community in Franklin's time, published in the *Bulletin de la Société Historique d'Auteuil et de Passy*, "lay the Bois de Boulogne, then a very small forest, the remains of the great forest of Rouvroy; to the north it was girdled by great estates, nearby, woods, considerable parks, separating it from l'Etoile; to the south it dominated the slopes which declined very gently towards Auteuil, nearly entirely covered by vineyards and pastures; but, to the east, the houses were erected on a veritable cornice, little cliffs which raised themselves from the Seine and from which the view extended beyond the river and from the Isle of Swans, over the sequestered plain of Grenelle and the environs of the Invalides, the hills of Issy and Meudon. The little town was perched on a level place attached to the principal slopes, with small cottages, some ruins, some narrow streets, some of which were so steep that on rainy days the water flowed over the uneven paving-stones or washed out the clay from these little roads."

In the Château de Passy lived the Comte de Bouillainvilliers; in the castle the old and wealthy Boufflers family. The Château de Coq was the property of M. Joly de Fleury, soon to be minister of finance. Nearby, on a property from whose grounds there bubbled up what was then the famous Passy mineral water, there lived Louis Guillaume Le Veillard, soon to be one of Franklin's intimates. Beyond his estate there lived M. Donatien Le Ray de Chaumont, Franklin's host, owner of the Hôtel de Valentinois, with its courtyard, its gardens, its encircling terrace and its fine prospect of the river and the distant spires of Paris.

Born Jacques Donatien Le Ray, M. de Chaumont was an ambitious entrepreneur who had early in life made enough money to buy the Château de Chaumont in the Loire valley. He had become superintendent of the Hôtel des Invalides, overseer of the king's forests, and then the commissar of the French army for the supply of uniforms. Purchase of the Hôtel de Valentinois, conveniently situated on the route from Paris to Versailles, was a further step up the ladder. He had close connections with the government and it is likely that he was officially prodded into giving the Americans a home at Passy. Certainly it was easier for the French to keep them under surveillance there than in the heart of Paris.

Chaumont was closely involved in the supply of arms to America even before Franklin arrived in Paris. As far back as August 18, 1776, Silas Deane had written to the Committee of Secret Correspondence stating: "Mons. Chaumont, a very wealthy person, and intendant for providing clothes, etc., for the French army, has offered me a credit on account of the Colonies to the amount of one million of livres, which I have accepted."

Franklin and Deane at first occupied one of the pavilions in the grounds of the Hôtel de Valentinois, but later moved into a wing of the main building. To start with, M. de Chaumont refused to take rent, suggesting only that the Americans, when they had won their independence, might like to give him a grant of land; but eventually he agreed to take 20,000 livres for the past five years. When Franklin gave dinner parties, which was often, it was Mme. de Chaumont who organized them. His household accounts were made up by one of the Chaumont daughters, and the Chaumont staff looked after his coach and pair when he acquired it. In addition, Jacques Finck, M. de Chaumont's major-domo, undertook the regular feeding of the Franklin establishment for 1,300 francs a month. "Breakfast, at eight o'clock on weekdays, and nine or ten on Sundays, was to consist of bread and butter, honey, coffee or chocolate; dinner, at two, was to be a joint of beef or veal or mutton, followed by fowl or game in season, with two side dishes, two vegetables courses, pastry, plus, of course, hors d'oeuvres, butter, pickles, radishes, two kinds of fruit in winter and four in summer, two fruit compôtes, cheese, biscuits, bonbons, and ices twice a week in summer and once in winter."

M. de Chaumont lived on a far grander scale, and the environment in which Franklin now found himself is epitomized by a description from Elkanah Watson, a young visiting American whom Franklin took to dine with his host.

We entered a spacious room, I following the Doctor, where several well-dressed persons (to my unsophisticated American eyes, gentlemen) bowed to us profoundly. These were servants. A folding-door opened at our approach, and presented to my view a brilliant assembly, who all greeted the wise old man in the most cordial and affectionate manner. He introduced me as a young American just arrived. One of the young ladies approached him with the familiarity of a daughter, tapped him kindly on the cheek, and called him "Pa-pa Franklin."

I was enraptured, with the ease and freedom exhibited in the table intercourse in France. Instead of the cold ceremony and formal compliments, to which I had been accustomed on such occasions, here all appeared at ease, and well sustained. Some were amusing themselves with music; others, with singing. Some were waltzing; and others gathered in little groups, in conversation. At the table, the ladies and gentlemen were mingled together, and joined in cheerful conversation, each selecting the delicacies of various courses, and drinking of delicious light wines, but with neither toasts nor healths.

At Passy, Franklin had domestically fallen on his feet, as he usually did. His elder grandson quickly slipped into the role of secretary. The younger, Benjamin Franklin Bache, at first attended the local Passy school. Later he was sent to Geneva so that, as Franklin wrote, "he will be educated a Republican and a Protestant, which could not be so conveniently done at the Schools in France." Jonathan Williams, Junior, Franklin's grandnephew, soon came from London, before being sent down to Nantes to help supervise the shipment of supplies to America. Deane, Lee and others joined for varying periods what was, in effect, a European headquarters for managing the War of Independence.

But Passy offered something more than a conveniently serviced base. It is likely that Franklin would have found congenial women friends wherever he settled, since women were attracted to him as surely as iron filings to a magnet, a circumstance which men with less appeal tended to report with disapproval. But Passy had pleasant inhabitants and during his eight years there Franklin formed a number of close friendships. Notable among them were those with Mme. Brillon and Mme. Helvétius. Anne-Louise d'Hardancourt Brillon de Jouy lived in Passy itself with her elderly husband, M. Brillon de Jouy, and her children. Mme. Helvétius, living in nearby Auteuil, born Anne-Catherine de Ligniville d'Autricourt, was the widow of Claude Adrien Helvétius, one of the French Encyclopedists, whose De l'Esprit, published in 1758, had caused a furor with its claim that sensation was the source of all intellectual activity. Both women were famous for the salons to which they attracted distinguished members of French intellectual society.

Soon after his arrival at Passy, Franklin was dining regularly twice a week with the Brillon family at their home, Moulin Joli, and almost weekly with Mme. Helvétius at Auteuil. It was with Mme. Brillon that he was most obsessed. "She has, among other elegant accomplishments," he wrote, "that of an excellent musician, and, with her daughters, who sing prettily, and some friends who play, she kindly entertains me and my grandson with little concerts, a cup of tea, and a game of chess. I call this my Opera, for I rarely go to the Opera at Paris." Married to an amiable, dullish man more than twenty years her senior, strikingly good-looking, she might well have become Franklin's mistress. But she could not be persuaded—even when she discovered that her daughters' governess had become her husband's lover—and Franklin had to be content with a sincere, affectionate, but strictly platonic friendship. To Mme. Helvétius he almost certainly proposed marriage, but with no better luck than with his different proposition to Mme. Brillon.

Franklin's reputation as a lady-killer spread until he felt that it needed explanation, and to his stepniece in Boston, Elizabeth Hubbard Partridge, he explained: "You mention the Kindness of the French Ladies to me. I must explain that matter. This is the civilest Nation upon Earth. Your first Acquaintances endeavour to find out what you like, and they tell others. If 'tis understood that you like Mutton, dine where you will you find Mutton. Somebody, it seems, gave it out that I lov'd Ladies; and then every body presented me their Ladies (or the Ladies presented themselves) to be *embrac'd*, that is to have their Necks kiss'd. For as to kissing of Lips or Cheeks it is not the Mode here, the first, is reckon'd rude, & the other may rub off the Paint. The French Ladies have however 1000 other ways of rendering themselves agreable; by their various Attentions and Civilities, & their sensible Conversation. 'Tis a delightful People to live with."

If Franklin's attraction to women was one advantage in his efforts to make friends and influence people in France, another was his long devotion to Freemasonry. In Paris the lodge of the Nine Sisters admitted him to membership in 1777 and made him Grand Master two years later. It was politically influential and its members included Rochefoucauld, Condorcet and the Abbé Sieyès, who, years later being asked what he had done in the French Revolution, replied with the immortal: "Survived."

Franklin began to appreciate the complexity of his work in Paris from the first weeks in 1777. The France in which he was now to seek aid, ostensibly with high confidence, in fact with justified misgivings that the task would be long and difficult, was governed on a system even more class-ridden and corrupt than that which had finally shocked him in London. Under the *ancien régime* no less than one out of every 250 members of the population belonged to one of the convoluted grades of the nobility. All these nobles were exempt from payment of ordinary land tax, from charges for maintaining the public roads and from military conscription. Together with the clergy, they benefited from the national revenues while the lower classes bore the burden of labor and of paying the taxes. Over all, there ruled, with monarchal absolutism, King Louis XVI, young, well-meaning, weak and incapable of arresting his country's steady slide into bankruptcy. A wonder of the century was that Paris had to wait so long before it witnessed the storming of the Bastille, heard the early-morning clatter of the tumbrils on the pavé and watched the sunlight glisten on the heavy blade of M. Guillotin's ingenious machine as it dropped to sever yet another head from another pair of shoulders.

Few societies differed more from that which Franklin and his supporters were trying to build along the Eastern Seaboard of a country whose natural resources reached far out across the plains and forests of an unpeopled and largely unexplored continent. It is true that the Proprietary party and the Assembly of Pennsylvania had deep differences. So had the administrations and the Assemblies of the other Colonies strung out along the coast; but when compared to the differences between America and Catholic France, these were unimportant socially and theologically. If ever symbols were required, it was only necessary to consider the austere whitewashed Quaker meeting houses and the multicolored splendor of Notre Dame, in which organ and choir made passionate appeal to the emotions.

Franklin persuaded political need to subdue his feelings and made of the differences as little as he could. "They have some frivolities, but they are harmless," he wrote of the French to Josiah Quincy. "To dress their heads so that a hat cannot be put on them, and then wear their hats under their arms, and to fill their noses with tobacco, may be called follies perhaps, but they are not vices. They are only the effects of the tyranny of custom. In short, there is nothing wanting in the character of a Frenchman, that belongs to that of an agreeable and worthy man. There are only some trifles surplus, or which might be spared."

There was yet another contrast between the French and the Commissioners. Franklin appears to have regarded it with surprise, and some Americans still fail to appreciate it. "This is really a generous nation, fond of glory, and particularly that of protecting the oppressed," he wrote to Robert Livingston. "Trade is not the admiration of their noblesse, who always govern here. Telling them their *commerce* will be advantaged by our success, and that it is their *interest* to help us, seems as much as to say, help us, and we shall not be obliged to you. Such indiscreet and improper language has been sometimes held here by some of our people, and produced no good effects." Yet Franklin himself, the quintessential businessman, so sank his mercenary instincts into the common cause that Vergennes, noting that the Americans had "a terrible mania for commerce," could add: "This reproach cannot apply to Mr. Franklin—I believe his hands and heart are equally pure."

As the Americans eventually persuaded the French to cobble together a program of aid, both peoples must have reflected on the old adage about necessity making strange bedfellows. After all, General Washington, now the military leader of the rebel Colonies, had for long been linked by the French with their expulsion from North America by the British. Now they were sending arms to Washington. Yet Count Ségur could write: "Nothing was more striking than the great contrast between the luxury of our capital, the elegance of our fashions, the magnificence of Versailles, the living evidence of the royal pride of Louis XIV, the polished dignity of our aristocracy, with the almost rustic attire, the simple but proud attitude, the free and direct language, the hair-style without trappings or powder, and with that ancient air which seemed suddenly to bring within our walls among the weak and servile civilisation of the 18th century, the wise contemporaries of Plato or republicans of the times of Caton and Fabius." Franklin knew the contrast, describing himself as "very plainly dressed, wearing my thin, gray straight hair, that peeps out under my only *coiffure,* a fine fur cap, which comes down my forehead almost to my spectacles. Think how this must appear among the powdered heads of Paris!" There was more than one point in favor of the fur cap, which he had picked up during his Canadian journey the previous spring. It was useful in concealing an eczema of the scalp, and it also had a propaganda value. Franklin may not have known that in Sweden, a country in whose foreign policy France was involved, there were both the aristocratic "Hats" and the opposing party, the popular, liberty-loving "Caps." What he did rightly assess was that the cap created a picture of simple rusticity which would charm the French. As a grand touch to the scene it was as successful as Napoleon putting his own lantern-lit shoulder to the artillery stuck in the mud the night before Marengo, Patton's pearl-handled guns or Montgomery, the nonsmoker, handing out cigarettes to the hard-pushed desert troops.

There were also Franklin's bifocal spectacles, a feature of his public appearances which became almost as famous as the fur cap. Previously he had carried two pairs of glasses but found the arrangement troublesome when on the move since in his coach he would wish sometimes to read, sometimes to look at the passing country. To overcome the inconvenience of constantly changing glasses he had special spectacles prepared, in effect combining the upper half of one pair with the lower half of the other. "By this means," he wrote, "as I wear my Spectacles constantly, I have only to move my Eyes up or down, as I want to see distinctly far or near, the proper Glasses being always ready. This I find more particularly convenient since my being in France, the Glasses that serve me best at Table to see what I eat, not being the best to see the Faces of those on the other Side of the Table who speak to me; and when one's Ears are not well accustomed to the Sounds of a Language, a Sight of the Movements in the Features of him that speaks helps to explain; so that I understand French better by the help of my Spectacles."

Franklin needed the help. He could read French with comparative ease but had more difficulty with the spoken word. There is a story, possibly apocryphal, that when attending one meeting of the Academy of Sciences he decided to clap whenever one of his Passy neighbors did so. The result was that he applauded most loudly when he himself was being praised.

Three weeks after he arrived in Paris it was being reported: "It is the mode today for everybody to have an engraving of M. Franklin over the mantelpiece." His face appeared on rings, bracelets, snuffboxes and even hats and coats. Canes, in imitation of his own, were carried, while in Nantes women began wearing wigs in the shape of the famous fur cap, a fashion called doing one's hair *à la Franklin.*

This extraordinary upsurge of popular French enthusiasm for Franklin cannot be entirely explained by his fame as the man who had tamed lightning. Two other factors were involved. The first was the instinctive sympathy of the ordinary people for a leader from the country which had defied the established order. Another decade was to pass before the fervor of men and women driven to desperation at last boiled over into revolution.

But the feudal tradition of land tenure, uncontrolled inflation and government by an out-of-date and out-of-touch nobility had for long been producing a population ripe for revolt. Who better to win their cheers than the man whose people had already taken up arms?

Gray-haired—and with not many of them—portly if not paunchy, crippled at times by gout and with sight none too good, Franklin yet radiated his own charismatic charm. If the Americans had a secret weapon on the continent of Europe, it was Benjamin Franklin.

He himself considered the veneration with a mixture of amusement and approval. He had little respect for hero worship in general, even though he had no objection to it in particular. But, as he well knew, it was good for the cause. He had been in France only a few weeks when he was drawn by Charles Nicolas Cochin the younger; publication of a copperplate from the drawing, engraved by Augustin de Saint-Aubin, was announced in the *Journal de Paris* on June 16, and in the *Mercure de France* the next month. "The print is above all a news picture," it has been pointed out. "Because of it, the sensational fact of Franklin's arrival in France and the sensational costume which so effectively dramatized his role as envoy from the New World to the Old reached every part of Europe, creating an image of tremendous value to Franklin's purpose. It is an accurate likeness and a perceptive characterization but its importance and its contemporary impact is as news."

There were also, and affecting a different class among the population, the Franklin medallions incorporated in knickknacks of all sorts. It was difficult to realize how numerous they were, he wrote to his daughter, Sally, in Philadelphia. "These, with the pictures, busts and prints (of which copies upon copies are spread everywhere), have made your father's face as well known as that of the moon," he continued, "so that he durst not do anything that would oblige him to run away, as his phiz would discover him wherever he should venture to show it. It is said by learned etymologists that the name *doll,* for the images that children play with, is derived from the word idol. From the number of *dolls* now made of him he may be truly said, *in that sense,* to be *i-doll-ized* in this country."

The craze, curiously enough, was not restricted to France, and in England the Wedgwood pottery works turned out medallions and busts. "We have," Josiah Wedgwood himself wrote, "some good Doctr. Franklins (will the courtiers believe it?) . . . out of the Kiln today." These were the Franklin medallions which Wedgwood produced in eight sizes, the largest being a wall plaque eleven inches tall and eight inches wide, behind glass. Smaller examples were for use in rings, scarfpins, lockets and bracelets.

"All the painters and sculptors wish to make the portrait of Lincfran, without and with spectacles," wrote the French artist M. Nogaret. "One sees copies at every street corner. The importunity has reached the point where he has pled for mercy, saying that in eight days' time they have given him twenty cases of crick in the neck. So they resign themselves to taking him once and for all. They strike him in silver, they mould him in china; one sees him now, at the last, well and faithfully rendered in medallions, in bracelets on bonbon boxes, in medals and on every mantlepiece worshipped no less than a household god."

Yet however great his popularity, Franklin's long-term success would depend very largely on the success of the American forces in the field and on the high seas. However skillfully he worked, French assistance would be limited until it was obvious that the Americans would survive, and qualified until it was seen that they were likely to win. At first the prospects looked poor. While Franklin had been crossing the Atlantic, a series of defeats had forced Washington to retreat across New Jersey, and on December 20 Congress, having left Philadelphia, met in Baltimore. Many civilians moved west under the threat of occupation and among the letters which Franklin received in the early spring of 1777 was one from his daughter: "You had not left us long before we were obliged to leave town," he was told. "I shall never forget or forgive them for turning me out of house and home in the middle of winter. . . . Your library we sent out of town, well packed in boxes, a week before us; and all the valuable things, mahogany excepted, we brought with us." However, by the time that Franklin learned the depressing news, the situation had again been transformed, this time for the better. Washington had daringly recrossed the Delaware on Christmas Day, won his victory at the battle of Trenton in which more than nine hundred Hessians serving the British were captured, and occupied Trenton four days later. Disaster had been averted and

Washington was seen, at least for the moment, as more than a match for the larger but cumbersome British forces.

The work of the American Commissioners—predominantly of Franklin, since from the day of his arrival he was overwhelmingly the most important of the three men—and then of Franklin, minister plenipotentiary, was to fall into three sections. There was the period which began with his first meeting with Vergennes and which ended—after the American victory over Burgoyne in the autumn of 1777—with the signing of treaties between France and America, and, soon afterward, the formal outbreak of war between Britain and France. There then followed three and a half years of fluctuating encounters, ended by the British surrender at Yorktown in the closing weeks of 1781. This decisive American victory made peace inevitable, but nearly two more years were required before the British capitulated, granted full independence to the Colonies and formally ended the war.

One of Franklin's first tasks as he settled into Passy during the spring of 1777 was to cope with the developing argument between Arthur Lee and Silas Deane on the details of the Beaumarchais schemes. Some of the first shipments of arms had at last reached French ports for shipment across the Atlantic almost as Franklin was arriving, and more ships had sailed by the end of February. This first consignment suggests the extent to which the Americans were dependent on France. It contained, among other supplies: 8,750 pairs of shoes, 3,600 blankets, 4,000 dozen pairs stockings, 164 brass cannon, 153 carriages, 41,000 balls, 37,000 light muskets, 373,000 flints, 15,000 gun worms (screws used for withdrawing the charge from a muzzle-loading gun), 514,000 musket balls, nearly 20,000 pounds of lead, nearly 161,000 pounds of powder, plus mortar bombs, more than 11,000 grenades and some 4,000 tents. There were to be many more similar consignments.

A main threat to the arms supply came from Britain's Secret Intelligence Service. Run by William Eden, later Lord Auckland, it operated so successfully that it had been waiting for Silas Deane's arrival in Paris, while from 1777 onward one of its main agents operated from inside Franklin's headquarters at Passy. This agent was Franklin's old friend, the American Dr. Bancroft, the Fellow of the Royal Society who had written admiringly of

Franklin's stoic attitude during the Cockpit encounter which he had watched three years previously.

Bancroft, to be known within the British spy network as Dr. Edwards, was considered by Congress as a resolute supporter, and part of Deane's orders when leaving Philadelphia for Paris ran: "You will endeavor to procure a meeting with Mr. Bancroft by writing a letter to him, under cover to Mr. Griffiths, at Turnham Green, near London, and desiring him to come over to you in France, or Holland, on the score of old acquaintance."

In Paris it was not only Deane whom Bancroft met. Soon after arrival, he was approached by Paul Wentworth, one of Eden's men. Wentworth "having induced me to believe that the British Ministry [knew why I was in Paris]," Bancroft later wrote, "I at length consented to meet the then Secretaries of State, Lords Weymouth and Suffolk and give them all the information in my power which I did with the most disinterested views." Having agreed to work for the British as well as the Americans, Bancroft found an excuse to visit London again, and here received his instructions. There was nothing equivocal about them. He was engaged to provide information on a number of subjects including "Franklin's & Dean's Correspondence with the Congress, & their Agents: & the secret, as well as ostensible, Letters from the Congress to them," also "Copys of any transactions, committed to Paper, & an exact account of all intercourse & the subject matter treated of, between the Courts of Versailles & Madrid, and the Agents from the Congress." And to Lord Stormont he was to provide intimate shipping information.

The means of passing on this information was laid down in some detail.

For Lord Stormont—All Letters directed to Mr Richardson—written on Gallantry—but the white Parts of the paper to contain the intelligence written with invisible Ink—the Wash to make which appear, is given to Ld. St.

In these Letters, or the Covers not visibly written on, will be contained what Ld. St. will be pleased to fold up, & direct in a Cover to Mr. Wentworth—& send it by messenger.

All packetts which M. Mary may send to Lord Stormont, to be sent unopened to M^r W——— by Messenger only.

Mr. Deans will call every Tuesday Evening after half past nine at the Tree pointed out on the S^o[uth] Terrace of the Tuilleries & take from the Hole at the root—the Bottle containing a Letter:—and place under the Box-Tree agreed on, a bottle containing any Communications from Lord Stormont to Dr. Edwards. All letters to be numbered with white Ink. The bottle to be sealed—& tyed by the Neck with a common twyne, about half a yard in length—the other end of which to be fastned to a peg of wood, split at top to receive a very small piece of a Card—this bottle to be thrust under the Tree, & the Peg into the Ground on the west side.

Once he had received his instructions, Bancroft left London for Paris—it being officially put about that he was under suspicion of involvement in the firing of naval stores at Portsmouth. Franklin was delighted to welcome his old friend, who was taken into the Passy household and remained there until Franklin left France in 1785. Two years later Deane was reporting to Congress that in Paris Bancroft "most assiduously devoted his time and abilities to the service of his country, and assisted the Commissioners in writing for them, and by keeping up a correspondence with his friends in London, from whom good and useful intelligence was obtained." Ironically, he added that "it will not be improper to say here, that the correspondence carried on between us was never intercepted."

Bancroft was the most successful of the spies who surrounded Franklin in Paris and who reported to London on his daily doings. He was, however, only one of a large number, and the thick volumes of the Auckland Papers in the British Library in London contain hundreds of letters showing the extent of British penetration. Interception of correspondence was efficient and regular. A typical note from one man in British employ, the Reverend John Vardill, asks for an urgent meeting with Eden since he "has Letters from America to communicate which must be given soon [to] the Persons to whom they are directed."

Much of the espionage activity was conducted, on both sides, at a simple, somewhat Boy Scout, level. Paul Wentworth traveled under twenty different identities, most of which were probably known to the French police, and usually carried in his jacket a private cipher and recipes for various secret inks. "The brownest of the two tinctures," he was to tell the Earl of Suffolk on one occasion, "is to be used like a wash, by means of a brush to be rubbed over the whole surface of the paper where no writing appears—presently the paper takes a dirty yellow colour, & the letters written with the white Ink (in the other bottle) assume a reddish hue & become very legible."

There were times when an air of mild farce crept in. Thus on some occasions Bancroft would copy out the list of cargoes it was planned to ship from France to America. The details would be passed on to Lord Stormont, who would object to Vergennes. But the friendly Vergennes would then pass on to the Commissioners details of the British objections, which would often list cargo items in the order they had been given in the Commissioners' minutes. It should have been obvious that some enemy had access to those minutes.

Franklin himself cannot be absolved from being overcasual. While he was still at the Hôtel d'Hambourg a friend had given him a comradely warning. "Forgive me, dear Doctor," wrote William Alexander, a Scotsman whom Franklin had known in Britain and who now lived in Saint-Germain, "for noticing that your papers seem to lye a little loosely about your house. You ought to consider yourself as surrounded by spies and amidst people who can make a cable from a thread. Would not a spare half-hour per day enable your grandson to arrange all your papers, useless or not, so that you could come at them sooner, and not one be visible to a prying eye?"

The answer can be judged from one which Franklin gave to another friend who had warned him of spies soon after his arrival in Paris. "As it is impossible to discover in every case the falsity of pretended friends who would know our affairs; and more so to prevent being watched by spies when interested people may think proper to place them for that purpose; I have long observed one rule which prevents any inconvenience from such practices. It is simply this: to be concerned in no affairs that I should blush to have made public, and to do nothing but what spies may see and welcome. When a man's actions are just and honorable, the more they are known, the more his reputation is increased and established. If I was sure, therefore, that my *valet de place* was a spy, as probably he is, I think I should not discharge him for that, if in other respects I liked him." The attitude may have been excusable in a provincial politician; it was potentially disastrous when running a war, and it was to guide more than one desperately needed shipload of supplies into the hands of the enemy.

Franklin had his own sources of intelligence but they seem to have been inferior to those of the British. There was, for instance, Mrs. Patience Lovell Wright, a Philadelphian living in London during the 1770s who appears to have crossed and recrossed the Channel without hindrance.

Mrs. Wright had first met Franklin when in March 1772 she arrived at Craven Street with an introduction from his sister Jane Mecom and a waxwork head of Cadwallader Colden. She was already well known in Philadelphia as a modeler of waxwork figures, and Franklin was ready to give her helpful introductions in London. However, he was somewhat cautious about the lady and adopted the same attitude when she arrived in Passy. It was only after considerable efforts that he was persuaded to sit as a model. Shortly afterward she arrived with a lifelike bust and placed it beside Franklin with the words: "There! are twin brothers."

The effigy was to have an unusual history. It came into the hands of Elkanah Watson, who borrowed a suit of Franklin's clothes from his grandson and, on a visit to Jonathan Williams, took it to Nantes. "I had the figure placed in the corner of a large room, near a closet, and behind a table," he later explained. "Before him I laid an open atlas, his arm resting upon the table, and mathematical instruments strewn upon it. A handkerchief was thrown over the arm stumps; and wires were extended to the closet, by which means the body could be elevated or depressed, and placed in various positions. Thus arranged, some ladies and gentlemen were invited to pay their respects to Dr. Franklin, by candle-light. For a moment, they were completely deceived, and all profoundly bowed and curtsied, which was reciprocated by the figure. Not a word being uttered, the trick was soon revealed. A report soon circulated that Doctor Franklin was at Monsieur Watson's. . . . At eleven o'clock the next morning, the Mayor of Nantes came in full dress, to call on the renowned philosopher. Cossoul, my worthy partner, being acquainted with the Mayor, favored the joke, for a moment, after their mutual salutations. Others came in, and all were disposed to gull their friends in the same manner."

Watson later took the effigy to London and unwisely placed it in the windows of his lodgings, where it was seen by a number of passers-by. He was soon having to deny reports in the London papers that Benjamin Franklin had arrived in London.

According to William Temple Franklin, Mrs. Wright had her

uses. "As soon as a general was appointed, or a squadron begun to be fitted out," he wrote, "the old lady found means of access to some family where she could gain information, and thus, without being at all suspected, she contrived to transmit an account of the number of troops and the place of the destination to her political friends abroad. She at one time had frequent access to Buckingham House [as Buckingham Palace was then known], and used, it was said, to speak her sentiments very freely to their Majesties, who were amused with her originality."

But, unknown to William Temple Franklin, Mrs. Wright's correspondence was as susceptible as anyone else's to interception by William Eden's employees. On one occasion her messages were to be taken across the Channel by Mrs. Bancroft, a lady presumably helping her husband when he was wearing his American rather than his British hat. A report to Eden said:

A Mr. Hake who has some particular Influence with Mrs. Bancroft, & who has occasionally been employed in other American Services, having offered to obtain the Papers with which she might be charged to Dieppe, Ld. Suffolk directed that he should not be discouraged; & he accordingly accompanied the Lady [Mrs. Bancroft] on Friday last to Brighthelmstone [Brighton], when he got Possession of all her Letters, which were carefully opened, & without any apparent alteration return'd to her as they did not appear to contain any thing material. The following extracts were taken:—

TO *Doctor Franklin* FROM *Mrs. Wright*

"The wicked Ministry have endeavoured to propagate that 5000 provincials had come over to Govr. Irzon & Genl. Howe. . . . The reason is that they had heard of a large additional number of foreign Troops —but as soon as they are convinced they are imposed on they will return again."

. . . . . .

TO *Doctor Franklin* FROM *Alderman Lee*

"I shall in the Course of a few Days be able to accomplish what I hinted to you on the 10th Instant relative to P———r & A———n—nothing I hope will transpire. Yrs. —L—"

P———r & A———n certainly mean "Powder & Ammunition"— some very extensive Scheme of this kind is carrying between Mr.

Magze–Adn. Lee & two Mr. Wistars one of whom is in London and the other in France in his way to Guadaloupe.

. . . . . .

TO *Dr. Bancroft Dieppe* FROM *Mrs. Wright*

"Mrs. Bancroft will deliver to you herself some Hints which I beg you will pay the greatest Attention to . . . inclosed I send you Newspapers & Pamphlets."

TO *Mr. Bronfield* FROM *Mrs. Bronfield*

"I wrote last Packet from Brighthelmston—I hope you & I.W. will arrive safe to the West Indies; & that the French fleet will convey you safe to S^O. Carolina & that your Cargoes will arrive safe. . . . Tis reported 7000 Provincials have join'd L^d. Percy in Rhode Island. Depend on it, it is only a Ministerial Lie."

Capt. Burton of the Dieppe Packet, to whom Mrs. Bancroft had been particularly recommended by Daniel Wistar, finding that Mr. Hake was an American, took occasion to intimate to him that he had a place in his vessel to conceal letters which the strictest search could never discover—& that it was constantly used for this purpose.

A great deal of Franklin's correspondence was thus intercepted, opened, copied and resealed. As Jonathan R. Dull has commented in his study, "Franklin the Diplomat: The French Mission," "The American mission was so full of people stealing information it is surprising they did not trip over each other." Much of the information the British gained was disappointing, as when one of Eden's employees was put on special duty to intercept a potentially interesting package being sent from London to a "Mrs. François," whose real identity was known. "I received your Commands at a little past 12," wrote Anthony Todd from London's General Post Office, "and after our Business Outwards was over, we set to work on the Job in question, apprehending it might contain more to copy than could in the morning be done, and especially if the Dutch Mail arrives, before the hour of 12 which you mention tomorrow; but the whole turns out to be nothing, for the large Packet to Mrs. François alias Doctor Franklin, is Newspapers only, and the rest is herewith, so good Night, or rather good Morning being 3 o'clock and believe me Dear Sir, Your honest Slave, Anthon. Todd."

The Americans made some use of codes and ciphers. For a while a simple transposition of numbers for names sufficed, one typical letter to Deane reading: "I am very glad that 105 is going to 156, and I am sure it will please 38 of 68." This was open to decoding, even though the numbers were regularly changed, and a cipher devised by Congressman James Lovell began to replace it.

Lovell's cipher was built upon the substitution of numerical equivalents for agreed-upon letters from a key word or phrase. "Each of the letters adopted for use served in turn as the initial element in alphabets arranged on a sheet in parallel vertical columns. A column of corresponding numbers placed alongside these columns of alphabets provided the equivalents for the letters of encoded words, the substitutions being made alternately from two alphabets, or if more than two then in strict rotation, forward or backward as desired. Since the alphabets normally included the ampersand as a final element, the numbers used in substitution were from 1 to 27. In the cipher's purest form the numbers 28 and 29 were used at the beginning of a passage as indication that the substitutions were being made in the normal or in a reverse order, and the number 30 was used as a blind. However, more frequently all three numbers (28–30) served as blinds. Any uncoded word or words broke the continuity, the next succeeding coded passage beginning with that alphabet used at the outset of the first encoded passage, unless 28 and 29 signaled reversal."

Neither Franklin nor his colleagues were accustomed to such devices and often thought them more nuisance than they were worth. "The cipher you have communicated," Franklin told Lovell, "either from some defect in your explanation, or in my comprehension, is not yet of use to me: for I can not understand by it the little specimen you have wrote in it. If you have that of M. Dumas, which I left with Mr. Morris, we may correspond by it when a few sentences are required only to be written in cipher, but it is too tedious for a whole letter."

Codes and ciphers were not very much hindrance to awareness of Franklin's activities, with Dr. Bancroft almost literally standing at his elbow, and only the time needed for a Channel crossing separating a decision in Paris and knowledge of it in London. Vigilance was something more than the natural reaction to an enemy whom the British knew, if they did not openly admit, had an alert political brain and a keen appreciation of political propaganda. Franklin had "tamed the lightning," a feat which comparatively few politicians could understand, and it was easy enough to see him in bogy-man proportions, an evil genius who unless carefully watched might produce all manner of unexpected devices. Like the extraordinary suggestions at the start of the twentieth century that flying machines might be used against an enemy or the later wild idea that the atom might be conscripted for battle purposes, such ideas were rarely taken seriously, but they could not be dismissed.

Early in March, for instance, one of Stormont's French agents reported:

We now entertain no doubt that the motive of Doctor Franklin's journey hither was entirely philosophical and that he is consulted daily by our own Ministry. Known then, that upon the principle of Archimedes the Doctor with the assistance of French mechanics is preparing a great number of reflecting mirrors which will reflect so much heat from the sun as will destroy anything by fire at a very considerable distance.

This apparatus is to be fixed at Calais on the French coast so as to command the English shore whereby they mean to burn and destroy the whole navy of Great Britain in our harbors.

During the conflagration the Doctor proposes to have a chain carried from Calais to Dover. He, standing at Calais, with a prodigious electrical machine of his own invention, will convey such a shock as will entirely overturn our whole island.

Some months later the New Jersey *Gazette* improved upon the story. "We are well assured," said the editor, "that Dr. Franklin, whose knowledge in philosophical sciences is universally allowed, and who has carried the powers of electricity to a greater length than any of his contemporaries, intends shortly to produce an *electrical machine* of such wonderful force that instead of giving a slight stroke to the elbows of fifty or a hundred thousand men, who are joined hand in hand, it will give a violent shock even to nature herself, so as to disunite kingdoms, join islands to continents, and render men of the same nation strangers and enemies to each other; and that by a certain chemical preparation from oil, he will be able to smooth the waves of the sea in one part of the globe, and raise tempests and whirlwinds in another, so as to be universally acknowledged for the greatest physician, politician, mathematician, and philosopher, this day living."

Throughout 1777 Franklin was concerned with more practical matters, notably contracts for arms and equipment. One, of which Paul Wentworth sent a verbatim translation to Eden, signed on June 6 by Franklin and Deane on one hand and Sieur de Montieu on the other, called for the following by the end of September: 10,000 uniform coats "one half in royal blue cloth, the other in brown cloth with red facings and trimmings, white buttons, vests and breeches of white double milled cloth according to the pattern agreed upon and delivered, at the rate of 38 livres per complete suit"; 100,000 weight of red copper for cannon: 20,000 weight of fine English tin: 200 tin boxes: 22,000 weight of copper "in sheets & in nails suitable for sheathing ships or for any other purpose reqd": 4 million gun flints: 8,000 "soldiers superior guns fitted with bayonets": and 10,000 "pairs of knitted woollen stockings suitable for soldiers use." The total cost—917,820 livres, or £35,500 at the estimated rate of exchange—was to be paid in installments ending in April of the following year.

The closeness with which Franklin and his staff were watched by the British is shown by the stream of intelligence reports which went back from Paris to London. One, typical of many, dated September 19, 1777, says: "About ten days ago *Mr. Chaumont* was sent for, by a special messenger, to Court. He went instantly, returned suddenly, tho' near midnight, & again next morning by Sunrise went to Versailles, & came back in the afternoon, sat about a Quarter of an Hour with Dr. Fr: & set off, saying he was going to his Country House, which is in the neighbourhood of the Duc de Choiseul. Dr. Fr. was very secret, saying to Mr. Deane, Mr. Ch. . . . only went on a Journey of Pleasure —we know eno' to convince us that neither his occupation nor his inclination allowed such a relaxation. We have since pumped out that he is gone to the Seaports with some extraordinary orders, & the Doctor says he is now sure of a War which will appear stronger when Cht. returns. Ld. St. . . . .t has made them very cautious of us, & now Dr. Fr: only is confided in which is a disagreeable circumstance."

There was a postscript the following day. "M. Chaumont is returned," London was informed, "but still too close for penetration, but he certainly went to & staid at Rochfort three days in close quarters. Mr. Dean could get nothing from him, & *Dr. Fr. complained also* that he could only get from him, that his Errand was favorable to America, & indeed to no other."

Wentworth also sent general accounts of the situation, which mixed the natural optimism of the spy with judgments on what Franklin or Deane was thinking. Franklin, he reported in October, "with his usual apathy says, He is not deceived by France —he dreaded their seizing the opportunity with too much warmth, & by relieving the necessities of America too liberally prevent their Industry, their ingenuity & the discovery of the Resources of a Country intended by Heaven for Independance in its utmost Latitude. He cannot bear the faintest Idea of reconciliation short of Indepency [*sic*]—& is averse, in his Conversations, to the necessity of incurring obligations from France, which may bind America beyond its true Interests. Civil Wars in the Political System, like bleeding to the Human body, or Thunder Storms in due Season are Salutary, etc. etc."

The British knew only too well that Franklin had preoccupations other than the supply of French arms to America. There was the diplomatic task of ensuring that Vergennes continued to believe that the short-term dangers of supporting the Americans would be outweighed by long-term dividends. The work of privateers had to be organized. When, moreover, this was successful, as it often was, the outcome was a mass of legal red tape concerning disposal of the prizes they had taken.

French army officers, soldiers of fortune and volunteers from the galaxy of minor European armies that then existed, all wished to be helped on their way to serve the United States. In addition, Franklin naturally indulged in his own specialty and by the middle of 1777 was operating an extensive publicity campaign not only in Europe but in Britain. Before much longer, moreover, he was developing, with considerable success, what the twentieth century was to know as "black propaganda," the practice, developed by the British and the Americans during the Second World War, of issuing news which appeared to come from the enemy. Little wonder that he was later to complain, "I retain my health *a merveille*; but what with bills of exchange, cruising ships, supplies, etc., besides the proper business of my station, I find I have too much to do."

There were numerous ad hoc problems. The Americans had soon captured a considerable number of British prisoners and

Franklin formally wrote to Stormont proposing their exchange for a similar number of Americans held by the British. "The king's ministers," Stormont replied, "receive no applications from rebels, unless when they come to implore his majesty's clemency." Eventually, small exchanges began and from then on Franklin became deeply involved not only in the slowly developing system but in the conditions of those Americans held in British prisons. "I apply not to the ambassador of America," Edmund Burke had written regarding one exchange, "but to Dr. Franklin the philosopher,—the friend, and the lover, of his species." In his reply Franklin commented: "Since the foolish part of mankind will make wars, from time to time, with each other, not having sense enough otherwise to settle their differences, it certainly become the wise part, who cannot prevent these wars, to alleviate as much as possible the calamities attending them."

Even more complicated than the problems of prisoner exchange were the complexities of passing on across the Atlantic the volunteers who arrived at Passy anxious to serve in the American forces, or who wrote to Franklin with long lists of their qualifications. The French had forbidden their own officers to serve in America and did their best to discourage others from doing so. This was no more than a minor impediment to Franklin. But before his arrival in Paris it had implicated Deane in a delicate situation involving the Marquis de Lafayette, the nineteen-year-old nephew of the Duc de Noailles, the French ambassador in London. With Deane's connivance, Lafayette started his journey, was discovered and brought back to Paris. The incident disturbed relations between the Americans and the French, and all Franklin's tact was needed before the situation was restored. Then, in April 1777, Lafayette succeeded, ostensibly without American aid, and embarked on the career that was to make him an intimate of Washington and a military commander famous throughout the world.

Franklin appears to have taken a fatherly interest in the young man, who in America was supported by money from friends in France. They wished to send him more. "But on Reflection," Franklin wrote in a draft letter to Washington himself, "knowing the extream Generosity of his disposition & fearing that some of his necessitous & artful countrymen may impose on his Kindness they wish to put his Money into the Hands of some discreet Friends, who may supply him from time to time; and by that means knowing his Expenses may take Occasion to advise him if necessary, with a friendly Affection, and Secure him from too much Imposition." Washington obliged.

Another professional who crossed the Atlantic to fight in the American forces was Baron von Steuben, whom Franklin raised from captain to general in his letter of recommendation to Congress. But not all men were of that caliber and not all were welcome when they arrived. There was, for instance, the party under a M. De Brétigney, who applied for a letter of recommendation from Franklin in the summer of 1777. He described himself as a captain of infantry who wished to fight for the United States with a group that included a German captain, a German adjutant, a subadjutant of the royal cavalry, and an engineer who had served in Alsace. The recommendation was given, and in return M. De Brétigney undertook "all expenses and promises to go with 125 guns and cartridge boxes which will be used in the service of the United States and for which M. de Brétigney will require no reimbursement."

The men eventually arrived in Philadelphia but from that vantage point it looked as if Franklin was doing his job too well. "A Monsr. Brétigney, with his suite, arrived here sometime ago, with arms and cloathing for 130 or 40 men, on his way to Congress to offer them his service for raising a Regiment, etc.," Henry Laurens, then president of the Continental Congress, was told by John Rutledge in Charleston. "He was accompanied by a Baron de Thuillierd and two Garangers who were engaged by General de Coudré. They have recommendations from Dr. Franklyn and Mr. Deane, but are not, actually, in the service of the United States. As usual they had no money and application was made to our inexhaustible Treasury for a supply. At length it was resolved to give permission for sending some of the public salt to Virginia and to desire Mr. Dorsius, who was to ship it, to send 'em in the vessel with it and supply 'em with what money may be necessary for forwarding 'em to Congress—whether this money will be repaid it is impossible to say. Be pleased, however, to obtain from Monsr. Brétigney an acc^t. of what he and the other Officers take up, and Repayment of it if it can be procured—if not we must lose it. I wish, however, to know explicitly as soon as you can inform me what we may expect from Congress on such occasions, for really we are so plagued with Sturdy Beggars, of Chevaliers and French adventurers com-

mended or recommended by the Congress's Commissioners at
Paris, that I am out of all Patience with 'em, and if we are not
to be reimbursed they will never have my vote for another sixpence."

Not all the men sent across the Atlantic by Franklin reached
their destination without trouble. In September 1777 it was
reported by the Admiralty Office in London: "Lord Mulgrave in
the 'Ardent' man of war, while cruising in the Channel, took a
vessel with 300 barrels of gunpowder not declared in her lading.
On board her were several French officers of distinction and a
German Count disguised as common mariners, who were discovered by their speaking such elegant French. They afterwards
came on deck dressed in their French uniforms and denied that
they were bound for America. Lord Mulgrave refused to release
them."

There were also the privateers, the privately owned armed
ships commissioned by Congress. When Franklin arrived in
Paris he carried with him a request to the French authorities for
the protection of American privateers in French ports and even
a request that their prizes might be sold there to avoid the
dangerous voyage to America. This was not readily granted,
since in many eyes the difference between privateer and pirate
could be seen only under a strong magnifying glass. Indeed, the
British were soon considering the hanging as pirates of all crew
captured when privateering; since they were levying war on
Britain, it was argued, they were in any case guilty of high treason. Fear of retaliation appears to have stayed the British hand.
A further complication arose when the captains of some ships
were found to be carrying three commissions—one from the
French, one from the British and one from Franklin. "The villains," Lord Dartmouth was told, "thus escape with impunity."

As early as June 1777 the Lords of the Admiralty had warned
Viscount Weymouth that "if the American privateers continue
to fit out in the Ports of France and to carry their Prizes thither,
it will not be in the power of this Board to give that Protection
to the Trade of His Majesty's Subjects which they will stand in
need of while so large a number of His Majesty's Ships are
employed in North America." The message included a somewhat panic-stricken report that the *Reprisal,* the *Lexington* and the
Dolphin were all cruising off the west of Ireland, and that fifteen
ships had been taken by these vessels within four days. Dr.

Franklin was the scapegoat, having allegedly ordered the commanders "to sink, burn and destroy" all they met.

By the first months of 1778 it was estimated in London that the privateers had cost Britain £1,800,633. Five hundred and fifty-nine British vessels had been captured and were thereafter used by the Americans. Many of the privateers were, as Franklin gleefully pointed out, "manned by old smugglers, who knew every creek on the coast of England, and, running all round the island, distressed the British coasting trade exceedingly." *The Black Prince* alone took no fewer than seventy-five ships in one year. Insurance on convoyed ships was twice what it had been, and on unconvoyed ships no less than six times. Moreover, the dangers of being boarded and captured by the Americans were so great that seamen's wages more than doubled.

After each capture Franklin had to study the papers, judge the legality of the action and then write to the admiralty of the French port to which the ship had been brought. A continuing problem was provided by the question of what to do with the privateers' prizes. Until the formal outbreak of war it was difficult for the French to condone their sale in French ports, and it was not always possible for the authorities to look the other way. Captain Wickes, who had brought Franklin to France, discovered one solution and it is difficult not to believe that he had been helped in the discovery by Franklin, who by the summer of 1777 was writing to a Cherbourg firm suggesting how they might evade the law. "The Prize cannot, as you observe," he said, "be sold & delivered in your Port, it being contrary to Treaties, & to Ordinances made in Conformity to those Treaties. But I suppose it may be done in the Road without the Port, or in some convenient Place on the Coast, where the Business may be transacted without much Observation & conducted with Discretion, so as to Occasion no trouble to the Ministers by Applications from the English Ambassador. I say I suppose this may be done, because I understand it has been practised in many Cases on the Coast of Brittany." The method was used increasingly. The privateer's captain would make contact with a suitable buyer, who would then be taken to a rendezvous at sea. The prize would change hands, be renamed, and then be brought into port under a disguise which would make any British protest to the French authorities exceedingly difficult.

But there was another side to the coin. "After seizing ships," it has been written, the privateers "found it easy to seize those of neutrals. Success brought luxury, extravagance, dissipation, and a loosening of the people's morals. Sailors were easily seduced from the public ships of war to the private ships of prey. By December 1776, there were, perhaps, ten thousand 'Yankees' aboard the privateers, badly cutting the numbers in the State militia, or the Continental Army and navy. [John] Paul Jones [the most famous American naval commander of the war] was disgusted and dismayed with the mania for privateering, which forced half the American fleet to lie empty and idle in the harbour."

There were other problems connected with the privateers which took up Franklin's time. It was to him that there came a letter from one hundred and fifty crew of the *Alliance* announcing that they would not sail until they were paid six months' wages and their prize money. Franklin explained that wages had to be paid, in effect, at their home station and that the intricate details of the prize money still remained to be settled. After the *Flora* had been seized by *The Black Prince,* it was Franklin who unraveled the facts for the French judges of admiralty and explained that while the ship belonged to the subjects of a neutral nation, the cargo belonged to British subjects despite the attempt to mask the fact by forms and registrations. Work of this kind increased as commissioned American ships began to operate regularly in European waters, and Franklin found himself embroiled in an almost continuous series of negotiations with the French judges of admiralty, with shipowners and with representatives at the French court of the countries whose vessels had been involved. It was work he thoroughly detested.

When the *Ariel* was bought and then found not big enough for the arms she was intended to carry, Franklin wrote two letters on the same day which aptly reveal his feelings. "And when I have once got rid of this Business," he wrote to John Paul Jones, "no Consideration shall tempt me to meddle again with such Matters." To his grandnephew Jonathan Williams, Jr., in Nantes, he maintained: "I will absolutely have nothing to do with any new Squadron Project. I have been too long in hot Water, plagu'd almost to Death with the Passions, Vagaries, and ill Humours and Madnesses of other People. I must have a little Repose." To Samuel Huntington, president of Congress, he complained that the trouble and vexation maritime affairs gave him was inconceivable, and he often asked Congress to relieve him of them. "I must repeat my motion that the Congress would appoint consuls in the principal ports to take care of their maritime and commercial affairs," he went on; "and beg earnestly that no more frigates may be sent here to my care." But a year later he was still pointing out to Williams: "It is a vexatious thing to have Business to do which one does not understand. I had resolved to have nothing more to do with Ship Affairs; but I have lately been persuaded into two. . . . I, in all these mercantile Matters, am like a Man walking in the Dark, I stumble often, and frequently get my Shins broke."

Successful as were the American ships in general, they would have been more so had it not been for William Eden's spy network. It is true that before the age of steam, weather played havoc with sailing times. But even after the entry of France into the war the Royal Navy commanded much of the Channel as well as the western approaches, and the constant stream of accurate information from France made the lives of John Paul Jones and his colleagues more dangerous, the success of their operations less likely. As early as April 1777 Bancroft could truthfully write to Wentworth: "I have papers of the first Consequence, & there are now, no secrets kept from me." And before the end of the year Wentworth, proposing to Lord North a special payment to Bancroft of £500 following news of a coming arms shipment, described as singularly important "the early information of such an armament, by which it may be prevented, or taken if it sails; and in either case distress the Congress to the degree of a successfull Campaign." But Bancroft was merely one among many in a band which the British seemed able to recruit with ease.

There was also Captain Hynson, stepbrother of the Captain Wickes who had brought Franklin to France. Hynson was originally selected as the potential captain of a privateer. Like most Americans who were not on the list of marked rebels, he seems to have traveled as he wished between France and England. In Paris, it was arranged that, instead of captaining a privateer, he should take over in Dover a vessel to be fitted out in France as a ship, speedy but armed, to carry dispatches to Philadelphia. But in London Hynson talked too openly about his work to a Mrs. Jump. Mrs. Jump also talked, and the plans came to the ears of the ever-listening William Eden. So important was the matter considered to be that in a minute prepared for George III Eden explained that he had been in touch with the Prime Minister and that two 16-gun vessels were to be stationed off the Channel Island of Jersey, presumably with orders to intercept Hynson and his dispatches. However, there was a fair prospect of the papers being cast overboard before the ship carrying them was boarded, and a more ingenious scheme was devised. Captain Hynson could be bought, although Stormont had his doubts. "I am more and more persuaded," he wrote to Eden, "that Hynson is, in some respects at least, an Instrument in Deane's Hands, but taking him upon that footing, some use may be made of him, as he is not a Man of real ability and may easily be drawn on to say more than he intends."

It was autumn before the British plans could be put into operation, since only then did the American Commissioners decide to give Congress the first long and detailed progress report of what they were doing and planning. At this point it appeared that the British scheme would go awry, since a vessel under a Captain Folger, a distant relative of Franklin, would be ready before Hynson's. But Deane, in Paris—with or without the encouragement of Dr. Bancroft—decided that Hynson should take the precious package of documents to Le Havre, whence Folger would be sailing.

"Captain Hynson, Sir," Deane wrote in his instructions, "The Commrs. are sending a Packet to America, & by this conveyance Captn. Folger has been wrote to, to take the Charge of it if not otherways engaged, but as it is of importance that this Packet goes by safe hands I have desired him, if he cannot go to give you the Letter directed to him. . . . I am in haste. Your sincere Friend and very [unclear] Sevt. S. Deane. P.S. You are desired not to mention any thing of your Voyage or of the Packet going to any one on any Acc^t whatever."

In Le Havre, Hynson noted that the package contained not only the official dispatches but a large bundle of private letters. He handed over the package to Folger; but not before he had opened it, abstracted the thick wad of official documents, replaced them with blank paper, and resealed the package.

While Folger was still on the Atlantic with the blank paper, George III in London was reading a note from William Eden. "The inclosed papers," it said, "were brought a few Hours ago by Lieut.-Col. Smith to Mr. Eden, who, as soon as he was left alone opened them carefully so as to preserve the covers, seals and functions for possible uses which may hereafter occurr. Mr. Eden sends them the first moment he can after placing them in convenient order for your Majesty's perusal. L.C. Smith does not know any of their contents & is enjoin'd the strictest secrecy as to their being obtain'd. Hynson has by his Conduct fully discharged his promises made some months ago. —He deserves his reward therefore; but it will be attempted make him of further use before he is discover'd." The reward was £200 a year, said Eden, before adding: "He was an honest rascal and no fool tho' apparently stupid."

There are two ironic footnotes to this incident, which brought the most detailed information of Franklin's early work in France to the British. The first is that before Hynson's full success was known, but when his defection had been revealed, he tried to transform the double cross into a treble cross. "I do not write you to reproach you for the ungrateful and treacherous part you have acted," Silas Deane wrote to him from Paris in a letter intercepted by the British. "I leave this to your own Reflections, but as you have had the Assurance to write to me, and to propose the betraying of your new Patrons, in the manner you have wickedly but in vain attempted to betray your former, & with them your Country, I must tell you that no letters from you will hereafter be received by Deane."

The second footnote concerns the one British regret: that Folger had not been intercepted, since in that case the package of "documents" would probably have been destroyed and the betrayal by Hynson need never have come to light. As it was, Franklin and his colleagues months later received a message from the Committee of Foreign Affairs. Its members, it reported, were "severely chagrined" when Folger "delivered only an enclosure of clean paper, with some familiar letters, none of which contained any political intelligence."

Had Franklin and his colleagues learned of Hynson's treachery earlier, the news would have added to the gloom that had been increasing during the second half of 1777. All Franklin's resolution was needed to keep up American spirits in Paris. His wit often helped. Thus when asked whether it was true, as claimed by the British ambassador, that six battalions under Washington had surrendered, he replied: "No, monsieur, it is not a truth; it is only a Stormont." And to the comment that

America presented a sublime spectacle, he replied: "Yes, but the spectators do not pay."

Silas Deane later summarized the position. "In September, 1777," he wrote, "I laid before my colleagues a general state of our expenditures and engagements, by which it appeared that they far exceeded our funds; and no remittances from America, but on the contrary bills were drawn on us from thence by order of Congress for large sums; we were greatly embarrassed; the most unfavorable intelligence arriving at the same time from America, we were well-nigh discouraged. It was proposed, even by Dr. Franklin, that we should dispose of a part of the clothing provided, and of the ships engaged, to extricate our affairs."

The financial problems were compounded by the progress of the British forces in America. Their plans for 1777 had apparently been simple. Howe's army in New York would move north up the Hudson and along the chain of lakes which had been followed by Franklin and the other members of the mission to Canada. At the same time another British army, under General Burgoyne—"Gentleman Johnny," who combined the careers of soldier and author—would march south from Canada and join the force moving up from New York. The operation would separate the Americans in New England from their compatriots in Philadelphia and signal the beginning of the end.

On the southern front Howe, instead of moving north, moved west. He was soon threatening, then occupying, Philadelphia, where before long a British Captain André was quartered in Franklin's house, "playing with his electrical apparatus, his musical glasses, his harps, harpsichords, viols and books." As the news filtered through to Paris the position looked increasingly grim. The prospects of more subsidies, or more arms, continued to shrink.

But meanwhile, on the northern half of what was intended to be a giant entrapping movement, the position was rather different. In midsummer Burgoyne's army of 8,000 men—plus wives, women and servants—moved out onto Lake Champlain, the Indians first in birchbark canoes and the British and German troops in galleys. The British were in red, blue or green regimental uniforms; some wore plumed cocked hats: the British grenadiers wore the high bearskin hat. The Germans' headgear was faced with metal. They wore high-spurred jackboots and carried a broadsword with a three-pound scabbard. Yet although this army was so totally unequipped to fight a war in the American wilderness, its first objective, Ticonderoga, was so lightly held that it was evacuated without a fight.

South of Ticonderoga, events began to repeat those of General Braddock's campaign more than two decades previously. Burgoyne, like Braddock, tried to fight parade-ground-style. When the British started to move artillery through the forests, the Americans felled enough timber to make that impossible. For the first time Burgoyne began to worry about supplies. The only consolation was that Howe, surely by now moving up the Hudson, would soon be crossing the watershed to meet him. But Howe, unknown to Burgoyne, was already confidently occupying Philadelphia, some 250 miles away.

Howe's extraordinary action has never been fully explained. But it was later claimed that when Lord Shelburne came into office with the change of government in 1782 he found Howe's instructions in a pigeonhole. They had, it was alleged, been put there by the then secretary of state for the Colonies, Lord George Germain, because he disliked the handwriting and therefore failed to send on the instructions.

Burgoyne was soon hard-pressed, although Franklin and his fellow Commissioners in Paris knew nothing of this and viewed the future with deepening gloom. Then, early in December, Jonathan Loring Austin, secretary of the Massachusetts Council's Board of War, arrived in France carrying Washington's dispatches. He posted to Paris without delay and arrived at Passy on December 4 while Franklin, Deane and Lee were in conference. Franklin rushed out and, before Austin had time to step from the coach, asked: "Sir, *is* Philadelphia taken?" On hearing the answer, "It is, sir," he turned back. As he did so, Austin continued, "But, sir, I have greater news than that. General Burgoyne and his whole army are prisoners of war." Here, in fact, were the first fruits of the arms shipments sent out months previously.

"Gentlemen," Washington's dispatch began, "The Brigantine Perch, John Harris, Commander, by whom you will receive this letter, has been taken up and fitted out for a voyage to France, solely with a view of conveying to you the authentic intelligence of the success of the American Arms in the Northern Department."

At first it was difficult to credit the extraordinary news. Then it became clear what had happened—the British had suffered a defeat which, the historian Lord Mahon was to say, had "not merely changed the relations of England and the feelings of Europe towards these insurgent colonies, but . . . has modified, for all times to come, the connexion between every colony and every parent state."

Burgoyne, unable to press on south, halted by the enemy, the country and the handicap of commanding an army equipped for a different continent, had slowly begun to retreat. Shortage of supplies forced him to put the troops on half-rations. At Saratoga a decision to continue the retreat by night was canceled: the surrounding forests were thick with the enemy; the British could move only under their watchful eyes, and in a series of sharp actions he not only failed to extricate himself but was badly beaten. After three council meetings, it was agreed that there was no alternative but capitulation. The American demand for unconditional surrender was refused. Instead, the Convention of Saratoga was signed, and under it a British army of more than 4,000 men—all that remained after the fighting of the previous months, laid down its arms on October 17, 1777. "About 10 o'clock," wrote Lieutenant William Digby, 53d Regiment, "we marched out, according to Treaty, with Drums beating & the honours of war; but the Drums seemed to have lost their former inspiring sounds, & though we beat the Grenadiers March, . . . it seemed by its last feeble effort, as if almost ashamed to be heard on such an occasion."

On hearing the news in Passy, Franklin immediately drafted a message to Vergennes. "We have the Honour," it began, "to acquaint your Excellency that we have just receiv'd an Express from Boston, in 30 days, with Advice of the total Reduction of the Force under General Burgoyne, himself & his whole Army having surrendered themselves Prisoners." He then listed the totals of those killed or captured and of the arms, a total, as he put it, of "37 together with 4 Members of Parliament." At Versailles, two days later, Louis XVI approved a note on his gilt-edged paper saying that he would no longer decline to hear any proposals that the Commissioners might put forward.

Franklin took care to ensure that those who wished the Americans well knew immediately of the British defeat. Among them was Mme. Brillon, to whom his grandson was sent with the good news as soon as it arrived. "My dear papa," she replied, "my

heart is too full, too moved to control itself; I yield to my over-
whelming desire to write you a word; that word is that we share
your joy as fully as we love you. . . . Farewell, I am about to
compose a triumphal march to enliven the way of General Bur-
goin [*sic*] and his men, wherever they may be heading."

The American victory at Saratoga had important diplomatic
repercussions in both Paris and London. To the French, the
defeat of a British army appeared as almost a defiance of the
natural laws, and certainly an omen that America would finally
emerge as an independent state. To the British, it was a re-
minder that some accommodation with the enemy might be less
dangerous than a continuation of the war.

Franklin was the first to move. "The commissioners from the
Congress of the United States of North America," he wrote with
Deane and Lee to Vergennes on December 8, "beg leave to
represent to your excellency, that it is near a year since they had
the honor of putting into your hands the propositions of Congress for a treaty of amity and commerce with this kingdom, to
which, with sundry other memorials requesting the aid of ships
of war, and offering engagements to unite the forces of the said
States with those of France and Spain in acting against the
dominions of Great Britain, and to make no peace but in con-
junction with those courts if Great Britain should declare war
against them, to all which they have received no determinate
answer."

The French were in fact by now considering open aid to
America, even though they realized it would mean war with
Britain. But action still hung upon the agreement of Spain, the
ally of the Bourbon family compact, and on the last day of 1777
it became known that Spain was not yet willing to come out in
open support. What was France to do?

What she in fact did was helped, quite fortuitously, by a move
from England and by the diplomatic use that Franklin made of
it. British reaction to the news of Burgoyne's defeat was an
attempt to patch up a peace with the Americans. What terms
would they accept, short of independence? Wentworth was sent
to France in an effort to find the answer. He left London on
December 3 but Franklin kept him cooling his heels in Paris until
January 6. And by that time Vergennes had made it known that
France was ready formally to recognize the Americans. When
the two men eventually met, Franklin found himself and Deane

offered safe-conduct passes if they would come to London to discuss possible peace terms. There were various inducements, including the offer of creating up to two hundred American peers. Franklin refused, on two counts. America would never consider peace before independence. And, in any case, he had no power to discuss negotiations. His decision was wise. Had he and Deane quitted Paris, Vergennes would have been left to the influence of Lord Stormont without any countervailing influence from the Americans. This was to be important, since the fact that the British were now putting out peace feelers could be presented to the French with considerable effect. Vergennes, now informed of the situation by Franklin, had to consider the possibility that if he waited for Spain's support, some rapprochement might come about between Britain and America. The British would be freed from the running sore that the French had no reason for healing. There seemed only one solution. On January 7 it was decided that a treaty should be signed with the Americans even without the support of Spain.

The next day a French plenipotentiary called on the Commissioners. He had one question to ask them and, with the answer, it is preserved in the French archives in Franklin's hand. "What is necessary to be done to give such Satisfaction to the American Commissioners, as to engage them not to listen to any Propositions from England for a new Connection with that Country?" The answer: "The Commissioners have long since propos'd a Treaty of Amity and Commerce, which is not yet concluded: the immediate Conclusion of that Treaty will remove the Uncertainty they are under with regard to it, and give them such a Reliance on the Friendship of France as to reject firmly all Propositions made to them of Peace from England, which have not for their Basis the entire Freedom & Independence of America, both in Matters of Government and Commerce."

The two treaties, of Alliance and Commerce, were signed on February 6. "I at my own Expence, by a special Messenger, and with unexampled dispatch, conveyed this intelligence to this City," Bancroft wrote in London on September 16, 1784, when asking the Marquis of Carmarthen, foreign secretary, for more money; "and to the King's Ministers within 42 hours, from the instant of their Signature, a piece of information, for which many individuals here, would, for purposes of Speculation, have given me more than all that I have received from Government."

What Bancroft did not know was that his assiduity on this occasion nearly betrayed him. Shortly after copies of the treaties had arrived in London, Charles James Fox announced in the House of Commons that they had been signed, and gave the date on which the signing had taken place. "This," in Deane's words, "caused many speculations and suspicions." But before any serious investigation was launched into how the British could have known so much so soon, the Duc de Noailles made a formal announcement of the treaty in London and the matter was dropped. Bancroft escaped suspicion and continued as before.

Three documents had been signed. One was the Treaty of Amity and Commerce. The second was the Treaty of Alliance, which was to come into force if war broke out between France and Britain. The third was a Secret Article providing for the admission of Spain to the alliance as soon as that country wished it. This was far more than Congress had hoped for, and it had come about, very largely, because of the ingenious way in which Franklin had played off Britain against France and France against Britain. Here was as great a triumph as any man could hope for.

It was mid-March before the formal treaties were ready for signature by the King and by the Commissioners. Franklin had a wig made for the occasion, found that it did not fit properly and decided to enter the royal presence without either wig or the sword that was normally worn. Instead, he dressed plainly, as though he were going to dine with the President of Congress, in a suit of plain dark velvet, with the usual snowy ruffles at wrist and bosom, white silk stockings and silver buckles. "But for his noble face," wrote Mme. Vigée-Le Brun, "I should have taken him for a big farmer, so great was his contrast with the other diplomats, who were all powdered, in full dress, and splashed all over with gold and ribbons." The rest of the Commissioners dressed as was expected of them.

Franklin arrived at Versailles shortly before noon with Silas Deane, Arthur Lee and two other Americans: Ralph Izard and Arthur Lee's brother William, who had been appointed Commissioners, respectively, to Tuscany (then an important grand duchy under the rule of Leopold I, later Leopold II, Holy Roman Emperor), and to Berlin and Austria. "The King, who had been at prayer, stopped and assumed a noble posture," wrote the Duc de Croÿ. "M. Vergennes introduced M. Franklin,

M. Deane, M. Lee and the two other Americans. The King spoke first, with more care and graciousness than I have ever heard him speak. He said: 'Assure Congress of my friendship. I hope this will be for the good of the two nations.' M. Franklin, very nobly thanked him in the name of America, and said: 'Your Majesty may count on the gratitude of Congress and its faithful observance of the pledges it now takes.' "

TWELVE

THE ROAD TO YORKTOWN

FTER THE SIGNING OF THE TREATIES between France and America early in 1778, more than three months passed before a naval encounter between British and French off the isle of Ushant, western France, led to war between the two countries. During these months Franklin's task was to be complicated by development of the internecine arguments between the Commissioners and by despairing British attempts to patch up a reconciliation with the Americans before the French formally came into the conflict.

The core of the argument between the Commissioners lay in the dispute over whether the early arms shipments arranged through Beaumarchais were gifts or had to be paid for in kind. Such was the undercover nature of the operation that there was scope for genuine confusion here. It might have been removed but for two factors. One was the venomous opposition to Deane which suffused Arthur Lee's actions. The other was the knowledge that Deane was acting in Paris not only for Congress but also for Willing & Morris, a firm of suppliers from which he earned 5 percent commission. Lee, soberly described in one biographical dictionary of the war as "American diplomat, trouble-maker," had influential friends in Congress and before the end of 1777 had engineered a demand for Deane's recall. Ostensibly, this was to report on affairs in Europe. In fact, it was to answer charges of peculation brought by Lee not only against Deane but against Franklin, who was accused, on Lee's information, with having "concurred with Mr. Deane in systems of profusion, disorder, and dissipation in the conduct of public affairs," and with not being "a proper person to be trusted with the management of the affairs of America; [being] haughty and self-sufficient, and not guided by principles of virtue or honour."

There is no satisfactory evidence that any of these charges rested on more than the jealousies and ingenuous suspicions of unsophisticated men who were out of their depth in the murky waters of arms procurement. Certainly in the early days, when Deane was working on his own, the prospects of securing any arms at all must have rested to a large extent on contracts that needed to be dubiously written and on personal arrangements and obligations that were never put into writing at all. So, too, with the privateers whose activities were sometimes claimed to have sustained Franklin and Deane as much as they sustained Congress. It would have been surprising if occasionally the captain of a privateer did not favor a Commissioner with a neat piece of the loot; it would have been equally surprising if such incidents were not enlarged from mouse-size to elephantine during transmission to Philadelphia.

The question was made more complex by the accepted practice of intermingling public position with private gain in ways less obvious than those which linked Silas Deane with Willing & Morris. Thus William Temple Franklin, his grandfather's secretary, was happy to turn a profit from the opportunities that the position offered. "Mr. de Chaumont having presst me much," he wrote to John Holker, Jr., in America, "I accepted his generous offer of taking a Share in a commercial operation, in which he had engaged his Children and one or two Friends & for which he was to make the necessary advances. I was put down in the Contract for an Interest of 25,000 [francs]; the whole amount of all our Shares was to be laid out here in Merchandise & sent to America on Several bottoms to your Address. The Profits arising from the Sale of sd Merchandise, after deducting the first

Cost, were to be Devided according to the amount of our Several Shares, & each person was at Liberty to order his Retirned in the manner he thoughts best. . . . This is therefore to request you would send me as soon as possible, in Loan Office or other Bills of Exchange on Paris payable at an early Date the whole amount of my Share of the Profits of Sale above mentioned."

It was within the climate of such happy dealings that Franklin the Commissioner handed Deane a letter to the President of Congress before he left France for America a few days after being received by Louis XVI. It read as follows: "My colleague, Mr. Deane, being recalled by Congress, and no reasons given that have yet appeared here, it is apprehended to be the effect of some misrepresentations from an enemy or two at Paris and at Nantes. I have no doubt that he will be able clearly to justify himself; but having lived intimately with him now fifteen months, the greatest part of the time in the same house, and been a constant witness of his public conduct, I can not omit giving this testimony, though unasked, in his behalf, that I esteem him a faithful, active and able minister, who, to my knowledge has done in various ways great and important service to his country, whose interests I wish may always by every one in her employ, be as much and as effectually promoted." Franklin nevertheless steered clear of Beaumarchais, whose contracts were at the center of the storm and whom he called "Mr. Figaro" even in official correspondence. The Frenchman was to claim that after a year in France Franklin had never set foot in his house.

Deane's testimonial from Franklin was viewed with some suspicion when he arrived in Philadelphia without the large collection of invoices, receipts and letters which Congress believed must have existed. He should, the committee considering his case later recorded, "have brought with him from France, and . . . laid before Congress, a fair abstract of all accounts and engagements on account of these States, so far as he had proceeded in them, which is the duty and the practice of every faithful agent acting for private persons or public bodies."

Congress split into pro-Deane and pro-Lee factions. Wild allegations were spread on both sides, and Arthur Lee told his brother Richard Henry Lee: "I am more and more satisfied that the old doctor is concerned in the plunder, and that in time we shall collect the proofs." The argument continued throughout

1778 and ended only the following year when Congress formally apologized to Beaumarchais and said that he would be paid. As far as Deane was concerned, nothing could—at that date—be proved against him.

Two years later Deane returned to Europe and renewed his friendship with Bancroft. By 1781 he had become disillusioned with American prospects and set out his views to a number of American friends. They were passed on by the ever-helpful Bancroft; but passed on to the British, who published them and, to conceal Bancroft's part in the affair, claimed that they had been captured on the high seas. "He resides at Ghent," Franklin wrote in 1782 of Deane, a man by that time thought of in America not only as a financial manipulator but also as a traitor, "is distressed both in mind and circumstances, raves and writes abundance, and I imagine it will end in his going over to join his friend Arnold in England [Benedict Arnold, who had tried to betray West Point]." Franklin's judgment was to be justified. A few years later Deane moved to England; he died in the autumn of 1789 while setting out for Canada. However, more than half a century later, in 1842, Congress partially cleared his name by voting $37,000 to his heirs.

With Deane's departure from Paris early in 1778, America's hopes in France were in the hands of two men whose relations can be judged by a note from Franklin to Arthur Lee as they manned the Paris station together. "If I have often receiv'd and borne your Magisterial Snubbings and Rebukes without Reply," this went, "ascribe it to the right Causes, my Concern for the Honour & Success of our Mission, which would be hurt by our Quarrelling, my Love of Peace, my Respect for your good Qualities, and my Pity of your Sick Mind, which is forever tormenting itself, with its Jealousies, Suspicions & Fancies that others mean you ill, wrong you, or fail in Respect for you. —If you do not cure your self of this Temper it will end in Insanity, of which it is the Symptomatick Forerunner, as I have seen in several Instances." Lee did not cure himself and two years later Franklin was thanking an acquaintance for "the extracts of Mr. Lee's philippics against me. Such they were intended," he continued, "but when I consider him as the most malicious enemy I ever had (though without the smallest cause), that he shows so clearly his abundant desire to accuse and defame me, and that all his charges are so frivolous, so ill-founded, and amount to so little,

I esteem them rather as panegyrics upon me and satires against himself."

These freely expressed feelings were not unusual among the band of brothers who strove in Paris to keep supplies flowing across the Atlantic. William Lee, brother of Arthur, and appointed Commissioner to Berlin and Vienna, found that neither court would accept him and therefore remained in Paris, supporting brother Arthur against Franklin until recalled in June 1779. Arthur, eventually making himself *persona non grata* with Vergennes, was recalled three months later. The same was true of Ralph Izard, since Tuscany was as unwilling to accept him as Berlin or Vienna was to accept William Lee. Remaining in Paris, he developed what the *Dictionary of American Biography* calls "a bitter antagonism" against Franklin and was also recalled in June 1779.

Deane's replacement arrived in April 1778. He was John Adams, who had retired from Congress only the previous November after serving on some ninety committees, over twenty-five of which he presided. This man of ferocious industry and impeccable integrity, traveling with his son John Quincy Adams, spent one night in Paris before joining the already overcrowded Franklin ménage at Passy. His reactions could easily have been forecast. "I found," he wrote,

that the Business of our Commission would never be done, unless I did it. My two Colleagues [Franklin and Arthur Lee] would agree in nothing. The Life of Dr. Franklin was a Scene of continual discipation [*sic*]. I could never obtain the favour of his Company in a Morning before Breakfast which would have been the most convenient time to read over the Letters and papers, deliberate on their contents, and decide upon the Substance of the Answers. It was late when he breakfasted, and as soon as Breakfast was over, a crowd of Carriges came to his Levee or if you like the term better to his Lodgings, with all Sorts of People; some Phylosophers, Accademicians and Economists; some of his small tribe of humble friends in the litterary Way whom he employed to translate some of his ancient Compositions, such as his Bonhomme Richard and for what I know his Polly Baker etc.; but by far the greater part were Women and Children, come to have the honour to see the great Franklin, and to have the pleasure of telling Stories about his Simplicity, his bald head and scattering strait hairs, among their Acquaintances. These Visitors occupied all the time, commonly, till it was time to dress to go to Dinner. He was invited to dine abroad every day and never declined unless when We had invited Company to dine with Us. I was always invited with him, till I found it necessary to send Apologies, that I might have some time to study the french Language and do the Business of the mission. Mr. Franklin kept a horn book always in his Pockett in which he minuted all his invitations to dinner, and Mr. Lee said it was the only thing in which he was punctual. It was the Custom in France to dine between one and two o'Clock: so that when the time came to dress, it was time for the Voiture to be ready to carry him to dinner. Mr. Lee came daily to my Appartment to attend to Business, but we could rarely obtain the Company of Dr. Franklin for a few minutes, and often when I had drawn the Papers and had them fairly copied for Signature, and Mr. Lee and I had signed them, I was frequently obliged to wait several days, before I could procure the Signature of Dr. Franklin to them. He went according to his Invitation to his Dinner and after that went sometimes to the Play, sometimes to the Philosophers but most commonly to visit those Ladies who were complaisant enough to depart from the custom of France so far as to procure Setts of Tea Geer as it is called and make Tea for him. Some of these Ladies I knew as Madam Hellvetius, Madam Brillon, Madam Chaumont, Madam Le Roy etc. and others whom I never knew and never enquired for. After Tea the Evening was spent, in hearing the Ladies sing and play upon their Piano Fortes and other instruments of Musick, and in various Games as Cards, Chess, Bakgammon, etc. etc. Mr. Franklin I believe however never play'd at any Thing but Chess or Checquers. In these Agreable and important Occupations and Amusements, the Afternoon and Evening was spent, and he came home at all hours from Nine to twelve O Clock at night. This Course of Life contributed to his Pleasure and I believe to his health and Longevity. He was now between Seventy and Eighty and I had so much respect and compassion for his Age, that I should have been happy to have done all the Business or rather all the Drudgery, if I could have been favoured with a few moments in a day to receive his Advice concerning the manner in which it ought to be done. But this condescention was not attainable. All that could be had was his Signature, after it was done, and this it is true he very rarely refused though he sometimes delayed.

Adams's attitude was quickly noted. So much so that Lafayette wrote to Washington imploring him to use his influence and popularity to cool the arguments in Paris. "For God's sake prevent their loudly disputing together," he pleaded. "Nothing hurts so much the interest and reputation of America, as to hear their intestine [sic] quarrels. On the other hand, there are two parties in France: MM Adams and Lee on one part, Doctor Franklin and his friends on the other. So great is the concern which these divisions give me, that I cannot wait on these gentlemen as much as I could wish, for fear of occasioning disputes and bringing them to a greater collision."

However, it was to Franklin that even Adams had to turn when it came to the complications of diplomatic expenses. "We are all new in these matters," Franklin wrote to him before showing that some were less new than others. In general, he went on, "where a Salary was given for Services and Expenses, the Expenses understood were merely those necessary to the Man, Housekeeping, Clothing and Coach: But the Rent of the Hotel in which he dwelt, the Payment of Couriers, the Postage of Letters, the Salaries of Clerks, the Stationery for his Bureau, with the Feasts and Illuminations made on publick Occasions were esteemed expenses of the Prince or State that appointed him."

Many if not most observers of Franklin at Passy took a view very different from that of John Adams. "[His] most original trait," wrote Pierre-Georges Cabanis, a scientific writer who was one of Madame Helvétius's circle, "the one that would have made him unique no matter in what century he lived, was his art of living in the best fashion for himself and for others, making the most effective use of all the tools nature has placed at the disposal of man. . . . He would eat, sleep, work whenever he saw fit, according to his needs, so that there never was a more leisurely man, though he certainly handles a tremendous amount of business. No matter when one asked for him, he was always available. His house in Passy, where he had chosen to live because he loved the country and fresh air, was always open for all visitors; he always had an hour for you."

The very different view held by John Adams was quickly passed on to Congress, which was also told by Adams of the difficulties that bedeviled business carried out by a triumvirate of Commissioners. One man, he declared, "would be obliged to incur no greater expense, and would be quite sufficient for all the business of a public minister." The reaction was hardly to his liking. The Commission was in effect dissolved and in September 1778 Franklin was appointed minister plenipotentiary to the Court of Versailles. Six months later Adams returned to Philadelphia.

Before this took place Franklin had dealt with a number of only vaguely linked attempts by unofficial British envoys to patch up a compromise between England and America. Although some were made with the covert approval of the Prime Minister, Lord North, they were made half-heartedly and with little prospect of success. They had begun late the previous year, as soon as Burgoyne's defeat became known in London. They had increased as the chances of a Franco-American treaty loomed nearer, and had continued even after the treaties had been signed. Franklin's old friend David Hartley came first; he was followed by two English Members of Parliament, David Hutton and William Pulteney, and a Mr. Chapman of the Irish Parliament. All their hopes foundered on the simple fact that Franklin was unwilling to enter into any discussions until the Colonies had irrevocably been granted independence. Hartley remained in contact until the autumn and Franklin's vehemence in reply to one of his letters is revealing. "I wish with you as much for the restoration of Peace as we both formerly did for the continuance of it," he wrote. "But it must now be a peace of a different kind. I was fond to a folly of our *British connections,* and it was with infinite regret that I saw the necessity you would force us into of breaking it. But the extreme cruelty with which we have been treated has now extinguished every thought of returning to it, and separated us for ever. You have thereby lost limbs that will never grow again."

In the meantime, the signing of the treaties between France and the Americans had suddenly awakened the British Government to the situation it was facing. In February 1778, Lord North pushed through Parliament a series of bills repealing virtually all the legislation to which the Americans had been objecting. The following month Parliament authorized him to offer the Americans a form of government almost identical with the idea of home rule within a British Empire which Franklin had been proposing for years. But the British still balked at independence. Nevertheless, in March Frederick Howard, the 5th Earl of Carlisle, was nominated head of a commission to be sent across the Atlantic "to treat, consult, and agree upon the means of quieting the disorders" in the Colonies. Other members were

William Eden, who more than most men understood the American situation; George Johnstone, an ex-governor of Florida; and almost inevitably, it must have seemed, the two Howe brothers. Carlisle himself was under no illusion about the gravity of the situation, writing: "The French interference gives a new colour to every thing that relates to the American contest. It changes it in every point of view that it can be placed. The Question is no longer which shall get the better, Gt. Britain or America, but whether Gt. Britain shall or shall not by every means in her power endeavour to hinder her colonies from becoming an accession of strength to her natural enemies and destroy a connection which is contrived for our ruin, and might possibly effect it, unless presented by the most vigourous exertions on our parts." Many were skeptical of success and Walpole noted that Carlisle was "very fit to make a treaty that will not be made."

Yet George III, genuinely anxious to end the war—but not willing to consider independence—feared Franklin as much as Franklin feared British intransigence. "The many instances of the inimical conduct of Franklin towards this country," he wrote to Lord North on March 26, 1778, "makes me aware that hatred to this Country is the constant object of his mind, and therefore I trust that fearing the Rebellious Colonies may accept the generous offers, I am enabled by Parliament to make them by the Commissioners now to be sent to America; that his chief aim in what he has thrown out is to prevent their going, or to draw out of Administration an inclination to go further lengths than the Act of Parliament will authorise, that information from him may prevent America from concluding with the Commissioners. Yet I think it so desirable to end the War with that Country, to be enabled with redoubled ardour to avenge the faithless and insolent conduct of France that I think it may be proper to keep open the channel of intercourse with that insidious man."

However, Walpole had been right. In America, Carlisle was challenged to a duel by Lafayette, who considered himself insulted by a statement issued by the Commissioners. Carlisle replied that his position prevented him from picking up the challenge. Congress refused to consider anything less than independence, and since this was quite outside the commission's brief, its members returned to Britain empty-handed.

By the time they were back in London in the autumn of 1778 it was beginning to appear that Burgoyne's defeat the previous year was merely a taste of things to come. On June 18 the British had evacuated Philadelphia and on July 2 Congress returned to the city. The British, Franklin's son-in-law wrote shortly after the Baches had come back, "stole and carried off with them some of your musical instruments, viz. a Welsh harp, ball harp, the set of tuned bells which were in a box, viol-de-gambs [sic], all the spare armonica glasses, and one or two spare cases; your armonica is safe. They took likewise the few books that were left behind, the chief of which were Temple's school-books, and the history of the Arts and Sciences in French, which is a great loss to the public; some of your electric apparatus is missing also. A Captain André also took with him the picture of you which hung in the dining-room."

Before Franklin received this account, Admiral Augustus Keppel, leading a British squadron out of Portsmouth, fell in on June 17 with two French frigates and fired to make them heave to. The French declaration of war which followed did not make an American victory inevitable; but it made an American defeat unlikely, if not impossible.

In Britain there was one unexpected and semifarcical result of the declaration of war: the argument between those who opted for blunt points for lightning conductors and those who took Franklin's view that sharp points gave greatest protection was transformed into a political issue. The rebel Franklin must be disobeyed, and all Loyalists therefore became blunt-enders. George III ordered that the pointed conductors at Kew Palace should be changed for blunt ones. And Sir John Pringle, pointing out that "the laws of nature were not changeable at Royal pleasure," was forced to resign from the presidency of the Royal Society and from his position as the Queen's physician. But even the ordinary people could not be bamboozled. Many rhymes circulated, among them: "While you, great George, for knowledge hunt / And sharp conductors change for blunt / The Empire's out of joint. / Franklin another course pursues / And all your thunder heedless views / By keeping to the point."

In France there was a change in the relationship with America, not only in big things but in small. Among the latter was the first mutual salute "between the flag of Liberty and that of France," an incident exultantly reported by John Paul Jones. Born John Paul in southwest Scotland, Jones had sailed to America as a boy and after a turbulent youth, during which he added "Jones" to his name, was commissioned in the new Continental navy in the autumn of 1775. In December 1777, he reached France in the 18-gun sloop *Ranger* and reported to Franklin in Passy. From the start the two men took to each other and henceforward Franklin did everything possible to encourage Jones's ambitious plans. The first of these was for a cutting-out expedition against the west coast of Britain. The idea was approved, and only a month after arriving in Passy Jones was instructed that "after equipping the 'Ranger' in the best manner for the cruise you propose, that you proceed with her in the best manner you shall judge best for distressing the Enemies of the United States, by sea or otherwise, consistent with the laws of war, and the terms of your commission."

It was before sailing for Britain that Jones, arriving in Quiberon Bay, in February 1778, found the French ship *Indépendance* waiting there. "I . . . immediately despatched my long boat to find out whether the Admiral would return my salute," he wrote. "He sent reply that he would return it as being that of the senior Officer of the American Continent, at present in Europe, with the same salute that he was authorised to give to an Admiral of Holland or any other republic, that is, with 4 guns less. I hesitated, for I had asked shot for shot, so I cast anchor at the entrance of the Bay, at a little distance from the French fleet. But seeing from some private information I received on the 14th that he had really spoken the truth, I accepted his offer the more readily as after all it was a recognition of our independence. The wind being contrary, and rather violent, it was only after sunset that the 'Ranger' could approach near enough to salute Lamothe Piquet with 13 guns; he returned it with 9. However, I did not allow the 'Independance' to salute him until the next morning, when I sent word to the Admiral that I wished to pass through his squadron, and to salute him again by daylight. He was singularly flattered by this, and again returned my salute with 9 guns. The officers of this squadron are extremely well bred and polite. They all visited my vessel the 'Ranger' and expressed the greatest satisfaction with it, saying, *it is a perfect jewel.* When we visited their vessels, they received us with every sign of pleasure and consideration, and saluted us with a *feu de joie*: their attentions and civilities were carried to such a point that, if these were not sincere, they must have been very well acted."

Two months later the *Ranger* set sail for Britain. Any doubts which Franklin might have retained about the operation would have been removed had he known—and he may well have known—of the instructions issued a few weeks earlier by Lord George Germain to Sir Henry Clinton, the new commander-in-chief in America. If unable to bring Washington to a decisive engagement, Sir Henry was told, he should organize amphibious operations "to attack the Ports on the Coast, from New York to Nova Scotia, and to seize or destroy every Ship or Vessel in the different Creeks or Harbours, wherever it is found practicable to penetrate; as also to destroy all Wharfs and Stores, and Materials for Ship-Building, so as to incapacitate them from raising a Marine, or continuing their Depradations upon the Trade of this Kingdom."

Jones's plan was far less ambitious, but its psychological impact on Britain was to be enormous. Sailing up the Irish Sea he arrived on April 22, 1778, off Whitehaven, a town on the southern shore of the Solway Firth which he had known as a boy. Two landing parties went ashore, fired a number of small ships in the harbor, and returned to the *Ranger* without casualties. The damage amounted to only a few hundred pounds, but the ability of an American ship to raid a British port made it necessary for the British drastically to revise their plans.

Nor was this all. From Whitehaven, Jones crossed the Solway Firth to St. Mary's Isle, one and one-half miles south of Kirkcudbright and today a peninsula. Here there lived the Earl of Selkirk, whom he intended to bring away and hold to ransom. However, the Earl was absent and the raiding party had to satisfy itself with the Selkirk family silver, which Jones subsequently returned. Then, as a concluding touch, the *Ranger* captured H.M.S. *Drake,* a Royal Navy vessel which she had encountered on her way to Whitehaven, and sailed her into Brest with the inverted English colors flying below the American flag.

Thus within a few days the British learned that an American raider could land parties on their shores, be stopped only by bad luck from kidnapping a highly ransomable member of the House of Lords and, worst indignity of all, capture one of His Majesty's vessels. Small wonder that as soon as men and ships were available—which was not until early the following year—Franklin was planning more ambitious raids and the taking of hostages for ready money.

"I should suppose, for example," he wrote to Lafayette, "that two millions sterling or forty-eight millions of livres might be demanded of Bristol for the town and shipping; twelve millions of livres from Bath; forty-eight millions from Liverpool; six millions from Lancaster, and twelve millions from Whitehaven." On the east coast there were also Newcastle, Scarborough, King's Lynn and Great Yarmouth. "And if among the troops there were a few horsemen to make sudden incursions at some little distance from the coast it would spread terror to much greater distances, and the whole would occasion movements and marches of troops that must put the enemy to a prodigious expense and harass them exceedingly."

One plan was for an amphibious assault on Liverpool, the naval operations to be in charge of Jones and the landing forces in charge of Lafayette. This was eventually abandoned for an equally audacious but purely naval operation which began on August 14, 1779, when a task force sailed from France.

Jones's flagship was the *Bon Homme Richard,* named in honor of Franklin's "Poor Richard" of the *Almanack.* Two other frigates, the *Alliance* and *La Pallas,* a corvette, a cutter and two privateers completed the force which sailed around Ireland and the north of Scotland, capturing a number of prizes on its way. Coming down the east coast of Scotland, Jones entered the Firth of Forth with the intention of attacking Leith, the port of Edinburgh. But a change in the wind kept him from the port, as it kept him from the port of Hull—officially Kingston-upon-Hull —a few days later.

Franklin was to gain some quite fortuitous praise as a result of this weather, since on September 28 *The London Evening Post,* after reporting that neither Leith nor Hull had been burned, went on: "What an example of honour and greatness does America thus show to us! While our troops are running about from town to town on their coast, and burning every thing, with a wanton, wicked, and deliberate barbarity, Dr. Franklin gives no orders to retaliate. He is above it. And there was a time when an English Minister would have disdained to make war in so villainous a mode. It is a disgrace to the nation. But notwithstanding the moderation hitherto shown by the Americans, upon our own coast, it is to be feared that moderation will cease in a little time."

Three days before the London paper had thus praised the

Americans for their moderation, Jones had fought one of the classic sea actions of the war. Off Flamborough Head the American squadron intercepted the Baltic merchant fleet, sailing under protection of the 54-gun *Serapis* and the 20-gun *Countess of Scarborough*. Jones engaged the *Serapis* and for three and a half hours of a moonlit night fought a close-quarter engagement with the two vessels yardarm to yardarm. The *Serapis*, badly on fire, eventually struck her colors. But by this time the *Bon Homme Richard* was sinking and Jones was forced to transfer his surviving crew to the British ship before his own vessel foundered. Then, accompanied by the *Countess of Scarborough*, which had been taken by *La Pallas*, he limped into Dutch waters.

The success of John Paul Jones's two forays increased still further Franklin's popularity in France. It had been boosted by the signing of the treaties between France and the Americans and then again by the outbreak of war between France and Britain. From then on he was the representative of a French ally, and fashionable French artists clamored to paint his portrait. "I have at the request of Friends sat so much and so often to painters and Statuaries, that I am perfectly sick of it," he was to write. "I know of nothing so tedious as sitting hours in one fix'd posture. I would nevertheless do it once more to oblige you if it was necessary, but there are already so many good Likenesses of the Face, that if the best of them is copied it will probably be better than a new one, and the body is only that of a lusty man which need not be drawn from the Life; any artist can add such a Body to the face."

Despite the slightly blasé attitude, Franklin maintained a keen interest in the techniques used by artists, particularly when they had a connection with printing. Thus he was a friend of Jean Claude Richard, Abbé de Saint-Non, one of the early practitioners of engraving in aquatint. "He was curious to know the ingenious and so expeditious method which Saint-Non used for his *gravure au lavis*," runs one account. "A day was set aside for it. Franklin came to lunch, and while tea was prepared the plate was arranged. All is in order: Saint-Non sets to work: he had provided himself with a press. He printed the plate and from it came a charming print, showing the genius, or spirit, of Franklin soaring above the hemisphere of the New World, crowned by the hands of Liberty." He visited the Louvre, where Fragonard had prepared an allegorical print in which Franklin protects the seated figure of America by apposing Minerva's shield to the lightning, and there accepted from the artist the first impression, which was printed as he watched.

Meeting Jean Claude Richard and Fragonard as equals was no more than expected of the man who had tamed lightning. Indeed, Franklin was to have two meetings with the great Voltaire himself. On the first occasion the honor was to all three of the American Commissioners. On their entry into his apartment, Voltaire raised himself from his couch and repeated some lines of poetry. Arthur Lee claimed that these were from James Thomson's "Liberty":

> Lo! swarming southward on rejoicing suns,
> Gay Colonies extend; the calm retreat
> Of undeserved distress, the better home
> Of those whom bigots chase from foreign lands.
> Not built on Rapine, Servitude, and Woe,
> And in their turn some petty tyrant's prey;
> But, bound by social Freedom, firm they rise.

Edward Hale and Edward Hale, Jr., maintain that Voltaire in fact quoted from Joseph Addison's poem, "A Letter from Italy to the Right Honourable Charles Lord Halifax, in the Year MDCCI":

> O Liberty, thou goddess heavenly bright,
> Profuse of bliss, and pregnant with delight!
> Eternal pleasures in thy presence reign,
> And smiling plenty leads thy wanton train;
> Eased of her load, subjection grows more light,
> And poverty looks cheerful in thy sight;
> Thou mak'st the gloomy face of nature gay,
> Giv'st beauty to the sun, and pleasure to the day.

"Franklin," Condorcet has said in his life of Voltaire, "was eager to see a man whose reputation had long been spread over both worlds; Voltaire, although he had lost the habit of speaking English, endeavoured to support the conversation in that language; and, afterwards reassuming French, he said: 'Je n'ai pu résister au désir de parler un moment la langue de M. Franklin.' ('I could not resist the desire of speaking the language of Mr.

Franklin for a moment.') The American philosopher presented his grandson to Voltaire, with a request that he would give him his benediction. 'God and liberty!' said Voltaire: 'it is the only benediction which can be given to the grandson of Franklin.' "

The second encounter came at a meeting of the Académie des Sciences. At a pause in the proceedings there arose a cry from those present calling for the two men, who sat near to one another, to be introduced. This was done. Then they shook hands. But this was not enough and the call came: "Il faut s'embrasser, à la Françoise." Then, says John Adams, "The two aged actors upon this great theatre of philosophy and frivolity then embraced each other by hugging one another in their arms, and kissing each other's cheeks, and then the tumult subsided. And the cry immediately spread through the whole kingdom, and, I suppose, over all Europe, 'Qu'il etait charmant de voir embrasser Solon et Sophocle!' ('How charming it was to see Solon and Sophocles embrace.')"—the Parisians hailing Franklin as Solon since they believed, incorrectly, that he had given America a constitution.

As France prepared to coordinate her military efforts with those of the Americans, Franklin was made minister plenipotentiary to the Court of Versailles, a post equal in status to those granted the states, kingdoms, principalities, duchies and dukedoms which then littered Europe in considerable numbers. However, accreditation brought its burdens. From now on, unless absolved by the King's secretary, he had to put in an appearance at Versailles every Tuesday. He also had to abide by the tedious court ceremonials, which included attendance in mourning as necessary. "Went to Versailles to assist at the ceremony of condolence on the death of the Empress Queen [Empress Maria Theresa]," he was later to record. "All the foreign ministers in deep mourning, —flopped hats and crape, long black cloaks, etc. The Nuncio pronounced the compliments to the king and afterwards to the Queen in her apartments. . . . Much fatigued by the going twice up and down the palace stairs, from the tenderness of my feet and the weakness of my knees; therefore did not go the rounds."

Usually, however, he did "go the rounds," the social rounds that might be enjoyable but took up time, that most precious of all commodities. Throughout 1779 and 1780, Franklin became increasingly short of the commodity as the Franco-American alliance produced a growing flow of arms across the Atlantic. At one level, it called for paying the bills for goods supplied to Congress. Franklin resented this strongly. It was, he wrote, "a business that requires being always at home, bills coming by post, from different ports and countries, and often requiring immediate answers, whether good or not; and to that end, it being necessary to examine by the books, exactly kept of all preceding acceptances, in order to detect double presentations, which happen very frequently. The great number of these bills makes almost sufficient business for one person, and the confinement they occasion is such, that we cannot allow ourselves a day's excursion into the country, and the want of exercise has hurt our healths in several instances." It was no more than the truth. During the eight and a half years he spent in Paris, Franklin rarely traveled, except to visit the court.

Quite apart from the official work which tied him to his Passy headquarters there was an extraordinary volume of other mail which had to be dealt with. Begging letters arrived by the score, asking for money, a post for a relative or preferential treatment on arrival in America. Ladies whose husbands, or other relatives, had crossed the Atlantic in the American cause and disappeared without trace frequently felt that recompense was their due. A Benedictine prior who had succumbed to gambling begged help from Franklin, who noted on his letter: "Wants me to pay his gaming debts and he will pray for success to our cause."

Inventors were generous, and to Passy there came offers of new methods of secret writing, a new gun carriage, a cannon which would fire twelve times a minute, a method of making gunpowder nonexplosive or explosive at will, an automatic chess-player and a process which could "kindle the lightning and cause the most tremendous explosions." A Lutheran clergyman wanting to emigrate noted that if he was unable to make a living by teaching, writing or farming, he could no doubt help the Americans by his knowledge of strategy. There were offers to write the history of the war, or of America. And there was the gentleman who wished Franklin to read his history of the beginning of the world, "proved by the agreement between the laws of physics and the book of Genesis." Among the requests for an interview with "the most illustrious man of his age" and for the gift of "one of the pens which traced the glory and safety of

America," there was the occasional request for information on erecting lightning conductors and a constant jogging of the mind about former acquaintanceship in Pennsylvania.

All this prevented Franklin from devoting much time to scientific speculation, a limitation which he much regretted. "If I were in a situation where I could be a little more master of my time," he wrote to one correspondent after describing an experiment to see whether the tides were affected by gravity, "I would, as you desire, write my ideas on the subject of chimneys: they might, I think, be useful. For by what I see everywhere the subject seems too little understood, which occasions much inconvenience and fruitless expense. But besides being harassed by too much business, I am exposed to numberless visits, some of kindness and civility, many of mere idle curiosity, from strangers of America and of different parts of Europe, as well as the inhabitants of the provinces who come to Paris. These devour my hours, and break my attention, and at night I often find myself fatigued without having done any thing. Celebrity may for a while flatter one's vanity, but its effects are troublesome. I have begun to write two or three things, which I wish to finish before I die; but I sometimes doubt the possibility."

Interruptions were frequent. "Near three years ago," he wrote to Edward Nairne, his friend the London instrument-maker, "I began a letter to you on the subject of hygrometers [instruments for measuring humidity]. I had written three folio pages of it, when I was interrupted by some business; and, before I had time to finish it, I had mislaid it. I have now found it, and, having added what I suppose I had intended to add, I enclose it."

Handling the bills with which Congress did its best to pay for military supplies was nevertheless a minor matter compared to the more and more intricate problems of supply itself. In March 1781, while the long drawn-out complexities of shipping arms across the Atlantic were still continuing, Franklin, aged seventy-five, offered his resignation to Congress. "I do not know that my mental faculties are impaired," he wrote; "perhaps I shall be the last to discover that; but I am sensible of great diminution of my activity, a quality I think particularly necessary in your Minister for this court. I am afraid, therefore that your affairs may, in some way or other, suffer by my deficiency."

His enemies made a meal of the idea. "He says perhaps he is

too Old," Alice Lee Shippen told Elizabeth Welles Adams, "but he does not perceive any thing like it himself; and then gives a strong Proof of it by recommending his Grandson as the Person who will, in a Year or two, be most fit for our Plenipotentiary. From this recommendation one or the other of these two things is clear, either Mr. F's faculties are impair'd, or he thinks ours are."

Although he was no doubt more than irked by the ceaseless bickerings among his suppliers, his captains and the other Commissioners, it is mildly surprising that he wished to retire from the scene at this stage of the game, and he may not have been entirely surprised when Congress ensured that he labored on for another four years.

At times it was difficult to believe that the war would ever reach a successful end, and on one occasion Franklin felt it necessary to warn Vergennes of what a British victory would mean. Congress had instructed him to ask for a further loan of 25 million francs and he took the opportunity to point out to Vergennes that the situation was critical. There was, he went on, "some danger lest the Congress should lose its influence over the people, if it is found unable to procure the aids that are wanted; and that the whole system of the new Government in America may thereby be shaken; that, if the English are suffered once to recover that country, such an opportunity of effectual separation as the present may not occur again in the course of ages; and that the possession of those fertile and extensive regions, and that vast seacoast, will afford them so broad a basis for future greatness, by the rapid growth of their commerce, and breed of seamen and soldiers, as will enable them to become the *terror of Europe,* and to exercise with impunity that insolence, which is so natural to their nation, and which will increase enormously with the increase of their power."

There was, indeed, good reason for worry. During the first weeks of 1780 the Americans were so short of money that even John Paul Jones received a discouraging reply to an appeal made to Franklin, being told that there was no chance at all of having his ship sheathed with copper. Nor could a second vessel be bought for him. As for refitting, Franklin had no money available and it was certain that the French would not pay for the work. All Jones got was approval for ordering repairs from a named firm. "But," Franklin told him, "let me repeat, for God's sake be sparing, unless you mean to make me bankrupt, or have your drafts dishonoured for want of money in my hands to pay them.''

Military affairs were no better than the financial. A French fleet had crossed the Atlantic in 1779 but had been too late to prevent the British from sending a force by sea from New York to invest the southern states. Savannah fell to it during the last days of December 1778, and before the end of January 1779 Augusta had also been captured. Little more than three months later Charleston was given up by the Americans and it appeared that the British were rolling back the Colonial forces with little difficulty.

Nevertheless, and despite whatever warnings he might give to Vergennes, Franklin himself refused to admit the possibility of defeat; or, perhaps more accurately, he refused to admit the possibility when writing to America. "I must soon quit this scene," he wrote to Washington on one of those later occasions when he felt he had little longer for this world, "but you may live to see our country flourish, as it will amazingly and rapidly after the war is over; like a field of young Indian corn, which long fair weather had enfeebled and discolored, and which in that weak state, by a thunder gust of violent wind, hail and rain, seemed to be threatened with absolute destruction; yet the storm being past, it recovers fresh verdure, shoots up with double vigor, and delights the eye, not of its owner only, but of every observing traveller." He was buttressed in his beliefs by the logistical argument: Britain, separated from the Colonies by 3,000 miles of sea, would never command the manpower or the finance to subdue perpetually a quickly growing nation whose natural wealth stretched across a rich and almost limitless interior. Even before the war had properly begun he had put the numerical argument to Priestley: "Britain, at the expense of three millions, has killed one hundred and fifty Yankees this campaign, which is twenty thousand pounds a head; and at Bunker's Hill she gained a mile of ground, half of which she lost again by our taking post on Ploughed Hill. During the same time 60,000 children have been born in America. From these *data* [your] mathematical head [that of Dr. Richard Price, the nonconformist minister and writer on economics whom Franklin had known at the Club of Honest Whigs] will easily calculate the time and expense necessary to kill us all, and conquer the whole of our territory.''

In his approach Franklin was the predecessor of the operational research experts of the Second World War. Like Professor P. M. S. Blackett, the British physicist who had helped to introduce radar in time for the Battle of Britain, he wished ''to avoid running the war by gusts of emotion.'' Instead, he judged every proposal on strictly utilitarian lines. Thus he defended the use of bows and arrows, when muskets were in short supply, on very commonsense grounds. A man could shoot as accurately with a bow as with a musket—possibly with greater accuracy—and could discharge four arrows in the time it took to charge and discharge a single bullet. The bow produced no obscuring smoke, while ''A flight of arrows, seen coming upon them, terrifies and disturbs the enemy's attention to their business.'' Moreover an arrow put a man *hors de combat* until it could be extracted and was in any case easier to provide than muskets and bullets. War with the Indians had taught a few lessons.

Franklin used the rational approach to all the problems which faced him in Passy, problems which if imperfectly solved could mean disaster or near-disaster. He himself had explained the method to Priestley years earlier. When there was much on either side of an argument, he said, he divided a sheet of paper into two columns and wrote ''pro'' over one of them and ''con'' over the other. ''Then during three or four Days Consideration,'' he continued, ''I put down under the different Heads short Hints of the different Motives that at different Times occur to me for or against the Measure. When I have thus got them all together in one View, I endeavour to estimate their respective Weights; and where I find two, one on each side, that seem equal, I strike them both out: If I find a Reason *pro* equal to some two Reasons *con,* I strike out the three. If I judge some two Reasons *con,* equal to some three Reasons *pro,* I strike out the five; and thus proceeding I find at length where the Balance lies; and if after a Day or two of farther Consideration, nothing new that is of Importance occurs on either side, I come to a Determination accordingly. And tho' the Weight of Reasons cannot be taken with the Precision of Algebraic Quantities, yet when each is thus considered separately and comparatively, and the whole lies before me, I think I can judge better, and am less likely to make a rash Step; and in fact I have found great Advantage from this kind of Equation, in what may be called *Moral* or *Prudential Algebra.*"

Beavering away in his Passy quarters, frequently plagued with the pains of gout when he had to take a carriage to Versailles or to some important function at which it was expedient to be present, Franklin never relaxed his objective prosecution of the war. Yet he was a man determined to limit its evils as far as possible. The most famous example is probably his call to commanders of armed ships on commission from Congress to treat Captain Cook and his crew "with all civility and kindness, affording them, as common friends to mankind, all the assistance in your power which they may happen to stand in need of." Cook, not known to have died in the spring of 1779, was thought to be returning from his voyage of discovery, and it was Franklin's plea that he should not be treated as an enemy.

These were the sentiments of a man who believed that the ships of neutral countries should be respected even when they were carrying British goods, and who maintained that surgeons should never be detained as prisoners of war but considered as friends to humanity.

War had already been "humanizing by degrees" over the centuries, he argued; surely it should be possible for nations to agree that the following categories of men should be left undisturbed:

1. Cultivators of the earth, because they labor for the subsistence of mankind. 2. Fishermen, for the same reason. 3. Merchants and traders, in unarmed ships, who accommodate different nations by communicating and exchanging the necessaries and conveniences of life. 4. Artists and mechanics, inhabiting and working in open towns.

It is hardly necessary to add that the hospitals of enemies should not be molested; they ought to be assisted.

In short, [he went on,] I would have nobody fought with, but those who are paid for fighting. If obliged to take corn from the farmer, friend or enemy, I would pay him for it; the same for the fish or goods of the others.

This once established, that encouragement to war which arises from spirit of rapine would be taken away, and peace therefore more likely to continue and be lasting.

The feeling came to the surface when he heard from David Hartley that plans were being made in England to safeguard theaters against the effects of fire. "Your concern for the security of life, even the lives of your enemies, does honor to your heart and your humanity," he wrote. "But what are the lives of a few idle haunters of play houses compared with the many thousands of worthy men and honest, industrious families butchered and destroyed by this devilish war? O! that we could find some happy invention to stop the spreading of the flames, and put an end to so horrid a conflagration!"

As the conflagration continued to blaze, Franklin grew increasingly bitter at the Americans' inability or unwillingness to tighten their belts. "The extravagant luxury of our country in the midst of all its distresses is to me amazing," he wrote on October 4, 1779, to John Jay, the president of Congress, just appointed minister to Spain. "When the difficulties are so great to find remittances to pay for the arms and ammunition necessary for our defense, I am astonished and vexed to find, upon inquiry, that much the greatest part of the Congress interest bills come to pay for tea, and a great part of the remainder is ordered to be laid out in gewgaws and superfluities."

Even his beloved daughter was not spared when she asked him to send her long black pins and lace and feathers. The request, he told her, "disgusted me as much as if you had put salt in my strawberries. . . . If you wear your cambric ruffles as I do, and take care not to mend the holes, they will come in time to be lace; and feathers, my dear girl, may be had in America from every cock's tail."

Franklin, better than any American then alive, realized how victory could be achieved only through a combined operation in which arms, economics and diplomacy were all utilized. There was also propaganda, a *specialité de la maison* with the U.S. ambassador to France since he had written for his brother's paper more than half a century before. In England he had raised one branch of this to a fine art. In Paris he also developed an early form of black propaganda, an outgrowth of the hoax which he had used more than once in England. The first opportunity occurred when the capture of the Hessians at the Battle of Trenton became known in Europe. It was common knowledge in France that at this time a Count Schaumburg was trying to hire

Hessian troops on behalf of George III, and there was an initial credibility about a letter which appeared in Paris, allegedly from "le Comte de Schaumberg" to the commander of the Hessians in America. Since a lump sum, it was claimed, was paid by the British for each Hessian killed, the Count congratulated the commander in America on the number who had died at Trenton. "I shall be sending you new recruits," the Count apparently continued. "Do not be economical with them. Remember glory before all things." He went on to suggest that there was no point in keeping the wounded alive, nor for too much medical care. "You know that I get paid for those who die of disease as much as I do for those who are killed [in battle], but I don't get a sou for deserters. My trip to Italy, which has cost me a very great deal, makes it desirable that there should be a great number of casualties." The hoax was quickly assessed by many for what it was. But it may have caused them to think, and it may have taken in the more gullible.

But this was only one side of the coin. The other was provided with the help of a printing press which Franklin had set up at Passy. On it he produced many of the forms required for congressional business. On it he printed items as different as passports and the *bagatelles* or *jeux d'esprit* with which he from time to time amused Parisian society. And on it he no doubt intended to print the book of British atrocities for which he began collecting details in 1779. "You being now upon the Spot," he wrote to Lafayette, "can easily obtain & send me all the authenticated Accounts of the Enemies Barbarity that are necessary for our Little Book, or What is better get some body there to write it, & send me a Copy that I may adapt the Cuts [illustrations] to it. I have found an excellent Engraver for the Purpose."

Atrocities material was eventually produced in a curious way, after peace negotiations with the British had begun, and with the aim of disillusioning still further an already disillusioned British public. It came as a forged supplement to Boston's *Independent Chronicle.*

For Franklin, master printer, there was little difficulty in finding type almost indistinguishable from that used in Boston. The outcome was a copy of the paper, complete with advertisements and similar material, that easily passed as genuine. Prominently included in it was the extract of a letter allegedly written by Captain Gerrish of the New England Militia, reporting that his troops had captured British material. "The possession of this Booty," he went on, "at first gave us Pleasure; but we were struck with Horror to find among the Packages 8 large ones, containing SCALPS of our unhappy Country-folks, taken in the three last Years by the Senneka Indians from the Inhabitants of the Frontiers of New York, New Jersey, Pennsylvania, and Virginia, and sent by them as a Present to Col. Haldimand, governor of Canada, in order to be by him transmitted to England." The eight packs contained a total of 954 scalps, it was alleged. Each was described, and of No. 8 it was said: "This package is a Mixture of all the Varieties above-mentioned; to the number of 122; with a Box of Birch Bark, containing 29 little Infants' Scalps of various Sizes; small white Hoops; white Ground; no Tears; and only a little black Knife in the Middle, to shew they were ript out of their Mothers' Bellies."

It had at first been proposed, the report went on, that the captured packages of scalps should be smuggled into England and hung up on "some dark Night on the Trees in St. James's Park, where they could be seen from the King and Queen's Palaces in the Morning." But this plan was changed. "It is now proposed," said the paper, "to make them up in decent little Packets, seal and direct them; one to the King, containing a Sample of every Sort for his Museum; one to the Queen, with some of Women and Little Children; the Rest to be distributed among both Houses of Parliament: a double Quantity to the Bishops."

Copies of the forged issue were soon circulating not only in Europe—"Make any use of them you may think proper to shame your Anglomanes, but do not let it be known through what hands they come," Franklin instructed Charles Dumas, who was sent a supply—but in England itself. And to John Adams he gave a justification not often available for those spreading atrocity propaganda. After saying that the numbers believed to have been scalped with British connivance was more than the 954 reported in the forged issue, he commented: "These being *substantial* Truths the Form is to be considered as Paper and Pack-thread," and concluded: "If it were republish'd in England it might make them a little asham'd of themselves."

The propaganda, the business routine, the multiplicity of

problems which came to Franklin's desk for solution, were all
dealt with against a background of sometimes crippling gout.
Franklin told Vergennes on one occasion that he had been "so
ill with the gout and a fever that I could neither write nor think
of anything." The President of Congress was told by Franklin
that he had been laid up with a long and severe fit of gout which
confined him to Passy for weeks and that even two months later
he had not quite recovered the full use of his feet.

All this could interfere with his duties, as he had once explained to John Adams. "My gout continues to disable me from
walking longer than formerly," he wrote, "but on Tuesday the
23rd past, I thought myself able to go through the ceremony,
and accordingly went to court, had my audience of the king in
the new character [of envoy extraordinary and minister plenipo-
tentiary] presented my letter of credence, and was received very
graciously, after which I went the rounds with the other foreign
ministers in visiting all the royal family. The fatigue, however,
was a little too much for my feet, and disabled me for near
another week."

With an honesty unusual among sufferers, Franklin admitted,
if obliquely, that he well knew the cause of the trouble, since
among the lighter pieces he wrote at Passy was *Dialogue between
Franklin and the Gout.* The essay begins with Franklin asking what
he has done to deserve it, a question to which the Gout replies:
"Many things; you have ate and drank too freely, and too much
indulged those legs of yours in their indolence." And, later:
"Yet you eat an inordinate breakfast, four dishes of tea, with
cream, and one or two buttered toasts, with slices of hung beef,
which I fancy are not things the most easily digested."

In words more candid than those of the *Dialogue*, Franklin
tended to confirm that good living was the cause of his gout, as
of most other men's. "On Monday the 15th [February 1779] I
dined and drank rather too freely at M. Darcy's," he noted.
"Tuesday morning I felt a little pain in my right great toe."
Quite apart from similar evenings, as when, he reported, "I ate
a hearty supper, much cheese and drank a good deal of champagne," there were the special occasions such as Independence
Day. One year a party of about fifty was invited to Passy. "An
elegant entertainment was prepared," Jonathan Loring Austin
wrote, "the table decorated with a variety of flowers in a pleasing
manner. The American flag, the Cap of Liberty, and many of the

useful arts were represented at this cheerful banquet. Each guest drew from a basket a handsome posy of flowers, having an inscription on it. Joy and festivity crowned the day. A number, say thirteen, toasts were drunk after dinner." Yet despite the apparent correlation between his gout and his enjoyment of food and drink there is another circumstance to be noted. The gout invariably seems to have arrived when Franklin was under the stress and strain of work.

Typical of the anxieties was the saga of a major cargo of military supplies which started in December 1779 when Franklin's grandnephew Jonathan Williams, Jr., began preparations. Delay followed delay—over money, the supplies themselves, the ships to carry them and the crews to man the ships—and a year later Franklin told Lafayette: "There has been a kind of Fatality attending the affair of sending out the Cloathing. A Number of unforeseen & unaccountable Accidents have delay'd and prevented it from time to time. Part of it is however at length gone; and the Rest in a fair Way of going soon, with the Arms, Powder, &c." On March 29, 1781, "the Rest" sailed in the *Alliance* and the *Lafayette,* and on May 14 Franklin wrote Lafayette saying that the ship bearing his name should have arrived by now. "She carried clothing for nearly twenty thousand men, with arms, ammunition &c. which will supply some of your wants." But the two ships were separated on the high seas by storms. The *Alliance* reached America. But the *Lafayette* was captured by three British men-of-war. Franklin learned of the loss in June, a few weeks before the captured cargoes were auctioned in London.

As Franklin wrestled with his problems, the war went on as inexorably as his gout. When France had signed the Treaty of Alliance with America it had at first seemed that this might, after a quick victory or two, drive the British into capitulation. Yet the French war machine, still affected by the defeats of the previous decade, and hampered by the crumbling financial situation, was slow in lumbering into action. At the start of 1780 victory looked as far away as ever.

But if the position appeared discouraging from Passy and from Philadelphia, it appeared little better from Whitehall. Discontent remained strong in Britain, where the constant draining away of men, money and materials was now increasingly criticized. In the summer of 1776 "the war" had been no more than a minor skirmish against a handful of armed Colonial rebels. By

1780 it had grown into a full-scale conflict against a formidable American army, a hornet's nest of privateers and the threatening military and naval forces of France.

Yet whatever discontents developed in Britain they were counteracted by events in the field. Here the British for long had reasons for confidence. They successfully remained in occupation of New York while their command of the sea had given them control of Georgia and South Carolina. Moreover in the early autumn the treachery of Benedict Arnold, who tried to betray West Point to the British for £20,000, sent a tremor through many Americans. "His Character is in the Sight of all Europe already on the Gibbet & will hang there in Chains for Ages" was Franklin's verdict to Lafayette. Certainly if a general who had heroically served the cause for five years could contemplate betraying one of the most important fortifications on the Hudson, what else might not happen? "I hope your Fears that there may be Arnolds at Paris are groundless," Franklin wrote to James Searle, who had been sent to Europe as Pennsylvania agent earlier in 1780. "But in such Time one cannot be too much on one's Guard, and I am obliged to you for the Caution." Dr. Bancroft no doubt took note of the warning.

Throughout 1780, the ebb and flow of battle had brought victories to both sides, but though none was decisive, the American surrender of Charleston had nearly been so. Then in 1781 the balance began to tilt, largely owing to the arrival off America of a formidable French fleet, which limited the freedom of action previously enjoyed by the British. In the south, now the center of action, the British commander, Lord Cornwallis, was forced into Yorktown, a coastal town from which he believed that evacuation under the protection of the British fleet was always available. But the vessels standing off Yorktown were the French ships of Admiral de Grasse. In the hinterland of Yorktown one American army under Lafayette was joined by a second under Washington. The trap finally closed, and on October 19, 1781, a British army of nearly 8,000 men surrendered to General Benjamin Lincoln, the Massachusetts farmer who in 1775 was only a lieutenant colonel in the militia but had become a major general in the Continental army two years later.

News of the British disaster, for it was no less, reached Europe in a month, a French vessel bringing the first reports to Vergennes on November 19. He at once wrote a note, timed 11:00

P.M., for Franklin at Passy. "The English garrison came out of Yorktown the 19th of October, with honors of war, and laid down their arms as prisoners," it ran. "About six thousand troops, eighteen hundred sailors, twenty-two stand of colors, and one hundred and seventy pieces of cannon—seventy-five of which are brass—are the trophies which signalize this victory; besides, a ship of fifty guns was burnt, also a frigate and a great number of transports."

Franklin immediately produced copies of Vergennes's note and sent them to friends and supporters throughout the city. The next day he exultantly proclaimed: "There is no parallel, in history, of two entire armies being captured from the same enemy in any one war."

But Franklin's excitement was so great that he forgot to inform Mme. Brillon, overwintering in Nice, as he had informed her of Burgoyne's defeat, an omission that led to a revealing exchange of letters. "Do you know, my dear papa, why I am sending you just a tiny, very tiny word? It is because I am sulking . . . yes, mister papa, sulking," she wrote. "What! You capture entire armies in America, you *burgoinize* Cornwallis, you capture guns, ships, ammunition, men, horses, etc. . . . and your friends have to learn it from the gazette. They get drunk on toasts to you, to Wasington [*sic*], to independence, to the King of France, to Marquis de Lafayette, Rochambault, Chatelux [*sic*], etc., etc., but from you, not a peep. . . . Surely you must feel twenty years younger after this good piece of news, which ought to give us a durable peace after a glorious war. . . . As I don't wish for the sinner's death, I shall compose a triumphal march, will send it to you, will write, and will even keep on loving you with all my heart."

Mme. Brillon did compose her triumphal march, the "Marche des Insurgents." And she received from Franklin a letter, written on Christmas Day, which gives a clue to his success in steering America to victory. "You are sulking, my dear friend, because I did not send you at once the story of our great victory," he began. "I am well aware of the magnitude of our advantage and of its possible good consequences, but I do not exult over it. Knowing that war is full of changes and uncertainty, in bad fortune I hope for good, and in good I fear bad. I play this game with almost the same equanimity as when you see me playing chess. You know that I never give up a game before it is finished, always hoping to win, or at least to get a move, and when I have a good game, I guard against presumption."

It was typical of Franklin that with the "business" side of the letter out of the way, he should remind Mme. Brillon of his personal infatuation. "I often pass in front of your house," he went on. "It seems desolate. In olden days, I broke a commandment, by coveting it, together with my neighbor's wife. Today, I don't covet it anymore, so that I am less of a sinner. But as far as the wife is concerned, I still think those commandments very bothersome and I am sorry that they ever were devised. If, in your travels, you ever come across the Holy Father, ask him to rescind them, as given only to the Jews and too much trouble for good Christians."

However cautious Franklin might be about Yorktown, there was little doubt of what the British defeat implied and he proposed striking a medal which would commemorate Saratoga and this second victory. His initial plan was to show, on one side of the medal, the infant Hercules in his cradle in the act of strangling the two serpents and, on the other, France as a Minerva sitting by the cradle with spear and helmet, clad in a robe flecked with fleurs-de-lis. As finally struck, one side of the medal showed the infant and also Minerva, who was fighting the British lion. Below was the motto NON SINE DIIS ANIMOSUS INFANS and the dates of Saratoga and Yorktown. On the other side was a head of Liberty, the date of the Declaration of Independence and the words LIBERTAS AMERICANA.

In Britain Lord George Germain, asked how Lord North had taken the news, replied to Sir Nathaniel William Wraxall: "As he would have taken a ball in his breast." In fact North, the minister more responsible than any other for the disastrous war, had groaned and exclaimed: "Oh, God, it is all over." It was not yet all over. But from the end of 1781 Franklin had the fresh burden of ensuring that peace negotiations did not transform victory into defeat.

THIRTEEN

INDEPENDENCE
WON

HE BRITISH FLEET WAS STILL IN EX-
istence but was now being successfully challenged by
the French. The war had been lost and the most sensible course would have been for Britain to admit the fact and
open peace negotiations, as quickly as possible and with the
minimum number of qualifications. However, this was a difficult
operation for a nation which only a generation before had humbled the French and which still considered itself the leader of the
Western world. Negotiations were therefore to be grudging,
marked by a dogged attempt to split the Americans from the
French and by a niggling over individual points which did Britain little credit at the time and which in the backward glance of
history does her even less. Surely—shades of Franklin's earlier
ideas!—the British could deal with the Colonies as partners in
a federation? Or surely a parallel might be drawn with the Irish,
for whom the British Government was about to repeal Poyning's
law, which for nearly three hundred years had ensured that no
legislation could be carried out by the Irish Parliament until it

had been approved by the king of England and the English council? It is just possible that some such compromise, well packaged and disguised, might have been slipped past the Americans but for the single-mindedness of Franklin. Peace was important—he knew that better than anyone—but first there must be the guarantee of independence, complete and unqualified. And peace would have been even longer delayed without the links which he had continued to maintain with Britain during the war years, and without his mastery of both the tactics and the strategy of diplomatic battle.

Earlier there had been attempts on both sides to arrange some kind of compromise peace. The Carlisle Mission of 1778, crossing the Atlantic from Britain in the wake of Burgoyne's defeat, had failed ignominiously. The following year John Adams was given the task of sounding out peace negotiations with Britain. But on arrival in Paris he found the French considered the situation unripe for negotiations. The operation was stillborn and by the end of the year Adams had been established in The Hague, minister to the United Provinces (Holland).

Only in June 1781—four months before the British disaster at Yorktown—did Congress nominate a five-man committee that was to try to negotiate a peace with Britain. Franklin was one member, John Adams another, a double choice which surprised members of the anti-Franklin faction in Philadelphia who knew of the bickering between the two men. "Can harmony be expected by joining a man's calumniator with him?" Alice Lee Shippen asked Abigail Adams. "It is certainly putting your friend [i.e., John Adams] in a disagreable situation, 'tis most probable if an advantageous peace should be negociated, Dr. Franklin will take the credit: if otherwise, he will throw the blame on him he has already marked out; but my dear Madam, the slander of corrupt men in a corrupt age, is better than their praise. The Dr. appears to be no respecter of persons, he breaks through every tye of gratitude, and of Country, all his affections centre in one character. He loves a knave wherever he finds him."

As well as Franklin and Adams, three other men were nominated: Thomas Jefferson, who could not accept because of his wife's illness; John Jay, by then minister to Spain; and Henry Laurens. But unknown to Congress, Laurens had been captured on the high seas by the British and was now incarcerated in the

Tower of London. His capture had been doubly unfortunate, since he had been unable to destroy a document which he carried and which appeared to be a draft treaty drawn up between the Americans and Holland. It was, in fact, an unofficial draft produced by the egregious William Lee, who had visited Holland while kicking his heels in Paris. But it was sufficient to bring about a British declaration of war on that country.

The committee of 1781 was instructed by Congress to demand independence and sovereignty, but was allowed to use its discretion on other points to be raised with the British. Quite as important, the Americans were instructed to act only with the knowledge and concurrence of the French authorities; and they had also to govern themselves by French advice and opinion. Although barely agreeable to most members of the committee, these instructions were acceptable to the semi-Europeanized Franklin. Indeed, when he received a letter from his friend David Hartley, proposing a meeting at which they could talk about peace, he had sent a copy to Vergennes with a covering letter which said: "I have not as yet made him any Answer, and will make him such as your Excellency's Prudence may advise."

The unnegotiable demand for independence still ruled out any chance of peace, since a disaster of epic proportions was required before the British would even consider it. Yorktown provided that disaster. Nevertheless, a suitable opportunity still had to be found for exploiting it. Luckily, as Franklin himself was to write, "Great Affairs sometimes take their rise from small Circumstances."

One of the circumstances was the very fact that Mme. Brillon had been wintering in the south of France. Nearby in Nice there were staying early in 1782 a number of her English friends, including the widow of William Pitt, Earl of Chatham; the Duchess of Ancaster, who was a close friend of the Queen of England; as well as Lord Cholmondeley, a gentleman of enlightened views who proudly boasted ownership of a Franklin medallion. It was suggested that Cholmondeley call on Franklin when returning to England through Paris, and on March 21 a note arrived in Passy suggesting a meeting the following morning.

The timing was more appropriate than either Franklin or Cholmondeley realized. The growing division of feeling in Britain had been demonstrated the previous December when a motion demanding that the government should seek peace with

America had been lost by only 179 votes to 220. The war party dramatically lost support as the significance of the surrender at Yorktown became apparent, and when General Conway, who had moved the repeal of the Stamp Act, prepared on February 22 a motion for ending the war, this was lost by a single vote. Five days later the sheriffs of London presented at the bar of the House of Commons a petition of the lord mayor, aldermen and commons of the city of London. Sitting in common council they had been impelled, it said, "to implore this honourable House to interpose, in such manner as to their wisdom shall seem most effectual, for preventing the continuance of the unfortunate war with America." The city of London was being hit by the disastrous business repercussions that Franklin had forecast years earlier.

On the same day the North ministry was compared in the House to Don Quixote, "the American war to Dulcinea del Toboso, the new Secretary to Sancha Pancha, or rather . . . the old Rosinante on which Don Quixote would ride in order to fight the windmill." And General Conway's motion against the war was won by 19 votes.

"I congratulate you, as the friend of America; I trust as not the enemy of England; I am sure as the friend of mankind," Edmund Burke wrote to Franklin immediately. "I trust [the vote] will lead to a speedy peace between the two branches of the English nation; perhaps to a general peace; and that our happiness may be an introduction to that of the world at large. I most sincerely congratulate you on the event."

Building on success, Conway moved five days later, on March 4, a motion for ending the war and recommending: "this House will consider as enemies to his Majesty and this country, all those who shall endeavour to frustrate his Majesty's paternal care for the ease and happiness of his people, by advising, or by any means attempting, the farther prosecution of offensive war on the continent of North America, for the purpose of reducing the revolted colonies to obedience by force." The motion was carried without division. George III had himself already made two despairing personal efforts. One was a proposal that peace might be made with individual American Colonies. The second was an attempt to negotiate with Vergennes and obtain a separate peace with the French. Both attempts failed so ignominiously that the King talked of abdication and even prepared an abdication statement.

After the vote on March 4 the Earl of Surrey moved a motion for the dismissal of Lord North and his government. It was marked down for debate on the twentieth, the day before Cholmondeley's arrival in Paris. When proceedings began in the House of Commons the Earl of Surrey rose. So did Lord North. "Each noble Lord seemed determined not to give way to the other," said the parliamentary report; "this created a great deal of confusion, one side of the House crying out loudly for Earl Surrey to speak first, the other side as loudly calling out Lord North."

Eventually, North held the floor, announcing, says the report, that: "*His Majesty's ministers were no more*; and therefore the object being already attained, the means by which gentlemen had intended to obtain it, could no longer be necessary." Eight years earlier a British secretary of state had claimed "that while Britain had a ship that could swim, or a man able to carry a musket, she ought never in sound policy to abandon her pretensions to dominion over her Colonies." Now the Colonies had humbled the great Lord North and brought George III to the edge of abdication.

Franklin did not know of this latest development as he sat in Passy discussing possible peace moves with Lord Cholmondeley on March 22. But he referred to the earlier House of Commons vote when he now, on Cholmondeley's suggestion, wrote to Lord Shelburne. "I hope," he said, "it will produce a *General Peace,* which I am sure your Lord^P, with all good Men, desires, which I wish to see before I die, and to which I shall, with infinite Pleasure, contribute everything in my power."

Shelburne was a better man to write to than Franklin knew. In the reorganization which followed Lord North's dramatic resignation and his replacement as prime minister by Lord Rockingham, Shelburne became secretary for the Colonies. "I answered [Dr. Franklin's] letter on the 6th April, expressing my Readiness to promote it upon Grounds of the utmost Simplicity & Good Faith," Shelburne later wrote in a "Secret & Confidential" report. He sent his reply by Richard Oswald, a Scots arms contractor and slave merchant. But anxious that Oswald should not be rebuffed, and perhaps wondering where his emissary stood in Franklin's opinion, Shelburne sent with him from London Caleb Whitefoord, whom Franklin had known for twenty years as a next-door neighbor in Craven Street.

The precaution was apparently necessary. Whitefoord called upon Franklin, asking if he would meet Oswald. But, says the editor of the Whitefoord papers, "Dr. Franklin having been much teized with People who came to him from London, and who afterwards gave unfaithful Reports of his Conversation, was very unwilling to receive any new acquaintance from England. But at Mr. Whitefoord's earnest Request, and from the high Character he gave of Mr. Oswald, the Doctor agreed to receive him; And thus the Parties being brought together and prepossessed in favour of each other, the negotiation commenced in the most amicable manner."

If the British were willing to grant independence, Oswald pointed out, surely the Americans would not wish to have such a solution imperiled by any demands from France? If demands were made, and Britain was forced to reject them, then the chance would be lost and the war would continue. Franklin scotched this attempt to drive a wedge between the Americans and the French by taking Oswald to see Vergennes. The French Foreign Minister pointed out that peace could not be based merely on a truce with the Americans. "He added," Shelburne later reported, "that the War could not be closed but by a general Treaty, in which Spain must be a Party, & that Holland also was to be included in the Negotiation."

Vergennes was thus keeping to his part of the bargain that peace negotiations should be conducted by America and France as allies, neither keeping any relevant fact from the other. Franklin tried to do the same. But before Oswald returned to London, Franklin had broached to him the delicate idea that Canada and Nova Scotia might be ceded to America as part of the peace settlement, a proposition of which Vergennes was not informed. However, as a man who had signed the Declaration of Independence, Franklin believed that his duty lay toward the new and still infant United States rather than to any agreement that had been made with the French.

Oswald arrived back in London before the end of April, his second journey on what was to become something of a shuttle service during the next few months. It must have been clear even to Shelburne—who, although benign toward the Americans, still clung to the hope that they might settle for some form of federation—that independence was inevitable. And despite Franklin's ambiguities over Canada, it was unlikely that the Americans would negotiate without the French. Oswald, it was decided, should therefore be dispatched back to Paris with authority to settle with Franklin the details of serious peace negotiations. It would take a little time and there was always the chance that something would turn up to alter the situation.

Something had already turned up, although neither London nor Paris had yet received news of it. Even while Oswald was preparing for his first meeting with Franklin a French fleet under Admiral de Grasse sailed from Martinique to attack Jamaica. It was intercepted in the Sainte Passage between the islands of Dominica and Guadeloupe by the British fleet under Admiral George Rodney, possibly Britain's finest seaman of the day. In the action that followed, on April 9–12, 1782, the French suffered a disastrous defeat, losing seven ships captured, including Admiral de Grasse's 110-gun flagship, the *Ville de Paris*, taken with her commander. There would, the British were confident, be no more Yorktowns.

Oswald arrived in Paris on May 4, the emissary of Shelburne, secretary for the Colonies. He was followed a few days later by Thomas Greville, sent by Charles James Fox, Britain's new foreign secretary and a man unwilling to let Shelburne take too much of the limelight.

There then came two months of making ready for real negotiations during which everyone became very wary of everyone else. Franklin was experienced enough to know that he, in practice the real American negotiator, would later come under attack whatever he did. The main complaint, he foresaw, would be that he was too compliant to the French. "Those who have been in Europe on Publick business," a Commodore Alexander Gillon wrote to Arthur Lee before the end of the year, "saw *with pain* the plans in embryo which now seem on the verge of execution; & it was the general opinion of every American Patriot in Europe, at that time, that the *Old Mercenary Fox* of Passy had voluntarily acceded to the project. It was then in general circulation there, that it was not the design, as it had not been the interest of the French ministry, that America should *too soon* be at Peace *with England* or that the United States sho'd *too soon* become a naval power, or that these States sho'd be recognized as Independent by any European power; but through *the favour & agency* of France."

Franklin, under pressure from Adams and Jay, actually leaned the other way. But he nevertheless took care to build his defenses as he went along and kept a detailed diary of the events which slowly drew those involved nearer to the conference table.

Then, on July 1, 1782, Lord Rockingham died. Shelburne took his place as prime minister. While this should, on the face of things, have helped the American cause, the effects of the change were limited by George III's suspicion that Shelburne would lean too much toward the American side. Nevertheless, Rockingham's death marked the start of the six-month negotiations which finally ended the war.

Franklin realized that the time had come to strike and drew up a confidential memorandum which listed four points necessary for peace and four which were advisable. The necessary points consisted of complete independence for the Colonies and the withdrawal of all British troops; settlement of the boundaries of the Colonies; confinement of Canadian boundaries at least to what they had been before their extension by the Quebec Act of 1774; and freedom for Americans to fish for both fish and whales on the Newfoundland Banks.

In addition he thought it advisable that the British should pay reparations for the burning of American towns; that Parliament should admit its error "in distressing those countries so much by the way in which it had waged the war; that American and British ships should trade on an equal footing with each other; and that Britain should cede the whole of Canada."

The necessary proposals, which were taken to London with those merely advisable without Vergennes having been informed, were to become the basis of the peace which was eventually signed. But there were numerous delays, misunderstandings and examples of sheer bad luck which at times seemed likely to draw out negotiations indefinitely. John Jay, former president of Congress and patrician lawyer, arrived in Paris from Spain, where he had been unsuccessful in obtaining a loan. John Adams was still in The Hague, but both men lacked Franklin's long practical experience of how diplomatic matters are managed and objected to the wording of Oswald's commission, which empowered him to deal with "commissioners named by the said colonies or plantations." There were no longer colonies and plantations, both men insisted, but only the free United States of America. Franklin maintained that this was being overlegalistic. Vergennes pointed out that the British, when dealing with the French, still used out-of-date language and described George III as king of England and king of France.

Then Franklin went ill of a kidney stone, and for the two months of September and October matters fell mainly into the hands of Jay. On August 29 the British Cabinet formally agreed to American independence and authorized Oswald to negotiate with the Americans—but only on the basis of Franklin's first four necessary proposals. There were further delays and it was not until October 5 that Jay, soon to be joined in Paris by Adams, replied with the American terms.

When Oswald reached London with these terms on October 11, news had already arrived of the repulse of a major Franco-Spanish assault on Gibraltar. The two countries had for long been hoping to wrest from the British the base which, controlling the Straits of Gibraltar, thus controlled the western entrance to the Mediterranean. Their failure strengthened the British hand in the delicate bargaining over details that was now to take place.

Oswald returned to Paris in mid-October, strengthened by Henry Strachey, secretary to Lord Howe during the abortive meeting with Franklin on Staten Island and now an undersecretary of state in the colonial office. Strachey had been sent by Shelburne because of his fear that Oswald was too anxious to conciliate the Americans. John Jay and John Adams believed for their part that Franklin had been too eager to conciliate the French. He had, of course, merely been sticking to the letter of the agreements made by the Americans when the French alone stood between them and defeat, and to the instructions he had received.

But there is a limit to most things. Late in October, Adams, Jay and Franklin met Oswald and Strachey, and Franklin told his fellow commissioners: "I am of your opinion, and will go on with these gentlemen in the business without consulting this Court." Making peace with the British was more important than keeping one's word with the French.

Americans and British met every morning. William Temple Franklin was secretary to the Americans, Caleb Whitefoord to the British. Whitefoord had remained in Paris with only one break since his arrival with Oswald in March, and was to remain there until March 1783. His work is outlined in his papers, where he says that each of the three commissioners "required separate copies of many official Papers, and also Copies must be made of all papers delivered by them to us: Besides this, Mr. Oswald being of a very active and speculative Mind, was much employed in drawing up Schemes and Plans either on behalf of the Loyalists, and the mother Country, or for annoying our Enemies. Some of those Plans were very long, and Mr. Whitefoord generally made two Copies of each; so that he had more writing there in *one* year than he ever had in his own Business in six."

This laborious work was due, Whitefoord noted, to the need for secrecy, since no outsider could be employed. Its effectiveness can be judged from an entry in the diary of one young American in Paris at the time: "Dined at Passy with Mr. and Mrs. Jay—Mr. Oswald—Mr. Whifford [*sic*], Dr. Bancroft, etc." To the end, Bancroft remained unchallenged and unsuspected. After the war he settled in London and died in 1821, a respected if minor British scientist, still thought by the Americans to have been a faithful friend. The truth came out only in the closing years of the century with the discovery of previously unknown documents.

By November 5, the two sides had hammered out the details of a peace agreement that Strachey was able to take to London. There was still argument, notably over compensation which the British averred should be paid to those Loyalists who had been driven from America. But after three weeks Strachey returned with a provisional treaty. It was signed on the morning of November 30 in the hotel where Oswald was staying and was to come into effect when terms of peace were agreed between Great Britain and France.

The signing produced its legend—that Franklin had worn the suit of figured Manchester velvet he had worn in the confrontation with Wedderburn in the Cockpit almost nine years previously. It had been started by a letter in the *Public Advertiser*. Franklin, on hearing the story, was quick to point out that the French court was in mourning for a German prince and that he, as ambassador, was naturally wearing a suit of black cloth.

The fact that the treaty only came into operation on the conclusion of a Franco-British peace was soon to be of use to Franklin. He had informed Vergennes that the articles were to be signed and once this had been done he sent the French Minister a copy. But the final lap of the negotiations had been carried out in defiance of the instructions from Congress that the French were to be fully informed. At first Vergennes made no protest, well knowing the pressure that Adams and Jay had exercised on Franklin. But when a request for a further 6 million livres was made by the Americans to the French, and when Franklin suggested that the money might be sent on a ship for which the British had already given a safe-conduct pass, Vergennes not unnaturally complained: "I am at a loss, sir, to explain your conduct and that of your colleagues on this occasion. You have concluded your preliminary articles without any communication between us, although the instructions from Congress prescribe that nothing shall be done without the participation of the King. You are about to hold out a certain hope of peace to America without even informing yourself on the state of the negociation on our part. You are wise and discreet, sir; you perfectly understand what is due to propriety; you have all your life performed your duties. I pray you to consider how you fulfill those which are due to the King? I am not desirous of enlarging these reflections; I commit them to your own integrity. When you shall be pleased to relieve my uncertainty I will entreat the King to enable me to answer your demands."

Even Franklin had to stretch his powers to explain the committee's double-dealing. This he did by stressing the—largely irrelevant—fact that the Anglo-American treaty would not come into operation until an Anglo-French treaty had been signed. Then he admitted the American fault—"Your observation is, however, apparently just, that in not consulting you before they were signed, we have been guilty of neglecting a point of *bien-séance*"—and he concluded with the sentences: *"The English, I just now learn, flatter themselves they have already divided us.* I hope this little misunderstanding will therefore be kept a secret, and that they will find themselves totally mistaken." Even at the age of seventy-six, Franklin was still one of the most competent diplomats on the scene.

Vergennes responded with a first installment of 600,000 livres and the promise of more to come. The year 1782 ended satisfactorily, while before the end of January 1783, Franklin was able to tell Robert R. Livingston, secretary of the department for foreign affairs, that "the preliminaries of peace between France, Spain and England were yesterday signed, and a cessation of arms agreed to by the ministers of those powers, and by us in behalf of the United States, of which act, so far as relates to us, I enclose a copy." But the Treaty of Paris was not signed until September 3 and another eight months were to pass before it was ratified by all the countries concerned. Only then did Franklin feel confident enough to write to Charles Thomson, the Pennsylvanian who had been secretary of the First Continental Congress: "Thus the great and hazardous enterprise we have been engaged in, is, God be praised, happily completed; an event I hardly expected I should live to see."

As ever, Franklin was cautious, looking not to the immediate future but to the next century, when, as he rightly feared, America and Britain would once again be at each other's throats. "A few years of peace, well improved, will restore and increase our strength; but our future safety will depend on our union and our virtue," he warned. "Britain will be long watching for advantages to recover what she has lost. If we do not convince the world that we are a nation to be depended on for fidelity in treaties, if we appear negligent in paying our debts, and ungrateful to those who have served and befriended us, our reputation and all the strength it is capable of procuring will be lost, and fresh attacks upon us will be encouraged and promoted by better prospects of success. Let us, therefore, beware of being lulled into a dangerous security, and of being both enervated and impoverished by luxury; of being weakened by internal contentions and divisions; of being shamefully extravagant in contracting private debts, while we are backward in discharging honorably those of the public; of neglect in military exercises and discipline, and in providing stores of arms and munitions of war to be ready on occasion; for all these are circumstances that give confidence to enemies and diffidence to friends; and the expenses required to prevent a war are much lighter than those that will, if not prevented, be absolutely necessary to maintain it."

From the start of 1783 the pressure on Franklin decreased. An officer was sent from Philadelphia to take over consular duties. The end of hostilities meant, also, an end to the ceaseless flow of paper work raised by the exploits of the privateers. Still more important, there was no longer the nagging fear that a diplo-

matic slip, either by himself or by one of the other commissioners, might injure the cause and demand weeks of careful repair.

But although the pressure eased, Franklin was by no means
unemployed. Anthony Todd, with whom he had discussed his
postmastership more than a decade before, and who had until
recently been intercepting his mail, was still secretary of the Post
Office and now wished to work out with him how communications between America and Europe could most effectively be
restored. There were suggestions for trade treaties from European countries, which now realized that a giant had been born
on the far side of the Atlantic. Franklin was involved in most of
them and it is significant that his last official act in France,
carried out only a few days before leaving Passy for good, was
the signing of an agreement with Prussia.

The easing of official pressure in 1783 gave him more spare
time. Some of it was to be spent on continuing the autobiography he had begun a dozen years earlier, although it is questionable whether he would have resumed it without some prodding.
This started when he received a letter from Abel James, a
Quaker friend in Philadelphia who enclosed a copy of the first
part of the manuscript Franklin had begun at Twyford. Before
sailing for France in 1776 he had entrusted a chest of his papers
to his old friend Joseph Galloway. But in the winter of 1775
Galloway had supported the British and had later become head
of Philadelphia's civil government when the British occupied the
city. Subsequently he crossed the Atlantic to England. Mrs. Galloway died in 1782. Abel James was one of her executors and it
has been assumed that the manuscript then came into his hands.
James urged Franklin to carry on with his memoirs. So did M.
Le Veillard and Benjamin Vaughan, an acquaintance of Franklin's, a British merchant, and friend of the Americans who had
been sent to Paris by the British opposition some months earlier. In 1784 Franklin took up his story again, continuing it to
1757 and his arrival in London.

But he no longer had his old dash, and a few months later
admitted to Dr. Ingenhousz: "Writing becomes more and more
irksome to me: I grow more indolent: philosophic discussions,
not being urgent like business, are postponed from time to time
till they are forgotten; besides, I have been these twenty months
past afflicted with the stone, which is always giving me more or
less uneasiness, unless when I am laid in bed; and when I would

write, it interrupts my train of thinking, so that I lay down my pen, and seek some light amusement."

Included in the amusement there was the activity of his Passy printing press, to which he apprenticed his younger grandson, Benjamin Franklin Bache, now returned from his schooling in Switzerland. Franklin still kept an alert eye on anything connected with printing or with books and book production, and expressed to Benjamin Vaughan commendable exasperation with publishers on a disagreeable feature of theirs not entirely unknown even today. "One can scarce see a new book," he wrote, "without observing the excessive artifices made use of to puff up a paper of verses into a pamphlet, a pamphlet into an octavo, and an octavo into a quarto, with scab-boardings, white-lines, sparse titles of chapters, and exorbitant margins, to such a degree, that the selling of paper seems now the object, and printing on it only the pretence. I inclose the copy of a page in a late comedy. Between every two lines there is a white space equal to another line. You have a law, I think, against butchers blowing of veal to make it look fatter; why not one against booksellers' blowing of books to make them look bigger."

But it was science, and more particularly its practical applications, which occupied his thoughts. Thus he appears to have been within an ace of utilizing the idea later developed by Aimé Argand, the Genevese physician and chemist. In the Argand burner, oil, passing up a circular hollow wick, was burned with greater efficiency. "The idea had occurred to him," writes Benjamin Vaughan; "but he had tried a bullrush as a wick, which did not succeed. His occupations did not permit him to repeat and extend his trials to the introduction of a larger column of air, than could pass through the stem of a bullrush."

Even at the height of the war he had regularly attended meetings of the Academy of Sciences and visited the royal château of La Muette, where there was a laboratory built by Louis XV and enlarged by his successor. Where science was concerned he had always been an optimist and at the height of the fighting had written to Priestley, "The rapid Progress *true* Science now makes, occasions my regretting that I was born so soon. It is impossible to imagine the Height to which may be carried, in a thousand years, the Power of Man over Matter. We may perhaps learn to deprive Masses of their Gravity and give them an absolute Levity, for the sake of easy Transport. Agriculture may diminish its Labour and double its Produce; all Diseases may by sure means be prevented or cured, not excepting even that of Old Age, and our Lives lengthened at pleasure even beyond the antediluvian Standard. O that moral Science were in as fair a way of Improvement, that Men would cease to be Wolves to one another, and that human Beings would at length learn what they now improperly call Humanity!"

His mind, as always, was attracted to the application of scientific knowledge and he was delighted to watch the demonstration at Javelle, on the Seine below Paris, in which "a clumsy boat was moved across that river in three minutes by rowing, not in the water, but in the air, that is, by whirling round a set of windmill vanes fixed to a horizontal axis, parallel to the keel, and placed at the head of the boat." Franklin watched as two men took it in turns to operate the four five-foot-long vanes. "The weather was calm," he reported. "The labor appeared to be great for one man, as the two several times relieved each other. But the action upon the air by the oblique surfaces of the vanes must have been considerable, as the motion of the boat appeared tolerably quick going and returning; and she returned to the same place whence she first set out, notwithstanding the current."

However, Franklin was a spectator in Paris of something more exciting than the vane-powered boat. This was the birth of ballooning, a new art whose daring appealed to him almost as much as the uses his quick mind envisaged for it. The Montgolfier brothers had sent up the first hot-air balloon from Annonay in the south of France in June 1783. In August Jacques-Alexandre-César Charles, professor of Experimental Philosophy in Paris, prepared to repeat the performance in the capital and Franklin was one of the thousands who gathered to watch the scene in the Champ de Mars, between the Military School and the river.

"There," he reported to Sir Joseph Banks, president of the Royal Society, the balloon "was held down by a Cord till 5 in the afternoon, when it was to be let loose. . . . At 5 o'clock Notice was given to the Spectators by the Firing of two Cannon, that the Cord was about to be cut. And presently the Globe was seen to rise, and that as fast as a Body of 12 feet Diameter, with a force of only 39 Pounds, could be supposed to move the resisting Air out of its way. There was some Wind, but not very strong. A little Rain had wet it, so that it shone, and made an agreable Appearance. It diminished in Apparent Magnitude as it rose, till it enter'd the Clouds, when it seem'd to me scarce bigger than an orange, and soon after becoming invisible, the Clouds concealing it."

Sir Joseph was told that there were many extravagant speculations among the crowd, while Franklin himself thought that the event might "pave the Way to some Discoveries in Natural Philosophy of which at present we have no Conception." And it was here, watching among the crowd, that according to Baron Grimm Franklin heard a man ask what use a balloon would ever be. "What use is a new-born baby?" he replied—a natural enough response, since only a fortnight earlier John Jay's wife had given birth to a daughter at Passy. In effect, wrote Baron Grimm, the newly born might die in its cradle, perhaps grow up an imbecile or on the other hand become the glory of its country, the light of its age and a benefactor of humanity. Franklin was apparently fond of the analogy, since he was quoted by the Duc de Croÿ as saying of ballooning: "It's still a child. Perhaps it won't come to anything, perhaps it will develop into something big. It's necessary to complete its education, and see."

In a postscript to his letter to Sir Joseph, Franklin reported where the balloon had landed, as well as further plans of the Montgolfiers, and added that it was being proposed to send up a man in a gondola slung beneath a balloon. It was enough to set his imagination on the move, and he was obviously glad to tell Sir Joseph of the possibilities. "Some suppose Flying to be now invented, and since Men may be supported in the Air, nothing is wanted but some light handy Instruments to give and direct Motion. Some think Progressive Motion on the Earth may be advanc'd by it, and that a Running Footman or a Horse hung and suspended under such a Globe so as to leave no more of Weight pressing the Earth with their Feet, than Perhaps 8 or 10 Pounds, might with a fair Wind run in a Straight Line across Countries as fast as the Wind, and over Hedges, Ditches & even Waters. It has been even fancied that in time People will keep such Globes anchored in the Air, to which by Pullies they may draw up Game to be preserved in the Cool, & Water to frozen when Ice is wanted. And that to get Money, it will be contrived to give People an extraordinary View of the Country by running them up in an Elbow Chair a Mile high for a Guinea, &c., &c."

This was merely the start of Franklin's enthusiasm. In October he reported to Banks how the Duc de Crillon, a neighbor in the Bois de Boulogne, had ended a firework display by sending up a balloon at night. "It carried under it," he wrote, "a large Lanthorn with inscriptions on its sides. The Night was quite calm and clear, so that it went right up. The appearance of the light diminished gradually till it appeared no bigger than one of the stars and in about twenty minutes I lost sight of it entirely."

The following month Franklin witnessed the first balloon ascent by man, made by M. Pilâtre de Rozier and the Marquis d'Arlandes from the Bois de Boulogne; and, early in December, yet another in which Charles and one of the brothers Robert were carried up over the rooftops of Paris and landed safely almost seven leagues away. It was after this ascent that he speculated on how these events might give a fresh turn to human affairs. "Convincing sovereigns of the folly of wars may perhaps be one effect of it," he wrote, "since it will be impracticable for the most potent of them to guard his dominions. Five thousand balloons, capable of raising two men each, could not cost more than five ships of the line; and where is the prince who can afford so to cover his country with troops for its defence as that ten thousand men descending from the clouds might not in many places do an infinite deal of mischief before a force could be brought together to repel them?"

And it was now Franklin who grasped that Britain was no longer an island in the old sense of the word. Charles and Robert, he told Henry Laurens, had made a trip through the air "to a place further distant than Dover is from Calais, and could have gone much farther if there had been more wind and daylight." He added that they had perfect command of the balloon and could apparently make it rise or descend at will, a lesson driven home when, in 1785, he received the first "air mail" letter, brought from London to Paris by the ballooning Dr. John Jeffries, who with Jean-Pierre Blanchard crossed the English Channel in a balloon from Dover to the Forest of Guines, twelve miles from Calais. But Franklin doubted if the balloon would become a common carriage in his time, "though being the easiest of all *voitures* it would be extremely convenient to me, now that my malady forbids the use of the old ones over a pavement."

With his interest in science, Franklin was naturally one of those whose experience was conscripted when, in March 1784, the King decided that the claims of Franz Anton Mesmer should be investigated. The Austrian had arrived in Paris six years previously and his method of treating a variety of diseases by what he described as animal magnetism—carried out on his behalf by a French doctor, Charles Deslon, since Mesmer himself was not qualified—quickly became fashionable. It also became suspect, partly because the treatment, which consisted of the healer walking among groups of patients and pointing an iron rod at each, was distinctly unconventional; partly because no really clear evidence of cures appeared available.

Five doctors were ordered to investigate Mesmer's claim, and Franklin was shortly afterward asked for his own views by M. de la Condamine. "I think that, in general, maladies caused by obstructions may be treated by electricity with advantage," he replied. "As to the animal magnetism so much talked of, I must doubt its existence till I can see or feel some effect of it. None of the cures said to have been performed by it have fallen under my observation, and there being so many disorders which cure themselves, and such a disposition in mankind to deceive themselves and one another on these occasions, and living long has given me so frequent opportunity of seeing certain remedies cried up as curing everything, and yet soon after totally laid aside as useless, I cannot but fear that the expectation of great advantage from this new method of treating diseases will prove a delusion. That delusion may, however, and in some cases, be of use while it lasts. There are in every great, rich city a number of persons who are never in health, because they are fond of medicines and always taking them, whereby they derange the natural functions and hurt their constitution. If these people can be persuaded to forbear their drugs, in expectation of being cured by only the physician's finger, or an iron rod pointing at them, they may possibly find good effects, though they mistake the cause." The letter showed an unusual impartiality, the normal reaction to Mesmer being either idolatry or strong condemnation, and Franklin was shortly afterward appointed, with four other members of the Académie des Sciences, to join the doctors.

During April and May the investigators attended sessions at which Mesmer's doctor went through the motions of treating patients. Some were held at Passy, where Franklin, his secretary, his two grandsons and a visiting American officer were allegedly brought under the influence of animal magnetism—but without feeling anything. The verdict of two reports issued in August and September, to the King and the Académie des Sciences respectively, failed to substantiate Mesmer's claims and the Austrian soon afterward left Paris for Switzerland. However, it is significant that Franklin himself ascribed such cures as were effected to the powers of suggestion, and discussed the matter in almost modern psychosomatic terms, while there is little doubt that Mesmer affected the development of dynamic psychiatry. To his elder grandson, Franklin pointed out that as a result of mesmerism non-Christians might try "to weaken our Faith in some of the Miracles of the New Testament."

While speculating on the mysteries of mesmerism, Franklin received an unexpected letter from his son, William. The ex-Governor, more Loyalist than the King, as he was described, had been arrested in New Jersey in June 1776 but two years later had been handed to the British in exchange for an American they held. The ex-Governor now became president of the Associated Loyalists but in August 1782 left America for England. By 1785 he had been separated from his father for roughly a decade, wanted to renew their former friendly relations and now proposed that he visit Passy to discuss family affairs.

Franklin was friendly but cautious. "It will be very agreable to me," he replied. "Indeed nothing has ever hurt me so much and affected me with such keen Sensations, as to find my self deserted in my old Age by my only Son; and not only deserted, but to find him taking up Arms against me, in a Cause wherein my good Fame, Fortune and Life were all at Stake. You conceived, you say, that your Duty to your King & Regard for your Country requir'd this. I ought not to blame you for differing in Sentiment with me in Public Affairs. We are Men, all subject to Errors. Our Opinions are not in our own Power; they are form'd and gov-ern'd much by Circumstances that are often as inexplicable as they are irresistible. Your Situation was such that few would have censured your remaining Neuter, tho' *there are Natural Duties which precede political Ones, and cannot be extinguish'd by them.* This is a disagreable Subject. I drop it. And we will endeavour as you propose mutually to forget what has happened relating to it, as well as we can."

However, Franklin was by no means willing that son William should come to Passy, perhaps wondering at the reception he would get from his French friends. But William's son, Temple, could well go to see his father in London. "You may confide to [him] the Family Affairs you wished to confer upon with me," Franklin added, "for he is discreet. And I trust that you will prudently avoid introducing him to Company that it may be improper for him to be seen with."

Franklin's grandson had another mission when he left France late in the summer of 1784: that of persuading Mary Hewson, whose mother, Mrs. Stevenson, had died the previous year, to spend the autumn and winter with his grandfather in Passy. Franklin had first invited her early in 1783. "Spring is coming on when travelling will be delightful," he had said. "Can you not, when your children are all at school, make a little party and take a trip hither? I have now a large house, delightfully situated, in which I could accommodate you and two or three friends, and I am but half an hour's drive from Paris." Mary Hewson had turned down the offer.

In 1784 she was at first uncertain, although responsive to Temple, whom Franklin, in his letter of invitation, openly acknowledged as his grandson for the first time. "We are all pleased with our old Friend Temple changed into young Franklin," Mary Hewson replied. "We see a strong resemblance of you, and indeed saw it when we did not think ourselves at liberty to say we did, as we pretended to be as ignorant as you supposed we were, or chose we should be. I believe you may have been handsomer than your Grandson is, but then you were never so genteel; and if he has a little less philosophy he has more polish. To have such a young man to run off with one, and yet to stay behind, argues great virtue or great stupidity. *Les belles Francoises* will be at no loss which to term it; my country women will not marvel so much, as at forty-five we are expected to be prudent."

Her indecision was exemplified by the tone of Temple's first eagerly awaited report back to Passy, which said that Mary Hewson had not yet said no. Then she accepted. Then she changed her mind. Temple, anxious to please and no doubt enjoying London, asked for more time and was given it by his grandfather; but only on two conditions—that he visit Bishop Shipley and his family and that he bring back samples of iron tiles which Franklin wished to use on his Philadelphia home when he returned. Eventually, but only on November 9, Temple wrote with the news that the widowed Mary Hewson would be coming to Paris with her children. There was one further hitch but on the nineteenth Franklin was informed that she was definitely coming, with a family of five, including a maid.

They all crossed the Channel before the end of the month and during the first days of December Mary Hewson and her children settled into Passy. Franklin's pleasure was reflected in a letter he wrote to her after the family returned to England five months later. "You talk of obligations to me, when in fact I am the person obliged," he said. "I passed a long winter, which appeared the shortest of any I ever past."

She had left only a few days before he received the order of release from Congress. As soon as the news arrived he began preparations to leave. They were to take him some ten weeks and it was July 12 before he was ready to depart.

Before he left he received a letter from his old friend Thomas Pownall in London. The two men had first met at the Albany Congress some thirty years earlier. Pownall had expanded his Albany views in *The Administration of the Colonies,* which proposed the union of all the American Colonies into one dominion. His beliefs had been against the grain of the times and he now wrote to Franklin with a sad mixture of envy and personal regret. "I am told you are on the point of returning to your own country; a country which you have not only saved but formed into a State, independent and sovereign," he said. "You must excuse me when I say what I feel—that I envy you. God has not only made you an instrument of good to your country, but has given you the most supreme of all happiness in the world—that of seeing your country and all the world acknowledging your deeds. . . . Adieu, my dear friend. . . . You are going to a new world formed to exhibit a scene which the old world never yet saw. You leave me here in the old world which, like myself, begins to feel as Asia hath felt—that it is wearing out apace."

FOURTEEN

LAST DAYS
OF A SAGE

HEN ON MAY 2, 1785, FRANKLIN AT LAST received permission to return to the United States, he informed Vergennes within a matter of hours and almost as soon began preparations for the major upheaval that the journey would involve. Yet he now, at the age of seventy-nine, felt ambivalent about the uprooting. Just as two decades earlier he had been intellectually torn between pride in the British Empire and dismay at the treatment of the Colonies, so now he felt the emotional pull of France as well as homesickness for the sights and sounds of Philadelphia. "The French are an amiable People to live with," he wrote to Captain Falconer. "They love me and I love them. Yet I do not feel myself at home, & I wish to die in my own country."

At Passy there were not only the personal belongings he had acquired in eight and a half years but also his printing press and a great variety of fonts cast there on his own instructions. Franklin the master printer did not intend to leave them in a foreign land and they filled many of the 128 heavy packages which his two grandsons helped him make ready for the journey by barge down the Seine to Le Havre. With them went a crated supply of M. Le Veillard's Passy water, later much appreciated by the Franklin family in Philadelphia.

Franklin himself had wished to travel downriver from Paris but by July, when he set out, drought was severely disturbing river traffic. The stone from which he was suffering made coach riding painful but the ever-helpful M. de Chaumont came to the rescue, had a few words with the Duc de Coigny, and was able to borrow for the occasion one of Marie Antoinette's litters with the two mules to carry it and a third animal for the muleteer.

As preparations for the journey were being made, Franklin wrote to Mary Hewson with the first of many attempts—eventually successful—to coax her to America. He would be happy when he was back home in Philadelphia, he said, before continuing: "But, however happy that circumstance may make me, your joining me there will surely make me happier, provided your change of country may be for the advantage of your dear little family. When you have made up your mind on the subject, let me know by a line, that I may prepare a house for you as near me, and otherwise as convenient for you, as possible."

He continued the persuasion after he had finally arranged for passage to Philadelphia in a ship which would leave London in mid-July and take him and his grandsons on board either at Le Havre or at a port in southern England. "The ship," Mary Hewson was told, "has a large, convenient cabin, with good lodging-places. The whole to be at my disposition, and there is plenty of room for you and yours. You may never have so good an opportunity of passing to America, if it is your intention. Think of it, and take your resolution."

In more than one of his letters during the last weeks at Passy there were hints of regret that he was leaving, as when he wrote to David Hartley: "I cannot quit the coasts of Europe without taking leave of my ever dear friend Mr. Hartley. We were long fellow laborers in the best of all works, the work of peace. I leave you still in the field, but, having finished my day's task, I am going home *to go to bed.* Wish me a good night's rest as I do you a pleasant evening." While friends and enemies alike tended to emphasize his success in the Europe he was about to leave, Franklin himself took a different view, as when he wrote to Francis Masères on the previous system under which the British

Empire allowed the Colonies to govern and tax themselves. "I used to consider that system as a large and beautiful porcelain vase," he wrote; "I lamented the measures that I saw likely to break it, and strove to prevent them; because, once broken, I saw no probability of its ever being repaired. My endeavours did not succeed; we are broken, and the parts must now do as well as they can for themselves. We may still do well, though separated. I have great hopes of our side, and good wishes for yours."

The note of melancholy which sounds through so much of his correspondence from the last weeks at Passy was increased by his French friends, none of whom wanted him to go, all of whom implored him to remain. Mme. Brillon, accepting that he could not be induced to stay, had his portrait painted by Joseph-Sifzède Duplessis. Vergennes regretted that France was losing such a man, and sent, with the compliments of the King, a miniature of the monarch framed with 408 diamonds, the usual gift to a minister plenipotentiary who had signed a treaty with the French court. Franklin, as was the custom, responded with a gift to the King of a gold snuffbox.

While he was unwilling to let his precious printing fonts remain in France, he realized that he could not take with him all that he had accumulated since 1776. So his "doctoral chair" was gifted to the Abbé Morellet, his tea table went to Mme. Le Veillard and a special table which could be raised or lowered to a variety of heights was presented to M. de Chaumont. He bundled up into a single parcel, which his elder grandson would later formally hand to the President of Congress, the originals of the various treaties and agreements with which he had been concerned. He again, and no doubt with mixed feelings, rejected appeals from both Mme. Brillon and Mme. Helvétius to abandon his projected journey and remain in Passy for the rest of his life.

By mid-July all was ready and at 4:00 A.M. on the twelfth there arrived in the courtyard at Passy the curtained litter, and coaches for those who were to accompany the doctor part of the way. They were to have a long wait. M. de Chaumont insisted that the Franklins join him in a farewell meal. Then most of the inhabitants of Passy turned out to salute the departure of their famous man. But Mme. Brillon was missing, unable to face the farewell. Instead she had written him an affectionate letter to which her husband had added a postscript that ran: "My very dear Papa, I have nothing to add, and even if I wanted to, my tears would not let me see." There were farewells and yet more farewells, and it was 4:00 P.M. when the convoy at last got under way. "When he left Passy," wrote Benjamin Vaughan, "it seemed as if the village had lost its patriarch." M. de Chaumont and his daughter Sophie rode beside the litter as far as Nanterre, then an old country town seven miles from the center of Paris. M. Le Veillard had decided to accompany Franklin as far as Le Havre, but in fact traveled on to England with him.

The 146-mile journey from Paris to Le Havre was a leisurely five-day affair. The first evening they stopped at St. Germain-en-Laye, where the wife of Franklin's grandnephew Jonathan Williams, Jr., also preparing to leave for America, had arranged accommodations for them. "I found that the motion of the litter," Franklin was able to record in his diary, ". . . did not much incommode me." The next day they continued down the valley to Mantes, where they spent the night. Here they were met by a messenger from Cardinal de la Rochefoucauld, "with an invitation to us to stop at his house at Gaillon the next day; acquainting us at the same time, that he would take no excuse; for, being all-powerful in his archbishopric, he would stop us *nolens volens* at his habitation, and not permit us to lodge anywhere else. We consented. . . . Found myself very little fatigued with the day's journey, the mules going only foot pace."

This was Franklin's reaction throughout the whole journey back to America. He bore the strains of travel better than his younger companions, and instead of snoozing behind the curtains of his litter made notes on the passing landscape. After the night at the Cardinal's château, they passed on the way to Rouen the towering white walls of Les Andelys, which make such an impressive display above the serpentine curves of the Seine, "a chain of chalk mountains, very high, with strata of flints," as Franklin recorded. "The quantity that appears to have been washed away on one side of these mountains, leaving precipices of three hundred feet high, gives an idea of extreme antiquity. It seems as if done by the beating of the sea."

At Rouen, he reported "a great company of genteel people at supper, which was our dinner." Here he was greeted by the President of the Département and received a deputation from the Academy of Rouen, whose members presented him with a magic square which was supposed to express his name. "I have perused it since," he observed, "but I do not comprehend it."

Eventually they arrived at the port of Le Havre. Here Franklin found waiting for him a final plea from Mme. Helvétius. "I can picture you in your litter, further from us at every step, already lost to me and to your friends who loved you so much and regret you so. I fear you are in pain, that the road will tire you and make you more uncomfortable. If such is the case, come back, my dear friend, come back to us. My little retreat will be the better for your presence. . . . You will make our life happier, we shall contribute to your happiness, such are the things that you must know for sure, that you have read in my heart and that of our friends."

Meanwhile, in nearby Passy, Mme. Brillon was writing her own farewell regrets. "My husband, my two daughters bid me tell you that they shall love you, respect you, cherish you always," they went; "as for me, my good Papa, your kindnesses to me will be prized by me even in the tomb. I shall recall them unceasingly, and if in another life we are destined to recover all that was dearest to us in this one, I shall fall in the arms of my good Papa, never to part again. Accept my best wishes for a pleasant voyage, never cease loving her who will always love you with all the strength of her affections; think of her once in a while, and remember most of all that she will never cease thinking of you, of your happiness, of all that concerns you; yes, my worthy friend, all the days of my life you will fill my thoughts and my heart; it is and ever shall be devotedly yours."

In Le Havre, Franklin turned to the best means of crossing the Channel. Several vessels were available—one reason why the matter had not been settled in advance—but all were considered too dear and they arranged to wait for the Southampton packet, which would take them across on the twenty-first.

In Le Havre there was plenty to do. The Governor and various military authorities arrived to present their compliments. So did Jean-Antoine Houdon, the sculptor who had been commissioned by the French to sculpt a statue of Washington and who would be traveling to America with Franklin. There was a day's delay due to adverse winds, and it was only at ten-thirty on the morning of the twenty-second that they finally went aboard.

It was a bad crossing, with a northwest wind fighting against the packet. Franklin weathered it well. "I was not in the least incommoded by the voyage," he recorded, "but my [grand] children and my friend M. Veillard were very sick." At two in the afternoon of the twenty-third the wind slackened off and in the evening the shadow of the Isle of Wight was discernible to the north. The following morning wind and tide made it difficult for the ship to run into Cowes, and the packet sailed up to Southampton, which it reached before nine.

Franklin and his party went at once to the Star Inn, where his son, who had arrived the previous night, was already staying. Their meeting was businesslike but cool and Franklin appears to have been more concerned with meeting English friends again than with discussing politics with the unrepentant ex-Governor. He now began a vigorous session of letter-writing without any pause after the turbulent forty-five-hour Channel crossing. First was a note to Jonathan Shipley, only eight miles away at Twyford. There was a letter to Benjamin Vaughan, another to Dr. Lettsom, F.R.S., a medical acquaintance, another to Jonathan Williams, Jr., who had booked Franklin's place on the Philadelphia packet but who had, unknown to Franklin, already arrived in Southampton.

Within a few hours a reply arrived from Twyford. Some of his friends, wrote Shipley, were "come most untimely to dine with us. As soon as we are rid of them, my wife, and I, and the only daughter that is now with us, will hasten to welcome you, and to enjoy, till the last moment of your departure, as much of the blessing of your conversation, as we can without being tiresome." They arrived that evening but were to have only three days with their friend, since by the twenty-seventh the Philadelphia packet was anchored in Southampton waters.

By the twenty-fifth Franklin was reacting to the stress and strain of the journey. To recover, he went to a well-known saltwater hot bath in the town and, as he wrote in his diary, "floating on my back, fell asleep, and slept near an hour by my watch, without sinking or turning! A thing I never did before, and should hardly have thought possible. Water is the easiest bed that can be." Soon he was occupied, once more, with the business that seemed to accumulate around him wherever he was. He protested about the exorbitant price being charged for the transfer of his 128 boxes on their journey down the Seine and at the same time appears to have discovered that he had been cheated by M. Finck, M. de Chaumont's maître d'hôtel who for nearly eight years had also been his. "He was continually saying of himself 'Je suis honnête homme; je suis honnête homme.' But I always suspected he was mistaken; and so it proves." He had business affairs to settle with his son. Mary Hewson had not, as he had half-hoped, arrived to sail to America with him. But he now wrote to her saying that she would always be welcome in Philadelphia, adding, "instead of being hurt by the journey or voyage, I really find myself very much better, not having suffered so little for the time these two years past." And when he knew that his stay in Europe was now counted in hours, he wrote to Mme. Helvétius. "Our ship arrived here yesterday from London," he said. "We are sailing today. Farewell, my very, very, very dear friend. Wish me a good crossing and tell the abbés to pray for us, that, after all, *being their profession.* I feel very well. If I arrive in America, you shall soon hear from me. I shall always love you. Think of me sometimes and write sometimes to your Benjamin Franklin."

On the twenty-seventh he and the Shipleys dined together onshore. Then they accepted Franklin's invitation to be taken out to the ship, on which Captain Thomas Truxtun entertained them all to supper. The Shipleys, it was arranged, would stay on board overnight, while Franklin slept, then say their farewells before leaving the ship in the morning.

But events went differently. "When I waked in the morning, found the company gone, and the ship under sail," Franklin noted in his diary. Wind and tide had been right for weighing anchor and the Shipleys had gone ashore without waking him. "I do assure you," Louisa later wrote, "we all left your ship with a heavy heart; but the taking leave was a scene we wished to save you as well as ourselves." She and her parents, riding back to Twyford, had only a mile behind them that early July morning when they met David Hartley. He had been away from London but had hastened to Southampton when he heard Franklin was there. Now he learned that his friend was already heading down Southampton Water for the Channel and the open sea.

Franklin apparently left no record of his intimate feelings as he watched the gray line of England dissolve into the mists on the morning of July 28. Only six weeks later, as he approached America, did he carry on with his diary. However, he was by no means unemployed. Instead of lazing his time away, as well he might, free now of official duties, he was only two days out when he recommenced the soundings which had enabled him to plot the course of the Gulf Stream with greater accuracy than before. Jonathan Williams, Jr., sailing to the start of a new life in America and soon to be followed by the wife whom Franklin had last met a few days earlier at St. Germain-en-Laye, helped him with the work. As on earlier transatlantic crossings, Franklin used bottles and kegs for the soundings, and noted temperature and color of the water at different depths.

That was not all. Between July 28 and September 14, he wrote three substantial papers, a considerable enough achievement for any man, let alone one in his eightieth year, incapacitated by the stone and writing in the rolling cabin of a 400-ton ship. The first was in the form of a long letter to Julien-David Le Roy, brother of Jean-Baptiste Le Roy, who was in charge of the King's laboratory at La Muette. Entitled "Maritime Observations," it ranged across the whole subject of life at sea, from the use of swimming anchors to a diet for sailors, and from the value of watertight compartments to the best forms of rigging. This epistle, written so late in life, was a good example of Franklin's ability to combine theory with practice, to write penetratingly of scientific possibilities and of day-to-day problems and their solution. He dealt with the ways in which the Gulf Stream might be generated; but he also dealt with very different problems, writing: "The accidents I have seen at sea with large dishes of soup upon a table, from the motion of the ship, have made me wish that our potters or pewterers would make soup dishes in divisions, like a set of small bowls united together, each containing about sufficient for one person, . . . for then, when the ship should make a sudden heel, the soup would not in a body flow over one side, and fall into people's laps and scald them, as is sometimes the case, but would be retained in the separate divisions." He was also proud to record that he had adapted his lightning conductor for use at sea. The device, consisting of the usual rod and a long chain which was dropped into the sea, was, he noted, "sold at a reasonable price by Nairne & Co., in London, and there are several instances of success attending the use of them. They are kept in a box, and may be run up and fixed in about five minutes, on the apparent approach of a thunder gust."

With "Maritime Observations" finished, he "embrace[d] willingly this leisure afforded by my present situation" to answer a request from his friend in Vienna, Jan Ingenhousz, for his views on the cure of smoky chimneys. The answer came in a paper later published in the *Transactions of the American Philosophical Society.* Dealing with both the theoretical and the practical side of the subject, it allowed Franklin to ride his old hobby-horse, the connection between ventilation and health. He no longer believed in the dangers of moist air, he declared, adding: "I am at this present writing in a ship with above forty persons, who have had no other than moist air to breathe for six weeks past; every thing we touch is damp, and nothing dries, yet we are all as healthy as we should be on the mountains of Switzerland, whose inhabitants are not more so than those of Bermuda or St. Helena, islands on whose rocks the waves are dashed into millions of particles, which fill the air with damp but produce no diseases, the moisture being pure, unmixed with the poisonous vapors arising from putrid marshes and stagnant pools, in which many insects die and corrupt the water." The dissertation to Dr. Ingenhousz was a natural predecessor to his third paper, which described an improved stove for burning coal which he had invented in London in 1771 and had later used in both Philadelphia and Passy.

When the third paper was finished, Captain Truxtun was already approaching landfall and on the morning of September 13 Franklin found himself passing between Capes Henlopen and May into Delaware Bay, "water smooth, air cool, day fair and fine." They sailed up past New Castle and anchored before tide and wind failed.

The following day Franklin made the last entry in his diary. "With the flood in the morning came a light breeze, which brought us above Gloucester Point, in full view of dear Philadelphia! when we again cast anchor, to wait for the health officer, who, having made his visit and finding no sickness, gave us leave to land."

His son-in-law, Richard Bache, came out to meet him, and a few moments later Franklin stepped ashore at the Market Street Wharf where he had arrived as a threadbare boy more than sixty years previously. "We were," he noted, "received by a crowd of people with huzzas, and accompanied with acclamations quite to my door."

For the week and more following his return to Philadelphia, Franklin was the magnet for every attention. The Speaker of the

Assembly called on him with a welcoming address. The Provost of the University, which he had helped to create some forty years before, also called. He was welcomed by the American Philosophical Society on taking the chair at its first assembly after his return. He met the members of the Union Fire Company which he had founded almost half a century earlier and declared that he would have his bucket and equipment ready in time for the next meeting. He was waited upon, moreover, by members of the Constitutional Society, and by the Anti-Constitutionalists, both of whom were to nominate him as a candidate in elections for the Supreme Executive Council the following month.

Yet although Franklin was to live for more than another four years, he was to perform only one further vital service to America. This was the result partly of age and ailments, partly of inclination. On being told by Congress that he could leave Paris, he had written to his friend Jan Ingenhousz: "I shall now be free of Politicks for the Rest of my Life. Welcome again my dear Philosophical Amusements." But he thought it his duty to accept election to the Supreme Executive Council of Pennsylvania, and then to its presidency, an appointment he held for three years. His impact here was not particularly great and his magisterial influence was to be exercised for the last time at the Constitutional Convention which in 1787 hammered out the laws under which the United States was to be governed, with few major changes, until the present day.

Despite his physical infirmities, Franklin settled down to what was to be a comparatively contented life, "drinking every day *les eaux épurées de Passy* with great satisfaction," he told M. Le Veillard, "as they kept well, and seem to be rendered more agreeable by the long voyage." He idolized his daughter, got on well with his son-in-law, and was as happy with his Bache grandchildren as he was with most youngsters. "I enjoy many comfortable Intervals," he wrote to a relative, Elizabeth Partridge, "in which I forget all my Ills, and amuse myself in Reading or Writing, or in Conversation with Friends, joking, laughing, and telling merry Stories, as when you first knew me, a young Man about Fifty."

Soon after his return he began enlarging the house he had acquired some two decades previously, and transforming the grounds from vegetable gardens "into grass plots and gravel walks, with trees and flowering shrubs." "I propose to have in it," he wrote to Jane Mecom of the enlarged building, "a long Room for my Library and Instruments, with two good Bedchambers and Two Garrets. The Library is to be even with the Floor of my best old Chamber: & the Story under it will for the present be employ'd only to hold Wood, but may be made into Rooms hereafter. This Addition is on the Side next the River. I hardly know how to justify building a Library at an Age that will so soon oblige me to quit it; but we are apt to forget that we are grown old, and Building is an Amusement." Franklin kept a tight hand on all the works. As he wrote to M. Le Veillard, "The affairs in dealing with so many workmen and furnishers of materials, such as bricklayers, carpenters, stone-cutters, painters, glaziers, lime-burners, timber-merchants, copper-smiths, carters, labourers, etc., etc., have added not a little to the fatiguing business I have gone through in the last year."

Soon after his return he found that his most famous invention, the lightning conductor, had been of some use to the inventor. While he was in France, the Franklin family had been frightened by a loud explosion during a thunderstorm. No damage was done, but it was thought that the house must have been struck by lightning. Now, during the rebuilding, the old lightning conductor was taken down. "I found," Franklin wrote, "that the copper point which had been nine inches long, and in its thickest part about one-third of an inch in diameter, had been almost all melted and blown away, very little of it remaining attached to the iron rod."

Quite apart from keeping an eye on the rebuilding, he found enough public business to keep him busy. Among his self-imposed tasks was that of combating, as far as he was able, the exaggerated accounts about life in the United States now being published in England. Just as British papers had reported that his ship had been captured by Algerian pirates and that he himself had been sold into slavery, so they now reported life in parts of America as breaking down into anarchy. Every minor trouble was magnified, while it was at least implied and often stated that huge numbers of the Colonial population regretted their independence.

"Our domestic misunderstandings, when we have them, are of small extent, tho' monstrously magnified by your microscopic newspapers," Franklin stressed to David Hartley. "He who judges from them, that we are falling into anarchy, or returning to the obedience of Britain, is like one who being shewn some spots in the Sun, shou'd fancy, that the whole Disk would soon be overspread by them, and that there wou'd be an end of Daylight. The great body of Intelligence among our people surrounds and overpowers our petty dissensions, as the Sun's great mass of fire diminishes and destroys his Spots."

Life in Philadelphia was, as he emphasized to Mary Hewson, exceedingly pleasant. "Cards we sometimes play here, in long winter evenings," he wrote, "but it is as they play at chess, not for money, but for honour, or the pleasure of beating one another. . . . As to public amusements, we have neither plays nor operas, but we had yesterday a kind of oratorio, as you will see by the enclosed paper; and we have assemblies, balls, and concerts, besides little parties at one another's houses, in which there is sometimes dancing, and frequently good music; so that we jog on in life as pleasantly as you do in England; anywhere but in London, for there you have plays performed by good actors. That, however, is, I think, the only advantage London has over Philadelphia."

The description was part of Franklin's campaign to coax Mary Hewson to Pennsylvania. Before the end of 1786 he had succeeded, receiving a note from her in October saying that she would be arriving soon and asking him to find temporary accommodations for herself, her three children and a maid—"that and one room to eat in is all we care for."

Mary Hewson soon settled into a home near Franklin's. In his own home, she found, he had contrived gadgets as ingenious as any he had devised at her mother's house in Craven Street a quarter of a century before. Since he was by now finding it difficult to get books from his higher library shelves, he had a simple machine, which he called the Long Arm. This was an eight-foot-long piece of one-inch-square wood, to one end of which were attached two thin lathes which he called the thumb and the finger. A knotted cord running through both enabled the user of the device to secure and hold the chosen book, which was then easily brought within reach.

His study chair not only incorporated a fan, which, during the heat of the summer, he could operate by a slight movement of one foot; the seat itself, when reversed, became a stepladder. And for a clock he had his own ingenious invention which, with only three wheels and two pinions, provided hours, minutes and seconds. In his bedroom two cords, like bellpulls, hung at the head of his bed. One was in fact a bellpull; the other, when pulled, raised an iron bolt, an inch square and nine or ten inches long, which dropped through staples on the door when this was shut and securely locked it. Even his bath was designed to provide maximum comfort, both physical and intellectual. A copper affair, it was—like the bath in which Marat was killed by Charlotte Corday—shaped like a shoe, thus enabling him to sit in the "heel" and enjoy his hot bath to the full; but at just the right place there was a bookrest so that he could read while soaking.

Washington, who visited Franklin while the Constitutional Convention was being held in Philadelphia, admired his machine "for smoothing clothes instead of ironing them." He was also very proud of a duplicating machine he had invented. When Dr. Manasseh Cutler, ex-army chaplain and property promoter, was commissioned to return to a neighbor in Philadelphia a letter that Franklin had received, together with a copy of it, his visitor recorded: "Dr. Franklin . . . desired him to compare them and see if there was a letter, or stroke, or point of the pen that did not perfectly correspond, and assured him that he had made out that copy in less than half a minute. Dr. Stiles was exceedingly puzzled; he knew not how to account for it."

However, the apparatus that Franklin most enjoyed demonstrating was an adaptation of equipment he had first seen in Germany. "He showed us," Dr. Cutler wrote in his diary, "a glass machine for exhibiting the circulation of the blood in the arteries and veins of the human body. The circulation is exhibited by the passing of a red fluid from a reservoir into numerous capillary tubes of glass, ramified in every direction, and then returning in similar tubes to the reservoir, which was done with great velocity, without any power to act visibly on the fluid, and had the appearance of perpetual motion."

From his comfortable base Franklin sallied out in his old age to do his civic duty, feeling that he could still benefit the people among whom he had returned to live. "Otherwise," he told Mme. Helvétius, "I shall wish I had accepted your friendly invitation to pass the rest of my days with you."

It was not easy. "I have sometimes wished I had brought with me from France, a balloon sufficiently large to raise me from the ground," he told a friend. "In my malady it would have been the most easy carriage for me, being led by a string held by a man walking on the ground." For some while after his return to Philadelphia he was able to walk the short distance to the Assembly chamber in the State House, a figure, so far as most Philadelphians were concerned, whose tale went back to a distant past that they knew only from stories told round the fire. He was twice reelected president of the Council, and the Pennsylvanians "engrossed the prime of my life," as he told his friends. "They have eaten my flesh, and seem resolved now to pick my bones."

Franklin's influence on Pennsylvania was exercised by his presence rather than by any changes or innovations which he set in motion. Thus the revision of the Test Act, which had been introduced in 1776, and under which all voters had to swear allegiance to the Constitution, was a motion which Franklin supported, and was known to support, but which had been proposed before he left for France in 1776. It was, by contrast, in the Constitutional Convention, which sat in Philadelphia from mid-May until September 17, 1787, that his final work for America was done, work which, as he explained to M. Le Veillard, once again held up his autobiography. "As to the little history I promised you," he wrote in April 1787, "my purpose still continues of compleating it, and I hoped to do it this summer, having built an addition to my house, in which I have plac'd my library, and where I can write without being disturb'd by the noise of the children, but the General Assembly having lately desired my assistance in a great convention to be held here in May next for amending the Federal Constitution, I begin to doubt whether I can make any progress in it till that business is over."

The previous September a meeting in Annapolis, originally called to settle a dispute between Maryland and Virginia on navigation of the Potomac, had recommended to Congress that the thirteen states should send delegates to Philadelphia on the second of May to consider the trade and commerce of the United States. Five months later Congress had sanctioned the Convention for revising the Articles of Confederation.

Franklin was inevitably elected a member of the Pennsylvania delegation and it was to his house in Market Street that Washington made his first visit on arriving in Philadelphia on May 13. The Convention opened the following day in the East Room of the State House where the Second Continental Congress had sat in May 1775 and where the Declaration of Independence had been signed. Not until the twenty-fifth was a quorum of seven states represented. During the intervening period, delegates began to arrive from a dozen states—Rhode Island not being represented, since its farmers feared that centralized government would remove their privileges. The newspapers announced the arrivals with due punctilio, giving state governors the title of Excellency, justices and chancellors that of Honorable, Congressmen an honorable with a small "h," and the also-rans as "the following respectable characters."

With the exceptions of the first day, when bad weather kept him away, of two days over the July 4 holiday and of ten days from July 26 until August 6, when the Committee of Detail was preparing its report, Franklin sat through all the Convention's sessions. According to Benjamin Rush, he exhibited daily "a spectacle of transcendent benevolence by attending the Convention punctually, and even taking part in its business and deliberations." He was, in fact, to be more than an onlooker. His absence on the first day of the Convention prevented him from personally proposing Washington as its president, but he ensured that the other members of the Pennsylvania delegation did so for him.

His interventions in the debates were not particularly numerous; his influence was exercised more by playing the ever-alert man of experience who would counter unwise proposals or break the logjams which were inevitable as the representatives of a dozen states tried to work out results that suited them all.

When Franklin did intervene he was able to produce from the past apposite examples which, if they did not sway the Convention—and indeed it was rare that they did—at least gave it a background to what it was deciding. After recommending that the national legislature should have the power to veto certain state laws—one of his proposals which was accepted, and which sprang from his treaty-making experience in France—he proposed that the executive should not receive salaries, a proposal which he supported by referring to his long experience in Britain. "Sir," said his proposal, which was read for him by his friend James Wilson, "there are two passions which have a powerful influence on the affairs of men. These are ambition and avarice; the love of power and the love of money. Separately, each of these has great force in prompting men to action; but when united in view of the same object, they have in many minds the most violent effects. Place before the eyes of such men a post of *honour* that shall at the same time be a place of *profit,* and they will move heaven and earth to obtain it. The vast number of such places it is that renders the British Government so tempestuous. The struggles for them are the true sources of all those factions which are perpetually dividing the Nation, distracting its councils, hurrying sometimes into fruitless & mischievous wars, and often compelling a submission to dishonorable terms of peace." Voting was postponed indefinitely and although the motion was treated with respect, it was noted that this was "rather for the author of it than from any conviction of its expediency or practicability."

It was in the crucial discussion over how the separate states, big and small, should be represented in the future Congress, that Franklin played his most important role. Should representation be proportional to population? If so, then surely the smaller states, which regarded their rights as equal to those of the more populous states, would be swamped in Congress.

Argument grew heated and on June 28 Franklin moved an unexpected motion: that future sessions should be opened with prayers. At the beginning of the War of Independence, he said, there had been considerable disunity. But the Congress had opened with prayers each day, in the very room in which they were now debating. Once again they needed to invoke God's help. Without it, he went on, "We shall be divided by our little partial local interests; our projects will be confounded, and we ourselves shall become a reproach and bye word down to future ages. And what is worse, mankind may hereafter from this unfortunate instance, despair of establishing Governments by Human Wisdom, and leave it to chance, war and conquest."

The motion for daily prayers was rejected. But it sobered the Convention, which two days later accepted Franklin's proposal that a compromise be sought. A committee on which one member from each state was represented was set up and eventually drew up a working agreement on all the points at issue—very roughly the Constitution as it is today. Franklin did not like the outcome, but he accepted it. He had, moreover, saved the Convention. The long wrangle as to how strong each state representation was to be had neared bursting point. Almost alone, Franklin had held together the debating concourse of opposites.

The Convention attracted to Philadelphia a succession of lobbyists, each anxious that his special interests should not be endangered by the outcome of discussions in the State House. Among them was Manasseh Cutler, who has left a graphic account of Franklin in the last few years of his life. He arrived in Philadelphia in mid-July, having just pushed through Congress in New York the Northwest Ordinance, with its grant of some five million acres. "We found [Franklin] in his garden, sitting upon a grass plat under a very large Mulberry, with several other gentlemen and two or three ladies," he later wrote, ". . . a short, fat, trunched old man, in a plain Quaker dress, bald pate, and short white locks, sitting without his hat under the tree. . . . The tea-table was spread under the tree, and Mrs. Bache, a very gross and rather homely lady, who is the only daughter of the Doctor and lives with him, served it out to the company. She had three of her children about her, over whom she seemed to have no kind of command, but who appeared to be excessively fond of their Grandpapa."

Tea finished, Cutler was shown Franklin's library, reputed to be the largest private library in America and, being as ardent a botanist as businessman, was intrigued by a copy of Linnaeus's *Systema Vegetabilium*. The book was so big that Franklin could hardly move it onto the table for display. "With that senile ambition common to old people, he insisted on doing it himself, and would permit no person to assist him, merely to show us how much strength he had remaining," Cutler commented. His manners were "perfectly easy, and every thing about him seems to diffuse an unrestrained freedom and happiness. He has an incessant vein of humor, accompanied with an uncommon vivacity, which seems as natural and involuntary as his breathing."

Cutler does not appear to have talked business with Franklin. But it would be surprising if he had not passed into the doctor's ear his own view of what the Convention should, and should not, decide. Although its first session had been held some two months previously, another two months of argument were required before the details were settled. And only on Sunday, September 16, was the Constitution engrossed. The following day it was read to the Convention.

Then Franklin rose, paper in hand. But he was too infirm to deliver its message, which was, once again, read by James Wilson. The Constitution, Franklin felt confident, was the best they could expect. "For when you assemble a number of men to have the advantage of their joint wisdom, you inevitably assemble with those men, all their prejudices, their passions, their errors of opinion, their local interests, and their selfish views. From such an assembly can a perfect production be expected? It therefore astonishes me, Sir, to find this system approaching so near to perfection as it does. . . . On the whole, Sir, I cannot help expressing a wish that every member of the Convention who may still have objections to it, would with me, on this occasion doubt a little of his own infallibility, and to make manifest our unanimity, put his name to this instrument."

As the document was being signed Franklin looked up to the chair on which Washington was sitting and behind which a sun was painted. Artists, he remarked, often had difficulty in differentiating between a rising and a setting sun. "But now at length," he said to those near him, "I have the happiness to know that it is a rising and not a setting Sun."

Three days later Franklin wrote to his sister Jane, telling her with obvious satisfaction that he had attended the sessions for five hours a day. "You may judge from thence," he went on, "that my Health continues; some tell me I look better, and they suppose the daily Exercise of going & returning from the Statehouse has done me good. You will see the Constitution we have propos'd in the Papers. The Forming of it so as to accommodate all the different Interests and Views was a difficult Task; and perhaps after all it may not be receiv'd with the same unanimity in the different States that the Convention have given the Example of in delivering it out for their Consideration. We have however done our best, and it must take its Chance."

He had survived remarkably well. But before the end of the year there was a setback. He fell down the steps leading to his garden, bruised himself, sprained his right wrist and suffered a severe attack of the stone. Once again, he snapped back and was able to write to Mme. Brillon in April that his health "continues the same, or rather better than when I left Passy."

But by the summer of 1788 he was beginning to realize that his time was at last running out. In July he made his will and a few weeks later began a serious effort to continue his autobiography. He had told more than one of his friends that when his presidency ended in October—three one-year terms only being allowed—he would return to this much-delayed project. As it was, he began before he was entirely free, writing in the margin of the manuscript: "I am now about to write at home, August,

1788." He carried on throughout the year. But he wrote slowly. His stone was so bad that now he was taking opium to deaden the pain; he could scarcely move and was carried in a sedan chair by two men from the local prison. By the middle of 1789 it was clear that he would never finish the work. He conscripted his grandson Benjamin Franklin Bache and the copying machine which he had devised, and during the autumn two copies were made of the autobiography: part one, which had been written in Jonathan Shipley's garden in 1771; part two, written in Passy; and the rest, which he had recently written. One copy was sent to Benjamin Vaughan with the request that it be shown to Richard Price. The second went to M. Le Veillard, who had so often implored him to go on with it. "I send you what is done of the Memoirs under this express Condition, however," Franklin wrote, "that you do not suffer any Copy to be taken of them, or any Part of them, on any Account whatever, and that you will, with your excellent friend the Duc de la Rochefoucauld, read them over carefully, examine them critically, and send me your friendly, candid Opinion of the Parts you would advise me to correct or expunge; this in Case you should be of Opinion that they are generally proper to be published; and if you judge otherwise, that you would send me that Opinion as soon as possible, and prevent my taking farther Trouble in endeavouring to finish them."

He was by now virtually confined to his bed and instead of writing letters dictated them to his grandson, a method which he wished he had begun earlier. Then, he told Benjamin Vaughan on November 2, 1789, "I might by this time have finished my Memoirs."

Toward the end of 1789, he reflected more than once in letters to friends on the political situation he had helped to create in the United States. On the whole, he was satisfied, telling Jean-Baptiste Le Roy that he was satisfied with the new American Constitution, which had the appearance of permanency; but adding, "in this world nothing can be said to be certain, except death and taxes." Even the French Revolution, which had already merged the red and blue of the city of Paris with the white of the Bourbons to form the tricolor of a new France, gave hope despite its horrors. "God grant," Franklin wrote to David Hartley in commenting on it, "that not only the love of liberty, but a thorough knowledge of the rights of man, may pervade all the nations of the earth, so that a philosopher may set his foot anywhere on its surface, and say, 'This is my country.' "

Franklin appears to have had little premonition of the explosion which was to drive the mob into the Bastille and so many tumbrils to the guillotine. This is hardly surprising. As minister in Paris he had the task of cultivating the King and his advisers, and his diplomatic friends were the very people who preferred to avert their thoughts from the wrath that might be coming. So were most of his personal acquaintances and cronies, and his neighbor at Passy, the harmless old M. Le Veillard, was only one member of his circle who was to lose a head in the Terror. The gulf between "them" and "us" was immeasurably greater in France than it was in America, and even greater than it was in England; Franklin had only limited opportunities for bridging the gulf.

Early in 1790 he put down for Ezra Stiles, president of Yale, his views on Christianity. They are an interesting epilogue to the somewhat varied ideas he had expressed over the years. "As to Jesus of Nazareth," he wrote, "my Opinion of whom you particularly desire, I think his system of morals and his religion, as he left them to us, the best the world ever saw or is like to see; but I apprehend it has received various corrupting changes, and I have, with most of the present Dissenters in England, some doubts as to his Divinity; though it is a question I do not dogmatize upon, having never studied it, and think it needless to busy myself with it now, when I expect soon an opportunity of knowing the truth with less trouble. I see no harm, however, in its being believed, if that belief has the good consequence, as probably it has, of making his doctrines more respected and more observed; especially as I do not perceive, that the Supreme takes it amiss, by distinguishing the unbelievers in his government of the world with any peculiar marks of his displeasure."

If Franklin's reply to Stiles exemplified his lack of dogmatism, his last essay showed that he still retained the wit which had served him so well in his early political campaigns. In Congress James Jackson, later governor of Georgia, had delivered an impassioned speech against any interference with the practice of slavery. Reading it, Franklin wrote in a letter to the *Federal Gazette*, had reminded him of a similar speech "made about 100 years since by Sidi Mehemet Ibrahim, a member of the Divan of

Algiers, which may be seen in Martin's Account of his Consul-ship, *anno* 1687." The Algerians had been petitioned, Franklin went on, to stop their piratical capture of Christians, who were snatched from ships in the Mediterranean and taken into slav-ery. He then quoted the Algerian answer, matching Jackson's support for slavery point by point with those from Sidi Mehemet Ibrahim, who concluded: "The Doctrine, that Plundering and Enslaving the Christians is unjust, is at best *problematical*; but that it is the Interest of this State to continue the Practice, is clear; therefore let the Petition be rejected." But the petition was, of course, just as imaginary as the "Comte de Schaumberg" who wanted his Hessians killed or the packages of scalps being sent as a gift to George III.

The previous month, Pennsylvania's antislavery organization had presented to the House of Representatives a petition for abolition, which Franklin had signed. Now, in March, the *Federal Gazette* published his polemic holding Congressman Jackson's ideas up to ridicule. As in his political heyday he signed it with a pseudonym which deceived only a few: "Historicus."

He was now in almost constant pain. But in the intervals, his doctor, John Jones, has said, "he not only amused himself with reading and conversing chearfully with his family and a few friends, who visited him, but was often employed in doing busi-ness of a public as well as private nature, with various persons, who waited on him for that purpose." One of them was Jeffer-son, from whom he inquired of events in France, which Jefferson had just left, and to whom he gave what he called "a sample" of his autobiography. "I found him in bed where he remains almost constantly," Thomas Jefferson wrote to M. Le Veillard after a visit to Philadelphia. "He had been clear of pain for some days and was chearful & in good spirits. He listened with a glow of interest to the details of your revolution & of his friends which I gave him. He is much emaciated. I pressed him to continue the narration of his life, & perhaps he will."

Toward the end of March he became feverish, possibly the result, Dr. Jones felt, of indulging his love of fresh air by sitting at an open window for some hours with the cold air blowing in. A few days later he complained of a pain in the left breast, and a cough made his breathing difficult. He still had periods of comparative ease, and the members of the family who had been doing turn and turn about at his bedside believed he was about to recover. When he asked his daughter to remake his bed so that he might die in a decent manner, she replied that she hoped he would live a long while yet. *"I hope not,"* he replied. And when advised to move his position so that he could breathe more easily, he replied: *"A dying man can do nothing easy."*

The end came when an abscess which had formed on a lung finally burst. "The organs of respiration became gradually oppressed—" his doctor wrote, "a calm lethargic state succeeded —and on the 17th [of April, 1790,] about eleven o'clock at night, he quietly expired, closing a long and useful life of eighty-four years and three months."

Mary Hewson, being called to perform the last offices for the corpse, was surprised to see at the foot of the bed an old picture of the Day of Judgment. The nurse told her that the picture had been in a garret for many years but that when Franklin had become confined to his bed he asked that it should be placed where it was always within his view.

In Congress the House of Representatives voted to wear mourning for a month. The Senate refused, despite an appeal to Washington by Thomas Jefferson, that the executive department should wear mourning; "he declined it," Jefferson later told Dr. Benjamin Rush, "because he said he should not know where to draw the line, if he once began that ceremony." In Paris, Mirabeau announced to the National Assembly: "Gentlemen, Franklin is dead—he has returned to the bosom of God— the genius who has liberated America, and shed over Europe the torrents of his light." The Assembly carried by acclamation a vote that mourning should be worn for three days.

What had Franklin achieved? At a local level he had, almost alone, given Philadelphia the library, the hospital and above all the American Philosophical Society, which were to help raise it to a preeminence among American cities.

More important—and not only because of the political influence it was to give Franklin in Europe during the American War of Independence—was his achievement in helping to solve the problems raised by electricity. Scientists in England, Germany and France were all working on them and all contributed to the answers; as in most sciences, discoveries were complexly interrelated rather than separately clean-cut. Yet Franklin in Philadelphia was quick to conceive of electricity as a single fluid rather than two. He thought in terms of "positive" and "negative" electricity rather than vitreous and resinous. And in a single experiment he demonstrated the law of conservation of charge. As for the experiment to show that lightning was electricity writ bold, that alone was enough to give him a place in the history of science.

There was also his extraordinary output as journalist, pamphleteer and author. His works were important for their political influence, just as those of earlier American writers—John Smith, John Hammond, Thomas Ash and Daniel Denton—were important in outlining the attractions of the country to potential colonists. Franklin's books were limited to two: *Experiments and Observations on Electricity,* which, in a series of letters outlining Franklin's investigation of electricity, went through numerous editions in the second half of the eighteenth century, and the *Autobiography.* This remarkable example of self-revelation is basically a book of sober advice for personal advancement, strung out along the account of a well-spent life. But a careful reading reveals numerous sly comments, as though the author is pointing fun at his own worthy recommendations. Written years after the events recorded, it has at places a gay imprecision; and throughout it has an understanding of human frailty which gives at least one clue to Franklin's success.

One feature of the *Autobiography* can be seen also in Franklin's political precepts, his scientific explanations and his lively trivia exhibited in private letters or correspondence with the more influential journals and papers. In all of them he seized firmly what he wished to say, then pinned it down with a minimum of words and a maximum of clarity. Both the riddles of electricity and the subtleties of politics should, he believed, be explicable to the uninitiated.

In business he was "sharp" in the dictionary definition of being quick to seize an advantage. But the sharpness could be qualified by a genuine liking for humanity and he wished, like Francis Drake, to have "the gentleman to haul and draw with the mariner, and the mariner with the gentleman. What! Let us show ourselves all to be of a company and let us not give occasion to the enemy to rejoice at our decay and overthrow."

Above all, Franklin had made possible the survival of an independent United States, a concept that until middle age he considered no more attractive than a confederation of states within a greater British Empire. Once battle was joined with Britain,

Franklin, as dominant in the political sphere as Washington in the military, became, in Europe, the organizer of victory. But if this was the greatest of his achievements it had as a by-product the injection into Europe of a realization that America could produce figures very different from the backwoodsmen of popular image. The early Colonists bred scientists other than Benjamin Franklin and men as deft politically. But his unusual combination of scientific flair and popular exposition revealed, particularly to France and to Britain, the intellectual potential already developed across the Atlantic. Returning to Europe in 1776 on the raft of his electrical reputation, old and plump yet still urged on by the mysterious impetus of genius, he had talked and intrigued, wheedled and borrowed, and helped to provide the troops in the field with the sinews of success. Franklin himself would have been among the first to agree that it was an admirable record.

REFERENCES

BIBLIOGRAPHY

INDEX

REFERENCES

Full details of the printed sources quoted are given with bibliographical information in the Bibliography, pp. 483–99.

1. PRINTER'S APPRENTICE

"I repeated the experiment": Thomas-François Dalibard, "Expériences et Observations sur le Tonnerre, Relatives à celles de Philadelphie, Mémoire Lû à l'Académie Royale des Sciences, le 13 Mai 1752, par M. Dalibard," printed Thomas-François Dalibard, *Expériences et Observations sur L'Electricité faites à Philadelphie en Amérique par M. Benjamin Franklin,* 2d ed., 2 vols., 2:99–125; here p. 112 [afterward referred to as Dalibard].

"M. Franklin's idea has ceased": ibid., p. 120.

"a stormy cloud having passed over": "Letters of the Abbé [Guillaume] Mazéas, F.R.S., to Rev. Stephen Hales, D.D., F.R.S., concerning the Success of the late Experiments in France. Translated from the French by James Parsons, M.D. F.R.S. May 20, 1752; read May 28, 1752," The Royal Society. *Philosophical Transactions, giving some Account of the Present Undertakings, Studies, and Labours, of the Ingenious, in many Considerable Parts of the World,* 47 (1751 and 1752): 535 [afterward referred to as *Phil. Trans.*].

"trying Mr. Franklin's experiment": John Canton–William Watson, July 21, 1752, quoted "A Letter of Mr. W. Watson, F.R.S. to the Royal Society, concerning the electrical Experiments in England upon Thunder-Clouds, Dec. 20, 1732 [*sic*], read Dec. 21, 1752," *Phil. Trans.*, 47 (1751 and 1752): 568.

"no other apparatus than an iron curtain-rod": Benjamin Wilson–William Watson, Aug. 12, 1752, quoted ibid., p. 569.

"You must remember, Sir": "A Letter from a Gentleman at Paris to his friend at Toulon, concerning a very extraordinary Experiment in Electricity, dated May 14, 1752," *The Gentleman's Magazine & Historical Chronicle*, 22 (June 1752): 263.

"Mean while you may assure": ibid., p. 264.

"God helps them that help themselves": "Richard Saunders, *Poor Richard, 1736. An Almanack for the Year of Christ 1736,*" Leonard W. Labaree and William B. Willcox et al. (eds.), *The Papers of Benjamin Franklin,* sponsored by the American Philosophical Society and Yale University, 22 vols. to date; here 2:140 [afterward referred to as Yale]. The sources of material used in *The Papers of Benjamin Franklin* are given in parentheses: here (Yale University Library, afterward referred to as Y.U.L.).

"Having been poor is no shame": "Richard Saunders, *Poor Richard improved: Being an Almanack and Ephemeris . . . for the Year of our Lord 1749,*" Yale 3:342 (Y.U.L.).

"a shade of thrift": Charles Francis Adams, *The Works of John Adams, Second President of the United States,* 10 vols.; here 1:319 [afterward referred to as Adams, *Works*].

"sprang from a defective early education": Adams, *Works,* 1:319.

"of more general use to young readers": BF–Duc de la Rochefoucauld, Oct. 22, 1788, quoted Jared Sparks (ed.), *The Works of Benjamin Franklin,* 10 vols.; here 10:360 [afterward referred to as Sparks].

"By that Register I perceiv'd": Max Farrand (ed.), *Benjamin Franklin's Memoirs* [Original MS.], *Parallel Text Edition,* p. 8 [afterward referred to as *Auto.*].

"Your uncle Benjamin": Josiah Franklin–Benjamin Franklin, May 26, 1739, Yale 2:229 (William Duane, *The Works of Dr. Benjamin Franklin,* 6 vols.; here 1:4–5; afterward referred to as Duane, *Works*).

"When I am living in the Midlands": H. Belloc, "The South Country," *Sonnets and Verse,* p. 42.

"They had got an English Bible": *Auto.,* p. 14.

"If Franklin says he knows": BF–Deborah Franklin, Sept. 6, 1758, Yale 8:137 (Duane, *Works,* 6:36–39).

"The houses are for the most part": John Josselyn, *An Account of two Voyages to New-England,* p. 162 [afterward referred to as Josselyn].

"make a kind of Wood of Trees": Daniel Neal, *The History of New-England*, 2 vols.; here 2:587.

"There are even wild ones": E. T. Fisher, *Report of a French Protestant Refugee, in Boston, 1687*, pp. 22 and 38.

"to take up loose people": Josselyn, p. 162.

"propos'd to give me": *Auto.*, p. 18.

"He had an excellent Constitution": ibid., pp. 22 and 24.

"from a View of the Expence": ibid., pp. 18 and 20.

"Dr. Franklin, when a child": "Supplement to the Memoirs: comprising Characters, Eulogiums, and Anecdotes of Dr. Franklin," William Temple Franklin (ed.), *Memoirs of the Life and Writings of Benjamin Franklin*, 4to ed., 3 vols.; here 1:447 [afterward referred to as W.T.F.].

"in cutting Wick for the Candles": *Auto.*, p. 20.

"good, just, & prudent": ibid., p. 24.

"little or no Notice was ever taken": ibid.

"I remember that, when I was a boxing boy": BF–Robert Morris, March 7, 1782, Albert H. Smyth (ed.), *The Writings of Benjamin Franklin*, 10 vols.; here 8:397 [afterward referred to as Smyth].

"It will sink to the bottom": BF–Mr. O.N., n.d., Letter LV, BF, *Experiments and Observations on Electricity* (1769), p. 464 [afterward referred to as *Exp. and Obs.* (1769)].

"I made two oval pallets": BF–M. [Jacques] Barbeu Dubourg, n.d., W.T.F., 3:408.

"I think it not impossible": ibid., p. 409.

"The printer hereof, prints linens": *Boston Gazette*, April 25, 1760, quoted James Parton, *Life and Times of Benjamin Franklin*, 2 vols.; here 1:52 [afterward referred to as Parton].

"a pair of deerskin breeches": John F. Watson, *Annals of Philadelphia and Pennsylvania, in the Olden Time*, 2 vols.; here 1:254 [afterward referred to as Watson].

"The Body of B. Franklin, Printer": "Fac-simile of an Epitaph on 'Benjamin Franklin,' written by himself, 1728, from Mr. Upcott's Collection," Charles John Smith, *Historical and Literary Curiosities*, Plate No. 18.

"I, Benjamin Franklin, of Philadelphia, printer": BF, Last Will and Testament, July 17, 1788, Sparks, vol. 1, App. 9, p. 599.

"I now had Access to better Books": *Auto.*, p. 30.

"of expressing my self in Terms": ibid., p. 42.

"wretched Stuff, in the Grubstreet Ballad Stile": ibid., p. 32.

"flatter'd my Vanity": ibid.

"on which we move": BF, *Articles of Belief and Acts of Religion,* in Two Parts, Part I: *First Principles,* Nov. 20, 1728, Library of Congress.

"perhaps the greatest single influence": J. A. Leo Lemay, "Franklin and the 'Autobiography,' " p. 193.

"The small-pox, so fatal": Lady Mary Wortley Montagu–Mrs. S. C. [Miss Sarah Chiswell], April 1, O.S. [1717], *The Letters and Works of Lady Mary Wortley Montagu,* 2 vols.; here 1:308.

"Notwithstanding God's hand is against us": Cotton Mather in *The Boston News-Letter,* quoted Smyth, 10:150.

"Whereas a wicked Libel": Rev. Increase Mather, "Advice to the Publick from Dr. Increase Mather," *The Boston News-Letter,* quoted John Clyde Oswald, *Benjamin Franklin, Printer,* p. 24 [afterward referred to as Oswald].

"I have always set a greater value": BF–Samuel Mather, May 12, 1784, Smyth, 9:208.

"Stoop, stoop": ibid., p. 209.

"This advice, thus beat into my head": ibid.

"I was excited to try my Hand": *Auto.,* p. 46.

"They read it": ibid.

"deliver'd at his Printing-House": Printer's note at end of Silence Dogood— Author of the "New-England Courant," *The New-England Courant,* No. 35, from Monday, March 26, to Monday, April 2, 1722, copy marked up by BF with contributors' names or initials, Burney Collection, British Library.

"My writing. Mrs. Dogood's letters": John Bigelow (ed.), *Autobiography of Benjamin Franklin,* p. 61.

"Were I endow'd": Silence Dogood, No. XI—Author of the "New-England Courant," *The New-England Courant,* No. 55, from Monday, Aug. 13, to Monday, Aug. 20, 1722.

"James Franklin should no longer print the Paper": *Auto.,* pp. 48 and 50.

"By private letters from Boston": quoted Parton, 1:91.

"There was a Consultation held": *Auto.,* p. 50.

"Long has the press groaned": quoted Parton, 1:91.

"The two made up an ill-mated pair": John Bach McMaster, "A Short Biography of Benjamin Franklin," p. 166.

"Perhaps I was too saucy": *Auto.,* p. 50.

"It was not fair in me": ibid.

"my indiscrete Disputations about Religion": *Auto.,* p. 52.

"without Victuals, or any Drink": ibid., p. 56.

"I was in my Working Dress": ibid., p. 60.

"These two Printers I found poorly Qualified": ibid., p. 68.

"Reasons for quitting Boston fully": ibid., p. 70.

"I was not a little surpriz'd": ibid., p. 72.

"many flattering things of me to my Father": ibid., p. 74.

"And since he will not set you up": ibid., p. 86.

"The Governor was there": ibid., p. 100.

"let me into Keith's Character": ibid., p. 104.

"He propos'd to take me over as his Clerk": ibid., p. 126.

"I was grown tired of London": ibid.

"I grew fond of her Company": *Auto.*, p. 112.

"Some of his Reasonings": ibid., p. 108.

"*present* Thoughts of the *general State of Things*": [BF], *A Dissertation on Liberty and Necessity, Pleasure and Pain*, p. 3. British Library.

"down to an Equality": ibid., p. 32.

"In our Return, at the Request of the Company": *Auto.*, pp. 122 and 124.

"He had two Sons about to set out": ibid., pp. 126 and 128.

"the chief dependence of the people": BF, Entry for Friday, July 22, 1726, "Journal of Occurrences in my Voyage to Philadelphia on board the Berkshire, Henry Clark, Master, from London," W.T.F., vol. 1, app. 1, p. i.

"I rise in the morning": BF, Entry for Thursday, Aug. 25, 1726, ibid., p. x.

"*Plan* . . . for regulating my future Conduct": *Auto.*, p. 128.

"1. It is necessary for me to be extremely frugal": quoted Mr. Walsh, "Life of Benjamin Franklin," Joseph Delaplaine, *Delaplaine's Repository of the Lives and Portraits of Distinguished American Characters*, vol. 2, pt. 1, pp. 51–52, quoted Sparks, 1:104–5n.

"pretty faithfully adhered to": *Auto.*, p. 128.

"I could not discern it so soon": BF, Entry for Sunday, Oct. 9, 1726, W.T.F., vol. 1, app. 1, p. xviii.

2. A TALENT TO SUCCEED

"divers Sorts, some for Food": William Penn–Committee of The Free Society of Traders of [Pennsylvania] Residing in London, 1683, quoted Horace

Mather Lippincott, *Early Philadelphia,* p. 26 [afterward referred to as Lippincott].

"were like clouds": Watson, 1:17.

"peaches by cartloads": Mahlon Stacy–[?], n.d., quoted Watson, 1:17.

"room enough for a House": William Penn–Society of Traders, 1683, quoted Lippincott, p. 27.

"I attended the Business diligently": *Auto.,* p. 130.

"I contriv'd a Copper-Plate Press for it": ibid., p. 142.

"My Mind having been much more improv'd": ibid.

"We admire, I think": John William Ward, "Who Was Benjamin Franklin?," p. 553.

"I think it would be highly commendable": BF, *A Modest Enquiry into the Nature and Necessity of a Paper-Currency,* April 3, 1729, Yale 1:157 (Historical Society of Pennsylvania, afterward referred to as H.S.P.).

"but the Rich Men dislik'd it": *Auto.,* p. 170.

"My Friends there who conceiv'd": ibid.

"In order to secure my Credit": *Auto.,* pp. 172 and 174.

"a whole Book of Devotions": BF–Jane Mecom, July 28, 1743, Carl Van Doren (ed.), *The Letters of Benjamin Franklin & Jane Mecom,* p. 38 [afterward referred to as *Franklin & Mecom Letters*].

"since Men are endued with Reason": BF, *Articles of Belief and Acts of Religion,* in Two Parts, Part I: *First Principles,* Nov. 20, 1728, Library of Congress.

"You have a fast and prayer day": BF–John Franklin, [May ?] 1745, Sparks, 7:16.

"a paltry thing": *Auto.,* p. 158.

"To wreck his rival's enterprise": Smyth, 2:100n.

"By this means the Attention of the Publick": *Auto.,* p. 160.

"The Author of a Gazette": *The Pennsylvania Gazette,* No. XL, from Thursday, Sept. 25, to Thursday, Oct. 2, 1729.

"Their happy Mother Country": *The Pennsylvania Gazette,* No. XLI, from Thursday, Oct. 2, to Thursday, Oct. 9, 1729.

"The Drinker's Dictionary": *The Pennsylvania Gazette,* No. 422, from Jan. 6 to Jan. 13, 1736/7.

"had established about 18 mills": J. P. Brissot de Warville, *New Travels in the United States of America,* p. 225n [afterward referred to as Brissot de Warville].

"a serious Courtship on my Part ensu'd": *Auto.,* p. 176.

"I let her [Mrs. Godfrey] know": ibid.

"that hard-to-be-govern'd Passion of Youth": *Auto.*, p. 178.

"The issue is whether or not": Robert E. Spiller, review of *Benjamin Franklin,* by Carl Van Doren, p. 231.

"had this son by an oyster wench": "Characters of Some of the Leading Men in the present American Rebellion," *The Morning Post, and Daily Advertiser,* No. 2068, June 1, 1779.

"the law of bastardy": John Bach McMaster, *Benjamin Franklin as a Man of Letters,* p. 45 [afterward referred to as McMaster].

"made some Courtship during this time": *Auto.*, p. 92.

"I had a great Respect & Affection": ibid.

"I by degrees [forgot] my Engagements": *Auto.*, p. 108.

"Our mutual Affection was revived": ibid., p. 180.

"a good & faithful Helpmate": ibid.

"I do hereby sincerely declare": *The Pennsylvania Gazette,* No. 420, from Dec. 23 to Dec. 30, 1736.

"removed from the House": *The Pennsylvania Gazette,* No. 526, Jan. 11, 1738.

"By the Death of a Gentleman": *The Pennsylvania Gazette,* No. 108, from Thursday, Dec. 3, to Tuesday, Dec. 8, 1730.

"Bibles, Testaments, Psalters": *The Pennsylvania Gazette,* No. XLIV, from Thursday, Oct. 23, to Monday, Oct. 27, 1729.

"I would not have you be too nice": BF–William Strahan, Feb. 12, 1744/5, quoted S. G. W. Benjamin, "Unpublished Letters of Franklin to Strahan," p. 22 [afterward referred to as "Franklin & Strahan Letters"].

"This however is a Matter": BF–Jan Ingenhousz, Oct. 2, 1781, Library of Congress.

"It was a shop which defies description": McMaster, p. 96.

in his business books were loans: Wilbur C. Plummer, "Consumer Credit in Colonial Philadelphia," p. 395.

"There is a FERRY": Advertisement, May 10, 1741, *The General Magazine and Historical Chronicle for all the British Plantations in America,* vol. 1, no. 5 (May 1741), p. 356.

"Do not be astonished, Sirs": quoted Smyth, 8:336n.

"I have heard that once": Richard Saunders, *Poor Richard improved: Being an Almanack and Ephemeris . . . for the Year of our Lord 1750,* Yale 3:438 (Y.U.L.).

"POOR RICHARD: AN ALMANACK": *The Pennsylvania Gazette,* No. 213, from Dec. 19 to Dec. 28, 1732.

"Daring and prodigality": Dixon Wecter, *The Hero in America,* p. 57 [afterward referred to as Wecter].

"He's a Fool": Richard Saunders, *Poor Richard, 1733. An Almanack For the Year of Christ 1733,* Yale 1:312 (Rosenbach Foundation).

"He that drinks fast": ibid., p. 315.

"The Bell calls others": Richard Saunders, *Poor Richard improved: Being an Almanack and Ephemeris . . . for the Year of our Lord 1754,* Yale 5:184 (Y.U.L.).

"To be intimate with": ibid., p. 185.

"*Mine* is better than *Ours*": Richard Saunders, *Poor Richard improved: Being an Almanack and Ephemeris . . . for the Year of our Lord 1756,* Yale 6:320 (Y.U.L.).

"Love your Enemies": ibid., p. 321.

"A Change of *Fortune*": ibid., p. 319.

"Be civil to *all*": ibid., p. 322.

"I consider'd it as a proper Vehicle": *Auto.,* p. 242.

"When the type was set": Paul A. W. Wallace, *Conrad Weiser, 1696–1760,* p. 103.

"saved the publication": ibid.

"Printers are educated in the Belief": *The Pennsylvania Gazette,* No. 134, from Thursday, June 3, to Thursday, June 10, 1731.

"The person returned at the time": Isaiah Thomas, *The History of Printing in America,* 2 vols.; here 1:237.

"a Club for mutual Improvement": *Auto.,* p. 152.

"produce one or more Queries on any Point of Morals": ibid.

"Have you lately heard": BF, "Rules for a Club formerly established in Philadelphia," Benjamin Vaughan (ed.), *Political, Miscellaneous, and Philosophical Pieces . . . written by Benj. Franklin, L.L.D. and F.R.S.,* pp. 534, 535 and 536 [afterward referred to as Vaughan].

"But my giving this Account": *Auto.,* p. 156.

"it might be convenient to us": ibid., p. 180.

"for want of due Care": ibid., p. 182.

"I conceiv'd to want Regulation": ibid., p. 260.

"for a little Drink": ibid., p. 262.

"& spend a social Evening together": ibid., p. 264.

"a Voluntary Society for the advancing of Knowledge": Cadwallader Colden–Dr. William Douglass, n.d. [1728], *The Letters and Papers of Cadwallader*

Colden 1711–1775, 9 vols.; here 1:272 [afterward referred to as *Colden Letters*].

"That One Society be formed of Virtuosi": BF, *A Proposal for Promoting USEFUL KNOWLEDGE among the British Plantations in America*, May 14, 1743, Royal Society of Arts, London.

"all philosophical Experiments": ibid.

"rather ashamed to have it known": BF–James Logan, Jan. 20, 1749/50, Sparks, 6:100n.

"In point of fact, most American scientists": I. Bernard Cohen, *Franklin and Newton*, p. 29 [afterward referred to as Cohen].

"Peace being concluded": *Auto.*, pp. 294 and 296.

"This reconcil'd me": ibid., p. 272.

"by a North-East storm": BF–Alexander Small, May 12, 1760, Letter XXXVI, *Exp. and Obs.* (1769), p. 381.

"your whole room is equally warmed": BF, "An Account of the new-invented Pensylvanian Fire-Places" (1744), *Exp. and Obs.* (1769), p. 304.

"That as we enjoy great Advantages": *Auto.*, p. 294.

"An Account of the New-Invented Pennsylvania Fire Places": ibid.

"to damage the eyes": BF, "An Account of the new-invented Pensylvanian Fire-Places" (1744), *Exp. and Obs.* (1769), p. 290.

"But if you will not take this Counsel": BF, "Advice to a Young Man on the Choice of a Mistress," June 25, 1745, printed "Why a Young Man should choose an Old Mistress," in Paul McPharlin (ed.), *Benjamin Franklin: Satires & Bagatelles*, pp. 33–34.

"To discover some Drug": BF, "A Letter to the Royal Academy at Brussels," printed "A Prize Question," ibid., pp. 38 and 39.

"I . . . found it of great Advantage": *Auto.*, p. 260.

"secur'd to [him] the Business": ibid., p. 258.

The royal grants: Dr. William Douglass, *A Summary, Historical and Political, . . . of the British Settlements in North-America*, 2 vols.; here vol. 2, pt. 1.

"I felt obliged to solicit the ministry": Thomas Penn–Governor Thomas, 1743, quoted Arthur Pound, *The Penns of Pennsylvania and England*, p. 278.

"By order of the House": Sister Joan de Lourdes Leonard, C.S.J., "The Organization and Procedure of the Pennsylvania Assembly, 1682–1776," p. 235.

"and, at length, had acquired such a knack": BF–Peter Collinson, n.d., Letter XXVII, *Exp. and Obs.* (1769), p. 351 [Yale 4:393 suggests date of this letter is 1752].

3. THE PROFESSIONAL AMATEUR

"I [have] remov'd to a more quiet Part": BF–Cadwallader Colden, Sept. 29, 1748, *Colden Letters*, 4:78.

"Thus you see I am in a fair Way": ibid., p. 79.

"At present I pass my time": BF–Abiah Franklin, April 12, 1750, Yale 3:475 (Boston Athenaeum).

"On one occasion [Franklin] saw her": Mrs. E. D. Gillespie, *A Book of Remembrance*, p. 17.

"we turn the sphere like a common grindstone": BF–Peter Collinson, Sept. 1, 1747, Letter II, BF, *Experiments and Observations on Electricity* (1751), p. 18 [afterward referred to as *Exp. and Obs.* (1751)]. [Yale 3:126 suggests correct date of this letter is that of the Bowdoin MS., May 25, 1747.]

"Altho' these Effects are at present but in *minimis*": "Experiments and Observations upon the Light that is produced by communicating Electrical Attraction to animal or inanimate Bodies, together with some of its most surprising Effects; communicated in a Letter from Mr. Stephen Gray, F.R.S. to Cromwell Mortimer, M.D. R.S. Secr., Jan. 28, 1734–5," *Phil. Trans.*, 39 (1735 and 1736): 24.

"One caught an urchin": John L. Heilbron, "Franklin's Physics," p. 32.

"This Principle is, that there are two distinct Electricities": "A Letter from Mons. Du Fay, F.R.S., and of the Royal Academy of Sciences at Paris to his Grace Charles, Duke of Richmond and Lenox, concerning Electricity. Translated from the French by T.S., M.D.," Dec. 27, 1733, *Phil Trans.*, 38 (1733 and 1734): 263.

"increased the electric sparks": M. l'Abbé [Jean Antoine] Nollet, *Recherches sur les Causes Particulières des Phénomènes Electriques*, p. 171.

"He invited guests": Park Benjamin, *The Intellectual Rise in Electricity*, p. 495 [afterward referred to as Benjamin].

"I wish to inform you of a new": Pieter van Musschenbroek–René de Réaumur, Jan. 1746, quoted M. l'Abbé Nollet, "Observations sur quelques nouveaux phénomènes d'Electricité," April 20, 1746, *Mémoires de Mathématique et de Physique, tirés des Registres de l'Académie Royale des Sciences, De l'Année MDCCXLVI* (Paris: de l'Imprimérie Royale, 1751), pp. 1–23; here p. 2.

"The exclamations of surprise": ibid., p. 18.

"It is no exaggeration to say that Watson": Cohen, p. 390.

"In 1746, being at Boston": *Auto.*, p. 380.

"sent an account of the new German experiments": BF–Michael Collinson, n.d. [1768], Norman G. Brett-James, *The Life of Peter Collinson, F.R.S., F.S.A.*, p. 186.

"Spencer introduced Franklin to an experiment": N. H. de V. Heathcote, "Franklin's Introduction to Electricity," p. 35.

"the work of Leipzig academicians": J. L. Heilbron, *Electricity in the 17th and 18th Centuries*, p. 325.

"And from the year 1743": Albrecht von Haller, "An historical account of the wonderful discoveries, made in Germany, &c. concerning Electricity," p. 194 [afterward referred to as von Haller].

reprinted in the Colonies: *American Magazine and Historical Chronicle*, 2 (December 1745): 530–37.

"fixed a Machine": *Boston Evening Post*, March 3, 1746, quoted J. A. Leo Lemay, *Ebenezer Kinnersley: Franklin's Friend*, p. 58 [afterward referred to as Lemay].

"at last succeeded": *Boston Evening Post*, Dec. 29, 1746, quoted ibid., p. 59.

"was continually full": *Auto.*, p. 380.

"We say B": BF–Peter Collinson, Sept. 1, 1747 [May 25, 1747], Letter II, *Exp. and Obs.* (1751), p. 15.

"I never was before engaged in": BF–Peter Collinson, March 28, 1747. Letter I, *Exp. and Obs.* (1769), p. 2.

"Some Gentlemen here are desirous": Cadwallader Colden–BF, Aug. 3, 1747, *Colden Letters*, 3:410.

"He could make an experiment": *Works of Henry Lord Brougham*, 11 vols.; here 6:253.

"He has endeavoured to remove": Sir Humphry Davy, quoted William Cabell Bruce, *Benjamin Franklin Self-Revealed*, 2 vols.; here 2:362 [afterward referred to as Bruce].

"The Force of the Electrical Spark": Ebenezer Kinnersley's advertisement, *The Maryland Gazette*, May 10, 17 and 24, 1749, quoted Lemay, p. 69.

"I taught him the use of the tube": BF–Dr. [John] L[ining], March 18, 1755, Letter XXIV, *Exp. and Obs.* (1769), p. 320 [Yale 5:521 suggests addressee is John Lining].

"The first [matter to be noted]": BF–Peter Collinson, Sept. 1, 1747 [May 25, 1747], Letter II, *Exp. and Obs.* (1751), p. 10.

"A curious Machine": *The Pennsylvania Gazette*, No. 1165, April 11, 1751.

"We suspend by fine silk thread": BF–Peter Collinson, Sept. 1, 1747 [May 25, 1747], Letter II, *Exp. and Obs.* (1751), p. 16.

"If now the picture be moderately electrified": BF–Peter Collinson, April 29, 1749, Letter III, ibid., p. 27.

"what we call'd an *electrical-battery*": ibid., p. 26.

"operate as a motive": BF–Messrs. Dubourg and Dalibard, n.d., W.T.F., 3:406.

"eat uncommonly tender": Appendix, *Experiments and Observations on Electricity, made at Philadelphia in America* (1774), p. 160 [afterward referred to as *Exp. and Obs.* (1774)].

"the operator must be very circumspect": BF–Messrs. Dubourg and Dalibard, n.d., W.T.F., 3:407.

"I was obliged to quit": BF–Dr. [Jan] Ingenhousz, April 29, 1785, entitled "On Electricity. A Three Wheeled Clock—Gravitation of Bodies affected by Sun and Moon—Conjecture on Tides," ibid., p. 476.

"I have lately made an Experiment": BF–[?], Dec. 25, 1750, Yale 4:82 [which suggests possible and probable recipient was John Franklin] (American Academy of Arts and Sciences).

"The knocking down of the six men": BF–Dr. [John] L[ining], March 18, 1755, Letter XXIV, *Exp. and Obs.* (1769), p. 324.

"Too great a charge": ibid., p. 325.

"Spirits, at the same time": BF–Peter Collinson, April 29, 1749, Letter III, *Exp. and Obs.* (1751), p. 34.

"As the possibility of this experiment": BF–Peter Collinson, April 29, 1749, Letter IV, *Exp. and Obs.* (1769), p. 37n.

"the *electrified bottle*": BF–Peter Collinson, April 29, 1749, Letter III, *Exp. and Obs.* (1751), p. 35.

"must have some practical use": Krüger, quoted Benjamin, p. 501.

"3 Instances of the Electrical power": Peter Collinson–BF, April 12, 1747/8, Yale 3:284 (Library Company of Philadelphia).

"My method was, to place the patient": BF–John Pringle, Dec. 21, 1757, Letter XXX, *Exp. and Obs.* (1769), p. 359.

"A man, for instance": ibid., p. 360.

"by the electric flame": "A Letter from Mr. Franklin to Mr. Peter Collinson, F.R.S., concerning the Effects of Lightning," June 20, 1751, read Nov. 14, 1751, *Phil. Trans.*, 47 (1751 and 1752): 291.

"A small cartridge is fill'd with dry powder": ibid.

"darted thick from the Crown": F. Hauksbee, *Physico-Mechanical Experiments on Various Subjects*, p. 9.

"it produc'd a Light but no Crackling": "Experiments of the Luminous Qualities of Amber, Diamonds, and Gum Lac, by Dr. Wall, in a Letter to Dr. Sloane, R. S. Secr.," *Phil. Trans.*, 26 (1708 and 1709): 71.

"intirely the same with Electricity": John Freke, *An Essay to shew the Cause of Electricity*, p. 28.

"the only difference exists": Johann Heinrich Winkler, *Die Stärke der electrischen Kraft des Wassers in gläsernen Gefässen etc.* (Leipzig, 1746), quoted Benjamin, p. 572.

"Lightening has pretty much the same qualities": von Haller, p. 193.

"Electricity in our hands": L'Abbé [Jean Antoine] Nollet, *Leçons de Physique experimentale*, 5 vols; here 4:314.

"fire . . . like a flash of lightning": BF–Peter Collinson, Sept. 1, 1747 [May 25, 1747], Letter II, *Exp. and Obs.* (1751), p. 17.

"a vivid flame": BF–Peter Collinson, July 28, 1747, Letter I, ibid., p. 9.

"jostled and mixed by the winds": BF–[?], n.d., Letter IV, ibid., p. 44 [Yale 3:372 suggests addressee is John Mitchell and date April 29, 1749].

"When the gun-barrel": ibid.

"subsisting" and "The electric fluid is attracted by points": BF notebook entry for Nov. 7, 1749, quoted BF–Dr. [John] L[ining], March 18, 1755, Letter XXIV, *Exp. and Obs.* (1769), p. 323.

"I cannot answer better": BF–Dr. [John] L[ining], March 18, 1755, Letter XXIV, ibid., p. 322.

"if these things are so": BF, "Opinions and Conjectures, Concerning the Properties and Effects of the Electrical Matter, arising from Experiments and Observations, made in Philadelphia, 1749," enclosed BF–Peter Collinson, July 29, 1750, *Exp. and Obs.* (1751), p. 62.

"upon the other Side of the *Atlantic Ocean*": "Some further Inquiries into the Nature and Properties of Electricity; by William Watson, F.R.S., read Jan. 21, 1747/8," *Phil. Trans.*, 45 (1748): 98.

"Part of a paper containing a new theory": *Journal Book* of the Royal Society, Nov. 9, 1749.

"The remainder of a paper": *Journal Book* of the Royal Society, Nov. 16, 1749.

"lately made in Philadelphia": Edward Cave, "By a Number of Experiments, lately made in Philadelphia, several of the principal Properties of the Electrical Fire were demonstrated, and its effects shewn," *The Gentleman's Magazine and Historical Chronicle*, 20 (January 1750): 34.

"A curious Remark on ELECTRICITY": *The Gentleman's Magazine and Historical Chronicle*, 20 (May 1750): 208.

"said more sensible things": Dr. John Fothergill–Dr. William Cuming, May 18, 1751, Betsy C. Corner and Christopher C. Booth, *Chain of Friendship: Selected Letters of Dr. John Fothergill of London, 1735–1780*, p. 143 [afterward referred to as *Fothergill Letters*].

"Perhaps only a hundred or so iron rods": Dalibard, 2:125.

"If any of thy Friends": Peter Collinson–BF [n.d.], quoted BF–Jared Eliot, April 12, 1753, Yale 4:466 (Y.U.L.).

"With Franklin grasp the lightning's fiery wing": Thomas Campbell, "The Pleasures of Hope," pt. 1, p. 12.

"While Franklin's quiet memory climbs to heaven": George Gordon Noel, Lord Byron, "The Age of Bronze," *The Works of Lord Byron,* 7 vols.; here 6:13.

"And stoic Franklin's energetic shade": ibid., p. 19.

"snatched the lightning shaft from heaven": Anne Robert Jacques Turgot, Epigram: "Eripuit Coelo fulmen, sceptrumque tyrannis," 1781.

"Some write in blood a name": Gordon Forrest, quoted Wecter, p. 64.

"particulars which I have": Joseph Priestley, *The History and Present State of Electricity, with Original Experiments,"* p. 180 [afterward referred to as Priestley, *History*].

"he could have a readier and better access": ibid.

"Preparing, therefore, a large silk handkerchief": ibid.

"As frequent Mention is made": *The Pennsylvania Gazette,* No. 1243, Oct. 19, 1752.

"I hope a more perfect & particular account": Cadwallader Colden–BF, Oct. 29 [24], 1752, *Colden Letters,* 4:353.

"The Professor, judging from the Needle": Extract of a Letter from Moscow, dated August 23, *The Pennsylvania Gazette,* No. 1315, March 5, 1754.

"his body [being] found": Parton, 1:292.

"justly envied": quoted ibid.

"How to secure Houses &c. from LIGHTNING": Richard Saunders, *Poor Richard improved: Being an Almanack and Ephemeris . . . for the Year of our Lord 1753,* Yale 4:408 (Y.U.L.).

"not chargeable with presumption": Kinnersley, quoted Lemay, p. 90.

"I found the bells rang sometimes": BF–Peter Collinson, September 1753, Letter XII, *Exp. and Obs.* (1769), p. 112.

"exactly as they should do": BF–Cadwallader Colden, Jan. 1, 1753, *Colden Letters,* 4:359.

"In one or two Places": BF–Cadwallader Colden, April 12, 1753, ibid., p. 382.

"preparing an Answer": BF–James Bowdoin, Dec. 13, 1753, Yale 5:156 (Massachusetts Historical Society, afterward referred to as M.H.S.).

"a phaenomenon hitherto almost inaccessible": "An Account of a Treatise presented to the Royal Society, intituled Letters concerning electricity in which the latest discoveries upon this subject, and the consequences which may be deduced from them, are examined; by the Abbé Nollet, extracted and translated from the French, by Mr. William Watson," read May 17, 1753, *Phil. Trans.*, vol. 48, pt. 1 (1753), p. 202.

"From this epoch": Alexander von Humboldt, *Cosmos: Sketch of a Physical Description of the Universe*, 2 vols.; here 2:341.

"could not overlook the merit": *Journal Book* of the Royal Society, 22:414.

"by a unanimous vote": BF–William Franklin, Dec. 19, 1767, Smyth, 5:77.

4. "TRIBUNE OF THE PEOPLE"

"Now I mention Mountains": BF–Jared Eliot, July 16, 1747, Yale 3:149 (Y.U.L.).

"The slate, which forms the roof": BF–Jacques Barbeu-Dubourg, n.d., entitled "On the Nature of Sea-Coal," W.T.F., 3:407.

"part of the high county of Derby": BF–Abbé Soulavie, Sept. 22, 1782, entitled "On the Theory of the Earth and its Magnetism," ibid., p. 454.

"It is evident from the quantities": BF–Mr. P[eter] F[ranklin], May 7, 1760, Letter XXXV, *Exp. and Obs.* (1769), p. 379.

"Bread, Beef, Port, Flour": Samuel Hazard et al. (eds.), *Pennsylvania Archives*, 9 series; here ser. 8, vol. 4, p. 3042 [afterward referred to as *Penn. Arch.*], quoted Yale 3:195 n4.

"If we fail, let us move the Purchase": *Auto.*, p. 290.

"I determined to try": ibid., p. 278.

" 'Till of late I could scarce believe": [BF], *Plain Truth: or, Serious Considerations On the Present State of the City of Philadelphia, and Province of Pennsylvania. By a Tradesman of Philadelphia*, p. 18.

"wealthy and powerful Body of People": ibid., p. 15.

"*Protection* is as truly": ibid., p. 15.

"Great and rich Men": ibid., p. 17.

"The House was pretty full": *Auto.*, p. 278.

"He at first refus'd us peremptorily": ibid., p. 280.

"It is proposed to breed gunners": BF–James Logan, Dec. 4, 1747, Sparks, 7:28.

"My Activity in these Operations": *Auto.*, pp. 280 and 282.

"The paper called 'Plain Truth' ": Thomas Penn–Lt. Lynford Lardner, March 29, 1748, quoted Hubertis Cummings, *Richard Peters, Provincial Secretary and Cleric*, p. 133.

"Mr. Franklin's doctrine that obedience": Thomas Penn–Richard Peters, June 9, 1748, quoted William Robert Shepherd, *History of Proprietary Government in Pennsylvania,* p. 222n.

"a Prospect of being more at Ease": BF–Peter Collinson, Oct. 18, 1748, Yale 3:320 (Pierpont Morgan Library, afterward referred to as P.M.L.).

"to treat with the said Indians": George II per Governor James Hamilton, Commission to Richard Peters, Isaac Norris and Benjamin Franklyn, Sept. 22, 1753, *Minutes of the Provincial Council of Pennsylvania, fro:1 the Organization to the Termination of the Proprietary Government,* 16 vols.; here 5:658 [afterward referred to as *Minutes*].

"He looked after them all": Smyth, 10:173.

"to regulate the Post offices": BF–Peter Collinson, May 28, 1754, Yale 5:333 (American Philosophical Society, afterward referred to as A.P.S.).

"Were there a general council": BF–James Parker, March 20, 1751, printed Archibald Kennedy, *The Importance of Gaining and Preserving the Friendship of the Indians to the British Interest, considered,* p. 41.

"the greatest political structure": BF–Lord Kames, Jan. 3, 1760, Abercairney Muniments (GD24), Scottish Record Office, Edinburgh [afterward referred to as S.R.O.].

"In some of the uninhabited Parts": *The Pennsylvania Gazette,* No. 1169, May 9, 1751.

"ill consequence to be apprehended": Conference with the Speaker, Claremont, Sept. 9, 1754, Newcastle Papers, Vol. CCCX, Add. MS. 32995, fo. 309, British Library.

"enter into articles of union": Mrs. L. K. Mathews, "Benjamin Franklin's Plans for a Colonial Union, 1750–1775," p. 397.

"Mr. *Ward,* Ensign of Capt. *Trent*'s Company": Enclosure, BF–Mr. Partridge, May 8, 1754, CO. 5 : 14, Pt. I, fo. 160, Public Record Office, London [afterward referred to as P.R.O.].

" 'Tis farther said": ibid.

"Join, or Die": *The Pennsylvania Gazette,* No. 1324, May 9, 1754.

"forward the whole to Albany": BF–James Alexander, June 8, 1754, John Bigelow (ed.), *The Complete Works of Benjamin Franklin,* 10 vols.; here 2:347 n1 [afterward referred to as Bigelow].

"to digest them into one general Plan": "Proceedings of the Congress held at Albany, by the Hon. James De Lancey, Esq., Lt. Gov. and Commander in Chief of the Province of New York, and the Commissioners of the several Provinces, met in the said City of Albany, the 19th of June, 1754, entered Provincial Council Resolution, June 24, 1754," *Minutes,* 6:66.

"That humble Application": *Minutes,* 6:105–6.

"tho' I projected the Plan": BF–Peter Collinson, Dec. 29, 1754, Yale 5:454 (P.M.L.).

"One large step over the mountains": Thomas Pownall–Lord Halifax, 1754, quoted Thomas Pownall, *The Administration of the British Colonies,* 2 vols.; here 2:230 and n.

"I doubt not but they will make a good [plan]": BF–Peter Collinson, Dec. 29, 1754, Yale 5:454 (P.M.L.).

"There is a Representation": Lord Newcastle–The Hon. Mr. Charles Townshend, Nov. 2, 1754, Newcastle Papers, Vol. LII, Add. MS. 32737, fo. 249, British Library.

"On Reflexion, it now seems probable": BF, "Albany Plan of Union," *The American Museum: or Repository of Ancient and Modern Fugitive Pieces &c. Prose and Poetical,* 5 (February, March and April 1789): 190–94, 285–87 and 365–68; here April 9, 1789, p. 368.

"the rashest and most indiscreet Governor": BF–Peter Collinson, Aug. 27, 1755, Yale 6:169 (P.M.L.).

"Mr. Morris asked me if I thought": quoted J. Bennett Nolan, *General Benjamin Franklin: The Military Career of a Philosopher,* p. 8 [afterward referred to as Nolan, *General BF*].

"reasonable" and "I should hope too": BF–William Shirley, Dec. 22, 1754, *The London Chronicle: or, Universal Evening Post,* XIX, No. 1426, from Thursday, Feb. 6, to Saturday, Feb. 8, 1766, p. 133.

"I saw an Instance": BF–James Birkett, March 1, 1755, Yale 5:500 (Y.U.L.).

"soothing fiction": C. Grant Robertson, *England under the Hanoverians,* p. 123 [afterward referred to as Robertson].

"I think with you": Thomas Penn–Governor [Robert Hunter] Morris, Sept. 19, 1755, *Penn. Arch.,* ser. 1, vol. 2, p. 420.

"*No, not at all common*": quoted BF–Peter Collinson, Aug. 25, 1755, Letter XXIX, *Exp. and Obs.* (1769), p. 359.

"Then you, Sir, who are a Man": General Edward Braddock–BF, *Auto.,* p. 338.

"Friends and Countrymen," "plac'd where they can be" and "If this Method": BF–To the Inhabitants of the Counties of Lancaster, York & Cumberland, Advertisement B. Franklin for Waggons, April 26, 1755, *Penn. Arch.,* ser. 1, vol. 2, p. 295.

"I can but honour, Franklin": William Shirley, Jr.–Governor Morris, May 14, 1755, *Penn. Arch.,* ser. 1, vol. 2, p. 311.

"which tho' so much out of his Way": Deborah Franklin–Peter Collinson, April 30, 1755, Yale 6:24 (Huntington Library).

"the Disposition of some public Money": *Auto.,* p. 346.

"gave sweetmeats, Horses and Presents": William Smith–Thomas Penn, 1755, quoted William S. Hanna, *Benjamin Franklin and Pennsylvania Politics,* p. 80 [afterward referred to as Hanna].

"I have bought fifty fat Oxen": Governor Morris–General Braddock, June 4, 1755, *Minutes,* 6:408.

"I am to proceed to Niagara": quoted *Auto.,* p. 350.

"He smil'd at my Ignorance": *Auto.,* pp. 350 and 352.

"success [was] long doubtful": "An Account of the Battle of the Monongahela, 9th July, 1755," E. B. O'Callaghan (ed.), *Documents relative to the Colonial History of the State of New York,* 14 vols.; here 10:304 [afterward referred to as O'Callaghan].

"*We shall better know*": quoted *Auto.,* pp. 354 and 356.

"The rout was complete": O'Callaghan, 10:304.

"The shocking news of the strange": quoted Smyth, 10:182.

"[We] have lost a Number of brave Men": BF–Jared Eliot, Aug. 31, 1755, Yale 6:172 (Y.U.L.).

"gave us Americans the first Suspicion": *Auto.,* p. 354.

"I am supposed to have had": BF–Peter Collinson, Aug. 27, 1755, Yale 6:171 (P.M.L.).

"The Removal of the Army from the Frontiers": Robert Hunter Morris–the Assembly, July 28, 1755, quoted *The Pennsylvania Gazette,* No. 1390, Aug. 14, 1755.

"We are once more": *The Pennsylvania Gazette,* No. 1397, Oct. 2, 1755.

"We have this Day the bad News": BF–Richard Partridge, Oct. 25, 1755, Yale 6:231 (A.P.S.).

an ingenious contribution: *The Pennsylvania Gazette,* No. 1408, Dec. 18, 1755.

"a Defence and Explanation by way of Dialogue": Extract, William Peters–Thomas Penn, n.d., enclosed Conrad Weiser–Governor Morris, Dec. 22, 1755, CO. 5 : 17, Pt. I, fo. 103, P.R.O.

"Since Mr. Franklin has put himself at the head": Governor Morris–Thomas Penn, Nov. 22, 1755, *Minutes,* 6:739.

"impossible to carry it into execution": Extract of letter, Governor Morris–Thomas Penn, Nov. 28, 1755, CO. 5 : 17, Pt. I, fo. 92, P.R.O.

"I think it my Duty to observe to You": Governor Morris–Sir Thomas Robinson, Aug. 28, 1755, *Minutes,* 6:600.

"prevail'd with me to take Charge": *Auto.,* p. 362.

"This Day the Honourable James Hamilton, Esq.": *The Pennsylvania Gazette*, No. 1408, Dec. 18, 1755.

"Part of our Route, this day": Ensign Thomas Lloyd–[?], Jan. 18, 1756, Sparks, 7:111n [Yale 6:380 suggests date is Jan. 30 or 31, 1756].

"Opposite them, across the swiftly coursing Lehigh": Nolan, *General BF*, p. 25.

"We found the Country under the greatest Consternation": James Hamilton–Governor Morris, Dec. 25, 1755, *Minutes*, 6:764.

"If Dogs are carried out with any Party": BF–James Read, Nov. 3, 1755, Yale 6:235 (Morris Duane, Philadelphia, on deposit in H.S.P.).

"a flourishing Town full of people": Richard Peters–Thomas Penn, n.d., quoted Nolan, *General BF*, p. 48.

"chosen over the heads of younger men": Nolan, *General BF*, p. 53.

"I do hereby authorize and empower you": Robert Hunter Morris, Lieutenant Governor and Commander in Chief, Commission to BF, Jan. 5, 1756, Yale 6:347 (A.P.S.).

"As we drew near this Place": BF–Robert Hunter Morris, Jan. 14, 1756, Yale 6:357 (H.S.P.).

"We arrived . . . about 12 o'clock": Ensign Thomas Lloyd–[?], Jan. 18 [Jan. 30 or 31], 1756, Sparks, 7:111n.

"[we] had inclosed our Camp": BF–Governor Morris, Jan. 25, 1756, *Minutes*, 7:15.

"We have enjoyed your roast beef": BF–Deborah Franklin, Jan. 25, 1756, Smyth, 3:324.

"at present the Expence in this County": BF–Governor Robert Hunter Morris, Jan. 26, 1756, *Minutes*, 7:17.

"The People happen to love me": BF–Peter Collinson, Nov. 5, 1756, Yale 7:13 (P.M.L.).

"You cannot but have heard of the Zeal": BF–Col. Henry Bouquet, Aug. 16, 1764, Bouquet Papers, Add. MS. 21650, fo. 402, British Library.

"audit, liquidate, adjust and settle": Governor Robert H. Morris–Commission to Edward Shippen, Samuel Morris, Alexander Stedman and Samuel McCall, Jnr., Jan. 31, 1756, *Penn. Arch.*, ser. 1, vol. 2, p. 599.

"The Governor will, I think, lose all character": Richard Peters–Thomas Penn, Feb. 18, 1756, quoted Nolan, *General BF*, p. 45.

"I much wonder the Governor would appoint Mr. Franklin": Thomas Penn–Richard Peters, May 8, 1756, quoted ibid., p. 45.

"I think Mr. Franklin will not engage": Thomas Penn–Richard Peters, n.d., quoted ibid., p. 89.

"I shall entrust you with a secret": Thomas Penn–William Peters, Feb. 17, 1756, quoted ibid., p. 90.

"the proprietaries who could take away": Parton, 1:369.

"Change of devils": William Franklin, quoted Smyth, 10:185n.

"By this compromise": Stanley McCrory Pargellis, *Lord Loudoun in North America*, p. 57.

"I know not whether": BF–The President and Council of the Royal Society, May 29, 1754, The Royal Society.

"He said much to me also": *Auto.*, pp. 388 and 390.

"he would not give his consent to it": quoted Parton, 1:379.

"That a Commissioner, or Commissioners": Pennsylvania Assembly Resolution, Jan. 28, 1757, Senate of Pennsylvania, *Votes and Proceedings of the House of Representatives*, 4:681 [afterward referred to as *Votes and Proc.*].

"Our Assembly talk of sending me to England": BF–William Strahan, Jan. 31, 1757, quoted J. A. Cochrane, *Dr. Johnson's Printer: The Life of William Strahan*, p. 100 [afterward referred to as Cochrane].

"so abridged and restricted": Pennsylvania Assembly, Report of the Committee of Grievances, Feb. 22, 1757, *Votes and Proc.*, 4:697.

"good Behaviour, and no longer" and "Will and Pleasure": ibid., p. 699.

"They talk of Sending the Electrician": Dr. John Kearsley, Jr.–Robert Hunter Morris, Feb. 8, 1757, Yale 7:110 n9 (Y.U.L.).

"might be of service to me": BF–Abiah Franklin, Sept. 7, 1749, Sparks, 7:41.

"if nothing extraordinary occurs": BF–William Strahan, Oct. 23, 1749, Bigelow, 10:254.

"In behalf of the Assembly": *Auto.*, pp. 392 and 394.

"I leave Home": BF–Deborah Franklin, April 5, 1757, Yale 7:175 (A.P.S.).

5. FIGHTING THE PROPRIETORS

"a constant supply of fuel in a chimney": BF–Dr. [John] L[ining], April 14, 1757, Letter XXVI, *Exp. and Obs.* (1769), p. 347 [Yale 7:184 suggests addressee is John Lining].

"The cooks [of those vessels]": [Captain Walter Lutwidge of *The General Wall*], quoted BF–Dr. William Brownrigg, Nov. 7, 1773, "Of the stilling of Waves by means of oil. Extracted from sundry Letters between Benjamin Franklin LL.D., F.R.S., William Brownrigg, M.D., F.R.S. and the Rev. Mr. Farish," *Phil. Trans.*, vol. 64, pt. 2 (1774), p. 448.

"For a new appearance": BF–Dr. [John] P[ringle], Dec. 1, 1762, Letter XLV, *Exp. and Obs.* (1769), p. 440 [Yale 10:158 suggests addressee is John Pringle].

"I saw it spread itself": BF–Dr. William Brownrigg, Nov. 7, 1773, *Phil. Trans.*, vol. 64, pt. 2 (1774), p. 449.

"ascended a couple of hundred paces": Pierre Edouard Lémontey, *Mémoires (inédits) de L'Abbé Morellet suivis de sa Correspondance avec M. le Comte R***, Ministre des Finances à Naples,* 2 vols.; here 1:204 [afterward referred to as *Morellet Memoirs*].

"astonished the rural philosophers": William Small–BF, n.d., quoted Bruce, 2:394–95.

"Methinks I hear some of you say": Richard Saunders, July 7, 1757, "Curious preliminary Address prefixed to the Pensylvania Almanac, entitled Poor Richard improved: for the Year 1758," *The Grand Magazine of Universal Intelligence, and Monthly Chronicle of our own Times,* 1 (March 1758): 123–27; here p. 125.

"About 9 a'Clock the Fog": *Auto.*, p. 410.

"Dr. Fothergill, London": R. Hingston Fox, *Dr. John Fothergill and His Friends,* p. 30.

"It gives me great pleasure": BF–William Strahan, Jan. 31, 1757, quoted Cochrane, p. 100.

"For my own part" and "one of the prettiest": William Strahan–Deborah Franklin, n.d., quoted Cochrane, p. 101 [Yale 7:295 gives date as Dec. 13, 1757].

"For the Lawyers are just at the top of the street": quoted J. Bennett Nolan, *Benjamin Franklin in Scotland and Ireland, 1759 and 1771,* pp. 11–12 [afterward referred to as Nolan, *Scotland and Ireland*].

"Our Friendship has been all clear Sunshine": BF–Mrs. Mary Hewson, Jan. 27, 1783, Whitfield J. Bell, Jr., " 'All Clear Sunshine': New Letters of Franklin and Mary Stevenson Hewson," p. 521 [afterward referred to as "Franklin & Stevenson Hewson Letters"].

"For some Time after my Arrival": William Franklin–Elizabeth Graeme, Dec. 9, 1757, Yale 7:288 (Harvard College Library).

his account book for August 1757: George Simpson Eddy, "Account Book of Benjamin Franklin kept by him during his First Mission to England as Provincial Agent, 1757–1762," p. 103 [afterward referred to as Eddy].

"Success to Printing": Smyth, 10:199.

"I have made your Compliments to Mrs. Stevenson": BF–Deborah Franklin, Feb. 19, 1758, Yale 7:384 (A.P.S.).

"of my Son Franky": BF–Jane Mecom, Jan. 13, 1772, *Franklin & Mecom Letters,* p. 134.

"Send it me with your small Picture": BF–Deborah Franklin, Nov. 22, 1757, Yale 7:278 (A.P.S.).

"never look well": BF–Deborah Franklin, June 10, 1758, Yale 8:91 (A.P.S.).

"gave prints, paintings and sculptures": Charles Coleman Sellers, *Benjamin Franklin in Portraiture,* p. 46 [afterward referred to as Sellers].

"I am sure there is no inducement": BF–Deborah Franklin, Jan. 14, 1758, Yale 7:359 (Duane, *Works,* 6:28–29).

"I have received Mrs. Franklin's Letter": William Strahan–David Hall, July 11, 1758, quoted Cochrane, p. 106.

"neither dated, Signed or addressed": Thomas Penn and Richard Penn–House of Representatives of the Province of Pennsylvania, Nov. 28, 1758, *Minutes,* 8:276.

"cupped me on the back of the head": BF–Deborah Franklin, Nov. 22, 1757, Yale 7:273 (Duane, *Works,* 7:20–24).

"Yes! but if my father": quoted BF–[Isaac Norris], Jan. 14, 1758, T. Balch (ed), *Letters and Papers, relating chiefly to the Provincial History of Pennsylvania, with some Notices of the Writers,* p. 111.

"I said, if then your father": ibid.

"I make no doubt but Reports": BF–Deborah Franklin, Nov. 22, 1757, Yale 7:275 (A.P.S.).

"is well qualified": William Smith, "Account of the College and Academy of Philadelphia"–the Proprietor, n.d., *The American Magazine and Monthly Chronicle for the British Colonies,* p. 639.

"As to [Franklin's] *not being careful*": "Ebenezer Kinnersley to the Author of the Account of the College and Academy of Philadelphia, published in the 'American Magazine' for October, 1758," *The Pennsylvania Gazette,* No. 1562, Nov. 30, 1758.

"It was to have been kept a Secret": BF–Deborah Franklin, June 10, 1758, Yale 8:95 (A.P.S.).

"Reason is heard with fear": John Fothergill–Israel Pemberton, Jr., June 12, 1758, *Fothergill Letters,* p. 195.

"Your kind Advice about getting a Chariot": BF–Deborah Franklin, Feb. 19, 1758, Yale 7:380 (A.P.S.).

"Pray remember to make me as happy": BF–Deborah Franklin, June 10, 1758, Yale 8:93 (A.P.S.).

"To show the Difference of Workmanship": BF–Deborah Franklin, Feb. 19, 1758, Yale 7:381 (A.P.S.).

"tie a Piece of Wire from one Bell to the other": BF–Deborah Franklin, June 10, 1758, Yale 8:94 (A.P.S.).

"being myself honour'd with visits": BF–Isaac Norris, Pennsylvania Assembly Committee of Accounts, Feb. 9, 1763, Smyth, 10:213.

"that God wants us to tipple": BF–Abbé Morellet, n.d., *Morellet Memoirs*, 1:305.

"I am at present meditating": BF–Deborah Franklin, Aug. 5, 1767, Yale 14:225 (A.P.S.).

"I had enjoyed continued health": BF Journal [Passy], Oct. 4, 1778, quoted Edward E. Hale and Edward E. Hale, Jr., *Franklin in France*, 2 vols.; here 1:247 [afterward referred to as Hale].

"entertained with great kindness": BF–Deborah Franklin, Sept. 6, 1758, Yale 8:134 (Duane, *Works*, 6:36–39).

"advantageous to my health": ibid., p. 134.

"They are wealthy": ibid., p. 135.

"had some Thoughts of re-purchasing": BF–Jane Mecom, March 1, 1766, *Franklin & Mecom Letters*, p. 91.

"The Proprietor is enrag'd": BF–Isaac Norris, June 9, 1759, quoted Eddy, p. 121.

"I have no doubt": Mrs. Deborah Logan–a friend, 1829, quoted "Doctor Franklin, Charles Thompson and Mrs. Logan," communicated by the Hon. William Willis, LL.D., of Portland, Maine, *The Historical Magazine*, p. 280 [afterward referred to as "Logan"].

"and will probably be many ways of use to me": BF–Deborah Franklin, Aug. 29, 1759, Yale 8:431 (A.P.S.).

"a Means of blinding all the Readers in the Nation": BF–John Baskerville [1760?], quoted, Advertisement for Baskerville's Folio Bible, *The London Chronicle: or, Universal Evening Post*, XIV, No. 1035, from Thursday, Aug. 11, to Saturday, Aug. 13, 1763, p. 146.

"He readily undertook [the task]": ibid.

"Dr. Franklin once told": Mrs. Deborah Logan–a friend, 1829, "Logan," p. 280.

"Franklin's son was open and communicative": *Autobiography of the Rev. Dr. Alexander Carlyle, Minister of Inveresk*, p. 395.

"Who knows but St. James's": quoted Parton, 1:403.

"Joys of Prestonfield Adieu!": "Verses by Dr. Franklin to Sir Alexander Dick, wrote at Coldstream on his return to England," October 1759, Mrs. Janet Dick-Cunyngham, Dick-Cunyngham MS., S.R.O.

"I have lately made a Tour": BF–Dr. Joshua Babcock, Jan. 13, 1772, Smyth, 5:362.

"Some are for keeping Canada": quoted Horace Walpole, *Memoirs of the Reign of King George the Third,* 4 vols.; here 1:34 [afterward referred to as *George III Memoirs*].

"No one can rejoice more sincerely": BF–Lord Kames, Jan. 3, 1760, Abercairney Muniments (GD24), S.R.O.

"If [the Colonies] could not agree": [BF], *The Interest of Great Britain Considered, With Regard to her Colonies, And the Acquisitions of Canada and Guadaloupe,* p. 39.

"When I say such an union": ibid., p. 40.

"This million doubling": [B.F.], *Observations Concerning the Increase of Mankind,* p. 56.

"Had such Power been lodged here": Ferdinand John Paris, "Answer to the Heads of Complaint"–BF, Nov. 27, 1758, *Minutes,* 8:281.

"fundamentally wrong and unjust": "His Majesty's Order in Council on the Report of the Lords of the Committee of Council for Plantation Affairs," Sept. 2, 1760, Privy Council Register, PC2/107, p. 483, and vide pp. 474–79; here p. 476, P.R.O. [afterward referred to as H.M. Order in Council, Sept. 2, 1760].

"the Assembly did not think them necessary": *Auto.,* p. 416.

"be able to fix a Time for [his] Return": BF–Deborah Franklin [March 28 (?), 1760], Yale 9:39 (A.P.S.).

"One, my Affection to Pensilvania": BF–Deborah Franklin, March 5, 1760, Yale 9:33 (A.P.S.).

"This instrument is played upon": BF–Rev. Father [Giambatista] Beccaria, July 13, 1762, Letter XLII, *Exp. and Obs.* (1769), p. 433.

"He has spent most of his time": Thomas Penn–Governor Hamilton, April 13, 1761, quoted Hanna, p. 145.

"Att Brussels we were at Prince Charles of Lorrains": William Franklin–Sarah Franklin, Oct. 10, 17[61], Yale 9:366 (A.P.S.).

"every one travell'd" and "The cities were well built": BF–Jared Ingersoll, Dec. 11, 1762, Yale 10:175 (New Haven Colony Historical Society).

"to walk in the Procession": William Franklin–Sarah Franklin, Oct. 10, 17[61], Yale 9:368 (A.P.S.).

"I am of Opinion that his Virtue": BF–William Strahan, Dec. 19, 1763, Yale 10:407 (P.M.L.).

the belief that he would be coming back: John Pringle–BF [May (?) 1763], Yale 10:268 (A.P.S.).

"One would fain hope": Chief Justice William Allen–D. Barclay & Sons, Feb. 15, 1762, Lewis Burd Walker, *The Burd Papers: Extracts from Chief Justice William Allen's Letter Book,"* p. 49 [afterward referred to as *Burd Papers*].

"I fancy I feel a little": BF–Mary Stevenson, June 7, 1762, Smyth, 4:158.

"I am very sorry, that you intend soon to leave": David Hume–BF, May 10, 1762, Yale 10:81 (A.P.S.).

6. A PENNSYLVANIA INTERLUDE

"I cannot I assure you": BF–William Strahan, Aug. 23, 1762, quoted Cochrane, p. 107.

"I shall only mention": BF–Richard Jackson, Dec. 6, 1762, Carl Van Doren (ed.), *Letters and Papers of Benjamin Franklin and Richard Jackson, 1753–1785*, p. 87 [afterward referred to as *Franklin & Jackson Letters*].

"had pleasant Weather and fair Winds": BF–William Strahan, Dec. 7, 1762, Yale 10:167 (P.M.L.).

"like travelling in a moving Village": BF–Lord Kames, June 2, 1765, Abercairney Muniments (GD24), S.R.O.

"Your Friend Mr. Franklin": James Hamilton–Jared Ingersoll, July 8, 1762, Yale 10:113 (M.H.S.).

"Every body concludes that this must have been": James Hamilton–Thomas Penn, Nov. 21, 1762, quoted Hanna, p. 148.

"It is no less amazing": John Penn–Earl of Stirling, Sept. 3, 1762, William Alexander Duer, *The Life of William Alexander, Earl of Stirling*, p. 70.

"I am told you will find": Thomas Penn–James Hamilton, n.d. [Sept. 1762], quoted Smyth, 10:212.

"Of all the enviable Things England has": BF–Mary Stevenson, March 25, 1763, Yale 10:232 (Y.U.L.).

"no Friend can wish me more in England": BF–William Strahan, Aug. 8, 1763, Yale 10:320 (Y.U.L.).

"If the stupid brutal Opposition": ibid.

"God bless you and let me find you": BF–William Strahan, Dec. 7, 1762, Yale 10:169 (P.M.L.).

"Don't let them tell you": Mary Stevenson–BF, May 24, 1764, "Franklin & Stevenson Hewson Letters," p. 527.

"the Governor offer'd me the Command": BF–John Fothergill, March 14, 1764, Yale 11:103 (Y.U.L.).

"You may judge": BF–Richard Jackson, Feb. 11, 1764, *Franklin & Jackson Letters*, p. 141.

"I have a great Opinion": BF–William Strahan, Dec. 19, 1763, Yale 10:406 (P.M.L.).

"send me an Invoice": BF–Deborah Franklin, June 16, 1763, Yale 10:291 (A.P.S.).

"What could Children of a Year old": BF, *A Narrative of the Late Massacres, in Lancaster County, of a Number of Indians, Friends of this Province, By Persons Unknown, With some Observations on the same, Printed in the Year M.DCC.LXIV,* Yale 11:65 (Y.U.L.).

"much the Butt of Party Rage and Malice": BF–William Strahan, Sept. 1, 1764, Yale 11:332 (P.M.L.).

the exact terms which Franklin had guaranteed: Original undertaking by Benjamin Franklin dated Aug. 28, 1760, Privy Council Register, PC.2/107, p. 505, P.R.O.

"the Located uncultivated Lands": Article II, H.M. Order in Council, Sept. 2, 1760, p. 476.

"that load of Obloquy": House of Representatives–Governor John Penn, March 24, 1764, *Votes and Proc.,* 5:336.

"thirteen verses of scurrilous billingsgate": J. Philip Gleason, "A Scurrilous Colonial Election and Franklin's Reputation," p. 82.

"London fishwives, huckstering salt sellers": ibid., p. 82.

"A Letcher" who "Needs nothing": ibid., p. 79.

"measuring how many quarts of fire": ibid., p. 76.

"Fight dog, fight bear": ibid., p. 74.

"The poll was opened": Charles Pettit–Joseph Reed, Nov. 3, 1764, William B. Reed, *Life and Correspondence of Joseph Reed,* 2 vols.; here 1:36 [afterward referred to as Reed].

"Resolved That Benjamin Franklin Esq. be": Pennsylvania Assembly Resolution, Oct. 26, 1764, *Votes and Proc.,* 5:383.

"That the Expence attending the Voyage": ibid.

"any Sum is to be had": BF–Jonathan Williams, Nov. 3, 1764, Yale 11:427 (Y.U.L.).

a seven-point protest: George S. Wykoff (ed.), "Peter Collinson's Letter concerning Franklin's 'Vindication,' " p. 102.

"I am now to take Leave": B.F., "Remarks on a Late Protest Against the Appointment of Mr. Franklin an Agent for this Province," Nov. 5, 1764, Vaughan, pp. 403–17; here p. 417.

"great Riots . . . armed Mobs": Pennsylvania Assembly—Petition to the King for changing the Proprietary Government of Pennsylvania into a Royal Government, signed B.F., May 26, 1764, CO. 5 : 1280, fo. 151, P.R.O.

"graciously pleased to resume the Government": ibid.

"accompanied by a great Number": *The Pennsylvania Gazette,* No. 1872, Nov. 8, 1764.

"very bitter ones; and you must expect": BF–Sarah Franklin, Nov. 8, 1764, Yale 11:449 (A.P.S.).

"I have hereby drawn on me": Chief Justice William Allen–D. Barclay & Sons, Nov. 20, 1764, *Burd Papers,* p. 63.

7. HOLDING THE SCALES

"a miserable vessel": "Sketch of the Services of B. Franklin to the United States of America," enclosed BF–Charles Thomson, Dec. 29, 1788, Smyth, 9:696.

"scarce strength to stand": ibid.

"Your good Mama was not at home": BF–Mary Stevenson [December 1764], "Franklin & Stevenson Hewson Letters," p. 527 [Yale 11:521 suggests letter was written between Dec. 12 and Dec. 16, 1764].

"wishes you would come over": BF–Deborah Franklin, Feb. 9, 1765, Yale 12:42 (A.P.S.).

"to be able to return about the End of Summer": ibid.

"A few Months, I hope": BF–Deborah Franklin, Feb. 14, 1765 (II), Yale 12:64 (A.P.S.).

"How could there be a reconciliation": Clarence Walworth Alvord, *The Mississippi Valley in British Politics,* 2 vols.; here Preface, 1:15 [afterward referred to as Alvord].

"In times of crisis": C. P. Snow, *Science and Government,* p. 43.

"mistaken Notion . . . that the Colonies": BF–Lord Kames, Feb. 25, 1767, Abercairney Muniments (GD24), S.R.O.

"had not been conquer'd by either King or Parliament": ibid.

"We might as well have hinder'd": [BF–Charles Thomson], "Extract of a Letter from a North American in London, to his Friend in America, dated July 11, 1765," *The London Chronicle,* XVIII, No. 1391, from Thursday, Nov. 14, to Saturday, Nov. 16, 1765, p. 471.

"notwithstanding all I could do": BF–David Hall, Aug. 9, 1765, Yale 12:234 (H.S.P.).

"would have had great Advantage": ibid, p. 233.

"may make you unpopular": BF–John Hughes, Aug. 9, 1765, Yale 12:234 (H.S.P.).

"In short, there seems to be": David Hall–BF, Sept. 6, 1765, Yale 12:257 (A.P.S.).

"I am so verey poor a writer": Deborah Franklin–BF, Sept. 22, 1765, Yale 12:270 (A.P.S.).

"This day the Letters per the August packet": Thomas Wharton–BF, Oct. 5, 1765, Yale 12:291 (A.P.S.).

"black Cloud seems to hang over us": James Parker–BF, Oct. 10, 1765, "Letters from James Parker to Benjamin Franklin," communicated by Worthington C. Ford, p. 201.

"The Matter of the Prop^y Party": William Franklin–William Strahan, Feb. 18, 1765, Smyth, 10:220.

"Thee shall be agent, Ben": quoted Parton, 1:465.

"I was for 9 day keep in one Contineued hurrey": Deborah Franklin–BF, Sept. 22, 1765, Yale 12:271 (A.P.S.).

"In the Heat of Party": BF–David Hall, Sept. 14, 1765, Yale 12:267 (Princeton University Library).

"*Liberty* aetas 145, *Stamp'd*": Esmond Wright, *Benjamin Franklin and American Independence,* p. 83.

"He who for a Post or Base": quoted ibid., p. 84.

"No *Stamped Paper*": [*The Pennsylvania Gazette,* for No. 1924, Nov. 7, 1765.]

"Remarkable *Occurrences*": [*The Pennsylvania Gazette,* for No. 1925, Nov. 14, 1765.]

"I saw Dr. Franklin yesterday": William Strahan–David Hall, Dec. 14, 1765, quoted Cochrane, p. 112.

"The very Tails of the American Sheep," BF–the Printer of *The Public Advertiser,* May 20, 1765, signed "A Traveller," *The Public Advertiser,* No. 9587, May 22, 1765.

"like other Fish, when attacked": ibid.

"He was fat, square built": Mrs. Deborah Logan–a friend, 1829, quoted "Logan," p. 280.

"No, never, unless compelled": "The Examination of Doctor Benjamin Franklin," Jan. 21, 1766, William Cobbett and Thomas C. Hansard (eds.), *The Parliamentary History of England, from the Earliest Period to 1803,* 36 vols.; here vol. 16 (1765–1771), col. 140 [afterward referred to as *Parl. Hist.*].

"The best in the world": ibid., col. 140.

"What used to be the pride": ibid., col. 160.

"My dear child": BF–Deborah Franklin, Feb. 22, 1766, Yale 13:165 (Y.U.L.).

"The Marquis of Rockingham told a Friend": William Strahan–David Hall, May 10, 1766, "Correspondence between William Strahan and David Hall, 1763–1777," 10:220 [afterward referred to as "Strahan & Hall Corr."].

"We have heard by a round about way": Sarah Franklin–BF, March 25 [1766], Yale 13:199 (A.P.S.).

"Upon its Arrival": Joseph Galloway–BF, May 23, 1766, Yale 13: 284 (A.P.S.).

"When the news of 'Stamp Act Repealed' ": Watson, 2:270.

he told Joseph Galloway: BF–Joseph Galloway, Aug. 8, 1767, Yale 14:230 (William L. Clements Library).

"I am preparing for my return": BF–Joseph Galloway, May 14, 1768, W.T.F., 2:164.

"gone in a few weeks": BF–William Franklin, July 2, 1768, W.T.F., 2:165.

"I purpose returning to America": BF–Pierre Samuel Du Pont de Nemours, Oct. 2, 1770, Yale 17:234 (Henry Francis Du Pont Winterthur Museum).

"I purpose it firmly": BF–Deborah Franklin, July 4, 1771, Yale 18:162 (A.P.S.).

"visiting": BF–Jonathan Shipley [June (?) 1773], Yale 20:256 (Y.U.L.).

"some Events in our Colony Affairs": BF–Jan Ingenhousz, Sept. 30, 1773, Yale 20:432 (A.P.S.).

"positively nothing shall prevent": BF–Deborah Franklin, Oct. 6, 1773, Yale 20:436 (A.P.S.).

"I have of late great Debates with my self": BF–William Franklin, Jan. 30, 1772, Yale 19:52 (A.P.S.).

"Now for the room we Cale yours": Deborah Franklin–BF [Oct. 6–13 (?), 1765], Yale 12:294 (A.P.S.).

"I could have wished to have been present": BF–Deborah Franklin, June 4, 1765, Yale 12:167 (A.P.S.).

"Let me have the Breadth of the Pier": BF–Deborah Franklin [August 1765], Yale 12:250 (A.P.S.).

"as I partake of none of the divershons": Deborah Franklin–BF, Feb. 10 [1765], Yale 12:44 (A.P.S.).

"You require the reason": BF–Dr. [John] L[ining], March 18, 1755, Letter XXIV, *Exp. and Obs.* (1769), p. 326.

"May we not infer from this experiment": Priestley, *History,* p. 732.

"Probably the vestries of our English churches": BF–John Winthrop, July 2, 1768, W.T.F., 3:372.

"Many country seats are provided": BF–John Winthrop, July 25, 1773, ibid., p. 423.

"As to my situation here": BF–William Franklin, Aug. 19, 1772, W.T.F., 2:172.

"grown so old as to feel": BF–William Franklin, July 2, 1768, ibid., p. 168.

"if I chose rather to reside in England": ibid., p. 165.

"inclination to be at home": ibid., p. 167.

"(which I still say to every body": ibid., p. 166.

"I took the liberty": John Fothergill–James Pemberton, Sept. 16, 1768, *Fothergill Letters,* p. 286.

"more and more convinced": BF–Thomas Cushing, n.d., quoted Nolan, *Scotland and Ireland,* p. 94.

"enrich'd by its industry": BF–Committee of Merchants in Philadelphia, July 9, 1769, Yale 16:175 (Y.U.L.).

"pledged himself to find": A. F. Pollard, "Charles Townshend," in Leslie Stephen et al. (eds.), *Dictionary of National Biography,* 63 vols.; here 57:119 [afterward referred to as Pollard].

"champagne speech": Charles Townshend, Chancellor of Exchequer, May 8, 1767, *George III Memoirs,* 3:23–25; here p. 25.

"[He] was one of those statesmen": Pollard, p. 119.

"drawn the teeth": BF–William Franklin, Jan. 9, 1768, W.T.F., 2:151.

"written to palliate a little": BF–Lord Kames, Feb. 28, 1768, Abercairney Muniments (GD24), S.R.O.

"Let us unite": [BF, "The Causes of the American Discontents before 1768"] [BF] F+S–the Printer of the London Chronicle, "The Waves never rise but when the Winds blow. Prov.," *The London Chronicle,* XXIII, No. 1725, from Tuesday, Jan. 5, to Thursday, Jan. 7, 1768, p. 18.

"It seems like setting up a smith's forge": BF–Rev. George Whitefield [before Sept. 2, 1769], quoted Joseph Belcher, *George Whitefield,* p. 415.

"With muskets charged": Josiah Quincy, *Memoir of the Life of Josiah Quincy, Jun., of Massachusetts,* p. 17 [afterward referred to as Quincy].

"But the Assiduity of our Friend": William Strahan–David Hall, Jan. 11, 1766, "Strahan & Hall Corr.," 10:92.

"An Act for the better Ordering and Governing Negroes": The Georgia Assembly Committee of Correspondence–BF, May 19, 1768, "The Commissions of Georgia to Benjamin Franklin to act as Colonial Agent," *The Georgia Historical Quarterly,* vol. 2, no. 3 (September 1918), p. 154.

"He told me he believed the fact": BF–Alphonse [Julien-David] Le Roy, August 1785, entitled "On Improvements in Navigation," W.T.F., 3:533.

"I have something remarkable": Marc Lescarbot, *Histoire de la Nouvelle France,* p. 531.

"I procured it to be engraved": BF–Alphonse [Julien-David] Le Roy, August 1785, entitled "On Improvements in Navigation," W.T.F., 3:534.

"The weather being perfectly calm": BF, "Observations On the Gulph Stream," ibid., p. 550.

"This Excursion tho' otherwise well": William Strahan–David Hall, June 14, 1766, "Strahan & Hall Corr.," 10:228.

"I am now nearly well again": BF–Deborah Franklin, June 13, 1766, quoted William Pepper, *The Medical Side of Benjamin Franklin,* p. 45.

"I said that when I was in London": Note on flyleaf of *Biography of John D. Michaelis,* quoted J. G. Rosengarten, "Franklin in Germany," p. 129.

"I think it a Duty": Mrs. Margaret Stevenson–Deborah Franklin, Sept. 18, 1767, "Franklin & Stevenson Hewson Letters," p. 528.

"They would previously make a hearty breakfast": BF–Mary Stevenson, Sept. 14, 1767, Library of Congress.

"has desired to have all my political writings": BF–William Franklin, Aug. 28, 1767, W.T.F., 2:144.

"transformed [him] into a Frenchman": BF–Mary Stevenson, Sept. 14, 1767, Library of Congress.

"That's saying enough": ibid.

"Versailles has had infinite Sums": ibid.

"seems now to me like a pleasing Dream": BF–Thomas-François Dalibard, Jan. 31, 1768, Yale 15:35 (A.P.S.).

"These I could not reconcile to my notion": BF–Benjamin Vaughan, July 31, 1786, entitled "On the pernicious quality of Lead," W.T.F., 3:553.

"To crown your work": Joseph Etienne Bertier–BF, Feb. 27, 1769, quoted Hale, 1:15.

"When I was there": BF–Samuel Rhoads, June 26, 1770, Yale 17:182 (H.S.P.).

"In short, all Europe": BF–Rev. Dr. Samuel Cooper, Sept. 30, 1769, Original Letters from Dr. Franklin to the Rev[d]. Dr. Cooper on American Politics, Kings MS. 201, fo. 5, British Library.

"being born and bred": Verner Winslow Crane, *Benjamin Franklin, Englishman and American,* p. 3.

"I live here as frugally as possible": BF–Deborah Franklin, June 22, 1767, Yale 14:193 (A.P.S.).

"The Buckwheat and Indian Meal are come": BF–Deborah Franklin, Jan. 28, 1772, Yale 19:44 (A.P.S.).

"As to my own Head": BF–Mary Stevenson, Jan. 22, 1770, Yale 17:32 (A.P.S.).

"The dumb bell is another of the latter": BF–William Franklin, Aug. 19, 1772, Library of Congress.

"In the Easter Holidays": BF–Deborah Franklin, June 10, 1770, Yale 17:167 (A.P.S.).

"Eat light Foods": BF–Deborah Franklin, Dec. 1, 1772, Yale 19:395 (A.P.S.).

"I have found it much more agreeable": BF–Jacques Barbeu-Dubourg, July 28, 1768, W.T.F., 3:374.

"This morning Queen Margaret": *The Craven Street Gazette*, No. 113, Sept. 22, 1770, app. 4, Parton, 1:622.

"this morning a certain great person": *The Craven Street Gazette*, No. 113, Sept. 25, 1770, app. 4, Parton, 1:624.

"My writing. Mrs. Dogoods Letters": "Franklin's Outline for his Memoirs," app., *Auto.*, p. 419.

"Dear Son, I have ever had a pleasure": *Auto.*, p. 2.

"a matter of keeping an eye": Theodore Hornberger, *Benjamin Franklin*, p. 6.

"At Dinner, among other nice Things": BF–Deborah Franklin, Aug. 14, 1771, Yale 18:204 (A.P.S.).

"How happy I was in the sweet retirement of Twyford": BF–[Jonathan Shipley,] Lord Bishop of St. Asaph, Sept. 13, 1775, J. L. Peyton, *Rambling Reminiscences of a Residence Abroad: England—Guernsey*, app. B, p. 288 [afterward referred to as Peyton].

8. THE FATAL ERROR

"Possibly we may not at first obtain": BF–Noble Wymberley Jones, June 7, 1769, quoted Alfred Owen Aldridge, "Benjamin Franklin as Georgia Agent," p. 168.

"I think one may clearly see": BF–The Committee of Correspondence, Massachusetts House of Representatives, May 15, 1771, Sparks, 7:521.

"The Council have renewed their choice of Mr. Bollan": Governor Thomas Hutchinson–Earl of Hillsborough, Nov. 20, 1770, CO. 5 : 759, fo. 335, P.R.O.

"The two Houses renewed their grants": Governor Thomas Hutchinson–Earl of Hillsborough, July 15, 1772, CO. 5 : 761, fo. 169, P.R.O.

"not only on bad Terms": William Strahan–William Franklin, April 3, 1771, Yale 18:65 (A.P.S.).

"me a Round of Forty Miles": BF–Thomas Cushing, Jan. 13, 1772, CO. 5 : 118, fo. 36, P.R.O.

"But if he takes no Step": ibid., fo. 37.

"I sometimes wish that you and I": BF–Rev. George Whitefield, July 2, 1756, Smyth, 3:339.

"As I have some Money to spare": BF–Richard Jackson, May 1, 1764, quoted *Franklin & Jackson Letters*, p. 18.

"humbly [prayed] that His Majesty": BF Petition to Privy Council, recorded Feb. 10, 1766, in Privy Council Register, PC.2/112, p. 479, P.R.O.

"such Gentlemen of Character": William Franklin–BF, April 30, 1766, Yale 13:257 (A.P.S.).

"I took the opportunity of urging": BF–William Franklin, Aug. 28, 1767, W.T.F., 2:143.

"many things happen between the Cup & the Lip": BF–William Franklin, April 20, 1771, Yale 18:76 (A.P.S.).

"if we were to consider the principal actors": Edmund Burke–James De Lancey, Aug. 20, 1772, Wentworth Woodhouse Muniments, Sheffield City Libraries.

"at least one white Protestant person": Clarence Walworth Alvord and Clarence Edwin Carter, *The New Regime, 1765–1767*, p. 256.

"The Removing": BF–Deborah Franklin, Nov. 4, 1772, Library of Congress.

"Politicians on our Side the Water": BF–Thomas Cushing, July 7, 1773, Draft in Library of Congress, quoted Yale 20:272 n7.

"mainly conduced to the civil war [of Independence]": John, Lord Campbell, *The Lives of the Lord Chancellors and Keepers of the Great Seal of England from the Earliest Times till the Reign of King George IV*, 8 vols.; here 6:104 [afterward referred to as Campbell].

"a gentleman of character and distinction": Tract relative to the Affair of Hutchinson's Letters [1774], W.T.F., 1:189.

"my *duty* to give my constituents intelligence": ibid.

"I can only allow them to be seen by yourself": BF–Thomas Cushing, Dec. 2, 1772, CO. 5 : 118, fo. 41, P.R.O.

"that they may be shown or read": BF–Thomas Cushing, July 7, 1773, CO. 5 : 118, fo. 61, P.R.O.

"I was permitted to carry": John Adams–David Hosack, Jan. 28, 1820, Note No. III to David Hosack, "A Biographical Memoir of Hugh Williamson, M.D., LL.D.," p. 179.

"three gentlemen here": Tract relative to the Affair of Hutchinson's Letters [1774], W.T.F., 1:191.

"ought to be retained on this side": Thomas Cushing–BF, April 20, 1773, Library of Congress.

"You mention the Surprize of Gentlemen": BF–Rev. Dr. Samuel Cooper, July 7, 1773, Kings MS. 201, fo. 28, British Library.

"was inform'd by one of its Members": Extract from the Journal of the House of Representatives of the Province of the Massachusetts Bay, June 2, 1773 [enclosure to Governor Thomas Hutchinson–Earl of Dartmouth, June 26, 1773], CO. 5 : 762, fo. 319, P.R.O.

"the tendency and design of the letters": ibid.

"many *dark* things to *light*": *The Massachusetts Spy,* June 3, 1773, quoted Bernard Bailyn, *The Ordeal of Thomas Hutchinson,* p. 240 [afterward referred to as Bailyn].

"the judicious Reader will discover": Introduction, *Copy of Letters sent to Great Britain by his Excellency Thomas Hutchinson, the Hon. Andrew Oliver and several other persons born and educated among us,* Printed by Edes & Gill, in Queen-Street, Boston, 1773, CO. 5 : 762, fo. 329, P.R.O.

"Considering the Number of Persons who were to see": Thomas Cushing–BF, June 14, 1773, Library of Congress.

"Nothing could have been more seasonable": Rev. Dr. Samuel Cooper–BF, June 14, 1773, Kings MS. 203, fo. 11, British Library.

"I never think of the measures necessary": Thomas Hutchinson–Thomas Whately, Jan. 20, 1769, *Copy of Letters . . .,* Printed by Edes & Gill, p. 16, CO. 5 : 762, fo. 336, P.R.O.

"To a candid mind": Lawrence S. Mayo (ed.), Thomas Hutchinson, *The History of the Colony and Province of Massachusetts Bay,* 3 vols.; here 3:294n.

"Resolved that if His Majesty in his great Goodness": Massachusetts House of Representatives, June 25, 1773 [enclosure to Governor Thomas Hutchinson–Earl of Dartmouth, June 26, 1773], CO. 5 : 762, fo. 323, P.R.O.

"The greatest part of the present session": Thomas Hutchinson–Earl of Dartmouth, June 26, 1773, CO. 5 : 762, fo. 317–18, P.R.O.

"I have the pleasure of hearing": BF–Earl of Dartmouth, Aug. 21, 1773, Yale 20:372 (M.H.S.).

"the next time I shall have the Honor" and "I cannot help expressing": Earl of Dartmouth–BF, Aug. 25, 1773, Yale 20:376 (Library of Congress, afterward referred to as L.C.).

"The Executive Government ought quietly": Campbell, 6:105.

"With regard to those proceedings & resolutions": Earl of Dartmouth–Thomas Hutchinson, Aug. 17, 1773, CO. 5 : 762, fo. 350, P.R.O.

"The flame which was raised": Thomas Hutchinson–Earl of Dartmouth, Aug. 7, 1773, CO. 5 : 762, fo. 382, P.R.O.

"Rules by which a Great Empire may be reduced to a Small One": *The Public Advertiser,* No. 11982, Sept. 11, 1773.

"An Edict by the King of Prussia": Potsdam, Aug. 25, 1773, *The Public Advertiser*, No. 11990, Sept. 22, 1773.

"was almost as busy": Editors of Yale 20: xxxiii.

"like a great Cake"; "never regard the heavy Burthens"; "Convert the brave honest Officers" and "Invest the General of your Army": Rules, I, IX, XV and XX, Q.E.D., "Rules by which a Great Empire may be reduced to a Small One," *The Public Advertiser*, No. 11982, Sept. 11, 1773.

"flourished under the Protection": "An Edict by the King of Prussia," Potsdam, Aug. 25, 1773, *The Public Advertiser*, No. 11990, Sept. 22, 1773.

"Here's news for ye!" and "I as much as any body": BF–William Franklin, Oct. 6, 1773, W.T.F., 2:198.

"designed to expose the conduct": ibid., p. 197.

"Such papers may seem to have a tendency": BF–William Franklin, Nov. 3, 1773, ibid., p. 209.

"I have held up a Looking-Glass": BF–Jane Mecom, Nov. 1, 1773, *Franklin & Mecom Letters*, p. 143.

"I imagine that it will hardly be complied with": BF–Thomas Cushing, Nov. 1, 1773, W.T.F., 2:199.

"Mr. Temple assured me in Terms the most precise": William Whately–The Printer of *The Public Advertiser*, Dec. 9, 1773, *The Public Advertiser*, No. 12056, Dec. 11, 1773.

"Temple, who was not unskilled in the use": Parton, 1:575.

"Finding that two Gentlemen": BF–The Printer of *The Public Advertiser*, Dec. 25, 1773, *The Public Advertiser*, No. 12069, Dec. 27, 1773.

John Pownall told the clerk of the Privy Council: John Pownall–Clerk of the Council in Waiting, Dec. 3, 1773, CO. 5 : 133, fo. 191, P.R.O.

"No subsequent step had yet been taken": BF–Thomas Cushing, Jan. 5, 1774, W.T.F., 2:209.

"sharp, unprincipled . . . destined to scale": Parton, 1:578.

"have a hearing in their own justification": Israel Maudit at Preliminary Hearing before the Privy Council Committee for Plantation Affairs, Jan. 11, 1774, printed in [Israel Maudit], *The Letters of Governor Hutchinson, and Lieut. Governor Oliver*, pp. 77–80; here p. 79.

"Under these Apprehensions, the Teas": Massachusetts House of Representatives Committee of Correspondence–BF, Dec. 21, 1773, Yale 20:511 (L.C.).

"if War is finally to be made": BF–Massachusetts House of Representatives Committee of Correspondence, Feb. 2, 1774, Yale, 21:76 (New York Public Library).

"I still think it would have been wise": BF–David Hartley, Feb. 2, 1780, Sparks, 8:414.

"When we got to the anti-room": J. Priestley–The Editor of *The Monthly Magazine*, Nov. 10, 1802, *The Monthly Magazine; or, British Register*, no. 1 of vol. 15, no. 97 (Feb. 1, 1803), pp. 1–2; here p. 2.

"Of the President's chair": John Bowring, *The Works of Jeremy Bentham*, 11 vols.; here 10:59.

"The Doctor was dressed in a full dress suit": Edward Bancroft, quoted William Temple Franklin (ed.), *Memoirs of the Life and Writings of Benjamin Franklin*, 8vo ed., 3 vols.; here 1:358n.

"the energy of a bold, bad man": Parton, 1:587.

"The writers did not give them to him": Alexander Wedderburn's Speech before the Privy Council, Jan. 29, 1774, Vaughan, p. 341.

"a most scurrilous invective": Earl of Shelburne–Earl of Chatham, Feb. 3, 1774, William Stanhope Taylor and Capt. John Henry Pringle (eds.), *Correspondence of William Pitt, Earl of Chatham*, 4 vols.; here 4:323.

"Amidst these tranquil events": editorial footnote, ibid., p. 323.

"The methods by which [Franklin]": Robertson, p. 258.

"The Lords of the Committee do agree humbly to Report": The Report of the Privy Council Committee, Jan. 29, 1774, Privy Council Register, PC.2/117, pp. 422–25, here p. 425, P.R.O.

"how all men tossed up their hats": quoted Campbell, 6:110.

"Sarcastic Sawney": A. Francis Steuart (ed.), *The Last Journals of Horace Walpole during the Reign of George III from 1771–1783*, 2 vols.; here 2:77.

"replied in a very well-performed invective": Edmund Burke–Marquis of Rockingham, Feb. 2, 1774, Wentworth Woodhouse Muniments, Sheffield City Libraries.

"I suppose no Man's Conduct and Character": General Gage–Thomas Hutchinson, Feb. 2, 1774, Correspondence of the Family of Hutchinson, 1741–1880, Vol. I, Egerton MS. 2659, fo. 69, British Library.

"Pray, what strange Accounts are these": David Hume–Adam Smith, Feb. 13, 1774, Hume MS., Royal Society of Edinburgh Library.

"had sufficient self-command": John Adolphus, *The History of England, from the Accession to the Decease of King George The Third*, 7 vols.; here 2:47.

"You know that in England": BF–Jan Ingenhousz, March 18, 1774, Yale 21:148 (Harvard University Library).

"if he had not considered the thing": BF–Joseph Priestley, quoted J. Priestley–The Editor of *The Monthly Magazine*, Nov. 10, 1802, *The Monthly Magazine; or, British Register*, no. 1 of vol. 15, no. 97 (Feb. 1, 1803), pp. 1–2; here p. 2.

"found it necessary": Anthony Todd–BF, Jan. 31, 1774, General Post Office, London [Letterbook copy].

"seems to have been the object": Charles William Fitzwilliam, Earl, and Lt.-Gen. Sir Richard Bourke, K.C.B. (eds.), *Correspondence of the Right Honourable Edmund Burke; between the Year 1744, and the Period of His Decease, in 1797*, 4 vols.; here 1:453 n8.

"In the meantime it will be a satisfaction": Earl of Dartmouth–Governor Thomas Hutchinson, Feb. 5, 1774, CO. 5 : 763, fo. 29, P.R.O.

"You will have heard": *The Pennsylvania Gazette*, No. 2367, May 4, 1774.

"Yesterday, about Four o'clock": ibid.

"seems to me to be a pretty extraordinary attempt": Governor Sir James Wright–Earl of Dartmouth, March 12, 1774, CO. 5 : 663, fo. 71, P.R.O.

"I am now upon the Continent": John Temple–BF, July 9, 1781, Library of Congress.

"My Lord, After a solemn declaration": Thomas Hutchinson–Earl of Dartmouth, Aug. 16, 1774, Dartmouth Papers, D(W)1778 : 946, Staffordshire Record Office, Stafford [afterward referred to as Dartmouth Papers].

"They fell into my hands": BF–William Franklin, Sept. 1, 1773, Yale 20:387 (Duane, *Works*, 6:329–31).

"I am now seriously preparing for my departure": BF–William Franklin, Jan. 5, 1774, W.T.F., 2:211.

"I hoped to have been on the Sea": BF–Deborah Franklin, April 28, 1774, Yale 21:205 (Y.U.L.).

"under a kind of Necessity": BF–Thomas Cushing, June 1, 1774, CO. 5 : 118, fo. 76, P.R.O.

"thought by the great Friends": BF–William Franklin, Sept. 7, 1774, Original Letters, Add. MS. 9828, fo. 172, British Library.

"dangerous and unwarrantable"; "the Leaders of the Faction at Boston"; "by a confidential communication" and "Both these Letters have": Earl of Dartmouth–General Gage, June 3, 1774, CO. 5 : 763, fo. 174, P.R.O.

"best and fairest for the Colonies": BF–Thomas Cushing, July 7, 1773, Dartmouth Papers, D(W)1778 : I/ii/867.

"a printed extract" and "I mention another letter": General Gage–Earl of Dartmouth, Dec. 15, 1774, Dartmouth Papers, D(W)1778 : 1020.

"I transmit your Lordship": Lt. General Thomas Gage–Earl of Dartmouth, Oct. 15, 1775, CO. 5 : 92, Pt. III, fo. 303, P.R.O.

"The enclosed are original Letters": General [William] Howe–Earl of Dartmouth, Nov. 30, 1775, CO. 5 : 92, Pt. III, fo. 341, P.R.O.

"These letters are perhaps now only precious": P.R.O. note, CO. 5 : 118, fo. 1, P.R.O.

"A Scurrilous and very wicked letter": P.R.O. comment on BF–Thomas Cushing, June 10, 1771, CO. 5 : 118, fo. 33, P.R.O.

"Removal of Province's powder": Benjamin Hallowell–Grey Cooper, Sept. 5, 1774, CO. 5 : 175, fo. 52–60d, P.R.O., summarized in K. G. Davies (ed.), *Documents of the American Revolution, 1770–1783*, 21 vols.; here 7:167.

"The learned gentleman's speech": quoted Campbell, 6:113.

Taxation no Tyranny: An Answer to the Resolutions and Address of the American Congress, 1775: Dr. Samuel Johnson, in *The Patriot*, printed Sir John Hawkins (ed.), *The Works of Samuel Johnson, LL.D.*, 11 vols.; here 10:93–143.

"are a race of convicts": *"Sir,"* said Dr. Johnson—, *Some sayings arranged by H. C. Biron*, p. 157.

"willing to love all mankind": ibid., p. 158.

"When I consider the extreme corruption": BF–Joseph Galloway, Feb. 25, 1775, Sparks, 8:146.

"have had a merit": The Rt. Hon. Sir George Otto Trevelyan, *The American Revolution*, 5 pts.; here pt. 1 *(1766–1776)*, p. 302.

"How much might have been done": BF–David Barclay, Feb. 12, 1781, Sparks, 8:532.

"Historians relate, not so much": Richard Saunders, *Poor Richard, 1739. An Almanack For the Year of Christ 1739 . . .* , Yale 2:220 (Y.U.L.).

"not to suffer, by their little misunderstandings": BF [Journal of Negotiations in London]–William Franklin, March 22, 1775, Sparks, 5:3.

"having more than once travelled": ibid., p. 7.

"HINTS FOR CONVERSATION upon the Subject of Terms that might probably produce a Durable Union between Britain and the Colonies," ibid., pp. 12–14.

"They were to meet today": Thomas Pownall–Earl of Dartmouth, Dec. 20, 1774, Dartmouth Papers, D(W)1778:1088.

"might with reason expect any reward": BF [Journal of Negotiations in London]–William Franklin, March 22, 1775, Sparks, 5:37.

"What the French vulgarly call": ibid.

"that immediate orders may be despatched": Lord Chatham's motion to withdraw the Troops from Boston, Jan. 20, 1775, *Parl. Hist.*, vol. 18 *(1774–1777)*, col. 160.

"The nation of America": Lord Chatham's speech, Jan. 20, 1775, ibid., col. 158.

"If the Ministers thus persevere": Report of Lord Chatham's speech by Mr. Hugh Boyd, *Genuine Abstracts from Two Speeches of the late Earl of Chatham and His Reply to the Earl of Suffolk, with some Introductory Observations and Notes*, p. 21.

"Sixteen Scotch peers, and twenty-four bishops": BF [Journal of Negotiations in London]–William Franklin, March 22, 1775, Sparks, 5:46.

"on the very day twelve months": ibid., p. 49.

"He stayed with me": ibid., p. 48.

"said, he fancied he had in his eye": Earl of Sandwich quoted ibid., p. 52.

"I wish it had been in my power": Dr. John Fothergill–Earl of Dartmouth, Feb. 6, 1775, Dartmouth Papers, D(W)1778 : II, 1133.

"if any supposed I could prevail": BF [Journal of Negotiations in London]– William Franklin, March 22, 1775, Sparks, 5:76.

9. INDEPENDENCE CLAIMED

"I am in perpetual Anxiety": BF–Thomas Cushing, Oct. 6, 1774, Smyth, 6:250.

"I was seldom many days without seeing him": *Memoirs of Dr. Joseph Priestley, to the Year 1795*, p. 88 [afterward referred to as *Priestley Memoirs*].

"Once upon a time an eagle": Adams, *Works,* 9:269.

"more and more unfit to be left alone": William Franklin–BF, Aug. 3, 1771, Yale 18:195 (A.P.S.).

"too much impair'd": BF–Deborah Franklin, May 1, 1771, Yale 18:91 (A.P.S.).

"She told me . . . that she never expected": William Franklin–BF, Dec. 24, 1774, William Duane (ed.), *Letters to Benjamin Franklin, from His Family and Friends, 1751–1790*, p. 60 [afterward referred to as Duane, *Letters*].

"The married state is, after all our jokes": BF–John Sargent, Jan. 27, 1783, Sparks, 9:478.

"If there was any prospect": William Franklin–BF, Dec, 24, 1774, Duane, *Letters*, p. 60.

"in whose hands": BF [Journal of Negotiations in London]–William Franklin, March 22, 1775, Sparks, 5:73.

"was employed in reading": *Priestley Memoirs*, p. 89.

"The tears may not have been": Editors of Yale 21:xli.

"Farewel, and befriend this infant": Dr. John Fothergill–BF [March 19, 1775], Yale 21:538 (L.C.).

"When you intend a long voyage": BF, Paper written on board the Pennsylvania packet, April 5, 1775, W.T.F., 3:539.

The authorities had refused: Peter Orlando Hutchinson (ed.), *The Diary and Letters of His Excellency Thomas Hutchinson Esq.*, 2 vols.; here 1:81–93.

"the weather constantly so moderate": BF–Joseph Priestley, May 16, 1775, John Towill Rutt, *Life and Correspondence of Joseph Priestley, LL.D., F.R.S.*, 2 vols.; here 1:269 [afterward referred to as Rutt].

"The next gale that sweeps from the north": William Wirt, *Sketches of the Life and Character of Patrick Henry*, p. 123.

"shot heard round the world": Ralph Waldo Emerson, "Hymn Sung at the Completion of the Concord Monument."

"and a war is commenced": BF–Jonathan Shipley, May 15, 1775, Peyton, p. 283.

"I found at my arrival all America": BF–Jonathan Shipley, July 7, 1775, ibid.

"banished from his mind": Reed, 1:100.

"Welcome! Once more": *Pennsylvania Packet*, May 8, 1775, quoted Parton, 2:73–74.

"My time was never more fully employed": BF–Joseph Priestley, July 7, 1775, Rutt, 1:271.

"frequent giddinesses": BF, Journal [Passy], Oct. 4, 1778, quoted Hale, 1:247.

"I don't understand it as any favour to me": BF–William Franklin, May 7, 1775, Original Letters, Add. MS. 9829, fo. 175, British Library.

"I did then [in March 1775]": BF–Thomas Life, June 5, 1775, Dartmouth Papers, D(W)1778 : II, 1291.

"I strongly hope however, that the ill success": Edward Bancroft–BF, Aug. 7, 1775, "Some Letters of Franklin's Correspondents," p. 162.

"You will see by the papers": BF–Edmund Burke, May 15, 1775, Wentworth Woodhouse Muniments, Sheffield City Libraries.

"What say you to your friend": Edmund Burke–Count Patrick D'Arcy, Oct. 5, 1775, ibid.

"It may possibly soon be all": BF–John Sargent, June 27, 1775, Smyth, 6:407.

"has begun to burn our seaport towns": BF–Joseph Priestley, July 7, 1775, Rutt, 1:270.

"All my prejudices are against": John Wesley–Earl of Dartmouth, June 14, 1775, Dartmouth Papers, D(W)1778 : I/i/1135.

"By all I can learn": Sir Henry Barkly–Grey Cooper, June 19, 1775, Geoffrey Seed, "A British Spy in Philadelphia, 1775–1777," p. 12 [afterward referred to as Seed].

"They say that Doctor Franklin": Hugh Finlay–Ingram, May 29, 1775, CO. 5: 135, fo. 35, P.R.O.

"and I differ widely": William Strahan–David Hall, Nov. 7, 1770, "Strahan & Hall Corr.," 11: 357.

"Mr. Strahan: You are a Member of Parliament": BF–William Strahan, July 5, 1775, W.T.F., 2: frontispiece.

"The suspicions against Dr. Franklin": William Bradford, Jr.–James Madison, July 1775, quoted David Hawke, *In the Midst of a Revolution*, p. 89.

"invested with full Powers": William Strahan–BF, June 7, 1775, Dartmouth Papers, D(W)1778 : II, 1299.

"the Amount of all the Taxes": William Strahan–BF, Sept. 6, 1775, Dartmouth Papers, D(W)1778 : II, 1495.

"I am still of the opinion": William Strahan–BF, Oct. 4, 1775, Dartmouth Papers, D(W)1778 : II, 1552.

"Since my arrival here": BF–William Strahan, Oct. 3, 1775, CO. 5 : 134, fo. 125, P.R.O.

"I think the storm thickens": John Antill–Anthony Todd, Aug. 5, 1775, CO. 5 : 134, fo. 180, P.R.O.

"a daring arteful insinuating incendiary" and "to use the greatest precaution": Sir Henry Barkly–Grey Cooper, Sept. 11, 1775, Seed, p. 20.

"The disguise Mr. Franklin put on": Sir Henry Barkly–Grey Cooper, Oct. 5, 1779 [1775], Seed, p. 23.

"I am persuaded the body": BF–David Hartley, Oct. 3, 1775, Vaughan, p. 555.

"If the Boston Port Bill": Lt.-Gen. Thomas Gage–Earl of Dartmouth, Oct. 15, 1775, CO. 5 : 92, Pt. III, fo. 302, P.R.O.

"We cannot in this country conceive": John Adams–William Lee, Oct. 4, 1775, CO. 5 : 134, fo. 106, P.R.O.

"I had the honor to be introduced to that very great man": George Washington Greene, *The Life of Nathanael Greene*, 3 vols.; here 1:116.

"corresponding with our friends in Great Britain": Resolution, Nov. 29, 1775, Francis Wharton (ed.), *The Revolutionary Diplomatic Correspondence of the United States*, 6 vols.; here 2:61 [afterward referred to as Wharton].

"yet a warm, a firm, a zealous Supporter": John Adams–Abigail Adams, Feb. 18, 1776, Charles Francis Adams, *Familiar Letters of John Adams and his wife, Abigail Adams, during the Revolution*, p. 135 [afterward referred to as Adams, *Familiar Letters*].

"I have just heard that two": William Franklin–Lord George Germain, March 28, 1776, CO. 5 : 993, fo. 79, P.R.O.

"The sending of this man": M. Garnier–Comte de Vergennes, May 17, 1776, Correspondance politique, Angleterre, vol. 516, no. 47, fo. 160, Ministère des Relations Extérieures, République Française, Paris.

"no more the gay, polite place": John Carroll–Eleanor Carroll, May 1, 1776, Peter Guilday, *The Life and Times of John Carroll*, p. 102 [afterward referred to as Guilday].

"I am here on my way to Canada": BF–Josiah Quincy, April 15, 1776, Quincy, p. 491.

"We . . . were received at the landing": John Carroll–Eleanor Carroll, May 1, 1776, Guilday, p. 101.

"On the passage I suffered": BF, Journal [Passy], Oct. 4, 1778, quoted Hale, 1:247.

"Our misfortunes in Canada": John Adams–Abigail Adams, June 26, 1776, L. H. Butterfield et al. (eds.), *The Adams Papers*, Series II, *Adams Family Correspondence, 1761–1782*, 4 vols.; here 2:23 [afterward referred to as *Adams Family Correspondence*].

"We have tried in vain to borrow some hard money": quoted Parton, 2:121.

"A Triumvirate": Capt. Charles Douglas, *Isis*–Philip Stephens for my Lords Commissioners of the Admiralty, May 25, 1776, CO. 5 : 124, fo. 305, P.R.O.

"As to myself, I find I grow daily more feeble": BF–Charles Carroll and Samuel Chase, May 27, 1776, Wharton, 2:94.

"little of what has pass'd": BF–George Washington, June 21, 1776, Smyth, 6:450.

Franklin wrote a note: BF–Richard Bache, Sept. 30, 1774, Sparks, 8:137.

"a Grub Street writer in London": Ambrose Serle–Earl of Dartmouth, June 11, 1777, Dartmouth Papers, D(W)1778 : II, 1763.

"sacred & undeniable" and "self-evident": Carl Becker, *The Declaration of Independence*, p. 142.

"We must be unanimous": Hancock, quoted Sparks, 1:408.

"Yes, we must, indeed, all hang together": BF, quoted ibid.

"another anecdote related of Franklin": Sparks, 1:408.

"would be made within ten days": Vice-Admiral Howe–Admiral Arbuthnot, quoted Paul Leicester Ford, "Lord Howe's Commission to Pacify the Colonies," p. 758.

"I could not with any satisfaction": David Barclay–BF, March 31, 1776, "Some Letters of Franklin's Correspondents," p. 175.

"Directing pardons to be offered the Colonies": BF–Admiral Howe, July 20, 1776, Wharton, 2:103.

"I know your great motive": ibid., p. 104.

"I will only add": Lord Howe–BF, Aug. 16, 1776, Yale 22:565 (L.C.).

"it was improper to appoint any of their Members": quoted John Adams–Abigail Adams, Sept. 6, 1776, Adams, *Familiar Letters*, p. 223.

"The Window was open": L. H. Butterfield et al. (eds.), *The Adams Papers*, Series I, *Diaries, The Diary and Autobiography of John Adams*, 4 vols.; here 3:418 [afterward referred to as Adams, *Diary & Auto.*].

"The Three Gentlemen": Viscount Howe–Lord George Germain, Sept. 20, 1776, CO. 5 : 177, fo. 39, P.R.O.

"Forces have been sent out": BF at Conference with Viscount Howe, Sept. 11, 1776, quoted Parton 2:148.

"to grant Pardons": John Adams–Abigail Adams, Sept. 14, 1776, *Adams Family Correspondence*, 2:124.

"for very obvious Reasons": Viscount Howe–Lord George Germain, Sept. 20, 1776, CO. 5 : 177, fo. 39, P.R.O.

"They met, they talked": quoted Ira D. Gruber, *The Howe Brothers and the American Revolution*, p. 119.

"It was an agreable Excursion": John Adams–Abigail Adams, Sept. 14, 1776, *Adams Family Correspondence*, 2:124.

10. BATTLE FOR ARMS

"But, the operation must have": Vergennes–Beaumarchais, n.d., quoted Hale, 1:39.

"By conversing with them": Committee of Correspondence–Silas Deane, March 3, 1776, George L. Clark, *Silas Deane: A Connecticut Leader in the American Revolution*, p. 44 [afterward referred to as *Silas Deane*].

"I arrived at Bordeaux": Deane's narrative, T. Balch (ed.), *Papers in Relation to the Case of Silas Deane*, p. 19 [afterward referred to as Balch].

"Unknown and unconnected in Europe": Deane's narrative, ibid., p. 20.

"Were it possible I would attempt": Silas Deane–Committee of Correspondence, Aug. 16, 1776, *Silas Deane*, p. 50.

"open his mouth before English-speaking people": Douglas Southall Freeman, *George Washington*, 7 vols.; here 4:421.

"would not say nay": ibid.

"difficult and in code": Caron de Beaumarchais–Silas Deane, July 18, 1776, Brian N. Morton (ed.), *Beaumarchais Correspondance*, 4 vols.; here 2:228 [afterward referred to as *Beaumarchais Correspondance*].

"I made out an invoice": Deane's narrative, Balch, p. 25.

"Sir, I am deeply touched": Vergennes–Lord Stormont, Charles J. Stillé, "The Marquis de La Fayette in the American Revolution," p. 10.

"one of the most curious specimens": ibid.

"I should never have completed": Silas Deane–Committee of Secret Correspondence, Nov. 29, 1776, Jared Sparks, *The Diplomatic Correspondence of the American Revolution*, 12 vols.; here 1:74 [afterward referred to as Sparks, *Dipl. Corr.*].

"I am old and good for nothing": BF–Dr. Benjamin Rush, Sept. 27, 1776, quoted Wharton, 1:473.

"in the negotiation of our loans from France": Wharton, 1:251.

"there was scarcely a peasant or a citizen": John Adams, *The Boston Patriot*, May 15, 1811, App. B, Adams, *Works*, 1:660.

"As to our public affairs": BF–a friend, possibly Joseph Priestley, quoted Parton, 2:204.

"Dear Temple, I hope you will return hither": BF–William Temple Franklin, Sept. 28, 1776, quoted William Bell Clark, *Lambert Wickes, Sea Raider and Diplomat*, p. 77 [afterward referred to as *Wickes*].

"renounce and disclaim all pretence of right": "Sketch of Propositions for a Peace," Smyth, 6:452.

"with all their adjoining and intermediate territories": ibid., p. 453.

"The Honourable Doctor Franklin being appointed": Committee of Secret Correspondence–Captain Lambert Wickes, Oct. 24, 1776, quoted *Wickes*, p. 89.

"The Arch ——— Dr. Franklin": Sir Grey Cooper–unknown correspondent, Oct. 28, 1776, quoted Parton, 2:205.

"boils continued to vex me": BF, Journal [Passy], Oct. 4, 1778, quoted Hale, 1:248.

"The carriage was a miserable one": BF, Journal [Dec. 4, 1776], quoted Parton, 2:207.

"Our voyage though not long": BF–John Hancock, Dec. 8, 1776, Wharton, 2:222.

"Nothing has, for a long time": Silas Deane–Committee of Secret Correspondence, Dec. 12, 1776, Sparks, *Dipl. Corr.*, 1:101.

"Does the appointment of a number of agents": Caron de Beaumarchais–Silas Deane, Dec. 17, 1776, *Beaumarchais Correspondence*, 3:19.

"no equivocal step" and "natural to conclude": Horace Walpole–Sir Horace Mann, Dec. 20, 1776, Peter Cunningham (ed.), *The Letters of Horace Walpole*, 9 vols.; here 6:398 [afterward referred to as *Walpole Letters*].

"The enemy, though much depressed": General William Howe–Lord George Germain, Nov. 30, 1776, CO. 5 : 93, Pt. II, fo. 305, P.R.O.

"In regard to this event": Marquis of Rockingham–[?], Dec. [n.d.], 1776, George Thomas, Earl of Albemarle, *Memoirs of the Marquis of Rockingham and his Contemporaries,* 2 vols.; here 2:301.

"I learnt Yesterday Evening": Lord Stormont–Lord Weymouth, Dec. 11, 1776, State Papers Foreign, S.P. 78/300 fo. 382, P.R.O.

"If the doctor were once in Paris": Comte de Vergennes–Lord Stormont, quoted Hale, 1:74.

"I recollect that conversing with him": Charles James Fox, Sir Nathaniel William Wraxall, *Historical Memoirs of my own time from 1772 to 1784,* 2 vols [afterward referred to as *Wraxall Memoirs*], quoted Parton, 2:218.

"Sir, We beg leave to acquaint": BF, Silas Deane and Arthur Lee–Comte de Vergennes, Dec. 23, 1776, Wharton, 2:239.

"In our first conversation with the minister": BF and Silas Deane–Committee of Secret Correspondence, March 12, 1777, ibid., p. 283.

"The Congress, the better to defend their coasts": BF, Silas Deane and Arthur Lee–Comte de Vergennes, Jan. 5, 1777, ibid., p. 245.

"I tell you nothing": Comte de Vergennes–Marquis de Noailles, Jan. 10, 1777, Correspondance politique, Angleterre, vol. 521, fo. 31, Ministère des Relations Extérieures, République Française, Paris.

11. FIGHT FOR SURVIVAL

"I have taken a lodging at Passy": BF–Charles Dumas, Jan. 29, 1777, quoted Wharton, 2:255.

"To the west lay the Bois de Boulogne": L. Madelin, "Franklin à Passy, 1777–1785," p. 79, quoted Richard E. Amacher (ed.), *Franklin's Wit & Folly*, p. 9.

"Mons. Chaumont, a very wealthy person": Silas Deane–Committee of Secret Correspondence, Aug. 18, 1776, Wharton, 2:119.

"Breakfast, at eight o'clock": Claude-Anne Lopez, *Mon Cher Papa: Franklin and the Ladies of Paris,* p. 132 [afterward referred to as Lopez].

"We entered a spacious room": Winslow C. Watson (ed.), *Men and Times of the Revolution; or Memoirs of Elkanah Watson,* p. 87 [afterward referred to as *Elkanah Watson Memoirs*].

"he will be educated a Republican": BF–Jane Mecom, April 22, 1779, *Franklin & Mecom Letters,* p. 191.

"She has, among other elegant accomplishments": BF–William Carmichael, June 17, 1780, Sparks, 8:473.

"You mention the Kindness": BF–Elizabeth [Hubbard] Partridge, Oct. 11, 1779, William Greene Roelker (ed.), *Benjamin Franklin and Catharine Ray Greene, Their Correspondence, 1755–1790*, p. 102.

"Survived": M. [François Auguste Marie] Mignet, "Notice Historique sur la Vie et les Travaux de M. le Comte Sieyès," *Receuil des Lectures, faites dans la Séance publique annuelle de L'Académie des Sciences Morales et Politiques*, Dec. 28, 1836, Institut Royal de France, p. 70.

"They have some frivolities": BF–Josiah Quincy, April 22, 1779, Quincy, p. 494.

"This is really a generous nation": BF–Robert Livingston, March 4, 1782, Wharton, 5:215.

"a terrible mania for commerce" and "This reproach cannot apply": Comte de Vergennes–Lafayette, Aug. 7, 1780, quoted Stanley J. Idzerda et al. (eds.), *Lafayette in the Age of the American Revolution: Selected Letters and Papers, 1776–1790*, 4 vols.; here 3:130 [afterward referred to as *Lafayette Letters*].

"Nothing was more striking": M. le Comte de Ségur, *Mémoires ou Souvenirs et Anecdotes*, 3 vols.; here 1:116–17.

"very plainly dressed": quoted Parton, 2:212.

"By this means as I wear my Spectacles constantly": BF–George Whatley, Aug. 21, 1784, Library of Congress.

"It is the mode today": quoted Hale, 1:70.

"The print is above all a news picture": Sellers, p. 228.

"These, with the pictures": BF–Sarah Franklin Bache, June 3, 1779, Wharton, 3:205.

"We have some good Doctr. Franklins": Josiah Wedgwood–Thomas Bentley, April 19, 1777, *Letters of Josiah Wedgwood*, 2 vols.; here 2:238.

"All the painters and sculptors": François Felix Nogaret, "L'Isle des sages," pp. 118–19 [Paris, 5785], quoted Sellers, p. 137 n28.

"You had not left us long": Sarah Franklin Bache–BF, Feb. 23, 1777, Duane, *Letters*, p. 74.

"You will endeavor to procure a meeting": Committee of Secret Correspondence–Silas Deane, March 3, 1776, Wharton, 2:80.

"having induced me to believe": Edward Bancroft, "State of Facts," Sept. 16, 1784 [enclosure (for Mr. Pitt) in Edward Bancroft–Marquis of Carmarthen, Sept. 17, 1784], F.O. 4 : 3, Part I, fo. 94, P.R.O. [afterward referred to as Bancroft].

"Franklin's & Dean's Correspondence with the Congress" and "Copys of any transactions": Engagement of Dr. Edwards to correspond with Paul Wentworth and Lord Stormont and the Means of conducting that Correspondence [in the hand of Paul Wentworth, Dec. 1776], Auckland Papers, Vol. II, Add. MS. 34413, fo. 107, British Library.

"For Lord Stormont": ibid., fo. 108.

"most assiduously devoted his time": Balch, p. 52.

"it will not be improper": ibid., p. 24.

"has Letters from America": Rev. John Vardill–William Eden, 1777, Auckland Papers, Vol. II, Add. MS. 34413, fo. 418, British Library.

"The brownest of the two tinctures": Paul Wentworth–[Earl of Suffolk], Aug. [Sept.] 2, 1777, Auckland Papers, Vol. III, Add. MS. 34414, fo. 98, British Library.

"Forgive me, dear Doctor": William Alexander–BF, March 1, 1777, quoted Hale, 1:87.

"As it is impossible to discover": BF–Mrs. Juliana Ritchie, Jan. 19, 1777, quoted ibid., p. 88.

"There! are twin brothers": Elkanah Watson Memoirs, p. 120.

"I had the figure placed": ibid., p. 121.

"As soon as a general was appointed": William Temple Franklin, quoted Bigelow, 8:60.

"A Mr. Hake who has some particular Influence": William Eden, "Statement concerning the Opening of Letters carried by Mrs. Bancroft . . ." n.d. [1777], Auckland Papers, Vol. II, Add. MS. 34413, fo. 423, British Library.

"The American mission": Jonathan R. Dull, "Franklin the Diplomat: The French Mission," p. 38.

"I received your Commands": Anthony Todd–William Eden, Friday [1777], Auckland Papers, Vol. III, Add. MS. 34414, fo. 533, British Library.

"I am very glad that 105": [?]–Silas Deane, Feb. 7, 1777, France, Archives des Affaires étrangères, Etats Unis, vol. 2, nos. 43, 44, Benjamin Franklin Stevens (ed.), Facsimiles of Manuscripts in European Archives Relating to America, 1773–1783, 25 vols.; here vol. 6, no. 635 [afterward referred to as Stevens].

"Each of the letters": "The Lovell Cipher and Its Derivatives," app., Adams Family Correspondence, 4:395.

"The cipher you have communicated": BF–James Lovell, Aug. 10, 1780, quoted Wharton, 4:27.

"We now entertain no doubt": one of Stormont's agents, March 4, 1777, quoted J. Bennett Nolan, "A British Editor Reports the American Revolution," p. 104 [afterward referred to as Nolan, "British Editor"].

"We are well assured": Editor, New Jersey *Gazette* [Oct. 2, 1777], quoted Parton, 2:252n.

"one half in royal blue cloth": Sieur de Montieu, "Contract with the American Commissioners to supply Stores for the Service of the United Colonies of North America, June 6, 1777," Auckland Papers, Vol. III, Add. MS. 34414, fo. 10, British Library.

"in sheets & in nails": ibid.

"soldiers superior guns": ibid.

"pairs of knitted woollen stockings": ibid.

"About ten days ago *Mr. Chaumont*": Paul Wentworth–[Earl of Suffolk], Sept. 19, 1777, Auckland Papers, Vol. III, Add. MS. 34414, fo. 162, British Library.

"M. Chaumont is returned": Paul Wentworth–[Earl of Suffolk], Sept. 20, 1777, ibid., fo. 166.

"with his usual apathy says": General Intelligence & Observations [about Oct. 21, 1777, in the hand of Paul Wentworth], ibid., fo. 244.

"I retain my health *a merveille*": BF–William Carmichael, April 7, 1780, quoted Wharton, 3:587.

"The king's ministers receive no applications": Lord Stormont–BF, April/May 1777, quoted BF–David Hartley, Feb. 16, 1782, Wharton, 5:170.

"I apply not to the ambassador of America": Edmund Burke–BF, August 1781, Wentworth Woodhouse Muniments, Sheffield City Libraries.

"Since the foolish part of mankind": BF–Edmund Burke, Oct. 15, 1781, ibid.

"But on Reflection": BF–General Washington, n.d., Library of Congress.

"all expenses and promises": M. De Brétigney, Terms of engagement on entering the Service of the United States, May 28, 1777, Auckland Papers, Vol. II, Add. MS. 34413, fo. 471, British Library.

"A Monsr. Brétigney with his suite": John Rutledge–Henry Laurens, Nov. 7, 1777, CO. 5 : 558, fo. 76, P.R.O.

"Lord Mulgrave in the 'Ardent' man of war": *Cumberland Chronicle and White-haven Advertiser*, Sept. 6, 1777, quoted Nolan, "British Editor," p. 97.

"The villains thus escape": W. Rawlings–Earl of Dartmouth, n.d. [June/July 1779], Dartmouth Papers, D(W)1778 : II, 1888.

"if the American privateers continue": Lords of the Admiralty [Sandwich, Lisburne and Palliser]–Viscount Weymouth, June 28, 1777, CO. 5 : 140, fo. 184, P.R.O.

"to sink, burn and destroy": Letter from Whitehaven dated June 26, 1777, enclosure Lords of the Admiralty–Viscount Weymouth, June 28, 1777, CO. 5 : 140, fo. 188, P.R.O.

"manned by old smugglers": "Sketch of the Services of B. Franklin to the United States of America," enclosed BF–Charles Thomson, Dec. 29, 1788, Smyth, 9:697.

"The Prize cannot, as you observe": BF–French firm at Cherbourg, June 12, 1777, quoted *Wickes*, p. 215.

"After seizing ships": Claude H. Van X. Tyne, *The War of Independence: American Phase*, p. 482.

"And when I have once got rid of this Business": BF–John Paul Jones, June 27, 1780, Smyth, 8: 112.

"I will absolutely have nothing to do": BF–Jonathan Williams, Jr., June 27, 1780, ibid., p. 113.

"I must repeat my motion": BF–Samuel Huntington, president of Congress, Aug. 10, 1780, Wharton, 4:26.

"It is a vexatious thing": BF–Jonathan Williams, Jr., June 15, 1781, Smyth, 8:270 and 271.

"I have papers of the first Consequence": Dr. B[ancroft]–Mr. W[entworth], April 24, 1777, Auckland Papers, Vol. II, Add. MS. 34413, fo. 402, British Library.

"the early information": Paul Wentworth–Lord North, Nov. 21, 1777, Auckland Papers, Vol. III, Add. MS. 34414, fo. 380, British Library.

"I am more and more persuaded": Lord Stormont–William Eden, April 16, 1777, Auckland Papers, Vol. II, Add. MS. 34413, fo. 401, British Library.

"Captain Hynson, Sir, The Commrs. are sending a Packet": Silas Deane–Capt. Joseph Hynson, Oct. 7, 1777, Auckland Papers, Vol. III, Add. MS. 34414, fo. 225, British Library.

"The inclosed papers were brought" and "He was an honest rascal": William Eden–George III, Oct. 20, 1777, ibid., fo. 239.

"I do not write you to reproach you": Silas Deane–Capt. Joseph Hynson, Oct. 26, 1777, ibid., fo. 261.

"severely chagrined" and "delivered only an enclosure": Committee of Foreign Affairs–the Commissioners [BF, Silas Deane and Arthur Lee], Jan. 12, 1778, Sparks, *Dipl. Corr.*, 1:359 and 360.

"No, monsieur, it is not a truth": quoted Parton, 2:228.

"Yes, but the spectators": quoted ibid., p. 229.

"In September, 1777 I laid before my colleagues": Silas Deane's narrative, Balch, p. 50.

"playing with his electrical apparatus": Parton, 2:281.

"Sir, *is* Philadelphia taken?": BF–Jonathan Loring Austin on Dec. 4, 1777, quoted Hale, 1:159.

"It is, sir," and "But, sir, I have greater news": Austin–BF, ibid.

"Gentlemen, The Brigantine Perch": Washington's dispatch, Oct. 24, 1777, quoted Hale, 1:155.

"not merely changed the relations": Lord Mahon, *History of England from the Peace of Utrecht to the Peace of Versailles, 1713–1783*, 7 vols.; here 6:288.

"About 10 o'clock we marched out": William Digby, Lieut., 53 Regt., Entry for Oct. 17, 1777, "Diary in the American War, 1776–1777," Add. MS. 32413, fo. 91, British Library.

"We have the Honour to acquaint your Excellency": American Commissioners–Comte de Vergennes, Dec. 4, 1777, France, Archives des Affaires étrangères, Etats Unis, vol. 2, no. 148, fo. 279, Stevens, vol. 7, no. 716.

Louis XVI approved a note: dated Dec. 6, 1777, Henri Doniol, *Histoire de la Participation de la France à l'établissement des Etats-Unis d'Amérique*, 5 vols.; here 2:625–26.

"My dear papa": Madame Brillon–BF, n.d., quoted Lopez, p. 36.

"The commissioners from the Congress": BF, Silas Deane and Arthur Lee–Vergennes, Dec. 8, 1777, Wharton, 2:444.

"What is necessary to be done": "Dr. Franklin's Answer to Question," Jan. 8, 1778, France, Archives des Affaires étrangères, Etats Unis, vol. 3, no. 4, Stevens, vol. 8, no. 774.

"The Commissioners have long since propos'd a Treaty": ibid.

"I at my own Expence, by a special Messenger": Bancroft fo. 94.

"This caused many speculations": Silas Deane's narrative, Balch, p. 54.

"But for his noble face": Mme. Vigée-Le Brun, March 23, 1779, *The Memoirs of Mme. Elisabeth Louise Vigée-Le Brun, 1755–1789*, p. 170.

"The King, who had been at prayer": Duc de Croÿ, Journal Entry for March 20, 1778, Le Vte. de Grouchy and Paul Cottin, *Journal inédit du Duc De Croÿ, 1718–1784*, 4 vols.; here 4:78 [afterward referred to as *De Croÿ Journal inédit*].

12. THE ROAD TO YORKTOWN

"American diplomat, trouble-maker": Mark Mayo Boatner, *Cassell's Biographical Dictionary of the American War of Independence, 1763–1783*, p. 603.

"concurred with Mr. Deane": "Charges against Mr. Benjamin Franklin with the Evidence," Balch, p. 89.

"a proper person to be trusted": ibid.

"Mr. de Chaumont having presst me much": William Temple Franklin–John Holker, Jr., Feb. 19, 1781, Library of Congress.

"My colleague, Mr. Deane": BF–Henry Laurens, March 31, 1778, Wharton, 2:528.

"have brought with him from France": Balch, p. 83.

"I am more and more satisfied": Arthur Lee–Richard Henry Lee, Sept. 12, 1778, Richard Henry Lee, *Life of Arthur Lee*, 2 vols.; here 2:148.

"He resides at Ghent": BF–Robert R. Livingston, March 4, 1782, Wharton, 5:216.

"If I have often receiv'd and borne": BF–Arthur Lee, April 3, 1778, Smyth, 7:132.

"the extracts of Mr. Lee's philippics against me": BF–William Carmichael, March 31, 1780, Wharton, 3:585.

"a bitter antagonism": Mabel L. Webber, "Ralph Izard," Allen Johnson et al. (eds.), *Dictionary of American Biography*, 20 vols.; here 9:524.

"I found that the Business of our Commission": John Adams's Autobiography, May 27, 1778, Adams, *Diary & Auto.*, 4:118.

"For God's sake prevent": Lafayette–George Washington, June 12, 1779, Charlemagne Tower, *The Marquis de La Fayette in the American Revolution*, 2 vols.; here 2:74.

"We are all new": BF–John Adams, June 11, 1781, Library of Congress.

"[His] most original trait": Pierre-Georges Cabanis, *Oeuvres complètes*, 5 vols.; here 5:269.

"would be obliged to incur no greater expense": John Adams–Samuel Adams, May 21, 1778, Adams, *Works*, 3:160.

"I wish with you as much for the restoration": BF–David Hartley, Sept. 3, 1778, quoted Hale, 1:226.

"to treat, consult, and agree upon the means": *London Gazette*, No. 11865, March 1778.

"The French interference gives a new colour": Earl of Carlisle, Minute, Sept. 29, 1778, Auckland Papers, Vol. V, Add. MS. 34416, fo. 33, British Library.

"very fit to make a treaty": Horace Walpole–Rev. William Mason, March 4, 1778, *Walpole Letters*, 7:37.

"The many instances of the inimical conduct": George III–Lord North, March 26, 1778, Letter No. 2251, Sir John Fortescue (ed.), *The Correspondence of King George the Third, from 1760 to December 1783*, 6 vols.; here 4:80.

"stole and carried off with them": Richard Bache–BF, July 14, 1778, Duane, *Letters*, p. 78.

"While you, great George": Smyth, 1:108.

"between the flag of Liberty": Captain John Paul Jones–Silas Deane, Feb. 26, 1778, Correspondance politique, Etats Unis, vol. 3, no. 45, fo. 108, Ministère des Relations Extérieures, République Française, Paris.

"after equipping the 'Ranger' ": Commissioners–Capt. John Paul Jones, Jan. 16, 1778, quoted Samuel Eliot Morison, *John Paul Jones: A Sailor's Biography*, p. 125.

"I . . . immediately despatched my long boat": Capt. John Paul Jones–Silas Deane, Feb. 26, 1778, Correspondance politique, Etats Unis, vol. 3, no. 45, fo. 108, Ministère des Relations Extérieures, République Française, Paris.

"to attack the Ports on the Coast": Lord George Germain–Sir Henry Clinton, March 8, 1778, H.Q. Papers of the British Army in America, vol. 9, no. 996(8) in Carleton Papers, P.R.O. 30/33:9, P.R.O.

"I should suppose, for example": BF–Lafayette, March 22, 1779, Wharton, 3:91.

"And if among the troops": ibid.

"What an example of honour": *The London Evening Post*, Sept. 28, 1779, quoted Don Carlos Seitz, *Paul Jones, His Exploits in English Seas During 1778–1780*, p. 51.

"I have at the request of Friends": Francis Lyn [BF]–Thomas Digges, June 25, 1780, Smyth, 8:110.

"He was curious to know the ingenious": Baron Roger Portalis and Henri Béraldi, *Les Graveurs de dix-huitième siècle*, 3 vols.; here 3:491ff.

"Lo! swarming southward on rejoicing suns": James Thomson, "Liberty," Rev. George Gilfillan (ed.), *Thomson's Poetical Works*, p. 274.

Edward Hale and Edward Hale, Jr., maintain: Hale 1:167–68.

"O Liberty, thou goddess heavenly bright": Joseph Addison, "A Letter from Italy to the Right Honourable Charles Lord Halifax, in the Year MDCCI," Richard Hurd, *The Works of Joseph Addison*, 6 vols.; here 1:35.

"Franklin was eager to see a man": The Marquis de Condorcet, *The Life of Voltaire*, 2 vols.; here 1:421.

"Il faut s'embrasser, à la Françoise": Adams, diary entry, April 29, 1778, Adams, *Works*, 3:147.

"The two aged actors": ibid.

"Went to Versailles to assist": BF, diary entry, Dec. 26, 1780, quoted Smyth, 10:339.

"a business that requires being always at home": BF–Robert R. Livingston, Sept. 3, 1782, Smyth, 8:588.

"Wants me to pay his gaming debts": BF note on Dom Bernard–BF, Sept. 14, 1778, I. Minis Hays (ed.), *Calendar of the Papers of Benjamin Franklin in the Library of the American Philosophical Society*, 5 vols.; here 1:496 [afterward referred to as Hays].

"kindle the lightning": Jacob–BF, July 30, 1784, Hays, 3:206.

"proved by the agreement": [Père Joseph Etienne] Bertier–BF, Feb. 18, 1783, ibid., p. 23.

"the most illustrious man": Sieur De Pommereuille–BF, Jan. 16, 1779, Hays, 2:8.

"one of the pens": Président Pigault de Lepinoy–BF, Sept. 11, 1782, ibid., p. 497.

"If I were in a situation where I could be": BF–Dr. Jan Ingenhousz, April 29, 1785, entitled "On Electricity. A Three wheeled Clock—Gravitation of Bodies affected by Sun and Moon—Conjecture on Tides," W.T.F., 3:478.

"Near three years ago": BF–Edward Nairne, Oct. 18, 1783, Smyth, 9:109.

"I do not know that my mental faculties": BF–Samuel Huntington, March 12, 1781, Smyth, 8:220.

"He says perhaps": Alice Lee Shippen–Elizabeth Welles Adams, June 17, 1781, *Adams Family Correspondence*, 4:154.

"some danger lest the Congress": BF–Vergennes, Feb. 13, 1781, Sparks, 8:536.

"But let me repeat, for God's sake be sparing": BF–John Paul Jones, Feb. 19, 1780, Library of Congress.

"I must soon quit this scene": BF–George Washington, March 4, 1780, Library of Congress.

"Britain, at the expense of three millions": BF–Joseph Priestley, Oct. 3, 1775, Rutt, 1:277.

"to avoid running the war": P. M. S. Blackett, "Scientists at the Operational Level," p. 28.

"A flight of arrows": BF–Charles Lee, Feb. 11, 1776, Wharton, 2:69.

"Then, during three or four Days Consideration": BF–Joseph Priestley, Sept. 19, 1772, Library of Congress.

"with all civility and kindness": BF–Captains and commanders of armed ships, March 10, 1779, Wharton, 3:76.

"humanizing by degrees" and "1. Cultivators of the earth": BF–Benjamin Vaughan, July 10, 1782, Wharton, 5:606.

"Your concern for the security of life": BF–David Hartley, Dec. 15, 1781, ibid., p. 51.

"The extravagant luxury of our country": BF–John Jay, President of Congress, Oct. 4, 1779, Wharton, 3:365.

"disgusted me as much as if you had put salt": BF–Sarah Franklin Bache, June 3, 1779, ibid., pp. 206 and 207.

"I shall be sending you new recruits" and "You know that I get paid": Le comte de Schaumberg–le baron d'Hohendorf, Feb. 18, 1777, printed as "Lettre douzième," M. de Lescure, *Correspondance secrète inédite,* 2 vols.; here 1:32.

"You being now upon the Spot": BF–Lafayette, Dec. 9, 1780, *Lafayette Letters,* 3:256.

"The possession of this Booty": Extract of letter from Captain Gerrish, of the New England Militia, dated Albany, March 7, 1782, Forged supplement to *Boston Independent Chronicle,* Smyth, 8:437.

"This package is a Mixture of all": ibid., p. 439.

"Some dark Night on the Trees": ibid., p. 441.

"It is now proposed": Boston report, ibid., p. 442.

"Make any use of them you may think proper": BF–Charles Dumas, May 3, 1782, Bigelow, 7:458.

"These being *substantial* Truths": BF–John Adams, April 22, 1782, Smyth, 8:433.

"so ill with the gout and a fever": BF–Vergennes, Feb. 25, 1779, Wharton, 3:63.

"My gout continues to disable me": BF–John Adams, April 3, 1779, ibid., p. 110.

Dialogue between Franklin and the Gout: BF, Oct. 22, 1780, W.T.F., 3:327–32.

"Many things; you have ate and drank" and "Yet you eat an inordinate breakfast": BF, *Dialogue between Franklin and the Gout,* ibid., p. 327.

"On Monday the 15th": BF, Journal [Passy], Feb. 28, 1779, quoted Hale, 1:250.

"I ate a hearty supper": BF Journal [Passy], Oct. 4, 1778, quoted ibid., p. 249.

"An elegant entertainment was prepared": Jonathan Loring Austin Journal, July 4 [1778], quoted ibid., p. 251.

"There has been a kind of Fatality": BF–Lafayette, Dec. 9, 1780, *Lafayette Letters,* 3:256.

"She carried clothing": BF–Lafayette, May 14, 1781, Library of Congress.

"His Character is in the Sight of all Europe": ibid.

"I hope your Fears that there may be Arnolds": BF–James Searle, Nov. 30, 1780, Smyth, 8:179.

"The English garrison came out of Yorktown": Vergennes–BF, 11:00 P.M., Nov. 19, 1781, quoted *Elkanah Watson Memoirs*, p. 134.

"There is no parallel": BF on Nov. 20, 1781, quoted ibid.

"Do you know, my dear papa": Mme. Brillon–BF, Dec. 11, 1781, quoted Lopez, p. 109.

"You are sulking, my dear friend": BF–Mme. Brillon, Dec. 25, 1781, quoted ibid., p. 110.

"I often pass in front of your house": BF–Mme. Brillon, Dec. 25, 1781, quoted ibid., p. 104.

"As he would have taken a ball": Lord George Germain–Sir N. William Wraxall, November 1781, *Wraxall Memoirs*, 2:100.

"Oh, God, it is all over": Lord North, quoted ibid.

13. INDEPENDENCE WON

"Can harmony be expected": Alice Lee Shippen–Abigail Adams, August 1781, *Adams Family Correspondence*, 4:203.

"I have not as yet": BF–Vergennes, June 27, 1781, Library of Congress.

"Great Affairs sometimes take": BF entry for May 9, 1782, "Journal of the Negotiation for Peace with Great Britain," Sparks, *Dipl. Corr.*, 3:376.

"to implore this honourable House to interpose": Petition from the City of London against the American War, Feb. 27, 1782, *Parl. Hist.*, vol. 22, col. 1064.

"the American war to Dulcinea del Toboso": Mr. [Noel] Hill, Debate in the Commons on the motion moved by General Conway against the further Prosecution of Offensive War with America, Feb. 27, 1782, ibid., col. 1083.

"I congratulate you, as the friend of America": Edmund Burke–BF, Feb. 28, 1782, Wharton, 5:208.

"this House will consider": General Conway's motion declaring the Advisers of the further prosecution of Offensive War in America to be Enemies to the King and Country, March 4, 1782, *Parl. Hist.*, vol. 22, col. 1087–89.

"Each noble Lord seemed determined": Change of Ministry, March 20, 1782, ibid., col. 1214.

"*His Majesty's ministers were no more*": Lord North, Change of Ministry, March 20, 1782, ibid., col. 1215.

"that while Britain had a ship": British Secretary of State in 1774, quoted by Sir. P. J. Clerke, Debate on Mr. [David] Hartley's Motion for a Bill to restore Peace with America, May 30, 1781, ibid., col. 336.

"I hope it will produce": BF–Lord Shelburne, March 22, 1782, Sparks, *Dipl. Corr.*, 3:377.

"I answered [Dr. Franklin's] letter": Lord Shelburne, "Secret and Confidential"–Sir Guy Carleton, K.B., and Vice Admiral Digby, June 5, 1782, CO. 5 : 178, fo. 219, P.R.O.

"Dr. Franklin having been much teized with People": W. A. S. Hewins (ed.), *The Whitefoord Papers, being the Correspondence and other Manuscripts of Colonel Charles Whitefoord and Caleb Whitefoord from 1739 to 1810*, p. 193 [afterward referred to as *Whitefoord Papers*].

"He added that the War could not be closed": Lord Shelburne, "Secret and Confidential"–Sir Guy Carleton, K.B., and Vice Admiral Digby, June 5, 1782, CO. 5 : 178, fo. 220, P.R.O.

"Those who have been in Europe": Commodore Alexander Gillon–Arthur Lee, Dec. 1, 1782, quoted "Accessions," *Pennsylvania Magazine of History and Biography*, vol. 62, no. 3 (July 1938), p. 430 [afterward referred to as *Pa. Mag. H&B*].

"in distressing those countries": quoted Hale, 2:68.

"commissioners named by the said colonies": ibid.

"I am of your opinion, and will go on": BF–fellow commissioners, October 1782, quoted Adams diary entry for Nov. 30, 1782, Adams, *Works*, 3:336.

"required separate copies of many official Papers": *Whitefoord Papers*, p. 193.

"Dined at Passy with Mr. and Mrs. Jay": Matthew Ridley, diary entry for Oct. 4, 1782, Herbert E. Klingelhofer, "Matthew Ridley's Diary During the Peace Negotiations of 1782," p. 117.

"I am at a loss, sir, to explain your conduct": Vergennes–BF, Dec. 15, 1782, Wharton, 6:140.

"Your observation is, however": BF–Vergennes, Dec. 17, 1782, ibid., p. 144.

"the preliminaries of peace": BF–Robert R. Livingston, Jan. 21, 1783, Smyth, 9:9.

"Thus the great and hazardous enterprise" and "A few years of peace": BF–Charles Thomson, May 13, 1784, Wharton, 6:806.

"Writing becomes more and more irksome": BF–Dr. [Jan] Ingenhousz, April 29, 1785, entitled "On Electricity. A Three wheeled Clock—Gravitation of Bodies affected by Sun and Moon—Conjecture on Tides," W.T.F., 3:475.

"One can scarce see a new book": BF–Benjamin Vaughan, April 21, 1785, W.T.F., 2:70.

"The idea had occurred to him": Benjamin Vaughan (ed.), *The Life and Works of Benjamin Franklin*, p. iii [afterward referred to as Vaughan, *Life*].

"The rapid Progress *true* Science": BF–Joseph Priestley, Feb. 8, 1780, Smyth, 8:10.

"a clumsy boat was moved" and "The weather was calm": BF–M. Alphonse [Julien-David] Le Roy, August 1785, entitled "On Improvements in Navigation," W.T.F., 3:528.

"There" the balloon "was held down by a Cord" and "pave the Way to some Discoveries": BF–Sir Joseph Banks, Aug. 30, 1783, Royal Society.

"What use is a new-born baby?": Baron von Grimm, *Correspondance littéraire*, 16 vols.; here 13:349.

"It's still a child": *De Croÿ Journal inédit*, p. 310.

"Some suppose Flying to be now invented": BF, Postscript–Sir Joseph Banks, Aug. 30, 1783, Royal Society.

"It carried under it a large Lanthorn": BF–Sir Joseph Banks, Oct. 8, 1783, Royal Society.

"Convincing sovereigns of the folly of wars": BF–Jan Ingenhousz, Jan. 16, 1784, Library of Congress.

"to a place further distant" and "though being the easiest": BF–Henry Laurens, Dec. 6, 1783, Wharton, 6:737.

"I think that, in general, maladies": BF–M. de la Condamine, March 19, 1784, Bigelow, 8:460.

"to weaken our Faith in some of the Miracles": BF–William Temple Franklin, Aug. 25, 1784, Smyth, 9:268.

"It will be very agreable to me": BF–William Franklin, Aug. 16, 1784, Original Letters, Add. MS. 9828, fo. 173, British Library.

"You may confide to [him]": BF–William Franklin, Aug. 16, 1784, ibid., fo. 174.

"Spring is coming on": BF–Mary Hewson, Jan. 27, 1783, W.T.F., 2:41.

"We are all pleased with our old Friend Temple": Mary Hewson–BF, Oct. 25, 1784, "Franklin & Stevenson Hewson Letters," p. 535.

"You talk of obligations to me": BF–Mary Hewson, May 5, 1785, Sparks, 10:167.

"I am told you are on the point": Thomas Pownall–BF, July 3, 1785, quoted Charles A. W. Pownall, *Thomas Pownall, M.P., F.R.S., Governor of Massachusetts Bay, Author of The Letters of Junius*, p. 429.

14. LAST DAYS OF A SAGE

"The French are an amiable People": BF–Captain Nathaniel Falconer, July 28, 1783, Smyth, 9:77.

"But, however happy that circumstance may make me": BF–Mary Hewson, May 5, 1785, Sparks, 10:167.

"The ship has a large, convenient cabin": BF–Mary Hewson, July 4, 1785, ibid., p. 201.

"I cannot quit the coasts of Europe": BF–David Hartley, July 5, 1785, ibid., p. 208.

"I used to consider that system": BF–Francis Masères, June 26, 1785, Bigelow, 9:130.

"My very dear Papa": M. Brillon, Postscript to Mme. Brillon–BF, July 10, 1785, quoted Lopez, p. 121.

"When he left Passy": Vaughan, *Life,* p. iii.

"I found that the motion of the litter": BF, Journal entry, July 12, 1785, John Bigelow (ed.), *The Life of Benjamin Franklin,* 3 vols.; here 3:325 [afterward referred to as Bigelow, *Life*].

"with an invitation to us to stop": BF, Journal entry, July 13, 1785, ibid., p. 325.

"a chain of chalk mountains": BF, Journal entry, July 15, 1785, ibid., p. 326.

"a great company of genteel people at supper": BF, Journal entry, July 15, 1785, ibid., p. 327.

"I have perused it since": BF, Journal entry, July 16, 1785, ibid., p. 327.

"I can picture you in your litter": Mme. Helvétius–BF, n.d., quoted Lopez, p. 299.

"My husband, my two daughters": Mme. Brillon–BF, n.d., Albert H. Smyth, "Franklin's Social Life in France," p. 433.

"I was not in the least incommoded by the voyage": BF–M. Limozin, July 25, 1785, Bigelow, 9:150.

"come most untimely to dine with us": Jonathan Shipley–BF, July 24, 1785, Sparks, 10:218.

"floating on my back, fell asleep": BF, Journal entry, July 25, 1785, Bigelow, *Life,* 3:330.

"He was continually saying of himself": BF–Donatien Le Ray de Chaumont, Oct. 20, 1785, Smyth, 9:470.

"instead of being hurt by the journey or voyage": BF–Mary Hewson, July 26, 1785, Sparks, 10:219.

"Our ship arrived here yesterday": BF–Mme. Helvétius, July 27, 1785, Library of Congress.

"When I waked in the morning": BF, Journal entry, July 28, 1785, Bigelow, *Life*, 3:331.

"I do assure you": Catharine Louisa Shipley–BF, Aug. 2, 1785, Sparks, 10:219.

"Maritime Observations": BF–M. Alphonse [Julien-David] Le Roy, August 1785, entitled "On Improvements in Navigation," W.T.F., 3:518–42.

"The accidents I have seen at sea": BF–M. Alphonse [Julien-David] Le Roy, August 1785, entitled "On Improvements in Navigation," including paper written April 5, 1775, ibid., p. 541.

"sold at a reasonable price by Nairne & Co.": BF–M. Alphonse [Julien-David] Le Roy, August 1785, entitled "On Improvements in Navigation," ibid., p. 526.

"embrace[d] willingly this leisure": BF–Dr. Jan Ingenhousz, Aug. 28, 1785, entitled "On the Causes and Cure of Smoky Chimneys," ibid., p. 479.

"I am at this present writing in a ship": ibid., p. 494.

"water smooth, air cool": BF, Journal entry, Sept. 13, 1785, Bigelow, *Life*, 3:331.

"With the flood in the morning": BF, Journal entry, Sept. 14, 1785, ibid.

"We were received by a crowd of people": ibid.

"I shall now be free of Politicks": BF–Dr. Jan Ingenhousz, April 29, 1785, Smyth, 9:318.

"drinking every day *les eaux épurées de Passy*": BF–M. Le Veillard, March 6, 1786, Bigelow, *Life*, 3:358.

"I enjoy many comfortable Intervals": BF–Mrs. Elizabeth Partridge, Nov. 25, 1788, Smyth, 9:683.

"into grass plots and gravel walks": BF–Mary Hewson, May 6, 1786, ibid., p. 511.

"I propose to have in it": BF–Jane Mecom, Sept. 21, 1786, quoted Edward M. Riley, "Franklin's Home," p. 158.

"The affairs in dealing with so many workmen": BF–M. Le Veillard, April 15, 1787, Smyth, 9:561.

"I found that the copper point": BF–M. Landriani, Oct. 14, 1787, entitled "On the Utility of Lightning Conductors," W.T.F., 3:556.

"Our domestic misunderstandings": BF–David Hartley, Sept. 6, 1783, Smyth, 9:88.

"Cards we sometimes play here": BF–Mary Hewson, May 6, 1786, ibid., p. 512.

"that and one room to eat in": Mary Hewson–BF, Oct. 17, 1786, "Franklin & Stevenson Hewson Letters," p. 533.

In his bedroom two cords: "Personal Recollections of Benjamin Franklin by Col. Robert Carr of Philadelphia, Contributed by Frederick D. Stow, Esq., of Philadelphia," *The Historical Magazine, and Notes and Queries concerning the Antiquities, History, and Biography of America*, n.s., vol. 4, no. 2 (August 1868), pp. 59–60; here p. 60.

"for smoothing clothes": Washington diary entry, Sept. 4, 1787, "Extracts from Washington's Diary, Kept while Attending the Constitutional Convention of 1787," *Pa. Mag. H&B*, vol. 11, no. 3 (1887), p. 307.

"Dr. Franklin . . . desired him to compare them": Dr. Manasseh Cutler, Diary entry, July 30, 1787, William Parker Cutler and Julia Perkins Cutler, *Life, Journals and Correspondence of Rev. Manasseh Cutler, LL.D.*, 2 vols.; here 1:312 [afterward referred to as Cutler].

"He showed us a glass machine": Dr. Manasseh Cutler, Diary entry, July 13, 1787, ibid., p. 269.

"Otherwise I shall wish": BF–Mme. Helvétius, Oct. 20, 1785, Smyth, 9:471.

"I have sometimes wished I had brought with me": BF–M. Le Roy, April 18, 1787, entitled "On Balloons," W.T.F., 3:555.

"engrossed the prime of my life": BF–John and Mrs. Bard, Nov. 14, 1785, Sparks, 10:239.

"As to the little history I promised you": BF–M. Le Veillard, April 15, 1787, Bigelow, *Life*, 3:368.

"a spectacle of transcendent benevolence": Benjamin Rush–Richard Price, June 2, 1787, quoted Charles E. Norton, "The Price Letters, 1767–1790," p. 367.

"Sir, there are two passions" and "rather for the author of it": BF motion, June 2, 1787, Max Farrand (ed.), *The Records of the Federal Convention of 1787*, 4 vols.; here 1:82 [afterward referred to as Farrand, *Fed. Convention*].

"We shall be divided by our little partial local interests": BF motion, June 28, 1787, ibid., p. 451.

"We found [Franklin] in his garden": Dr. Manasseh Cutler, Diary entry, July 13, 1787, Cutler, 1:267–68.

"With that senile ambition common to old people" and "perfectly easy and every thing": Diary entry, July 13, 1787, ibid., p. 270.

"For when you assemble a number of men": BF's speech, Sept. 17, 1787, quoted Farrand, *Fed. Convention*, 2:642 and 643.

"But now at length I have the happiness": BF, Sept. 17, 1787, quoted ibid., p. 648.

"You may judge from thence": BF–Jane Mecom, Sept. 20, 1787, *Franklin & Mecom Letters*, p. 298.

"continues the same": BF–Mme. Brillon, April 19, 1788, Library of Congress.

"I am now about to write at home": BF, August 1788, in margin of Auto. MS., *Auto.*, xxiii.

"I send you what is done of the Memoirs": BF–M. Le Veillard, Nov. 13, 1789, Library of Congress.

"I might by this time have finished my Memoirs": BF–Benjamin Vaughan, Nov. 2, 1789, Sparks, 10:397.

"in this world nothing can be said to be certain": BF–Jean-Baptiste Le Roy, Nov. 13, 1789, ibid., p. 410.

"God grant, that not only the love of liberty": BF–David Hartley, Dec. 4, 1789, ibid., p. 411.

"As to Jesus of Nazareth": BF–Ezra Stiles, March 9, 1790, ibid., p. 424.

"made about a 100 Years since": Historicus [BF], Essay in *Federal Gazette*, March 25, 1790, Smyth, 10:87.

"The Doctrine, that Plundering": quoted ibid., p. 91.

"he not only amused himself with reading": Dr. John Jones, Report of Dr. Franklin's last illness, in *The Pennsylvania Gazette*, No. 3125, Wednesday, April 21, 1790, Hardwicke Papers, Vol. CCCVIII, Correspondence of W. Pollard, 1789–1812, Add. MS. 35656, fo. 90, British Library.

"a sample": Thomas Jefferson, "Autobiography," H. A. Washington (ed.), *The Writings of Thomas Jefferson*, 9 vols.; here 1:109 [afterward referred to as *Jefferson Writings*].

"I found him in bed": Thomas Jefferson–M. Le Veillard, April 5, 1790, Autographs of Modern Statesmen, Add. MS. 12099, fo. 23, British Library.

"*I hope not*": Sparks, 1:531.

"*A dying man can do nothing easy*": ibid.

"The organs of respiration": Dr. John Jones, Report of Dr. Franklin's last illness, in *The Pennsylvania Gazette*, No. 3125, Wednesday, April 21, 1790, Hardwicke Papers, Vol. CCCVIII, Correspondence of W. Pollard, 1789–1812, Add. MS. 35656, fo. 90, British Library.

he asked that it should be placed: "Anecdotes of Mary H———," *Pa. Mag. H&B*, vol. 19, no. 3 (1895), p. 409.

"he declined it": Thomas Jefferson–Dr. Benjamin Rush, Oct. 4, 1803, *Jefferson Writings*, 4:508.

"Gentlemen, Franklin is dead": M. Mirabeau–National Assembly in Paris, June 11, 1790, reported in *Gazette Nationale, ou le Moniteur universel,* June 12, 1790, quoted Brissot de Warville, p. 229.

"the gentleman to haul and draw": Francis Drake, quoted Julian S. Corbett, *Drake and the Tudor Navy,* 2 vols.; here 1:262.

BIBLIOGRAPHY

NOTE: The huge quarries containing the raw materials of Franklin's life have been worked over with ever-increasing attention since William Duane published his six-volume *The Works of Dr. Benjamin Franklin* between 1808 and 1818. William Temple Franklin quickly followed it in 1818 with the three-volume survey of his grandfather's life and work. Between 1836 and 1840 Jared Sparks edited a ten-volume selection of letters and ancillary material, and a quarter of a century later there came the first "life and times," a two-volume work by James Parton. It was followed, in 1887–89, by another ten-volume selection of works and letters by John Bigelow, and this was followed, during the first decade of the present century, by yet another ten-volume publication, Albert H. Smyth's *The Writings of Benjamin Franklin*. The result of these Herculean efforts is that many of Franklin's letters appear in two, three, four or even more different records of his life. All these efforts, which drew upon slightly differing selections from the same huge body of material, are now being overshadowed by *The Papers of Benjamin Franklin*, published by Yale University Press under the auspices of the American Philosophical Society and Yale University. Twenty-two volumes have been published, and it is already clear that to write of Franklin without paying unqualified tribute to this remarkable feat of scholarship and industry would be comparable to discussing the Bible without mentioning God.

The 1,500-page *Calendars* of the American Philosophical Society's Franklin holdings were published early in the century, while for the last few years those in the Library of Congress have been available on microfilm to scholars throughout the world. The very numerous printings of Franklin's *Autobiography* have been superseded by Max Farrand's variorum edition.

The manuscript material in the Public Record Office, Kew and London; in the British Library (formerly the British Museum Library), London; and in the Dartmouth Papers in the Staffordshire Record Office has, like the many published volumes of official Pennsylvania, been used for the numerous specialist articles in journals such as those mines of Frankliniana, the *Pennsylvania Magazine of History and Biography* and *The William and Mary Quarterly*.

The two massive collections of American diplomatic documents covering the War of Independence compiled by Wharton and by Sparks underpin the crucial role played by Franklin after 1776, as do the *American Archives*, compiled by Peter Force.

However, these are only a few among the major items which during more than two centuries have been providing ever more detailed facts about the most famous American of his age.

Adams, Charles Francis (ed.). *Familiar Letters of John Adams and his wife, Abigail Adams, during the Revolution, with a Memoir of Mrs. Adams.* New York: Hurd and Houghton; Cambridge: The Riverside Press, 1876.

———. *The Works of John Adams, Second President of the United States: with a Life of the Author, Notes and Illustrations, by his Grandson.* 10 vols. Boston: Little, Brown and Company, 1850–56.

Addison, Joseph. *The Works of Joseph Addison. See:* Hurd, Richard, D.D.

Adolphus, John. *The History of England, from the Accession to the Decease of King George The Third.* 7 vols. London: John Lee, 1840–45.

Albemarle, George Thomas, Earl of. *Memoirs of The Marquis of Rockingham and his contemporaries, with Original Letters and Documents now first published.* 2 vols. London: Richard Bentley, 1852.

Aldridge, Alfred Owen. "Benjamin Franklin as Georgia Agent." *The Georgia Review,* vol. 6, no. 2 (Summer 1952), pp. 161–73.

Almon, John. *Biographical, Literary, and Political Anecdotes, of several of The Most Eminent Persons of The Present Age, never before printed. With an Appendix consisting of Original, Explanatory, and Scarce Papers. By the Author of Anecdotes of the Late Earl of Chatham.* 3 vols. London: Printed for T. N. Longman and L. B. Seeley, 1797.

Alvord, Clarence Walworth. *The Mississippi Valley in British Politics: A Study of the Trade, Land Speculation, and Experiments in Imperialism culminating in the American Revolution.* 2 vols. Cleveland: The Arthur H. Clark Company, 1917.

———, and Carter, Clarence Edwin. *The New Regime, 1765–1767. Collections of the Illinois State Historical Library,* vol. 11 (British Series, vol. 2). Springfield: Trustees of the Illinois State Historical Library, 1916.

Amacher, Richard E. (ed.). *Franklin's Wit & Folly: The Bagatelles.* New Brunswick, N.J.: Rutgers University Press, 1953.

Bailyn, Bernard. *The Ordeal of Thomas Hutchinson.* Cambridge, Mass.: The Belknap Press of Harvard University Press, 1974.

Balch, T. (ed.). *Letters and Papers, relating chiefly to the Provincial History of Pennsyl-*

vania, with some Notices of the Writers. Philadelphia: Privately printed, Crissy and Markley, 1855.

————. *Papers in Relation to the Case of Silas Deane.* Philadelphia: Printed for the Seventy-six Society, 1855.

Becker, Carl. *The Declaration of Independence.* New York: Harcourt, Brace and Company, 1922.

Belcher, Joseph, D.D. *George Whitefield: A Biography, with Special Reference to his Labors in America.* New York: The American Tract Society, 1857.

Bell, Whitfield J., Jr. " 'All Clear Sunshine': New Letters of Franklin and Mary Stevenson Hewson." *Proceedings of the American Philosophical Society Held at Philadelphia for Promoting Useful Knowledge,* vol. 100, no. 6 (Dec. 17, 1956), pp. 521–36.

Belloc, H. *Sonnets and Verse.* London: Duckworth & Co., 1923.

Bemis, Samuel F. "British Secret Service and the French-American Alliance." *The American Historical Review,* vol. 29, no. 3 (April 1924), pp. 474–95.

————. *The Diplomacy of the American Revolution.* New York: D. Appleton-Century Co., Inc., 1935.

Benjamin, Park. *The Intellectual Rise in Electricity: A History.* London: Longmans, Green & Co., 1895.

Benjamin, S. G. W. "Unpublished Letters of Franklin to Strahan." *The Atlantic Monthly,* vol. 61, no. 363 (January 1888), pp. 21–36.

Benson, Adolph B. *Peter Kalm's Travels in North America. The English Version of 1770. Revised from the original Swedish and with a Translation of New Material from Kalm's Diary Notes.* 2 vols. New York: Wilson-Erickson, Inc., 1937.

Bigelow, John (ed.). *Autobiography of Benjamin Franklin. Edited from his Manuscript, with Notes and an Introduction.* Philadelphia: J. B. Lippincott & Co.; London: Trübner & Co., 1868.

————. *The Complete Works of Benjamin Franklin, including his private as well as official and scientific correspondence.* 10 vols. New York: G. P. Putnam's Sons, 1887–89.

————. *The Life of Benjamin Franklin, written by himself. Now first edited from original manuscripts and from his printed correspondence and other writings.* 3 vols. Philadelphia: J. B. Lippincott & Co., 1879.

Biron, H. C. *"Sir," said Dr. Johnson—. Some sayings arranged by H. C. Biron.* London: Duckworth and Co., 1911.

Blackett, P. M. S. "Scientists at the Operational level" (1941). *Document I: Operational Research. The Advancement of Science,* vol. 5, no. 17 (April 1948), pp. 26–38.

Boatner, Mark Mayo. *Cassell's Biographical Dictionary of the American War of Independence, 1763–1783.* London: Cassell, 1973.

Bowen, Katherine Drinker. *Miracle at Philadelphia: The Story of the Constitutional Convention, May to September, 1787.* London: Hamish Hamilton, 1967.

Bowring, John. *The Works of Jeremy Bentham, published under the superintendence of his Executor.* 11 vols. Edinburgh: William Tait; London: Simpkin, Marshall, & Co., 1843.

Boyd, Hugh. *Genuine Abstracts from Two Speeches of the late Earl of Chatham and His Reply to the Earl of Suffolk, with some Introductory Observations and Notes.* London: Printed for J. Dodsley in Pall-Mall, 1879.

Brissot de Warville, J. P. *New Travels in the United States of America performed in 1788. Translated from the French.* Dublin: Printed by W. Corbet for P. Byrnem, A. Grueber, W. M'Kenzie, J. Moore, W. Jones, R. M'Allister and J. Rice, 1792.

Brougham, Henry. *Works of Henry Lord Brougham.* 11 vols. Edinburgh: Adam and Charles Black, 1872.

Bruce, William Cabell. *Benjamin Franklin Self-Revealed: A Biographical and Critical Study Based Mainly on His Own Writings.* 2 vols. New York: G. P. Putnam's Sons, 1917.

Butterfield, Lyman H., et al. (eds.). *The Adams Papers.* Series I, *Diaries: Diary and Autobiography of John Adams.* 4 vols. Cambridge, Mass.: The Belknap Press of Harvard University Press, 1961.

————. *The Adams Papers.* Series II, *Adams Family Correspondence, 1761–1782.* 4 vols. Cambridge, Mass.: The Belknap Press of Harvard University Press, 1963 and 1973.

Byron, [George Gordon Noel] Lord. *The Works of Lord Byron.* 7 vols. London: Vols. 1–3, John Murray, 1819; vols. 4–7, Printed for John and Henry L. Hunt, Tavistock Street, 1819–25.

Cabanis, Pierre-Georges. *Oeuvres complètes.* 5 vols. Paris: Bossange, 1823–25.

Campbell, John, Lord. *The Lives of the Lord Chancellors and Keepers of the Great Seal of England from the Earliest Times till the Reign of King George IV.* 8 vols. London: John Murray, 1845–69.

Campbell, Thomas. *"The Pleasures of Hope," with other Poems.* Edinburgh: Printed for Mundell & Son; and for Longman & Rees and J. Wright, London, 1799.

Carlyle, Rev. Dr. Alexander. *Autobiography of the Rev. Dr. Alexander Carlyle, Minister of Inveresk, containing Memorials of the Men and Events of his Time.* Edinburgh and London: William Blackwood and Sons, 1860.

Clark, George L. *Silas Deane: A Connecticut Leader in the American Revolution.* New York: G. P. Putnam's Sons, 1913.

Clark, William Bell. *Lambert Wickes, Sea Raider and Diplomat: The Story of a Naval Captain of the Revolution.* New Haven: Yale University Press; London: Oxford University Press, 1932.

Cobbett, William, and Hansard, Thomas C. (eds.). *The Parliamentary History of England, from the Earliest Period to 1803.* 36 vols. London: Printed by T. C. Hansard for Longman, Hurst, Rees, Orme, & Brown; J. Richardson; Black, Parry, & Co.; J. Hatchard; J. Ridgway; E. Jeffery; J. Booker; J. Rodwell; Cradock & Joy; R. H. Evans; E. Budd; J. Booth; and T. C. Hansard, 1806–20.

Cochrane, J. A. *Dr. Johnson's Printer: The Life of William Strahan.* London: Routledge & Kegan Paul, 1964.

Cohen, I. Bernard. *Franklin and Newton: An Inquiry into Speculative Newtonian Experimental Science and Franklin's Work in Electricity as an Example Thereof.* Philadelphia: The American Philosophical Society, 1956.

Colden, Cadwallader. *The Letters and Papers of Cadwallader Colden, 1711–1775.* 9 vols. *Collections of The New-York Historical Society,* vols. 50–56, 67 and 68. New York: The New-York Historical Society, 1917–23, 1934–35.

Condorcet, The Marquis de. *The Life of Voltaire. To which are added Memoirs of*

Voltaire, written by himself. Translated from the French. 2 vols. London: Printed for G. G. J. and J. Robinson, Pater-noster-row, 1790.

Copeland, Thomas W., et al. (eds.). *The Correspondence of Edmund Burke.* 10 vols. Cambridge: At the University Press; Chicago: The University of Chicago Press, 1958–78.

Corbett, Julian S. *Drake and the Tudor Navy, with a History of the Rise of England as a Maritime Power.* 2 vols. London: Longmans, Green and Co., 1898.

Corner, Betsy C., and Booth, Christopher C. *Chain of Friendship: Selected Letters of Dr. John Fothergill of London, 1735–1780. With Introduction and Notes.* Cambridge, Mass.: The Belknap Press of Harvard University Press, 1971.

Crane, Verner Winslow. *Benjamin Franklin, Englishman and American.* Baltimore: The Williams & Wilkins Company, 1936.

Croÿ, Duc [Emmanuel] De. *Journal inédit. See:* Grouchy, [Emmanuel Henri] le Vte. de.

Cummings, Hubertis. *Richard Peters, Provincial Secretary and Cleric, 1704–1776.* Philadelphia: University of Pennsylvania Press, 1944.

Cunningham, Peter (ed.). *The Letters of Horace Walpole, Fourth Earl of Orford.* 9 vols. London: Richard Bentley, 1858.

Cutler, William Parker, and Cutler, Julia Perkins. *Life, Journals and Correspondence of Rev. Manasseh Cutler, LL.D., by his grandchildren.* 2 vols. Cincinnati: Robert Clarke & Co., 1888.

Dalibard, Thomas-François. *Expériences et Observations sur L'Electricité faites A Philadelphie en Amérique par M. Benjamin Franklin & communiquées dans plusieurs Lettres à M. P. Collinson, de la Société Royale de Londres. Traduites de l'Anglois. Seconde Edition. Revue, corrigée & augmentée d'un Supplément considérable du même Auteur, avec des Notes & des Expériences nouvelles.* 2 vols. Paris: Chez Durand, rue du Foin, au Griffon, 1756.

Davies, K. G. (ed.). *Documents of the American Revolution, 1770–1783.* Colonial Office Series. 21 vols. Shannon: Irish University Press and [later] Dublin: Irish Academic Press, 1972–1981.

Doniol, Henri. *Histoire de la Participation de la France à l'établissement des Etats-Unis d'Amérique: Correspondance diplomatique et documents* (Alphonse Picard, ed.). 5 vols. Paris: Imprimerie Nationale, 1885–99.

Douglass, William, M.D. *A Summary, Historical and Political, Of the first Planting, progressive Improvements, and present State of the British Settlements in North-America.* 2 vols. Boston: Rogers and Fowle, 1747 and 1749; and Daniel Fowle, 1750.

Duane, William (ed.). *Letters to Benjamin Franklin, from His Family and Friends, 1751–1790.* New York: C. Benjamin Richardson, 1859.

———. *The Works of Dr. Benjamin Franklin.* 6 vols. Philadelphia: Printed and published by William Duane, 1808–18.

Duer, William Alexander. *The Life of William Alexander, Earl of Stirling; Major General in the Army of the United States, during the Revolution, with selections from his correspondence. By his grandson.* New York: Published for the New Jersey Historical Society by Wiley & Putnam, 1847.

Dull, Jonathan R. "Franklin the Diplomat: The French Mission." *Transactions of the American Philosophical Society Held at Philadelphia for Promoting Useful knowledge,* vol. 72, pt. 1 (1982), pp. 1–72.

Eddy, George Simpson. "Account Book of Benjamin Franklin, kept by him during his First Mission to England as Provincial Agent, 1757–1762." *Pennsylvania Magazine of History and Biography*, vol. 55, no. 2 (1931), pp. 97–133.

Einstein, Lewis. *Divided Loyalties: Americans in England during the War of Independence.* London: Cobden-Sanderson, 1933.

Farrand, Max (ed.). *Benjamin Franklin's Memoirs, Parallel Text Edition. Comprising the texts of Franklin's original manuscript, the French translation by Louis Guillaume le Veillard, the French translation published by Buisson, and the version edited by William Temple Franklin, his grandson. Edited, with an introduction and explanatory notes.* Berkeley and Los Angeles: University of California Press, 1949.

———. *The Records of the Federal Convention of 1787.* Rev. ed. 4 vols. New Haven: Yale University Press; London: Oxford University Press, 1937.

Faÿ, Bernard. *Franklin: The Apostle of Modern Times.* Boston: Little, Brown & Co., 1929.

Fisher, E. T. *Report of a French Protestant Refugee, in Boston, 1687, translated from the French by E. T. Fisher.* Brooklyn, N.Y.: Printed by Munsell, Albany (Edition 125 copies), 1868.

Fitzwilliam, Charles William, Earl, and Bourke, Lt. Gen. Sir Richard, K.C.B. (eds.). *Correspondence of the Right Honourable Edmund Burke; between the Year 1744, and the Period of His Decease, in 1797.* 4 vols. London: Francis and John Rivington, 1844.

Force, Peter (ed.). *American Archives: Consisting of a Collection of Authentic Records, State Papers, Debates, and Letters and Other Notices of Publick Affairs . . . Fourth Series, March 7, 1774–July 4, 1776.* 6 vols. Fifth Series, *July 4, 1776–Sept. 3, 1783.* 3 vols. Washington, D.C.: M. St. C. Clarke and P. Force, 1837–46 and 1848–53.

Ford, Paul Leicester. *Franklin Bibliography: A List of Books Written by or Relating to Benjamin Franklin.* Brooklyn, N.Y., 1889.

———. "Letters from James Parker to Benjamin Franklin." *Proceedings of the Massachusetts Historical Society*, 2d ser., vol. 16 (May Meeting, 1902), pp. 186–232.

———. "Lord Howe's Commission to Pacify the Colonies." *The Atlantic Monthly*, 77 (June 1896): 758–62.

Ford, Worthington C. "Franklin's *New England Courant.*" *Proceedings of the Massachusetts Historical Society*, 57 (1923–24): 336–53.

Fortescue, Sir John (ed.). *The Correspondence of King George The Third, from 1760 to December 1783. Printed from the Original Papers in the Royal Archives at Windsor Castle.* 6 vols. London: Macmillan & Co., 1927–28.

Fox, R. Hingston, M.D. *Dr. John Fothergill and His Friends: Chapters in Eighteenth-Century Life.* London: Macmillan and Co., 1919.

Franklin, Benjamin.

AUTOBIOGRAPHY: Numerous editions of Franklin's autobiography have been published. For those consulted, *see:* Bigelow, John (ed.), *Autobiography of Benjamin Franklin,* and Farrand, Max (ed.), *Benjamin Franklin's Memoirs.*

WORKS: *Experiments and Observations on Electricity, made at Philadelphia in America, by Mr. Benjamin Franklin, and communicated in several Letters to Mr. P. Collinson,* of London, F.R.S. London: Printed and sold by E. Cave, at St. John's Gate, 1751.

Subsequent editions included additional material.

COLLECTED WORKS: *See:* Bigelow, John (ed.), *The Complete Works of Benjamin Franklin;* Duane, William (ed.), *The Works of Dr. Benjamin Franklin;* Franklin, William Temple, *Memoirs of the Life and Writings of Benjamin Franklin;* Labaree, Leonard W., and Willcox, William B. et al. (eds.), *The Papers of Benjamin Franklin;* Smyth, Albert H. (ed.), *The Writings of Benjamin Franklin;* Sparks, Jared (ed.), *The Works of Benjamin Franklin;* and Vaughan, Benjamin (ed.), *The Life and Works of Benjamin Franklin* and *Political, Miscellaneous and Philosophical Pieces.*

LETTERS: *See:* Duane, William (ed.), *Letters to Benjamin Franklin . . . 1751–1790;* Roelker, William Greene (ed.), *Benjamin Franklin and Catharine Ray Greene;* Van Doren, Carl (ed.), *Letters and Papers of Benjamin Franklin and Richard Jackson, 1753–1785* and *The Letters of Benjamin Franklin & Jane Mecom.*

See also: Franklin, Benjamin, *Experiments and Observations,* describing his work on electricity in letters to Peter Collinson (*see* WORKS, *above*).

BIOGRAPHIES: For some of the numerous biographies of Benjamin Franklin describing part, or all, of his life, *see:* Bigelow, John (ed.), *The Life of Benjamin Franklin;* Faÿ, Bernard, *Franklin, the Apostle of Modern Times;* Hawke, David Freeman, *Franklin;* Parton, James, *Life and Times of Benjamin Franklin;* Russell, Phillips, *Benjamin Franklin: The First Civilised American;* Schoenbrun, David, *Triumph in Paris: The Exploits of Benjamin Franklin;* Tourtellot, Arthur Bernon, *Benjamin Franklin: The Shaping of Genius, The Boston Years;* and Van Doren, Carl, *Benjamin Franklin.*

INDIVIDUAL WRITINGS: A selection of the more significant of Franklin's writings includes the following:

A Dissertation on Liberty and Necessity, Pleasure and Pain. London, Printed in the Year 1725. (From the Ashbee Collection, British Library.)

A Modest Enquiry into the Nature and Necessity of a Paper Currency, April 3, 1729. In Leonard W. Labaree (ed.), *The Papers of Benjamin Franklin,* 1:141–57.

Proposals relating to the Education of Youth in Pensilvania By Benjamin Franklin. Facsimile reprint (of original edition of 1749) with an introduction by William Pepper. Philadelphia: University of Pennsylvania, 1931.

Advice on to a Young Man on the Choice of a Mistress. In Paul McPharlin (ed.), *Benjamin Franklin, Satires & Bagatelles,* pp. 32–34.

A Letter to the Royal Academy at Brussels. In Paul McPharlin (ed.), *Benjamin Franklin, Satires & Bagatelles,* pp. 37–39.

Plain Truth: or, Serious Considerations On the Present State of the City of Philadelphia, and Province of Pennsylvania, By a Tradesman of Philadelphia. [Philadelphia:] Printed [by B. Franklin] in the year 1747.

The Way to Wealth as clearly shewn in the preface of an old Pennsylvanian Almanack, intitled, Poor Richard Improved, 1758. Philadelphia: Printed and Sold by B. Franklin and D. Hall, 1758.

The Interest of Great Britain Considered, With Regard to her Colonies, And the Acquisition of Canada and Guadaloupe. To which are added, Observations concerning the Increase of Mankind, Peopling of Countries, &c. London: Printed for T. Becket at Tully's Head, near Surry Street in the Strand, 1760.

Hints for Conversation upon the Subject of Terms that might probably produce a Durable Union between Britain and the Colonies. In Jared Sparks (ed.), *The Works of Benjamin Franklin*, 5:12–14.

Poor Richard's Almanack, 1733–1758. Philadelphia: Printed and Sold by B. Franklin; [and later] by B. Franklin, and D. Hall, 1733–1758.

A Treaty held with the Ohio Indians, at Carlisle, In October, 1753. Philadelphia: Printed and Sold by B. Franklin and D. Hall, 1753.

A Narrative of the Late Massacres, in Lancaster County, of a Number of Indians, Friends of this Province, By Persons Unknown, With some Observations on the same. [Philadelphia:] Printed [by Anthony Armbruster] in the year 1764.

Cool Thoughts on the Present Situation of Our Public Affairs. In a Letter to a Friend in the Country. Philadelphia: Printed by W. Dunlap, 1764.

BIBLIOGRAPHY: *See:* Ford, Paul Leicester, *Franklin Bibliography.*

Franklin, William Temple. *Memoirs of the Life and Writings of Benjamin Franklin, LL.D., F.R.S., &c., Minister Plenipotentiary from the United States of America, at the Court of France, and for the Treaty of Peace and Independence with Great Britain, &c. &c. Written by himself to a late period, and continued to the time of his death, By his Grandson: William Temple Franklin. Now first published from the Original MSS, comprising the Private Correspondence and Public Negotiations of Dr. Franklin and a Selection from his Political, Philosophical, and Miscellaneous Works.* 3 vols. London: Printed for Henry Colburn, British and Foreign Public Library, Conduit Street, 1818. 4to edition and 8vo edition.

Freeman, Douglas Southall. *George Washington, a Biography.* 7 vols. New York: Charles Scribner's Sons, 1948–57.

Freke, John. *An Essay to shew the Cause of Electricity, and Why Some Things are Non-Electricable, In which is also Consider'd its Influence in the Blasts on Human Bodies, in the Blights on Trees, in the Damps in Mines; and as it may affect the Sensitive Plant &c. In a Letter to William Watson, F.R.S.* London: Printed for W. Irmys, in Paternoster Row, 1746.

Gilfillan, Rev. George (ed.). *Thomson's Poetical Works, With Life, Critical Dissertation and Explanatory Notes.* Edinburgh: James Nicol; London: James Nisbet; Dublin: W. Robertson, 1853.

Gillespie, Mrs. E. D. *A Book of Remembrance.* 3d ed. Philadelphia: J.B. Lippincott Company, 1901.

Gleason, J. Philip. "A Scurrilous Colonial Election and Franklin's Reputation." *The William and Mary Quarterly*, 3d ser., vol. 18, no. 1 (January 1961), pp. 68–84.

Greene, George Washington. *The Life of Nathanael Greene, Major-General in the Army of the Revolution.* 3 vols. New York: G. P. Putnam and Son, 1867–71.

Grimm, [Friedrich Melchior] Baron von. *Correspondance littéraire, philosophique et critique par Grimm, Diderot, Raynal, Meister, etc. revue sur les textes originaux.* 16 vols. Paris: Garnier frères, 1877–82.

Grouchy, [Emmanuel Henri] le Vte. de, and Cottin, Paul. *Journal inédit du Duc [Emmanuel] De Croÿ, 1718–1784, Publié d'après le manuscrit autographe conservé à la Bibliothèque de l'Institut, avec introduction, notes et index.* 4 vols. Paris: Ernest Flammarion, 1906–7.

Gruber, Ira D. *The Howe Brothers and the American Revolution*. Chapel Hill: University of North Carolina Press, 1974.

Guilday, Peter. *The Life and Times of John Carroll, Archbishop of Baltimore (1735–1815)*. New York: The Encyclopedia Press, 1922.

Hale, Edward E., and Hale, Edward E., Jr. *Franklin in France*. 2 vols. Boston: Roberts Brothers, 1887–88.

Hanna, William S. *Benjamin Franklin and Pennsylvania Politics*. Stanford, Cal.: Stanford University Press, 1964.

Hauksbee, F[rancis K.], F.R.S. *Physico-Mechanical Experiments on Various Subjects, containing An Account of Several Surprizing* Phenomena *touching Light and Electricity, Producible on the* Attrition *of Bodies. With many other Remarkable appearances, not before observ'd. Together with the Explanations of all the Machines, (the figures of which are Curiously Engrav'd on Copper) and other Apparatus us'd in making the Experiments*. London: Printed by R. Brugis, for the Author; and Sold only at his House in Wine-Office-Court in Fleet-Street, 1709.

Hawke, David Freeman. *Franklin*. New York: Harper & Row, 1976.

———. *In the Midst of a Revolution*. Philadelphia: University of Pennsylvania Press, 1961.

Hays, I. Minis (ed.). *Calendar of the Papers of Benjamin Franklin in the Library of the American Philosophical Society*. 5 vols. Philadelphia: American Philosophical Society, 1908.

Hazard, Samuel, et al. (eds.). *Pennsylvania Archives. Selected and Arranged from Original Documents in the Office of the Secretary of the Commonwealth, conformably to Acts of the General Assembly, February 15, 1851, & March 1, 1852. Commencing 1644*. 9 series. Philadelphia: Printed by Joseph Severns & Co., 1852; and Harrisburg, 1852–1935.

Heathcote, N. H. de V. "Franklin's Introduction to Electricity," *Isis*, vol. 46, pt. 1, no. 143 (March 1955), pp. 29–35.

Heilbron, John L. *Electricity in the 17th and 18th Centuries: A Study of Early Modern Physics*. Berkeley and Los Angeles: University of California Press, 1979.

———. "Franklin's Physics." *Physics Today*, vol. 29, no. 7 (July 1976), pp. 32–37.

Hewins, W. A. S. (ed.). *The Whitefoord Papers, being the Correspondence and other Manuscripts of Colonel Charles Whitefoord and Caleb Whitefoord from 1739 to 1810, edited with introduction and Notes*. Oxford: At the Clarendon Press, 1898.

Historical Manuscripts Commission, The. *The Manuscripts of the Earl of Dartmouth*. Dartmouth I: *1660–1843*, Eleventh Report, Appendix V; Dartmouth II: *American Papers, 1676–1839*, Fourteenth Report, Appendix X; Dartmouth III: *1559–1824*, Fifteenth Report, Appendix I. 3 vols. London: Printed for Her Majesty's Stationery Office by Eyre & Spottiswoode, 1887–96.

Hornberger, Theodore. *Benjamin Franklin*. Minneapolis: University of Minnesota Press, 1962.

Hosack, David. "A Biographical Memoir of Hugh Williamson, M.D., LL.D., delivered Nov. 1, 1819," *Collections of The New-York Historical Society*, vol. 3 *(For the Year 1821)*, pp. 125–79. New York: E. Bliss and E. White, 1821.

Humboldt, Alexander von. *Cosmos: Sketch of a Physical Description of the Universe. Translated under the Superintendence of Lieut-Col. Edward Sabine, R.A. For. Sec.*

R.S. 2 vols. London: Printed for Longman, Brown, Green, and Longmans, and John Murray, 1846 and 1848.

Hurd, Richard, D.D. *The Works of Joseph Addison, with Notes.* 6 vols. London: George Bell & Sons, 1901.

Hutchinson, Peter Orlando (ed.). *The Diary and Letters of His Excellency Thomas Hutchinson, Esq.* 2 vols. London: Sampson Low, Marston, Searle & Rivington, 1883 and 1886.

Hutchinson, Thomas. *The History of the Colony and Province of Massachusetts Bay. See:* Mayo, Lawrence S. (ed.).

Hutson, James H. "Benjamin Franklin and Pennsylvania Politics, 1751–1755, A Reappraisal." *Pennsylvania Magazine of History and Biography,* 93 (1969): 303–71.

———. *Pennsylvania Politics, 1746–1770: The Movement for Royal Government and Its Consequences.* Princeton: Princeton University Press, 1972.

Idzerda, Stanley J., et al. (eds.). *Lafayette in the Age of the American Revolution: Selected Letters and Papers, 1776–1790.* 4 vols. Ithaca, N.Y.: Cornell University Press, 1977–81.

James, Norman G. Brett-. *The Life of Peter Collinson, F.R.S., F.S.A.* London: Edgar G. Dunstan & Co., n.d. [1926].

Jefferson, Thomas. *The Writings of Thomas Jefferson. See:* Washington, H. A. (ed.).

Johnson, Allen, et al. (eds.). *Dictionary of American Biography.* 20 vols. London: Oxford University Press; New York: Charles Scribner's Sons, 1928–37.

Johnson, Samuel. *Taxation no Tyranny: An Answer to the Resolutions and Address of the American Congress, 1775.* In Sir John Hawkins (ed.), *The Works of Samuel Johnson.* 11 vols. London: Printed for J. Buckland et al., 1787.

Jones, R. V. "Benjamin Franklin." *Notes and Records of The Royal Society, London,* vol. 31, no. 2 (January 1977), pp. 201–25.

Josselyn, John, Gent. *An Account of two Voyages to New-England.* London: Printed for Giles Widdows, at the Green Dragon in St. Paul's Church-yard, 1674.

Kammen, Michael G. *A Rope of Sand: The Colonial Agents, British Politics, and the American Revolution.* Ithaca, N.Y.: Cornell University Press, 1968.

Kennedy, Archibald. *The Importance of Gaining and Preserving the Friendship of the Indians to the British Interest, considered.* London: Printed for E. Cave jun. at St. John's Gate, 1752.

Klingelhofer, Herbert E. "Matthew Ridley's Diary During the Peace Negotiations of 1782." *The William and Mary Quarterly,* vol. 20, 3d ser. (1963), pp. 95–133.

Labaree, Leonard W., et al. (eds.). *The Papers of Benjamin Franklin,* vols. 1–14. New Haven: Yale University Press, 1959–70. *See also:* Willcox, William B., et al. (eds.).

Lee, Richard Henry. *Life of Arthur Lee . . . with his correspondence, etc.* 2 vols. Boston: Wells and Lilly, 1829.

Lemay, J. A. Leo. *Ebenezer Kinnersley: Franklin's Friend.* Philadelphia: University of Pennsylvania Press, 1964.

———. "Franklin and the 'Autobiography': An Essay on Recent Scholarship." *Eighteenth-Century Studies: A Journal of Literature and the Arts,* vol. 1, no. 2 (December 1967), pp. 185–211.

Lémontey, Pierre Edouard. *Mémoires (inédits) de L'Abbé Morellet suivis de sa Corre-*

spondance avec M. le Comte R***, Ministre des Finances à Naples, précédés d'un Eloge Historique de l'Abbé Morellet. 2 vols. Paris: Baudouin Frères, Libraires Editeurs, 1823.

Leonard, Sister Joan de Lourdes, C.S.J. "The Organization and Procedure of the Pennsylvania Assembly, 1682–1776." *Pennsylvania Magazine of History and Biography,* vol. 72, no. 3 (July 1948), pp. 215–39.

Lescarbot, Marc. *Histoire de la Nouvelle France.* 2d ed. Paris: Chez Jean Millot, devant S. Barthelemi aux trois Coronnes: Et en sa boutique sur les degrez de la grand salle du Palais, 1611.

Lescure, M. [Mathurin François Adolphe] de. *Correspondance secrète inédite sur Louis XVI, Marie-Antoinette, la cour, et la ville de 1777 à 1792.* 2 vols. Paris: Henri Plon, Imprimeur-Editeur, 1866.

Lippincott, Horace Mather. *Early Philadelphia: Its People, Life and Progress.* Philadelphia: J. B. Lippincott Company, 1917.

Lopez, Claude-Anne. *Mon Cher Papa: Franklin and the Ladies of Paris.* New Haven: Yale University Press, 1966.

McMaster, John Bach. *Benjamin Franklin as a Man of Letters.* Boston: Houghton, Mifflin and Company, 1887.

———. "A Short Biography of Benjamin Franklin, read to the American Philosophical Society in commemoration of the One Hundredth Anniversary of the Decease of Benjamin Franklin, April 17, 1890." *Proceedings of the American Philosophical Society,* vol. 28, no. 133 (April 17, 1890), pp. 166–72.

McPharlin, Paul (ed.). *Benjamin Franklin: Satires & Bagatelles.* Detroit: Fine Book Circle, 1937.

Mahon, Lord. *History of England from the Peace of Utrecht to the Peace of Versailles, 1713–1783.* 7 vols. London: John Murray, 1836–54.

Mathews, Mrs. L. K. "Benjamin Franklin's Plans for a Colonial Union, 1750–1775." *The American Political Science Review,* vol. 8, no. 3 (August 1914), pp. 393–412.

Maudit, Israel. *The Letters of Governor Hutchinson, and Lieut. Governor Oliver, &c. Printed at Boston. And Remarks Thereon. With the Assembly's Address, and the Proceedings of the Lords Committee of Council. Together with The Substance of Mr. Wedderburn's Speech relating to those Letters. And the Report of the Lords Committee to his Majesty in Council.* 2d ed. London: Printed for J. Wilkie, at Number 71, in St. Paul's Church-yard, 1774.

Mayo, Lawrence S. (ed.). Thomas Hutchinson, *The History of the Colony and Province of Massachusetts Bay. Edited from the author's own copies of Vols. I and II and his manuscript copy of Vol. III, with a memoir and additional notes.* Cambridge, Mass.: Harvard University Press, 1936.

Montagu, Lady Mary Wortley. *The Letters and Works of Lady Mary Wortley Montagu edited by her great-grandson Lord Wharncliffe.* Standard Edition in 2 vols. London: Swan Sonnenschein & Co.; New York: Macmillan & Co., 1893.

Morison, Samuel Eliot. *John Paul Jones: A Sailor's Biography.* Boston: Little, Brown and Company, 1959.

Morton, Brian N. (ed.). *Beaumarchais Correspondance.* 4 vols. Paris: Editions A.-G. Nizet, 1969–78.

Mottelay, Paul Fleury. *Bibliographical History of Electricity & Magnetism chronologically arranged.* London: Charles Griffin & Company Limited, 1922.

Munro, James, and Grant, W. L. (eds.). *Acts of the Privy Council of England, Colonial Series, 1613–1783.* 6 vols. London: H.M.S.O., 1908–12.

Neal, Daniel. *The History of New-England containing an Impartial Account of the Civil and Ecclesiastical Affairs of the Country to the Year of our Lord, 1700, To which is added the Present State of New-England, with a New and Accurate Map of the Country, and an Appendix Containing their Present Charter, their Ecclesiastical Discipline, and their Municipal-Laws.* 2 vols. London: Printed for J. Clark, at the Bible and Crown, in the Poultry, R. Ford, at the Angel in the Poultry, and R. Crutten-den, at the Bible and Three Crowns in Cheapside, 1720.

Nolan, J. Bennett. *Benjamin Franklin in Scotland and Ireland, 1759 and 1771.* Philadelphia: University of Pennsylvania Press; London: Oxford University Press, 1938.

———. "A British Editor Reports the American Revolution, with Curious Side Lights on Benjamin Franklin." *Pennsylvania Magazine of History and Biography,* vol. 80, no. 1 (January 1956), pp. 92–112.

———. *General Benjamin Franklin: The Military Career of a Philosopher.* Philadelphia: University of Pennsylvania Press; London: Oxford University Press, 1936.

Nol[l]et, L'Abbé [Jean Antoine]. *Leçons de Physique expérimentale.* 5 vols. Amsterdam and Leipzig: Chez Arkste's & Merkus, 1754.

———. *Recherches sur les Causes Particulières des Phénomènes Electriques, et sur les effets nuisibles ou avantageux qu'on peut en attendre.* Paris: Chez les Frères Guerin, 1749.

Norton, Charles E. "The Price Letters, 1767–1790." *Proceedings of Massachusetts Historical Society,* 2d ser., vol. 17 (May 1903), pp. 262–377.

O'Callaghan, E. B. (ed.). *Documents relative to the Colonial History of the State of New York; procured in Holland, England and France, by John Romeyn Brodhead, Esq., Agent, under and by virtue of an act of the Legislature, entitled "An Act to Appoint an Agent to procure and transcribe Documents in Europe relative to the Colonial History of the State, passed May 2, 1839."* 14 vols. Albany: Weed, Parsons and Company, Printers, 1856–83.

Olson, Alison Gilbert. "The British Government and Colonial Union." *The William and Mary Quarterly,* 3d ser., vol. 17, no. 1 (January 1960), pp. 22–34.

Oswald, John Clyde. *Benjamin Franklin, Printer.* New York: Doubleday, Page and Company for The Associated Advertising Clubs of the World, 1917.

Pargellis, Stanley McCrory. *Lord Loudoun in North America.* New Haven: Yale University Press; London: Oxford University Press, 1933.

Parton, James. *Life and Times of Benjamin Franklin.* 2 vols. New York: Mason Brothers; Boston: Mason & Hamlin; Philadelphia: J. B. Lippincott & Co.; Chicago: S. C. Griggs & Co.; London: Trübner & Co., 1864.

Pennsylvania Archives. See: Hazard, Samuel, et al. (eds.).

Pennsylvania Gazette, The, 1728–1789. A Reprint Edition, in Cooperation with the Historical Society of Pennsylvania. 25 vols. Philadelphia: Microsurance, Inc., 1968.

Pennsylvania Historical & Museum Commission—Division of Public Records. *Minutes of the Provincial Council of Pennsylvania, from the Organization to the Termination of the Proprietary Government.* 16 vols. Harrisburg: Published by the State, 1851–53.

Pennsylvania, Senate of. *Votes and Proceedings of the House of Representatives of the Province of Pennsylvania*. Vol. 4, *Beginning 15 Oct. 1744*. Vol. 5, *Beginning 14 Oct. 1758*. Philadelphia: Printed and sold by Henry Miller in Race-St., 1774 and 1775.

Pepper, William. *The Medical Side of Benjamin Franklin*. Philadelphia: William J. Campbell, 1911.

Peyton, J. L. *Rambling Reminiscences of a Residence Abroad: England—Guernsey*. Staunton, Va.: S. M. Yost & Son, 1888.

Pitt, William, Earl of Chatham. *Correspondence of William Pitt*. See: Taylor, William Stanhope, and Pringle, Capt. John Henry (eds.).

Plummer, Wilbur C. "Consumer Credit in Colonial Philadelphia." *Pennsylvania Magazine of History and Biography*, vol. 66, no. 4 (October 1942), pp. 385–409.

Portalis, Baron Roger, and Béraldi, Henri. *Les Graveurs de dix-huitième siècle*. 3 vols. Paris: D. Morgand et C. Fatout, 1880–82.

Pound, Arthur. *The Penns of Pennsylvania and England*. New York: The Macmillan Company, 1932.

Pownall, Charles A. W. *Thomas Pownall, M.P., F.R.S., Governor of Massachusetts Bay, Author of The Letters of Junius: with a Supplement comparing the Colonies of Kings George III and Edward VII*. London: Henry Stevens, Son & Stiles, 1908.

Pownall, Thomas. *The Administration of the British Colonies*. 5th ed. 2 vols. London: Printed for J. Walter at Homer's Head, Charing-Cross, 1774.

Priestley, Joseph, LL.D., F.R.S. *The History and Present State of Electricity, with Original Experiments*. London: Printed for J. Dodsley in Pall-Mall, J. Johnson and B. Davenport in Pater-noster Row, and T. Cadell (Successor to Mr. Millar) in the Strand, 1767.

———. *Memoirs of Dr. Joseph Priestley, to the Year 1795, written by himself, with a continuation, to the time of his Decease, by his son, Joseph Priestley*. London: Printed for J. Johnson, 1806.

Quincy, Josiah. *Memoir of the Life of Josiah Quincy, Jun., of Massachusetts, by his son, Josiah Quincy*. Boston: Cummings, Hilliard & Company, 1825.

Reed, William B. *Life and Correspondence of Joseph Reed by his Grandson*. 2 vols. Philadelphia: Lindsay and Blakiston, 1847.

Riley, Edward M. "Franklin's Home." *Transactions of the American Philosophical Society*, n.s., vol 43, pt. 1 (1953), pp. 148–60.

Roach, Hannah Benner. "Benjamin Franklin Slept Here." *Pennsylvania Magazine of History and Biography*, 84 (1960): 127–74.

Robertson, C. Grant. *England Under the Hanoverians*. London: Methuen & Co. Ltd., 1911.

Roelker, William Greene (ed.). *Benjamin Franklin and Catharine Ray Greene: Their Correspondence, 1755–1790*. Philadelphia: American Philosophical Society, 1949.

Rosengarten, J. G. "Franklin in Germany." *Lippincott's Monthly Magazine*, 71 (January 1903): 128–34.

Russell, Phillips. *Benjamin Franklin: The First Civilised American*. London: Ernest Benn, 1927.

Rutt, John Towill. *Life and Correspondence of Joseph Priestley, LL.D., F.R.S.* 2 vols. London: R. Hunter, 1831–32.

Schoenbrun, David. *Triumph in Paris: The Exploits of Benjamin Franklin.* New York: Harper & Row, 1976.

Seed, Geoffrey. "A British Spy in Philadelphia, 1775–1777." *Pennsylvania Magazine of History and Biography,* vol. 85, no. 1 (January 1961), pp. 3–37.

Ségur, M. [Louis Philippe] le Comte de. *Mémoires ou Souvenirs et Anecdotes.* 3 vols. Paris: Alexis Eymery, Libraire-Editeur, 1824–26.

Seitz, Don Carlos. *Paul Jones, His Exploits in English Seas During 1778–1780. Contemporary accounts collected from English newspapers, with a complete bibliography.* New York: E. P. Dutton & Co., 1917.

Sellers, Charles Coleman. *Benjamin Franklin in Portraiture.* New Haven: Yale University Press, 1962.

———. *Patience Wright: American Artist and Spy in George III's London.* Middletown, Conn.: Wesleyan University Press, 1976.

Shepherd, William Robert. *History of Proprietary Government in Pennsylvania.* New York: Columbia University Press, 1896.

Shurtleff, Nathaniel B. *A Topographical and Historical Description of Boston.* Boston: A. Williams & Co., 1871.

Simon, Grant Miles. "Houses and Early Life in Philadelphia." *Transactions of the American Philosophical Society,* n.s., 43 (1953): 280–88.

Smith, Charles John. *Historical and Literary Curiosities, consisting of Fac-similes of Original Documents; Scenes of Remarkable Events and Interesting Localities; and the Birth-places, Residences, Portraits and Monuments, of Eminent Literary Characters; with a Variety of Reliques and Antiquities connected with the same subjects. Selected and engraved by the late C. J. Smith, F.S.A.* London: Henry G. Bohn, Covent Garden, 1840.

Smith, William. "Account of the College and Academy of Philadelphia." *The American Magazine and Monthly Chronicle for the British Colonies,* vol. 1 (October 1757–October 1758) and Supplement (October 1758), pp. 630–40.

Smyth, Albert H. "Franklin's Social Life in France, with hitherto unpublished Letters." *Putnam's Monthly and The Critic: A Magazine of Literature, Art & Life,* vol. 1, no. 1 (October 1906), pp. 30–41; no. 2 (November 1906), pp. 167–73; no. 3 (December 1906), pp. 310–16; and no. 4 (January 1907), pp. 431–38.

——— (ed.). *The Writings of Benjamin Franklin. Collected and edited with a life and introduction.* 10 vols. New York: The Macmillan Co., 1905–7.

Snow, C. P. *Science and Government.* London: Oxford University Press, 1961.

"Some Letters of Franklin's Correspondents." *Pennyslvania Magazine of History and Biography,* vol. 27, no. 2 (1903), pp. 162–75.

Sparks, Jared. *The Diplomatic Correspondence of the American Revolution.* 12 vols. Boston: N. Hale and Gray & Bowen; New York: G. & C. & H. Carvill, 1829–30.

——— (ed.). *The Works of Benjamin Franklin, containing several political and historical tracts not included in any former edition . . . with notes and a life of the author.* 10 vols. Boston: Hilliard Gray and Company, 1836–40; Chicago: Townsend, MacCoun, 1882; and London: B. F. Stevens, 1882.

Spiller, Robert E. Review of *Benjamin Franklin,* by Carl Van Doren. *Pennsylvania Magazine of History and Biography,* vol. 63, no. 2 (April 1939), pp. 228–37.

Stephen, Leslie, et al. (eds.). *Dictionary of National Biography.* 63 vols. London: Smith, Elder, & Co., 1885–1900.

Steuart, A. Francis (ed.). *The Last Journals of Horace Walpole during the Reign of George III from 1771–1783, with notes by Dr. Doran, and with an introduction.* 2 vols. London: John Lane, The Bodley Head; New York: John Lane Company, 1910.

Stevens, Benjamin Franklin (ed.). *Facsimiles of Manuscripts in European Archives Relating to America, 1773–1783, with Descriptions, Editorial Notes, Collations, References, and Translations.* 25 vols. London: Issued only to Subscribers at 4, Trafalgar Square, Charing Cross, London, 1889–98.

Stillé, Charles J. "The Marquis de La Fayette in the American Revolution." *Pennsylvania Magazine of History and Biography*, vol. 19, no. 1 (1895), pp. 1–21.

Strahan, William. "Correspondence between William Strahan and David Hall, 1763–1777." *Pennsylvania Magazine of History and Biography*, vol. 10, nos. 1, 2, 3 and 4 (1886), pp. 86–99, 217–32, 322–33, 461–73; and vol. 11, nos. 1, 2, 3 and 4 (1887), pp. 98–111, 223–34, 346–57, 482–90.

Taylor, William Stanhope, and Pringle, Capt. John Henry (eds.). *Correspondence of William Pitt, Earl of Chatham.* 4 vols. London: John Murray, 1838–40.

Thomas, Isaiah, LL.D. *The History of Printing in America, with a Biography of Printers, and an Account of Newspapers.* 2 vols. 2d ed. Albany: Joel Munsell, Printer, 1874.

Thomson, James. *Thomson's Poetical Works. See:* Gilfillan, Rev. George (ed.).

Tourtellot, Arthur Bernon. *Benjamin Franklin: The Shaping of Genius, the Boston Years.* Garden City, N.Y.: Doubleday & Co., 1977.

Tower, Charlemagne. *The Marquis de La Fayette in the American Revolution, with some account of the Attitude of France toward the War of Independence.* 2 vols. Philadelphia: J. B. Lippincott Company, 1895.

Trevelyan, The Rt. Hon. Sir George Otto. *The American Revolution.* 4 parts in 6 vols. London: Longmans, Green, and Co., 1899–1914.

Tyne, Claude H. Van X. *The War of Independence: American Phase.* London: Constable & Co., 1929.

Van Doren, Carl. *Benjamin Franklin.* New York: The Viking Press, 1938.

────── (ed.). *Letters and Papers of Benjamin Franklin and Richard Jackson, 1753–1785.* Philadelphia: The American Philosophical Society, 1947.

──────. *The Letters of Benjamin Franklin & Jane Mecom, with an Introduction.* Princeton: Princeton University Press, 1950.

Vaughan, Benjamin (ed.). *The Life and Works of Benjamin Franklin.* Bungay: Printed and Published by Brightly and Childs [c. 1800].

──────. *Political, Miscellaneous, and Philosophical Pieces . . . Written by Benj. Franklin, LL.D. and F.R.S., now first collected with explanatory plates, Notes, And an Index to the Whole.* London: Printed for J. Johnson, No. 72, St. Paul's Church-Yard, 1779.

Vigée-Le Brun, Mme. Elisabeth Louise. *The Memoirs of Mme. Elisabeth Louise Vigée-Le Brun, 1755–1789.* Translated by Gerard Shelley. London: John Hamilton Ltd., n.d. [1926].

von Haller, Albrecht. "An historical account of the wonderful discoveries made in Germany, &c. concerning Electricity." *The Gentleman's Magazine & Historical Chronicle*, 15 (April 1745): 193–97.

Walker, Lewis Burd. *The Burd Papers: Extracts from Chief Justice William Allen's*

Letter Book, Together with an Appendix containing Pamphlets in the Controversy with Franklin. 3 vols. Pottsville, Pa.: Standard Publishing Company, 1897–99.

Wallace, Paul A. W. *Conrad Weiser, 1696–1760: Friend of Colonist and Mohawk*. Philadelphia: University of Pennsylvania Press; London: Oxford University Press, 1945.

Walpole, Horace. *The Last Journals of Horace Walpole*. See: Steuart, A. Francis (ed.).

———. *Memoirs of the Reign of King George the Third. Now First published from the Original MSS, Edited, with Notes, By Sir Denis Le Marchant, Bart*. 4 vols. London: Richard Bentley, 1845.

Ward, John William. "Who Was Benjamin Franklin?" *The American Scholar*, vol. 32, no. 4 (Autumn 1963), pp. 541–53.

Washington, H. A. (ed.). *The Writings of Thomas Jefferson, being his Autobiography, Correspondence, Reports, Messages, Addresses, and Other Writings, Official and Private*. 9 vols. Washington, D.C.: Published by order of the Joint Committee of Congress on the Library from the Original MS. in the Department of State, Taylor & Maury, 1853–54.

Watson, John F. *Annals of Philadelphia and Pennsylvania, in the Olden Time; being a collection of Memoirs, Anecdotes, and Incidents of the City and its Inhabitants, and of the Earliest Settlements of the Inland Part of Pennsylvania, from The Days of the Founders, intended to preserve the recollections of olden time, and to exhibit society in its changes of manners and customs, and the city and country in their local changes and improvements. Embellished with engravings by T. H. Mumford*. 2 vols. Philadelphia: Printed and published for the author, and for sale by John Penington and Uriah Hunt; New York: Baker & Crane, 1844.

Watson, Winslow C. (ed.). *Men and Times of the Revolution; or Memoirs of Elkanah Watson*. New York: Dana and Company, 1856.

Wecter, Dixon. *The Hero in America: A Chronicle of Hero-Worship*. Ann Arbor: Ann Arbor Paperbacks, The University of Michigan, 1963.

Wedgwood, Josiah. *Letters of Josiah Wedgwood*. 2 vols., *1762–1772* and *1772–1780*, for private circulation. London: Printed by The Women's Prtg Soc. Ltd, 1903.

Weld, Charles Richard. *A History of the Royal Society, with Memoirs of the Presidents, Compiled from Authentic Documents*. 2 vols. London: John W. Parker, West Strand, 1848.

Wharton, Francis (ed.). *The Revolutionary Diplomatic Correspondence of the United States*. 6 vols. Washington, D.C.: Government Printing Office, 1889.

Willcox, William B., et al. (eds.). *The Papers of Benjamin Franklin*, vols. 15–22 to date. New Haven: Yale University Press, 1971– [in progress]. *See also:* Labaree, Leonard W., et al. (eds.).

Willis, The Hon. William. "Doctor Franklin, Charles Thompson and Mrs. Logan." *The Historical Magazine, and Notes and Queries concerning the Antiquities, History and Biography of America*, new (2d) ser., vol. 4, no. 6 (December 1868), pp. 280–82.

Wirt, William. *Sketches of the Life and Character of Patrick Henry*. Philadelphia: James Webster, 1818.

Wraxall, Sir Nathaniel William, Bart. *Historical Memoirs of my own time from 1772 to 1784*. 2 vols. London: T. Cordell & W. Davies, 1815.

Wright, Esmond. *Benjamin Franklin and American Independence.* London: The English Universities Press Ltd., 1966.

Wykoff, George S. (ed.). "Peter Collinson's Letter concerning Franklin's 'Vindication': Notes and Documents—II." *Pennsylvania Magazine of History and Biography,* vol. 66, no. 1 (January 1942), pp. 99–105.

INDEX

ABOUT THE AUTHOR

Born in London, the late Ronald W. Clark was a World War II war correspondent; he landed in France on D-Day and later covered the Nuremberg trials. His other books include widely acclaimed biographies of Einstein, Freud, Darwin, Bertrand Russell, the Huxleys, and Lenin.

Other DACAPO titles of interest

EINSTEIN
His Life and Times
Philipp Frank
354 pp., 17 photos
80358-5 $12.95

LOUIS PASTEUR
Free Lance of Science
René Dubos
462 pp., 25 photos
80262-7 $11.95

MEMOIRS OF
HARRY S. TRUMAN
Volume I. 1945: Year of Decisions
608 pp.
80266-X $14.95

MEMOIRS OF
HARRY S. TRUMAN
Volume II. 1946-1952:
Years of Trial and Hope
608 pp.
80297-X $14.95

MICHAEL FARADAY
L. Pearce Williams
531 pp., 32 pp. of photos
80299-6 $13.95

REBELS AND REDCOATS
The American Revolution
Through the Eyes of Those
Who Fought and Lived It
George F. Scheer and
Hugh F. Rankin
572 pp., 19 illus.
80307-0 $14.95

ROBERT H. GODDARD
Pioneer of Space Research
Milton Lehman
New preface by Frederick Durant
488 pp., 40 pp. of photos
80331-3 $12.95

THOMAS A. EDISON
A Streak of Luck
Robert Conot
608 pp., 35 photos
80261-9 $13.95

A TRANSACTION OF FREE MEN
The Birth and Course of the
Declaration of Independence
New introduction by the author
David Freeman Hawke
296 pp., 11 illus.
80352-6 $12.95

Available at your bookstore

OR ORDER DIRECTLY FROM

DA CAPO PRESS, INC.

233 Spring Street, New York, New York 10013